THE
BLAIR
EFFECT

THE
BLAIR
EFFECT

Edited by
Anthony Seldon

LITTLE, BROWN AND COMPANY

A *Little, Brown* Book

First published in Great Britain in 2001
by Little, Brown and Company

Typeset in Sabon by M Rules
Printed and bound in Great Britain by
Clays Ltd, St Ives plc

Little, Brown and Company (UK)
Brettenham House
Lancaster Place
London WC2E 7EN

CONTENTS

PREFACE

THIS IS THE third volume in a series sponsored by The Institute of Contemporary British History which analyses the impact of different governments. The earlier volumes, *The Thatcher Effect* and *The Major Effect*, both edited with Dennis Kavanagh, were published in 1989 and 1994 respectively. This will be the first volume which will be coming out assessing the full impact of one full term of government.

The approach in all three volumes is the same. Leading authorities from academe and the media address common themes in their specialist area.

- What was the state of the area when the Tories fell in May 1997?
- What was the state of the area in early 2001?
- What changed and why?
- How successful or effective have the changes been?
- To what extent was the change driven by the Prime Minister himself, and how far from Number 10 in general, by ministers, departments, ideology, circumstances or other influences?

Within this common framework, authors are encouraged to develop their own particular approaches. Some followed the rubric precisely, others ranged more freely. The aim is to cover the main waterfront of the Blair government's policies. In a concluding chapter, I examine which areas saw the most significant changes and assess how effective the changes were that Britain saw from 1997 to 2001. I also examine Tony Blair's personal impact, and assess the prospects for a second Labour government after 2001.

The book overall seeks to be studiously non party political. Where individual authors have particular political persuasions, I sought to balance them by others with alternative outlooks. The Institute, which was set up in 1986, endeavours not only to make contemporary British history accessible, but also it does not shun taking on difficult challenges. Few have been more difficult than assessing objectively the impact of a government which has done so much to influence opinion and which, at the same time, has suffered from initially an overly friendly and then an overly critical media. It is all the more important, therefore, that we have an authoritative audit of the work of the first Blair government, produced on the cusp of the events themselves.

Anthony Seldon
February 2001

ACKNOWLEDGEMENTS

FIRST AND FOREMOST, I would like to thank the chapter writers, who have been unfailingly prompt and responsive. Special thanks go to Christopher Foster, Robert Hewison and Geoffrey Owen, all of whom joined the team late in the day (in the case of the last, extremely late!). An editor has a role very similar to that of a football manager. He chooses the team and gives them instructions but he is utterly dependent on their performance on the day. It was a great relief that they worked so well together as a team and gave such strong performances.

David Butler hosted a conference to discuss the Blair government and the book in September 2000. My thanks to him and the Warden and Fellows of Nuffield College. At the Institute of Contemporary British History, Harriet Jones, Michael Kandiah and Virginia Preston were unfailingly supportive and helpful.

I would like to thank Chris Riddell for the cartoons, all of which appeared in the contemporary press and all of which are important historical documents in their own right. They serve not just to punctuate but to inform the text. The choice of cartoons is wholly the editor's: authors might or might not like the cartoons appearing in front of their chapters. Chris donated the cartoons *gratis*. All profits from the book will be given to the Institute of Contemporary British History.

At Little, Brown, I would like to thank Becky Quintavalle for being one of the best and most enthusiastic editors with whom I have ever worked. My colleagues Mary-Anne Brightwell and Teresa Goudie helped oversee the book's production, the latter produced the bibliography and Stephen Williams produced the chronology. John Beaton was an excellent copy-editor, and Peter Snowdon a helpful editorial assistant, as ever. My former ICBH colleague, Brian Brivati, suggested I edit the book, and my thanks to him. At Brighton College, my thanks, as always, go to my wonderful colleagues and to the pupils, who are such a source of delight and stimulation.

Politics and Government

THAT SINKING FEELING

© Chris Riddell

Chapter 1

NEW LABOUR, NEW MILLENNIUM, NEW PREMIERSHIP

Dennis Kavanagh

ASSESSMENT OF TONY Blair's relatively short premiership is inevitably of work in progress. Blair's tenure, by May 2001, will have been exceeded by ten of the eighteen other men and women who began their premierships in the twentieth century. A four year term places him behind Lloyd George (five years ten months) and ahead of Ted Heath (three years eight months). The first won the 1914–18 war, the second took Britain into the European Community, both major landmarks in the twentieth century and both in less than three years into their premierships. Blair cannot yet point to anything comparable.

For all his impatience with tradition and rhetorical invocations of the new and the modern, Blair has a sense of the premiership's history and wants to make his mark on it. He has often told aides that his agenda is '. . . to achieve peace in Northern Ireland, sort out health, education and welfare, and improve relations with Europe', commenting: 'If I can do those, then I won't have done so badly.' He might have further added that he wants to make the present century one in which the centre left becomes the normal party of government.

Achieving any one of these will be significant, and none are entirely in his control. There is still a lot to do, to quote one of his slogans. Hence the importance of achievements in the second term for his reputation (but it is likely to require at least another term to accomplish).

A New Kind of Leader

I shall argue that Blair is turning out to be a distinctive Prime Minister. Commentators have already compared him to Thatcher, Bonaparte, Clinton and even Stalin: the term 'Presidential' has become almost a

Pavlovian adjective when his leadership is discussed. Having reformed his party and the constitution and embarked on a series of steps to modernise the Whitehall machine, it is not surprising that he has ideas about refashioning the premiership. He wants to make his office an animating force across Whitehall. His successors in the new century are likely to seek to emulate a number of his practices. Some of the latter are part of a long-term trend, but some are new.

Blair has undoubtedly already had a significant impact on his party. The reinvention of the party as New Labour, the change to clause 4 in 1995 – where previous leaders had either failed or considered the task too daunting – and the stunning general election victory in 1997 were very much his achievements. Hugh Gaitskell's biographer, Philip Williams (1982), once distinguished between Labour leaders who were stabilisers (Wilson), problem solvers (Attlee) and pathfinders (Gaitskell). The last type seek to lead the party in a new direction, have their own vision and may not appeal to all followers. Blair (like Thatcher for the Conservative party) belongs to this category, although Labour's culture of solidarity has meant that pathfinder leaders have rarely come to the fore.

There is no doubt that, in professional and public assessments, the outstanding political leaders in Britain have been pathfinders. Winning a war has been the route to greatness. A BBC survey among historians and commentators at the end of 1999 ranked Winston Churchill and Lloyd George, largely on account of their success as dynamic war leaders, as the two greatest Prime Ministers of the twentieth century. Thatcher (for tackling relative economic decline and industrial conflict), Asquith (facing constitutional crises), and Attlee (handling the retreat from Empire and post-war reconstruction) occupied the next three places. Indeed, both Attlee and Thatcher re-shaped the domestic political agenda for years after they had left office. Blair has yet to be tested by crises comparable to those which the outstanding leaders faced and his long-term influence on the agenda can only be judged after he leaves office.

Both Lloyd George in 1916 and Winston Churchill in 1940 provoked controversy by their importation of teams of personal advisers and had distinctive approaches to being Prime Minister. But they left no institutional legacy, apart from Lloyd George's creation of the Cabinet Office. Mrs Thatcher provided a model of how a Prime Minister, blessed with great reserves of energy, conviction and self-confidence, could stretch the powers of the office to their limits. Again, however, what remains is a memory of a style not an institutional legacy. Blair has done more.

The office and role of the Prime Minister have hardly changed in the past eighty years or so, and the formal powers remain largely the same. But the world has changed greatly, as has Britain's place in it, and the responsibilities and public expectations of government have been transformed. Number 10 Downing Street, denoting both the Prime Minister and the office, may have grown potentially more powerful in the Whitehall–Westminster village, but its influence has shrunk in the world outside. Since 1945 Britain's loss of Empire and decline in relative international standing, the government's diminished control over the economy and utilities (in the wake of privatisation) and 'the hollowing out' of the state because of the loss of powers to the EU and the Scottish Parliament have reduced the writ of the Prime Minister. Peter Hennessy (2000) quotes William Rees-Mogg as saying that today a British Prime Minister '. . . cannot have the world impact of a Pitt, a Disraeli, a Gladstone, a Lloyd George or a Churchill'. Indeed, Richard Rose's new study (2001) argues that Blair's emphasis on style and presentation represents a devaluing of the concern with policy and conflicts of interest which was central for his predecessors. A good press is not the same as a good policy.

Political leaders do not operate in contexts chosen by themselves; they are inheritors more than they are choosers. In May 1997, Blair inherited a more favourable legacy than any of the above leaders or indeed of any other Labour Prime Minister. He was backed by a huge parliamentary majority, goodwill from the media, a united Labour party or at least one which was less faction-ridden than at any time in memory, a weak and divided opposition (for all of which he can claim credit) and relatively sound public finances, falling unemployment and low inflation. He also arrived at a time when centre-left parties were in office in all but a handful of West European capitals, although only one had an outright majority of seats, and a kindred political spirit occupied the White House. When he became party leader in July 1994, the Conservative government had already self-destructed and he began a long political honeymoon. His aides claim that none of the above make problems easier to resolve. They might try to operate with their opposites.

Blair's approach to the premiership has been shaped by a number of negative and positive influences. It is remarkable how often new Prime Ministers are or strive to be unlike their predecessors in exercising leadership. It is almost a pendulum trend in British politics (Ingham, 1999). One thinks of Bonar Law and Stanley Baldwin following Lloyd George, Attlee following Churchill, Thatcher following Callaghan, Major following Thatcher. Major was a negative model for Blair. For all the difficulties that faced Major in the 1992 Parliament, Blair regarded him as a Prime Minister who failed to give leadership, in the sense of taming party critics, managing the media, or sticking to a clear line. But previous Labour Party leaders and Prime Ministers also provided an example to be avoided; they had often found themselves undermined by internal divisions and damaging attacks by party critics. Operating in a culture of inner party democracy they had had to possess 'fixing' and consensus building skills of a high order and take account of which policies the annual party conference, big trade unions or party factions would accept. The result was often elaborately negotiated and fudged policies and party appointments balanced between left and right factions. Labour leaders consequently found it difficult to project themselves as strong figures on the national stage.

Opposition Leader

Blair was a remarkably successful opposition leader between 1994 and 1997. He consolidated Neil Kinnock's party changes which had weakened the policy role of conference and NEC, with the aim of making Labour more disciplined and facilitating his personal leadership. Much of the hard work had been done by Kinnock and the gains were having an impact when Blair became leader. Blair gave presentation and media management a higher priority and downgraded the role of party activists and party institutions in communicating with the public. He transformed the public image (and reality) of the party and impressed his own personality on voters and the media. For purposes of making Labour electable, Blair considered that being seen to be in charge was as important as actually being in charge. This Millbank (the party headquarters are located in Millbank Towers, an office block in Westminster) model of party management emphasised the authority of the leader and his office, centralised control of communications, and disciplined adherence to the Blair-defined 'message'.

After the excesses of party democracy and triumphs of the left in the 1980s, Blair was boldly reviving the oligarchical model of Robert Michels. According to this, regardless of how democratic was the constitution, party elites, even in a socialist party, would get their own way. But could Blair effectively translate this model, so successful for campaigning and opposition, to government? Armed with the authority and resources of government, perhaps yes. But, faced by the ministerial barons in their departments, perhaps not.

Blair has been criticised for destroying the checks and balances of the 'old' constitution. It is wrong, however, to regard Labour's inner party democracy as the genuine article; it excused a number of unsavoury practices. Party members in trade unions or constituencies were rarely balloted over conference motions, unrepresentative activists dominated decaying local parties, resolutions were cooked with little reference or answerability to party members and the block vote gave unaccountable power to the trade unions. Robert McKenzie, author of the classic *British Political Parties*, a study of the distribution of power in the parties, described Labour as a 'living lie', because of the gap between its democratic constitution and actual practice in taking decisions.

From the time of Labour's first Prime Minister, Ramsay MacDonald, down to Harold Wilson and James Callaghan, Labour premiers have been conscious of the need to appeal to voters beyond those in the working class and trade unions. But becoming a catchall, or more broadly based, party had become even more urgent for Labour by the 1980s and 1990s. Social and economic changes were expanding traditional non-Labour voting groups and reducing the party's core vote. In private, Blair talked eloquently of his belief that centre-left parties in the West were facing common problems. Increasingly, voters were resistant to paying more taxes, disliked strikes by trade unions, demanded public services which were more consumer-oriented and provided greater opportunity to exercise choice, and did not identify with many state-owned enterprises. The Labour Party had to respond to people's aspirations for themselves and their families, becoming a party for the gainers as well as the casualties of social and economic change. He thought that politics at the end of the twentieth century had moved beyond battles between socialism and capitalism, between left and right. Successful politics was about occupying the centre ground and backing policies because they worked, not because they were ideologically correct (Butler and Kavanagh, 1997: 51). Centre-left parties across much of the EU were turning away from state ownership of industries and policies of tax and spend, and seeking to encourage more flexible labour markets and a welfare system that distinguished between the deserving and the undeserving poor (Sassoon, 2000).

With no family background in the Labour movement, or the usual connections with the public sector or the trade unions, Blair could personify New Labour in a way that was hardly possible for his immediate predecessors. As an outsider he was not burdened with much of the baggage that his predecessors brought with them, and was openly impatient with many of the party's structures and much of its ethos. What is more, most of his fellow-modernisers openly shared his views and backed his leadership. The key elements of his approach to the premiership were largely in place before 1 May 1997.

Prime Minister

If Blair's premiership was to be terminated today, his government's major achievement would be the wide range of constitutional reforms. Devolution, a Human Rights Act, an elected London Mayor, proportional representation for non-Westminster elections, and ending voting rights for hereditary peers in the Lords, is an impressive record. In the first two sessions of the 1997 Parliament, thirteen statutes relating to the constitution were passed. Some of this was unfinished business from the last Labour government in the 1970s, and even from Gladstone. There is no doubt, however, that the scale of constitutional reform has provided the significant discontinuity with the Thatcher–Major years. Another achievement has been the sustained economic growth and stability, which has enabled the Chancellor to announce in November 2000 an extra £71 billion spending on public services over the next three years, with hardly a murmur from the financial markets. This would have been unthinkable for a previous Labour Chancellor. Gordon Brown's budget measures and welfare reforms have been redistributive; with the minimum wage and working family tax credit targeted to benefit the poor in work.

Critics on the constitutional front have complained variously about the absence of an over-arching theme to the reforms, or the lack of a major Blair speech on the constitution, or the contrast between the pluralism and de-centralisation of the constitutional reforms and the tight control of the party and government (Barnett, 2000; Marquand, 2000). The paradoxical result has been that a Prime Minister whose constitutional reforms are inclusive and de-centralising is also a control freak on matters closer to home. Blair has provided a schizoid response to the politics of the 1980s – constitutional reform as a reaction to Thatcher's elective dictatorship, and a stronger centre in the party and government as a reaction to Labour's internal divisions. Critics are also disappointed at the lack of action, or at least positive signals, on a referendum for PR for Westminster elections, and creation of a 'modern' (i.e. largely non-nominated) second chamber. And on the economy much of the credit must be shared, at least, with the Chancellor.

In many other areas there has been broad continuity with the Major government. This is particularly the case in the acceptance of neo-liberal ideas of economic management, flexible labour markets, public–private partnerships (hardly different from the previous government's private finance initiative) for the London underground and air traffic control, peace in Northern Ireland, indirect taxes, and a wait and see line on membership of the Euro, as well as exclusion from the Franco-German axis of the EU. In each of these areas, there have been developments from Major, e.g. flexible labour markets but with a minimum wage and more bargaining rights for unions; the Northern Ireland peace process was stalled by May 1997 but has been rescued by a public willingness of ministers to talk to Sinn Fein, and an Assembly has been set up; on the European single currency 'wait and see' has been replaced by 'prepare and decide', and there seems little doubt that Blair's approach is more positive than Major's; and by 2000 public spending had become a higher priority than tax cuts. In opposition, Blair and Brown accepted Conservative income tax rates and spending plans for the first two years of the Parliament. By 2001, the mood has altered compared to the Thatcherite era. Then Labour was on the defensive over its planned spending increases ('where's the money coming from'; was the complaint). Today, the Conservatives are on the same back foot with their promised tax cuts ('where are the cuts in services to be made?' is the charge).

Blair has also become painfully aware that reforming the public services is for the long term – who now recalls his claim that 1999 would be the year of 'delivery'? The measure of his government's radicalism may not be the provision of extra funds now allocated by Gordon Brown but the degree to which structural changes are made in the core services of education and health. To date, Blair has largely been a 'preference-accommodator' rather than a 'shaper' of the public mood. His outlook reflected the durability of much of Thatcher's legacy and what he regards as economic and social reality.

To a remarkable degree, Blair actually carried the Millbank model through. Key appointments in Downing Street were given to the many people who had worked in his political office in opposition. They constitute the core of his key 9 a.m. Monday morning office meeting, his first and agenda-setting meeting for the week (Kavanagh and Seldon, 2001). His political strategist and pollster, Philip Gould, has continued to have regular access to him (the first time a pollster has had such access to a British Prime Minister). Blair formed a stronger Prime Minister's office than any of his predecessors, maintained the emphasis on proactive communications, attached as little importance to the Cabinet as a forum for taking decisions or even testing them, as he had to the Shadow Cabinet, and gave a wide brief on domestic policies to Gordon Brown at the Treasury. What Philip Gould, in opposition, called a system of unitary command (Gould, 1998), with all power flowing from the leader and his office, has been established in government.

Blair has used membership ballots as a plebiscitary device to disempower the annual conference and the activists. Never a tribal politician, he has looked beyond Labour to project himself and his government. One Labour moderniser advised the author that in Number 10 one had to understand that Blair was surrounded by 'party people' and 'Tony's people', with the latter more important. His Number 10 aides include a number of former Social Democrats and he has rewarded several successful businessmen with peerages and ministerial office. The chairmanships of important committees have been given to non-Labour figures, like Chris Patten, Lord Wakeham and Lord Jenkins. And, remarkably, the Liberal Democrats have been given membership of a joint Cabinet committee. The 'Big Tent' has certainly been extended to members of other parties and none, but some of his own party do not feel so included. As one close associate commented: 'He is leader of his party, but not *of* it' (cited in Foley, 2000: 106).

The 179-seat majority has meant that, unlike John Major after 1992, Blair has not had to bargain with his back-benchers to make fine calculations about how he can get his legislation through the Commons. Every previous Labour Prime Minister has experienced a period of either minority government or one in which the majority was not assured. This was the case for MacDonald in his two spells as a Labour Prime Minister (1924, 1929–31), Attlee (1950–51), Wilson (1964–66 and 1974) and Callaghan (1977–79). Under Blair the Chief Whip has become a less significant figure in Number 10.

Blair's approach to party management is a function in part of the parliamentary arithmetic, but also of changes in the party institutions and of his personal style. He has never been a tea-room man – contrast this with Jim Callaghan regularly lunching with Welsh Labour MPs in the House of Commons on Tuesdays and Thursdays before PMQs. But Parliament itself has declined, losing powers to the European Union and the Scottish

Parliament. Politicians make a larger public impact outside the chamber, on the *Today* programme, for instance. Traditionally, Prime Ministers spent much time in Parliament, often (until 1940) combining the post with being Leader of the House of Commons. Research by a team at the London School of Economics shows a steady decline in Prime Minister's participation, in the form of making statements and taking part in debates, in the Commons over the century. Blair has voted in only 5 per cent of House of Commons divisions since May 1997, a much lower figure than his predecessors. The reduction of PMQs to one weekly slot – as well as his infrequent appearance for votes – reduces the opportunities for MPs to have a word with him or for him to sense the atmosphere in the Commons. Although Parliament still counts for the Prime Minister on the days of PMQs, or when his government lacks an assured majority, he is increasingly drawn back to *his* office in Number 10 where *his* staff work for *him*.

More broadly, Blair's courting of business, the Murdoch press and middle England have been part of a strategy of inclusiveness and making Labour a catch-all electoral party. The so-called Blair 'project' is above all the search for electoral hegemony. Inevitably, there has been some relegation of the importance of the trade unions and Labour's heartlands. Compared with the ever-present influence of the unions on Labour Prime Ministers between 1964 and 1970, and 1974 and 1979, contacts between Blair and the TUC are now modest. Unions and activists, as well as a number of back-bench MPs, feel neglected. The party members' lack of empathy with the project was seen in the response to the leadership's strenuous efforts to 'manage' the selection of the party candidates for London Mayor and First Minister in Wales. Ultimately, both were unsuccessful. To be the candidate of either 'Tony' or Millbank was a death certificate in the search for votes. Of course, previous party leaders have also seen their favoured candidates for party posts turned down. But what was striking about the London and Welsh campaigns was the open relish with which party members repudiated Blair's preferred candidate.

The decline of Cabinet (and its occasional recovery) has been a staple of debate for many years. Interestingly, the same trend has been noted in other Westminster-type systems in Canada, New Zealand and Australia. Under Blair, the Cabinet system (including Cabinet committees) has declined further. Mrs Thatcher often used the Cabinet as a discursive (or argumentative) body (James, 1999: 83) and Major used it to get key ministers in line, for example, over the Maastricht negotiations and ending the poll tax. Blair's Cabinets are too short – less than an hour – to be discursive. After 1977, when the Cabinet ceased to meet twice weekly, Thatcher and Major held around fifty meetings a year. The figure has fallen further under Blair. Attlee's Cabinet met for some ninety hours a year and usually had five or six papers before it at each session. Blair's Cabinets total about thirty hours a year and rarely receive papers. The Cabinet is now part of a network of powerful figures and units in Whitehall. Blair's Chief of Staff,

Jonathan Powell, spoke before and after May 1997 about the favoured approach: 'We want to move to a Napoleonic system and away from feudal baronies'. Presumably, the 'we' meant that he was not speaking for himself alone. After all, that is the way Blair had worked in opposition.

When taxed about the Napoleonic allegation by *Guardian* interviewers at Chequers on 24 September 1999, Blair replied:

> You have got to run an efficient government and you have got to run an effective centre . . . I want to make sure we are driving [the programme] through. I just think you live with this. You are either a strong Prime Minister in which case you are a control freak or you are a weak Prime Minister in which case you are weak really and I think in the end I know which I would like to be accused of.

If the Commons and Cabinet do not loom large for Blair, then what does? Clearly, his Number 10 staff are important. Blair's aides, Jonathan Powell, Charles Falconer, Alastair Campbell, Sally Morgan, Anji Hunter and Policy Unit are all 'fixing' with ministers, civil servants, the party and the media on his behalf. Like a US President, he chooses teams of people he trusts to work on projects he is interested in. It is a fluid, task-orientated system, one that has echoes of Mrs Thatcher's and Lloyd George's approaches. 'Rather than refer an issue to a Cabinet committee, he sees a problem and sets up a group and he is not very interested in their turf and titles', according to a senior civil servant. Prime Ministers have long had regular bilaterals (usually weekly) with the Foreign Secretary and Chancellor of the Exchequer. Blair also has weekly sessions with John Prescott, the DPM, and several meetings with his Chancellor. He has regular – every two months or so – so-called 'stock taking' bilaterals with ministers for the key issues of education, health, crime and, more recently, transport. They consider output data which is used to monitor progress in achieving agreed outcomes. In a further twist, senior departmental officials accompany their minister at these sessions. The presence of the senior civil servants, including Permanent Secretaries, and revisions of their job remits and regular appraisals linked to performance pay are a reminder of the importance which Number 10 attaches to outcomes. No doubt there is give and take between Blair and the Cabinet Minister, but clearly Number 10 gains leverage from setting targets and monitoring them.

Blair and his Number 10 team began with a fear of departmentalism. In opposition, shadow ministers, except for Gordon Brown, had been effectively under his thumb. Their discussions on policy with civil servants in the run up to Labour entering government had to be cleared beforehand with his Chief of Staff, Jonathan Powell. Blair continues to be concerned that ministers who want to make a personal mark or who go native in the departments can easily lose sight of their role in contributing to the wider government programme. Prime Ministers are dependent on ministers to carry through a programme. The minister after all has the budgets, staff, access to expertise and policy networks, and statutory powers are vested in him as the Secretary of State. Blair has tried to combat this tendency with an emphasis on 'joined up' policy making, getting departments to work together to provide solutions to the so-called 'wicked issues' which are not the responsibility of any one department but cut across a number of them. This is an old theme in British government (Kavanagh and Richards, 2000). Blair has tried to go further by introducing joint budgets for projects in the 1998 and 2000 comprehensive spending reviews, creating new units in the Cabinet Office, notably the Performance and Innovation Unit and the Social Exclusion Unit, both explicitly designed to work across departmental boundaries, and reforming the senior Civil Service to create a greater sense of corporacy. He decides the units' tasks and they report to him.

The emphasis on bilateralism has its dangers as well as its uses. As Nigel Lawson (1992) appreciated, it excludes the Cabinet from the bigger picture and allows the Prime Minister to step in as and when he wishes. It is understandable that Blair has been heavily involved in Northern Ireland, Kosovo and the EU. But, when crises allow, he has also become personally engaged with health, schools and transport. As Professor Peter Hennessy observed to the House of Commons Public Administration Committee in May 2000, Blair's in and out interventionist style, depending on the pressures on his time, defies analysis and produces disjointed government. One cost of the Blair approach has been a loss of collegiality. Previous Labour government's suffered similarly, but the lack of strong ideological divisions since 1997 has allowed ministers' personal grudges and rivalries to be fully expressed, often via their assistance for biographers and commentators.

Blair has also looked to the Cabinet Office to be more than an 'honest broker' between departments and to promote the government's (effectively Number 10's) programme across Whitehall. An interventionalist premier makes work for a Cabinet Secretary. One of Blair's staff said that the Cabinet Secretary '. . . should be our Chief Whip in Whitehall'. Sir Richard Wilson, the Cabinet Secretary and head of the Civil Service since January 1998, has instigated some and acquiesced in other parts of the accretion of power to Number 10. Indeed, eyebrows in Whitehall were raised at his willingness as a civil servant to act as Blair's emissary and reportedly seek the resignation of at least two ministers – Frank Field and Geoffrey Robinson.

Blair, more than any other recent Prime Minister, has been his government's communicator-in-chief. As with Presidents Reagan and Clinton he has sought not only to gain favourable media coverage but, when this fails, to by-pass the political reporters, going 'direct' to the voters. In the age of pro-active media management, the politician's publicity ideal is to shape the news environment so that journalists are driven to focus on the issues, themes, messages and spokesperson that he or she wishes. Compared with Major, the number of people with media skills in Number 10 has almost trebled. The Press Secretary, Alastair Campbell, is very close to Blair and his views on presentation, speechwriting and the performance of colleagues carry weight. Significantly, a few days into the life of the government, he (and Jonathan Powell) was empowered by an order-in-council, to give instructions to civil servants. Campbell quickly strengthened the convention that ministers' announcements should be cleared beforehand with Number 10, and that their media appearances and interviews be similarly approved. The Press Office and Policy Unit have been joined by a Strategic Communications Unit which plans the 'grid' or scheduling of government announcements, including ministerial press conferences, policy launches, speeches and green papers. The 'grid' for the following week is distributed to the Cabinet and reported as a separate item. Blair himself has written a record number of syndicated columns for the regional and national press in addition to giving numerous press conferences, interviews and speeches (Kavanagh and Seldon, 2001). It is difficult to recall a more media conscious British government. Blair has also readily adapted to the requirements of 'infotainment' programmes such as David Frost, Des O'Connor or Richard and Judy to satisfy the human interest concerns of the audience. Like Clinton he believes that with the decline of parties political leaders today have to 'connect' or empathise with the public.

Over the past three decades the Prime Minister's office has expanded in size and become more specialised. Until 1974 the Civil Service had successfully resisted the introduction of more than a handful of political aides in Number 10 and marginalised those who were recruited. The growth in staff in recent years has been in response to the changing demands on Prime Ministers from the growing burden of foreign affairs (including the EU, summitry and crises) and from an expanding and more intrusive mass media, as well as the preferences of leaders (particularly Harold Wilson and Tony Blair). Until 1964 no more than seventy people were employed in different capacities in Number 10 and probably no more than a handful worked on policy and political matters for the Prime Minister. When John Major left office in May 1997 the total figure had grown to 130. By late 2000 over two hundred people worked in Number 10 and nearly forty on policy and party matters.

The staffs of the Press Office, Political Office, Private Office are at an all-time high and new units for Strategic Communications and Research and Information were added in 1998 and 1999 respectively. Compared to John Major, Tony Blair has doubled the number of staff working directly for him. The Policy Unit, with fourteen members, has doubled in size and in late 1999 each member was given the research support of a civil servant. Civil servants and political appointments work side by side in the Policy Unit, Press Office and the new Strategic Communications Unit and political appointments have been added to many units which were traditionally the preserve of civil servants. His political Chief of Staff, Jonathan Powell, is based in the Private Office as was, until recently, his deputy, Pat

McFadden. In a new departure, in 1999, Blair's Head of the Policy Unit and his Principal Private Secretary, attended the autumn summit meetings of Permanent Secretaries at Sunningdale.

Blair has shown as little respect for many of the traditions of Number 10 as he has for those of his party and the constitution. The strengthening of Number 10, in large part to oversee strategy and monitor departments, has provoked controversy. But one needs to keep a sense of proportion. All strong Prime Ministers have faced charges of neglecting the Cabinet, building up a 'kitchen cabinet', and politicising the civil service – Lloyd George, Wilson and Thatcher spring readily to mind as examples. Blair has certainly tilted the balance to Number 10 from the Cabinet and there has been a blurring of the lines between politics and administration. But the record number of seventy-eight special advisers in Whitehall has to be compared with over 3,000 senior civil servants, and the Number 10 staff still remains modest in comparison with that for many other Western leaders.

With the exception of Gordon Brown, Blair's Cabinet ministers appear to be subordinates, there to implement the policies largely agreed with Number 10. The previous Labour Cabinets of Attlee, Wilson (post–1966, and 1974–76, and Callaghan) all contained a large number of heavyweight ministers, who commanded followings among MPs, and whose resignations would have rocked the government. This applies only to a handful of Blair's ministers. Brown's position is interesting. It is only since the 1960s that the Chancellor has overtaken the Foreign Secretary or Home Secretary as the normal second most powerful member of the Cabinet. Blair, unlike Thatcher, has not sought independent economic advice and, unusually, allows Gordon Brown to chair the key Economic Affairs Committee of Cabinet. The frequency with which the two men meet, often without officials and therefore without a written record of what they discuss, Brown's influence over a large part of domestic policy via the Public Spending Agreements between the Treasury and the departments, and his recruitment of his own team at the Treasury, has led to talk of there being a dual premiership. The two men have a closer relationship than existed even between Howe and Thatcher and Lawson and Thatcher and this has certainly helped to create a strong centre in government (Deakin and Parry, 2000; Lipsey, 2000). The relationship has been helped by Brown's successful management of the economy. It has been easier to agree on spending the extra increments from economic growth and falling unemployment than sharing the burdens from cut backs. But this success has not prevented Brown from being regarded as uncollegial and being the target of complaints from Cabinet ministers that he should not act as though he is Prime Minister.

It is possible to see Blair as a new kind of leader, responding to a different context than faced his predecessors. There has been a decline in recent years in the membership and activity of political parties, less popular identification with them, a dissolution of the ties of social class, a weakening of ties between political parties and the press, which has become more adversarial, and a more shallow relationship between voters and political leaders. Much has been made of US pollster Dick Morris's (1999) injunction that the media's search for new stories or new angles on existing stories, the public's short attention span, and the regular reports of opinion polls and focus groups, as well as other tools of dipstick politics like radio phone-ins and television question times, make each day like polling day. In fact, Tony Blair and Philip Gould were exchanging memos about the need for permanent campaigning long before Blair's leaked memo in July 2000, calling on his aides to present him with headline catching initiatives. Philip Gould (1998: 294) explained the importance in modern politics of being proactive and taking the news initiative: 'You must always seek to gain and keep momentum, or it will pass immediately to your opponent. Gaining momentum means dominating the news agenda, entering the new cycle at the earliest possible time, and repeatedly re-entering it, with stories and initiatives so that subsequent news coverage is set on your terms.'

Blair's concern with chasing the daily headlines and constantly unveiling initiatives, however, has had its downside. The frequent announcements of plans, task forces and working parties, and targets and over-hyped funding allocations, appear to have been driven more by communication imperatives than considerations of good policy. Many of the claimed achievements, as well as the Blair rhetoric, are often at odds with the personal experiences of voters. In turn, a sceptical media has devoted resources to 'unmasking' the spin behind the stories. Cynical reporters, for example, interpreted the announcement of Mrs Blair's pregnancy as a device to distract attention from unwelcome news about Ken Livingstone, and for a time speculated that an embarrassing memo of Philip Gould's was deliberately leaked to the *Sunday Times* in May 2000, to serve as a wake-up call to the party. A *Times* analysis of press coverage of government figures during 1998 found that Peter Mandelson and Alastair Campbell together received more mentions than the Foreign Secretary, Home Secretary, or Deputy Prime Minister (Rose, 2001). The remorseless concentration on spinning and staying on message has incurred costs in terms of a decline in public trust of Blair and his reputation for integrity. Recent surveys show that levels of political cynicism and distrust of ministers have returned to those prevailing at the close of Major's premiership. The initial goodwill and trust have dissipated. It is difficult to believe that this is largely the result of a cynical press. His political strategist reported that Blair is increasingly seen by the public as 'all spin and presentation, he just says things to please people not because he believes them'.

Blair is no doubt frustrated at the lack of media appreciation for what has been done so far. Such, however, is the lot eventually of all democratic leaders. Consider the diminished standing of such dominant figures as Asquith, Lloyd George, Attlee, Macmillan, Heath and Thatcher when their premierships ended. Blair has set his heart on a second term, during which, it is implied, he will be more radical. Perhaps. But power is often a wasting asset; the public gets bored with ministers' repeated promises and exhortations; the media likes a change of face in Number 10; the growing number of disappointed office-seekers and embittered former ministers on the back-benches are a source of trouble, and there is no guarantee that events will continue to be as favourable. Moreover, very few governments (Thatcher's 1983 administration is one exception) have become more successful or radical over a second term. Blair should be modest about his expectations of the second term: the future may not be better; the best may be in the past.

Labour's 1997 general election promises were cautious but the public goodwill and sense of euphoria at the change of government were immense. The huge swing of votes in the 1997 general election and the scale of the Labour victory suggested that there was a sea change of mood. Blair appears to have regarded it, however, as a vote for a change of government and for politics conducted with competence and integrity, but not for a change of direction. Public disappointment is probably less a reaction to what has not been delivered – improving the public services will take many years – than to the gap between grandiose claims and modest achievements. This is another example of the downside of translating the campaign mode of politics to government.

Historically, Labour has been an 'outsider' party in terms of its proximity to and connections with established elites, particularly in the media, City, industry, the professions, the Church of England and South East England. Blair has done much to reverse that. Responding to the decline of Labour's traditional core constituencies he has successfully courted some of these groups, particularly business and Labour is now less of an outside party than at any time in its history. Previous Labour leaders have also felt bound to prove their competence, particularly in economic management, and on terms largely defined by conservative forces. By 1997, some of this inferiority complex had declined because of the Conservative mishandling of the ERM and the damage to its reputation for economic competence.

The charge of presidentialism has been revived under Blair. Commentators usually invoke the term as code for criticism of a Prime Minister who has become too big for his or her boots, or exercises power in such a personal way as to verge on the unconstitutional. Blair certainly learnt lessons from President Clinton, notably in election campaigning, presenting himself to the public, and proactive media communications. But beyond that, comparisons with the US President have limited usefulness. In passing legislation and budgets and getting appointments approved, a Prime Minister with an assured parliamentary majority is more powerful than a US President. On the other hand, a Prime Minister's greater influence in Whitehall and Westminster is offset by the political decline of these arenas because of devolution, the EU and globalisation. In the EU the Prime Minister is just one of fifteen national leaders and over the years on many key issues in the Council of Ministers Britain has been on the losing side. The growing integration of international finance imposes additional constraints on the independence of a British government. A Prime Minister operates in a shrinking world (Rose, 2001).

In Blair's case, the presidential analogy has encompassed the strengthening of Number 10, his elevation above his colleagues, successful public appeal across the political spectrum, and *his* high media profile. One can see how the growth of media coverage of personalities and the increase in summitry contribute to the distancing of the Prime Minister from his colleagues. In the United States, Presidents Reagan and Clinton and in Britain, Thatcher and Blair have been exponents of this *spatial* leadership (Foley, 2000). Effective national leaders, it is argued, now use the media to present themselves as above-party figures. It has also coincided with a (temporary?) decline in the checks and balances traditionally provided by the House of Commons, Cabinet and Labour party institutions, and the reaction against John Major's weakness. Perhaps it is possible that there may be a swing of the pendulum again and a return to a more collegial Cabinet, a more balanced party system in the House of Commons and stronger departments. The key words in Whitehall today, 'Tony wants' will no longer count for so much.

Conclusion

Blair's long-term impact on the premiership will depend in part on how successful he is judged to be in changing the agenda and delivering promised improvements. This will be for the second term. However, it is likely that future Prime Ministers will retain a large Policy Unit and staff in order to monitor departments and exercise strategic oversight from the centre and maintain a strong communications presence as a response to the growing importance of the media. The decline of Prime Ministerial activity in Parliament and of the Cabinet appear to be part of a longer-term trend. Prime Ministers have also long wanted the Cabinet Office to move beyond its remit of acting as an honest broker and ensuring that the Cabinet system works smoothly; it is unlikely that Blair's use of the Cabinet Office to encourage policy innovation and better implementation will be reversed.

The above trends are largely a step-wise reinforcement of what some predecessors have done or considered. What has been new under Blair has been the willingness to create so many new bodies – the Strategic Communications Unit and Research and Information Unit in Number 10, the Performance and Innovation Unit and Social Exclusion Unit in the Cabinet Office and the three hundred or so task forces – all in the first two years. Also new has been placing a political Chief of Staff in the Private Office, for so long the inner sanctum of the civil service, and the mix of political appointees and officials in the various Number 10 units. Blair has, in effect, created a Prime Minister's Department without calling it such.

Blair has fashioned a stronger role for the Prime Minister in the British system. I have argued that this has been a response shaped partly by his own ideas about effective political leadership preference and partly by certain trends in politics and the media coverage. But this is no guarantee of compliance from departments or colleagues, or support from the media or voters. The more distinctive the Prime Minister becomes from the party, Parliament or Cabinet, the more he/she becomes exposed when things go wrong and blame is allocated. Blair had early intimations of his political mortality in 2000 in the hostile reaction to his W.I. speech and the public support in September for the fuel protestors and his own tumbling personal ratings. In the past century only a handful of Prime Ministers have left office at a time of their own choosing and with their political authority not at a low point. A spectacular fall has been the fate of the outstanding figures like Lloyd George, Churchill in 1945 and Thatcher. Indeed, it seems to be a badge of being a great Prime Minister.

References

A. Barnett (2000) 'Corporate Populism and Party Democracy', *New Left Review*.

D. Butler and D. Kavanagh (1997) *The British General Election of 1997*, London, Macmillan.

N. Deakin and R. Party (2000) *The Treasury and Social Policy. The Struggle for the Control of Welfare Strategy*, London, Macmillan.

N. Fairclough (2000) *New Labour, New Language*, London, Routledge.

M. Foley (2000) *The British Presidency*, Manchester, Manchester University Press.

A. Gamble and T.I. Wright (2000) (ed.) *The New Social Democracy*, Oxford, Blackwell.

P. Gould (1998) *The Unfinished Revolution*, London, Little Brown.

P. Hennessy (2000) *The Prime Minister. The Office and its Holders since 1945*, London, HarperCollins.

B. Ingham (1999) 'Ra ra Rasputin', *New Statesman*, 6 December, pp. 72–73.

S. James (1999) *British Cabinet Government*, London, Routledge.

D. Kavanagh and A. Seldon (2001) *The Powers Behind The Prime Minister. The Hidden Influence of Number Ten*, 2nd edn, London, HarperCollins.

D. Kavanagh and D. Richards (2000) 'Departmentalism and Joined-up Government. Back to the Future', *Parliamentary Affairs*.

N. Lawson (1992) *The View From Number Ten*, London, Bantam.

D. Lipsey (2000) *The Secret Treasury*, London, Viking.

D. Marquand (2000) 'Premature obsequies: Social democracy comes in from the cold' in A. Gamble and T. Wright.

D. Morris (1999) *The New Prince*, Los Angeles, Renaissance Books.

R. Rose (2001) *The Prime Minister in a Shrinking World*, Cambridge, Polity.

D. Sassoon (2000) 'European Social Democracy and New Labour' in A. Gamble and T. Wright (eds), pp. 19–36.

P. Williams (1982) 'Changing styles of Labour leadership' in D. Kavanagh (ed.) The Politics of the Labour Party, London, Allen and Unwin.

© Chris Riddell

Chapter 2

BLAIR AS PRIME MINISTER

Peter Riddell

TONY BLAIR IS the outsider as Prime Minister. His lack of experience of government in May 1997, shared by most other senior ministers and their closest advisers, and his distance from the traditional Labour Party have meant that his approach has differed from any of his recent predecessors. Power has been exercised as much informally as through the familiar formal means. That has explained much of the distinctive, and often controversial, way he has behaved as Prime Minister and has run his Cabinet.

Mr Blair's attempt to behave differently – partly as a deliberate decision, partly through unfamiliarity and most importantly by bringing the habits of Opposition into government – has fuelled talk of a 'Blair presidency'. This has always been more a matter of style than substance, of presentation than policy, as Mr Blair and his team tried to find the levers of power and use them to change the direction of Whitehall. In practice, they have had to come to terms with the inter-departmental nature of Whitehall. But the centre, both in 10 Downing Street and in the Cabinet Office, has been strengthened. This has raised the question about how far Mr Blair has moved in the direction of what Professor Peter Hennessy[1] has called a 'command and control' premiership away from a more collective and collegial approach.

The office of Prime Minister is, as Asquith famously remarked in his memoirs, 'what its holder chooses and is able to make of it'. That has, however, often led to a confusion between the institution and the behaviour of the current holder at a particular time. It is an easy, though generally fallacious, leap from describing a particularly strong or assertive Prime Minister, such as Lady Thatcher in the mid-1980s or Tony Blair from 1997 until 1999, to the conclusion that the office itself has changed permanently. Or, alternatively, that a change of Prime Ministers will mean a switch back from an allegedly presidential to a more collective style of running a government. The reality is usually in between – a balance of long-term changes in the institution towards a strengthening of the centre and short-term variations based on the power of a particular Prime Minister, which also varies during their period in Downing Street.

A Prime Minister's direct executive powers are limited: appointing and dismissing ministers; chairing and summoning meetings of ministers and others; and being responsible for the civil service. Most legal powers, and organisational responsibilities, lie with various Secretaries of State. The less formal, but nonetheless very important, duties and responsibilities of the post have evolved and broadened over time, as Hennessy described in updating Bagehot's list of roles,[2] notably, for the past fifty years, over the use of the nuclear deterrent and, from early 1970s, the time-consuming work of handling Northern Ireland and relations with other European heads of government. Perhaps most significant of all as a constraining factor is the geography of 10 Downing Street. The old Georgian house, or rather houses, may have been extended, but they provide a physical limit on the size of a Prime Minister's operations, however open the green baize door to the Cabinet Office sometimes is.

This familiar definition, of course, begs the key questions about how Prime Ministers operate. As Sir Richard Wilson, Cabinet Secretary from January 1998, noted in evidence to the Public Administration Committee of the Commons that June:[3] 'Every Prime Minister has a different style, a different approach to the job.' What may be described as the informal powers, derived from authority, public reputation and media image, matter as much for a Prime Minister as the formal powers. Indeed, they matter more for a Prime Minister than, say, for a Chancellor who has no end of formal powers at his command. The influence of the holder depends more on his or her personal authority over ministerial and parliamentary colleagues, public standing and popularity. This varies not only between Prime Ministers but also within their terms of office.

In Mr Blair's case, the institution of the Prime Ministership he inherited was functioning smoothly, despite adverse political circumstances, as shown in part by the ease of the transition. John Major was punctilious as Prime Minister in handling the office and made few organisational changes. After Mr Major took over in November 1990, there was much comment about the apparent revival of the Cabinet, and its committees, as forums for collective discussion compared with Lady Thatcher's preference for small ad hoc groups of ministers.

The significance of the change between the Thatcher and Major years was much exaggerated. Under Mr Major, few decisions were taken in the full Cabinet, or even in its main committees. The greater use of the Cabinet during the Major years was mainly for political discussions rather than government decisions, partly in the 'political' sessions without civil servants.

Far more important was the decline in Mr Major's authority – his informal powers – as a result of the infighting over Europe within his Cabinet and the Conservative parliamentary party. This grew steadily worse from 1992 onwards and was not halted by Mr Major's decision to seek re-election as Conservative leader in June/July 1995. So, while institutionally little changed, Mr Major was seen as a weak Prime Minister with little control over his political colleagues or respect in the country.

Inexperience

The scale of the Labour election victory on 1 May 1997, immediately transformed the political position of the new Prime Minister and his ability to use the familiar powers of the office. But as important was that Mr Blair, his senior ministerial colleagues and their close group of advisers were the most inexperienced team to move into Downing Street and the main Whitehall departments, at least since the formation of the MacDonald government in 1924, and, arguably, since the first Derby administration in 1852. Apart from MacDonald, no previous Prime Minister in the last century had less than five to six years experience as minister, and the average was ten years. This is more than a historical curiosity since it meant that Mr Blair and all his immediate colleagues and advisers were wholly unfamiliar with the workings of Whitehall.

There had admittedly been extensive contacts during 1996–97 between senior civil service and Labour leaders under the Douglas-Home convention. Sir Robin, now Lord, Butler had sought to educate the Blair team about life in Whitehall. But neither these meetings nor seminars at Templeton College, Oxford, involving retired civil servants, former Labour ministers and academics were later seen by ministers as a full preparation for the realities of government. Jonathan Powell, Mr Blair's Chief of Staff in Opposition and government, and a former middle-ranking diplomat in the British Embassy in Washington, had tried to prepare Mr Blair by giving him boxes to read in the evenings and over the weekend. Yet Mr Blair still arrived in Downing Street on 2 May 1997, as a stranger to what would have been second nature to his predecessors.

Mr Blair has also never been a conventional party politician. His poor voting record in the Commons as Prime Minister – voting in many fewer divisions than any of his peacetime predecessors apart from the ageing Winston Churchill in the 1950s – in part reflected his general lack of interest in Parliament. He is not a House of Commons man. He has never particularly enjoyed the world of the tea room and the smoking room and has always been an adequate rather than sparkling performer in exchanges in the chamber itself. As a back-bencher (briefly) and Labour spokesman from 1983 onwards, Mr Blair preferred to return to his young family in Islington rather than hang around the House for late night votes. While several previous Prime Ministers had had older teenage children when in Downing Street, Mr Blair was the first since Asquith to have young children there. This was both a source of media interest and a strain both for him and his wife Cherie – as shown by the huge media interest in the birth of his fourth child, Leo, in May 2000 and then by the arrest of his elder son, Euan, after being found drunk in Leicester Square. His wife also became a figure of controversy with some newspapers and Tory MPs for her continued activity as a lawyer, particularly on human rights issues. His concern for his family, and their privacy, led to repeated tensions with the press, feeding speculation about how long he would wish to remain Prime Minister if re-elected for a second term.

In an echo of Gladstone, and unlike his recent predecessors in Downing Street, Mr Blair's approach to politics has deep moral and ethical rather than ideological roots. He has taken a close interest in religious matters since his days as an Oxford undergraduate. As Prime Minister, he has been more likely to take a book about religion on holiday with him as a heavyweight volume on policy. As Prime Minister, he has developed an interest in Islam and on his holidays in 1999 and 2000 read books about Islam, which he discussed with visiting Arab leaders.[4] His moralism has been seen in his repeated references to the importance of family and in his approach to the Kosovo conflict in spring 1999. This emphasis jarred with a number of Labour supporters, and fellow ministers, who disliked his apparent moralising. And while by age he was part of the baby boom generation, playing his guitar for relaxation and more of a fan of rock than classical music, he was otherwise more puritan in style than his racier contemporaries like President Bill Clinton or Chancellor Gerhard Schroeder.

New Labour

Mr Blair has frequently said that he chose Labour, and was not born into the party. His father was an active Conservative before his political career was cut short by a stroke and he only joined Labour when his son became party leader. Mr Blair's remarks were intended to demonstrate his commitment to the party, but, in practice, were more often seen as double-edged, as evidence of Mr Blair, the outsider, striving too hard to prove his Labour credentials. While always fiercely anti-Conservative – both in public and private conversation – Mr Blair has never been a tribal Labour loyalist. He has seen Labour's history as much as a warning as an inspiration (apart from the achievements of the post-war Attlee government, especially founding the NHS). He was noticeably uncomfortable at the celebrations at the Old Vic to mark the anniversary of the foundation of the party in early 2000. Even before becoming Labour leader in July 1994, he did not disguise his impatience with party traditionalists, and particularly with the trade unions. As leader, he not only successfully forced the rewriting of the clause 4 statement of party's aims in 1994–95, but he also developed close relations with big business, and with media groups previously hostile to the party, notably Rupert Murdoch, chairman of News Corporation, the owner of the *Sun* and other Wapping titles. Mr Blair hardly disguised his preference for meeting company chairmen rather than trade union leaders.

Mr Blair also advocated policy approaches distinct from the collectivism of 'old' Labour under the umbrella of the Third Way, marrying economic competitiveness with social justice. While the precise meaning has always been rather fuzzy, the Third Way has amounted to a case for active, though not big, government in the era of globalisation. This approach was reinforced by the close links Mr Blair developed with President Bill Clinton and the New Democrats in the United States. A number of seminars were held about the Third Way involving the younger generation of centre-left leaders in Europe as well as the USA, though the French socialists rarely attended because of their dislike of such Anglo-American revisionism. Domestically, also, as the first volume of Paddy Ashdown's diaries shows,[5] Mr Blair has sought to broaden out the political boundaries of Labour, no longer talking about socialism but about the progressive centre left, valuing Keynes and Beveridge equally with Tawney and Crosland. Blair seriously considered the possibility of bringing the Liberal Democrats into a coalition government as part of the so-called 'project' of ending the century-old rift on the centre left between Labour and the Liberals. But, in the end, he was blocked by the opposition to proportional representation of a majority of his Shadow Cabinet and then Cabinet, including such key figures as Gordon Brown, John Prescott and Jack Straw, all of whom were suspicious about the reliability of the Liberal Democrats.

Yet, as Mr Ashdown has argued, his pluralist aspirations have run alongside what became known as 'control freak' tendencies. Mr Blair's self-consciously 'big tent' approach has been linked to a much more exclusive style of operation by Mr Blair and his close advisers. Some talk almost as if they staged a coup d'etat to seize control of the machinery of the Labour Party in 1994. Dennis Kavanagh and Anthony Seldon[6] remark about how this led to a determination to carry on the centralised operation of Opposition into government. Mr Blair has retained the same tight group of aides he brought together in the six months after he became Labour leader in July 1994.

The Blairites have operated like a Leninist vanguard both in relation to the Labour Party and to government. This was initially marked by the use of the term 'new' Labour as a deliberate contrast to 'old' Labour. There have been echoes of the 'one of us' attitude of Thatcherites in the mid 1980s. That mood has existed alongside the factionalism within 'new' Labour between allies of Mr Blair and Gordon Brown, and between the latter and Peter Mandelson, at least until the latter's second resignation in

January 2001.[7] Each of the factions agreed on the need for tight discipline, both in Opposition and Government.

Another key characteristic has been the high priority attached to presentation. This is not just a technical matter of media handling, with the use of focus groups to test opinion, but, more importantly, represents a strategic belief that a party, and a government, are only successful if they dominate the news agenda. An election victory is not enough. The public is no longer loyal or deeply committed to a party. Rather, their support has constantly to be courted and won. This 'permanent campaign' view of politics, so familiar from the United States, involves continual looking over your shoulder – and can work against risk-taking and produce excessive caution on policy. This has permeated the whole way Mr Blair and his allies have operated in Downing Street.

Strengthening the Centre

Mr Blair himself was loathe to discuss his approach to government when still in Opposition. This was partly because of a lack of interest in the machinery of government. As a barrister, Mr Blair had never run or been part of a large organisation. Mr Powell did do a lot of preparatory work. The main conclusion drawn by the Blair team was that the centre needed to be strengthened. Mr Powell commented at a seminar of civil servants and industrialists in early 1997 that: 'You may see a change from a feudal system of barons to a more Napoleonic system.'[8]

Some of the Blairites' thinking was revealed in the book by Peter Mandelson and Roger Liddle.[9] In describing what a Blair Downing Street would be like, they wrote: 'He has to get personal control of the central-government machine and drive it hard, in the knowledge that if the government does not run the machine the machine will run the government.' They urged a 'more formalised strengthening of the centre of government and a stronger political presence in Number 10'. They envisaged both an expanded Policy Unit and a strong political figure to direct and co-ordinate strategy. While opinions varied about the desirability of a Prime Minister's Department, this was rejected by Mr Powell.[10] His preference was for 'the Cabinet Office taking on a more active role in pushing forward the government's programme, rather merely brokering and co-ordinating departmental views'. At that stage, the option of creating a strategy and legislative priorities committee was considered, though rejected, on the familiar grounds that those left out would be resentful and, as happened under Harold Wilson, the smaller inner group would eventually expand to include all or most of the whole Cabinet. The idea of a strategy committee or inner Cabinet was revived by Lord Simon of Highbury when he considered the matter on behalf of Mr Blair after leaving government in 1999. Just before the election, in March 1997, Mr Blair summed up his attitude to office by saying that: 'People have to know that we will run from the centre, govern from the centre.' This was, however, as much a matter of style as of machinery.

When Mr Blair walked up Downing Street to be cheered by a carefully arranged crowd of Labour Party supporters, he and his close advisers were still largely unfamiliar with the normal workings of Whitehall and determined to adopt a new approach. Some of this was a different style, a Prime Minister clearly in charge and dominating his party, unlike the increasingly isolated John Major. But there were also several initiatives intended to change the institution of 10 Downing Street.

The first, and most contentious, evidence of the strengthening of the centre was the big increase in the number of special advisers. The total throughout Whitehall roughly doubled to seventy-four over the 1997–99 period, but roughly half the increase was in 10 Downing Street where the number of special advisers rose from eight to twenty-five. The bald figures mask different types of adviser from the very partisan political/media adviser like Charlie Whelan at the Treasury (from June 1997 to January 1999) to what are properly called special, even specialist, advisers like Michael Barber at education and Keith Hallawell, the drugs 'czar'. The budget for special advisers doubled to nearly £4 million a year by 2000. The increase was examined by the Committee on Standards in Public Life (chaired by Lord Neill of Bladen) during an inquiry in summer 1998.[11] In face of Opposition and press criticisms, Sir Richard Wilson said: 'I do not think that the Senior Civil Service of 3700 people is in danger of being swamped by seventy-odd special advisers. This is not what is happening and I do not see it as creeping politicisation.'

An Order in Council was introduced allowing up to three special advisers, all in 10 Downing Street, to be appointed who would have executive powers over civil servants. In practice, only two were initially appointed – Mr Powell as Chief of Staff, and Alastair Campbell as Chief Press Secretary. In evidence to the Neill Committee,[12] Sir Robin Butler, or Lord Butler of Brockwell as he had become on retirement, explained the change as almost a technicality since it had been doubted whether a special adviser could do the things required of a Chief Press Secretary. Some concern was expressed by retired civil servants and Opposition politicians (in evidence to the Neill Committee) that giving special advisers the authority to give directions to civil servants had created a bad precedent by blurring traditional lines of impartiality. But the government was careful to stress that there was no intention of increasing the number beyond three. The Neill Committee reported[13] having had 'no testimony to the effect that the exercise of executive powers by special advisers at Number 10 was causing problems at the moment'. But the committee suggested that any increase in the number of special advisers with executive powers – like the number of special advisers generally – should be subject to parliamentary approval under a proposed Civil Service Act.

However, the appointments of both Mr Powell and Mr Campbell have caused controversy. There was lengthy wrangling, both before and after the general election, about Mr Powell's role within 10 Downing Street. David (Lord) Wolfson served as Chief of Staff in the early years of the Thatcher administration, but he was, in effect, a special/political adviser separate from the main private office. But Mr Powell immediately moved to the centre of the Downing Street operation, in the Private Secretary's office, and there were proposals to make him the Principal Private Secretary, then Alex Allan, who had extended his already long stay to cover the election. This idea was resisted by Sir Robin, not least because the Principal Private Secretary is the main channel of communication to both Buckingham Palace and to the Opposition parties, and also handles sensitive intelligence matters. The occupant of this post should therefore not be a party appointee. Eventually, a compromise was agreed whereby the title of Principal Private Secretary and these functions were taken by the other senior private secretary, at first John Holmes, the foreign affairs secretary, and then from 1998, Jeremy Heywood, after his promotion from being the private secretary handling economic affairs. In practice, these two worked closely alongside Mr Powell who was responsible for the overall management of 10 Downing Street.

Presentation

The appointment of a politically committed person as the Prime Minister's Official Spokesman is not new, and Mr Campbell's status as a special adviser has made little practical difference. After all, Joe Haines, who served Harold Wilson, was as fiercely partisan as Mr Campbell, while many of the civil servants who have been press spokesmen have in time become closely identified with the Prime Minister, if not their parties, and have left office with them, as Sir Bernard Ingham did in 1990. Mr Campbell has been controversial partly for his combative style, in time becoming the story rather than simply messenger, notably after he agreed to a fly-on-the-wall BBC documentary by Michael Cockerell. Mr Campbell took a prominent role in the Downing Street meetings leading up to the resignation of Peter Mandelson in January 2001, underlining the media-driven nature of the Government's working.

As significant has been Mr Campbell's shake-up of the government's media organisation. In Opposition, New Labour had run a tight media operation based at Millbank Tower with carefully co-ordinated themes and messages sent to spokesmen and MPs, reinforced by twenty-four hour rebuttal. Mr Campbell and his colleagues were shocked by what they saw as the amateurism of the existing set-up in Whitehall. The change of government led to the retirement, often unhappily, of a large number of long-serving heads of information in departments. There were several stories about poor relations with ministers. This involved a clash of cultures as well as of personalities. There were 'some bumpy moments', as Sir Robin Butler admitted in October 1997,[14] a couple of months before his retirement. Opposition spokesmen and advisers brought their habits of Opposition to Whitehall and many information officers were hostile or attached to their traditional ways. Many of the new heads of information were former journalists sympathetic to Labour who could easily have been special advisers rather than civil servants. It was hard to see any of them working for Conservative ministers.

An inquiry into the Government Information Service was set up, involving Mr Campbell. Chaired by Sir Robin Mountfield, Permanent Secretary at the Office of Public Service, the report recommended a far-reaching shake-up of the service. There was a lot of talk about 'raising its game' and the changes were linked with an attempt to centralise day-to-day control in Downing Street. The existing co-ordination function was hardening by new language in the post-election edition of the 'Ministerial Code', as 'Questions of Procedure for Ministers' was re-named. Its new paragraph 88 said:[15]

> In order to ensure the effective presentation of government policy, all major interviews and media appearances, both print and broadsheet, should be agreed with the Number 10 Press Office before any commitments are entered into. The policy content of all major speeches, press releases and new policy initiatives should be cleared in good time with the Number 10 Private Office; the timing and form of announcements should be cleared with the Number 10 Press Office. Each Department should keep a record of media contacts by both Ministers and Officials.

On the face of it, this paragraph amounted to 'the biggest centralisation of power seen in Whitehall in peacetime', as I argued at the time, August 1997,[16] with the punchy, and only slightly over-the-top, introduction 'Goodbye Cabinet Government. Welcome the Blair Presidency'. This new wording represented a step change from co-ordination by the centre to control by the centre. The Downing Street defence of the change was revealing: 'It is the strategic and message discipline we operated in Opposition as translated to government.' In the early months of the government's life, there was a sense of Big Brother looking over everyone's shoulder from Downing Street as contacts between ministers and journalists were reported to Number 10. That close monitoring, in time, predictably broke down under the pressure of events and the operations of a departmental system.

More significant, and permanent, was the creation, following the Mountfield report, of the Strategic Communications Unit within 10 Downing Street to plan longer-term communications and to write speeches and newspaper articles under the Prime Minister's name. This activity was so prolific that the Blair by-line appeared for a time more often than even the most active columnist. The initial head of the unit was a civil servant and its six strong staff included two former Labour supporting journalists. The unit also developed the Number 10 website and prepared the government's annual report which was first issued in July 1998. These reports have been widely criticised for being vacuous and for making unaudited assertions which would never have been acceptable in the report of a private sector company. The unit's activities have been different in scale from earlier Downing Street media operations and have frequently come near to, and sometimes crossed, the line between explaining the government's case and propaganda on behalf of New Labour. Later, a Research and Information Unit was established under Bill Bush, a former researcher from the BBC. These innovations are the clearest illustration of how the 'permanent campaign' has changed Downing Street. There was continual friction, particularly in the first two years, between senior civil servants and political appointees over the boundaries between government and party – reflecting both the inexperience of Whitehall of the New Labour team and their 'permanent campaign' style of operating.

Policy

If these changes attracted most attention, potentially more significant was the attempt to strengthen the direction of the government's strategy from the centre. The Downing Street Policy Unit was expanded from eight to a dozen under the direction of David Miliband, Blair's chief policy adviser in Opposition. While previously a mixture of civil servants and outsiders, the unit under Labour consisted mainly of special advisers, with only one or two exceptions from the civil service.

In addition, outside 10 Downing Street itself, the centre has been strengthened following a review carried out during the first half of 1998 by Sir Richard Wilson after he became Cabinet Secretary. Two of the most important innovations on the policy side were the creation in December 1997 of the Social Exclusion Unit (SEU) and, a year later, of the Performance and Innovation Unit (PIU). Their remit was to look at issues which cut across departmental boundaries and their work was similar to some of the studies carried out from 1970 until 1983 by the original think tank, the Central Policy Review Staff (CPRS). The SEU produced reports on, for example, homelessness, truancy, teenage pregnancy and neighbourhood renewal. A review of its operations in autumn 1999 concluded that there was a gap between analysis and implementation, and in the unit's relations with departments, reflecting the problems of co-ordinating new policies across Whitehall. The PIU – very much a son of the CPRS – looked at issues facing government and the public sector. Its reports covered electronic commerce, the implications of an ageing population, recovering the proceeds of crime, rural policy (fiercely resisted by the Ministry of Agriculture), adoption, the health, environmental and employment implications of trade policy. In an echo of the wide-ranging studies carried out by the CPRS in its early days under Lord Rothschild, one of the most interesting PIU reports discussed some of the big long-term strategic challenges facing government from demographic, technological, genetic, economic and political changes. But because of the sensitivity of some of the implications – for example on immigration – 10 Downing Street opposed publication of the full report and only a partial version appeared.

These units were staffed by civil servants and outsiders, and not by politically appointed special advisers. But members of the Policy Unit were closely involved in each of the projects, so the units, and reorganised Cabinet Office, became, in effect, part of Downing Street's attempt to drive forward change throughout Whitehall. Revealingly, when a vacancy occurred to head PIU, it was taken by Geoff Mulgan, a private member of the Downing Street Policy Unit. Moreover, within the Cabinet Office, first Peter Mandelson and, from July 1998, Lord Falconer of Thoroton, an old flatmate of Mr Blair's, acted as the Prime Minister's progress chasers, sorting out problems between departments. As ministers of state, they had far more influence than their nominal superiors in the Cabinet Office – David Clark, Jack Cunningham and Mo Mowlam. The last two of whom were widely, but misleadingly, described as the Cabinet 'enforcers'. Lord Falconer was an example also of Mr Blair's tendency to appoint Blairites as ministers in the Lords with real ministerial responsibilities, as opposed to their traditional role of mainly being just departmental spokesmen. Other examples of Lords ministers in policymaking positions were Baroness Jay, Leader of the Lords; Lord Williams of Mostyn, initially a Home Office minister and then Attorney General; Lord Macdonald of Tradeston on Transport; Baroness Symons, first at the Foreign Office then Defence; Baroness Blackstone at Higher Education; and Baroness Hayman, at Transport then Health and Agriculture.

The Cabinet

For all the talk about strengthening the centre, Mr Blair has been keen to avoid any suggestion that a Prime Minister's Department is being created – largely to avoid fuelling charges of presidentialism and in order to preserve the constitutional conventions of departmental responsibility and control. Of course, this is partly a matter of semantics. The distinction between a Prime Minister's Office and a Prime Minister's Department is artificial. There is no absolute line between the two. But successive Cabinet Secretaries from Lord Hunt of Tamworth in the 1970s to Sir Richard Wilson now, have been strongly opposed to crossing the line. This is both to avoid opening up broader constitutional questions about the balance

10474

between Downing Street and departments and to retain the politically neutral position of the Cabinet Office. The Number 10 operation is still small by comparison with the executive offices in presidential systems, such as the United States and Germany, and even in prime ministerial systems, such as Australia and Canada. But the changes introduced since June 1997 have significantly changed the scale and scope of the Downing Street operation, particularly in handling presentation and communications.

Tony Blair has used the levers of power in both traditional and novel ways – using informal as much as formal power. Cabinet meetings have seldom lasted longer than an hour and often much less. The agenda has been informal rather than the formal list of items of the past, on domestic, foreign and parliamentary business. Instead, Mr Blair has preferred to raise a topic of the moment, as well as to discuss forthcoming announcements and policy initiatives. That, as in other ways, reflected his style in Opposition when the Shadow Cabinet was downgraded and policy initiatives were decided jointly by him and Gordon Brown in conjunction with the relevant spokesman. This is not as radical a constitutional change as it appears since, as successive Cabinet Secretaries have pointed out, the role of the full Cabinet as a decision-making body has declined steadily over the past fifty years under Prime Ministers of both parties. As Lord Butler of Brockwell has pointed out, the Cabinet has reverted to its original eighteenth-century role of a weekly discussion among political friends. In Mr Blair's case, really important topics were usually discussed amongst a much smaller group of real friends and advisers.

The change in the role of the Cabinet has reflected the absence of a collegial style under Mr Blair. Senior ministers, even those counting themselves as New Labour, have privately complained about feeling on the outside and not part of a joint enterprise. For instance, after Mr Blair had over-ridden the hostility of many Cabinet members in summer 1997 by going ahead with the Dome, many ministers, including Chris Smith, the Culture Secretary, did not feel tied by collective responsibility in criticising the project when it ran into serious trouble in the summer of 2000.

The Cabinet committee system has remained in place, with a larger number of committees being set up, but its use has been patchy. As Lord Irvine of Lairg, the Lord Chancellor, has been fond of pointing out, the committees were used in a classic way to discuss and develop the legislation on devolution as part of the extensive constitutional reform programme. But these issues involved several departments whose interests had to be reconciled. Similarly, Mr Blair was scrupulous in working through the Defence and Overseas Policy Committee of the Cabinet during the military actions against Iraq in December 1998 and during the Kosovo conflict from March to June 1999. The full Cabinet was also kept informed in both these cases. The PSX public spending committee, chaired by Gordon Brown, has also cross-questioned departments during the comprehensive spending reviews – though as one Cabinet minister remarked, 'everyone knows that one only member of the committee really matters and that is Gordon'. Mr Brown has largely ignored the economic strategy committee, which he chairs.

On the wide range of other issues, however, Mr Blair has not used Cabinet committees and has either worked through ad hoc groups, like previous Prime Ministers have done, or bilaterally with relevant departmental ministers. Mr Blair has had a regular series of one-on-one sessions with secretaries of state to monitor annual work programmes, attended by the relevant members of the Policy Unit. Depending on the particular department, members of the unit have acted as the advance guard expressing the Prime Minister's views and working with Blairite ministers and advisers to advance a self-consciously modernising agenda. The phrase 'Tony wants' has become widely used in Whitehall as members of the unit and other advisers have used his name. Sometimes this has involved working with the Secretary of State, in other cases with rising middle-ranking or junior ministers. For instance, any discussion of the review of NHS policy over the 1999–2000 winter could not omit Robert Hill of the Policy Unit, working closely with Alan Milburn and his team at the Department of Health. Similarly, Andrew Adonis has been closely involved alongside David Blunkett and Estelle Morris, and Michael Barber, in the development of the government's policy on secondary schools, towards accepting greater diversity and breaking down the monopoly of local authority provision. David Miliband, the head of the unit, and Geoff Mulgan, before he became head of the Performance and Innovation Unit in September 2000, were closely involved in developing policies on social exclusion and poverty. Relations between the Policy Unit and departments have varied considerably. John Prescott was particularly prickly over the involvement of Geoff Norris in his department, especially over transport policy, and he made public complaints about Downing Street advisers.

Yet there is a limit to what even the most assiduous member of the Policy Unit is able to do, even in the name of the Prime Minister. There are several levels of involvement – first, what a Prime Minister himself sees and influences; second, what a member of the Policy Unit or private secretary can monitor; and, third, what happens in departments and among local authorities and other providers in the country. This is rather like a pyramid with fewer and fewer issues being considered the closer you get to the Blair study at the top.

Prime Ministerial Time

The key has been prime ministerial time, and energy. Mr Blair came to office saying he wanted to concentrate on the big picture and a few big issues: education, welfare reform (less in later years), health (more in later years), and improving relations with business and Europe. But he quickly found both how much of his time was occupied with unforeseen events (Iraq, Kosovo etc.) and also how demanding were both Europe and Northern Ireland. Kosovo turned out to be the longest single call on Mr Blair's time, and political capital. From late March until mid-June 1999, he concentrated on taking a leading role in pressing for tough action to force the Serbs out of Kosovo. He often faced criticism from European allies and, unusually, from the Clinton White House for his outspokenness, particularly over the use of ground troops.

European relations have proved to be the most consistently demanding item in his diary – not just what have become four summits of EU leaders a year (two in each half-yearly presidency), but also frequent one- or two-day trips to the main European capitals. Mr Blair has been keen to build alliances on particular issues, especially as Britain was outside the main European initiative of the post-1997 period, the launch of the euro in January 1999. He developed particularly close relations on economic reform with the Spanish and Portuguese Prime Ministers and sought to keep in close touch with the German Chancellor, French President and Prime Minister (especially following the surprise victory of Lionel Jospin within weeks of his own) and the various Italian Prime Ministers with regular visits.

Mr Blair came to office having said little about Northern Ireland but he soon committed himself to trying to relaunch the peace talks, leading up to the Good Friday Agreement of 1998. All Irish matters are very demanding. Leaders of the various groups want to deal with the Prime Minister personally and no conversation is ever short. Both John Major and Tony Blair talked in almost identical terms about how unexpectedly demanding these talks were – disproportionately so in relation to the level of public interest on the mainland of Britain or their electoral significance. As Mr Major discovered, few British political leaders benefit from even partial success in Northern Ireland. But Prime Ministers realise that Northern Ireland remains an important national interest which requires time because of its potential to go wrong and affect both security and international relations. The demands and frustrations of constantly dealing with Northern Ireland were one reason for the appointment of such a senior and trusted figure as Peter Mandelson as Northern Ireland Secretary in October 1999, to take some of the daily burden off Tony Blair.

From time to time, some domestic issues have become a major demand on Mr Blair, most unexpectedly and, for a few days, threateningly, the fuel protests of mid-September 2000. The government thought it had responded to concerns over fuel duties in the March 2000 Budget and, following the failure of boycotts in June/July, ministers were not inclined to take the threat of further direct action seriously. When the blockades at oil refineries by militant hauliers and farmers spread over the weekend of 9/10 September, Mr Blair was anyway distracted by the military operation to rescue British troops captured in Sierra Leone. Even on the following day, ministers were slow to respond, and they subsequently admitted[17] that they were at the mercy of events for at least another couple of days. Tony Blair himself appeared ineffective when he gave assurances at a Downing Street news conference on the Tuesday evening that oil would start moving again within twenty-four hours – and nothing much happened. This was a big, though partly temporary, blow to Mr Blair's prestige and, afterwards, both Mr Blair's advisers and senior civil servants acknowledged that the affair exposed serious shortcomings in the civil contingencies preparations. This inter-departmental machinery has been shown to work well in dealing with terrorism, hijackings and organised demonstrations, but was almost wholly unprepared for the type of semi-organised protests seen in September. This was partly because changes in the structure of the economy (just-in-time ordering and the disappearance of previous corporate hierarchies).

These events limited the amount of time Mr Blair could spend on day-to-day domestic issues, to his frequent frustration. Unlike Margaret Thatcher or even John Major, Mr Blair did not have an all-consuming interest in the details of policy. He has preferred to focus on a few big questions. But when necessary, in a way familiar from his days as a barrister, he could master a brief and be persuasive on the details in negotiations and meetings.

One of the main features of his Prime Ministership has been the deliberate linking of policy and presentation. This has not only been reflected in the establishment of the Strategic Communications Unit but also in day-to-day operations. Mr Blair has spent a good deal of time attending carefully staged visits to promote this or that government initiative. There is hardly a school, hospital or rundown council estate within a couple of miles of Downing Street – and hence within easy reach of television cameras – that has not had such a media event. Anji Hunter, one of his oldest friends and gatekeeper to the world outside Whitehall, has spent a lot of time organising such road-shows. All of which has taken up time which previous Prime Ministers would have spent in meetings or ministerial committees. That, and the smaller amount of time he has spent at Westminster, are the main differences from the way his predecessors have spent their days as Prime Minister.

Ministers and civil servants report that whenever a difficult issue comes up, presentation is always considered. Alastair Campbell is much more than just a spokesman. That is why comparisons of his role to Sir Bernard Ingham's are misleading. Sir Bernard was always the interpreter of His Mistress's voice to the outside world, but he was outside her inner circle. He did not attend meetings of the Cabinet or join her inner circle for late night whiskys in the Downing Street flat. Sir Bernard was always below stairs, while Mr Campbell is definitely above stairs. He is part of the inner circle, advising on strategy as well as its presentation. His influence – in conjunction with Anji Hunter – was seen particularly in handling relations with Buckingham Palace after the death of Diana, Princess of Wales and then in advising on the overhaul of the Nato media operation during the Kosovo conflict, as related in Rawnsley, 2000.[18]

Bilateral or Trilateral?

However, even this qualified picture of Prime Ministerial leadership sees Whitehall too much in terms of who goes in and out of the door of 10 Downing Street. While there is no longer collective decision making, and has not been for a long time, a simple presidential model does not fit either, except perhaps in handling of presentation. A better description is bilateral with 10 Downing Street and the Treasury, on the one side, and departments on the other. He gradually discovered, however, how hard it is to implement change. A Prime Minister may say what he wants, and he can make a difference on a few important issues. But departments remain in charge of implementation and details and they, in turn, are dependent on attitudes on the ground. Mr Blair has admitted[19] that the main lessons he has learnt in office have been about the difficulties of achieving change in the public sector and how to use the civil service machine. This has been a mutual process of education as senior civil servants have had to learn how to cope with the 'permanent campaign' style of New Labour.

Mr Blair and his advisers in time recognised that they had to go beyond their initial cautious policies – typified by the five pre-election pledges – and adopt more radical approaches, particularly to education and health. Having dubbed 1999 'the year of delivery', the government had to deal with the public's belief that standards had not improved. One of Mr Blair's most frequent complaints, particularly from 1999 onwards, has been about the difficulty of delivering change. He caused controversy by making an off-the-cuff remark in a speech in July 1999 about the 'scars' on his back from trying to achieve in the public services in the face of conservatism in the public sector. Mr Blair was often torn between bemoaning obstructive attitudes in the public sector and needing to enlist the support of demoralised teachers, nurses, doctors and policemen.

The real power relationships have been more trilateral than bilateral since the Treasury has usually been involved as a central player. Mr Brown has deliberately taken on the role of overlord over a wide range of domestic policy, particularly welfare reform. This has gone beyond the usual Treasury interest in all policies involving spending. Mr Brown has also taken a leading role in the design of the whole New Deal welfare-to-work programme and over changes in pensions policy. The Treasury was also worried about Sir Richard Wilson's review of the 'centre' in the first half of 1998, particularly about suggestions that a strengthened centre concentrated on Downing Street and the Cabinet Office would have a wide remit over domestic policy. The Treasury sought to strengthen its influence over domestic policy, both via Mr Brown's personal involvement and via the introduction of public service agreements in the first comprehensive spending review of 1998. This gave the Treasury an explicit role in agreeing a series of performance targets with departments in exchange for the provision of more money.

Reflecting their close long-term relationship, Mr Blair has, in practice, accepted the supremacy of Mr Brown on economic policy. Officials initially found it hard to penetrate the frequent Blair/Brown relationship and it was only after the arrival of Jeremy Heywood that a record was kept of their discussions. Mr Heywood, and David Miliband, head of the Downing Street Policy Unit, were closely involved in the two comprehensive spending reviews in 1998 and 2000, working with Ed Balls, Mr Brown's chief adviser. But Downing Street advisers were often excluded from discussion of other matters, particularly taxation. The Treasury's near contempt for 10 Downing Street's involvement in these matters is a consistent theme of Geoffrey Robinson's memoirs.[20] The rivalry between 10 Downing Street and the Treasury has been a constant theme of the Blair government. The recurrent stories in various books about the feuding at the top of New Labour has had a cumulative debilitating effect. The picture painted by Andrew Rawnsley in his widely noticed book of October 2000[21] may be over-the-top in detail, and in some of the specific quotations, but vividly conveys the dysfunctional and corrosive relationships at the top of the government, with mutual suspicion and tensions, particularly between Gordon Brown and Peter Mandelson, and their advisers. Tony Blair has often had to placate the two other members of the mutually dependent triangle.

So far from being a dominant presidential figure, Mr Blair emerges as a more cautious leader – sharing power with his Chancellor on many issues, keen to set a broad strategic direction except when his personal involvement is needed, reluctant to take risks, and frustrated by the difficulties of achieving change. To the disappointment of some of his early supporters on the centre left, notably Lord Jenkins of Hillhead, Mr Blair was very cautious over entry to the euro and about proportional representation. On the former, his private view was that the priority for a first term should be to prove that Labour could again be a competent government, notably in managing the economy, and put itself in a position to win a second full term. So the euro was seen as just too big a gamble for a first term. Mr Blair's caution was reinforced by his desire not to alienate some of his press supporters and by his anxiety about winning the promised referendum in face of the hostility of a large section of the press. His critics saw this as a missed opportunity since they believed that a referendum on euro entry could easily have been won within a year of the 1997 election. In February 2001, he promised an assessment within two years of an election. Second, after setting up an independent commission to examine the voting system under Lord Jenkins, he gave a guarded reception to its report in autumn 1998 and was reluctant to have a confrontation with many members of his Cabinet who opposed closer links with the Liberal Democrats and PR.

The two significant exceptions to this risk averse approach have been Northern Ireland and Kosovo. In the latter case, Mr Blair took a considerable risk – notably to Britain's relations with other countries – and was fortunate that Serbian troops were withdrawn from Kosovo before a decision had to be taken on deploying ground troops in a combat role. What was striking about Kosovo was that the episode seemed almost out of character, though was partly explained by his moralistic view of some international issues.

A Beleaguered Centre?

Mr Blair has been stronger on values and images than detailed policies – with little interest in process compared with results. Mr Blair was, for instance, hardly involved in the civil service reforms launched by Sir Richard Wilson. He approved what Sir Richard was doing and gave his nod to the detailed plans after an hour long session in Downing Street in late 1999. After Sir Richard and his fellow permanent secretaries had made their presentation, he turned to Lord Simon of Highbury, who, by then, had left the government, but had become a roving adviser on modernising government. He asked Lord Simon his opinion as a former chairman of BP about how the proposals looked from a private sector perspective. He duly approved and that was enough for Mr Blair.[22] Mr Blair was a sceptic about shifting departmental responsibilities around Whitehall, believing that the possible benefits were generally not worth the costs and upheavals involved in any changes in Whitehall. The picture is not of an all-powerful centre, but of an often beleaguered and isolated Prime Minister. That was underlined by the government's apparent impotence in face not only of the fuel protests of September 2000 but also of the floods and severe rail disruption of October and November 2000. The fuel protests exposed the weaknesses of Whitehall's preparations for civil contingencies, with the centre struggling to cope with a fragmented fuel distribution system.

Philip Gould, the Blairites' campaign adviser, complained in the 1999 paperback edition of his revealingly titled *The Unfinished Revolution*[23] that:

> The centre actually has far less power than is typically ascribed to it. Anyone who spends any time at Number 10 quickly realises that it is a tiny corner of a huge government machine, staffed with talented people but lacking the resources necessary to be a commanding and dominating nerve centre. The idea that officials at Number 10 headquarters are smoothly pulling strings and levers, effortlessly controlling events, is ridiculous.

That image would be familiar to many former Prime Ministers and their private office staff and advisers. In that sense, Mr Blair's changes to the Downing Street operation seem less significant than his use of informal power which has varied since 1997, depending on circumstance. Indeed, when the government ran into political trouble in the first half of 2000, the institutional changes, such as the Strategic Communications Unit and the expanded resources on presentation, made no difference. What mattered was that Mr Blair was less successful in the use of informal power. He was less respected, and had lost the authority and confidence of voters. That was epitomised by the heckling and slow handclap he faced from some members of the Women's Institute when he made an ill-judged speech to them in June 2000. The limits on the exercise of his power were brought out in a series of leaked memos from Philip Gould[24] which reported on how the New Labour brand had been 'badly contaminated' and the sense that the government had been drifting, undermining Mr Blair's authority. One of the Gould memos said that his research showed that 'TB is not believed to be real. He lacks conviction; he is all spin and presentation; he says things to please people, not because he believes them.'

The constraints on Prime Ministerial power have become more apparent over time. That has raised two key questions: how long the Blairite vanguard can maintain its coherence and the drawbacks of the bilateral/trilateral style of decision making? The inner group of advisers around Mr Blair has been largely constant since 1994. Mr Blair has relied heavily on a small inner circle of advisers (Alastair Campbell, Jonathan Powell, David Miliband and Anji Hunter), and close political allies (notably Gordon Brown), as well as his immediate staff of private secretaries (notably Jeremy Heywood). These have been supplemented by longstanding friends who have become ministers, especially Lord Irvine of Lairg and Lord Falconer of Thoroton. Some other successful ministers, such as David Blunkett and Jack Straw, have had Mr Blair's ear, and, via Anji Hunter, he has kept contacts with a fluctuating group of outsiders – in business, religion, journalism etc. But the cast list has hardly changed since 1997. However, will the Blair team be able to renew itself in a second term or will, over time, Mr Blair's radicalism lose its edge? The resignation of Peter Mandelson in January 2001 broke up the original partnership that created New Labour and left Mr Blair looking an increasingly isolated standard bearer of Blairism. Second, the problem about Mr Blair's style of running his government is less the absence of collective decision making than the lack of any sense of collective involvement in what happens. There is little sense of a joint enterprise and more of a distance from Mr Blair. That could mean that when troubles arrive, as they did during 2000, Mr Blair is on his own. One of the virtues of a more collective approach is as a form of political insurance, to tie ministerial colleagues in more. As his premiership developed, Mr Blair showed few signs of wanting to adopt a more collective style. He was more concerned with improving the links between decision making and implementation, to ensure Whitehall was more responsive.

If the Blair premiership is seen in time as different from previous ones, it will be more through his personal exercise of power rather than because he has changed the way that Downing Street operates. The changes that have been introduced – the greater number of special advisers, the expansion of the Policy Unit and the strengthening of the Cabinet Office – are unlikely to be jettisoned, though a later Prime Minister may be less interested in retaining the more symbolically contentious Strategic Communications Unit. If Mr Blair has been a Napoleonic figure, he has been a frustrated rather than a commanding one. The Downing Street he leaves to his successor will be much less changed than France was after Napoleon.

Notes

1 Peter Hennessy *The Prime Minister – the Office and Its Holders Since 1945*, 2000, chapter 18.
2 Peter Hennessy *The Hidden Wiring*, 1995, chapter 3.
3 Sir Richard Wilson, evidence to Public Administration Committee, 16 June 1998, in *The Government Information and Communication Service*, House of Commons Paper 770.
4 Information from Downing Street.
5 Paddy Ashdown *The Ashdown Diaries. Volume One 1988–97*, 2000.
6 Dennis Kavanagh and Anthony Seldon *Powers Behind the Prime Minister*, 1999, p. 245.
7 Vividly brought out in Paul Routledge *Mandy* (1999); Donald Macintyre *Mandelson* (1999); Andrew Rawnsley *Servants of the People* (2000) and Geoffrey Robinson *The Unconventional Minister* (2000).
8 Initially reported by Hennessy who chaired the meeting (2000) with Powell's identity by Rawnsley, 2000, p. 27.
9 Peter Mandelson and Roger Liddle *The Blair Revolution: Can New Labour Deliver?* 1996, p. 235.
10 Peter Riddell, 'How will Blair play it?' *The Times*, 20 May 1996.
11 Committee on Standards in Public Life *Reinforcing Standards*, Sixth Report, Command 4557–1, 2000, chapter six, paragraph 6.35.
12 Ibid., paragraph 6.36.
13 Ibid., paragraph 6.57.
14 Sir Robin Butler, interview in *The Times*, 29 October 1997.
15 Ministerial Code, July 1997, paragraph 88.
16 Peter Riddell, 'Tories should focus on what really matters', *The Times*, 1 August 1997.
17 Information from Downing Street.
18 Rawnsley, 2000, chapters 4 and 14.
19 Information from Downing Street.
20 Robinson, 2000.
21 Rawnsley, 2000.
22 Peter Riddell, 'Politics has a proper place in Whitehall', *The Times*, 16 December 1999.
23 Philip Gould *The Unfinished Revolution*, p. xxiii.
24 Gould memos as reported in *The Times*, 19 July 2000, and *Sunday Times*, 12 June 2000.

Chapter 3

PARLIAMENT

Philip Norton

THE PERCEPTION OF a Parliament in 'decline' has been a feature of much literature on British politics since the late nineteenth and early twentieth centuries. Though the existence of a 'golden age' of Parliament has been disputed, there have been repeated claims that Parliament is not as strong as it could and should be in questioning government and forcing it to answer for its actions. The period since the 1960s has seen demands for reform of parliamentary structures and procedures in order to strengthen Parliament as an institution capable of scrutinising and influencing government. Some changes to procedures were made in the 1966–70 Parliament when Richard Crossman was Leader of the House of Commons. The most significant reform of the last half of the twentieth century occurred in 1979, when the House approved the establishment of a series of select committees 'to examine the expenditure, administration and policy in the principal government departments . . . and associated public bodies'. The reform was only one of several agreed in the 1979–83 Parliament. Pressure for further change continued. In 1992 the Hansard Society published proposals for radical reform of the way in which Parliament scrutinised legislation. In late 1994, the House approved recommendations from a Select Committee on the Sittings of the House for some changes in the sitting hours of the House and in the way in which business was conducted. The effect of these changes varied but, in combination, they failed to change significantly the relationship between the executive and Parliament.

The period since the 1960s also witnessed a change in behaviour. In the quarter century after 1945, party cohesion was a marked feature of parliamentary life. MPs voted loyally with their parties. The distinguished American observer of British politics, Samuel H. Beer, argued that since voting cohesion was so close to one hundred per cent on both sides of the

House, there was little point in measuring it. There were actually two parliamentary sessions in the 1950s when not one Conservative MP cast a dissenting vote against the whips. The situation changed markedly in the 1970s. Conservative back-benchers voted against their own side on more occasions than before, in greater numbers and with more effect.[1] For the first time in post-war history, a government was defeated in the division lobbies of the House of Commons because of cross-voting by some of its own supporters. Increased levels of cross-voting by government back-benchers were experienced by the Labour government of 1974–79. The minority Labour government suffered forty-two defeats in the Parliament, twenty-three of them because Labour MPs voted in the Opposition lobby.[2]

Most of the period of Conservative government from 1979 to 1997 saw a government with a sizeable overall parliamentary majority, especially in the period from 1983 to 1992. Though cross-voting by Conservative MPs continued, the size of the government's majority was sufficient to absorb almost, though not quite all, occasions of cross-voting by dissident back-benchers. The situation was to change in the 1992–97 Parliament, when the Conservative government of John Major faced serious dissension by back-benchers in a Parliament in which the government had a small and, at times, non-existent overall majority. The party was badly divided on the issue of European integration and suffered a number of high-profile defeats in the House of Commons on the issue, notably on the Maastricht treaty in 1993 and VAT on fuel in 1994. There was a perception of a party in disarray, badly divided and being held hostage by dissident back-benchers and by Ulster Unionist MPs (supporting the government in return for concessions on policy affecting Northern Ireland). The perception was, in many respects, exaggerated. The parliamentary Conservative party was divided on fewer issues than the parliamentary Labour party (PLP) and the defeats it suffered were remarkable for their scarcity rather than their extent, especially when compared with the period of Conservative government from 1970 to 1974. The perception, though, was important. The government appeared badly divided and in the eyes of many critics – including on the government back-benches – drifting. It gave the impression, in Norman Lamont's memorable phrase, of being in office but not in power.

By 1997, Parliament appeared in need of reform. Television cameras had been allowed to record proceedings in the House of Commons since 1989. What viewers saw reinforced the impression of a body with archaic and inefficient procedures and a membership that was rowdy and partisan. The cameras recorded Conservative back-benchers attacking their own government. Parliament appeared to be failing in doing its job. The government appeared unable to govern effectively.

The reputation of the House of Commons was also undermined by allegations of misconduct by ministers and MPs. The issue became a prominent political issue in 1994 following claims of MPs being willing to accept cash in return for tabling parliamentary questions. Two MPs were briefly suspended from the service of the House; two ministers left their posts. The Prime Minister, John Major, established the Committee on Standards in Public Life, chaired by a judge, Lord Nolan, and in 1995, after some acrimonious debates, the House of Commons approved various recommendations from the Committee on the regulation of Members' conduct. Investigations of misconduct by MPs continued to attract the headlines, including in the run-up to, and during, the 1997 general election campaign. The campaign in the constituency of Tatton, defended by one of the Conservative MPs caught up in allegations of 'sleaze', drew the attention of the national media.

By 1997, Parliament was the subject of calls from some MPs, journalists and academics to reform its practices and procedures to make it a more effective body of scrutiny and influence. For some, changes within the institution would not be enough to make a difference: they wanted radical constitutional change. The issue of 'sleaze' undermined the standing of Parliament. There was a general recognition, at both mass and elite level, that Parliament was not performing well. In the 1991 MORI State of the Nation poll, fifty-eight per cent of those questioned thought that Parliament worked 'very well' or 'fairly well', against sixteen per cent who thought it worked 'fairly badly' or 'very badly'. In the 1995 State of the Nation poll, forty-three per cent thought it worked very or fairly well, against thirty per cent who thought it worked fairly or very badly. Though it would be an exaggeration to claim that there was a crisis of Parliament, the institution was under pressure to change.

How, then, has Parliament changed under the Blair government? The changes, and explanations for change, can be considered under two heads: reform and behaviour. The first encompasses changes to the structures, practices and procedures of the institution. The second considers changes in the behaviour of members.

Reform

The need for some reform of Parliament has been conceded by the main political parties in succeeding general elections. All three parties committed themselves to some reform in their 1992 manifestos. They did so again in their 1997 manifestos. The 1997 Conservative manifesto declared that 'We have . . . already done much to improve the way Parliament works and will do more'. There was an emphasis on the publication of bills in draft to allow for more parliamentary scrutiny. The Liberal Democrats asserted that they would modernise the House of Commons by improving drafting and consultation on legislation, reduce the number of MPs and introduce tougher rules for conduct. They would 'strengthen MPs' ability to hold the government to account'. The manifesto also advocated reform of the House of Lords, with a two-Parliament programme of reform designed to produce a predominantly-elected second chamber. However, neither party was to have the opportunity to implement their proposals. Labour, as the 'out' party for eighteen years, now had the opportunity to implement reform proposals and to show that what may be attractive to a party in Opposition – a more critical House of Commons – could prove acceptable to a party in government. The Labour manifesto in 1997 attacked the Conservative government for appearing 'opposed to the very idea of democracy'. 'There is,' it declared, 'unquestionably a crisis of confidence in our political system, to which Labour will respond in a measured and sensible way.' This 'measured' response included parliamentary reform. The House of Lords was to be subject to major change:

> As an initial, self-contained reform, not dependent on further reform in the future, the right of hereditary peers to sit and vote in the House of Lords will be ended by statue. This will be the first stage in a process of reform to make the House of Lords more democratic and representative.

A committee of both Houses would be appointed to undertake 'a wide-ranging review of possible further change and then to bring forward proposals for reform'.

The section on 'A modern House of Lords' was followed by one on 'An effective House of Commons'. It declared that 'the House of Commons is in need of modernisation' and said that a Labour government would ask the House of Commons to establish a special select committee to review its procedures:

> Prime Minister's Questions will be made more effective. Ministerial accountability will be reviewed so as to remove recent abuses. The process for scrutinising European legislation will be overhauled.

After three sessions, the government could make some claim to have carried out much of what it promised. The House of Lords Act 1999 removed all but ninety-two hereditary peers from membership of the House of Lords. The bill dominated the second session of Parliament and the government accepted the 'Weatherill amendment', retaining ninety-two hereditary members, in order to facilitate its passage and to prevent the Lords blocking other bills in protest. The government also appointed a Royal Commission on Reform of the House of Lords, under the Conservative peer Lord Wakeham, a former Leader of the House of Commons and of the House of Lords, to make recommendations for the second stage of Lords reform. The Commission was asked to complete its work by the end of 1999 and, to the surprise of many, managed to keep to its tight timetable, delivering its report to the Queen on 28 December 1999. The report, *A House for the Future* (Cm 4534), was published the following month. It made 132 wide-ranging proposals on the recruitment of peers and changes to the procedures of the House. It recommended a part-elected House of approximately 550 members, offering three options for the number to be elected – sixty-five, eighty-seven or 195 – the preferred option being eighty-seven. The Leader of the House of Lords, Baroness Jay, announced on 7 March 2000 that the government was minded to accept 'the broad outlines' of the report.

In the House of Commons, the Prime Minister decided to answer questions during one thirty-minute slot each week instead of two fifteen-minute sessions. This took effect on Wednesday, 21 May 1997. The House moved quickly to appoint a Select Committee on the Modernisation of the House of Commons. Established on 4 June 1997, its remit was 'to consider how the practices and procedures of the House should be modernised, and to make recommendations thereon'. It was charged with making a first report to the House before the summer adjournment on ways in which 'the procedure for examining legislation could be improved'. The Committee duly obliged and the following month, on 29 July, published its report, *The Legislative Process*. The report included a memorandum submitted by its chairman, the Leader of the House, Ann Taylor. 'For all its strengths, the House of Commons is not as effective as it might be,' she wrote. '[I]n the Government's view the time has come to draw the threads together and embark on a significant programme of change.' The Committee recommended a range of reforms, most to be tried on an experimental basis. These included programming the passage of legislation, greater pre-legislative scrutiny and consultation, and provision for some bills to carry over from one session to another.

The Committee proceeded to publish reports on other aspects of reform. Within a year of its appointment, seven reports had been published. By the summer recess 2000, it had published a total of twelve substantive reports. Among the more substantial were those on the scrutiny of European business, the creation of a parallel chamber, and conduct in the chamber. Not all were debated, but when the recommendations of various reports were placed before the House, they were agreed. As a consequence, various changes in legislative scrutiny were made. The Financial Services and Markets Bill was the first bill of the Parliament to be carried over from one session to another. The Grand Committee Room off Westminster Hall was converted into a mini, or parallel, chamber to discuss issues not involving votes: known as 'sittings in Westminster Hall', the sessions allowed matters for which there was little or no time in the chamber to be considered. There were changes to procedure in the chamber. The wearing of a collapsible opera hat to raise points of order during a division was no longer required. The order paper was made more comprehensible. The procedures for scrutinising European documents were strengthened, with scrutiny extended to the second and third pillars of the European Union.

Taken together, the changes suggested that much progress had been made by the government in implementing its manifesto pledges. In a debate on relations between Parliament and the executive on 13 July 2000, the Prime Minister listed the changes that had been made. 'We have taken major steps,' he declared, 'to modernise the other place and to improve the ways in which the House can work.'[3] The government, he indicated, would be willing to consider other proposals for improvement. The Leader of the House, Margaret Beckett, made similar points in her winding-up speech. The government could claim that it had reformed Parliament in line with its vision of modernising the constitution.

However, when put in a wider political context, the changes appeared limited and failed to change significantly the relationship between the legislature and the executive. There was a perception, not confined to the Opposition, that Parliament had, if anything, been further marginalised. 'The Blair government,' declared Peter Riddell, 'has neglected Parliament.'[4] Far from correcting the problems identified in its 1997 manifesto, the government had, if anything, exacerbated them. In the spring of 2000, the Speaker, Betty Boothroyd, wrote to the Cabinet Secretary, Sir Richard Wilson, and to the Leader of the House of Commons, Margaret Beckett, complaining that ministers and civil servants had by-passed the House of Commons. The Cabinet Secretary set up special training for staff in units that had regular dealings with Parliament 'to deal with the main rubbing points'. The Leader of the House sent a memo to her Cabinet colleagues:

> Repeated complaints from both members and the Speaker, where they are unfortunately justified, lend unnecessary credence to the Opposition's generalised complaints that the Government is treating Parliament with contempt.[5]

The Liaison Committee of the House of Commons, comprising principally the chairmen of select committees, issued a report in March 2000, entitled *Shifting the Balance: Select Committees and the Executive*. Though arguing that departmental select committees had been a success, it conceded that 'it is time for some further reform and modernisation'.[6] It made several recommendations for strengthening select committees, including creating an alternative career to that of ministerial office for select committee chairmen. The government issued a fairly brusque response, essentially dismissing the committee's recommendations. The committee responded by summoning the Leader of the House to appear before it to give evidence, the first time that the committee had decided to take evidence. The public session took place on 10 July 2000, Margaret Beckett adopting a stonewalling position in the face of critical questioning from the committee. Her most critical questioner was Labour MP Gwyneth Dunwoody. In the light of the minister's performance, the committee decided to issue a special report. The government's response, it declared, was 'both disappointing and surprising'.

We found it disappointing because our proposals were modest . . . And
we found it surprising that a Government which has made so much of
its policy of modernising Parliament should apparently take so
different a view when its own accountability and freedom of action
are at issue.[7]

The committee provided a detailed response to the main proposals in its
report. It rebutted the arguments advanced by the government, doing so in
fairly robust terms. In so doing, it drew attention (p. xiv) to continuing dissatisfaction with the way present procedures were operating.

In its Reply, the Government says that the present means of selecting
Members to serve on Select Committees 'have stood the test of time'.
This is not so. There is widespread disquiet, both amongst Members
and outside the House, about a system which is not open, and which
is not clearly independent of the Government and the party managers.
Those being scrutinised should not have a say in the selection of the
scrutineers. We believe that the present system does not, and should
not, have the confidence of the House and the public.

Criticism of the government's approach to Parliament was also voiced by a
number of Labour back-benchers. When the government brought forward
a timetable motion in November 2000 to limit debate on motions to provide for the timetabling of bills and for some votes to be held over until the
following Wednesday, some Labour MPs expressed their discontent. Ian
Pearson, the Member for Dudley South, rose to express his opposition:

I was not put here to have an easy job; I was put here to scrutinise the
Government, and I believe in doing that. It is imprudent for the
Government to timetable a motion on a fundamental change to my
terms and conditions of employment that will make life easier for the
Government and for back-benchers, but which will produce a result
which is far worse for democracy.[8]

Overall, the 'Blair effect' on Parliament appeared to have been to weaken
rather than strengthen it. Parliament did not suddenly become a marginal
institution on 2 May 1997. It had difficulty in calling government to
account before 1997. However, the institution has been further weakened
during the Blair premiership. There are four variously inter-linking explanations for this development.

Uncertainty of purpose

The commitment to modernise the House of Commons was part of
Labour's wider theme of modernisation. 'We have modernised the Labour

Party and we will modernise Britain', declared Tony Blair in the introduction to the 1997 manifesto. The theme was reflected in the title of the Select Committee on Modernisation. However, the term itself is a broad one, dictating no clear approach to parliamentary reform. In 1999, William Hague established a Commission to Strengthen Parliament. (I chaired the Commission.) In its report published in July 2000, the Commission drew attention to the fact parliamentary reform may be enacted for different purposes. It may be carried out to expedite the passage of government business. It may be enacted in order to get rid of cumbersome or archaic procedures. It may be introduced for the convenience of Members. Or it may be introduced in order to strengthen Parliament in calling government to account.[9] These purposes are not mutually exclusive nor are they mutually compatible. The term 'modernisation' may be taken to encompass all of them. As such, it covers everything and consequently means nothing. It left it open to the Select Committee on Modernisation to roam widely, and it did so. It looked at ways that the House could be strengthened in scrutinising government legislation. It looked at ways of getting rid of procedures that no longer served any great purpose. It looked at ways of making the House more family-friendly. In so doing, it lacked a clear focus and, in the view of some, failed to give priority to any one purpose. The point was made both by the Liaison Committee and by Speaker Betty Boothroyd in her farewell address to MPs. In its report in July 2000, the Liaison Committee concluded (p. xxv) with the words:

> There has been much discussion about shorter sitting hours, and more family-friendly scheduling of business in the House. This may be all very well; but any real modernisation of Parliament must provide better accountability and tougher scrutiny of the Government of the day. This is our aim. We believe it is the test by which the public will judge the effectiveness and value of Parliament. This is not something that will go away.

And addressing MPs on 26 July 2000, Betty Boothroyd declared:

> Let us start by remembering that the function of Parliament is to hold the Executive to account . . . It is the core task of Members . . . Furthermore, the House must be prepared to put in the hours necessary to carry out effective examination of the Government's legislative programme. If that means long days, or rearrangement of the parliamentary year, so be it. Of course, I have been here long enough to recognise the importance of enabling parliamentarians to enjoy a domestic life; it should not be impossible to meet both objectives – but where there is a clash, the requirements of effective scrutiny and the democratic process must take priority over the convenience of Members.[10]

The failure to focus on strengthening Parliament in calling government to account can be attributed in part to the emphasis on the nebulous concept of modernisation. It may also be ascribed to conflicting pressures within the parliamentary Labour party and the government. The PLP witnessed an unprecedented influx of new Members, including a record number of women. There was pressure from many new Labour MPs for the House to sit earlier and to have more Member-friendly procedures. One bone of contention for some MPs was the method of voting, trooping through the division lobbies in order to vote on a motion. Some pushed for a move away from the present system in favour of electronic voting. This was one of the issues that was explored by the Modernisation Committee. In its sixth report published in June 1998, it reported the results of a survey of MPs. Of those who responded, just over half (53 per cent) opted to retain the present system. However, of those Members first elected in 1997, only 33 per cent favoured the status quo. In July 2000, the Modernisation Committee published a report, *Programming of Legislation and Timing of Votes*, advocating that certain votes after 10.00 p.m. (as on statutory instruments) be held over to the following day, a proposal very much for the convenience of MPs but, in the view of opponents, one that would help government get its measures. The report, according to one former member of the committee, was 'in response to determined pressure from Labour back-benchers, and perhaps from some Conservative and Liberal Democrat back-benchers'. The MP, Dr Phyllis Starkey, went on:

> Although I welcome the report, as a back-bencher I do not think it has gone far enough, and I for one will continue to keep up the pressure on the Modernisation Committee to modernise with rather more will and effectiveness than it has shown already.[11]

These pressures from MPs ensured that the Modernisation Committee covered several areas. It was not able to focus on strengthening Parliament in calling government to account. However desirable the disparate changes that were recommended and implemented, the approach taken by the Modernisation Committee lacked coherence.

Need to get its business

Any government needs to get its measures approved by Parliament. The job of the Chief Whip is to help the government get its business. The Blair government was notable, but hardly unique, in being keen to ensure that it got its business as expeditiously as possible. (The Conservative government under Edward Heath in 1970–74 had been equally keen to get its measures through.) What made it distinctive was the combination of its parliamentary majority and the person appointed as Chief Whip in May 1997. The size of the majority was significant because it meant that it could absorb significant defections without jeopardising the capacity of the government to win. Any government with an overall majority will usually get its measures. For most of the time, the size of the overall majority is irrelevant: the government will win. It matters only in exceptional circumstances. An overall majority of 179 meant that the Blair government was not likely to face exceptional circumstances.

In forming his government, Tony Blair appointed Nick Brown as Government Chief Whip. Brown had spent two years as Deputy Chief Whip in Opposition. As Chief Whip in government, he acquired a reputation for firmness. This encompassed also his relationship with the Leader of the House of Commons, Ann Taylor.

MPs of the governing party have dual and not necessarily compatible roles. They are elected to support and to sustain their party in government. As members of the House of Commons, they are members of an institution that is meant to question and if necessary say no to the very body they are elected to support and sustain. There is thus an inherent conflict, one that is usually resolved in favour of the party. The Chief Whip and Leader of the House of Commons are both members of the government but with somewhat different roles. The Chief Whip is concerned principally with the party aspect of getting the government's business. The Leader of the House, in many respects, embodies the dual role of the back-bench MP. She is a government minister, with a responsibility for defending the government and organising business in such a way that the government gets its measures. At the same time, she has a responsibility to the whole House, representing the views of the House (not just the government side) to government as well as of the government to the House.

In the first year of the Labour government, there was an apparent clash between Nick Brown and Ann Taylor. Brown was determined to get the government's business through as expeditiously as possible. He was oriented, in short, to the executive and not the legislature. Ann Taylor had been Shadow Leader of the House in the previous Parliament and had worked with the Conservative Leader of the House, Tony Newton, to achieve changes in procedure. The changes had been agreed, though only after the Labour Whips' Office under Derek Foster had agreed to withdraw its opposition to implementing the proposals of the Select Committee on the Sittings of the House. Taylor had shown some understanding of the need to reform procedures in order to ensure that the House of Commons was more effective in calling government to account. When she became Leader of the House, she worked with the Shadow Leader, Gillian Shephard, in order to try to reach a consensus within the Modernisation Committee.

Taylor favoured some changes that would strengthen the House of Commons in scrutinising government. As the government introduced the measures it had promised in its manifesto, ministers became less interested in seeing procedural changes implemented. For Brown, the priority was to ensure that Labour MPs voted through the government's bills and did not cause too much trouble. He exhibited what was described as an 'air of quiet menace . . . in order to keep Labour MPs in line during crucial Commons votes'.[12] He was reportedly not enamoured of attempts to strengthen the House in any way that might threaten the government's position. A consequence of the clash between the Leader of the House and the Chief Whip was that there were no coherent proposals to strengthen the House of Commons in calling government to account.

In 1998, Nick Brown ceased to be Chief Whip and was replaced by Ann Taylor. Taylor was replaced as Leader of the House by Margaret Beckett, who moved from her post as Trade and Industry Secretary. Taylor thus assumed Brown's responsibility for ensuring that government got its business. Her replacement was not an advocate of reform and, during her tenure of the office, the Modernisation Committee produced its report advocating holding votes over to the following day, viewed by the Opposition as an executive-oriented approach. As we have seen, Beckett also took a negative view of the Liaison Committee report advocating reform to the departmental select committees. In November 2000, she brought motions before the House to give effect to deferred voting and also to the programming of bills. The same week she led for the government in a debate on the Liaison Committee's report. She attracted criticism for the fact that the report was being debated on an adjournment motion, denying MPs an opportunity to vote on the Committee's recommendations. Beckett refused to give an assurance that there would be an opportunity to vote on the recommendations. The two debates, which occurred in the same week, showed clearly that there was no longer any pressure from within government favouring significant reform.

The need to get its business also provides an explanation for the government's approach to reform of the second chamber. It was opposed to hereditary peers serving in the House of Lords. It thus proposed legislation that was directed at the composition of the second chamber. The government showed little enthusiasm for changing, certainly not for increasing, the powers of the second chamber. It moved in the second session to implement its commitment to the 'self-contained' reform, removing hereditary peers from membership. It showed little motivation to move quickly, if at all, to the expected 'stage two' of reform. It was put under pressure by the Opposition, especially the Opposition leader in the Lords, Lord Cranborne, to say what it planned to do, and under pressure from the Opposition announced the creation of the Royal Commission. The Commission was not a manifesto commitment. The Labour Party submission to the Commission reflected Labour's lack of enthusiasm for an elected second chamber, one that could claim the legitimacy of election to challenge the first chamber. After the Royal Commission reported, the government moved slowly in seeking to implement its manifesto commitment to establish a joint committee of the two Houses and there was disagreement between the two sides of the House in the Lords as to what the purpose of the joint committee would be. The Opposition thought it should look at the wider issues of power and composition. The government view was that it was to consider the procedural consequences for the House of the recommendations of the Royal Commission. Both sides recognised that the joint committee, once in being, would not be in a position to make recommendations that could be implemented during the lifetime of the Parliament.

Absence of leadership

Parliamentary reform requires leadership. The leadership that was given from the top in the Parliament was geared primarily to ensuring that government got its measures. There was little appreciation of the need for changes in parliamentary procedure. This brings us back to the point made by Peter Riddell: the Blair government ignored Parliament. As critics were quick to point out, the Prime Minister in particular ignored Parliament.

The priorities of the Prime Minister were clearly demonstrated when he spoke to the PLP after the 1997 election victory. Because of the size of the new parliamentary party, the meeting was held in Church House, Westminster. Tony Blair stressed that the party was elected on the basis of the manifesto and that was what the party had to deliver. Loyalty was expected. 'We ran as New Labour, we govern as New Labour, but the extra majority places an added responsibility on us to do that,' said a party spokesman.[13] It was made clear that MPs were expected to toe the party line.

The Prime Minister's attitude towards Parliament was revealed both in his behaviour and in his remarks in the House of Commons on parliamentary reform. Prime Ministerial activity in the House of Commons has declined since the 1860s.[14] Tony Blair devoted less time to parliamentary activity than his predecessors. Though turning up regularly to participate in Prime Minister's Question Time and to make statements, Blair rarely participated in debates or in divisions. In the first two sessions of the Parliament, he led for the government in only three debates, less often than any Prime Minister in recent history.[15] His voting record was the worst of any modern Prime Minister. In the first two sessions, he voted in less than one in ten divisions. Most of his immediate predecessors usually managed to vote in 20 per cent or more of divisions; some managed to vote in more than 40 per cent of the votes in some sessions.

His actions appeared to derive from a dismissive attitude towards Parliament, seeing it as not central to the task of governing. This attitude found some expression when he took part in a debate on the relationship between Parliament and the executive in July 2000. The motion had been tabled by the Opposition on one of its Opposition Days. The Prime Minister attacked the Leader of the Opposition, William Hague, for a partisan speech and for the choice of topic:

Instead of making that eccentric speech on the first occasion of his calling a debate as the Leader of the Opposition, he could have discussed jobs, the economy, schools, hospitals or even crime. I do not know whether people in his pubs and clubs are talking about pre-legislative scrutiny, but they are not in mine.[16]

Issues dealing with the size of the Cabinet and matters such as the ministerial code, he declared, 'were good issues for academics and constitutional experts, but they are not the big issues that Parliament should debate'. Instead, he went on to focus on 'the big constitutional questions relating to the fundamental relationship between Parliament and the executive'. Changes taking place within Parliament were thus seen as marginal to the 'big constitutional questions' that were being addressed by government.

The Prime Minister's attitude towards Parliament was not necessarily shared by all ministers. Some developed reputations for being seen in the House and for being willing to listen and negotiate with back-benchers – a point to which we shall return – but the Prime Minister's attitude appeared to dictate a government approach that was essentially dismissive of Parliament. One consequence was the number of occasions on which policy statements were made at press conferences rather than in the House of Commons, thus incurring the ire of the Speaker. 'It seems to me that there is a situation developing in some Departments,' she said on 5 April 2000, 'in which the interest of Parliament is regarded as secondary to media presentation, or is overlooked altogether.'[17] There was no leadership provided to shift this particular focus.

Commitment to constitutional change

The Blair government was committed to various major constitutional changes. These are the focus of other chapters in this volume. Their relevance for our purposes is twofold. The first is that the measures implementing them took priority over any proposal for reform within Parliament itself. That is apparent from what has been said already. Ministers were keen to get their measures on to the statute book. This took precedence over consideration of parliamentary reform. The second is that the measures of constitutional change had implications for Parliament. The constitutional change having the most immediate impact was the creation of elected assemblies in Scotland and Wales. There were two implications for the House. One was in terms of attendance. The other was procedural.

The creation of new bases of power in Edinburgh and Cardiff proved attractive to many parliamentarians at Westminster. They sought election to the new assemblies. Those who were successful retained a dual mandate, indicating their intention to leave the House of Commons only at the succeeding election. (Fourteen announced their intention to give up their seats.) A number of Westminster parliamentarians achieved official positions in the new bodies. The Scottish, Welsh and Northern Ireland assemblies each selected a peer as presiding officer. The First and Deputy First Ministers in all three assemblies were MPs. When Alun Michael resigned as First Minister in Wales, he was replaced by another Westminster MP. The consequence was a denuding of the House of Commons of attendance by many Scottish and Welsh MPs. Priority was given to Edinburgh or Cardiff.

Changes in the procedures of the House encouraged this process. Once the Scottish and Welsh executives were in place, questions about devolved matters were no longer answered by ministers at the dispatch box. Following recommendations from the Select Committee on Procedure, the House resolved in October 1999 that, subject to the discretion on the chair, questions could not be tabled on matters for which responsibility had been devolved, unless the question sought information which the UK government was empowered to require of the devolved executive or related to certain specified matters, such as concordats or other instruments of liaison between the UK government and the devolved executive. Question time for Scottish questions was also limited to thirty minutes, though still coming up on the rota at monthly intervals. Scottish and Welsh question times became notable for the number of times ministers disclaimed responsibility for the matters raised. Recognising the situation faced by MPs sitting for English seats, the government brought forward a motion to establish a new thirteen-member Standing Committee on Regional Affairs. The motion, empowering the committee to discuss 'any matter relating to regional affairs in England which may be referred to it', was approved by the House on 11 April 2000.

The constitutional changes also raised more fundamental questions about the consequences for Parliament. One was the West Lothian question, raised previously by Labour MP Tam Dalyell, which queried why MPs sitting for Scottish seats should be permitted to vote on measures affecting England when MPs sitting for English seats could not vote on equivalent measures affecting Scotland. Another related issue was the size of the House of Commons. Given the creation of elected assemblies in Scotland and Wales, there was a case for reducing the number of MPs returned from each, as had happened in the case of Northern Ireland Parliament from 1922 to 1972. (When it ceased to exist, the number of MPs returned from the province had been increased.) The government conceded the case for bringing the electoral quota in Scotland in line with that of England, and asked the Boundary Commission to bring it into line in its next review. However, it showed no willingness to go further and made no commitment to changes in the number of MPs returned from Wales.

The combined effect of these developments was that there was no developed or coherent approach to parliamentary reform. Though conceding the

case for some change, that change was approached on a piecemeal basis –
deriving from no single purpose – and was not allowed to get in the way of
government's legislative priorities.

Behaviour

Claims of government arrogance in its stance towards Parliament were
reinforced by perceptions of Labour MPs being forced into unthinking
compliance with the government's wishes. Labour MPs were portrayed as
supine loyalists,[18] doing whatever was dictated by the messages on their
pagers. The standing orders of the PLP were revised in the 1992–97
Parliament to limit the opportunities for expressions of dissent from PLP
decisions. According to the new standing orders, 'members shall consult the
Chief Whip before tabling any motion, amendment or prayer'. They also
stipulate: 'A reprimand may be given by the Chief Whip in writing, and
reported . . . to the constituency Labour party of the member concerned.'
In the new Parliament, the whips refined their use of the pager. The story is
variously recounted of Labour MPs receiving a pager message for one vote
saying 'Labour MPs vote aye', followed a few moments later by
'Correction: Free Vote'. The use of the pager was not confined to Labour
MPs. In any gathering of MPs, there would be a mass reaching for the
waistband or handbag shortly before a vote as pagers started vibrating or
bleeping.

The perception of supine loyalty was reinforced by Labour MPs using
the floor of the House of Commons, especially during Prime Minister's
Question Time, to congratulate the government on its policies and actions.
The incidence of congratulatory questions has increased over time. In the
1971–72 session, for example, the Prime Minister was congratulated on
average once in every sixteen Prime Minister's Question Times. In the
1992–93 session, it was one in every three.[19] The activity of some Labour
MPs in questioning Tony Blair led to accusations that Labour MPs were
more sycophantic than ever before. One study found that the use of phrases
such as 'astonishing', 'brilliant', 'remarkable' and 'excellent', were common
in questions to the Prime Minister.[20] The loyalty shown especially by female
Labour MPs, both in vote and speech, led to one misogynist Labour MP
characterising them as 'The Stepford Wives'.[21] In the press they were regularly described as 'Blair's Babes'.

These perceptions had some basis in fact. Labour MPs, especially female
MPs, proved remarkably loyal. In the period from 7 May 1997 to 20 June
2000, there were 941 votes in the House of Commons, well over 90 per
cent of them whipped votes. One or more Labour MPs voted against the
whips in sixty-two of them. This represents less than 7 per cent of the
total number. Expressed in terms of the number of votes experiencing dissent by Labour MPs, the Parliament can be characterised as the most loyal

of the 'modern' era: that is, post 1970. Indeed, the PLP was even more loyal in the first three sessions of the Parliament than it had been in the 1945 Parliament and (albeit marginally more so) than in the 1966 Parliament.[22] Of those Labour MPs who did vote against the whips, they were frequently MPs who had served in previous Parliaments and who had rebelled before. There was a notable coterie of 'serial dissenters'. (Among the most prominent were Jeremy Corbyn, Tony Benn, Dennis Skinner and Audrey Wise.) MPs elected for the first time in 1997 were less likely to rebel than those elected in earlier Parliaments. Of pre-1997 entrants, 32 per cent rebelled once or more in the first three sessions. Of 1997 entrants, only 25 per cent did so.[23] The new female entrants were the least likely to rebel. Only 14 per cent of the new women entrants voted against the whips, as against 31 per cent of the newly-elected men. The comparable figures for pre-1997 entrants are 28 per cent and 33 per cent respectively. There was also some evidence to support the perception of increased sycophancy in questioning the Prime Minister. According to one study, there were more congratulatory questions asked in the first three sessions of the 1997 Parliament than in the equivalent period in preceding Parliaments. Newly-elected MPs were more likely to ask such questions than was the case with newly-elected Conservative MPs in the 1992 Parliament.[24]

The Parliament was thus notable for the extent of loyalty displayed by government back-benchers. This was in line with popular perception. However, the loyalty was not total. As we have seen, there were sixty-two occasions on which one or more Labour MPs voted against the government. Furthermore, when they did vote against the whips, they did so in some numbers. The average dissenting lobby was twenty-one Members. Only three post-war Parliaments (1966, February 1974 and October 1974) have seen a larger average. The largest rebellion took place in May 1999 when sixty-seven Labour MPs voted against the government over its proposals for incapacity benefit contained in the Welfare Reform and Pensions Bill. This was the eleventh largest dissenting lobby in the period since 1945. Forty-seven Labour MPs voted against a reduction in lone-parent benefits contained in the Social Security Bill. In total, during the first three sessions (up to June 2000), one hundred and twenty-two Labour MPs voted against the whips on one or more occasions. This represents over one-third of back-benchers.[25]

Also in terms of questions to the Prime Minister, the number of congratulatory questions was not that much different from that for the equivalent period in the 1992 Parliament. Tony Blair was congratulated twenty-one times compared with sixteen for Major. As the author of the study noted: 'New Labour's back-benchers have congratulated the Prime Minister or the government on more occasions this Parliament than Conservative back-benchers did in the last – but certainly not to the extent that we would expect from the unfavourable press coverage that they have received since the election.'[26]

Relative to what appears to have been the public perception, the PLP was not exclusively loyal and sycophantic. However, compared to previous Parliaments, government back-benchers *were* notably more willing to comply with the requests of the whips. Cohesion not only remained a feature of parliamentary voting behaviour, it was a particularly marked feature of Parliament under the Blair premiership. This loyalty is somewhat counter-intuitive, given the trend of dissent in past Parliaments and given the history of divisiveness within the ranks of the Labour Party. Even in the preceding 1992–97 Parliament, Labour MPs were divided on more issues than Conservative MPs.[27] However, because the Conservatives were then in power and were badly split on the issue of European integration, it was the Conservative split that attracted media attention.

What, then, explains the high level of cohesion among Labour MPs during the Parliament? Was it simply the use of pressure from the whips and instructions from Number 10 that ensured Labour MPs trooped loyally into the same division lobby? Though, as we have seen, Chief Whips are capable of exuding an 'air of quiet menace', and some MPs fall into the category of unthinking loyalists, neither feature is peculiar to Parliament under Blair. What, then, makes this Parliament distinctive? Philip Cowley and Mark Stuart have advanced three variables that combined to produce such high levels of cohesion.

The first is that of agreement. More so than in previous Parliaments, Labour MPs were more likely actually to agree with the policies of the leadership. This was borne out by the surveys conducted by the British Representation Panel and the Members of Parliament Project. There was a shift to a more Blairite position among Labour MPs. Though the PLP remained a left-of-centre body, it is less so than before, and various MPs on the left conceded that the government was doing a reasonable job or at least much better than the alternative on offer.

The second variable is that of self-discipline. The party had been the 'out' party for eighteen years and was desperate for office. Having got office, it did not want to lose it. Labour MPs were conscious of the effect that a divided party had on the electorate. Electors do not reward a divided party. Labour candidates had seen what had happened to the Conservative Party in the 1997 election and attributed it in part to the splits within the party over European integration. They did not want to jeopardise the chances of Labour being re-elected by kicking over the traces themselves. If they disagreed with the government, they frequently kept their dissent low-key.

The third variable is that of consultation. Though the Prime Minister was portrayed as arrogant, heading an administration that treated Parliament with contempt, ministers were on occasion willing to listen to back-benchers and to make concessions. Some ministers made particular efforts to keep in touch with back-benchers. Some attended meetings of the relevant back-bench departmental committee. Some (often the same) were seen around the tea room. Among those with a reputation for keeping in touch with back-benchers was Home Secretary Jack Straw – a technique he learned from Barbara Castle when he was her special adviser, according to one former Cabinet minister.[28] Such contact helped build up goodwill and also ensured that there were channels of communication if problems arose. When there were difficulties, concessions were variously made.

Two other variables may also have come into play. One is touched upon by Cowley and Stuart in discussing the self-discipline of members. That is a change in the parliamentary culture deriving from the large influx of new MPs. The size of the new intake was exceptional: a third of the MPs in the new Parliament had not sat in the previous Parliament. Whereas in previous Parliaments, new MPs – being in a notable minority – could absorb the culture of the existing Members, on this occasion the new MPs were so numerous that they could influence the culture. As Cowley and Stuart note, the need to avoid appearing divided was felt especially strongly by the new intake. As one MP told them: 'The younger ones are the product of the party and they were, they think, elected because of the party. The older ones know that they survived despite the party.' New MPs also had no experience of anything other than the 'pager' culture.

The other, and arguably less plausible, variable is that advanced by Labour MP Bob Marshall-Andrews. He has argued that potential rebels remained silent because they believed they could leave it to the House of Lords to cause trouble on the issue. The Upper House provided them with an alibi.

> When we no longer have that alibi, Members who, at this stage are content – because the second chamber exists – to adhere to the Whip in circumstances where they do not agree and where they may wish to be a check on the executive may, in due course, change.[29]

The argument is questionable even though the fact that the House of Lords caused more problems for government than the House of Commons is demonstrable. The government faced no defeats in the House of Commons. In the first three sessions of the Parliament, the government suffered over one hundred defeats·in the House of Lords. These included the rejection of four bills at second reading. Some of the defeats may have provided alibis for some MPs, though the effect of the activity of the House encouraged some to favour more radical reform of the Upper House.

There was thus some dissension in the Parliament, though not on the scale of preceding Parliaments. A similar point may be made about allegations of improper conduct by MPs. Having attacked the Conservative Party for 'sleaze', the government saw some of its own back-benchers under investigation for falling foul of the rules of conduct. The party suspended two Members while they were under police investigation or facing criminal charges. Both were later cleared. One MP, Fiona Jones, the Member for

Newark, was convicted in March 1999 of an offence in relation to her election expenses and disqualified from sitting. The judgement was overturned in the High Court the following month and she was allowed to re-take her seat. Allegations of misuse of parliamentary and ministerial contacts (including the leaking of drafts of select committee reports and offering access to key ministers) by former Labour advisers turned lobbyists attracted at times extensive, and negative, media coverage. Those caught up in the coverage included the son of the Scottish Secretary, Dr John Reid, and Derek Draper, former aide to Peter Mandelson. One lobbyist claimed that many Labour back-benchers were accessible to lobbyists because they were keen to be seen to be active and wanted something to do.

The behaviour of government back-benchers differed from that of back-benchers in previous Parliaments, though not massively. They were somewhat more loyal, both in voice and vote, and did not attract quite the attention of Conservative MPs in the preceding Parliament for personal or political misconduct. However, the difference in voting behaviour – coupled with the size of the government's overall majority – was sufficient to fuel perceptions of a major difference between this and the preceding Parliament. Whereas John Major was seen as facing an unruly Parliament, making his life difficult if not impossible, Tony Blair was seen as standing aloof from a docile House of Commons. According to former Chief Whip Derek Foster: 'I said this place must never be the Prime Minister's poodle. Unfortunately, it has become so.'

Conclusion

By the end of the Parliament, what had changed? The most significant change had taken place in the Upper House. In November 1999, its membership was effectively halved, with all but ninety-two hereditary peers ceasing to be members. The Upper House showed a greater willingness to defeat government bills on second reading – contrary to the convention (the Salisbury Convention) enunciated in 1945 – though the number of defeats in the first session of the 'reformed' House showed no great increase on previous sessions. In part, this reflected the loss of a sizeable proportion of Conservative hereditary peers, the government being able to survive votes now with the support of the Liberal Democrats.

One other change in the Upper House attracted less attention. It became as hard-working as the House of Commons. It sat usually as many days as the House of Commons. In 1999 it sat for 157 days and for longer hours than in any twelve-month period in its history. In 1999 the average time for the rising of the House was after 10.00 p.m. Average daily attendance exceeded four hundred. After the summer recess in 2000, the House returned on 25 September to complete the stages of several bills that had not yet completed their passage. The House of Commons did not return until 23 October. The experience of the House of Lords, especially in the 1999–2000 session, illustrated two important points. One was that the Upper House was fulfilling an important role in the legislative process, undertaking revision of legislation that the Commons had not been able to complete. The other was that the government itself had little grasp of the parliamentary process, especially that in the Lords, and was prone to miscalculate the time needed to get its measures through. This resulted in the 1999–2000 session being an unduly long one, the Queen's Speech for the new session not taking place until 6 December 2000: the latest it had been held since 1921. Though some Labour MPs claimed the delay was because of filibustering by Conservative peers, the Government Chief Whip in the Lords, Lord Carter, conceded that no such filibustering had taken place.

Whereas peers became busier in the Parliament, the trend in the House of Commons was in the other direction. Though sittings in the House of Commons were supplemented by meetings in Westminster Hall, both were marked by low attendance. Few MPs bothered to attend sittings in Westminster Hall. Empty green benches also became a feature of the chamber. The parliamentary 'week' for many MPs, especially those who travelled from some distance, was principally two days – Tuesdays and Wednesdays. Much work was done through committees, though the small size of the parliamentary Conservative party appears to have been responsible for Conservatives having difficulty maintaining a high attendance record in select committees and having a low or non-existent record of attending back-bench party committees. Departmental select committees remained the main mechanism for structured and regular scrutiny of government. Some achieved a relatively high profile, including the Culture, Media and Sport Committee under Gerald Kaufman, and the Transport Sub-Committee under the redoubtable Gwyneth Dunwoody. In this respect, though, they marked no great change from preceding Parliaments and, if anything, collectively attracted less attention than before. There were various changes to the procedures and legislative process, though nothing that could be construed as paradigmatic change.

Modest advances in how Parliament conducted itself in scrutinising the actions and measures of government were overshadowed by the appearance of a dominant and aloof government. Conservative ministers in the Thatcher and Major governments had acquired reputations for arrogance in their relationship with Parliament. Some ministers in the new Labour government appeared to be arrogant from the time of taking office. The accusation of arrogance was levelled especially at the Prime Minister. 'Every Prime Minister,' declared veteran Labour MP Tony Benn in the Commons on 9 November 1999, 'can do what he likes, and the current one certainly does.' A number of independent-minded MPs on both sides of the House, led by Labour MPs Tony Benn and Alan Simpson, Independent Labour MP Dennis Canavan, Independent Martin Bell, and

Conservatives David Davis and Richard Shepherd, tabled an early day motion in the House noting 'the emergence of a semi-presidential style of government, by-passing the Cabinet and taking this House for granted, with few effective checks and balances on the power of the executive', and urging all Members, while honouring personal and political obligations and loyalty to party manifestos,

> to speak and vote more freely in the House on the proposals put before them, and by doing so to re-assert their historic role as elected representatives, their right and duty to express their own deeply-held convictions and the responsibility for maintaining the role of this House as a democratic legislature holding all governments to account, having been elected by the people for that purpose.

As the motion recognised, the problem lay as much with private Members as with ministers. If the political will to achieve change did not exist, then no reform would take place. As we have seen, many government supporters appeared unwilling to challenge government, taking a partisan stance in preference to one favouring the institution of Parliament. Labour backbenchers flexed their muscle on 23 October 2000 in electing Michael Martin, a Labour deputy speaker, as Speaker of the House. The election was interpreted by some as Labour MPs showing their independence of ministers, the candidate favoured by leading figures on both front benches – former Conservative Cabinet minister, Sir George Young – failing to be elected. Many Conservative MPs interpreted the result instead as demonstrating the arrogance of a governing party, Labour MPs electing one of their own. Martin was the only one of twelve candidates for the Speakership not to have a proposer and seconder drawn from different parties. The actions of government back-benchers, as much as those of ministers, caused some MPs to worry about the prospect of ever achieving change that would allow the House of Commons to undertake effective scrutiny of government.

During the Parliament, the effect of growing disquiet among Members was not to achieve any significant change. However, somewhat ironically, government ministers did by their actions serve to put parliamentary reform on the political agenda. The Conservative Party – the party in Opposition – established a Commission to Strengthen Parliament. The Hansard Society set up a commission on the scrutinising role of Parliament. These actions were not that surprising. What is remarkable is the coverage that they received. Growing unease, especially among politicians and the media, ensured that the issue achieved a greater political profile than in earlier years would have been possible. The perception of executive arrogance may have been greater than the reality, but the perception proved a powerful one. Parliament under Blair was seen as a Parliament under threat.

Notes

1　Philip Norton, *Dissension in the House of Commons 1945–74*, Macmillan, 1974; Philip Norton, *Conservative Dissidents*, Temple Smith, 1978.

2　Philip Norton, *Dissension in the House of Commons 1974–1979*, Oxford University Press, 1980.

3　*House of Commons Debates, Official Report*, Vol. 353, col. 1099.

4　Peter Riddell, *Parliament Under Blair*, Politico's, 2000, p. 245.

5　Quoted by Riddell, p. 245.

6　Liaison Committee, *Shifting the Balance: Select Committees and the Executive*, First Report, Session, 1999–2000, HC 300, p. vii.

7　Liaison Committee, *Independence or Control?* Second Report, Session 1999–2000, HC748, p. vii.

8　*House of Commons, Official Report*, Vol. 356, col. 177.

9　*Strengthening Parliament: The Report of the Commission to Strengthen Parliament*, Conservative Party, 2000, p. 7.

10　*House of Commons Debates, Official Report*, Vol. 354, col. 1114.

11　*House of Commons Debates, Official Report*, Vol. 353, col. 1128.

12　'Profile: Nick Brown' BBC News On-Line, 8 November 1998.

13　Jon Hibbs, 'Don't step out of line, Blair will tell MPs'. *Daily Telegraph*, 7 May 1997.

14　P. Dunleavy and G. W. Jones, 'Leaders, Politics and Institutional Change: The Decline of Prime Ministerial Accountability in the House of commons, 1868–1990', *British Journal of Political Studies*, vol. 23, 1993, pp. 267–98.

15　Andrew Tyrie, *Mr Blair's Poodle*, Centre for Policy Studies, 2000, pp. 29–30.

16　*House of Commons, Official Report*, Vol. 353, col. 1097.

17　*House of Commons, Official Report*, Vol. 347, col. 975.

18　See, for example, *Sunday Times*, 29 March 1998.

19　Mark Shephard, 'Prime Minister's Question Time – Functions, Flux, Causes and Consequences: A Behavioural Analysis', Unpublished PhD thesis, University of Houston, Texas, USA, 1999, p. 75.

20　Richard C. V. Nash, 'New Labour and the marginalisation of Parliament', Unpublished BA thesis, University of Hull, 2000, p. 42.

21　*The Times*, 7 February 1998.

22　Philip Cowley and Mark Stuart, 'Can Sheep Bark? British Labour MPs and the modification of Government policy', Paper presented at the Fourth Workshop of Parliamentary Scholars and Parliamentarians, Wroxton College, 2000, p. 8.

23　Cowley and Stuart, p. 10.

24　Nash, p. 41.

25　Cowley and Stuart, pp. 9–11.

26　Nash, p. 41.

27　Philip Cowley and Philip Norton, 'Are Conservative MPs Revolting?' *Research Papers in Legislative Studies, No. 2*, University of Hull: Centre for Legislative Studies, 1996.

28　Member of the 1974–79 Cabinet to author, 2000.

29　*HC Debates*, Vol. 306, cols 779–780.

THE
CAMPAIGNS
OF TONY

© Chris Riddell

Chapter 4

ELECTIONS AND PUBLIC OPINION

Ivor Crewe

The Blair Effect in 1997

ALTHOUGH THEIR POLITICAL careers depend on it, few party leaders devote much thought or energy to electoral strategy. They encourage or discourage policy ideas; they have the final say on the election manifesto; they lead the campaign and respond incessantly to the media; if they happen to be Prime Minister they agonise over their choice of election date. They shape short-term tactics but not long-term strategy.

Tony Blair was the exception. No party leader in modern British history prepared his party for an election with as thought-through, coherent and radical an electoral strategy as Tony Blair did between his becoming leader in 1994 and the general election three years later. No party leader in modern times has attempted, let alone succeeded, in persuading a reluctant party to abandon long-established policies and structures for the sake of electoral victory. After four successive election defeats, the acute disappointment of 1992 and eighteen years in Opposition, a desperate party was ready to respond; but John Smith, his short-lived predecessor, would not have led the party in the same direction.

There were three, connected, elements in Blair's electoral strategy. The first was the single-minded conversion of non-Labour voters rather than the mobilisation of traditional Labour supporters. The former were assumed to be concentrated in the growing ranks of middle-income, economically aspiring, home-owning, tax-paying (but public service consuming), selfish, decent and moderate Middle England. Many belonged to the lost generation of Labour supporters who had voted Conservative or SDP in the Thatcher years. They would make the crucial difference in dozens of marginal seats, particularly in the Midlands and the South. Long-standing Labour loyalists were assumed to be too small in number to guarantee Labour victory yet to share sufficient of the values of Middle England not to desert the party; but anyway, they lived largely in safe Labour seats and when it came to voting had nowhere else to go.

The second component of the strategy was the repositioning of the party on the centre-right of the ideological spectrum. Old Labour policies that frightened the target non-Labour voter were abandoned, notably income tax rises, nationalisation, the strengthening of trade unions and any hint of liberal tenderness on crime, welfare 'scroungers' and immigration. To make it clear to voters that the Labour Party had re-invented itself, the Blairites replaced clause 4 of the party constitution and reduced the trade unions' power and role in the party. The Blairite project made a virtue of fiscal responsibility, appeared to be more pro-business than pro-labour and cultivated institutions that traditionally supported the Right, such as the press, the City and the police, with the aim of at least neutralising their hostility. It also set out to convince Liberal Democrats that Labour was closer than the Conservatives to their values, by embracing constitutional and electoral reform, in order to soften them up for a tactical vote for Labour in the two-party marginals.

The third part of the strategy was the modernisation of the party machine, which where necessary meant centralisation at the expense of local constituency parties. National headquarters was to target marginal seats to the neglect of safe and hopeless seats and to exercise maximum influence over candidate selection to avoid the embarrassing publicity of left-wingers being selected. Highly professional and experienced teams would deal with the media, manage public relations, create an advertising campaign and measure voters' views through polls and focus groups.

In May 1997 Tony Blair led the Labour Party to the greatest electoral triumph in its history. A swing of over 10 per cent, easily the biggest since 1945, delivered the Labour Party 419 seats and a huge overall majority of 179 in the House of Commons, more than at any previous election. Of course the scale of the 1997 victory cannot be attributed to Blair's electoral strategy alone. It owed as much, perhaps more, to the exceptionally dismal performance of the Conservatives as it did to the achievement of Labour. At 44.4 per cent Labour's share of the national vote was not particularly impressive by historical standards, being lower than in any post-war election up to 1966, including those it lost. The relatively low turnout also needs to be taken into account. Less than a third of the registered electorate – only 30.9 per cent – turned out to vote Labour, hardly a mass mobilisation for political renewal. What gave Labour its huge majority was the catastrophic decline of the Conservative vote to 31.5 per cent, its lowest ebb since 1832. The monthly opinion polls demonstrate that the electoral rot for the Conservatives set in with Black Wednesday in September 1992, before Tony Blair became Labour leader, and spread with splits, sleaze and (perceived) public spending cuts in the course of the Parliament. The 1997 result signified the voters' rejection of the Conservative government more than its endorsement of New Labour. Yet Blair did make a significant contribution: he turned Labour into an acceptable and preferable alternative.

Nor did every element of Blair's electoral strategy contribute to Labour's win. The 'Millbank Machine', invariably depicted by the media as professional, slick and ruthless, while undoubtedly superior to Labour's national campaign organisation at any previous election, appears to have made little difference to the result. Most significantly, it failed to mobilise anything like Labour's full potential support. Nationally turnout declined to 71.3 per cent, the lowest level since 1935, despite six weeks of intensive media coverage, the emergence of a fourth national party in the form of the Referendum Party, a record number of candidates, fine weather and a relatively young register. Turnout declined particularly sharply in Labour's own heartlands, in contrast to Labour's previous election landslide of 1945.[1] Part of the explanation may have been Millbank's hard-nosed concentration of campaign resources on a hundred marginal seats at the expense of safe Labour areas. But this tactic failed: Labour's share of the vote increased on average by 12.5 percentage points in its target seats, but by 13.4 percentage points in its non-target seats,[2] while denuding traditional Labour areas of any serious campaigning on the ground. And despite Millbank's tight control of media relations and the sophistication of its campaign materials, Labour's lead in the opinion polls, while always large, steadily slipped in the course of the campaign, from 22 percentage points in the first two weeks to sixteen points in the last few days (and thirteen points in the actual vote) – a 'loss' of over two million voters.[3]

Nevertheless, some of the distinctive features of the 1997 election result occurred as a result of Blair's electoral strategy. There *was* a 'Blair effect', or rather, three Blair effects. The first was the rebranding of the Labour Party in the eyes of the electorate. Old Labour had had its heart in the right place but could not be trusted to manage the economy or govern with competence and discipline; in particular it would put up taxes and cave in to trade union pressure. New Labour, led by Blair, was perceived as different: the British Election Study shows that in 1997 voters placed the Labour Party closer to their own positions on critical Left-Right issues (and the Conservatives further away) than they did in 1992.[4] Policy areas in which voters had preferred the Conservatives for a generation, irrespective of the Conservatives' overall popularity – such as taxation, law and order and Europe – were 'captured' by New Labour.[5] Most important of all, for the first time in its history, Labour came to be regarded as the more competent at managing the economy. This was partly by default after Britain's humiliating withdrawal from the ERM and effective devaluation in September 1992 and partly through Gordon Brown's repeated pledges to limit public expenditure to the Conservative government's targets, to desist from raising income tax, and to adopt pro-business principles and policies. Gallup regularly asks its respondents which party can best handle Britain's economic difficulties. In April 1992, despite the recession over which John Major's government was presiding, respondents split 45 to 38 per cent in favour of the Conservatives. In April 1997, respondents split 48 to 39 per cent in favour of Labour. Under Blair, Labour had become safe, sensible and united.

The second Blair effect followed from the first: Labour's stunning success in 'Middle England'. In the 1980s, the Thatcher government's appeal to the 'new working class' of relatively affluent and ambitious technicians and office workers, especially in the economically buoyant Midlands and South, drove Labour back into its industrial and urban fastnesses of the North, Wales and Scotland. In 1983 and 1987 Labour was no longer a national party but the party of a substantial but declining socio-geographic sector, the old industrial working class. Outside Inner London, it barely won any seats below the line running from the Wash to the Severn. In 1997 the strongest swings from Conservative to Labour were in the prosperous regions of Outer London (14.3 per cent), the South East (12.5 per cent) and East Anglia (11.4 per cent) and the weakest swings were in the relatively deprived regions of Wales (7.1 per cent), Scotland (7.2 per cent) and Yorkshire and Humberside (8.8 per cent). On election night the drumbeat of Labour gains was a roll-call of the suburban and small town Home Counties: Brighton, Braintree, Hastings, Harrow, Hendon, Hemel Hempstead, Hove, Putney, St Albans, Southgate, Watford. The middle classes and mortgage payers swung much more strongly to solid and respectable New Labour than the working class and council tenants did.

The third Blair effect was the growth in anti-Conservative tactical voting. It had emerged on a limited scale in the 1987 and 1992 elections, but accelerated in 1997. The main reason was the deepening unpopularity of the Conservatives and thus the greater determination of non-Conservatives to cast their vote for whichever candidate appeared to have the best prospect of defeating the local Conservative MP. But the readiness of the Liberal Democrats to vote Labour in Con–Lab marginals and of Labour supporters to reciprocate in Con–Lib Dem marginals would almost certainly have been on a smaller scale had Blair not moved the Labour Party closer to the Liberal Democrats on the issue of constitutional reform. It tipped the balance in an additional twenty-five to thirty-five Conservative seats, providing Labour with an additional fifteen to twenty-one seats and the Liberal Democrats with an extra ten to fourteen.[6] Tactical voting created the largest Liberal parliamentary group since the 1920s and turned what would have been an emphatic Labour majority of 140 or so into a landslide of 179. It also reinforced the pro-Labour bias in the electoral system.

A footnote needs to be added on what the Blair Effect was not: it was nothing to do with Tony Blair's personality. Certainly, his creation of New Labour was crucial for making Labour electable, and the determination with which he drove through reforms no doubt reflected elements of his personality. But the direct impact of both his and John Major's personal attributes and qualities on the election result was tiny.[7] To be sure, in 1997 voters told the polls that they preferred Tony Blair to John Major as the next Prime Minister, but that was because, for quite separate reasons, they wanted a Labour rather than Conservative government. The media focused on the party leaders during the campaign and often depicted the election as a choice between Blair and Major. But that was not the primary basis on which people voted.

The Blair Effect Since 1997: Evidence and Evaluation

Tony Blair and his closest supporters are acutely aware that the Left's past election triumphs have been particularly short-lived. No Labour government has managed to get re-elected with a sufficient majority to last a full second parliamentary term. Labour's massive majority of 146 in 1945 (8.4 per cent lead in the vote) crumbled to an unsustainable five in 1950 and was overturned in 1951; Harold Wilson's two-stage advance to a majority of 102 in 1966 (6 per cent lead in the vote) was wiped out four years later. The New Labour project was intended to reunite the Centre-Left and put it in power for a generation; the electoral strategy was designed not simply to win the 1997 election but to set voting patterns in a new mould so that Labour could win a second and third term.

The dramatic shifts in voting that led to the 1997 result are not in themselves evidence of the fundamental shift in party support sought by the Blairites. What in fact characterised the 1997 election was not realignment but dealignment. The British Election Study, conducted after every general election since 1964, has recorded an unremitting weakening of party loyalties – 'a partisan dealignment' – at every election, and 1997 was no exception. Indeed, the most pronounced weakening has occurred at those elections which have ushered in long-lasting changes to the shape of the party system: February 1974, 1979 – and 1997. By 1997 only 16 per cent declared themselves to be 'very strong' party identifiers while 42 per cent acknowledged having a weak identification or none at all.[8] Of course, the weaker the electorate's partisan loyalties, the more volatile its voting decisions and the greater the opportunity for a new or reconstituted party to capture support that was hitherto beyond its reach. But the same conditions offer the Opposition the opportunity to rapidly recover the supporters it lost and bounce back.

It is impossible to know until the next election (at the earliest) whether Blair has succeeded in forging an enduring realignment of the electorate. In the meantime we can examine the preliminary evidence provided by the opinion polls and various elections that have taken place since 1997 – by-elections, local elections, the European elections and elections for the Scottish, Welsh and London Assemblies. In all of these elections the Labour vote has declined, absolutely and proportionately, since 1997 but that fact alone signifies little. Almost every postwar government has gone through a cycle of honeymoon, disappointment, disillusion and reconciliation in its relations with the electorate in the course of a full Parliament. To interpret the trends in support for the Blair government the benchmark that counts is not the 1997 general election but the cycles of decline and recovery under previous governments. Do the graph lines of Labour support in the first three years of the Blair government resemble those for the 1966 Wilson government, which crashed to defeat in 1970, or those for the 1979, 1983 and 1987 Thatcher governments, which bounced back from mid-term slumps to win the subsequent election? Or do they reveal a unique profile, unprecedented under any previous recent government, indicating a new electoral era?

The Blair Effect, 1997–2000: The Evidence

What the opinion polls show

The possibility that Blair's electoral strategy produced an enduring transformation of Labour's prospects was supported by the polls from 1997 to the autumn of 2000. For over three years the government basked in the longest period of electoral sunshine that any government has enjoyed since records began. It then hit a huge and sudden storm during the fuel crisis of September 2000, but still entered the (probably) final year before the election in a stronger position than most of its predecessors.

The three-year honeymoon: May 1997 to August 2000

Figure 1 shows the trend in the parties' standing (measured by voting intentions) during the three years after the election. In one respect the pattern since 1997 looks familiar: the popularity of the Blair government, like that of its predecessors, gradually drifted down from an immediate post-election boost; the new government's initial gloss had clearly worn off before the fuel crisis.

In all other respects the level and stability of support for the Blair government – at least as expressed in the polls – was unparalleled in modern times. Four features of the opinion poll trends stand out. The first is the huge surge of popularity that Labour's election victory brought with it. Labour won 44.5 per cent of the vote at the election but in the polls that followed saw its support jump to the high fifties. A sizeable number of sympathisers whose residual doubts stopped them short of voting Labour at the election must have swung to Labour once it appeared that a Blair administration was safe and respectable. Secondly, as Figure 2 shows, the downward drift in Labour's popularity that inevitably followed was much gentler than for any previous recent government (except for the

Figure I Vote intentions, July 1997–June 2000

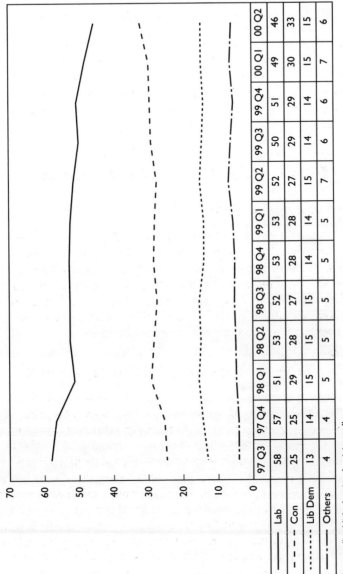

	97 Q3	97 Q4	98 Q1	98 Q2	98 Q3	98 Q4	99 Q1	99 Q2	99 Q3	99 Q4	00 Q1	00 Q2
Lab	58	57	51	53	52	53	53	52	50	51	49	46
Con	25	25	29	28	27	28	28	27	29	29	30	33
Lib Dem	13	14	15	15	15	14	14	15	14	14	15	15
Others	4	4	5	5	5	5	5	7	6	6	7	6

Source: all published national opinion polls.

Figure 2 Government's share of vote at election and in opinion polls three years later

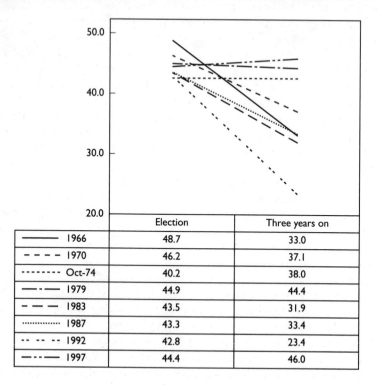

	Election	Three years on
—————— 1966	48.7	33.0
– – – – 1970	46.2	37.1
·········· Oct-74	40.2	38.0
——·—— 1979	44.9	44.4
– – – 1983	43.5	31.9
············ 1987	43.3	33.4
·· ·· ·· 1992	42.8	23.4
——··—— 1997	44.4	46.0

Wilson/Callaghan government of 1974–79, when the gradient was similar, but from a much lower starting point). The popularity of the 1979, 1983 and 1987 Conservative governments, each of which was eventually re-elected, declined in each case by about 15–16 percentage points by the third year of the Parliament. The popularity of Tony Blair's administration fell by only 12 percentage points in its worst quarter, and then from a far higher starting point. Thirdly, the sheer scale of support for the government was unprecedented. Throughout 1998 and 1999 Labour's standing in the polls exceeded 50 per cent and at its lowest point before the fuel crisis, in Spring 2000, was still a little higher, at 46 per cent, than at the general election. No previous government in recent memory has reached even 40 per cent in the polls in its third year (except for the Conservatives, briefly, at the time of the Falklands War in summer 1982).

Finally, with Conservative support stuck in the low thirties (at best) until autumn 2000, the Labour government remained comfortably ahead of the Conservative Opposition through its first three years. Again, this is unmatched by any previous post-war government. The three Conservative governments of the 1980s all trailed behind Labour in their third year but went on to win. The Blair government, by contrast, was ahead by 20 percentage points for most of the first three years. The polls were indicating, in the starkest terms, that Labour was on course to another massive majority.

The government's exceptional popularity appeared to owe something to a personal Blair effect. When asked to say which of Tony Blair, William Hague or Paddy Ashdown (and after July 1999, Charles Kennedy) they would prefer as Prime Minister, people overwhelmingly chose Blair and on a scale quite without historical parallel (see Figure 3). At the height of her popularity, Mrs Thatcher was preferred as Prime Minister by majorities of 25 to 30 percentage points over Neil Kinnock.[9] In March 1991, only four months into his premiership and in the afterglow of victory in the Gulf War, John Major was 33 points ahead of Neil Kinnock. Tony Blair, however, was preferred to William Hague or Paddy Ashdown by majorities of never less than 40 percentage points throughout 1997, 1998 and 1999. Personal errors of judgement, made much of in the media, such as the Ecclestone affair, appeared to have no impact. His halo slipped a little in 2000 but he remained the voters' preference over Hague by huge majorities of 38 points in the first quarter and 29 points in the second. Hague's inability to look the part of a Prime Minister in voters' eyes was part of the explanation, but only a small part. Throughout Blair's first three years as Prime Minister, his popularity ran about 12 points ahead of his party's. In the popularity stakes Labour owed more to Blair than Blair owed to Labour. He was a very considerable electoral asset.

Voters' preferences between the parties to manage the economy are a crucial influence on an election outcome. The reversal after 1992 of the deep-rooted assumption that the Conservatives are the more competent economic managers was a significant electoral turning point for the Labour Party. Labour's striking 20 point advantage on the issue at the election narrowed over the following three years but it was still preferred by a comfortable 10 point margin (45 to 35 per cent) at the lowest point of the government's popularity. At the same stage of the 1987–92 Conservative government, the Conservatives were preferred by only 4 per cent. The buoyant state of the economy was no doubt partly responsible. The Labour government inherited and then sustained an economy with historically low levels of inflation and unemployment and an above-average growth rate; when the spectre of recession loomed in 1998 it managed a 'soft landing' and avoided a new round of stop-go. But the healthy fundamentals of the economy were not reflected in voters' view of the country's economic prospects, or of their own. In the summer of 1997, after Labour's win, MORI reported that optimists about the economy outnumbered pessimists by 8 percentage points; three years later pessimists outnumbered optimists by 13 points. Similarly personal economic optimism (the 'feel good' factor) declined slightly from −3 to −9. Perhaps voters had become accustomed to the new prosperity or perhaps they believed it could not last. Whatever the case they continued to trust New Labour more than the Conservatives on the economy – a historical first for a Labour government.

Figure 3 'Who would make the best Prime Minister?'

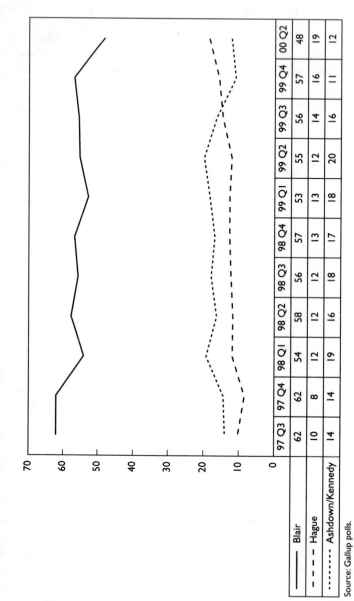

	97 Q3	97 Q4	98 Q1	98 Q2	98 Q3	98 Q4	99 Q1	99 Q2	99 Q3	99 Q4	00 Q2
Blair	62	62	54	58	56	57	53	55	56	57	48
Hague	10	8	12	12	12	13	13	12	14	16	19
Ashdown/Kennedy	14	14	19	16	18	17	18	20	16	11	12

Source: Gallup polls.

The Blair effect persisted in one other respect. After the election Labour's standing improved most in the social groups that New Labour deliberately targeted while it stagnated in its traditional base (see Table 1). Between the election and the second quarter of 2000 there was a (further) national swing from the Conservatives to Labour of 3.5 per cent. Among the white collar AB and C1 social classes, however, the swing was 6.5 and 5 per cent respectively, whereas among the unskilled workers and welfare dependants comprising the DE class it was a mere 0.5 per cent. By 2000 the traditional class basis of the vote had virtually disappeared.[10] There were parallel regional differences. After the election the Labour government extended the inroads it had already made into the South and Midlands with above-average swings of 8 per cent in the East Midlands, 7 per cent in East Anglia, 6 per cent in the South West and 4.5 per cent in the South East. In Wales, by contrast, the swing was only 0.5 per cent and in the North and North West regions there was a small swing back to the Conservatives. Middle England rallied to New Labour; the Traditional Heartlands slunk away. This gradual shift in the socio-geographic axis of Labour support in the polls was reflected, indeed magnified, in some of the actual elections held after 1997.

Table 1 Swing since general election

Social class		Region	
AB	6.5 to Lab	Scotland	5.0 to Lab
C1	5.0 to Lab	North	2.0 to Con
C2	2.0 to Lab	North West	1.0 to Con
DE	0.5 to Lab	Yorks & Humb	2.0 to Lab
		Wales	0.5 to Lab
TU member	0.5 to Con	West Midlands	1.0 to Lab
Non-member	4.0 to Lab	East Midlands	8.0 to Lab
		East Anglia	7.0 to Lab
		South East	4.5 to Lab
		London	3.0 to Lab
Age		South West	6.0 to Lab
18–24	7.0 to Lab		
25–34	7.0 to Lab		
55–64	0.5 to Lab		
65+	3.5 to Con		

Source: MORI polls in Market & Opinion Research International, British Public Opinion, Vol. XXIII (6), August, 2000.

The impact of the fuel crisis, September 2000

On Friday 8 September, hauliers and farmers picketed fuel distribution depots in protest at the rising cost of petrol and diesel. Motorists rushed to fill their tanks and by the following Tuesday most garages had run dry. Stranded without petrol many motorists could not get to work and deliveries were disrupted. In a televised statement, after crisis talks with the oil companies, an apparently rattled Prime Minister prematurely promised that the situation had been resolved and that petrol tanker deliveries were already returning to normal.

The speed with which the unexpected fuel shortages disrupted people's everyday lives, albeit very temporarily, was matched by the ferocity with which voters turned against the government, and Tony Blair in particular. According to a mid-September *Guardian*/ICM poll, for example, 63 per cent of respondents blamed the government rather than OPEC or the petrol companies for petrol price rises; 59 per cent thought Blair wrong to refuse concessions to the protestors; 76 per cent opposed high petrol prices as an anti-pollution measure and 71 per cent disagreed that Labour was a 'listening government'.[11]

The government paid an immediate electoral price (see Figure 4). In two MORI polls conducted in mid-August Labour support had stood at 51 per cent, and Conservative support at 29–32 per cent, in line with much of the previous three years. In two MORI polls conducted in mid-September, immediately after the fuel crisis, Labour support slumped to 36 per cent, while Conservative support jumped to 36–38 per cent. Altogether five polls were conducted that week: the Conservatives drew level with Labour in two and nudged ahead in three – the first time they had taken the lead in eight years. An NOP poll for Channel 4 conducted in the following week put the Conservatives as far as 8 points ahead.

Blair's popularity fell even more sharply than the government's. His 'satisfaction rating' in the *Guardian*/ICM poll plummeted from +2 in July 2000 to −34 and in poll after poll people described him as 'arrogant', 'out of touch' and 'untrustworthy'. A MORI/Carlton TV poll found that Hague was regarded as marginally less 'out of touch with ordinary people' than Blair – although not by much.[12] For the first time in his leadership he was a liability rather than asset to his party.

The voters who in overwhelming numbers described Blair and his government as 'out of touch' were right. By ignoring the growing signs of discontent over fuel prices – hauliers had lobbied and demonstrated over the summer – the government was neglecting the Middle England that had been central to its pre-1997 electoral strategy. Ordinary households, especially in the provinces and countryside, depend on their car to get to work, shops and schools. In 1998–99 the average car-owning household spent £72 a week on motoring, and that was before the petrol price increases.[13] Motoring costs are a major item in their budget and they considered the high price of petrol as an unavoidable tax on necessity, as unfair as the poll tax. Voters without cars were just as aggrieved. For many, the issue was about more than petrol prices. It stood for an accumulating list of resentments – the government's apparent indifference to the special problems of rural areas; its lack of sympathy for small businesses; its failure to deliver essential services (of which affordable fuel was considered one); the

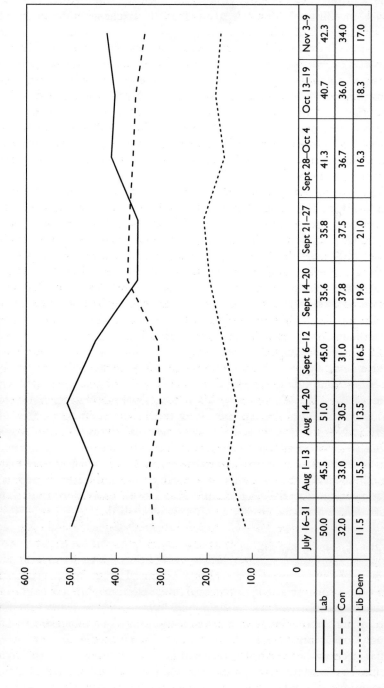

Figure 4 Opinion polls before and after the September 2000 fuel crisis

	July 16–31	Aug 1–13	Aug 14–20	Sept 6–12	Sept 14–20	Sept 21–27	Sept 28–Oct 4	Oct 13–19	Nov 3–9
Lab	50.0	45.5	51.0	45.0	35.6	35.8	41.3	40.7	42.3
Con	32.0	33.0	30.5	31.0	37.8	37.5	36.7	36.0	34.0
Lib Dem	11.5	15.5	13.5	16.5	19.6	21.0	16.3	18.3	17.0

growing burden of indirect tax. It stood for the remoteness of a metropolitan elite from the day-to-day concerns of Mondeo Man.

Not since Britain's forced departure from the Exchange Rate Mechanism in September 1992 and, before that, the Winter of Discontent in January 1979, has a government suffered such a sudden and massive collapse in support. On those two previous occasions the government of the day never recovered and went on to lose the following election. Will the Blair government suffer the same fate or will its dip in the polls prove as shortlived as the fuel crisis itself?

The Blair Government looks unlikely to suffer the same fate. The dip in the polls, although astonishingly sharp and sudden, was almost as shortlived as the fuel crisis itself. By mid November Labour had recovered most of the support it had lost at the height of the crisis as petrol supplies and day-to-day life returned to normal. Support for the parties consolidated at an average of Labour 42, Conservative 34, Liberal Democrat 18. Blair remained the first choice for prime minister by a clear margin and voters still regarded Labour as more capable, united, and likely to make voters better off than the Conservatives.[14] Nevertheless, even after the announcement on 8 November of a freeze on fuel duty and lower excise duty for farmers and hauliers (and substantial rises in the old age pension) the majority of voters remained dissatisfied.[15] The price of petrol, and in particular the level of duty, still rankled deeply. It did appear that the Government's marathon honeymoon was truly over and that its row with the electorate was more than a tiff.

Yet by the new year, it was clear that the tiff was not an irrevocable bust-up. Labour had fully recovered its losses: in the six polls of January 2001 Labour led the Conservatives by, on average, 49 to 32 per cent. Its 17 point lead was identical to the lead it enjoyed at the same point before the 1997 election. No post-war government has been so far ahead four months before an election, not even the post-Falklands Thatcher Government in early 1983. And no Opposition party has come anywhere near to closing a gap of that size in the run-up to the election. Short of a successful repeat of the protests close to the election the fuel tax revolt appears to have left the Blair Government shaken, but completely unscathed.

Parliamentary by-elections 1997–2000

Opinion polls are not the same as real elections. They record the responses of hypothetical voters at a hypothetical future election who may not be perfectly representative of the voting public. In both 1992 and 1997 the final forecast polls overestimated the actual Labour vote and underestimated the actual Conservative vote. This phenomenon repeatedly recurred in the actual elections held after 1997, which failed, sometimes dramatically, to paint as rosy a picture of the Labour government's standing or prospects as the opinion polls did.

By-elections are real elections but they are not general elections. With no government at stake, but opportunities for well-organised minor parties to target a campaign, they are the perfect pretext for voters to indulge in protest and tactical voting. Governments typically lose seats, including hitherto safe seats, at by-elections, only to regain them at the following general election. The three Conservative governments of the 1980s lost a total of thirteen seats at by-elections but regained eleven of them when re-elected at the subsequent general election. By-election gains and losses therefore signify little in themselves. However, the scale and pattern of the anti-government swing at by-elections, when placed in historical perspective, does provide a rough guide to the depth of popular dissatisfaction with the government and of popular confidence in the Opposition.

Twelve by-elections were held between May 1997 and September 2000. Only one changed party hands – Romsey in plush and rural Hampshire, where the second-placed Liberal Democrats, aided by thousands of Labour switchers, overcame a Conservative majority of 8585 (17 per cent). It was a reminder that the anti-Conservative tactical voting tacitly encouraged by New Labour remained a potent force. By a stroke of luck the by-election seats Labour found itself defending were all ultra-safe; it held onto them but in every case with slashed majorities and a substantially reduced share of the vote. In Hamilton South, for example, the Labour majority plunged from 19,409 to a mere 556, on a swing of 23 per cent to the Scottish Nationalists; in Leeds Central it crumbled from 20,689 to 2293 on a 21 per cent swing to the Liberal Democrats. But haemorrhaging on this scale is quite common for the government party at by-elections, especially to third parties. The critical test of by-election performance is the average net swing from government to opposition party and how it compares with previous administrations.

The answer is provided by Table 2, which compares the pattern of vote changes in by-elections in the first three years of every full-term Parliament since 1964. Three features of the post-1997 by-elections stand out. The first is the smallness of the average swing from Labour to Conservative: a mere 4 per cent. This is weak by comparison with the average swing of 12 per cent in the Labour governments of 1966–70 and 1974–79 and of between 7 and 10 per cent (from Conservative to Labour) during the three Conservative governments of 1979, 1983 and 1987 – which were all re-elected. The modesty of the swing back to the Conservatives arises partly from Labour's success in containing its average loss of votes (8 percentage points compared with 14 in 1966–70 and 12 in 1974–79). It owes more, however, to the second notable characteristic of the post-1997 by-elections: the failure of the Conservatives to recover more than marginally from their dismal performance in 1997. On average the Conservative share of the vote at by-elections rose by less than 1 per cent, corroborating the findings of the opinion polls. In the previous two Labour governments, 10 to 12 percentage points was typically added to the Conservative vote, starting from a higher base. By-elections echo the polls in suggesting that well into the second half

Table 2 By-elections in the first three years of full-Parliament governments: 1966–2000

Date	Number of by-elections	Con % point change since GE	Lab % point change since GE	Lib % point change since GE	Con-Lab swing %	% turnout (mean)	Change in turnout % point change since GE
First 3 years of Cons governments							
1970–74	10	–8.5	–5.0	9.3	1.8 to Lab	56.5	–12.0
1979–82	8	–12.0	–9.9	11.9	1.1 to Lab	56.8	–14.5
1983–86	11	–13.9	0.3	12.3	7.1 to Lab	63.4	–9.6
1987–90	6	–15.6	4.7	–2.2	10.2 to Lab	53.7	–17.8
1992–95	10	–23.9	9.1	11.6	16.5 to Lab	53.0	–23.6
First 3 years of Labour governments							
1966–69	11	10.4	–14.1	1.9	12.3 to Con	62.1	–12.5
1974–77	17	11.5	–12.3	–5.4	11.9 to Con	57.5	–12.6
1997–2000	12	–0.7	–8.3	7.5	3.8 to Con	42.0	–26.7

Notes

Change in party support: restricted to by-elections with three-cornered contests at both by-election and preceding general election. First three years of Parliament only.

Turnout: all by elections in whole Parliament.

of the Blair government there had been no serious recovery by the Conservative Opposition.

The third feature of the by-elections was the generally abysmal turnout. Turnout at by-elections has always been lower than at general elections, but whereas it averaged just under 60 per cent in the 1960s, 1970s and 1980s, it fell to 53 per cent in the 1992–97 Parliament, and to a mere 42 per cent after 1997. This was not because the by-elections happened to fall in traditionally low turnout areas: the decline in the constituency turnout compared with the preceding general election was twice as steep in the 1997 Parliament (down 26 percentage points) than it had been in the 1960s to 1980s (down about 13 points). It was because the two main parties were no longer able to mobilise their traditional but passive supporters. This was particularly true for the Labour Party in its own heartlands. In industrial Wigan turnout fell to 25.1 per cent; in multi-ethnic Tottenham to 24.4 per cent, and in inner city Leeds Central a mere 19.6 per cent, the lowest at a by-election since the war. The mass apathy was not quite sufficient to rob Labour of any of the seats, but it was a graphic warning that the government could not count on an automatic vote from its traditional supporters. New Labour blamed ramshackle Old Labour local parties; Old Labour blamed newfangled New Labour 'modernisation', which, they claimed, alienated Labour's working-class supporters and left them dangerously exposed to the blandishments of the smaller parties. It was a Blair Effect that the Blairites would not admit to, and it recurred in other elections too.

The local elections, 1998–2000

Local elections were held each year of the Parliament: for the counties in 1997 on the same day as the election, for the London boroughs in 1998, for the 'whole-council' district councils in 1999, and for the 'one-third' district councils and metropolitan boroughs in each of 1998, 1999 and 2000. Assessments of their significance for the national standing of the parties are notoriously tricky. For one thing, turnout is typically only half that of a general election and tends to decline disproportionately among traditional supporters of the party in government. For another, although council elections are used by voters to express a verdict on the Westminster government, large deviations from the underlying national swing occur in particular wards or authorities as a result of local circumstances. Moreover a minority deliberately 'split their ticket' between local and general elections. The Liberal Democrats do consistently better in local than general elections, especially at Labour's expense.[16]

Interpretation of the national situation is complicated further by the pattern of party changeover of wards and councils, which depends on the situation four years previously when the seats were last defended (and which in turn depends on the situation four years previous to that, ad infinitum). The seats contested in the local elections of 1998 to 2000 were last contested in 1994 to 1996, when Conservative fortunes were at a historical nadir. By 1996, the Conservatives had fewer elected councillors than the Liberal Democrats and controlled only thirteen councils. Apparently dramatic Conservative gains turned out to be no more than recovery of territory which normally would not have been ceded in the first place. In the 1999 local elections, for example, the Conservatives made a net gain of 1437 seats while Labour incurred a net loss of 1346. But in 1995, when the seats were previously contested, the Conservatives lost 2018 and Labour gained 1807; in other words, in 1999 the Conservatives only recovered two thirds of the ground it had forfeited in 1995.[17]

The most telling evidence from local elections is the parties' estimated national share of the vote (see Table 3) and the most useful way of drawing conclusions for a general election is a comparison with the equivalent stage of previous Parliaments. By these standards the local elections of both 1998 and 1999 confirmed the indications from by-elections: Labour was losing support, but by much less than normal for the party in office; and the Conservatives were barely advancing on their historically low base of 31.5 per cent at the general election. In the equivalent years of the 1983–87 and 1987–92 Conservative governments, the Conservatives lagged behind Labour by 5 and 3 per cent respectively, but were eventually re-elected. Blair's government was doing noticeably better: it remained 3 to 4 per cent ahead of the Conservatives.

Table 3 Parties' share of the national vote at local elections

	Con	Lab	Lib Dem	% lead for government	Fall in government support since GE	Swing since GE
1984	37	38	22	−1	−5	7.5 to Lab
1985	32	37	27	−5	−10	9.5 to Lab
1986	34	37	27	−3	−8	8.5 to Lab
1988	40	40	18	0	−2	5.5 to Lab
1989	37	40	21	−3	−5	7.0 to Lab
1990	32	40	18	−8	−10	9.5 to Lab
1993	31	41	24	−10	−10	8.0 to Lab
1994	27	41	28	−14	−14	10.0 to Lab
1995	25	46	25	−21	−16	13.5 to Lab
1998	33	37	24	4	−6.5	4.0 to Con
1999	33	36	25	3	−7.5	3.5 to Con
2000	37	29	28	−8	−16.5	11.0 to Con

Source: BBC Political Research Unit.

The local elections in 2000 were a different matter. They translated into a national vote of Conservative 37 per cent, Labour 29 per cent, Liberal Democrat 28 per cent, by no means an abnormal result for a government in its third year, but clearly signifying that disillusion with the government had set in among voters. The vote was startlingly at odds with where the parties stood in the opinion polls: Conservative 30 per cent, Labour 49 per cent and Liberal Democrat 14 per cent. Re-election, let alone comfortable re-election, was not a foregone conclusion.

Quite what precipitated the sharp fall in Labour support compared with the local elections a year earlier is difficult to fathom. There were no obvious crises, scandals, splits or policy failures to alienate the voters. The decline had in fact been signalled in the national polls: Labour support was drifting down at a rate of half a per cent a month over the preceding year, the result presumably of apathy more than active antagonism. And what explained the huge discrepancy with the opinion polls was primarily the exceptionally poor turnout. As for by-elections, so for local elections: after 1997 turnout receded further from its already low level. Since 1945 it had oscillated between 40 and 50 per cent; in 1998, 1999 and 2000 it averaged a mere 29–30 per cent. It was lower still – barely above 20 per cent – in Merseyside, Hull, Salford and other solidly working-class areas. When turnout falls so low in Labour's natural strongholds it has a distorting effect on national vote shares. It also enabled the Liberal Democrats to take urban seats from Labour where they mounted an effective local campaign: they captured Liverpool council in 1998, Sheffield in 1999 and Oldham in 2000. Indeed after 1997 the pattern of Liberal Democrat fortunes went into reverse: they were steadily losing seats to the Conservatives and gaining seats from Labour. At local level the Blair Effect was not working. New Labour was leaving Old Labour voters indifferent, not inspired. And the Liberal Democrats were turning into competitors, not partners.

The elections to the Scottish Parliament and Welsh Assembly

On the day of the 1999 local elections, the Welsh and Scots also went to the polls to elect the members of their newly formed Parliaments. These elections differed from both local and general elections because of their regional focus and because they adopted the 'Additional Member' electoral system – the first time proportional representation has been adopted on the British mainland. Yet the outcome contained many of the features of the local elections (see Table 4).

Once again, the Labour vote[18] not only fell from its general election level but was wholly at variance with the levels reported in the regional polls conducted at the time.[19] In Scotland it declined by a relatively modest 7 percentage points but in Wales it plunged by as much as 17 percentage points.

Table 4 The parties' performance in the 1999 elections to the Scottish Parliament, Welsh Assembly and European Parliament and in the 2000 election to the London Assembly

	Labour % vote	Cons % vote	Lib Dem % vote	SNP/Plaid % vote	Others % vote	Lab maj over Con % vote	Swing since 1997	Turnout	Electoral system used
General election, May 1997	44	31	17	3	5	13	n.a.	71%	First-past-the-post
Scot. Parl. election, May 1999	39	16	14	29	3	21	3.5% to Con 7% to SNP	58%	PR additional member
% change since 1997	-7	-2	1	7	1	-7			
Welsh Assembly election, May 1999	38	16	14	28	4	22	6.5% to Con 17.5% to Plaid	46%	PR member
% change since 1997	-17	-4	2	18	-1	-13			
Euro elections, June 1999	28	36	13	5	19	-8	10.5% to Con	23%	PR regional list
% change since 1997	-16	5	-4	2	14	-21			
London Assembly election, May 2000	32	33	19		16	-1	10% to Con	31%	PR additional member
% change since 1997	-18	2	5		12				

The government was relieved in Scotland, where the polls had been showing the Scottish Nationalists level pegging or even ahead six months earlier; but in Wales it was taken wholly unawares. Once again, the Conservatives were unable to capitalise on the government's unpopularity. In Scotland, where they had been wiped out at the 1997 general election, their vote slipped further in the regional election and they again failed to win a single seat on the constituency ballot (but were allocated 18 'additional members' from the regional list to obtain proportional representation). In Wales, too, they had not won a single seat in 1997 and managed to win just one on the constituency ballots in 1999.

The beneficiaries of voters' dissatisfaction with the government were the nationalist parties. Both performed better than in the simultaneous local elections, which suggests that many voters believed that the nationalist parties had a special role as champions of the region against London. In Scotland the SNP has been the main if usually distant challenger to Labour in its city and industrial heartlands since the 1970s; the regional elections consolidated the SNP's position as Scotland's main Opposition party, albeit at Edinburgh, not Westminster. In Wales, Plaid Cymru broke out of its redoubts in the rural Welsh-speaking West, making substantial inroads into industrial South Wales, and capturing such hitherto impregnable Labour seats as Islwyn, Llanelli and Rhondda. It was suddenly propelled from being a permanent minor party to the main Opposition party in Wales, a position it will probably retain over the long term, in parallel with the SNP in Scotland.

Why did Labour's support fall so much below expectations, especially in Wales? Once again, low turnout – at only 46 per cent – was a factor. Traditional Labour supporters (and Conservatives) turned out in much lower proportions than Plaid Cymru supporters and Liberal Democrats.[20] Plaid supporters, by contrast, were much keener to vote in elections to Wales' own assembly. What kept Labour supporters at home? New Labour's pro-business rhetoric and policies of income tax cuts and public expenditure controls probably played less well in Wales, where unemployment and farm bankruptcies are much more in evidence than the new economy. Labour also paid a price for Downing Street's heavy-handed attempt to impose a trusted Blairite, Alun Michael, as leader of the Welsh Labour Party and thus prospective First Minister, in preference to the wayward but Welsh-speaking Rhodri Morgan, who was preferred by local party members. It was notable that a similarly clumsy attempt by the Labour Party in Scotland to deny the veteran left-winger, Dennis Canavan, a Labour nomination for the Scottish Parliament, exploded in the party's face, when he was handsomely re-elected as an Independent in his Falkirk West constituency. Not surprisingly, perhaps, New Labour's electoral strategy made little headway in a region for which it was not designed. Much more surprising was the strength of the backlash it provoked.

The election to the European Parliament

Throughout the Blair administration Labour's standing was much lower in the polling stations than in the polls. Of no election was this more starkly true than that for the European Parliament, held in June 1999, using for the first time the regional closed-list system of proportional representation. In the polls Labour led the Conservatives by a massive 51 to 27 per cent. In the Euro-election the Conservatives outpolled Labour by 36 to 28 per cent, winning thirty-six of the eighty-four seats to Labour's twenty-nine. It was the first nationwide election won by the Conservatives since 1992. The Labour-to-Conservative swing since the 1997 general election was 10.5 per cent, sufficient if repeated at a general election to return the Conservatives to office as the single largest party. No election shook the confidence of the Labour government as much. William Hague hailed it as a sure sign of Conservative recovery and victories to come; it undoubtedly secured his hitherto ambiguous position as party leader. Critics of New Labour, led by John Prescott, used the result to renew their attack on proportional representation, a curious argument in view of the fact that Labour's tally of seats would have been even lower under the old first-past-the-post system.

What, in fact, did this wholly unexpected rebuff for the government signify? Any interpretation must incorporate the extraordinarily low turnout of 23 per cent. The vote on which the Conservatives 'won' represented a mere 8 per cent of the electorate. The factors that produced such high levels of abstention in by-elections and local elections were also present in the Euro-elections – the sense that little was at stake, apathy about New Labour, moribund local party organisation, scepticism about politics in general. But there were additional factors. Voters were increasingly hostile to 'Europe', could see little connection between the European Parliament and their own interests, and were left cold by an exceptionally low-key campaign in huge regional constituencies with which they had no identity. Turnout fell particularly steeply, compared with both the 1994 Euro-election and the 1997 general election, in strong Labour areas. Thus the Conservatives 'won' by default: their supporters did not stay at home on quite the same scale as Labour's. Yet the majority of them did.

Differential abstention explains most of Labour's poor showing, but a second factor was the defection of some regular Labour supporters to the Nationalists in Scotland and Wales, to the Greens in England and even to the anti-European UK Independence Party in England. The regional list system, combined with voters' sense that little of consequence was at stake, provided the ideal conditions for protest and whimsical voting. The UK Independence Party and the Greens won seats for the first time. The minor parties' combined share of the vote amounted to 23.5 per cent (compared with 7.0 per cent at the general election) and more of it was at the expense of Labour than of the Conservatives.

European elections may be nationwide elections but they too are not general elections. At the next general election the composition of the government will be at stake; a clear choice of governments will be offered; a substantial majority will turn out to vote; and they will do so using the familiar first-past-the-post system. The operation of that system will have changed since 1997, almost certainly to Labour's advantage.

The London elections, May 2000

The outcome of the London elections in May 2000 repeated the pattern of the regional and European elections of the previous year and brought into sharp relief the weakness of a key element in the Blairite strategy, central control of candidate selection. The national party failed to learn the lesson of the Welsh elections. Its crude attempt to deny the Labour nomination to the party members' evident first choice, Ken Livingstone, by the discredited mechanism of the trade union block vote and various other underhand methods, revived memories of Old Labour's discredited ways, publicised Labour divisions, made Blair look shifty, and left a general bad taste. Moreover, it failed: denied the nomination, Livingstone stood as an Independent, and won comfortably, reducing the liked but hapless Frank Dobson, the official Labour candidate, to a poor third place with only 13 per cent of the vote. He might have done even worse, if the Conservative candidate, Steve Norris, had been the united and early choice of the London Conservatives, rather than the latterday and disputed replacement for the disgraced Lord Archer.

The Assembly election, which lacked the colour of the mayoral race, offers the better indicator of the parties' standing (see Table 4 above). The pattern was familiar. The turnout was a dismal 33 per cent, despite the wide choice of parties, party election broadcasts, a free mailshot for every mayoral candidate, and the sheer entertainment value of the mayoral con-test, relayed in every detail by the national media as well as London's *Evening Standard*. Turnout was lowest – below 30 per cent – in Labour's four safest Assembly constituencies, in three of which Labour's share of the vote fell particularly sharply. It declined by 25 percentage points in the largely working class North East constituency covering Hackney, Islington and Walthamstow, for example, and by 21 points in inner city Lambeth and Southwark. Overall, Labour's share of the London vote plunged by 18 percentage points from its 1997 general election level, a very similar decline to that in Wales (17 points) and the European elections (16 points) a year earlier. Yet the Conservatives failed to profit from Londoners' indifference to the Labour Party. They won slightly more constituency votes than Labour (but fewer list votes) but advanced by a mere 2 percentage points on their paltry 1997 general election level. It was the minor parties that were able to take advantage of proportional representation, and the lack of significant and in particular tax-raising powers of the London Assembly: the Greens won 11 per cent of the list vote and three 'top up' members of the Assembly and fringe parties of the far Right and Left did relatively well, especially in working-class areas. Fewer than one in three Londoners voted for their own mayor or Assembly; fewer than one in ten came out to vote either Labour or Conservative. No election better illustrated the new depths of indifference the British electorate felt towards conventional party politics under the Blair government. Whatever else it achieved, the Blair government's programme of constitutional reform did not usher in the democratic renewal it was meant to produce.

The pro-Labour bias of the electoral system

For the last decade the electoral system has been strongly biased in favour of the Labour Party at the expense of the Conservatives. It delivers considerably more seats to Labour than to the Conservatives for the same share of the national vote and as a result Labour needs a considerably lower share of that vote than the Conservatives do to secure an overall majority.

Two factors have created the bias. First, Labour seats have smaller electorates than Conservative seats. This is partly because Labour dominates Scotland and Wales where statue requires the parliamentary constituencies to be smaller, and partly because Labour is strong in the de-populating industrial and inner city areas while the Conservatives are strong in the outer suburban and rural areas, which are growing in population. Despite the changes to the constituency boundaries, which were based on 1991 population figures, by 1997 Labour seats contained 6500 fewer electors on average than Conservative seats (and 9000 fewer voters because of lower turnout). Second, the first-past-the-post system rewards parties with a geographically concentrated vote and penalises parties with an evenly distributed vote. In 1997 the Conservatives lost most votes in seats where they were strong in 1992 and thus had seats to lose. Combined with anti-Conservative tactical voting this produced a much more even spread of the Conservative vote than of the Labour vote.[21]

The degree of bias in the electoral system in 1997 can be illustrated by the following facts about the Conservatives' handicap and Labour's cushion at the next election. On the assumption of a uniform national swing across constituencies, and no change in the Liberal Democrat vote, then:

- Even if the Labour lead at the next election is reduced to 5 per cent of the vote, as polls at the time of writing indicate, its overall majority would be a very comfortable eighty-five to ninety.
- Even if the Conservatives drew level with Labour at 38 per cent apiece, Labour would have an overall majority of seventeen in Parliament.
- Even if the Conservatives drew 6 percentage points ahead of Labour (i.e. 41 to 35 per cent) Labour would remain the largest party in the Commons and would head a minority administration.

- To obtain an overall majority of one the Conservatives would need a 10 percentage point lead in the national vote and a swing of 11.5 per cent.

Would the bias weaken if voters swung strongly back to the Conservatives at the next election? Without an unpopular Conservative government to vote against, anti-Conservative tactical voting might fade. On the other hand, Liberal Democrats and Labour supporters will probably continue to see their parties as closer to each other than to the Conservatives on the key issues of Europe, taxation, social spending and constitutional reform, so anti-Conservative tactical voting is unlikely to disappear altogether. However, other pro-Labour biases will get stronger. Continuing migration from cities to countryside and from inner-city to outer suburb will produce an even larger discrepancy in the size of Labour and Conservative constituencies. Moreover, there will be a new pro-Labour bias: on past record, new MPs in marginal seats (very largely Labour) build up a small personal vote by the following election, which protects them from the full force of an anti-government swing. A swing back to the Conservatives on a wholly unprecedented scale will be required to overcome the electoral system's bias and eject Labour from office. No measure of the electorate's mood during the first Blair government, not even the polls at the height of the fuel crisis, suggests that that will happen.

Blair's Electoral Strategy: A Report Card

Blair's electoral strategy has had mixed success. On the credit side, he has retained much of his new support from Middle England, by a strong economy, non-doctrinaire policies, an amorphous rhetoric of 'inclusion' and, until the fuel crisis, the avoidance of major cock-ups. Even in its chastened state Labour remains the preferred party for leadership and competence and on the public service issues of health, education and social security. Its centrist policies and discourse have left Hague with little room to manoeuvre frontal attacks on the main battlefield of taxing and spending; instead he has had to content himself with guerilla assaults on such popular issues as asylum seekers; rural crime and the Dome. Oscillating between 'compassionate' Conservatism and tax-cutting radicalism, the Conservatives have been unable to convince the electorate that they are an alternative government in waiting and have struggled to add much to the core of support to which they were reduced in 1997. Even on the single European currency, the one big issue on which the Conservatives are close to majority public opinion, Blair's commitment to a referendum, but procrastination on the date, is likely to draw the issue's electoral sting. Finally, Blair has steered Labour close enough to the Liberal Democrats, as their sharing of government in Scotland and Wales shows, to be confident that anti-

Conservative tactical voting will operate again next time, if on a slightly lower scale.

On the debit side, Blair was unable to mobilise widespread enthusiasm for New Labour at the general election. He has since failed to convert the fragile goodwill that followed the rejection of an exceptionally disliked Conservative government into something more solid. He has not turned dealignment into realignment. By neglecting Labour's traditional supporters in its home territory – if not substantively, then symbolically and organisationally – the Blairites have left Labour exposed to widespread apathy and to the blandishments of smaller parties. They have allowed their bedrock to erode without replacing it by equally solid foundations elsewhere. The Blair government cannot match the fervent commitment that the Thatcher governments inspired among a sizeable minority of the electorate. It might well be damaged by adverse differential turnout in its marginal seats; more significantly, it is vulnerable to volatile swings among voters to whom it has provided no political or social anchors.

The electoral conundrum of the first Blair government is that it has done remarkably well *in* the polls but, by-elections aside, remarkably badly *at* the polls. The polls offer one verdict on Blair's electoral strategy; actual elections quite another. Both cast light on Blair's electoral strategy but neither is a reliable pointer to the next election result. A strong economy, a hamstrung Opposition and, above all, an advantageous electoral system will probably see Blair through to a second term. None of these factors were a central part of his electoral strategy, but they may well give him a second opportunity to improve upon it.

Notes

1 John Curtice and Michael Steed, 'The Results Analysed', in David Butler and Dennis Kavanagh, *The British General Election of 1997*, Macmillan, 1997, pp. 295–325 (p. 299).

2 Ibid., p. 312. A different analysis concludes that their target seats swung to Labour by 1 percentage point more than the non-target seats. See David Denver, Gordon Hands and Simon Henig, 'Triumph of Targeting? Constituency Campaigning in the 1997 Election', in David Denver *et al.*, *British Elections & Parties Review (Volume 8: The 1997 General Election)*, Frank Cass, 1998, pp. 171–190 (p. 186).

3 Ivor Crewe, 'The opinion polls: confidence restored?', *Parliamentary Affairs*, 50(4), 1997, pp. 569–85.

4 David Sanders, 'The Impact of Left-Right Ideology', in Geoffrey Evans and Pippa Norris, eds., *Critical Elections: British Parties and Voters in Long-Term Perspective*, Sage Publications, 1999, pp. 181–206.

5 *Gallup Political & Economic Index*, No. 440, May 1997, New Malden, Surrey: The Gallup Organisation.

6 Curtice and Steed, *loc. cit.*, p. 313.
7 John Bartle and Ivor Crewe, 'The Impact of Party Leaders in Britain: Strong Assumptions, Weak Evidence', in Anthony King, ed., *Leaders' Personalities and the Outcome of Democratic Elections*, Oxford University Press, 2001, forthcoming.
8 Ivor Crewe and Katarina Thomson, 'Party Loyalties: Realignment or Dealignment?', in Geoffrey Evans and Pippa Norris, eds, *op. cit.*, pp. 64–86 (p. 17).
9 The 'best for Prime Minister' question was not asked by the opinion polls in 1982 at the height of Mrs Thatcher's popularity after victory in the Falklands War. But at the 1983 election, which she won so handsomely, the BBC/Gallup election-day survey reported that she was preferred by a relatively modest majority of 11 percentage points over David Steel, the leader of the Liberals. See Ivor Crewe, 'How to Win a Landslide Without Really Trying: Why the Conservatives Won in 1983', in Austin Ranney, ed., *Britain At The Polls, 1983*, N.C. Durham: Duke University Press/ American Enterprise Institute, 1985, pp. 155–96 (p. 176).
10 David Sanders, 'How important is Labour's "heartland" vote?' in P. Diamond, ed., *Must Labour Choose? Contributions to the Heartlands Debate*, Progress, 2000, forthcoming.
11 *The Guardian*, 19 September 2000, p. 4.
12 'Polls Archive', MORI website. Respondents were asked 'Do you think that the Prime Minister, Tony Blair [Conservative leader, William Hague] is or is not in touch with what ordinary people think? The figures were: 'in touch': Blair 35 per cent, Hague 37 per cent; 'not in touch': Blair 62 per cent, Hague 55 per cent. The telephone poll was conducted on 13–14 October.
13 Pamela Meadows, 'Against London', *Prospect*, November 2000, p. 15.
14 In the MORI/Carlton poll (see note 12 for details) Labour was described as united by 41 per cent; the Conservatives by 26 per cent. An NOP/*Sunday Times* poll conducted on 11–13 October reported that Labour was preferred to the Conservatives by 39 to 31 per cent as the party 'you would trust to make you and your family better off' and by 37 to 25 per cent as the party 'with the best team of ministers'. Blair was preferred to Hague by 36 to 25 per cent as 'the better prime minister'.
15 A Gallup poll published in the *Daily Telegraph* on 11 November 2000 reported that 56 per cent regarded the measures as inadequate and 59 per cent said that the government 'had not shown a willingness to listen to the public's concerns'.
16 The following figures for the joint general and local election of 1997 make the point:

	Con %	Lab %	Lib Dem %	Others %
General election, 1 May 1997	32	45	17	6
Local elections, 1 May 1997	29	40	26	5
Difference	–3%	–5%	9%	–1%

See Colin Rallings and Michael Thrasher, 'Split-Ticket Voting at the 1997

British General and Local Elections: An Aggregate Analysis', in David Denver, *et. al., op. cit.*, pp. 111–34 (p. 116).

17 Colin Rallings and Michael Thrasher, 'Election Report: 1999 Local Elections', *Politics Review*, 9(1), September 1999, pp. 23–25.

18 All voting figures for the Scottish and Welsh elections refer to the constituency ballots, not the regional list ballots used to produce the additional members.

19 An NOP/*HTV* poll and a Scottish Opinion/*Daily Record* poll, both conducted immediately before the regional elections, overestimated the Labour vote in Wales and Scotland by 9 and 8 percentage points respectively.

20 See Richard Wyn Jones and Dafydd Tristan, 'A "Quiet Earthquake": The First Elections to the National Assembly for Wales', Institute of Welsh Politics, University of Aberystwyth, *mimeo*, 2000, p. 6.

21 John Curtice and Michael Steed, *loc. cit.*, pp. 314–18.

© Chris Riddell

Chapter 5

THE CIVIL SERVICE

Rod Rhodes

Introduction

NEW LABOUR WAS slow to get under way in modernising the civil service. Initially, the government promised a White Paper on 'Better Government' for autumn 1997. It would clean up politics; root out waste and inefficiency; improve regulation; listen to the people in developing services; provide greater transparency and accountability; use the potential of IT to deliver services, not just information; and break down institutional barriers to working together. The (then) Chancellor of the Duchy of Lancaster, David Clark, promised a radical initiative which would set out the vision of what government would look like in fifteen years. It was repeatedly delayed from 'early in 1998' to June or July. The White Paper *Modernising Government* (Cm 4310 1999) finally emerged in March 1999. I err on the side of understatement when I infer public sector reform was not a priority.[1]

The government wants joined-up and strategic policy making; a focus on the users of public services; high quality and efficient public services; and new information technology to meet the needs of citizens and business. It is also committed to the public sector and its staff. The phrases roll off the tongue. The reforms lag behind. The easy assessment is that government policy was pragmatic and we got more of the same. In fact, the drip, drip style of reform obscured an important shift of emphasis from markets to networks.

In this chapter, I describe the main strands of civil service reform, discuss the problems inherited by New Labour and assess whether their reforms will deal with these problems. I argue there has been a shift from the providing state of Old Labour and the minimal state of 'Thatcherism' to New Labour's enabling state characterised by joined-up government. If Margaret

Thatcher's reform saw the coming of the can-do manager, Tony Blair's call for joined-up government signals a further switch from management to diplomacy.

Varieties of Reform

Reform has taken many forms over the past two decades: privatisation, marketisation, corporate management, regulation, decentralisation and political control. I describe the changes briefly, concentrating on New Labour and on the effects on the civil service in particular rather than the public sector in general.

Privatisation

Privatisation refers to the sale of public assets to the private sector. Whether the policy was a success, and one can argue about its several objectives and the extent to which they were achieved, there can be no doubt about the scale of the programme. The government sold over fifty major organisations, raising some £64 billion to pay for tax cuts. The scale of privatisation will necessarily decline under New Labour simply because so many public assets have been sold already. However, the government do not rule it out on ideological grounds – for example it sold 60 per cent of the equity in the Commonwealth Development Corporation.

Privatisation had one obvious result for the civil service; numbers fell sharply. From a high of 762,000 in 1976, numbers fell to 481,000 in 1998 (a fall of 38 per cent). Most significant, non-industrial civil servants fell from 571,000 to 430,000 (a fall of 25 per cent) whereas industrial civil servants fell from 209,000 to 33,000 (a fall of 84 per cent which accounts for 63 per cent of the total fall in civil service numbers).

Marketisation

Marketisation refers to the use of market mechanisms in the delivery of public services. In the UK, the term covers mainly contracting-out (for example, compulsory competitive tendering in local government); quasi-markets in the guise of the purchaser–provider split (for example, the National Health Service (NHS); and experiments with voucher schemes (for example, nursery education). New Labour curbed marketisation. The government ended the purchaser–provider split in health and abolished nursery vouchers. However, the proposed moratorium on contracting-out (*Hansard* 22 May 1996 col. 311) did not happen. New Labour is no enemy of the private sector and public–private partnerships will continue and expand. For example, the private finance initiative (PFI) in health involves the private sector building hospitals and leasing them back to the public sector for up to sixty years. Some thirty-one hospitals will be so financed. According to the *Modernising Government* White Paper, the policy is that marketisation 'has a role to play, again not out of dogmatism but out of pragmatism, because we want the best value for money'.

Corporate management

Corporate management refers to introducing private sector management in the public sector. It stresses: hands-on, professional management; explicit targets, standards and measures of performance; managing by results; value for money; and more recently closeness to the consumer. There are many variations on this list and most have their roots in a preference for private sector management styles, stressing performance measurement in general and output measurement in particular. For example, civil servants now have contracts and build their own CV rather than having their careers managed for them.

Corporate management has a long history in the UK. Its present-day hallmark is the '3Es' of economy, efficiency and effectiveness with economy ever present. This first emphasis shifted to making services transparent to their consumers through such mechanisms as the Citizen's Charter. New Labour's policy is pragmatic, with the government supporting initiatives such as 'Benchmarking', which aims to measure and improve quality; and 'Investor in People', which sets standards for human resources management. Both continue the mini-tradition of importing private sector management practices into the public sector. New Labour has 'reinvented' the Citizen's Charter as 'Service First'. For example, the government has set up a People's Panel comprising 5000 people from all walks of life to give their views on improving service delivery. It also has a touching faith in the ability of information technology to improve the quality and responsiveness of local service delivery. Sir Richard Wilson's Report to the Prime Minister on *Civil Service Reform* (1999) clearly shows the importance New Labour attaches to getting high levels of performance and value for money from the civil service. Managerialism marches into the new millennium in a flurry of jargon.

Regulation

As the boundaries of the state were redrawn in the 1980s, the British state sought to strengthen its ability to regulate and audit institutions, their policies and implementation of those policies. The government substituted regulation for ownership, and so multiplied the watchdogs of the new private sector monopolies. The 'audit explosion' also refers to all forms of internal and external regulation. It covers management and financial audit and evaluation. The emphasis falls on administrative control, not trust, and on quantified, external, retrospective forms of control.

It is internal regulation that has the greatest effect on the civil service and the increase is massive. Christopher Hood and his colleagues identify 134 such bodies spending £776 million a year in running costs and incurring roughly the same amount in compliance costs. Examples of such bodies range from the National Audit Office, the Prisons Inspectorate, the Parliamentary Commissioner for Administration, the Office of Public Service and the Higher Education Funding Council. If anything the growth has speeded up under New Labour. Hood identifies at least twelve major new organisations created or announced by March 1999. They include: the Benefit Fraud Inspectorate (eighty-six people and £3.4 million); and the Commission for Health Improvement and the National Institute of Clinical Excellence for the National Health Service. Hood estimates the cost of New Labour's changes as at least £20 million a year.

Hood also detects a significant shift in regulatory philosophy under New Labour with a growing awareness of the costs of regulation and the need for consistency of practice between regulators. For example, the government has set up the Public Audit Forum to share ideas about good practice. Most significant is the trend to 'enforced self-regulation'; that is more formal, external regulation for poor performers but what Tony Blair calls 'light touch inspection regimes' for good performers.[2]

The strict financial climate saw the Treasury become more powerful. The Conservative government introduced several changes in budgeting and financial management to strengthen its control of total spending while ostensibly increasing financial delegation. However, financial discretion was an illusion. The brute reality of everyday life was the financial control that lies at the core of the UK reform package. It remains so under New Labour. Public spending plans are set for three years. Resource accounting seeks to link resources to policy outputs. The comprehensive spending review identifies the government's spending priorities. The strategy is to have targets and other measures to ensure that these priorities are translated into services. So, spending patterns were changed and 'Public Service Agreements' were introduced to impose the necessary discipline.

Decentralisation

Decentralisation encompasses both deconcentration and devolution. Deconcentration refers to the redistribution of administrative responsibilities in central government. Devolution refers to the exercise of political authority by lay, elected, institutions within areas defined by community characteristics. The UK reforms of the 1980s and 1990s sought to deconcentrate managerial authority; for example, to agencies. With New Labour, devolution became a political priority in Britain.

Deconcentration

Agencification means creating semi-autonomous agencies responsible for operational management. The key notion is to separate operational management from the policy-making core or central department so the agency has freedom to manage. It is a classical doctrine of public administration. By January 1998, there were 138 agencies employing 77 per cent of the civil service and the programme was almost complete.

New Labour accepted agencies after early doubts. The only issue is whether they will resist interfering. They seem certain to succumb to temptation, just like their predecessors. Thus, Jack Straw, Home Secretary, assumed responsibility for answering questions on the prison service instead of the agency's director-general. There is no consensus about the extent of deconcentration to agencies. For the chief executives of many agencies the reality of everyday life is constant interference by parent department, Treasury and Cabinet Office. As one chief executive pointed out: 'I am a civil servant and cannot say no.' There are now agencies aplenty. Ministerial ability to leave them alone remains, as ever, variable. Decentralisation continues to be elusive.

Devolution

On devolution, Scottish civil servants transferred to the Parliament but, as staff of the Scottish Executive, continue to be part of a unified civil service. There are obvious tensions in such dual loyalties. The government recognises there is a problem, asserting the 'ultimate loyalty of civil servants will remain to the Crown'. However, 'in practice the loyalty of individual civil servants will be to whichever administration they are serving' and they 'will continue to take their instructions from their departmental ministers'. It seems certain the UK civil service will become less unified.

Scotland is now embedded in a changed and changing set of institutional links. A Joint Ministerial Committee (JMC) consisting of ministers of the UK government, Scottish ministers, members of the Cabinet of the Welsh Assembly and ministers in the Northern Ireland Executive Committee will provide central co-ordination. It will consider non-devolved matters which impinge on devolved responsibilities and conversely. For Europe, the JMC will co-ordinate the devolved administrations, which may have offices in Brussels but will 'support and advance the single UK negotiating line'. Sir Richard Wilson, in a speech to a Senior Civil Service Conference in October 1998, commented the civil service 'are going to have to learn skills that we haven't learned before'. As one insider commented: 'We have a knack of taking decisions under anaesthetic and it hasn't worn off yet' (private information).

Before 1972, local government could be described as part of the constitution. No such claim would be made today. British central government has exerted ever-greater control over local authorities, especially their spending. Policy was centralising even if the outcomes were not always as intended. After much procrastination, the New Labour government decided there would be no regional assemblies for England. It is also nervous about devolving power to local government because it wants to keep control over public spending. The proposals for elected mayors are the centrepiece of the government's White Paper, *Modern Local Government. In Touch with the People* (Cm 4014 1998). The core theme is the renewal of democracy but the government displays a marked reluctance to empower local authorities.

It is unusual for a discussion of the civil service to talk about local government but it is necessary because the clarion call for joined-up government is the distinctive strand in New Labour's reforms. Tony Blair stated the aims succinctly: 'joined-up problems need joined-up solutions' and this theme runs through the *Modernising Government* White Paper with its frequent references to 'joined-up' government and 'holistic governance'. The terms cover both horizontal joining-up between central departments and vertical joining-up between all the agencies involved in delivering services. So services must be effective and co-ordinated and the principles of joined-up government apply across the public sector and to voluntary and private sector organisations.

Joining-up takes various forms. For example, there are area-based programmes or 'action zones' (twenty-six in health, twenty-five in education) linking central and local government, health authorities, the private sector and voluntary organisations; and group focused programmes such as the 'Better Government for Older People' pilot. The state is an enabling partner that joins and steers flexible networks and the civil service must adapt. Already the jargon breeds – diplomats, boundary-spanning roles – but whatever the label, the task is to build bridges between the organisations involved in designing policies and delivering services. In future civil servants will manage packages of services, packages of organisations and packages of governments.

Political control

The efforts of ministers to reassert political control over the civil service is a common feature of recent public sector reform in Westminster systems. Before the 1997 general election, there was concern that the civil service had worked under one-party rule for too long. Such fears were misplaced. The transition to New Labour went smoothly and the Prime Minister wrote to the (then) Head of the Home Civil Service, Sir Robin Butler, congratulating him on the handover. There was no night of the long knives for permanent secretaries, although several will retire over the next few years, so the Prime Minister will have plentiful opportunity to make changes.

There was a notable increase in political advisers from thirty-eight under John Major to seventy-four under Tony Blair with the costs rising from £1.8 billion to £3.9 billion (see the chapters by Riddell and Seldon). The most notable increase was in the Number 10 Policy Unit with twenty-five advisers. The most notable cull took place in the Government Information and Communication Service where twenty-five heads or deputies either resigned or were replaced, prompting the Select Committee on Public

Administration to wonder if there was now a two-tier system of information in which the civil servants played a subordinate role.[3] The aim was better co-ordination of government policy. Sir Richard Wilson conducted a review of the Cabinet Office, which aimed to make it the corporate heart of the civil service and strengthen cross-departmental co-ordination. Specific innovations include: merging the Office of Public Service with the rest of the Cabinet Office; setting up a Performance and Innovation Unit to improve co-ordination; and incorporating the Civil Service College to a new Centre for Management and Policy Studies which will, for example, jointly train ministers and civil servants.

The Treasury and Number 10 are the nexus of New Labour's policy making (see the chapter by Stephens). Recent changes aim to support that process and should be interpreted as centralisation because the linking theme is better policy co-ordination by Number 10 and stronger corporate management of the civil service by the Cabinet Office. As Peter Hennessy argues, the Number 10 Unit and the Cabinet Office drive government policy making with (initially) Peter Mandelson as the Cabinet enforcer. This proactive core is supported by some two hundred task forces, advisory groups and reviews designed to tackle, for example, the 'wicked issues' that cut across departmental boundaries. So, 'Number 10 is omnipresent in the serious policy reviews'. One exemplar of the new centralisation is the *Ministerial Code* with its injunctions that all major interviews, press releases and policy statements should be cleared with Number 10.[4]

The *Modernising Government* White Paper concludes the civil service faces seven challenges:

- Implementing constitutional reform in a way that preserves a unified civil service and ensures close working between the UK government and the devolved administrations.
- Getting staff in all departments to integrate the EU dimension into policy thinking.
- Focusing work on public services so as to improve their quality, make them more innovative and responsive to users and ensure that they are delivered in an efficient and joined-up way.
- Creating a more innovative and less risk averse culture in the civil service.
- Improving collaborative working across organisational boundaries.
- Managing the civil service so as to equip it to meet these challenges.
- Thinking ahead strategically to future priorities (p. 56).

There is an Action Plan for implementing the White Paper's proposals and the government will publish regularly the various 'milestones' as targets are achieved. The Performance and Innovation Unit in the Cabinet Office has published its manual on *Wiring It Up* (2000), setting out how to manage cross-cutting policies and services. The Modernising Government secretariat of the Cabinet Office published *Professional Policy Making for the Twenty-First Century* (1999) which resuscitated the rational policy making model so beloved of earlier generations of reformers. If the volume of publications is a relevant indicator, there is reform aplenty. But statements of intent are not enough. Now I need to answer two questions. Do these reforms overcome the unintended consequences of previous reforms? Will the reforms enable the government to meet its stated objectives?

Unintended Consequences

The Conservative government's public sector reforms created many problems, namely: fragmentation, steering, accountability, politicisation and managerial roles.

Fragmentation

The most obvious result of the new system is institutional fragmentation. Typically, services are now delivered through a combination of local government, special-purpose bodies, the voluntary sector and the private sector. The scale of the change is not always appreciated; for example, the special-purpose bodies sector is now larger than local government! The *Modernising Government* White Paper provides its own illustration of the large number of organisations involved in providing long-term domiciliary care. Service delivery depends as never before, therefore, on linking organisations and the White Paper's focus on joined-up government is a direct response to the problem.

Steering

The government did not strengthen strategic capacity with the other changes and concern about the effectiveness of central policy making predates the election of New Labour. So, the (then) Head of the Home Civil Service, Sir Robin Butler, commented:

> it is essential that it does not reach the point where individual
> Departments and their Agencies become simply different unconnected
> elements in the overall public sector, with . . . *no real working
> mechanisms for policy co-ordination* (emphasis added).[5]

The former Yorkshire Regional Health provides a good example of the limits to the centre's ability to steer. The parliamentary Committee of Public Accounts investigated the Yorkshire Regional Health Authority (RHA). It found that, for example, to choose one out of a litany, the RHA awarded a contract to Yorkshire Water for clinical waste incineration worth £7.2

million of capital and £2 million a year in revenue. It was not let competitively. It was for *fifteen* years. The Authority did not get NHS Executive approval. The problem was interorganisational; the central NHS Executive could not steer. Government policy is compulsory competitive tendering. EU policy requires all major public sector contracts to be open to member states. But Yorkshire is exempt, it would seem.[6]

There are two limits to central steering. First, the centre has rubber levers; pulling the central policy lever does not necessarily mean something happens at the bottom. Such frustrations lead to colourful language. So, for the Department of Health, instilling financial discipline in doctors is likened to 'herding cats'. Despite several attempts over the year to strengthen central control over such departmental policy silos, the problem persists. Second, ministerial or baronial government is a long-standing feature of British government. 'Ministers are like medieval barons in that they preside over their own, sometimes vast, policy territory. Within that territory they are largely supreme . . . The ministers have their own policy space . . . The ministers fight – or form alliances – with other barons in order to get what they want. They resent interference in their territory by other barons and will fight to defend it.'[7] Power-dependence characterises the links between both barons and the barons and Prime Minister and forms the fault line at the heart of the machine. So, New Labour criticises central departments for acting as iron cages frustrating action on the wicked issues. It calls for a corporate approach, stronger horizontal policy making, reforms of the Cabinet Office and a Prime Minister's department. These calls are not new. For the umpteenth time, a government confronts the problem of the centre's strategic capability. Co-ordination is a central theme not only of the *Modernising Government* White Paper but of the Prime Minister's search to control government policy making.

Accountability

Fragmentation erodes accountability because sheer institutional complexity obscures who is accountable to whom for what. Special-purpose, nominated bodies have multiplied in place of central departments and elected local councils for the delivery of some services. Again, Yorkshire RHA dramatically illustrates the point; the catalogue of misdeeds is eye-catching. The Committee of Public Accounts was 'concerned' about a further eight instances of 'unacceptable' behaviour which they noted 'with surprise' and 'serious concern', including on one occasion, an 'appalled'. They also consider the remedial action 'deeply unsatisfactory'. It paints the picture of an Authority that embraced the culture of the day, neglected its classical stewardship role, and got away with 'blue murder' for several years. Control was exerted – later, much later. No one was brought to book for the substantial waste of public money. The money was not recovered. Nor can Yorkshire RHA be dismissed as a single, aberrant organisation. It is an example of both private government in action and the problem of holding networks to account.

There is confusion at the heart of policy between responsiveness and accountability and it matters for two reasons. First, responsive service delivery as envisaged by such innovations as the Citizen's Charter supplements but does not replace political accountability because the consumer has no powers to hold a government agency to account. Citizens have become consumers of services. The Citizen's Charter is the government's equivalent of the Consumer Association's magazine, *Which*, but I doubt that it is as, let alone more, effective than *Which*. There is a larger debate about empowering citizens to exercise democratic control. It was a muted debate in British government and none of the policies discussed in this chapter offer a significant role to citizens.

Second, agencification aggravated the accountability 'gap' because the government introduced no new arrangements to preserve the constitutional convention of ministerial responsibility. William Waldegrave tried to justify this inaction by drawing a distinction between 'responsibility, which can be delegated, and accountability, which remains firmly with the minister'. On this view, agencies and the other reforms clarified responsibility but left 'the Minister properly accountable for the policies he settles'. The distinction hinges on clear definitions of both policy and management and of the respective roles and responsibilities of ministers, senior civil servants and agency chief executives. They do not exist. Current arrangements allow the minister to take the credit when the policy goes well but to blame the chief executive when things go wrong and examples abound. There is no clear dividing line between policy and operations, undermining ministerial accountability to Parliament by helping ministers avoid blame.[8]

In short, British government has undergone a significant decrease in political accountability. It is a major problem. It is not confined to agencies. The Public Service Committee wanted a more direct line of accountability between Parliament, civil servants and the chief executives of agencies. The (then) Conservative government rejected its proposals. New Labour remains largely silent on the topic. The *Modernising Government* White Paper emphasises 'responsiveness' to citizens as service users. Accountability covers: extending the remit of the Parliamentary Ombudsman; strengthening audit; and the claim that ministerial appointments strengthen accountability. Waldegrave's distinction between managerial responsibility for delivering services and ministerial accountability to Parliament is alive and well and the White Paper addresses only the former.

Politicisation

The civil service no longer has a monopoly of policy advice. Ministers now insist on and get advice from many sources. So far, however, there has been no overt politicisation of appointments to the senior civil service. Mrs

Thatcher's appointments led Hugo Young to describe the service as 'a thoroughly Thatcherised satrapy' but the Royal Institute of Public Administration's working group concluded there had been 'personalisation not politicisation' in senior appointments. There may have been no overt party politicisation of the higher civil service, but we have lost 'institutional scepticism'. Margaret Thatcher was determined to appoint 'can-do' managers.[9]

When New Labour appointed seventy-four political advisers, it threw petrol on the dying embers of the politicisation debate, as did the (abandoned) attempt to appoint Jonathan Powell, Blair's Chief of Staff, as his Principal Private Secretary (a post normally filled by a civil servant). But again, the search is for officials who can deliver government policies, although some senior civil servants fear that, with open competition and contracts, the era of political appointments to the top job is already with us (private information).

Managerial roles

The senior civil service has three main roles: political advice (to ministers), management (of their departments) and diplomacy (or managing external relations). Advising the minister cannot be reduced to giving policy advice. It is also about support and fire fighting and can extend to the grey area of party politics. Ministers now draw on several sources of policy advice; political advisers, think tanks, consultants. The senior civil service must also ensure the department 'delivers', a phrase which covers both organising the department and managing its human resources. The focus is strategic management and operational management, or the day-to-day running of the department, is increasingly and extensively delegated. Finally, diplomacy covers all the external relations of the department, that is, other central departments, other public agencies (including local authorities), Parliament, the media and the EU. As Sir Douglas Wass noted, 'finesse and diplomacy are an essential ingredient in public service'.

Views differ on the extent to which political advisers have eroded the senior civil service's role in providing policy advice. Political advisers rule OK. But it is not OK for some senior civil servants who believe the advisers give poor advice and are not accountable (private information). The Neill Committee on Standards in Public Life agreed that the framework for appointing advisers could be improved to promote accountability.[10] Clearly, the civil service no longer has a monopoly. As obvious, there is great variation between departments; for example, many ministers have only one adviser while five Cabinet ministers have more than two. The senior civil service is not bypassed, nor is their role reduced to that of second stringers to political advisers. Rather, they put together packages of advice from many sources (private information). New Labour may have accelerated this trend but it did not initiate it.

Sceptics doubt that the senior civil service has picked up more than a veneer of the new managerialism. Theakston concludes that reforms have affected the senior civil service in three ways. First, 'there is now less group self-confidence'. Second, they are rarely policy initiators; 'they are much less active in pushing their own policy views'. Third, they have a much higher public profile. They are no longer 'statesmen in disguise'. He stresses their role as 'administrative conservators' who guard the institutions, processes and staff of government and the distinctive values and principles of public service. However, so far, the key shift has been for senior civil servants to become policy managers.[11]

Recent public sector reforms, especially corporate management and the '3Es', challenge the culture of Whitehall. Many fear an erosion of public service ethics. With the spread of patronage, and one-party government for eighteen years, worries grew about standards of conduct. Allegedly, management reforms undermine the generalist tradition and lead to the demise of public duty. Agencies fragment the civil service. Civil servants are no longer socialised into its shared traditions. The principles of the Citizen's Charter replace the public service ethos but businesslike methods are no substitute for traditional values.

Corporate management, open competition and macho-ministers add up to a challenge to the public service ethos. So, interest in a code of ethics grew. The Conservative government drafted a code and New Labour proposes to give it statutory force, although parliamentary times has still not been made for the measure. Its *Ministerial Code* states that ministers have 'a duty to uphold the political impartiality of the Civil Service' and 'to ensure that influence over appointments is not abused for partisan purposes'. The *Modernising Government* White Paper also asserts its commitment to public services and public servants although it will 'not tolerate mediocrity'. So, the glue still holds at least for the senior civil service.

Will Government be Modernised?

Will the government's reforms resolve any of these problems and meet the stated objectives? Its policy is more of the same, with a twist – and the twist is joined-up government. Four issues remain unresolved: co-ordination; the mix of governing structures; accountability; and top management reviews.

The holy grail of co-ordination

The search for horizontal co-ordination between departments and vertical co-ordination between public sector organisations lies at the heart of New Labour's reforms. As Kavanagh and Seldon point out, we have seen prime ministerial centralisation in the guises of institutional innovation and more resources for Number 10 and the Cabinet Office. There is also strong political and policy direction as the Treasury and Number 10 seek a strong grip on the government machine. The pendulum swings yet again as the centre promotes co-ordination and strategic oversight to combat Whitehall's departmentalism. Such 'power grabs' are 'a reaction to felt weakness, a frustration with the inability to pull effective levers'.[12]

However, despite strong pressures for more co-ordination throughout Western Europe:

> 'the co-ordination activities of the core remain in practice modest in scope: most internal co-ordination takes place at lower levels of the state hierarchy; is rarely strategic or even directive, but selective, issue oriented and reactive; is negative in the sense that it is characterised by the toleration of heavily compartmentalised units pursuing mutual avoidance strategies to reduce tensions' . . . All governments have resorted to a variety of measures to reduce the burden of co-ordination . . . but with only limited success and . . . many of the measures adopted have served only to complicate and even increase co-ordination requirements.

Co-ordination is the philosopher's stone of modern government, ever sought, but always just beyond reach.[13]

There are some obvious problems facing efforts to improve both horizontal and vertical co-ordination. Many commentators have noted the fall from grace of the traditional mechanisms of horizontal co-ordination; the Cabinet and Cabinet committees. However, one of the disadvantages of such new horizontal mechanisms as task forces is that they do not necessarily involve ministers. But if action is to follow, ministerial support and commitment will probably be necessary. So, recently, there has been a revival of Cabinet committees because they are the traditional mechanism for getting that support and commitment. Also, the reforms have created competing power centres in the Cabinet Office; for example, the Performance and Innovation Unit reports direct to the Prime Minister. Finally, although ministerial baronies may have been in retreat, they have not been vanquished and their compliance with the wishes of the centre cannot be taken for granted.

Action zones show the limits to vertical co-ordination. There is an epidemic of zones, to the point where the solution (to fragmentation) becomes part of the problem (by adding to the bodies to be co-ordinated). For example, John Denham, when a junior minister in the Department of Health, conceded that 'zones can sometimes make government look more, rather than less, complicated to the citizen'. There is the danger of 'initiative overload' because the zones do not join up.

Zones show the government adopting an instrumental approach to network management, assuming the centre can devise and impose tools to

foster integration in and between networks and realise central government's objectives. It is an example of imposed consensual technocracy,
which will not solve the problem of co-ordination. The reforms have a centralising thrust. They seek to co-ordinate departments and local authorities
by imposing a new style of management on other agencies. So, they 'do not
want to run local services from the centre' but 'The Government is not
afraid to take action where standards slip'; an obvious instance of a command operating code. The centre owns zones and local agendas are
recognised only in as far as they promote the central agenda. Such a code,
no matter how well disguised, runs the ever-present risk of recalcitrance
from key actors and a loss of flexibility in dealing with localised problems.
Gentle pressure relentlessly applied is still a command operating code in a
velvet glove. When you are sat at the top of a pyramid and you cannot see
the bottom, control deficits are an ever-present unintended consequence.
Network structures are characterised by a decentralised negotiating style
that trades off control for agreement. Management by negotiation means
agreeing with the objectives of others not just persuading them that you
were right all along or resorting to sanctions when they disagree.

It's the mix that matters

All governing structures fail. Bureaucracy and red tape is an old litany. We
also become increasingly aware of the limits to marketisation. If contracting-out remains, the purchaser–provider split has gone and PFI stores up
problems. The Treasury may avoid capital spending but there is a problem
because hospital trusts do not have the resources to pay the private sector's
charges. As with the previous government, the full costs of this policy
emerge slowly. Similarly there are limits to networks. For example, they are
effective when: professional discretion and expertise are core values; flexibility to meet localised, varied service demands is needed; and cross-sector,
multi-agency co-operation and production is required. Equally networks,
like all other resource allocation mechanisms, are not cost free because, for
example, they can be: inefficient as co-operation causes delay; and unaccountable for their actions. Also, network negotiation and co-ordination
can be confounded by their political context when, for example, party
political interests undermine negotiations and the search for an agreed
course of action.

   One clear effect of marketisation is that it undermines the effectiveness
of networks. The government promoted competition and contracting-out.
The result was to 'corrode common values and commitments' and 'to
create an atmosphere of mistrust'. Market relations had 'corrosive effects'
on 'professional networks, which depend on co-operation, reciprocity and
interdependence'. In short, contracts undermine trust, reciprocity, infor-
mality and co-operation. It's the mix of governing structures that matters
but that mix can be of oil and water.[14]

Finally, before this catalogue of qualifications and defects suggests that joined-up government and networks are unworkable, it is important to remember that *all* governing structures fail. Networks have distinct advantages. First, markets and hierarchies fail. Networks work in conditions where they do not. Second, networks bring together policy makers and the implementing agencies, and by so doing increase the available expertise and information. Third, networks bring together many actors to negotiate about a policy, increasing the acceptability of that policy and improving the likelihood of compliance. Fourth, networks increase the resources available for policy making by drawing together the public, private and voluntary sectors.

What system of accountability?

The *Modernising Government* White Paper pays no heed to the question of political accountability. The government has no proposals to strengthen ministerial accountability to Parliament. The emphasis falls on central political control of priorities and managerial control of implementation. *Modernising Government* proposes a technological fix. Devolution apart, political caution pervades the government's distrust of local authorities, the decision to shelve regional assemblies in England and the proposals on 'freedom' of information.

Finally, New Labour's reforms may worsen the problem of accountability. Hogwood, Judge and McVicar show that agencies and special-purpose bodies have multiple constituencies, each seeking to hold them to account, and there is no system, just disparate, overlapping demands.[15] In zones, the constituent organisations may hold their officials and politicians to account but to whom is the set of organisations accountable. As Hood and his colleagues show, joined-up government does not extend to joined-up regulation and no one regulates the regulators. The next generation of Yorkshire RHAs will thrive in these conditions.[16]

Everybody but us

Speaking in May 1999, on 'The Civil Service in the New Millennium', Sir Richard Wilson, Head of the Home Civil Service, commented:

> I mentioned earlier the pride which the Civil Service has traditionally taken at its more senior levels in its ability to advise Ministers on policy. But we are now beginning to question among ourselves quite how good we were in fact at this skill. Were we talking about devising policies which could be managed effectively to deliver the outcomes which the government of the day wanted? Or were we more concerned with devising policies which the Minister could get through his Cabinet colleagues and Parliament and present successfully to the press? And how often have we in practice gone back later and evaluated the success

with which policies have delivered what was claimed for them at the time when they were launched, rather than simply move on to devising the next policy which helps the Minister through a difficult moment?

Questions there may be. Change is less obvious. In 2000, a permanent secretary is white, over fifty, with an Oxbridge degree in the humanities who has worked in the civil service for twenty-five to thirty years. He will have served in a central as well as a functional ministry, and will retire at sixty after five to ten years in the top job. And, of course, he is male; between 1970 and 1998 there were only five female permanent secretaries and two are in post. Their task remain a mix of policy advice, management and diplomacy, although the balance shifts. The 1980s saw the senior civil service lose its monopoly over policy advice. There was a change of emphasis from policy advice to management. Joined-up government envisages a further shift to diplomacy. Civil service recruitment has become more diverse. Their background is less socially exclusive. Recent changes gradually work their way through to the top job. In 1998 just under half of the recruits for top jobs were from Oxbridge and two-thirds had arts degrees. Patterns of and procedures for recruitment began to change in the 1990s. Departments and agencies need only 'consider' open competition and not all vacancies are open to external candidates. About 30 per cent of all senior vacancies are now open to external candidates, although Sir Richard Wilson's report envisages another push to make the service more diverse. The apt cliché is 'evolution not revolution' and change affects 'everyone but us'. The *Modernising Government* White Paper will not lead to a dramatic increase in the rate of change. It contains no proposals for evaluating policy advice to ministers and the work of top civil servants. Sir Richard Wilson envisages 'rigorous reviews involving all managers' but after twenty years of continual reform, by December 1999 there were still no systematic procedures for evaluating the policy, management or diplomatic work of top administrators.

Summing-up Joining-up

There was no grand design for reforming the civil service in particular or the public sector in general. It may have been true, as one insider remarked, that the Prime Minister did not know what he wanted from the Whitehall machine:

> They say, in effect, 'Tell me, Prime Minister, what *you* want and *we'll* do it'. But he keeps saying different things. Richard Wilson finds it very difficult the way the Prime Minister jumps around. It's a succession of knee jerks . . . They are not standing back and defining what they mean. Phrases like 'joined-up government' and the 'Third Way' don't mean anything.[17]

But increasingly the emperor's new clothes become visible. New Labour rejects the command bureaucracy model of Old Labour with its emphasis on hierarchy, authority and rules. At first sight, it accepts the Conservative government's policy of marketising public services but it pragmatically accepts such reforms as the Citizen's Charter while rejecting others. Distinctively, it favours joined-up government or delivering public services by steering networks of organisations where the currency is not authority (bureaucracy) or price competition (markets) but trust. In the parlance of the chattering classes, it is the 'Third Way' in action. It typifies the shift from the providing state of Old Labour and the minimal state of Thatcherism to the enabling state and the long-standing Labour commitment to making the state work. Civil servants still combine policy advice, management and diplomacy but the arrival of joined-up government signals a further switch from management to diplomacy.

The new centralisation, whether referred to as the command premiership, the Blair presidency of Bonapartism, is discussed elsewhere in this volume (see the chapter by Riddell). But this chapter's analysis of joined-up government is directly relevant to any assessment of Blair's incumbency. Institutional fragmentation in general and devolution in particular can undermine the search for central control. Baronial government will reassert itself. Implementing agencies will continue to act in their own interests. The pressure of events will crowd in on a centre that will run out of time, energy and resources to intervene. It is an old, old story.

There is much to welcome in New Labour's modernising programme for central, local and devolved government. But the government lacks the trust it seeks to inspire. It fears the independence it bestows. It recognises the need to manage networks but fails to recognise the limits to central intervention as it tries to balance independence with central control and the limits to networks as a fallible governing structure. Hands-off is the hardest lesson of all for British central government to learn. The command premiership still has not learnt it.

Notes

1 A conclusion reinforced by the modest proposals in P. Mandelson and R. Liddle, *The Blair Revolution. Can New Labour Deliver?* Faber and Faber, 1996, chapter 10.
2 C. Hood, O. James, G. Jones, C. Scott and T. Travers, 'Regulation Inside Government: Where New Public Management Meets the Audit Explosion', *Public Money and Management*, 18, No. 2, 1998, pp. 61–8; and C. Hood, O. James, O. and C. Scott, 'Regulation in Government: Has it increased, is it increasing, should it be diminished?', *Public Administration*, 78, 2000, pp. 283–304.

3 Select Committee on Public Administration, *The Government Information and Communication Service: Report and Proceedings of the Select Committee together with Minutes of Evidence and Appendices*, HC 770, The Stationery Office, 1998.

4 P. Hennessy, 'The Blair Style of Government', *Government and Opposition*, 33, 1998, p. 15. See also D. Kavanagh and A. Seldon, 'The Power Behind the Prime Minister: the hidden influence of No. 10', in R.A.W. Rhodes (ed.), *Transforming British Government. Volume 2. Changing Roles and Relationships*, Macmillan, 2000. To avoid overlap with chapters 2 and 10 of this volume, I merely note the reforms of Number 10. Of course, I recognise their importance for the roles of the senior civil service and note the effects at the appropriate points.

5 Sir Robin Butler, 'The Evolution of the Civil Service', *Public Administration*, 71, 1993, p. 404.

6 Committee of Public Accounts, *The Former Yorkshire Regional Health Authority: The Inquiry Commissioned by the NHS Chief Executive*, The Stationery Office, 1997.

7 P. Norton, 'Barons in a Shrinking Kingdom: senior ministers in British government', in R.A.W. Rhodes (ed.), *Transforming British Government. Volume 2. Changing Roles and Relationships*, Macmillan, 2000.

8 See W. Waldegrave, *Public Service and the Future: Reforming Britain's Bureaucracies*, Conservative Political Centre, 1993, p. 20.

9 Quoted in P. Hennessy, *Whitehall*, Secker & Warburg, 1989, p. 631. See also RIPA, *Top Jobs in Whitehall: Appointments and Promotions in the Senior Civil Service*, RIPA, 1987, p. 43.

10 Sixth Report of the Committee on Standards in Public Life, *Reinforcing Standards*. Cm 4557 – I, The Stationery Office, 2000, chapter 6. See also *The Government's Response to the Sixth Report from the Committee on Standards in Public Life*. Cm 4817, The Stationery Office, 2000).

11 K. Theakston, *Leadership in Whitehall*, Macmillan, 1999, pp. 257–9.

12 D. Kavanagh, D. and A. Seldon, 'The Power Behind the Prime Minister: the hidden influence of No. 10', in R.A.W. Rhodes (ed.), *Transforming British Government. Volume 2. Changing Roles and Relationships*, Macmillan, 2000. See also chapter 10 in this volume.

13 V. Wright and J.E.S. Hayward, 'Governing from the Centre: policy co-ordination in six European core executives', in R.A.W. Rhodes (ed.), *Transforming British Government. Volume 2. Changing Roles and Relationships*, Macmillan, 2000.

14 R. Flynn and others (1996), *Markets and Networks: contracting in community services*, Open University Press, pp. 115 and 136–7.

15 B.W. Hogwood, D. Judge and M. McVicar, 'Agencies and Accountability', in R.A.W. Rhodes (ed.), *Transforming British Government. Volume 2. Changing Roles and Relationships*, Macmillan, 2000.

16 One counterweight to this pessimistic judgement may be the BSE Inquiry Report. It criticises the government for withholding information from the public and for giving the public simple and misleading messages about the risks involved. It argues that government credibility depends on trust and trust depends on openness. *The BSE Inquiry. Volume 1. Findings and Conclusions* HC 887–I, The Stationery Office, 2000. Whether any one

report can change such long-standing civil service traditions as secrecy and protecting the minister from political embarrassment remains to be seen.

17 Cited in P. Hennessy, *The Blair Revolution in Government?* Institute for Politics and International Studies, University of Leeds, 2000, p. 9.

© Chris Riddell

Chapter 6

LOCAL GOVERNMENT

Tony Travers

Inheritance

LABOUR INHERITED A local government system that had endured almost
a quarter of a century of financial constraint, reorganisation and loss of
powers. Ever since Britain had experienced public expenditure and economic difficulties during the mid-1970s, successive governments had
sought to reduce (in real terms) local authority expenditure. The Thatcher
and Major administrations had devoted several major Acts of Parliament to
substantive change to local authority finance, functions and structure.[1] By
1997, there was a powerful demand (at least among local councillors and
officers) that a change of government should lead to a reversal of the long
attack on local autonomy.

In reality, local government in Britain had been in decline since the 1940s.[2]
Major provision such as health, water and other utilities had been removed
from local authority control and then nationalised. The municipal empires
that had been created in the late-nineteenth and early-twentieth centuries had
been significantly dismantled by the late 1990s. Demands for universal services and the development of the Welfare State had dealt huge blows to the
notion of local government's freedom to provide services that differed from
area to area. The National Health Service, for example, had been explicitly
founded with the intention of ensuring equal provision to people throughout
the country. Local government had become significantly 'nationalised'.[3]

But whatever the long-term background to the Blair administration's
local government inheritance, the activities of Labour-controlled local
authorities during the 1980s[4] more than anything else determined New
Labour's attitude to local democracy. The rotten apples of Liverpool and
Lambeth became the key stimulants of Blair's policy menu for the new
government.

Labour in Local Government

Labour was in a strong position in local government in 1997. After seventeen years of Conservative governments, both the Labour Party and the Liberal Democrats had won control of councils throughout Britain. The Tories' power-base in all parts of local government had been badly eroded, particularly in Scotland, Wales and urban England: they held no seats at all on councils such as Liverpool and Manchester and precious few in many other cities. The party had even lost its grip on most of the shire counties. Labour, by contrast, had won control of councils in rural areas and in many parts of the South East of England.

However, the activities of a small number of Labour councils (and council unions) between 1978 and 1990 had scorched a lasting impression on the memories of senior Labour politicians. Conservative party political broadcasts for years after the 'Winter of Discontent' of 1978–79 had used images of militant strikers, piles of rubbish in city parks and the unburied dead to alert the electorate of the dangers of left-wing control in local government.

The Thatcher government's legislation to force councils to contract-out – by competitive tendering – the provision of virtually all manual services (later followed by the Major government's similar action against white-collar services) had been designed to break the grip of the public sector unions. While Labour had always opposed compulsory competitive tendering, Tony Blair and his colleagues were alert to the dangers of re-kindling union power within local government.

But even more than the Winter of Discontent and the public sector unions, the activities of a number of left-dominated Labour councils during the 1980s came to influence the Blair government's approach to local government. During the dark hours of the Labour Party's near-death experience between 1979 and 1987, there had been radical Labour administrations in Liverpool, Lambeth, Sheffield, and most notoriously, the Greater London Council (GLC). These authorities had behaved in such a way as to convince most national Labour strategists that if and when they took power, legislation should be pushed through which once-and-for-all dealt with the risk of a return to the bad old days of the 1980s.

The GLC and its radical colleague authorities had pursued an approach to politics that embodied virtually everything that New Labour came to oppose about left-wing politics. A number of councils had come close to refusing to set a rate in opposition to the Conservative government's rate capping legislation: they delayed setting their local tax for many weeks. Councillors in two of these authorities – Liverpool and Lambeth – were surcharged by the District Auditor for wilful loss of ratepayers' money.

Many of the so-called loony-left councils gave grants to fringe minority organisations. Such actions enraged the tabloid press. The GLC's grants programme, which involved giving financial support to a range of gay, black and other minority groups, achieved almost daily media coverage. The GLC leadership appeared to support (or at least refused to condemn) IRA terrorism. Worst of all, service quality collapsed in a number of left-led councils as union domination of local politics removed the capacity of senior officers to manage their staff.

It is impossible to exaggerate the effect of the GLC, Liverpool and the other left-controlled councils on Labour thinking during the 1990s. Even though the bulk of Labour-controlled and other authorities were administered in much the same way they had been in the past, the actions of a handful of radical councils came to dominate Labour policy-making. The fact that many ministers, MPs and civil servants lived in a number of the more problematic London boroughs did not help matters.[5] It profoundly affected New Labour's approach to local government after 1997.

The 1997 Manifesto

Labour's 1997 manifesto[6] was an accurate predictor of the fundamentally cautious approach adopted by the party once it had won the general election. The main points of the proposals were:

- the removal of expenditure capping;
- councils to promote economic, social and environmental well-being;
- annual elections to all councils;
- experiments with elected mayors;
- introduction of 'best value' regime;
- the abolition of compulsory competitive tendering;
- the achievement of 'fair' grant distribution;
- directly-elected mayor and assembly for London.

Beyond local government, though clearly of relevance, Labour was committed to:

- a Scottish Parliament and Welsh Assembly;
- Regional Development Agencies for England.

The Labour Manifesto did not give any hint of enthusiasm for the use of local government as a key element in the policy implementation that lay ahead. There was no radicalism about local taxation, nor any commitment to transfer powers from either central government or quangos to local government. Rather, local authorities were once more to be the object of legislative change to improve their economy, effectiveness and accountability.

Labour in Office

One of Labour's early decisions was to merge the Department of the Environment (previously local government's sponsor) and the Department of Transport. This returned the Whitehall arrangements to those that had existed during the Heath government of 1970–74. The new Department of the Environment, Transport and the Regions was to be headed by John Prescott (also Deputy Prime Minister), with Hilary Armstrong as Minister of State with responsibility for local government. Nick Raynsford was given specific responsibility for London (and thus for the creation of the new local government structure there).

The new administration signalled its intention to change local government by the publication of a series of consultative papers, under the generic title 'Modernising local government'. The notion of 'modernisation' was to become key to the Blair government's approach to local authorities. Senior figures at the core of the new government believed the existing system of local government – and, indeed, many councillors – was antiquated and conservative. Wholesale modernisation was the order of the day.

Six consultative papers were produced. Three were about management, probity and effectiveness: *Local democracy and community leadership*; *Improving local services through best value*; and *A new ethical framework*. The remaining three tackled the perennial issue of finance: *Improving local financial accountability*; *Capital finance*; and *Business rates*. Between them they suggested government radicalism in its approach to the internal management of local authorities and deep conservatism about finance.

The papers on internal management and processes suggested that local government should move away from its traditional reliance on the committee system and instead split the 'executive' and 'non-executive' roles of councillors within each local authority. In particular, the possibility of introducing an executive mayor or a cabinet system was outlined.[7] The government argued that councils should provide more effective civil leadership. Concern was expressed at low electoral turnouts in local government. Potential reforms such as annual elections for all councils and ways of easing access to voting were put forward.

The proposed Best Value regime was a classic example of New Labour thinking. The government was determined to keep pressure on councils to deliver the kind of public service efficiencies and effectiveness that the previous Conservative administration had – with some success – striven for. However, ministers wanted to differentiate themselves from the Tories' preoccupation with 'value for money', thus the consultative papers explained:[8] 'Achieving Best Value is not just about economy and efficiency, but also about effectiveness and the quality of local services – the setting of targets and performance against these should therefore underpin the new regime.'

Best Value was to involve each authority in producing a performance plan which would then be independently audited. It was a highly-technical solution to the government's problem of how to ensure that (often Labour) authorities did not revert to the kind of behaviour and inefficiency commonplace in the bad old days before Mrs Thatcher's government had tamed them. But although the Blair government's motives were obvious, there was rather less certainty about how Best Value would actually operate.

Like John Major's government, Blair's was in no mood to unravel the system of local government finance. Mrs Thatcher had introduced a new, disliked, local government tax with disastrous results. No one within the Blair government had the stomach for the kind of radical reform of local authority finance that many in local government would have liked. Local Income Tax, which had for so long been the preferred tax reform for many Labour supporters within town halls, was a dead duck. So was a sales tax. The best that John Prescott could offer was the removal of 'crude and universal' expenditure capping, the possibility of a small local add-on to the National Non-Domestic Rate (which the Tories had nationalised in 1990) and some delegation of control over capital spending.

The final key element in Labour's approach was the proposal that all councils should adopt a 'new ethical framework', which would involve the adoption of a new Code of Conduct for councillors and officers, the creation of a 'standards committee' for each authority and an appeal mechanism involving independent members. Many decisions about possible standards breaches would be made by a nationally-appointed regional board. The perceived need for such reforms arose from the recommendations of the Nolan Report.[9]

The new government's approach was instantly seen by local authorities as a mixture of carrots and sticks. While the Local Government Association was happy enough with the abolition of capping and compulsory competitive tendering, it was less content with the performance-driven threat of Best Value (which it viewed as centralisation). There was virtually no support for the idea of elected mayors. In short, from local government's point of view the Blair administration was planning to be radical where councillors wanted no change (i.e. the internal workings of local government) and cautious where local authorities wanted reform (i.e. finance).

In one area of policy there was little or no opposition to Blair's approach to local government. The manifesto had promised a directly-elected mayor and assembly for the capital (to replace the Greater London Council (GLC), which had been abolished by the Conservatives in 1986). A green paper on London government was published in July 1997,[10] followed by the legislation required to test public opinion in a referendum to be held in May 1998. While the overall proposals for the capital were widely welcomed, there was some opposition to the idea of directly-elected mayors.

London politics had been highly-charged during the 1980s, not least because of the behaviour of a number of borough councils and the abolition of the GLC. But by the mid-1990s the vacuum left by the defunct GLC had to some extent been filled by an array of partnerships and, after 1994, by the new Government Office for London. Sweetness and light had overtaken the grim ideological struggles of the 1980s.[11] Moreover, the new Greater London Authority was not replacing any existing institution: there was no particular reason for any campaign to oppose a policy that opinion polls regularly showed had high levels of public support.

The introduction of a directly-elected mayor for London was extremely radical. The United Kingdom had no previous experience of such an elected executive. The proposed Scottish Parliament and Welsh Assembly were conventional administrations which involved the election of a number of members who would, between them, create an executive and elect a First Minister. But the London reform created an elected single-person executive subject only to scrutiny by a small assembly and who could not be removed between elections. The capital was an extraordinary place to attempt such an experiment: London's population was seven and a quarter million, compared with five million in Scotland and just three million in Wales.

What was the Blair Government Seeking to Do?

The single word most used by ministers within the Blair government to describe their approach to local authorities was 'modernisation'. It appeared again and again in green and white papers. It was used by supporters of the government and (as a term of abuse) by its opponents. Different parts of the government were rather more committed to this process of modernisation than others. Downing Street and the Treasury were strongly in favour of changing the culture of local councils and councillors, whereas the Department of the Environment, Transport and the Regions (local government's sponsoring department) was more modest in its aspirations. Many Labour supporters in local authorities and constituency parties were amongst modernisation's most bitter opponents.

Thus the Prime Minister and his policy unit were widely perceived as driving the agenda to change local government. Individual policy unit members, in particular Robert Hill, were seen as driving forward policies to apply cattle-prods to all parts of local government on a regular basis. DETR ministers, headed by Deputy Prime Minister John Prescott, were seen as being closer to 'old' Labour values and therefore less keen on the more radical policies advocated by Downing Street. Moreover, Prescott and Richard Caborn (who, with Hilary Armstrong, was one of the DETR's ministers of state during the early part of the Blair government) were far more interested in the development of Regional Development Agencies.

Unusually, for a Prime Minister, Mr Blair explained his own vision for local government in an Institute for Public Policy Research pamphlet published in 1998.[12] In it, Blair claimed change was needed because: (i) localities lacked a clear sense of direction; (ii) there was a lack of coherence and cohesion in delivering local services; and (iii) the quality of local services is too variable.

He went on to criticise local authorities for a number of failings before offering an olive branch. First: 'Britain comes bottom of the European league table for turnout in local elections'. Second: 'Most people do not know the name of the leader of their council.' Third: 'The committee system takes up an enormous amount of time . . . A radical reform is needed'. Fourth: 'The government will intervene if authorities are incapable of improving their performance' and finally 'Councils that are performing well could be given more freedom and powers'.

Notwithstanding that Parliamentary and central government performance in parallel spheres of political life (e.g. the turnout at the 1997 general election had been just 70 per cent – low by European standards) was dismal, Tony Blair was committed to reforming the culture of local government. Many of his ideas were not dissimilar from those of Michael Heseltine,[13] who had been Environment Secretary in both Thatcher and Major governments. Heseltine had been happy to support central intervention to improve local services and directly-elected mayors.

Detailed proposals for local government reform published during 1997 and 1998 (summarised in the previous section) did not look particularly radical. But they were strongly backed up by the kind of public rhetoric and private ministerial comment (elsewhere called 'spin') that amounted to a powerful critique of local government. Although the Prime Minister and his advisors believed in the constitutional importance of elected local authorities, they did not much like its current manifestations. That is, local government appeared to be acceptable in theory, but not in practice.

The Blair view of local government went well beyond the distaste felt by senior Labour politicians such as Neil Kinnock and John Cunningham as they had battled with the left during the 1980s.[14] By 1997, virtually the whole of local government – including former hot-spots of militancy such as Liverpool and Lambeth – was under the control of conventional party politicians, whether Labour, Conservative, Liberal Democrat, or otherwise.

Long before Tony Blair entered Downing Street the rigours of local politics – coupled with a raft of Tory legislation – had convinced Labour in the inner cities that the time for posturing and ideology was over. Cleaning the streets and improving school standards had become top priorities in virtually all areas. Paradoxically in many of the places where Labour had been most radical during the 1980s, e.g. Southwark, Camden, Greenwich, Brent, Manchester and, eventually, Lambeth, the transformation was greatest. The new realism gripped many councils – particularly in London – in such a way as radically to improve service standards and expectations.

New Labour found natural allies within the reformed councils in Manchester, Newham, Camden and Southwark. Hammersmith and Fulham was one of the first authorities to appoint an executive mayor (even before legislation allowing directly-elected mayors was passed). Lewisham committed itself to a referendum on whether or not to introduce a directly-elected mayor. The Liberal Democrat leader of Liverpool strongly supported an elected mayor for his city. Service improvements generally took place rapidly in authorities where collapse had been greatest during the 1980s.

The Blair government's concerns did not focus on the newly-efficient, newly-moderate authorities which had forsaken their wicked extremist pasts for the sunlit uplands of New Labour's inclusive modernised paradise. Instead Downing Street became almost obsessively concerned with the 'complacent average' authorities that appeared to coast along with outdated and inefficient political leadership and which were gradually, it was believed, losing public support.

At a stroke the many plodding, old-Labour, councils in places such as West Yorkshire, the West Midlands and South Wales became a problem. The coincidence that a number of new Labour ministers had constituencies in the north-east of England (where Old Labour was vastly powerful within local government) simply served to encourage the modernisers that something had to be done, and fast. To the party faithful in these areas, the fact that they had been the bedrock of traditional Labour local government during the turbulent 1980s created a massive sense of injustice when the Blair whizz-kids singled them out for a short, sharp, lesson in modernisation.

Best Value was resented within local councils as yet another technocratic, top-down, incursion into local democracy. The need to generate detailed service-by-service performance plans, including dozens of targets and key indicators, was viewed as bureaucratic and intrusive. After it started operating in the spring of 2000 many councillors found it difficult fully to understand how Best Value worked. Even in 2001 it is difficult with certainty to point to concrete improvements that come from the new regime.

Local government appeared more comfortable with the Local Public Service Agreements that were invented in 2000.[15] Local PSAs were designed to sign local authorities up to a national pattern of improved public service provision: the Treasury could negotiate with the Local Government Association about outputs and outcomes to be derived as a result of public spending increases. Though welcomed by local government, local PSAs were, undoubtedly another technocratic, top-down, effort by national government to control what went on within local councils (and, indeed, within Whitehall departments).

A further Blair government initiative designed to drive up quality was the beacon council scheme.[16] An independent panel was appointed by DETR ministers to select councils which excelled in particular services.

Such authorities were awarded beacon council status for a fixed period of years. A council that qualified as a beacon authority in a number of services could apply for overall beacon status. Such authorities were later, at an unspecified date, to be given wider discretion over service provision, e.g. to make capital investment, than other councils.

However, the topic of elected mayors stirred the most determined response from councillors of all parties. Most councillors believed that their existing pattern of committees, departments and service provision was reasonably effective. Thus, the idea that every council would be forced to choose between a cabinet, directly-elected mayor or mayor-plus-council-manager model eventually outlined by Labour in 1998[17] proved hugely unpopular within local government.[18] By early 2001 it appeared that only a handful of councils (Liverpool, Birmingham, Watford, Lewisham and Berwick) appeared likely to opt for holding the referendum that might lead to the election of a mayor.

The Blair agenda was enthusiastically supported by a number of key councillors, academics and commentators who broadly shared the view that local government was in need of reform. An organisation, the New Local Government Network (NLGN), was set up to promote modernisation through conferences and seminars that offered ministers a platform to explain their policies, and the publication of papers.[19] Leading members included Geoffrey (later Lord) Filkin, who had previously headed one of the local authority associations, Professor Gerry Stoker, of Strathclyde (later Manchester) University, and Professor Paul Corrigan of the University of North London. Councillors from all parties took part in the Network, as did a number of leading private companies. The NLGN worked closely with ministers, who regularly appeared at conferences to talk-up the full modernising agenda.

Other councillors and commentators were highly sceptical of modernisation. Academics such as John Stewart (University of Birmingham) and George Jones (London School of Economics) used their regular column in *Local Government Chronicle* to take the government to task for (what they saw as) centrally-imposed reform of local authorities. The Local Government Association, in particular its Chair, Sir Jeremy Beecham, sought to act as a constructive critic, though it was clear from many of its statements that the LGA was pretty unenthusiastic about the modernisation proposed. The LGA generally took the line that it accepted the need for change, then explained that the government's proposals were somehow inappropriate.[20]

One reform that provoked much less opposition than directly-elected mayors and Best Value was the effort to improve ethical standards in local government. Although local government had not been the origin of the problem of 'sleaze', it was certainly included in the solution. The Blair government proposed a series of improvements to the way in which councils conducted their business, including a new Standards Committee for each council, with the involvement of an appointed, regional, body.

Local authorities broadly supported the government's decision to give them a power to promote the 'social, environmental and economic well-being' of their populations. This change was partly real (it gave councils greater freedom to use resources for certain purposes) and partly symbolic (suggesting that, at least at the margin, local government could be trusted with additional freedoms). However, it was clear that the Blair government was not prepared to give local councils the kind of power of general competence enjoyed by local authorities in some other parts of Europe.

Financing Local Government

Few issues had taxed successive British governments more than the country's Byzantine local government finance system. The Thatcher and Major governments had undertaken three separate reviews of the subject. The introduction of the 'community charge', popularly known as the poll tax, in 1990 (1989 in Scotland) and its replacement (by council tax) in 1993 lived on in the memories of politicians as a terrible warning about the dangers of over-ambitious reforms of local taxation. Moreover, New Labour fought the 1997 election on a platform of fiscal rectitude. Every effort was made to convince the electorate and business that the election of a Labour government would not lead to a return to the Bad Old Days of the late 1970s.

Local authorities, on the other hand, had long imagined that if the Conservatives were vanquished from national government, it would be possible to return to a world of greater freedom over their finances. In particular, they wanted three financial reforms: the abolition of rate capping (Labour had long been committed to do so); the return of local control over the non-domestic rate; and a fairer system of distributing government grants to councils. Many Labour and Liberal Democrat councillors (and Nationalists in Scotland and Wales) also hoped that council tax would be reformed so as to make it more progressive.

Labour abandoned 'crude and universal' capping soon after taking office. However, in a sign of how far the Treasury intended to keep a grip over council finances, two conditions were set. First, the threat of selective capping would remain – if an authority spent excessively over time, it was likely to find itself punished by Whitehall. Second, an ingenious scheme of penalising councils that put up their council tax by more than a DETR-set figure (generally 4.5 per cent per year) was introduced: the government withdrew support for council tax benefit (paid to poorer residents) if the 4.5 per cent norm was exceeded. Thus, if councils put up their spending – and thus council tax – too much, local tax bills would have to bear the costs of additional council tax benefit.

The new council tax benefit penalty system instantly caused almost as much resentment within local government as the capping system it replaced. But the Treasury was adamant: if councils wanted to push their taxes up, then local people should feel the pinch. Nor was the Treasury willing to budge on the national non-domestic rate (NNDR). The control of the NNDR had shifted to Whitehall in 1990 and New Labour had no desire to be accused of favouring higher taxes on business (although it did, through the national tax system, put up such taxes).

In committing itself to making the Revenue Support Grant (RSG) fairer, Labour had made a promise that was to prove hard to keep. By the start of the 2001–02 financial year, no fundamental changes had been made to the grant system. In truth the English (and, separately, the Welsh and Scottish systems) were, by international standards, models of precision, transparency and objectivity. Indeed, the very openness of the RSG – in particular the process of calculating authorities' spending needs – led many councils to attack it.

A major review of the grant system took place during 1999 and 2000. International experience was researched. Other ways of allocating grants were considered, notably bid-based or performance-based systems. The Department for Education and Employment, in the person of Secretary of State David Blunkett, fought for ring-fenced education grants. There was even discussion in the press about removing education from local government altogether. Local government, which had long criticised the existing grant arrangements, was bitterly critical of any move away from formula-driven grants. Education was stoutly defended as a core local government service.

The conclusions of the government's review of finance were published in a green paper during the autumn of 2000.[21] None of the options for reforming the grant system was ruled out, though none was signalled as a particular priority. A future government might continue with formula-based general grants or, alternatively, move to bid-, performance-, or plan-based specific grants. No full reform of the system can take place before 2003–04.

The green paper made it clear that council tax would not be reformed: there would be no changes to make it more progressive. It was proposed that councils could in future set a small, locally-determined, non-domestic rate in addition to the national one. But the scale of any local business rate would be limited to a maximum level set by the government and would require extensive consultation with local non-domestic ratepayers.

The only element in the government's proposals that was mildly radical was the suggestion of moving to a system of control under which councils would be freer to incur capital expenditure. Labour had, early in its term of office, removed some of the restrictions (imposed by the previous government) that stopped councils using the receipts from sales of assets to re-invest in local infrastructure. The green paper proposed going further, with councils to be given far greater freedom to determine their pattern of spending. Overall limits on spending would, it was proposed, be determined in the longer term by prudential rules (such as the level of indebtedness or the debt to revenue ratio) rather than by Whitehall fiat. But even the capital reforms would have to wait until 2002 or 2003 for implementation.

Labour had not found a radical reform for local government finance. Like the previous administration, the thought of new taxes, or big increases in existing ones, was vetoed by the Treasury from day one. Even changes to council tax and the non-domestic rate were kept to limited proposals. Despite real terms increases in education and other public service spending plans flowing from the government's spending reviews, New Labour was determined that council spending should be seen to be under control.

London

Ever since the Thatcher government abolished the Greater London Council in 1986, the Labour Party had been committed to re-creating a system of London-wide government. In the 1987 and 1992 general election manifestos it was clear that any new authority for the capital would be a slimline version of an – admittedly large – conventional British local council. There would be direct elections to a number of wards throughout the city. Elected councillors would then select a leader from among their number. Although Neil Kinnock and his colleagues were at pains to stress their proposal was not a 'GLC Mark 2', there can be no doubt that this particular version of London government would have been closely related to the GLC model.

The death of John Smith and the election of Tony Blair as leader of the Labour Party led to a change in policy towards London government. Blair became convinced (after he had become leader) that the capital should have Britain's first directly-elected executive mayor. The leader's policy was adopted by his party, though the majority of the shadow cabinet were either opposed to it or neutral. In the run-up to the 1997 election Labour's environment shadow (Frank Dobson) was personally against the notion of a directly-elected mayor for London.

Immediately after Labour's 1997 victory a green paper[22] was published to flesh out the details of the London policy. The key points were:

- a directly-elected executive mayor;
- a small, elected, assembly to scrutinise the mayor;
- elections by a form of proportional representation;
- a small central staff to service the mayor and assembly;
- four functional bodies (wholly or partly appointed by the mayor) to run transport, police, the fire brigade and economic development;
- the power to set a council tax precept.

Following consultation on the outline scheme in the green paper, a white paper was published during the spring of 1998.[23] Immediately after a referendum was held (under new legislation) to test public opinion. Although the turnout was low (34 per cent), the result strongly endorsed the white paper proposals for a mayor and assembly (by 72 per cent to 28 per cent).

After a long and difficult Parliamentary process (during which the government decided to amend the legislation so as to introduce a complex public-private partnership to finance the re-construction of London Underground's infrastructure), the Greater London Authority was elected for the first time in May 2000. Although the legislation created a strong mayor (and a correspondingly weak assembly), it also left ministers a number of fall-back powers of intervention just in case a mayor indulged in too many policies that proved unacceptable to central government.

The process of electing the capital's first directly-elected chief executive was sufficiently exotic to have generated a separate book in its own right.[24] Both the Conservative and Labour parties became involved in spectacular and devious efforts to choose a candidate. In a country with no history of primary elections of the kind commonplace in the United States, both parties had to invent processes to select their candidates.

The Tories first chose Lord (Jeffrey) Archer, who later had to resign because of a newspaper allegation about a previous court case. A second attempt to find a mayoral candidate was thrown into disarray when the favourite – Steven Norris, who had been defeated by Archer first time round – was ruled out of the contest by the party selection committee. Eventually Norris was re-instated and went on to become the candidate.

However, the Conservatives' efforts were positively well-choreographed when compared with the Labour Party's. Ever since the 1997 election victory and the certainty that London would soon have a directly-elected mayor, there had been speculation that the last leader of the Greater London Council, Ken Livingstone, would stand as Labour candidate for the new role. But to Blair and the New Labour machine Livingstone embodied everything that was wrong with the party's previous image with the electorate. He was seen as extremist, oppositional and dangerous.[25]

To make matters more complex Livingstone and Archer became a kind of comedy double-act during the early stages of the mayoral election campaign. Whenever they both turned up to an event, a full battery of press and photographers accompanied them. Either man added a touch of glamour and excitement to the grey world of local government, but together they made it international news.

Blair and his core colleagues were determined to stop Livingstone. At first the possibility of ruling him out of the contest altogether was considered. A vetting procedure was set up, run nominally by the London Labour

Party, but with strong national input. But by use of an extraordinary capacity to generate favourable media coverage Livingstone managed to make it impossible for the party to rule him out of the contest. Millbank's (Labour's headquarters) next bright idea was to decide that the election to select the mayoral candidate should be by an electoral college, with one-third of the votes from party members, one-third from London MPs, MEPs and Greater London Authority candidates and one-third from the trades unions within the capital. This old-fashioned semi-democracy was seen as the best possible way of stopping Livingstone.

Three candidates stood for the Labour nomination: Livingstone, Glenda Jackson (MP for Hampstead) and Frank Dobson (MP for Holborn and St Pancras). Dobson, who had had to stand down from his job as Health Secretary, had been pressured by Blair and other senior colleagues to stand. Relying heavily on the trades unions and the MPs/MEPs/GLA candidates, Dobson just scraped in ahead of Livingstone. The latter, by contrast, won significant support among party members.

Ken Livingstone appeared to have been defeated by an old-style Labour machine effort. Steve Norris, by then the Tory candidate, memorably described the whole process as 'reminiscent of North Korea'. But press speculation mounted that Livingstone would stand as an independent – against the official Labour candidate. After more than two weeks of dithering Livingstone did indeed break with his party and ran for mayor of London as an independent candidate.

Blair's apparent efforts to martyr Livingstone, like those of Margaret Thatcher fifteen years before, proved utterly counter-productive. 'Ken', as he was universally known, was seen as an underdog and a London populist. He was also strangely glamorous. It was small wonder that, on 5 May 2000, Livingstone became London's first-ever directly-elected mayor.

It is impossible to know how much damage the Livingstone debacle did to Blair and his government. National opinion polls did not waver. But New Labour's image as a party of efficient and effective political fixers was dealt a major blow. The political fiasco over the selection and election of the London mayor became another bump on what proved to be a rocky road for Blair during 2000.

In his first year in office (from May 2000 to the spring of 2001) Ken Livingstone adopted a number of Blairite characteristics. He created an 'advisory cabinet' which included not only political friends but also non-aligned representatives, for example, of the City of London. Both his Conservative and Liberal Democrat opponents during the mayoral election contest (Steve Norris and Susan Kramer) became members of the board responsible for transport. Every effort was made to be consensual and, to use a favourite word of the Blair government, 'inclusive'. A leading New York transport manager – Robert Kiley – was imported by the new mayor to run the Underground, buses and roads. What became known by some as the 'kenocracy' proved, in many ways, to be the least-worst version of a Livingstone regime imaginable from Tony Blair's point of view. However, when efforts were made by Livingstone supporters to seek the mayor's re-admission to the Labour Party, the view within the party leadership remained one of 'wait and see'.

Despite the bizarre difficulties thrown up by the selection and election of Ken Livingstone, Blair and the Labour modernisers remained committed to elected mayors for other cities. Most of the party's activists saw such powerful, elected, executives as a serious threat to the traditional form of local government (and thus to the dominance of party politics within local government). The election of an independent as the country's first mayor, however unusual the circumstances, merely convinced them that elected mayors were a bad thing for party politics. Indeed, support or opposition to the idea of elected mayors became an almost perfect way of telling whether an individual party member was New or Old Labour.

By the time that Livingstone had completed his first year in office, it was clear there was unlikely to be a rush to be the second directly-elected mayor. While the leaders of Liverpool (Mike Storey, a Liberal Democrat) and Birmingham (Albert Bore, Labour) personally encouraged the move towards holding the referendum that could enable the move to a mayor, much of the rest of the political class in such cities remained opposed to reform.

Regional Government in England

Labour's approach to regional government in England outside London was muddled. Progress was made by the introduction, in 1998, of Regional Development Agencies (RDAs). They were appointed, not elected, institutions. RDAs were charged with improving the economic competitiveness and success of the regions. At the same time that RDAs were created, regional 'chambers' (which generally became known as 'assemblies') were set up to oversee them. These chambers or assemblies, which were intended to secure some form of local political accountability, were constituted from indirectly-elected members of local authorities within their area plus a minority of individuals from other representative organisations.

The Blair government made no move towards fully-fledged regional government in England. Despite a genuine shift of power to Scotland, Wales, Northern Ireland and London, devolution of England (apart from the capital) proved a reform too far for New Labour's constitutional modernisers. Press reports between 1997 and 2001 suggested the Cabinet remained split about the issue. On the one hand, Deputy Prime Minister John Prescott remained an enthusiast for regional power, while on the other, Home Secretary Jack Straw was highly sceptical. Local government, which had long suspected that any move towards regional government would have damaging consequences for (particularly county) councils, was not enthusiastic for change, except, perhaps in the North East.

By 2001, devolved government had arrived in three parts of Britain and, haltingly, in Northern Ireland, but it remained a shadow or compromise in the rest of the UK. The four new institutions set up in Edinburgh, Cardiff, Belfast and London had had the effect of reducing the importance and visibility of the UK Parliament at Westminster. The Scottish Parliament had taken over all responsibility for the country's local government structure, functions and finance. Possibly the consequences of a transfer of powers to Bristol, Birmingham, Manchester, Leeds and Newcastle was, at least during a first term of office, seen as providing Westminster with too many threats to its power. There may also have been a fear about the possible longer-term threat to England's territorial integrity.

Auditors, Inspectors and Regulators

A feature of the Blair government was its extraordinary faith in public-sector regulators of various kinds. John Major's government had built up the Office for Standards in Education (OFSTED) and had also required the publication of a large number of local authority performance indicators. Labour, who were keen to be seen as tough on public service failure, gave further powers to OFSTED (whose powers of inspection were extended from schools to local authorities and all forms of under-fives' provision), as well as creating a new Housing Inspectorate and a further inspectorate to enforce the Best Value regime.[26] Social services inspection was strengthened after a number of horrific child abuse scandals.

Significantly, Labour re-appointed Chris Woodhead as Chief Inspector of Schools (i.e. head of OFSTED). Woodhead had been a scourge of low attaining schools and local authority education departments under John Major's government. With his forthright and anti-progressive views, the Chief Inspector provided Tony Blair with an educational quality-guarantee. Many Labour-supporting teachers and commentators were horrified by New Labour's willingness to support Woodhead. Nevertheless, the Tory-appointed Chief Inspector survived in his role until he resigned at the end of 2000. His departure was cherished by liberals and greeted with alarm by conservatives.

The topsy-like growth in inspection and oversight was a further manifestation of Labour's deep suspicion of local government. Downing Street and the Treasury believed that unless local authorities were named-and-shamed, incentivised and scrutinised, they would slump into a relentless slough of mediocrity and failure. Blair and his ministers had no problem in sanctioning a central government take over of failing local authority services (e.g. schools administration in Hackney and in Islington). Indeed, they had no difficulty in giving the private sector a stake in the running of such failing council services. The ghosts of Labour's humiliations in the 1980s and early 1990s still caused enough fear to galvanise the government into full-scale national takeovers of poorly-performing local services.

Zones, One-off Initiatives and Special Funding

Another manifestation of the Blair government's desire to get things done from the top down – without the need to rely on existing elected local government – was the proliferation of zones and other new initiatives.[27] Ministers felt that quick action was needed to tackle low educational attainment, poor housing, health inequalities and other social and economic ills. Given the attitudes outlined above about local government (slow, inefficient, conservative) it was hardly surprising that education zones, housing zones, health zones and others were created with reckless abandon by individual ministers.

In addition to the various zones, the government funded initiatives designed to solve particular problems, e.g. low school achievement by children from poorer households; crime and social disorder on particular social housing estates; urban out-migration and the growing use of hard drugs. Such allocations of central government cash to individual councils, neighbourhoods or institutions led to a further proliferation of partnerships and one-off incursions into local public provision.

Urban funding schemes such as the Single Regeneration Budget (SRB), which were inherited by Labour from the Conservatives, continued with few alterations after 1997. The Blair government felt at home with SRB, which allowed central government to distribute regeneration resources only to those public-private partnerships that promised particular outcomes. SRB resources, and those previously administered by the government-appointed agency English Partnerships, were transferred to the Regional Development Agencies from April 1999.

Local authorities, as the sole democratically-elected institutions outside Parliament (apart from the new Scottish, Welsh, Northern Ireland and London institutions), found themselves having to take the lead in co-ordinating the activities of all the new zones, initiatives and funding programmes. By 1999 ministers' enthusiasms were generating far more new programmes and funding streams than could rationally be co-ordinated at the local level. This realisation led, in turn, to further nationally-led initiatives to encourage 'joined-up' provision.[28]

Urban and Rural Policy

The Blair government, like all previous Labour governments, consisted of a majority of MPs from urban constituencies. But because the party had also won a significant number of suburban and rural seats in 1997, it could not ignore the rural lobby that became so vocal during the period after the election. Falling agricultural incomes and Labour MP Mike Foster's efforts (using a Private Member's Bill) to ban fox hunting generated a powerful and visible rural lobby. During the autumn of 2000 this lobby also addressed the issue of rising vehicle fuel prices.

The plight of many northern and midlands cities, whose industrial base had largely disappeared during the 1980s, was even more pressing for the urban-based Labour Party. In 1998 the Deputy Prime Minister, John Prescott, appointed Lord (Richard) Rogers, the architect, to head an Urban Task Force (UTF), which was intended to come up with proposals to stop the flight from the cities. The UTF reported in 1999,[29] suggesting a number of spending and tax changes that were designed to bring about an 'urban renaissance'.

At the end of 2000, the government issued two consultative papers, one on urban[30] and the other on rural[31] policy. Both documents made modest proposals for ameliorating the conditions of the areas concerned. For the rural areas proposals included some protection against rising motoring costs, the need for improved public transport, more affordable housing for local people and protection for the countryside. The urban document outlined a number of tax changes and new neighbourhood initiatives designed to make city life more attractive. A cabinet committee for urban policy was proposed.

However, neither document was particularly radical. The problems which had generated the powerful rural lobby (mostly the collapse in farming incomes and the rise in fuel prices) were unlikely to be tackled by a single policy document. Indeed, none of the major political parties in Britain appeared to have a solution to the perennial difficulties of a rural economy that awkwardly combined demands for new housing and services (because of a rising number of people fleeing towns and cities) with wholly-different requirements for increased subsidy for the minority of poor, agriculture-dependent, individuals who made up the traditional country population.

Many of the larger cities – though not London – continued to suffer population decline. In all cities, including the capital, there were spectacular pockets of decay. Liverpool, Manchester and Newcastle-upon-Tyne in particular faced the need to maintain or improve public services against a backdrop of falling populations. Although the 1990s had seen a modest revival in the fortunes of most of the older city centres (by 2001 having a branch of chic department store Harvey Nichols in a city was generally seen as far more important than the condition of local manufacturing) the surrounding halo of the inner city often continued to decline.

Lottery-funded projects such as the Lowry Centre (Salford), Tate Modern (Southwark) and the Baltic Flour Mill (Gateshead) meant arts-based regeneration was added to the mix of urban funding schemes that the

Blair government had inherited from the Conservatives. Indeed, lottery-funded theatres, galleries and minor local improvements became a significant objective for local authorities throughout the Blair administration. Some of these schemes (e.g. Tate Modern) proved wildly successful, others will saddle local councils with debts for years to come. The Millennium Dome at Greenwich, which was by far the largest recipient of Lottery cash, was claimed by its supporters as a major contributor to regeneration in south-east London.

Conclusion

The Blair effect on local government was, in part, a cautious, inch-by-inch, effort to liberalise (at least some, well-behaved) councils. At the same time, the Blair administration took great care to extend the oversight and regulation of local authorities, which were seen as inherently wasteful and conservative. The transmission of such apparently contradictory messages to councillors and their officers had the inevitable effect of causing confusion and, privately, resentment.

There is no way of divorcing Labour's treatment of local government from the grim struggle between central and local government during the 1980s. None of Blair's ministers – Old or New Labour – wanted to miss the opportunity of ensuring that local government was kept compliant. Never again would the national party be held to ransom by a handful of radical mavericks in town and city halls. The attempt to thwart Ken Livingstone in his bid to become Labour candidate for Mayor of London was supported by senior figures from all parts of the party and by many individual members. Even today, characters such as Livingstone induce deep suspicion among virtually all Labour front-benchers and many other party members.

Yet the caution with which Blair treated local government stands in sharp contrast to the robust devolution of power from Westminster to Scotland, Wales and Northern Ireland. The creation of a Scottish Parliament, with full legislative powers, was a very large shift of control away from London. At the same time, the government was unwilling to allow councils even modest freedom to set their own business rates or (in effect) to decide how much to spend on schools.

At the end of the Blair government 96 per cent of all taxation in the United Kingdom remains in the hands of central government. The remaining 4 per cent is the council tax set by local government, though even this tax is subject to severe constraints and the annual threat of capping. The figure of 96 per cent is extraordinarily high by the standards of developed democracies. Yet the Blair government has made no efforts to reduce the centralised nature of taxation and public expenditure control. Nor do the Conservatives promise any change. Britain looks set to remain one of the most centrally-focused democracies in the world.

Tony Blair had never been a member of a local authority. He had no experience of town hall power before becoming an MP or Prime Minister. This lack of experience other than in national politics would be seen as very unusual in countries such as the United States, France or Germany, where holding office at other levels of government (sometimes simultaneously) is the norm. Perhaps Blair's suspicion of local government derived in part from this omission. His government sees local government as one of a number of vehicles for delivering centrally-determined objectives.

In retrospect, the 1997 Blair government can be seen to have been technocratic and inconsistent in its approach to local government. In common with the Thatcher and Major governments, there was no evidence of any particular end-point for the total of local authority reforms made. Unsure about just how much to trust local councils, the government chose to adopt 'safety first' policies. Keeping the electorate content with New Labour at a national level proved more important than any constitutional principles about local democracy.

To be fair, there was probably less additional centralisation than had taken place under the Thatcher administrations. This meant that the pace of developing central control slowed down after 1997, though it barely receded. The advent of new inspectors, Best Value and Local Public Service Agreements arguably extended central influence. By 2001 the Blair effect on local government was modest and, in parts, muddled. Many local authorities will have seen this as an improvement, though only just. A long war was over, but with no certainty about the peace.

Notes

1 For a brief analysis of these governments, see J. Stewart and G. Stoker, *Local Government in the 1990s*, Macmillan, 1995.

2 See M. Loughlin, D. Gelfand and K. Young (eds) *Half a Century of Municipal Decline*, George Allen & Unwin, 1985.

3 For an analysis of this nationalised version of local government see R. Rhodes, *The National World of Local Government*, Allen & Unwin, 1986.

4 For an analysis of the consequences of this background see J. Stewart and G. Stoker (eds) *The Future of Local Government*, Macmillan, 1989.

5 G.W. Jones and T. Travers, 'Central Government Perceptions of Local Government', in *Local Democracy and Local Government*, ed. L. Pratchett and D. Wilson, Macmillan, 1996.

6 Labour Party, *New Labour because Britain deserves better*, Labour Party, 1997, p. 34 and 35.

7 Department of the Environment, Transport and the Regions, *Modernising local government. Local democracy and community leadership*, HMSO, 1998, p. 33.

8 Department of the Environment, Transport and the Regions, *Modernising local government. Improving local services through best value*, HMSO, 1998, p. 9.

9 Committee on Standards in Public Life, *Standards of Conduct in Local Government in England, Scotland and Wales*, Third Report, 1997, Cm 3702.

10 Department of the Environment, Transport and the Regions, *New Leadership for London*, TSO, Cm 3724, 1997.

11 T. Travers and G.W. Jones, *The New Government of London*, Joseph Rowntree Foundation, 1997, pp. 22–31.

12 T. Blair, *Leading the Way. A new vision for local government*, IPPR, 1998.

13 Michael Heseltine, *Where There's a Will*, Hutchinson, 1987.

14 D. Butler, A. Adonis and T. Travers, *Failure in British Government. The Politics of the Poll Tax*, Oxford University Press, 1994, pp. 256–7.

15 HM Treasury, *Spending Review 2000. New Public Spending Plans 2001–2004*, 2000, Cm 4807, paragraph 33.3.

16 Department of the Environment, Transport and the Regions, *Modern Local Government In 'Touch with the People*, HMSO, Cm 4114, p. 21, 1998.

17 Department of the Environment, Transport and the Regions, *Modern Local Government In Touch with the People*, HMSO, 1998, Cm 4114, pp. 26–30.

18 Local Government Association, *Modern Local Government taking the initiative. A LGA survey of local authorities*, LGA, 1999, p. 21.

19 See, for example, G. Filkin, *Building Capacity for Best Value*, New Local Government Network, 1999.

20 A good example of this approach can be found in Local Government Association *Making Decisions Locally. Report of the LGA's hearing on political leadership and ethics*, LGA, paragraphs 13–31 1999.

21 Department of the Environment, Transport and the Regions, *Modernising Local Government Finance: A Green Paper*, DETR, 2000.

22 Department of the Environment, Transport and the Regions, *New Leadership for London*, Cm 3724, TSO, 1997.

23 Department of the Environment, Transport and the Regions, *A Mayor and Assembly for London*, Cm 3897, TSO, 1998.

24 M. Darcy and R. Maclean, (2000) *Nightmayor* London: Politicos.

25 See J. Carvel, *Citizen Ken*, Chatto & Windus, 1984.

26 C. Hood, C. Scott, G. Jones and T. Travers, *Regulation Inside Government. Wase-Watchers, Quality Police and Sleaze-Busters*, Oxford University Press, 1999.

27 Local Government Association, *Whose zone is it anyway? The guide to area based initiatives*, LGA, 1999.

28 Social Exclusion Unit, *A New Commitment to Neighbourhood Renewal*, Cabinet Office, 2001.

29 Urban Task Force, *Towards an Urban Renaissance*, E&FN Spon, 1999.

30 Department of the Environment, Transport and the Regions, *Our towns and cities: the future. Delivering an Urban Renaissance*, Cm 4911, TSO, 2000.

31 D-E-T-R, *Our Countryside: The future. A fair deal for rural England*, Cm 4909, TSO, 2000.

© Chris Riddell

Chapter 7

CONSTITUTIONAL REFORM

Vernon Bogdanor

I Labour and Constitutional Reform in the Twentieth Century

IN NO AREA of policy has the Blair effect been more radical and far-reaching than in that of the constitution. Between 1997 and 2001, the reforms of the Blair government provided for devolution to Scotland, Wales and Northern Ireland; new proportional election systems for the devolved bodies, for the European Parliament, and for the new London strategic authority and mayor; the removal of all but ninety-two of the hereditary peers from the House of Lords; a Human Rights Act; a Freedom of Information Act; radical reform of local government; the state funding of political parties; and widespread use of the referendum.

This remarkable plethora of constitutional reforms would hardly have been expected by anyone acquainted with the history of the Labour Party. For, since Labour became a national party in 1918, constitutional reform has rarely been one of its major priorities. Certainly no previous Labour government has put reform of the constitution at the centre of its programme. Labour's mission, after all, was to transform society and the economy, not to change the constitution. With the achievement of universal suffrage, constitutional issues would move into the background; the foreground would be occupied by economics and society. Indeed, from the time of the founding of the party, most socialists and social democrats tended to think in terms of a linear transition from political democracy, well on the way to being achieved by the beginning of the twentieth century, to social democracy.[1] 'The workman', Keir Hardie declared in 1907, 'will use the political freedom which his fathers won for him to win industrial freedom for his children. That is the real inward meaning of the Labour Party.'[2] The historic task of the Liberal Party had been to achieve political democracy; that of Labour was to establish social democracy. This perspective can be found both in the classic work by T.H. Marshall, *Citizenship and Social Class* (1950), and also in Anthony Crosland's 'revisionist' text, *The Future of Socialism* (1956).[3] Labour inherited a political democracy. Its task was to transform it into a social democracy. For this reason, Labour tended to regard constitutional reform as a distraction from its central aims, not as a contribution towards them.

The Labour Party, unlike most Continental socialist parties, never regarded the state as irredeemably hostile to its aspirations. It sought therefore to capture the main institutions of the state, not to transform them. No doubt part of the reason for its attitude was that the fledgling party had found it easy, at the beginning of the twentieth century, to come to an accommodation with one of the 'bourgeois' parties, the Liberals, through the Gladstone–MacDonald electoral pact of 1903. Thus, while almost every Continental socialist party came to support proportional representation, as the only way in which its minority 'socialist' vote could be properly reflected in the legislature, Labour, in large part due to the influence of MacDonald, refused to do so, believing, correctly, that it would one day be the majority party and so benefit from the system. This viewpoint was reflected at the 1926 Labour Party Conference by George Lansbury, from the Left of the party, who agreed with MacDonald on this if on little else. Seeking to rebut a speaker who had declared that the first-past-the-post system had worked in the interest of the capitalist parties, Lansbury declared that, 'Speaking quite personally he thought that the majority of the decisions under the present system had worked for the other people; but if they were wise they could now make it work for themselves'.[4] And so it proved to be.

Labour has, it is true, flirted on occasion with the alternative vote. It did so in 1918, and during the years of the second Labour government between 1929–31. It may well do so again in the twenty-first century. The report of the Commission on electoral reform, chaired by Lord Jenkins, and published in 1998, called for a system of proportional representation known as 'AV plus', comprising the alternative vote plus topping up on a county basis to secure proportionality. Labour, however, while it is unlikely to endorse proportional representation might well put to the electorate in a referendum the alternative vote without topping up as its preferred alternative to first-past-the-post. In each case – in 1918, in 1929–31, and in a possible future referendum – the motive is the same – to secure a realignment of the Left, a rapprochement between the Labour and Liberal parties, and a new 'progressive' coalition, which could become a permanent majority in British politics. It is the politics of the Gladstone–MacDonald pact adapted to changed conditions.

On the whole, though, Labour's heart, since 1914 at least, has lain with the first-past-the-post system. The Left, particularly, has supported that system, fearing contamination from any alliance with non-socialist elements and particularly the Liberal Party. When Roy Jenkins, during the hung parliament of March–October 1974, sought to persuade his Cabinet colleagues to consider 'the matter of the single transferable vote', Willie Ross, the Scottish Secretary, pointed out that 'If we were not too careful we could see the end of any possibility of a Labour Government',[5] while Ron Hayward, Secretary of the Labour Party, declared in 1976 that 'Proportional representation means coalition government at Westminster, on the lines of our European partners, and it is goodbye then to any dreams or aspirations for a democratic socialist Britain'.[6]

Nor was Labour better disposed to other constitutional reforms. When Churchill proposed that the question of the continuation of the wartime coalition government in 1945 be put to the people in a referendum, he was rebuffed by Attlee who declared it to be 'a device . . . alien to all our traditions', and went on to say that it 'has only too often been the instrument of Nazism and Fascism. Hitler's practices in the field of referenda and plebiscites can hardly have endeared these expedients to the British heart'.[7] The referendum, most Labour leaders believed, was a conservative if not a populist weapon, and its use would tend to retard the progress of social change. On this they were very much in accord with their Continental neighbours. Indeed, in Europe, it has been the Right, not the Left, which has tended to champion the referendum. The attitude of Continental social democrats to the referendum was well expressed by Swedish Prime Minister, Tage Erlander, in 1948, when he declared:

> It is obvious that referendums are a strongly conservative force. It seems much harder to pursue an effective reform policy if reactionaries are offered the opportunity to appeal to people's natural conservatism and natural resistance to change . . . The referendum system, . . . provides an instrument for blocking radical progressive policy.[8]

As for a bill of rights, Labour had been bitterly hostile to judicial intervention in politics ever since the series of judicial decisions at the beginning of the century, culminating in Taff Vale, took away from the trade unions' rights which they believed had long been recognised and accepted. Judges, Labour felt, came predominantly from the upper classes of society and held reactionary views. This view of the judiciary as class enemies was heightened in the 1970s when the judges were called upon to administer the Heath government's ill-fated Industrial Relations Act. 'If,' declared Michael Foot, in 1976, 'the freedom of the people of this country and especially the rights of trade unions – if these precious things of the past had been left to the good sense and fair-mindedness of the judges we would have few freedoms in this country at all.'[9]

Devolution, it is true, was supported by the Labour Party in its early years. Irish Home Rule, as well as Home Rule for Scotland and Wales were central planks in the policy of such early Labour leaders as Keir

Hardie and Ramsay MacDonald. But, as it came to maturity as a national party in the 1920s, so Labour dropped Home Rule; by the mid-1920s, devolution, for Labour, meant little more than local government reform. 'I do not think,' Labour's assistant general secretary, Jim Middleton, told a leading Scottish nationalist in 1924, 'all the large measures in which the Scottish, English and Welsh peoples are interested necessarily depend upon self-government for their success.'[10] Moreover, the post-war Attlee government was, as we shall see, particularly hostile to devolution, and hostile to it for socialist reasons.

Labour, as early as 1918, favoured, in its policy document, 'Labour and the New Social Order', a second chamber, albeit not one based upon the hereditary principle. Between 1922 and the late 1960s, however, Labour's policy seemed to be, in Richard Crossman's words, 'that an indefensible anachronism is preferable to a second Chamber with any real authority', a position which he found 'logical, but rather reactionary'.[11] Even when, in 1968–69, Labour proposed reform of the Lords, it was defeated, just as it was to be in the 1970s on devolution, by its own rebellious back-benchers rather than by the Conservatives.

Most of Labour's constitutional reforming impulses, then, had burnt themselves out by the 1920s, and the first two Labour governments, led by Ramsay MacDonald, were highly conservative on the constitution, as was Clement Attlee's great reforming government of 1945. For, by the 1920s, the battle for universal suffrage had clearly been won, and the newly mobilised electorate was interested less in the completion of the old liberal programme of constitutional reform, than in using the vote to improve social and economic conditions. Thus constitutional questions came to be eclipsed by socioeconomic issues at the heart of the political agenda. Moreover, some reforms, such as the referendum, would threaten the interests of the political parties themselves. It was indeed the development of tightly organised political parties which helped to fossilise the movement for constitutional change.[12] So it was that the old constitutional liberal movement seemed to have played itself out, and political structures came to be frozen. During the last part of the twentieth century, they began to become unfrozen again, as the old radical programme of constitutional change came once more to the forefront of politics. Until the 1990s, however, Labour's aim was to capture the state not to reform it.

II The Reform Agenda

Labour, then, has, at least since the 1920s, been distinctly sceptical if not downright hostile towards constitutional reform. This makes the sweep and scope of the Blair government's reforms even more astonishing. For, since the general election of 1997, the following major constitutional reforms have been enacted:

- Legislation providing for referendums on devolution in Scotland, Wales and Northern Ireland, and for a referendum on a directly-elected mayor for London with a strategic authority.
- Devolution to Scotland, providing for a directly-elected Parliament, elected by the additional member system of proportional representation, with legislative powers.
- Devolution to Wales, providing for a directly-elected National Assembly, elected by the additional member system of proportional representation, with executive powers.
- Devolution to Northern Ireland, providing for a directly-elected Assembly, elected by the single transferable vote system of proportional representation, with legislative powers, and requiring a partnership executive to be established to comprise members of both communities, the Unionist and the Nationalist.
- A new electoral system, the additional member system of proportional representation for elections to the European Parliament.
- A directly-elected mayor for London, elected by the supplementary vote, and a directly-elected strategic authority for London, elected by the additional member system of proportional representation.
- Legislation requiring every local authority in England and Wales to abandon the committee system, under which local authorities have been organised since 1835, in favour of a system with a separate executive. The two main models provide for either a Cabinet-type system or a directly-elected mayor. If, however, a local authority wishes to adopt this latter option, it must first secure assent through referendum. In addition, 5 per cent of locally registered elections can *require* the authority to hold a referendum on the mayor option.
- A Human Rights Act, allowing judges to declare that legislation is incompatible with the European Convention on Human Rights, and providing a fast track procedure for Parliament to alter such legislation if it so wishes.
- The removal of all but ninety-two hereditary peers from the House of Lords as the first phase of a wider reform of the second chamber.
- A Freedom of Information Act.
- Limits on campaign spending in the Elections, Political Parties and Referendums Act.

In addition, further referendums have been promised on whether Britain should adhere to the European common currency, and whether an alternative electoral system should be adopted for elections to Westminster.

There can be no doubt, then, that the Blair government has set in train the most radical programme of constitutional reform that Britain has seen since 1911 or 1832 – indeed it may be argued that the radicalism of the reforms is even greater, since both 1832 and 1911 were concerned with single, albeit major reforms – the reform of the franchise and the reform of the House of Lords.

There is a further striking feature of the reforms, namely that many of them have been validated by referendum which, until the 1970s, was widely thought to be unconstitutional. Even in 1975, when a referendum was held on Britain's entry into the European Community, it was alleged that this was a unique and exceptional issue, and that there would never be another. The devolution referendums of 1979 were forced on an unwilling Labour government by dissident back-benchers. Yet, in 1996, Blair insisted, against the wishes of many in Scotland, that referendums be held before devolution was again brought before Parliament.

Now that devolution is on the statute book, its achievement may seem to have been inevitable. Yet, every previous attempt by Parliament to leg-islate for devolution since Gladstone's first Home Rule bill of 1886 had failed. The 1886 bill was defeated in the Commons; the second bill was defeated in the Lords in 1893; the third bill reached the statute book in 1914 but was never implemented because of the war. The fourth bill, of 1920, was rejected by the twenty-six counties which now comprise the Republic of Ireland, and accepted, ironically, only by the six counties of Northern Ireland, which had steadfastly resisted Home Rule since 1886. The first bill providing for devolution in Scotland and Wales had to be withdrawn in 1977 when the Callaghan government failed to secure a majority for a guillotine motion. The second bill reached the statute book, but was massively repudiated in Wales in the referendum of 1979 by a majority of four to one against; while in the Scottish referendum of 1979, there was a narrow majority in favour of devolution, but insufficient to overcome the hurdle erected by Parliament that 40 per cent of the Scottish electorate had to vote 'Yes', for devolution to be implemented. Accordingly, the Thatcher government repealed both the Scotland Act and the Wales Act shortly after coming to power.

The positive results in the referendums of the 1990s on devolution and on the London authority, would seem to indicate that some, at least, of the constitutional reforms of the Blair era correspond with popular wishes. Yet it would be wrong to suggest that constitutional reform, except possibly in Scotland, arouses any popular excitement. Turnout for the referendums in Wales and London was low, at 50 per cent and 34 per cent respectively, and in Britain as a whole, constitutional reform came sixteenth out of sixteen in the concerns of voters during the 1997 election campaign.[13] Constitutional reform lies at the bottom of most voters' list of priorities. There is a great contrast in this regard with the years 1832 and 1911 when there was con-siderable popular excitement and indeed much pressure and agitation for constitutional change. The revolution of the 1990s has, by contrast, been a quiet one; but it has been a revolution all the same; and its consequences are likely to prove very profound.

III Towards a British Constitution

Validation of constitutional reform by means of the referendum shows that it is no longer true that the British constitution knows nothing of the people. Indeed, it has become almost a convention of the constitution that any major constitutional change, and especially any which involve a transfer of powers away from Westminster – whether to devolved bodies in Scotland and Wales or to the European Union – require a referendum to validate it. On matters such as these, a vote in Parliament is no longer sufficient to secure legitimacy.

Yet, until the 1970s, the referendum tended to be dismissed as unconstitutional, since Parliament was sovereign.[14] But of course if Parliament is sovereign, if Parliament can do as it likes, then Parliament can decide to call a referendum.

It is striking that, amidst the plethora of referendums which have been held, or are shortly to be held, the claim is still reiterated that the sovereignty of Parliament remains unaffected, since it supposedly remains with Parliament to decide whether to take account of the wishes of the people or to ignore them. Formally, of course, that remains true. In practice, however, a referendum which yields a clear outcome on a reasonable turnout binds Parliament. Anyone who doubts this should compare the debates on the Scotland bill of 1998, held *after* a referendum, with those on the Scotland bill of 1978, held *before* a referendum. In the case of the later bill, there were many back-bench opponents and sceptics, both in the Commons and the Lords. But none of their arguments could prevail against the fact that the Scots had indicated by a large majority that they wanted devolution.

The government has indeed been insistent that its reforms leave the sovereignty of Parliament intact. That is why it provided for devolution to Scotland, Wales and Northern Ireland and not a federal solution. With devolution, Parliament retains the right, in theory at least, to legislate for Scotland, Wales and Northern Ireland, even with regard to their domestic affairs. Moreover the Human Rights Act did not give judges the power to strike down Westminster legislation. It remains for Parliament to decide whether or not to repeal legislation which the judges declare to be incompatible with the European Convention. For this reason, indeed, it is a mistake to speak of the Human Rights Act incorporating the Convention, Article 13 of which provides for a remedy against breaches. The Human Rights Act, however, provides no remedy, since it remains a matter for Parliament to take action if a court declares legislation to be incompatible with the Convention. If Parliament decides not to take any action, the citizen has no redress other than to put his or her case before the European Court of Human Rights at Strasbourg.

In form, therefore, the constitutional reforms of the Blair era leave the sovereignty of Parliament and the fundamentals of the British constitution intact. They may thus seem to involve no more than a shifting of the institutional furniture which leave the conceptual foundations of the dwelling, as it were, untouched. In practice, however, these reforms revolutionise the constitution by undermining its foundations. Precisely because we can continue to use our traditional constitutional concepts, we can easily hide from ourselves the magnitude of the changes which have been made. Perhaps the Blair government had good reason to hide the revolutionary nature of its reforms. For it is difficult to persuade the British people to accept a change which is presented as one of principle. 'The British,' the constitutional historian, Peter Hennessy, told the Nolan Committee on Standards in Public Life, 'like to live in a series of half-way houses.'[15] Perhaps the only way to persuade the British people to accept radical change is to tell them that the change is evolutionary in nature, requiring the introduction of no new principle, but flowing from principles that have been already accepted in the past.

The crucial consequence of the reforms of the Blair era, however, is to give us, for the first time in our history, a constitution; and, moreover, a constitution which is quasi-federal in nature. It can hardly be denied that this is a revolutionary change.

IV Human Rights

The Human Rights Act, even though it does not go so far as to incorporate the European Convention into our domestic law, nevertheless alters very considerably the balance between Parliament and the judiciary. For it will be difficult, although not of course impossible, for Parliament not to respond to a declaration made by the judges that a particular item of legislation is incompatible with the Convention. Thus the judges are likely to build up a corpus of constitutional principles in the area of human rights. That will be something novel in our constitutional experience.

'There is,' declares Dicey, 'in the English constitution (*sic*), an absence of those declarations or definitions of rights so dear to foreign constitutionalists.' The principles defining our civil liberties are 'like all maxims established by judicial legislation, mere generalisations drawn either from the decisions or dicta of judges, or from statutes'. By contrast, Dicey, goes on, 'most foreign constitution-makers have begun with declarations of rights. For this they have often been in no wise to blame'.

The consequence, however, Dicey continues, is that 'the relation of the rights of individuals to the principles of the constitution is not quite the same in countries like Belgium, where the constitution is the result of a legislative act, as in England, where the constitution itself is based upon legal decisions – the difference in this matter between the constitutions of Belgium and the English constitution may be described by the statement that in Belgium individual rights are deductions drawn from the principles of the constitution, whilst in England the so-called principles of the constitution are inductions or generalistations based upon particular decisions pronounced by the courts as to the rights of given individuals.'[16]

The Human Rights Act is likely to transform this situation. In future, our civil liberties will no longer be in the form of specific inductive generalistations, but will instead be derived from 'principles of the constitution', principles of the European Convention. Matters hitherto the responsibility of Parliament will in future become, in large part, the responsibility of the courts. The European Convention provided European judges with a weapon. The Human Rights Act hands that weapon over to British judges. No one can be sure what British judges will do with it. In the United States, the Supreme Court has used the weapon of judicial review both to reaffirm and to do away with slavery, to require Jeohovah's Witnesses to salute the flag, and to allow them not to do so, to ban the Communist Party and to legalise it.

In 1998, in the *Bowman* case, the European Court of Human Rights declared that the provisions of the Representation of the People Act, by which third parties were restricted to local campaign expenditure of £5, violated the European Convention. In consequence, much of our law on political funding has to be rewritten. Might our own judges not decide in future that the legislation imposing a national cap on party spending, as provided for in the Elections, Political Parties and Referendums Act of 2000, violates the Convention, just as American judges decided, in the landmark case of *Buckley v Valeo* in 1974, that restrictions on campaign spending violated the First Amendment? Issues concerning the regulation of political spending raise complex and profound questions of political philosophy – to what extent should the freedom of individuals to give and of parties to spend be curtailed by the principle of equality requiring a level playing field between those parties which can gain support from wealthy interests and those which cannot? Such complex questions, previously resolved by Parliament, will now be answered by judges.

Inevitably, greater attention will come to be focused on who these judges are and how they are to be appointed. There are many who argue that judges come from too narrow a segment of society, that they are unrepresentative and out of touch. Many of the quality newspapers have begun to 'profile' the law lords, distinguishing between those who are 'liberal' and those who are 'conservative'. In the United States, decisions made by the Supreme Court between 1933 and 1953 were much affected by the fact that all appointments between these years were made by presidents belonging to the Democrat party. Between 1969 and 1993, by contrast, all appointments were made by presidents belonging to the Republican party; for, by chance, no Supreme Court vacancy arose during the presidency of Carter, the only president from the Democrat party during these years. In Britain, the removal of political influence over the appointment of judges occurred comparatively recently. In the nineteenth century, Lord Salisbury, the Conservative Prime Minister, was quite explicit about what he called 'the unwritten law of our party system'. 'There is no clearer statute in that unwritten law,' he wrote, 'than the rule that party claims should always weigh very heavily in the disposal of the highest legal appointments. In dealing with them you cannot ignore the party system as you do in the choice of a general or an archbishop. It would be a breach of the tacit convention on which politicians and lawyers have worked the British Constitution together for the last 200 years. Perhaps it is not an ideal system – some day no doubt the M.R. [Master of the Rolls] will be appointed by competitive examination in law Reports, but it is our system for the present: and we should give your party arrangements a wrench if we threw it aside.' He also believed that judges should be Conservatives since, 'within certain limits of intelligence, honesty and knowledge of the law, one man would make as good a judge as another, and a Tory mentality was *ipso facto* more trustworthy than a Liberal one'.[17]

In future, it will be the task of judges, however chosen, to interpret parliamentary legislation in terms of a higher law, the European Convention. Yet Dicey declared that, in Britain, 'There is no law which Parliament cannot change. There is no fundamental or so-called constitutional law.' There is no person or body 'which can pronounce void any enactment passed by the British Parliament on the ground of such enactment being opposed to the constitution'.[18] These propositions, though they may remain true in form, have now become in substance false. The Human Rights Act in effect makes the European Convention the fundamental law of the land. It is a law which Parliament in practice will not be able to alter, while the judges will be able, if not to pronounce legislation void, to put pressure on Parliament to alter any enactment which is contrary to the Convention.

'In England,' Tocqueville famously remarked, 'the Parliament has an acknowledged right to modify the constitution; as, therefore, the constitution may undergo perpetual change, it does not in reality exist; the Parliament is at once a legislative and constituent assembly.'[19] Parliament, however, insofar as human rights are concerned, is a constituent assembly no longer, although of course it retains the somewhat theoretical right of repealing the Human Rights Act.

V Devolution

With devolution, too, great concern was shown to preserve the shell of parliamentary sovereignty. Paragraph 42 of the White Paper on Scottish devolution, *Scotland's Parliament*, declared, in stern Diceyan tones, that 'The United Kingdom Parliament is and will remain sovereign in all matters'. Section 28(7) of the Scotland Act declares that 'This section,' which provides for the Scottish Parliament to make laws, 'does not affect the power of the Parliament of the United Kingdom to make laws for Scotland.' In practice, however, as was the case with the Northern Ireland Parliament, Stormont, between 1921 and 1972, Westminster will, by convention, not legislate with regard to devolved matters in Scotland without the consent of the Scottish Parliament; and the government will normally oppose any private Member's bill seeking to alter the law on devolved subjects in Scotland. Thus, with regard to Scotland, the sovereignty of Parliament now means something different from what it means with regard to England. For England, sovereignty continues to mean supremacy over all persons, matters and things. For Scotland, it means no more than a vague right of supervision over the Scottish Parliament. Sovereignty no longer corresponds to a real power to make laws regulating Scotland's domestic affairs.

Even in Wales, where devolution is limited to executive matters and Parliament retains full authority over all legislation for Wales, parliamentary sovereignty has come, in practice, to be limited. In the first post-devolution Question Time for Wales, on 7 July 1999, the Speaker, on three separate occasions, cautioned ministers not to answer questions on devolved matters.[20] The first occasion was when Welsh Office junior minister, Peter Hain, was asked a Question on tourism. He replied: 'I had responsibility for this matter until 1 July' (when the Welsh National Assembly came into existence).

The Speaker then declared: 'If it is a devolved matter, we must pass on.'

On the second occasion, Alun Michael, Secretary of State for Wales, was asked a Question about the beef industry, he replied, 'This is a matter for the National Assembly for Wales'.

The Speaker then declared: 'If the Minister announces that it is a matter for the National Assembly for Wales, I cannot allow the House to trespass on these responsibilities [Interruption] If the Minister tells me that it is a matter for the Assembly, it cannot be a matter for the House, correct?'

Alun Michael: 'Correct.'

On the third occasion, a Question was asked of Welsh Office junior minister, Jon Owen Jones, on abattoirs in Wales, he replied: 'This is a matter for my right Hon. Friend, the Minister of Agriculture, Fisheries and Food, or in Wales, for the National Assembly.'

The Speaker then declared: 'Order. In that case, it is a matter for the Welsh Assembly. It cannot be the responsibility of both this House and the Assembly.'

Thus, even in Wales, where only the power to make secondary legislation has been devolved, and where, therefore, no area of policy is strictly a devolved matter, large powers have been removed from the purview of ministers and Members of Parliament.

The consequence is that devolution has introduced a federal element into the working of Westminster from where it has hitherto been absent, with the de minimis exception of Northern Irish matters between 1921 and 1972.

Before devolution, every MP was responsible for scrutinising both the domestic and the non-domestic affairs of every part of the United Kingdom. Now, MPs will play no part at all in legislating for the domestic affairs of Scotland or Northern Ireland, and only a limited role, if at all, in legislating for the domestic affairs of Wales – for, as we have seen, ministers can refuse to accept Questions on Welsh domestic matters, even though responsibility for primary legislation for Wales still remains with Westminster.

Only with regard to England will MPs continue to enjoy the responsibility which hitherto they have enjoyed over the whole of the United Kingdom, of scrutinising both primary and secondary legislation. Even, with regard to England, however, this responsibility, though formally untrammelled, may in practice be limited by the advent of directly-elected mayors. With regard to London, for example, the mayor, Ken Livingstone, is likely to say that he alone, and not MPs representing London constituencies, has a mandate to speak for the people of London, since he alone has been directly-elected to represent the people of London. Similarly, a directly-elected mayor of, for example, Newcastle is likely to say that he or she alone, and not MPs representing Newcastle constituencies, is qualified to speak for the people of Newcastle.

What is clear is that Westminster is now a Parliament for England, a Parliament for primary legislation for Wales, and a federal Parliament for Northern Ireland and Scotland. MPs, therefore, have different responsibilities for different parts of the United Kingdom.

Moreover, Scottish and Northern Irish MPs, and perhaps also Welsh MPs, have lost their constituency responsibilities. They now have a lesser role to play at Westminster than their English counterparts.

In the Scottish Parliament, the parliamentary allowances for members elected through the list have been reduced on the grounds that they do not have any constituency responsibilities. Following devolution, MPs representing Scottish constituencies lose most of their constituency responsibilities, which are taken over by MSPs. Is there not a case in logic for reducing the pay and allowances of Westminster MPs from Scotland and Northern Ireland on the grounds that they too have hardly any constituency work? When this proposition was put to the Leader of the House, Margaret Beckett, in June 1999, she replied: 'I strongly hold the view . . . that there is not and should not be such a thing as two different kinds of Members of Parliament.'[21]

This reply, however, ignores the fact that there are, in reality, and for the first time in the history of Parliament, if we make an exception for the experiment in devolution in Northern Ireland between 1921 and 1972, two different kinds of Members of Parliament. The Scotland Act thus does more than devolve powers to Scotland. It divides power between Scotland and Westminster. In doing so, it establishes the constitution of a quasi-federal state.

A constitution, of course, and especially a federal constitution, generally requires a court to police it. The Scotland Act provides for such a constitutional court in the form of the Judicial Committee of the Privy Council. The Judicial Committee, of course, can only pronounce on Scottish legislation, not on Westminster legislation, so that formally the sovereignty of Parliament is, once again, preserved. In practice, however, if the Judicial Committee decides a dispute in Scotland's favour, it will be very difficult for Westminster to override its verdict. Thus, both Westminster and the Scottish Parliament will in practice depend upon the Judicial Committee for the demarcation of their respective spheres of action, a condition characteristic of a federal system of government, and Westminster in practice loses yet another of the characteristics of a sovereign Parliament, the right to make laws from which there is no appeal.

Dicey once declared that the British Constitution was a 'historic' constitution'.[22] By this he meant not only that it was very old, but also that it was original and spontaneous, the product not of deliberate design but of a long process of evolution. There is no inherent reason of course why the main elements of such a constitution should not have been brought together in a single codified document. The crucial provision of such a document, however, before 1997, would have had to be that any article in it could be amended or repealed in exactly the same way as any other Act of Parliament. Thus, to formulate the British constitution in writing would have been a fruitless exercise. It could have been formulated in just eight words: What the Queen in Parliament enacts is law. It is for this reason that it has always been thought to be pointless to rationalise our historic constitution in codified form. The Human Rights Act and the Scotland Act, however, have the characteristic of fundamental laws. They in practice limit the rights of Westminster as a sovereign Parliament, and provide for a constitution which is quasi-federal in nature. It would be difficult to imagine a more radical or long-lasting consequence of the Blair effect.

VI Socialism and the Constitution

The government has been much criticised because there seems to be a lack of connection between its various constitutional reforms. There seems to be no theme linking them together. David Marquand has declared:

> The old constitution is dissolving beneath our eyes. The only question is what will replace it. To that question the authors of the revolution have no answer.[23]

This lack of a grand plan, however, may be a virtue not a defect. The Blair government, after all, has introduced very radical constitutional changes not, as in many other democracies, following defeat in war, revolution, or the introduction of a new regime, but in response to what it perceives as

real and concrete needs – the desire of the citizen for constitutional protection and for greater information, and the desire of the Scottish and
Welsh people for a degree of autonomy in their domestic affairs. The
strength of feeling for devolution, after all, differs widely in different parts
of the country, being strong in Scotland, but much weaker in most regions
of England, and probably non-existent in the south-east. Asymmetrical
devolution, therefore, is a sensible response to popular needs, as revealed
by referendums.

There is, however, a conflict between the Blair government's constitutional reform programme, and other aspects of the New Labour
programme; and there is, in particular, a very profound conflict between
constitutional reform and socialism or social democracy.

The Blair government has placed a great deal of emphasis on joined-up
or holistic government. Only in this way, so it is suggested, will it be possible to provide coherent solutions to deep-seated problems such as that of
social exclusion. This requires, however, that there be an agreed diagnosis of
the causes of these problems, and agreed remedies. Devolution and the dispersal of power to local parliaments and assemblies, as well as the dispersal
of power to local mayors, will increase the difficulty of obtaining such
agreed solutions. For, after all, there is no reason why a First Minister in the
Scottish Parliament or the Mayor of London, should agree with the central
government's diagnosis of the problem or its proposed solutions. Suppose
that a Scottish Parliament is elected with a non-Labour majority, and decides
that it wishes to reintroduce selection in education, or to raise revenue for
the National Health Service in Scotland by charging patients for occupying
hospital beds. Such measures would be deeply distasteful to the Labour
Party, but a Labour government would not be able to prevent them.

Even with a Labour First Minister and Mayor, there is no reason to
expect automatic agreement with central government. Both Scotland and
London, after all, are far less New Labour than the Blair government. The
leaders of the authorities representing these areas might well have quite different diagnoses of the problems from that held by the Blair government,
and there is no way in which central government can impose its own diagnosis upon them. Devolution, after all, like the Human Rights Act, hands
a weapon to politicians in alternative centres of power. There is no way of
predicting what they will do with it. There is thus a profound conflict
between the dispersal of power and the search for holistic government
which seems inevitably to imply centralisation. Insofar as holistic government is concerned, devolution involves a dispersal of effort as well as a
dispersal of power. Indeed, much of the Blair project of social reform seems
to entail centralisation, not devolution.

In its heyday when Labour seemed to be a genuinely socialist party, the
Labour movement was a profoundly centralising force in British politics.
One of Labour's fundamental principles, which lay at the very heart of the
Welfare State created by the Attlee government in the late 1940s, was that

the benefits and burdens which individuals ought to bear, should depend upon need and not on geography. It would be wrong for a deprived child in Glasgow to receive a higher level of benefit than a deprived child in Liverpool, because Scotland enjoyed a Parliament of its own, while Merseyside did not. 'If comprehensive education is right in Glasgow,' a Labour MP declared during the devolution debates of the 1970s, 'it is right in the South of England.'[24] The very real problems, therefore, of the deprived areas of the country should be resolved, not by devolution, but by a strong socialist government at Westminster, the only body which could determine a fair distribution between different regions. The problems of the Scottish or the Welsh working class were thus also those of the English working class, and the remedy was the same, a strong socialist government which would be able to emancipate all the people in the whole of the United Kingdom.

It was for this reason that the Labour Party, and in particular the Labour left, was so sceptical of devolution in the 1970s. Separate assemblies, declared Neil Kinnock, as a rebellious back-bencher in 1976, 'could be an obituary notice for this movement'.[25] Labour was concerned less perhaps with the argument over *sovereignty*, that devolution would prove the slippery slope leading to the break-up of the United Kingdom, but, with quite a different argument, one based on *power*, that, with devolution, Westminster would lose the power to correct territorial disparities.

On the first Welsh Day debate in the House of Commons, Aneurin Bevan told MPs that: 'My colleagues, all of them members of the Miners' Federation of Great Britain, have no special solution for the Welsh coal industry which is not a solution for the whole of the mining industry of Great Britain. There is no Welsh problem.'[26] To those who called for devolution for Wales, Bevan had nothing but contempt.

> Is it not rather cruel to give the impression to the 50,000 unemployed men and women in Wales that their plight would be relieved and their distress removed by this constitutional change? It is not socialism. It is escapism. This is exactly the way in which nation after nation has been ruined in the last twenty-five to fifty years, trying to pretend that deep-seated economic difficulties can be removed by constitutional changes.[27]

It was because devolution so threatened the pursuit of socialist and social democratic aims that Bevan so strongly resisted the creation of a separate Welsh or Scottish health service. The service was to be a National Health Service, with treatment to depend upon need and not upon the accident of where one lived.

Devolution, then, threatens the Welfare State which Labour built up as its own during the Attlee years. And indeed, already, less than two years into the life of the Scottish Parliament, a divergence has appeared in one important plank of the Welfare State. For the Scottish Parliament has decided not to follow Westminster in charging tuition fees for university students. Instead it is proposing that Scottish graduates will pay a total of £2,000 in instalments once they earn £10,000 per year, the money to go to provide means-tested grants for students from low-income backgrounds.

Thus, a Scottish student attending a Scottish university will enjoy more generous financial arrangements than an English, Welsh or Northern Irish student. This poses a dilemma for socialists and social democrats. For, if the Blair government's introduction of student fees is right for England, why should it not also be right for Scotland, or, conversely, if the Scottish Parliament declares, as it did, that tuition fees were harming access to higher education, and were therefore socially damaging, why should not the same be true in England, Wales and Northern Ireland?

Much ink has been spilled on the speculative question of whether devolution makes the break-up of the United Kingdom more likely, or whether, by seeking to contain centrifugal forces, it is the policy most likely to hold the United Kingdom together. Whether or not, however, devolution means the end of the United Kingdom, it can be seen that it marks the end of one strand at least of socialism or social democracy, namely the belief that a benign government at Westminster can secure the distribution of benefits and burdens on the basis not of geography but of need.

The fundamental case for devolution, after all, is that of diversity, and diversity is more of a liberal value than a socialist one. Much is heard concerning the influence upon the Blair government of Liberalism. Yet the Liberalism to which Blair appeals is that of Beveridge and Keynes, and of Lloyd George. It is the so-called 'New Liberalism' of the early part of the twentieth century. That type of Liberalism, however, was, to almost the same extent as social democracy, a centralising force, because it was concerned with the politics of social reform. Lloyd George did, it is true, accept a 'national' Welsh, Scottish and Irish dimension to his National Insurance Act of 1911, but only because 'you have got to defer to sentiment'.[28] He was as sure as Aneurin Bevan was to be that an insurance scheme and a health service had to ignore 'national' boundaries within the United Kingdom if it was to be genuinely equitable. Beveridge, too, would have been quite horrified at 'national' or regional differences in welfare payments or in taxation.

In fact, the constitutional reform programme of New Labour has affinities less with New Liberalism, than with Gladstonian Old Liberalism, the Liberalism which prized diversity as an end in itself, and was highly sceptical of the benefits of 'constructivism', the idea that the state could engineer social outcomes. Thus, in one sense the constitutional reform programme of New Labour is not new at all, but very old, although of course, for the Labour Party to adopt a policy which goes so much against its raison d'être, is profoundly new for it.

It may seem that, when a movement comes to be more concerned with its procedures than with substance, it has lost belief in its ultimate aims.[29] A happy man, Bagehot says somewhere, is not forever worrying about improvements to his house. Perhaps by analogy a happy political party does not normally concern itself with the constitution. The Royal Society for the Protection of Birds now apparently has more members than all of the political parties put together. Were it suddenly to develop an interest in its constitution, in the rules by which its executive should be chosen, we should begin to suspect that the Society had lost confidence in its ornithological aims. Those who founded and fought for the Labour Party when socialism seemed the wave of the future were concerned less with changing the rules by which governments were formed and power exercised, than with changing society.

The general election of 1997, however, was the first since the Labour Party became a national party in 1918, in which nationalisation or state control was not an election issue, since Labour had abandoned it. Indeed, there were precious few differences on social and economic policy between the Conservatives and Labour, fewer than the differences between one wing of the Conservative Party, led by John Major, and the party's right wing, whose leading spokesman was John Redwood. Had Redwood won the leadership election of 1995, the social and economic consequences would have been far greater than those following New Labour's election victory in 1997, when the main differences between the parties seemed to lie in the area of constitutional reform. It was indeed a regression far beyond the twentieth century, back to the nineteenth, to the days when the main conflict between the party of the Left, the Liberals, and the party of the Right, the Conservatives, was over Home Rule. Perhaps the end of the twentieth century has seen the death of that 'constructivism' against which Gladstone railed. Perhaps the Left will once again be defined not by its attitude to social and economic issues, but by its approach to the constitution. It is too early to tell.

Labour's emphasis on constitutional reform does, however, tell us something quite profound not only about the constitution but about the contemporary condition of the Labour Party, and about socialism and social democracy, those prime ideological casualties of the twentieth century.

Notes

1 I find the attempt of Miles Taylor to argue otherwise in 'Labour and the Constitution', pp. 151–180, in Duncan Tanner, Pat Thane and Nick Tiratsoo (eds), *Labour's First Century*, Cambridge University Press, 2000, unconvincing.

2 Keir Hardie, *From Serfdom to Socialism* [1907], Harvester Press, Brighton, 1974, p. 77.

3 T.H. Marshall, *Citizenship and Social Class and Other Essays*, Cambridge University Press, 1950; C.A.R. Crosland, *the Future of Socialism*, Jonathan Cape, 1956.

4 Labour Party Conference Reports, 1926, p. 273.
5 Barbara Castle, *The Castle Diaries 1974–1976*, Weidenfeld and Nicolson, 1980, pp. 69–70.
6 Quoted in Vernon Bogdanor, *The People and the Party System*, Cambridge University Press, 1981, p. 55.
7 Quoted in Bogdanor, *The People and the Party System*, p. 35.
8 Quoted in Leif Lewin, *Ideology and Strategy: A Century of Swedish Politics*, Cambridge University Press, 1988, p. 235.
9 Quoted in Vernon Bogdanor, *Politics and the Constitution: Essays on British Government*, Dartmouth Press, Aldershot, 1996, p. 189.
10 Quoted in Miles Taylor, 'Labour and the Constitution' in Tanner, Thane and Tiratsoo, p. 159.
11 Quoted in Miles Taylor, *op. cit.* p. 169.
12 Michael Steed, 'Participation through Western Democratic Institutions', p. 96, in Geraint Parry, ed., *Participation in Politics*, Manchester University Press, 1972.
13 Robert Worcester and Roger Mortimore, *Explaining Labour's Landslide*, Politico's, 1999, p. 152.
14 Dicey, of course, never shared this view, being a fervent advocate of the referendum for major constitutional change, and especially for Home Rule, which he hoped would be defeated in a referendum. See the introduction to the 8th edition of the *Law of the Constitution*, published in 1915.
15 Peter Hennessy, *The Hidden Wiring: Unearthing the British Constitution*, Gollancz, 1995, p. 107.
16 A.V. Dicey, *Introduction to the Study of the Law of the Constitution* (1885), 10th edition, Macmillan, 1959, pp. 197–8.
17 R.F.V. Heuston, *Lives of the Lord Chancellors*, Clarendon Press, Oxford, 1964, pp. 52 and 36–37. I owe this reference to Robert Stevens.
18 Dicey, pp. 88, 91.
19 Alexis de Tocqueville, *Democracy in America*, Pt 1, ch. 6.
20 House of Commons Debates, 6th series, vol. 334, cc. 1013–5.
21 House of Commons Debates, 6th series, vol. 332, col. 795.
22 This comment occurs in his unpublished lectures on comparative constitutions to be found in the Codrington Library, All Souls College, Oxford, MS 323 LR 6 b 13.
23 Marquand, David, p. 269, 'Democracy in Britain' in *Political Quarterly*, 2000, pp. 269–270.
24 House of Commons Debates, 5th series, vol. 922, col. 1396, 13 December 1976.
25 Labour Party Conference, 1976, cited in Miles Taylor, 'Labour and the Constitution', loc. cit. p. 180.
26 House of Commons Debates, 5th series, vol. 403, col. 2312, 10 October 1944.
27 House of Commons Debates, 5th series, vol. 428, col. 405, 28 October 1946.
28 W.J. Braithwaite, *Lloyd George's Ambulance Wagon*, Methuen, 1957, p. 222.
29 I owe this thought to Raymond Plant.

© Chris Riddell

Chapter 8

THE PARTY SYSTEM

Lewis Baston

T HE 'PARTY SYSTEM' is only incidentally a policy area, and therefore
it poses rather different questions about the sources of change in the
period since 1997. This chapter is divided into four parts, each of
which relates to one aspect of the party system. The first is about the rules
under which party competition takes place, which have been evolving rapidly since 1994; the second concerns the internal organisation of the
political parties themselves. The third covers recent trends in pressure
group politics, and the fourth examines the biggest question of all –
whether 'The Project' of New Labour has managed to recast the party
system and escape from the Conservative Party dominance of the twentieth
century.

The Rules of the Game

British law and constitutional theory has been slow to adapt to the existence of political parties. Electoral law has been almost exclusively based
on the individual constituency campaigns – which are subject to stringent
spending controls and restrictions on permissible techniques of campaigning. National political finance has been completely unregulated. Secret
donations used to be the mainstay of Conservative Party finance.

This pattern started to change in 1994 after a series of eruptions of
sleaze.[1] John Major appointed the Nolan Committee to examine standards
of conduct in public life in October 1994 after the resignation of Neil
Hamilton. The House of Commons voted in 1995 to accept the first set of
recommendations and interpolated an additional ban on 'paid advocacy'
and a new code of conduct was thereby introduced for MPs. An external
Parliamentary Commissioner for Standards became responsible for

producing reports on allegations against MPs and the ineffective Select Committee on Privileges was replaced by a tougher Select Committee on Standards and Privileges.

The Political Parties, Referendums and Elections Act 2000 is a radical reform. This measure's genesis was in the Labour government's decision to extend the remit of the Committee on Standards in Public Life (chaired first by Lord Nolan and then by Sir Patrick Neill) to cover party and election finance, something the Conservative government always refused to do. The resulting inquiry reported in October 1998.[2] Its recommendations were surprisingly sweeping, forming what the committee called a 'substantial and interrelated' package that was designed to cope with future changes such as devolution and the possibility of electoral reform. The core of the report was transparency: all donations of over £5000 nationally and £1000 for a single constituency would be disclosed, foreign donations banned, anonymous donations exceeding £50 banned, clear rules on the auditing of political parties' accounts, more scrutiny of honours, shareholder consent for corporate donations, and controls on other organisations and individuals spending over £25,000 on political activity during an election campaign. The existing system of a ban on paid election advertising on TV and radio would be continued, as would the free party election broadcasts. There would be no state funding, but tax relief on donations of up to £500. A national spending limit of £20m was recommended. An independent Election Commission would oversee the conduct of elections.

The government's Bill followed the Neill recommendations quite closely. The spending limit is set at £15m, and intriguingly the campaign period is defined as the 365 days leading up to a general election.[3] The Conservatives spent a bit more in 1997, while Labour spent £13m and the Liberal Democrats spent less than £1m, so this aspect of the new law is unlikely to have a significant impact for some time, particularly as the Conservatives have not been able to raise the sort of sums they did while in government as beneficiaries of secret donations.

The framework of British election law was laid down when there was hardly a 'national campaign' to regulate, and pays scant attention to the role of political parties in elections. The new system at last does recognise the existence of parties, and the importance of their national campaigns in terms of propaganda, research, polling and spin. It also governs the expenditure on political matters of bodies not officially part of a political party. Such spending has been going on for a long time since it was legitimised by the legal ruling in the *Tronoh Mines* case of 1952, usually from businesses and front organisations favouring Conservative policy, and trade unions favouring Labour policy. It will be regulated by disclosure requirements, a spending cap and the oversight of the Elections Commission. Future elections will take place under a very different regulatory environment from the freewheeling days of the past, where enormous sums of unaccounted money sloshed around Central Office and a network of front organisations.

Local campaign law is only slightly affected, although there are clear signs that it is due for reform. The limits set under the Representation of the People Act – currently about £8000 per candidate – are widely evaded by all parties in marginal seats by a variety of creative accounting techniques, and were relaxed for by-elections under the Conservative government. No petition relating to expenses has been presented since 1929, although the Labour MP for Newark, Fiona Jones, was prosecuted for allegedly returning fraudulent election expenses. Her conviction was overturned on appeal. For the most part, the main parties choose to look the other way as far as imaginative expenses returns are considered, but it is a frequent cause of tension and ill-will at a local level. In contrast to the national 'campaign period' of a year, local expenses pertain only to the weeks immediately prior to the election. Parties usually hold a farcical 'adoption meeting' to effect the completely bogus transition from 'prospective candidate' to 'candidate' and for expenses purposes this is when the meter starts running.

A more minor but overdue reform was introduced in 1999 with the Registration of Political Parties Act, which established a national register of political parties, their names and emblems. The registration system at last gave parties control over their own names, preventing bogus candidates from using the same or similar names to deliberately confuse voters. The Act also allowed political parties to place their symbol on the ballot paper, an additional safeguard against unofficial candidates. Concern had been growing for some time about the use of spurious party titles as a wrecking tactic; in 1992 an unofficial 'Labour' candidate polled more than the Conservative majority in Slough, and in 1997 several 'New Labour' candidates stood without Tony Blair's blessing against official Labour. The most notorious spoiler was Richard Huggett, who called himself a 'Literal Democrat' in the 1994 Euro election and won 10,203 votes without a serious campaign, while the Conservative majority over the real Liberal Democrats was only 700. Huggett nearly managed it again as 'Liberal Democrat Top Choice' candidate in Winchester in 1997, but the authentic Lib Dem Mark Oaten squeaked ahead of the Conservative by a disputed two-vote margin. Registration of political parties worked relatively well in the Euro and GLA elections, although in the finest traditions of left-wing fringe politics there have been disputes over the ownership of the title 'socialist'.

One aspect of the Neill recommendations that was introduced was a massive increase in the 'Short money' funding to support the work of the opposition parties in Parliament. The government relies on an extended system of political advisers and of course the information resources of the civil service to assist its parliamentary responsibilities. The Conservatives now receive a tripled allocation of £3m to assist their duties as the parliamentary opposition, and support for other opposition parties was also up-rated. However, the Conservatives have attempted to stretch the definition of parliamentary duties and the use of such funds for a campaigning 'War Room' was investigated in winter 2000 and 2001, with the possibility of withdrawal of Short money misapplied to campaigning.

Party funding reform was definitely part of a Blair agenda; it would not have happened without the Labour government and it was a cause Blair backed in explicit terms in the 1997 Labour conference. It was one aspect of a general modernisation and reform of the British political system, which formed a central part of the New Labour ideology. It was also a linking idea with traditional Labour ideology. Complaints about the secrecy and inequality in the party funding system were previously more associated with the left of the party and the trade union funded *Labour Research* periodical. It was also a response to the climate of concern of sleaze that set in as the Conservative government disintegrated; although that in turn owed much to successful Labour campaigning on standards of conduct under John Smith and Tony Blair. Some of the other aspects of the change, such as the registration of political parties and the establishment of the Elections Commission owe more to internal deliberations within the Home Office and the Neill Committee. But the official recognition and regulation of the party system is a lasting result of the Blair effect.

Inside the Parties

The Labour Party

Blair's leadership has been acutely conscious of the lessons of history, and the reasons why past Labour governments have run into trouble and failed to win a full second term. The economic strategy has been shaped by the need to avoid the pitfalls of the past, and has succeeded in doing so. Party management has been affected no less, but the results have been rather mixed.

Past Labour Prime Ministers tended to neglect the Labour Party machinery, with baneful consequences in 1964–70 and 1974–79. Harold Wilson had a dismissive attitude to Transport House and took little interest in its activities. Under his leadership there were few significant reforms to the party's machinery, and a massive slump in membership between 1964 and 1969: the party claimed 830,000 members in 1964 and 680,000 in 1970, although the true figures were probably about half this.[4] In the 1970s the Labour Party was almost a hostile force to the Labour government. The government's policies and the plans developed by the NEC's policy making system were completely different. In 1976 the party conference called for the nationalisation of banking and insurance in the middle of a financial crisis that dragged Denis Healey back from Heathrow to confront a derisive assembly. Government policies were regularly repudiated in votes in the NEC and conference. The poor state of relations between party and government in each case had a bad effect. It presented an unattractive picture of a divided party, and in the 1970s in particular attracted accusations that Labour was becoming extreme. It also handicapped the party's organisational ability to present its case at general elections.

Since 1997 the Labour leadership has certainly not neglected the party; the 'Blair effect' has revolutionised the party's structures, ideology and methods since 1994 and there has been a permanent revolution in the party continuing since 1997.

Margaret McDonagh was appointed General Secretary of the party in October 1998, symbolising the change in style between Old and New Labour. All previous Labour General Secretaries have been men, often trade unionists, and many have come to the office quite late in life; some have represented the well-meaning inefficiency of the Labour movement. McDonagh, though a party organiser since the early 1980s, stands out as a young (late thirties) woman and as notoriously efficient and brisk. McDonagh has campaigned in the celebrated New Labour causes of the 1990s – the Clinton–Gore election in 1992, Blair's leadership campaign in 1994, the successful bid to rewrite clause 4 in 1994–95 and as General Election Co-ordinator in 1997.

Labour's National Executive Committee (NEC), which is technically the supreme authority within the party between conferences, was reformed in 1997. Its new composition is:

- The Leader and Deputy Leader
- The Leader of the Labour MEPs
- The Treasurer
- Three front bench MPs
- One youth member
- One member of the Black Socialists
- Twelve trade unionists
- One member of the socialist and co-op societies
- Six CLP representatives
- Two local government representatives
- Three back-bench MPs

MPs are now barred from standing in the CLP and trade union sections. The abolition of the women's section representatives on the NEC was accompanied by a 50 per cent quota for women representatives among the trade union, local government and PLP sections. Representation for ordinary members (what used to be called the 'rank and file'), local government and back-benchers has increased as a result of the restructuring of the NEC.

Elections for the six places elected by the party's individual membership have become contested between broad tendencies within the party. In 1998 the 'Grassroots Alliance' of left-wing members won four of the six; two successful candidates were Liz Davies, who had been denied selection by the NEC for the Leeds North East constituency, and Mark Seddon, editor of *Tribune*. The pro-leadership slate regained one of the four seats in 2000 although the new NEC member, the actor Tony Robinson, proved a sceptical loyalist. Voting in NEC elections, despite the restructuring which has potentially increased the possibilities for electing rebels, has tended to produce a supportive NEC. The leadership can command large majorities in contested votes on the NEC, a far cry from the position in 1970 or 1979 when the left was in control.

The party has turned its attention also to the structure of its constituency organisation, which has remained little altered since Labour became a national party in 1918. The 'Partnership in Power' task force has remained in operation after 1997 and was commissioned by the NEC in July 1999 to review constituency organisation. The team, chaired by Ian McCartney, produced a consultative document, *21st Century Party*,[5] in late 1999 and offered Constituency Labour Parties (CLPs) the chance to comment. *21st Century Party* drew attention to the social changes and the reforms to other areas of party operations, and suggested strongly that CLPs needed reform to make organisation stronger, more outward looking and part of the community. Experimental forms of organisation, such as all-member meetings of the CLP and policy-oriented membership groups, had already begun in parties such as Enfield Southgate and Bracknell, and were commended for wider use. The consultation exercise on *21st Century Party* revealed most CLPs were in favour of reforming existing procedures rather than a radical new structure, and for more transparent selection mechanisms. *21st Century Party* will return to the conference agenda in 2001 with a view to implementation in 2002.

Policy formation within the Labour Party has been under the auspices of the National Policy Forum rather than the previous process of NEC policy groups and resolutions to conference. While more amenable to leadership influence, the National Policy Forum process has channelled the grumbles of many party members about the speed and direction of government policy. There has been a fall-off in activism and a susurrus of critical resolutions from CLPs, but it has been very minor compared to the experience of 1964–70 and 1974–79. Perhaps the most dramatic indication of the change in the politics of the CLPs was at the Brighton conference in 2000, when they voted two to one in favour of the government line and against the re-establishment of the earnings indexation of pensions.[6]

The Brighton votes, and some straws in the wind – such as the selection of David Lammy rather than a more left-wing candidate for the Tottenham by-election in June 2000 – suggest that the Labour Party has been changed rather more profoundly than many commentators have suggested by the Blair effect. New Labour started out as a management buy-out of a once competitive firm that had been failing to keep its place in the market for some years. It was the project of a relatively small group of people at the centre.[7] The party leadership feared that the mass support won for the new clause 4 in 1995 among the party membership was merely a sign of desperation to win, but it appears that a genuine constituency for new, or newish, Labour, exists among the membership – although perhaps mainly the passive membership who do not regularly attend meetings.

The wary attitude among the leadership towards the party has been manifest in its extremely active, interventionist role in party management. As has often been commented, New Labour has devolved governmental power to new institutions but attempted to centralise it within the party. The efforts to impose central control have been punctuated by a number of high-profile failures. The first straw in the wind was the Uxbridge by-election of July 1997, in which the Millbank-approved candidate did worse than the local candidate had managed in the general election, despite the government's overwhelming popularity when the by-election took place. More embarrassing ructions took place in Scotland and Wales in 1999 and London in 2000.

The Scottish case was caused by the party's procedures for selecting candidates in the Scottish Parliament election of May 1999. There had been widespread concerns that sleaze, a problem affecting Labour councils particularly in the west of Scotland, might contaminate the new institution, and there was general assent to rigorous selection procedures. However, several MPs and leading activists failed to gain approval to be potential MSPs, more because of their left-wing political record than any stain on their character. Dennis Canavan, the MP for Falkirk West, was so put out by his rejection that he stood as an independent in the Scottish Parliament election and won the largest majority of any candidate.

The problem in Wales was more serious. The Welsh Secretary Ron Davies was the Labour leader in Wales until his 'moment of madness' on Clapham Common in October 1998. The Prime Minister chose Alun Michael as his successor at the Welsh Office, but there had to be another election to choose the new leader of the Labour Party in Wales. The resulting campaign between Michael and Rhodri Morgan was divisive and the electoral college system was widely regarded as a blatant fiddle. Michael's victory was narrow and tainted by heavy-handed central intervention.[8]

Labour's showing in the Welsh Assembly elections in May 1999 was poor. The party had been generally expected to win an overall majority despite the twenty out of sixty 'top up' seats, but ended up in a minority with twenty-eight seats. Labour crashed to defeat in its ex-mining heartland of Rhondda and Islwyn where Plaid Cymru capitalised on local authority issues and the perception that Welsh Labour was run from London. The only Labour candidate to improve on the party's 1997 showing was Rhodri Morgan in Cardiff West. Alun Michael resigned shortly before a no-confidence vote in February 2000 and was replaced as First Minister by

Rhodri Morgan. New Labour's fears about Morgan proved to be unjustified and he has refrained from 'disloyal' behaviour and run an effective Welsh executive, even to the extent of doing a deal with the Liberal Democrats to put the executive on a more stable footing. Tony Blair admitted in an interview in April 2000 that, 'I got that judgment wrong. Essentially you have got to let go of it with devolution.'[9]

Devolution was one matter, local government another. The party leadership intervened heavily again in the London mayoral Labour selection and despite winning the internal selection battle lost the electoral war to Ken Livingstone in May 2000.[10] Readmission of Livingstone to the Labour Party promptly became a *cause célèbre* for left-wing party members in London. The obsession the party leadership had with avoiding past mistakes, particularly anything associated with the early 1980s, has led it into a new set of mistakes and cemented the image of Blair as a 'control freak' into the public and media imagination.

Party discipline has also been tight inside the House of Commons, although in this case unity has been less costly to establish. Compared to past experience there have been relatively few large back-bench rebellions and ministerial resignations. Even in 1945–51 there were undercurrents of discontent expressed in rebellion on the National Service Bill in 1947 and the foundation of the 'Keep Left' group in 1948. Several MPs were thrown out of the party in 1948–49, mostly for pro-Soviet fellow travelling. The left-wing Tribune Group was founded at the start of the 1964 Parliament, and there was general discontent and flashpoint rebellions on prescription charges in 1968 and industrial relations in 1969. Twenty-four MPs had the Labour whip temporarily withdrawn in 1968. In 1974–79 rebellions led to government defeats on public spending plans, devolution, pay policy and even the level of income tax in 1978. So far since 1997 there have been big rebellions on several welfare issues and air traffic control but controversial measures on issues such as jury trial have gone through. Few of the 1997 intake have joined the left-wing Campaign Group, and no new large dissident back-bench groups have sprung up. The only ministerial resignations on issues of policy have been those of Malcolm Chisholm over lone parent benefit in 1997 and Peter Kilfoyle over a range of issues in 2000. Dennis Canavan and Ken Livingstone have been expelled for standing against official Labour candidates, and Tommy Graham of Renfrew expelled for his role in the political infighting of Paisley.

The unity of the Parliamentary Labour Party, in contrast to the divisions apparent under previous Labour governments – and the Tory splits during the Major years – is a tribute to the hunger for victory that Neil Kinnock tried hard to instil during the 1980s but Blair managed to foster and exploit. The New Labour buy-out of the Labour Party has attracted the conditional loyalty of a considerable segment of the party membership, although it still bears the imprint of its origins as a relatively small clique. The loyalty is conditional on continued electoral success. If Labour should lose the election, it seems unlikely that Blair would choose to continue as leader in such humiliating and disappointing circumstances, and would probably choose to assume personal responsibility for the defeat. However, the changes in ideology and party structure would be unlikely to be reversed. There would be no electoral mileage in returning to a more fundamentalist socialist approach and although a future leader might wish to take a more hands-off approach to the party's activities the new constitutional structure is here to stay. The most likely change would be at the tactical level; as with the Conservatives after 1997, Labour would be cast adrift and might resort to fishing the poisoned waters of populism for the sake of survival. An alternative would be to establish Labour more clearly as the party of personal liberty and jettison some of the social authoritarianism of Home Office and social security policy in 1997–2001.

The permanence of the changes that have been expressed in the Policy Review of 1989, the new clause 4 of 1995 and the economics of Blairism poses the question of whether New Labour is an essentially different sort of party from the Labour Party that existed for most of the twentieth century. The party has certainly abandoned its traditional commitment to a large-scale state role in the economy and has run a cautious set of fiscal and monetary policies. Labour is also more explicitly a catch-all party rather than the political arm of the working-class movement.[11] It has adapted in a similar fashion to the new Liberals who emerged in the early 1900s and the moderate takeover of the Conservative Party in the 1920s. The party system no longer presents the choice between a Labour Party theoretically committed to socialism and a Conservative Party theoretically committed to capitalism but having a varying amount in common in practice, from the convergence of 1955 and 1959 to the radical choice of 1983. Labour's 1997 manifesto was the first to acclaim the capitalist ethic of 'healthy profits as an essential motor of a dynamic market economy'.[12]

However, although the market economy is now common ground between the main parties, there is nothing recognisable as a wider consensus between Labour and the Conservatives.

The Conservative Party

The Conservative Party was sandbagged by the Blair effect during and after the general election of May 1997. It was reduced to an unprecedentedly weak electoral position and remained very badly off in opinion polls and by-elections for three years. Blair's astonishing popularity during 1997 and 1998 posed a difficult dilemma for the party, which compounded the usual problems facing an opposition. There are risks in new ideas – they beg the question of why they were not attempted while in power, and also (like Ann Widdecombe's cannabis policy) can fall apart through inadequate consultation and research. Dusting off old ideas is also unproductive, particularly if the party was badly defeated. The party has veered around in search of a solution since 1997.

Another inevitable problem of opposition is the big question of tax and spend. The 'tax guarantee' of 1999 was an obvious hostage to fortune and was rescinded in 2000, but the arithmetic problem arose again in a different form at the 2000 conference as the party made specific promises to spend more and tax less. Many Conservative policies designed to appeal to particular interest groups such as the countryside lobby will also cost money. In power, the Conservatives used Treasury 'costings' of opposition plans during election campaigns and are vulnerable to the same tactics from Labour.

The old internal Conservative problem of Europe has receded, but this is mainly to do with changes in Conservative politics than any changes of policy from the Blair government. After the victory of William Hague over Kenneth Clarke in June 1997 pro-European Conservatives became an increasingly embattled minority and two MEPs founded a breakaway pro-Euro Conservative Party. The failure of that party to make an impact on the June 1999 Euro elections, and the surprisingly good showing by the main Conservative Party in that election, set the Conservatives on an anti-Europe path that the compromises of government under Thatcher and Major had precluded. Michael Heseltine's appearance at a fringe meeting at the 1999 conference was disrupted by Eurosceptics throwing peanuts across a partition. 'Save the pound', despite the residual ambiguities of the party's policy, has become the principal campaigning slogan and outright hostility to the Euro plays well at Conservative selection meetings.[13] The Conservatives have also proposed constitutional reform of European institutions which may not be reconcilable with continued membership. For many Tories, withdrawal from the EU is 'the love that dare not speak its name'. The parties are further apart than they have been since 1983, with the Conservatives and Labour having swapped places. It remains to be seen how much importance the electorate attach to Europe in a general election, and whether the promise of a referendum in the event of a government recommendation to join the Euro will defuse the issue for Labour.

With the decline of Europe as a divisive issue, a previously subterranean division within the Conservative Party has emerged – what some call 'Mods and Rockers', or libertarians and authoritarians. The official party line has veered between the two approaches. The party tried to demonstrate a humble and inclusive approach at its 1997 conference, and Michael Portillo has continued to speak of the need to welcome women, ethnic minorities and gay people ever since. However, there was little sign of this after 1999, with the package of policies described as the 'Common Sense Revolution'. Battle was joined at the 2000 party conference, with Portillo making a daring plea for inclusiveness and Ann Widdecombe's call to step up punitive policies towards cannabis use rapidly being discredited.

Particularly during 2000, the temptation to reject the 'inclusiveness' line has been overwhelming. The party's most successful efforts have been when they capitalise on a populist line as and when a suitable issue arises, as with asylum seekers, clause 28 and the right to shoot burglars, at the price of an inclusive reputation. Exploitation of hot button issues has led to the defection of socially liberal Conservatives Shaun Woodward and Ivan Massow to Labour. After the 2000 conference Hague attempted to bridge the gap by praising inclusiveness while still maintaining populist policies. Blair's own reputation as a metropolitan moderniser, an Islington man who moves among the great and the good, has led to the Conservatives posing as the reverse: a party of the ordinary and non-metropolitan opposed to an elite (ironic, given the total absorption from an early age of Hague and his advisers into metropolitan political life). Farmers, hunters, homophobes and xenophobes have been appeased, and the refinery blockades commended as the conduct of 'fine upstanding citizens'. The Conservatives, the traditional 'court' party of the establishment, have been usurped by Blair and have adopted the classic oppositional technique of accumulating disgruntled, anti-modern interest groups in an inverse rainbow coalition. How this might fit, philosophically and practically, with the neo-liberal economics espoused by the Tories is anyone's guess.

The Conservatives have been forced to adapt to some Blair policies, such as the minimum wage and devolution, but promise to scrap others such as the bulk of the New Deal. As well as New Labour, the Conservatives have been influenced by American approaches. After defeat in April 1992, Labour sought out lessons from the successful November 1992 Clinton campaign. The Conservatives have also taken the Atlantic route since 1997. Hague's closest policy advisers, Rick Nye and Danny Finkelstein, are both keen students of American conservatism and the Tories have studied Wisconsin and New York in search of policies. The 1999 rhetoric of 'kitchen table Conservatism' was a direct lift from American discourse; 'Common Sense' copied Ontario; and the term 'compassionate conservatism' is much bandied about by the advisers of George W. Bush (although compassion is hard to find in Texas).

The Conservatives have attempted to play up English issues, as foreshadowed by Andrew Hargreaves, a Conservative MP who lost his seat in 1997:

> Should the Labour Party be in a position to implement its policy by undemocratic means, I guarantee that we shall hound it out of England as an undemocratic party of minorities, never standing up for the majority English interest. It would be a party of ethnic ghettos. In local government, it has made such ghettos of our great cities, for purely political advantage. It would be a party of minorities – never the party of an English majority in England. We shall never let the people of England forget the contempt with which the Labour Party treats an English electorate.[14]

By 'undemocratic means' Hargreaves was anticipating a Labour government reliant on Scottish votes under devolution. William Hague attempted to court an English anti-devolutionary backlash in his policy statement of 13 November 2000 promising 'English votes for English laws' but the issue seems to have little resonance.

Despite the incoherence and opportunism of much of the Conservatives' political approach, there has been a thorough overhaul of the party's institutions. Any management consultant, let alone one with the McKinsey's experience boasted by Hague, would have been horrified by the party's creaking structures. Hague, and his allies Archie Norman (Chief of Staff), Cecil Parkinson and Michael Ancram, have reshaped the party in the most radical way since Rab Butler and Lord Woolton's 1940s reforms. The unique and bizarre corporate structure of the party – Central Office and all its debts were previously the personal property of the party leader – has been changed and the National Union and Central Office have been merged. New units have been established relating to young people, ethnic minorities, young professionals and the religious right. However, party membership has fallen drastically short of the targets set in 1997 and has not risen in the way that Labour gained members in 1994–97.

The bureaucratic distinctions between research and press sections in Central Office have grown blurred as the Conservatives have adopted the 'War Room' campaigning approach used by Clinton and Blair. Hague has introduced plebiscitary – perhaps Napoleonic – democracy to the Conservative Party. There were two ballots of the party membership in 1998, the first to validate Hague's election as leader, and the second to approve the party's policy on the Euro. Both passed overwhelmingly. Another will take place on the draft manifesto. Hague has also been more ruthless about expelling dissidents, such as Peter Temple-Morris on the left and Adrian Rogers on the right. These techniques of party management are direct lifts from the methods used by New Labour, such as the 'Road to the Manifesto' ballot in late 1996.[15] The Conservatives have also reformed their leadership election procedure again, making it almost as difficult to mount a coup against a Tory leader as it is to overthrow a Labour leader. The Conservatives have implicitly acknowledged Tony Blair's approach to party management as an effective one worthy of emulation.

The Liberal Democrats

The centre parties made little electoral progress in the elections of 1987 and 1992, as their vote slipped back although without a significant loss of seats. They were held back by the stability of the Conservative vote and the Tories' ability to hold off Liberal Democrat challenges by raising the fear of letting in Labour by the 'back door'. The Conservative collapse of May 1997, and the success of Blair in dispelling fear of Labour, led to a series of Liberal Democrat victories. The party won forty-six seats, adding a forty-seventh with victory in the May 2000 Romsey by-election. Despite this success – the greatest haul of seats as an independent party since 1929 – Lib

Dem influence at Westminster has remained at the periphery because of Labour's overwhelming majority.

However, the Liberal Democrats, particularly through their relations with Labour, are an important element in the workings of the post-1997 party system. The most obvious features of the closer relationship between the parties have been the two coalition governments established in Scotland (May 1999) and Wales (October 2000). Only over student finance in Scotland was there a massive gap between the policies of the two parties. For the first time since 1945, Liberals have wielded executive power, and for the first time since 1931–32 governments have been formed from more than one party during peacetime.[16] Given the basis of politics in Scotland, Labour seems doomed to run the executive in a perpetual coalition with the Liberal Democrats; the Conservatives are too distant in their philosophy from the other Scottish parties. In the longer term, the SNP might downplay its aspirations for independence and thus become a feasible partner for the Lib Dems. Devolution, as well as hung local authorities in England such as Cheshire and (1993–99) Hertfordshire, has cured Labour of its fear and suspicion of coalition, and some of its tribalism, that has been an element in the party's culture at least since 1931.

A national coalition was a possibility under consideration before election day in 1997 if there was a hung Parliament, or even a small Labour majority. In the event, a special Cabinet committee was established in July 1997 to co-ordinate moves on constitutional reform, and its remit gradually expanded. Much of the government's early constitutional agenda fulfilled age-old Liberal hopes. Co-operation between the Liberals and a government is not unprecedented (there was informal contact in 1951–55, 1964–66 and a formal Pact in 1977–78) but the Cabinet committee system is a new departure and one not necessitated by a small majority in Parliament. There was further talk of full coalition in autumn 1997, and much behind the scenes contact between Number 10, Paddy Ashdown and the important linking presence of Lord Jenkins of Hillhead.[17]

Both Labour and the Liberal Democrats have internal differences on the wisdom of co-operation, which do not exactly parallel the left/right divisions on other political questions. Blair and Ashdown were rather extreme in the context of their own parties in actually liking and trusting each other and tending to see the good points in each other's parties. Ashdown in particular believed in the positive virtues of coalition and had moved his party towards closer relations with Labour since his Chard speech after the 1992 election. New Labour's final abandonment of any pretensions to effect a socialist change in society removed a symbolic barrier to co-operation, and actually placed the Liberal Democrats to the left of Labour on economic issues. However, John Prescott and many others in the Labour Party had little time for the Liberal Democrats and regarded them as an opposition force, or even an irresponsible rabble. Prescott threw up an obstacle to deeper co-operation, and Blair was not prepared to alienate him, or the strand of feeling he represents in the Labour Party, for intangible gains. Ashdown's replacement by Charles Kennedy in 1999 meant a slight distancing from Labour, and the Lib Dems have been critical on issues such as civil liberties and cannabis law. However, Blair has kept his 'third party insurance' up to date in case of a close result in the general election and coalition remains a possibility.

Building closer relations with the Liberal Democrats is a policy that shows a particularly dramatic example of the 'Blair effect'. Blair has an unusual lack of tribal feelings for a political leader: Lloyd George is probably the nearest comparison among past Prime Ministers. According to Rawnsley, the building of a broad pro-Blair consensus is known, according to taste, as 'Operation Hoover' or 'Operation Gobble'. It extends to pro-Europe Conservatives such as EU Commissioner Chris Patten and ex liberal Tories like Shaun Woodward (Patten and Woodward were the co-authors of the take-no-prisoners Conservative election campaign of 1992). The Liberal Democrats have also been quietly absorbing pro-Europe Conservatives such as defeated MPs Keith Raffan (now an MSP) and Hugh Dykes, and MEPs James Moorhouse and Bill Newton-Dunn. Underlying Blair's non-tribalism lies in part his own personal history – that he chose the Labour Party rather than being born into it – and his interest in historical analysis that blames much of the Conservative domination of the twentieth century on the division of progressive forces between Liberals and Labour. A large part of the Blair project in fact concerns the party system, and the priority is to forge a lasting progressive front in British politics of the sort that kept the Tories out in 1905–15.

The question for the Liberal Democrats, and Labour, is whether the progressive front apparent informally in the 1997 election can be sustained when there is not an unpopular Conservative government to eject. Many Liberal Democrat seats are in traditionally Conservative areas and the party risks losing these if it identifies too closely with Labour – as it did in 1924. It also needs to attract tactical votes and conversions from Labour sympathisers, who are more likely to vote for a party of constructive criticism than an outright opposition force. While maintaining this balance, the party needs to look over its shoulder at the often vicious battles with Labour in that party's former municipal heartlands that has produced Lib Dem controlled authorities in Liverpool and Sheffield. There is an inbuilt tension in the party between its parliamentary corps, most of whom won their seats from Conservatives and feel sympathy for the Labour agenda, and urban councillors who have battled against Labour and dislike the machine politics which characterises Labour at local level in some areas.

Outside the Parties

Despite its overwhelming victory in May 1997, Labour – and New Labour in particular – is a profoundly insecure party, conscious of Labour's exclusion from power and inability to win a second term, as well as its general unfamiliarity with the establishment and the 'state' it finds itself running. Blair would agree with Reggie Maudling's observation that, 'Britain is a Conservative country that votes Labour from time to time'. Labour is almost pathetically grateful for any support and praise it receives, particularly from business, and is anxious to please. The government is therefore a natural target for lobbying. This was helped by the cliquish nature of New Labour, in which Derek Draper's alleged boast in 1998 that 'there are seventeen people that count' in the Labour government was regarded by some commentators as a generous estimate. The expertise of insiders such as Draper was a scarce, and therefore valuable, commodity. Draper came to grief in a minor scandal in summer 1998, but the importance of lobbying and networking remains, despite the clean-up forced on the sector after the fall of Ian Greer in the mid 1990s. The interface of business and government is as troublesome as it ever was.

For much of its term, the Blair government has also been very insecure about the press. During the period of the Major government an axis developed between the right wing of the Conservative Party and the Tory press, which worked in concert to undermine his leadership. Blair reaped some of the benefits, but has faced a powerful, highly politicised press – particularly the *Daily Mail* and the *Daily Telegraph* – which now finds the Conservative Party leadership more to its taste. Part of the inclusive Blair project has been to win press support, or at least to moderate the hostility of the press, but after September 2000 the right-wing papers resumed the normal service suspended since 1994 and became venomous. Blair's patience was finally exhausted by an attack in the *Daily Mail* on the Chief of Defence Staff in November 2000 and he said:

> The problem with the right is that they cannot accept there's a Labour government and they will attack anyone who works in public service under a Labour government.

The most striking challenges to the government, which have spilled over into rhetoric that disputes its right to govern, have originated away from Westminster although they have found ready allies in the press and the Conservative Party. Right-wing campaign groups have sprung up in opposition to the Labour agenda. The first major manifestation of this was the campaign of opposition to the Private Member's Bill sponsored by Michael Foster, the Labour MP for Worcester, to ban hunting with hounds, in 1997. Opposition to hunting has long been the concern of animal welfare groups, but the 1997 Bill led to a more organised pro-hunting campaign.

The pro-hunting forces assembled in reaction to the Foster Bill were the core of what became the Countryside Alliance, which sponsored a 'Countryside March' in London on 1 March 1998. The agenda of the Alliance and the March was obscure and unclear; some claimed that it was in opposition to Labour policies primarily on hunting but also on other rural issues, but others – including Agriculture Secretary Nick Brown who took part – thought of it as a demonstration of general concern over the place of the 'countryside' in modern Britain. Farmers and hunters have formed a vocal anti-Labour chorus, assembling for example outside the 2000 Brighton conference and at refinery picket lines during the September 2000 fuel blockaide. That crisis illustrated the increased willingness of disgruntled interest groups – in that case principally truckers and farmers – to resort to direct action.

The September 2000 blockades reintroduced civil contingency planning to the lexicon of British politics. It was a familiar matter during the 1970s, when governments had to work out how to respond to strikes by workers in many strategic industries, but the last large-scale emergency was the 1984–85 miners' strike. The machinery seemed to have gone rusty. Action was rapidly taken and the government was able to see off the much-anticipated second round of fuel protests easily in November, but it appears to be an area in which constant review is necessary.

Direct action is also a prime technique of the diffuse 'anti-capitalist' campaign active in many countries and particularly apparent at the 'Battle of Seattle' during the World Trade Organization conference in 1999. A 'carnival against capitalism' in London followed, drawing together various anarchist, ecological and dissenting groups; it led to some civil disorder and a predictable chorus of outrage from the press. While against capitalism, particularly globalisation and multinational corporations (McDonalds is a special target), it is less easy to tell what the campaign is for.

While the main parties have both adopted variants of market economics and made unstable compromises between libertarianism and authoritarianism, opposition to this basis of party politics has increasingly moved into the streets. The countryside movement has a radical reactionary fringe, opposed to racial equality and gay rights, and the fuel blockades set a rather sinister precedent for a powerful interest group using brute force to achieve its aims. Anti-capitalism has occasionally resulted in the physical destruction of the manifestations of 'monopoly capitalism'. The undercurrents of discontent with the current neo-liberal order pose a threat and a challenge to the traditional parties. The last time we were supposed to have seen an 'end of ideology' was around 1960 but it was followed by a resurgence of ideological politics.

The Party System as a Whole

In broad terms there have been two eras of party politics since 1945. The first was from 1945 to 1970 and consisted of two dominant and quite closely competitive parties commanding 40 per cent or more of the vote, with relatively small swings at each election. The largest shift in support for one of the main parties was the six point fall in the Conservative vote between 1959 and 1964.

1945–70	Maximum	Mean	Minimum
Labour vote	48.8% (1951)	46.0%	43.0% (1970)
Conservative vote	49.7% (1955)	45.3%	39.8% (1945)
Liberal vote	11.2% (1964)	7.0%	2.5% (1951)
Turnout	84.0% (1950)	77.4%	72.0% (1970)

The second began in 1974 with the break up of the two party system and the rise of the Liberals, Nationalists and independent Ulster Unionists. The combined share of Labour and the Conservatives fell from 89.4 per cent in 1970 (and a peak of 96.8 per cent in 1951) to 75 per cent in February 1974, and has not subsequently gone over the 80.6 per cent reached in 1979. The Labour Party was particularly disadvantaged by the change in the nature of the party system; while Conservative support partially recovered after 1974, Labour's did not. Party support was more fluid in 1974–83 in particular than before; Conservative support rose 8.1 per cent in 1979 and Labour's fell 9.3 per cent in 1983, but from 1983 up to and including 1992 the British party system seemed to have settled down into a position of Conservative dominance on a minority vote, and Labour weakness.

1974–92	Maximum	Mean	Minimum
Labour vote	39.2% (1974)	34.3%	27.6% (1983)
Conservative vote	43.9% (1979)	40.7%	35.8% (1974)
Liberal &c vote	25.4% (1983)	19.5%	13.8% (1979)
Turnout	78.7% (1974)	75.5%	72.7% (1983)

The 1997 election result had relatively little in common with the run of results between 1974 and 1992; it was either 'deviating' or 'realigning' but cannot yet be categorised for the simple reason that such a judgement cannot be made before analysis of the 2001/2 election. Labour's share was well over the range achieved in 1974–92, and the Conservatives' well below. The Labour vote rose 8.8 per cent and the Conservatives' fell 11.2 per cent, even more dramatic changes than in February 1974, but declining turnout and an increasing share of the vote for minor parties have continued. There was clearly no reversion to the 1945–70 party system.

The Blair government has not restored much faith in the political process, still less the two party system. Turnout in 1997 (71.5 per cent) was the lowest since 1935. Participation in local elections, by-elections and most notably of all the Euro election (24.1 per cent turnout in 1999, compared to 36.8 per cent in 1989 and 1994) have hit very low levels. The government's concern at these developments is reflected in the experiments in more flexible and accessible voting methods, but few of these seem to have helped.[18] The most common expectation is for a general election turnout below 70 per cent – the worst ever with the exception of the chaotic election of December 1918.

The erosion of the two party system has continued. The devolved institutions of Scotland, and particularly Wales, have been the catalyst for strong challenges from the nationalist parties. In Scotland and London there have been significant challenges to Labour from the left. The Euro elections of June 1999 were notable for an extraordinarily high 'other' vote, cast principally for the anti-European UKIP and the Greens; 18.9 per cent voted for minor parties, the highest such figure ever. The long decline in party loyalty among the electorate has made the British party system more permeable to challenge than before, and the introduction of proportional representation for European and devolved elections has lowered the barriers to entry for minor parties.[19] The Liberal Democrats have made local government advances deep into former Labour territory in some cities, and proved resilient against Conservative recovery, at least outside the south west. The national political battle has continued to break into kaleidoscopic fragments – Labour v Lib Dem in many cities, Labour v Tory still in smaller towns, Lib Dem v Tory in suburban and rural areas, Labour v Plaid Cymru in the valleys, Labour v SNP in urban Scotland, four-way fights in rural Scotland . . . the party system has not been this plural and confusing since the 1920s.

The broad brush of mid term politics under the Blair government shows a government which has faced an unprecedented easy ride with public opinion. The Labour Party led in the polls for eight continuous years from September 1992 to September 2000. Even after the sudden swings of September and October 2000, the Blair government has the enviable record of having the shallowest mid term trough of any government – behind in the polls for a couple of weeks with the worst reading showing an 8 point deficit. Every other government since polling began, even the tranquil Churchill government of 1951–55, has been further behind than this. No government since Churchill's has had a similar unblemished record of holding its seats in by-elections. Blair's own popularity, and all the measures of approval in depth of the government's record, started from a very high level in 1997–98, eroded slowly in 1998–2000 and dipped more sharply in summer and autumn 2000.

Mid-term voting trends have indicated the intriguing possibility that two core features of the British political scene are losing their purchase on electors. Peter Kellner has analysed the opinion polls during the Conservative spike occasioned by the September 2000 fuel crisis, and found that something very unusual had happened:

	Middle class		Working class	
% share	May 1997	Sept 2000	May 1997	Sept 2000
Con	39	39	24	39
Lab	34	34	55	34
LD	20	20	14	19

Source: *Evening Standard* 9 October 2000.

The finding that voting intention did not vary between middle and working-class voters is astonishing, even at a rather freakish period in politics. The contrast between massive working-class disillusion with Labour and the loyalty of Labour's new middle-class support is striking.[20] Class has been the main feature of voting behaviour for a century, although its 'decline' since the 1970s has been a matter of extended academic debate. If anything like this pattern should continue, these debates will assume a radically different form. It would form a neat demonstration of Blair's transformation of the Labour Party from a class party into a catch-all party.

Another related deep structural feature of British politics seems to be fading somewhat. A glance at the electoral map of 1885, 1892 or 1910 shows the Conservatives to be the party of London and the south east,[21] the 'core' of England. The Liberals were the party of the periphery – Scotland, Wales, remote rural areas and heartlands of non-conformist Christianity as opposed to Anglicanism. Labour inherited the role of being the party of the periphery. The Conservatives have remained the party of the core for over a century but unusually Labour's showing in mid-term has been better in core than periphery (at least in England). The Euro election of 1999 and the local elections of 2000 illustrated this point well.

European election by parliamentary constituency[†]	Labour in 1999, Conservative in 1992	Conservative in 1999, Labour in 1992
London	10	0
South East	9	0
South West	1	2
East Midlands	1	1
West Midlands	0	6 (2)*
East Anglia	0	0
North West	2	5
Yorkshire – Humberside	0	8 (4)*
Northern	0	2 (1)*
Wales	0	0
Scotland	0	1

Source: 1999: House of Commons Library Research Paper 99/64 *Elections to the European Parliament – June 1999*; 1992: Rallings, Colin and Thrasher, Michael, *Media Guide to the New Parliamentary Constituencies* Plymouth: LGC, 1995.
* The number of seats that were Labour even in 1983.
† Regions are standard regions not the Euro constituencies.

Compared with 1992, therefore, Labour 'gained' nineteen constituencies from the Tories in London and the south east and 'lost' a net twenty-one to the Tories in the rest of the country in 1999. The affluent suburbs of Brent North voted Labour, while the former mining stronghold of Don Valley was Conservative. In May 2000 Labour still led in the Reading seats, unexpected gains of 1997, but were lagging in Bradford West and even Coventry North West, both of which had stayed loyal in the dark days of 1983.[22]

Alongside acquiring strength in new places, Labour has ebbed in its traditional strongholds, which have acquired the shorthand term 'heartlands' to describe them. In local elections in some areas such as Liverpool and Sheffield the Liberal Democrats have overrun these areas of traditional strength, and in the valleys of South Wales Plaid Cymru has achieved massive advances, but for the most part losses have been to apathy. Turnout has fallen to pitiful levels – in Liverpool Riverside only 10.3 per cent turned out for the Euro election. In the five constituencies of Liverpool only 17,417 voted Labour in that election, compared to 13,954 in the two constituencies of suburban Harrow. Turnout has also fallen badly in local elections and was already fairly low (51.9 per cent in Liverpool Riverside in 1997). This apathy has been the product of long social and political trends, but it is worth recalling that in 1950 the highest turnout was to be found in safe Labour areas.

While the 'heartlands' are not an immediate electoral problem for Labour – no other party is placed to win such seats – the lack of political participation is another pointer to the undercurrents of discontent with the seemingly placid political and policy scene. Peter Kilfoyle, whose resignation drew some attention to these issues, prefers to talk instead of Labour's 'core vote' – the disadvantaged people for whom Labour is supposed to exist. Kilfoyle points out that there is a core vote in every seat, for example even wealthy towns often have an isolated and run down estate, and if this more dispersed core vote fails to turn out it poses a threat to Labour seats.[23]

Conclusion

It seems most likely that Labour has established the same sort of dominant position previously enjoyed by the Conservatives from about 1975 until late 1992, but other possibilities are still just about open. Perhaps rather than the 1974–92 system in reverse, it could be similar to the 1918–29/1931–45 system, with Labour rather than the Conservatives in the dominant position in a generally low turnout environment, or 1906–15, with a Lib-Lab-Nationalist bloc driving a frustrated Tory party into wilder and wilder extremes of opposition. The Conservatives might hope that 1997 was just a deviating election and that the era that began in 1974–79 has not yet come to a close.

The origins of the change in electoral alignment were obviously in the collapse of the Conservative government's unity and its image of incompetence, but the accession of Blair in July 1994 does mark a step change in the polls – a second stage of realignment. It would seem churlish to deny that the 'Blair effect' – the rebranding of the party as New Labour, the ditching of clause 4, the changes in rhetoric and policy – was a vitally important part of Labour's ascendancy. Throughout most of 1993, despite the unpopularity of the Conservative government, more people thought the Tories likely to win the next election than Labour.[24] After 1994 the assumption that Labour would win set in, and this self-fulfilling confidence was closely associated with Blair and New Labour.

No firm judgement about the Blair effect on the party system can be made until the voters' (and non voters') reactions to the government are known. The cautious political historian will even then try to dodge the issue, and wait for yet another election before pronouncing. However, some interim conclusions are possible:

- The Labour government, through implementation of the Neill reforms and devolution, has produced radical change in the political and legal environment in which the party system operates.
- Conceptions about how to organise a political party have been radically changed for both Labour and the Conservatives, and this change owes its inspiration largely to Blair and New Labour (and thereby to Bill Clinton and Neil Kinnock at further remove).
- The party system has not reconnected with popular loyalty, and there is evidence that the basis of party politics has continued to erode in favour of apathy and the temptations of direct action.
- Blair's form of Labour politics may be a third stage in Labour's electoral evolution – from a class party, to a class party confined to the periphery, and now perhaps to a catch-all party appealing across class and geographical lines. If this comes to pass, it might be the most subtle and far reaching Blair effect of all.

Notes

1 Peter Riddell, *Parliament Under Blair*, Politico's, 2000, provides an admirable discussion of reforms both before and after 1997.
2 Fifth Report of the Committee on Standards in Public Life *The Funding of Political Parties in the United Kingdom*, HMSO, 1998, Cm 4057.
3 The Neill Report did not recommend a specified period. The government's Bill also did not include any tax relief on donations.
4 These numbers are misleading as the minimum affiliation for a CLP was 1,000 members. Most local parties claimed this thousand, although actual membership was lower. The real fall in membership was probably much worse than 150,000.
5 *21st Century Party*, Labour Party, 1999.
6 The vote went against the government because the trade union votes were

cast 3–1 against. Union votes were generally to bolster the party leadership against the CLPs in the 1950s and 1960s.

7 Philip Gould, *The Unfinished Revolution*, Little, Brown, 1998, is a revealing account of the small size and defensiveness of the group at the heart of New Labour. Its title is an explicit statement that the changes in Labour's policy and structures are a continuous process, not a once and for all change.

8 Paul Flynn, *Dragons Led By Poodles*, Politico's, 2000, is a blow-by-blow account, from a critical perspective, of the messy Labour politics in Wales of 1997–99.

9 *Observer* 9 April 2000.

10 Rory MacLean and Mark D'Arcy, *Nightmare: The race for London's Mayor*, Politico's, 2000.

11 Brian Brivati and Richard Heffernan, *The Labour Party: A Centenary History*, Macmillan, 2000, contains a range of essays touching on this theme, particularly Martin Smith's 'Tony Blair and the Transition to New Labour 1994–2000', pp. 143–162. See also Gould's *Unfinished Revolution* and Paul Anderson and Nyta Mann, *Safety First: The Making of New Labour*, Granta, 1997.

12 *New Labour: Because Britain Deserves Better*, Labour Party, 1997.

13 *Guardian* 16 October 2000.

14 House of Commons Debates, 20 February 1997, column 1120.

15 Although Labour came to this form of internal government from a ramshackle system of formal democracy, unlike the Conservatives which started as an autocracy.

16 The so-called Liberal Nationals, in the National coalition 1931–40, were a satellite party to the Conservatives.

17 Andrew Rawnsley, *Servants of the People*, Hamish Hamilton, 2000, pp. 192–209. Paddy Ashdown, *The Ashdown Diaries Volume 1 1988–97*, Penguin, 2000, is the most revealing account yet published.

18 House of Commons Library Research Paper 00/53 *The Local Elections and Elections for a London Mayor and Assembly May 2000* lists the experiments. Universal postal voting was the only method that seemed to lift turnout significantly.

19 David Butler and Martin Westlake, *British Politics and European Elections 1999*, Macmillan, 2000, particularly the appendix by John Curtice and Michael Steed, discusses the result and the impact of the electoral system. The form of PR used for the Euro election – regional lists with d'Hondt allocation – was relatively unkind to smaller parties but the Greens and UKIP polled well enough to win representation. Canavan won a constituency seat in the Scottish Parliament and Sheridan was elected from the Scottish Socialist Party top-up list.

20 Labour's subsequent recovery in the polls has, as one might expect, been concentrated in the volatile working-class vote, although the class gap that has opened up again is slight compared even to 1997.

21 In 1885 there was only one non-Conservative seat (Hastings) in the counties of Surrey, Sussex and Kent; there were none in 1970 and 1992.

22 Simon Henig and Lewis Baston, *Politico's Guide to the General Election*, Politico's, 2000.

23 Peter Kilfoyle, *Left Behind*, Politico's, 2000, is mainly a memoir of his role as a Labour Party official in Liverpool but has some reflections on this.
24 *Gallup Political Index* and David Butler and Gareth Butler, *Twentieth Century British Political Facts*, Macmillan, 2000.

SECTION 2

Economics and Finance

© Chris Riddell

Chapter 9

THE TREASURY UNDER LABOUR

Philip Stephens

ORDON BROWN WAS better prepared than any of his predecessors when he entered the Chancellor's office on the morning of 2 May 1997. He had shadowed the post for five years. During that time he had torn up and rewritten Labour's economic strategy. Dumping the ideological baggage that had seen his party languish in opposition for eighteen years, Brown had set out in meticulous detail his policies for government. He was the 'biggest' figure in Tony Blair's Cabinet. The partnership between the two men had been the foundation stone for Labour's sweeping election victory. As time passed, the relationship would become strained, notably over whether Britain should join the euro. But in the summer of 1997 no-one doubted the Chancellor's immense political authority. His economic strategy represented a momentous shift for a party of the left. In effect, it remade the landscape of post-war economic policymaking, erasing the old dividing lines between right and left. Brown was characteristically immodest in claiming that he had put an end to 'boom and bust'. The economic cycle is not so easily abolished. But his new frameworks for monetary and fiscal policy restored the discipline to policymaking that had once been provided by the Bretton Woods exchange rate regime. Here was Labour's reconciliation with the market economy and with the macro-economic orthodoxy of the times. Brown scorned the demand management on which previous Labour governments had relied in favour of macro-economic stability and a social policy rooted in welfare reform and higher spending on education and training. Explicit in all this was a recognition that the government's ambition of greater social cohesion was contingent on a demonstrable capacity to run the economy competently.

At the core of Brown's approach was the conviction that Britain's sad record of postwar economic mismanagement showed that politicians could not be trusted. In the new process of policymaking, discretion was to be replaced with rules: operational independence for the Bank of England in setting interest rates and a self-imposed straitjacket for fiscal policy codified in legislation. As the then Shadow Chancellor had remarked in January 1997: 'Policies for economic management must now recognise that in a global economy, there is no long-run trade-off between growth and inflation. In fact, low inflation is a precondition for economic growth.'[1] The approach was well-suited to the Chancellor's Presbyterian temperament.

The failures of his party's past loomed large. Brown had seen too many Labour Chancellors lurch from profligate post-election boom to fatal pre-election bust. Stability, rules, discipline, prudence, transparency: the mantras were more than election slogans. They were the means by which the New Labour government would exorcise the past. The party, as Blair would often remind his colleagues, had never secured two full terms in office. It had foundered instead on the rocks of successive economic crises. Stafford Cripps in 1948, James Callaghan in 1967, Denis Healey in 1976 – all had been humiliated by the financial markets. The sterling crises in those years had been symptom as much as cause of the failure of self-discipline. Subsequent election defeats were proof that the Labour way of governing had been bad politics as well as bad economics.

Brown decreed that efforts to generate faster growth in the economy would henceforth fall on micro-economic policy: measures to stimulate enterprise, to strengthen competition, raise productivity and, crucial for its social policy, to improve employability. The Chancellor's 'fairness agenda' was based on generous, though targeted, additional spending on the poorest families and pensioners and, crucial this, the determined use of compulsion and incentives to get those of working age back into employment. The first half of the Parliament saw a ferocious squeeze on public spending, but this was followed in the summer of 2000 with plans for large and sustained increases in the health, education and transport budgets in the early years of the new millennium. The famine was thus followed by something of a feast. Brown was rewarded for his initial prudence with steady, if occasionally faltering, economic growth, low inflation, a steep fall in unemployment and a sharp turnaround in the public finances.

There was luck as well as judgement in this. The Conservatives had bequeathed an economy that had been growing strongly. Brown was also to get caught in storms of his own making. By the autumn of 2000, for example, a popular revolt over fuel prices provided a sharp reminder that there were limits to Brown's use of what the Conservative opposition dubbed 'stealth taxes' to cut the fiscal deficit and fund higher public spending. In his March 2001 Budget, he was obliged to dig into his pre-election war chest to buy off the protesting road hauliers and farmers and to pay for an effective freeze in the duties on petrol and diesel. And throughout the 1997–2001 Parliament, a sharp and sustained rise in the value of sterling did significant damage to the country's manufacturing base. That meant that by the beginning of 2001, the prospect of British entry into the European single currency looked as difficult a prospect as ever.

The contrast, though, with the record of previous Labour administrations was indeed remarkable. Brown could boast of monetary and fiscal stability, growth running at between 2 and 3 per cent, and a steep fall in unemployment to levels last seen in the 1970s. A large budget surplus in the 2000/2001 financial year suggested that the planned step change in the funding of key public services, notably health and education, could be accomplished without compromising fatally the more rigorous fiscal framework. The New Deal for the unemployed, the introduction of the Working Families Tax Credit, a minimum wage, and the progressive tightening of benefit rules also signalled a structural and cultural shift in the operation of the welfare state. Getting more people into work was at the heart of Brown's strategy to bind economic efficiency with social cohesion. Many of these measures were borrowed from the new Chancellor's many friends in the Clinton Administration, as were a myriad of tax measures, incentives and changes in competition policy designed to nurture enterprise and reverse Britain's poor productivity record. In Brown's mind, the interests of the socially-excluded and the entrepreneur could be reconciled. Whether the avalanche of tax reforms will make much difference to Britain's long-term economic performance, however, is questionable. For many observers, such changes introduced needless new complexities into the tax system, while aspects of the tougher approach to competition policy – notably inquiries into banks and supermarkets – owed as much to the government's quest for favourable headlines as to good policy.

The officials who had applauded him on the steps of the Treasury were soon to discover that Brown was not the easiest of political masters. His style was impatient and imperious. Officials accustomed to a culture in which policy decisions were debated from first principle found the new Chancellor less than receptive. He had already taken the decisions that would set the new government's economic course. Many of these were shaped by Ed Balls, his young but highly influential adviser. The Treasury's task was to implement not question them. The real debates took place within the Chancellor's tight-knit circle of personal advisers, out of sight of the officials. At the outset Balls, Ed Miliband, the political adviser, Charlie Whelan, the press spokesman and Geoffrey Robinson, the Paymaster General, were the key figures. They would decide; the role of Treasury officials was to deliver. Whelan and Robinson were obliged to resign in the aftermath of the public revelation of Robinson's £370,000 loan to Peter Mandelson. But Brown would never fully embrace the official Treasury.

It was a style of policymaking that led to mistakes – the more so because Brown was equally dismissive of Cabinet colleagues. But to the Chancellor's mind it was the way to get things done. There was another paradox. Brown was a strategic thinker, a chess-player, one of those rare politicians whose decisions look well beyond the near horizon. He was a man of intellectual rigour. But the Chancellor was also intensely political, obsessed with tomorrow's headlines as well as his longer-term goals. To those who watched him at close quarters he was as privately insecure as publicly confident. The description offered by one senior Downing Street aide of the Chancellor during one of the periodic spats between Blair and Brown was of a politician with 'psychological flaws'. In so far as the phrase seemed to capture Brown's obsessive determination to maximise his own authority at the expense of others, it carried a certain truth. He was also careless of the traditional civil service boundaries between policy presentation and propaganda. Terence Burns, the permanent secretary, who had greeted him on the steps of the Treasury on 2 May, was soon marginalised within his own department. He left a year later. Andrew Turnbull, his successor, had only modest success in persuading Brown to adapt to the Whitehall way of doing business. For the Treasury, this created a curious paradox. The Chancellor's personal political authority gave the department an influence across Whitehall greater than at any time in the postwar period. Brown's control of the economic agenda extended well beyond the narrow boundaries of fiscal and monetary policy. The decision to fix Whitehall spending on a three-year basis – and to accompany those budgets with detailed performance targets set and monitored by the Treasury – extended the Chancellor's reach across Whitehall. He often seemed contemptuous of his colleagues' departmental responsibilities, pre-empting their own policy announcements in his own Budget and pre-Budget statements to Parliament. There were bitter rows with, among others, John Prescott and David Blunkett. It was Brown who forced upon Prescott what many Treasury officials regarded as the 'half-baked' scheme to part privatise London Transport. The irony here, though, was that, for all the Treasury's new authority across Whitehall, it was exercised by the Chancellor rather than by the institution. Within his own department Brown was remote – even from his junior ministers. One of those ministers privately complained that he saw more of the Prime Minister than of the Chancellor.

Rules Rule OK?

For those on the left, the break with Keynesian demand policies was New Labour's betrayal. For Brown, in his favourite phrase, it was prudence with a purpose. Social improvement was impossible without economic stability. 'Inflation,' as he had put it in 1995, was 'the enemy of the poor, the pensioner and the middle income family.'[2] Those who had thought before the 1997 election that the Chancellor's decision to worship at the altar of economic orthodoxy was born of the expediency of opposition soon learned otherwise. Brown was determined that Labour's conversion would be irreversible. If a single, overriding, feature defined the economic policy of the first Blair government, it was the Chancellor's construction of permanent monetary and fiscal frameworks to keep it on the path of virtue. There was an irony here. Nigel Lawson, the author of the late 1980s boom, had perished in the vain search for such a macro-economic straitjacket. 'Rules Rule OK', Lawson had once said, before proceeding to break most of them.

Brown judged, rightly, that the decisions Labour took at the outset would set the tone for the rest of the Parliament. The nation, and the financial markets, wanted immediate proof of the new government's intent. Credibility in financial markets, he knew, is a precious commodity for a left-of-centre government. In the US, the Clinton Administration, from which both Blair and Brown borrowed liberally, had secured it by taking aggressive action to reduce the budget deficit as part of a bargain with Alan Greenspan's Federal Reserve. Brown too intended to drive down the fiscal deficit. But the immediate focus of the financial markets would be on the new government's monetary policy.

The Chancellor acted swiftly. His decision to give operational independence to the Bank of England was the big surprise of the first week of the Blair government. But it was the timing rather than the decision itself that caught the nation unawares. Some two years earlier Brown had signalled that he was contemplating the transfer of monetary policy to the Bank.[3] He suggested then that a new Monetary Policy Committee should formulate the Bank's recommendations to the Treasury on the level of interest rates. That would de-personalise the 'Ken and Eddie' show, the monthly meeting at which Eddie George offered advice to Kenneth Clarke on interest rates. Once this new MPC was up and running Labour, Brown said in his speech in May 1995, would consider 'whether the operational role of the Bank of England should be extended beyond its advisory role in monetary policymaking'.

As the election loomed Brown hardened the commitment to this new arrangement, but signalled that operational independence would depend on the new MPC establishing a 'track record' of good advice on interest rates. He changed his mind just days before the May election, deciding that an immediate announcement would bring a windfall boost to the new government's credibility. It would also minimise the risk of political opposition within the Cabinet and on the Labour back-benches. Greenspan had urged just such a course on the then Chancellor-in-waiting when the two met in Washington in February 1997.[4] The economic situation also argued for speedy action. The economy was growing unsustainably fast but Kenneth Clarke had several times rejected the Bank of England's calls for higher interest rates before the election. Inflation, according to the Treasury's best guess, was heading for 4 per cent. On the Tuesday after the election, Brown authorised an immediate quarter point increase in rates to 6.25 per cent. (According to Geoffrey Robinson, the then Paymaster General, Blair objected to a proposed half-point rise.)[5] But there were obvious advantages in leaving the task of pushing borrowing costs higher still to the newly-independent Bank.

It was striking and illuminating that this decision – the biggest change in economic policymaking since the war – was not discussed in Cabinet. Only John Prescott and Robin Cook were informed of the move before Brown's press conference in the Treasury on the Tuesday following the election. Blair and Brown had discussed it two days earlier but had dismissed the suggestion of Robin Butler, the Cabinet Secretary, that such a momentous change deserved wider debate around the Cabinet table. The Chancellor also earned a strong rebuke from Betty Boothroyd, the Speaker, for his assumption that the announcement could be made at a press conference rather than on the floor of the House of Commons. Brown, though, was careless both of the sensitivities of his Cabinet colleagues and the traditions of the Commons.

The model chosen by Brown for the new Bank was something of a hybrid, melding elements taken from the Federal Reserve, the Bundesbank and New Zealand's central bank. As the then Shadow Chancellor had remarked in 1995, 'I am attracted to the openness of debate and decision-making which occurs in the US, the internal democracy of decision-making in the Bundesbank and the way in which the New Zealand government sets targets for the bank to pursue'. The new arrangements for the MPC duly borrowed from all three models.

The Chancellor set the inflation target at 2.5 per cent, with a provision that should the actual rate vary by more than one percentage point, the MPC would be required to explain itself publicly in a letter to Treasury. For his part the Chancellor would review and reset the target each year in the Budget. Crucially, the obligation on the MPC was 'symmetrical'. It was obliged to avoid deflation as well as inflation. The Chancellor's letter to Eddie George setting out the new arrangements made it clear that the MPC's overriding responsibility was to hit the target. But it should also 'take account' of the importance of economic growth. From Brown's perspective, the key point was the division of responsibilities between setting and meeting the target. The former remained under political and therefore democratic control. That allowed the Chancellor to claim that the new arrangements made the authorities accountable to Parliament. The proceedings would also be transparent, with the MPC obliged to publish the minutes of its monthly meetings and its members to appear regularly before the Commons select committee on Treasury Affairs. A quarterly Inflation Report provided some of the intellectual underpinning for interest rate decisions. As for the composition of the MPC, five permanent Bank officials, including the governor and deputy governor, were joined by four independent economists.

Putting the new system in place was not without its glitches. Delighted as he was with the transfer to the Bank of monetary policy, George fiercely objected to Brown's decision to transfer banking supervision to a new

Financial Services Authority. A row between the two came close to prompting George's resignation and was one of the issues that soured the relationship between the Chancellor and Terry Burns. In a clumsy attempt to destabilise him, Brown subsequently let it be known that he opposed George's reappointment for a second five-year term as governor. But the Chancellor on this occasion was over-ruled by Blair. George was given a second term early in 1998.[6] Reviews of the MPC's record during the following few years have been broadly favourable. The Bank's operational independence did win Brown the precious credibility he had hoped for. Inflationary expectations fell, as did long-term interest rates. Short-term rates peaked at 7.5 per cent in June 1998 and had fallen back to 6 per cent by the beginning of the new millennium. The ten-year bond differential with Germany fell from 1.7 percentage points in April 1997 to average just over 0.5 percentage points. Successive rises in short-term rates in the first year of the new government forestalled the threatened acceleration in price rises and subsequently the inflation rate tracked Brown's target within a range of 0.5 percentage points.

Whether this record reflected the unique wisdom of the Committee is more questionable. Many would argue it should have raised rates still more aggressively in 1997 and then cut them faster when the economy threatened to dip into recession in the second half of 1998. The replacement of discretion by rules also left the government powerless to respond to the steep – and ultimately unsustainable – rise in sterling's value. The structure of the Committee – with each of the nine members individually rather than collectively responsible for the monthly decisions on interests – created a bias towards hyper-activity. Interest rates were changed no fewer than twelve times in the first two years of the MPC's life – showing a disposition to activism scorned by central banks with a longer track record of independence. Ambiguities in the relationship between the MPC's 'insiders' and 'outsiders' also brought conflicts within the Committee and confusion outside it.[7] Against that, interest rate decisions had been removed from the arena of politics. That promised a decisive break with the less-than-glorious history of monetary policymaking in Britain.

Golden Rules

With monetary policy despatched to the Bank of England, Brown set about creating his 'platform of stability' for fiscal policy. Once again, most of the work had been done in opposition. The new rules were put in place by the July 1997 Budget and legislated into a new 'Code for Fiscal Stability' the following year. At their core were Brown's 'Golden Rule' – over the economic cycle the government would only borrow to invest and not to fund current expenditure – and a commitment that public debt as a proportion of national income would be held at a 'stable and prudent level'. The reasoning behind both sets of reforms were reviewed by the Chancellor in a lecture to the Royal Economics Society in July 2000.[9] The opening section is worth quoting at length because it encapsulates Brown's approach to macro-economic policymaking. Four lessons, he said, had been learned in the post-war period:

- Because there is no long-term trade off between inflation and unemployment demand management alone cannot deliver high and stable levels of unemployment.
- In an open economy rigid monetary rules that assume a fixed relationship between money and inflation do not produce reliable targets for policy.
- The discretion necessary for effective economic policy is possible only within an institutional framework that commands market credibility and public trust.
- That credibility depends on clearly defined long-term policy objectives, maximum openness and transparency, and clear and accountable divisions of responsibility.

Brown went on to say that the analysis of the operation of modern economy several decades previously by Milton Friedman had been right. Where Friedman had been mistaken was in his prescription of rigid monetary targets as the lodestar for policymakers. Even with that caveat, this nod in the direction of the father of modern monetarism was by any standards a pretty startling statement from a Labour Chancellor.

In reality, the new fiscal rules gave the Chancellor significant latitude in setting his spending and borrowing targets. The proviso that they applied over the economic cycle assured him of a measure of discretion in the annual Budget. And because his forecasts of revenue, spending and borrowing were deliberately conservative, Brown consistently outperformed against the targets. The framework, though, was sufficiently robust – and transparent – to serve Brown's purpose of reassurance for the markets. And the turnaround in the fiscal position inherited from the Conservatives was much faster than Brown had anticipated. In 1996–97 public sector net borrowing had amounted to 3.6 per cent of national income. Three years later the public finances had moved into sizeable surplus, with a net repayment of 2 per cent of GDP recorded in 1999–2000. In the same year the surplus on the current budget reached £20bn. The stock of public sector net debt meanwhile fell from fractionally over 44 per cent of national income in 1996–97 to below 35 per cent in 2000–01.

Several factors were at work here. The large tax increases announced by the previous Conservative government took their full effect as Brown entered the Treasury. The new Chancellor added several of his own to these – notably the abolition of dividend tax credits and advance corporation tax (two measures which were together generating an additional £7bn of annual receipts by 2000), a higher escalator on fuel duties, and the phasing out of such reliefs as the married couple's income tax allowance and mortgage interest relief.[10] These were Brown's Stealth Taxes. Just as importantly, economic growth was consistently faster, and employment higher, than the Treasury had predicted. In 1997–98 public borrowing was £8bn lower than the Treasury's initial Budget forecast and in the following year the surplus was £9bn more. In 1999–2000 the figures were £12bn better and estimates for 2000–01 were for an overshoot of £20bn relative to the Treasury's earlier forecast. Much of this reflected increased revenue from income and corporation taxes and lower expenditure on social security benefits, but there were also signs of a structural increase in receipts. Combined income and corporation tax receipts, for example, were over £8bn higher in the 1999–2000 financial year than had been predicted in the March 1999 Budget.[11] This surge in revenues also coincided with the squeeze on public spending during the two years after the 1997 election. The result was a cumulative fiscal tightening of £40bn or over 4 per cent of GDP between 1996–97 and 1999–2000.

Arguably Brown's Budgets should have been tighter still. The sharp rise in sterling's value that had begun in the latter half of 1996 gathered pace over the following two years. Against the D-Mark the pound reached DM3.30 in the early months of 2000, up from DM2.80 at the time of the 1997 election. The trade-weighted value of sterling rose by 10 per cent over the same period. Few at the Treasury believed the rise was sustainable, but Brown refused to acknowledge that a still tighter fiscal policy would have slowed the appreciation. The result was a level for the exchange rate which significantly eroded the competitiveness of much of British industry – undercutting Brown's supply-side measures to improve industrial performance. That said, in the early months of 2001 the government entered the campaign for its re-election with the public finances in healthier shape than at any point under a previous Labour government. For the first time in two generations Labour's manifesto for a second term was not one long mea culpa. Instead, in the words of one leading investment bank, Brown faced 'an embarrassment of riches'.[12] The Chancellor dipped into the pot in November 2000 to buy off protesting motorists and pensioners, but still he left himself room to deliver tax cuts for 'hard-working families' in his March 2001 Budget.

Prudence with a Purpose

If its first three years defined the economic prudence of the Blair government then the outcome of the Comprehensive Spending Review in the summer of 2000 offered the social purpose of Gordon Brown's strategy. After the famine came the promise of a feast. Previous Labour governments has spent first and cut later. This Chancellor did the reverse. Taxes were increased, but this time at the beginning rather than at the end of the Parliament. The government entered the campaign for a second term offering sizeable increases in spending on the welfare state and, for the less well-off, modest tax cuts.

Brown had watched in horror as Labour's tax and spending strategy had unravelled in the 1992 election campaign. He took an important lesson from the reception given by the voters to the late John Smith's shadow budget. However much the electorate might eventually accept higher taxes in return for better public services it did not trust Labour to deliver that bargain. The popular perception was that Labour wanted higher taxes for their own sake. The additional revenue raised would be frittered away rather than spent wisely. The nation would pay more in taxes and there would be little or no improvement in public services. Succeeding John Smith as Shadow Chancellor, Brown systematically purged the party of all its spending commitments. The process accelerated when Tony Blair became leader in 1994. By the time of the 1997 election campaign Labour was committed to sticking with the Conservatives' spending targets for the following two years. The one additional spending pledge Brown had made – the New Deal for the young unemployed – was to be financed by a £5bn windfall tax on the privatised utilities.

Stick to them it did. In real terms the overall level of spending (measured in 1999–2000 prices) fell from £343bn in 1996–97, the year before the election, to £340.7bn in 1999–2000. The squeeze was aptly described by the former Chancellor Kenneth Clarke as 'eye-wateringly tight'. In part, it reflected the steep decline in social security expenditure as the level of unemployment fell. But, in spite of one-off additions to the health and education budgets, Brown had imposed a spending regime tighter than would have been expected of the Conservatives. As a share of national income spending fell from 41.2 per cent of GDP in 1996–97 to 38.9 per cent in 1998–99. The reins were somewhat relaxed in the summer of 1998 when the outcome of the Treasury's first Comprehensive Spending Review promised large increases for health and education. But, as the Institute for Fiscal Studies pointed out, spending over the whole of the Parliament was expected to average less than 40 per cent of GDP. That compared with a ratio of 43 per cent for the Conservative administration of 1992–97 and of 44 per cent over the period 1979–97.[13]

The second spending review in July 2000, however, saw a different Gordon Brown appear at the Commons Despatch Box. His first three years in the Treasury had demonstrated his determination to remake the process of economic policymaking. These latest spending decisions marked an equally determined effort to demonstrate that a government committed to economic orthodoxy could nonetheless change the nature of society. Setting the targets for 2001 to 2004 he announced sustained rises of more than 6 per cent a year in real terms for health and education, with a still sharper increase for transport infrastructure.[14] Overall, the review projected real increases of 3.25 per cent a year in Whitehall's budgets – against a projected underlying growth rate for the economy of 2.5 per cent. The increase in discretionary spending was higher still because of a projected further deceleration in the growth of the social security budget. The loosening of the spending reins was accompanied by a commitment to the reform and modernisation of public services, above all of the National Health Service. But the political message was evident: the first three years of the Blair government had been about demonstrating that a party of the centre-left could run a modern market economy, but the Blair government made the distinction between a market economy and a market society. In the summer of 2000 the pitch was that the state could still make a difference by providing decent universal health, education and welfare provision and by rebuilding the nation's crumbling infrastructure.

There were strengths and weaknesses in that case. On the credit side, Mr Brown had indeed changed the political argument. For most of the 1980s and 1990s the Labour Party had been on the defensive over public spending. The smallest pledge of additional expenditure invited the Conservative retort that Labour planned to raise taxes. It was not until the 1997 election that Labour had an answer to that charge. Now the roles were reversed. Brown succeeded in the course of 1997–2001 in making a case for active if not big government. As the election approached, William Hague's Conservative opposition promised tax cuts. But now it was the Labour government demanding to know where the money would come from – that the voters be told which public services would be cut to finance lower taxes. Michael Portillo, the Shadow Chancellor, found himself in the awkward position of deploring the condition of public services while promising to spend less on them in future.

On the debit side, the lurch from famine to feast undermined the government's claim that it was presiding over a radical transformation of public services. The huge spending increases announced by Brown in the summer of 2000 were measured against the reality of a visible decline in the quality of services in the preceding years. The voters were being promised jam tomorrow. Unsurprisingly, many were sceptical.

Stealth Taxes

No new taxes. Such was Labour's promise at the 1997 election. So it might have seemed anyway to the voters. In fact the pledges were more circumscribed. Gordon Brown, under instruction from Tony Blair, said there would be no increase in either the basic or the top rates of income tax. He promised a reduction in the rate of VAT on fuel. There would be a windfall tax on the privatised utilities to pay for the New Deal welfare-to-work programme. And that was broadly it. The new Chancellor had plenty of room to find new sources of revenue. And he did.

The scene was set by the July 1997 Budget. As expected, the Chancellor raised a one-off £5.2bn through a windfall tax. But a much bigger slice of additional revenue came from the abolition of payable tax credits for pension schemes and UK companies. This apparently arcane but lucrative change yielded an annual £5.4bn in extra revenue by the time its full effect was felt in 1999–2000. Without a blush, Brown included this increase under the heading 'Encouraging long-term investment'.[15] Other significant sources of revenue included an increase in the fuel and tobacco duty escalators. In March of the following year Brown's second Budget saw the abolition of Advance Corporation Tax (yielding £2bn annually by 2000–01), increases in stamp duty on housing transactions and a cut in the married couple's allowance. In the following year the allowance was abolished as was mortgage interest relief. Meanwhile a new climate change levy promised an extra £1.75bn a year for the Treasury. There were tax cuts too – notably the introduction of a 10p starting rate of income tax and a steep reduction in the National Insurance Contributions of the low paid. But fiscal drag, the process by which economic growth automatically raises the tax burden, was also filling the Treasury's coffers. The share of national income taken by tax and National Insurance rose from about 36 per cent in the year before the election to 38 per cent three years later. It was a tax increase Brown resolutely refused to acknowledge, even though others in the government felt it could be justified by the need to restore the public finances to surplus.

The strategy of loading tax increases on the less immediately visible parts of the tax system was hardly novel. It had been pioneered by the Thatcher government in the early 1980s with the switch from income to value added tax. Kenneth Clarke 'invented' new taxes on insurance and air travel in his attempts to plug the fiscal deficit. But by the autumn of 2000 there were clear signs that the voters had tired of the trickery. Excise duties on tobacco and alcohol were being seriously undermined by large-scale smuggling across the Channel. And the popular revolt in September against the level of fuel taxes served as powerful warning that the voters are not fooled all of the time. Brown's response in his November 2000 Pre-Budget Report – reductions in the taxes paid by road hauliers and notional reductions in the excise duties paid by other motorists – severely dented his credibility. It also served as a warning that if the Blair government wanted to further raise taxes in its second term, it would have to be more honest with the electorate.

Work, Welfare and Enterprise

The Middle Britain so close to the heart of Tony Blair's politics rarely featured in Gordon Brown's political vocabulary. In the mind of his Chancellor, Blair's preoccupation with 'Sierra Man' and 'Worcester

Woman' focus groups spoke to the Prime Minister's political weakness. The two argued about the phasing out of the married couple's allowance and the scrapping of mortgage interest relief. On most counts Brown won the argument, though it was on Blair's insistence that he had ruled out before the election any increase in the 40p top rate of income tax. The Chancellor would have preferred a 50p rate for the richest.

Brown, though, confronted the bigger dilemma that had faced every Chancellor from the centre-left during the post-war period: how to lever up the life-chances of the poorest in society without imposing an intolerable tax burden on the middle classes. During the 1950s Anthony Crosland had answered that question with the proposition that rapid economic growth would pay for the welfare state while demand management would under-write full employment. Handing independence to the Bank of England and eschewing fiscal fine-tuning in favour of a long-term framework, Blair's government had surrendered those levers. Economic efficiency was all very well. But where was the social justice that gave the government its purpose?

Part of the answer came with the outcome of the second spending review with its hefty and sustained real increases in the education budget and generous provision for children and poorer pensioners. To Brown's mind, education equals employability equals greater equality. Welfare reform was also at the core of the strategy: state benefits should provide a supplement to, rather than a substitute for, income from employment. The passive welfare state cushioned the impact on those who lost their jobs. Brown's active alternative would equip them to find alternative employment. Overall, the Chancellor's approach to welfare had three distinct but con-nected strands: targeted assistance for those outside the employment market in the form of a minimum pension guarantee and significantly higher payments to low-income families with children; a minimum wage to put a floor under income from work; and tax credits and other incentives to make work pay at the bottom end of the income scale.

Employment, Brown declared, was the most important bridge between economic efficiency and social justice. As he had remarked just before the election in a lecture paying tribute to Crosland, 20 per cent of Britain's working-age families had no-one in employment: 'So while in Crosland's time, old age and disability were the over-riding causes of poverty, today it is unemployment and the absence of skills that is the biggest source of poverty.'[16] Work, he added, was 'central not just to economic prosperity but to individual fulfilment'.

The idea of the Working Families Tax Credit was borrowed, like much else, from the Clinton Administration. Brown's fascination with Washington's approach to the supply-side of the economy contrasted with a certain scorn for the continental European social model – even though the tougher demands put on unemployed welfare recipients had been pio-neered in Scandinavia and the Netherlands. Paid through the wage-packet, the credit provided an automatic top-up for those on low incomes. Its introduction was accompanied by a new minimum wage, by a sharp reduction in National Insurance Contributions at the bottom end of the income scale and the new 10p starting rate of income tax. Here was the carrot to get the long-term unemployed back into the labour market. The stick came in the form of a tightening of the benefits regime, with the gradual rolling out of the New Deal alternatives of work or training across all age groups.

These changes undoubtedly introduced new complexities into the welfare system. The extension of in-work benefits significantly increased the numbers in the so-called benefits trap. And the marrying of the tax and benefits systems in the WFTC muddied the distinctions between household and individual incomes. But critics generally missed the two overriding political objectives. The first was to foster a change in the culture among benefit recipients so that welfare was seen as a hand-up rather than handout. In Brown's description the issue would no longer be about what the state did for you but rather what the state could help you do for yourself. The second, often missed point, was that the replacement of handouts by tax breaks made the system far more acceptable to the middle income voters who paid for it. Put simply, benefits for people in work seem far more palatable to those who pay the bill.

There was another dimension to Gordon Brown's supply side reforms. One of the things that most struck visitors to 11 Downing Street during this first Blair Parliament was that they were as likely to meet a departing venture capitalist as a trade unionist. Brown was assiduous in cultivating his political base among what might be described as the Old Labour constituency. But he was also serious in his intent in rebranding his party as the friend of enterprise. Though more careful than Blair in heaping praise on those who profited most from a new economy of rapid technological innovation and globalisation, successive Budgets marked out the Chancellor as firmly on the side of the entrepreneurs and small businesses. Thus in unveiling his first Budget in July 1997, the Chancellor saw nothing odd in combining the New Deal for the unemployed with a raft of measures designed to cut the tax burden on small and medium-sized businesses. The same pattern was repeated in successive Budgets, which saw changes to the capital gains tax regime to encourage entrepreneurial investment, a 10p starting rate of corporation tax for small companies, and new employee share-ownership plans and tax reliefs for corporate venturing. It seemed curious to some that a Chancellor so obviously determined to raise the life-chances of the poor was as closely attentive to the new generation of internet entrepreneurs.

Prepare and Decide

On one issue pivotal to the economics and politics of the new government, Blair and Brown were caught off balance. The politics of the pound –

specifically the question of whether Britain should join the European single currency dogged the Prime Minister and his Chancellor throughout the 1997–2001 Parliament. Here economics collided with that most dangerous of issues for British governments, the politics of Europe. Once again it soured relations in Downing Street. The single currency became the lightning rod for the often bitter clashes of personality within the Cabinet and, according to some within that circle, a pawn in Brown's ambition to succeed Blair as Prime Minister. Four years beyond the 1997 election, it remained unclear whether and when sterling would be replaced by the euro. There was no constitutional bar, the government said. In principle, it was in favour of joining a successful euro. But public opinion remained firmly against the single currency and Blair had shown little willingness to invest the political capital required to confront a generally hostile press and a popular mood of scepticism.

Both Blair and Brown had promised that the election of a Labour government would allow Britain to turn its back on the civil war over Europe which had all but destroyed John Major's administration. In an important respect this was true. But it was not enough to defuse the corrosive politics of sterling. In most areas of economic policy the Blair government could claim decisiveness. On the single currency, there was malignant drift.

The Prime Minister led a pro-European administration – the first since Edward Heath's to be wholehearted in its commitment to play a leading role on the European stage. As the then Shadow Chancellor had said of Emu in a speech to a German audience in the summer of 1996, 'Britain should not once again risk standing aside and failing to influence a crucial phase in Europe's development.'[17] But while the Cabinet was largely free of the ideological fault lines which had broken the Conservatives, the debate over the future of sterling retained a lethal capacity to destabilise relationships at the highest levels of government. And the arguments over the euro badly strained Brown's relationship with Mr Blair, raising time and again the issue of whether the Chancellor would ever come to terms with his burning personal resentment over failing to secure the leadership on the death of John Smith in 1994.

Under the terms of the single currency 'opt-out' negotiated by John Major in the Maastricht treaty, the British government had until the end of 1997 – barely six months beyond the general election – to decide whether it wanted to be part of the first wave of Economic and Monetary Union in January 1999. Joining then was never a real prospect. Less certain, was whether the pound should or could be swapped for the euro in 2000 or 2001. This was the judgement that the Chancellor and Prime Minister had to take in the autumn of 1997.

A year before the election Brown had made it clear that British participation in the project would depend on a minimum level of economic convergence between the British and continental European economies. He had also called for a more transparent system of economic decision-making if and when Emu got underway. Both signalled a delay in British entry. But his subsequent hopes in the summer of 1997 that the whole single currency project might be put back – and Britain's dilemma deferred – by a failure of other European nations to meet the so-called Maastricht criteria were disappointed. Mr Brown raised with officials the possibility of seeking to persuade France and Germany to delay the launch of the project for two years. Sir Nigel Wicks, the senior Treasury official responsible for European affairs, advised him that was impossible. So too did the Foreign Office. The government had to make its choice.

Brown's statement to the House of Commons in October 1997[18] ruling out participation in Emu during the lifetime of the Parliament was framed with the intention of freeing the government from the constant speculation about if and when Britain might join. The new policy was christened Prepare and Decide – a phrase inadvertently borrowed from Michael Heseltine. It was a failure. Before long the Brown/Blair approach was more accurately characterised as Wait and See. Unkind officials in Whitehall preferred Dither and Delay.

Within days of entering the Treasury, Brown confirmed his judgement that the economics ruled out joining the first wave. Speaking on the Tuesday after the election, he offered a reminder that both he and Blair had said during the election campaign that 'it is highly unlikely that we will join Emu at the first date in 1999'.[19] To underline this delay, he acknowledged that the arrangements made to give the Bank of England operational independence did not meet the terms of the Maastricht treaty. Further legislation would be needed at a later stage to give the Bank the full independence required by Emu.

The judgement on 1999 was undoubtedly right. The UK economy had been growing fast while those of its European partners remained mired if not in recession then in sluggish growth. The disjunction in the economic cycles was reflected in the fact that short-term interest rates in the UK, soon at 7 per cent and rising, were at least 3 percentage points higher than in continental Europe. There was no prospect of sustainable convergence by the single currency launch date. Among Treasury officials scarcely a voice was heard in favour of early entry to Emu. As an institution, it was still badly scarred by the humiliating experience of sterling's ejection from the European exchange rate on Black Wednesday in September 1992. It had never been a pro-European institution. The post-war culture in Great George Street had been moulded by the relationship with the US and most particularly the reliance on US loans and support at the International Monetary Fund to underpin sterling through its regular crises. For the Treasury, Brussels was another country. Mr Brown found nothing by way of preparation had been done to keep open Mr Major's supposed option. The war within the Tory cabinet had effectively ruled out any serious work by officials.

If Blair and Brown then were agreed that the government would not be in at the beginning, little discussion had taken place on the crucial question of how that decision would be framed. Would the government seek to participate shortly afterwards, would it hold to a neutral stance allowing itself to react to events? And what did this mean for the timing of the referendum the government had promised the voters if it did decide the time was right to join? All these questions were unanswered when Brown asked a team of Treasury officials headed by Wicks to produce a series of papers covering no fewer than seven possible options. Though he was decided in his own mind against immediate entry, Brown stipulated that these papers should include an exploration of that possibility. He was determined that no-one would be able to say that an opportunity had been lost simply because the Treasury had not done the requisite work. Some officials took away the impression that he was keen Britain be part of Emu as soon as the economic conditions were right. That said, they were also asked to produce the arguments for staying out of the single currency more or less indefinitely. Brown intended to announce his position in the autumn of 1997. A speech to the Confederation of British Industry in November was pencilled in as the platform.

The timetable was telescoped by events. By September 1997 briefings and counter-briefings from ministers and their advisers had produced a series of conflicting press reports on the government's intentions. The financial markets were more than once thrown into turmoil by the front page speculation. In October, an attempt by Brown to steer the debate by telling *The Times* newspaper that the government would most likely stay outside Emu for the lifetime of the Parliament sparked sharp clashes within the Cabinet. Blair worried he was being 'bounced' by the Chancellor. Peter Mandelson, more influential than his middle-ranking ministerial position in the Cabinet Office indicated, pressed the Prime Minister to keep his options open. Even if actual entry into the single currency was delayed, the government might still consider an early referendum. This intervention inflamed Mandelson's already difficult relations with Brown which dated back to the 1994 leadership contest. The Chancellor had never forgiven Mandelson, then a close adviser, for backing Blair as the successor to Smith. The euro was henceforth a constant additional source of friction in a poisoned and poisonous relationship between the two – further complicated by the fact that both had privileged access to Blair.

The statement the Chancellor finally made in October was the product of an intense debate between Blair, Brown and Mandelson. It was replete with calculated ambiguities. Enthusiasts could claim subsequently that for the first time a British government had declared for the principle of the single currency. As Brown put it: 'I have said that, if a single currency works and is successful, Britain should join it. We should therefore begin now to prepare ourselves so that, should we meet the economic tests, we can make a decision to join a successful single currency early in the next Parliament'.[20] Preparations would be made – including work on a national changeover plan – to make that option real. This particular glass, though, was as half empty as it was half full. Ruling out participation during the Parliament, Brown said that before Britain could join the economic benefits of membership had to be 'clear and unambiguous'. At the insistence of Blair and Mandelson, he included one small caveat. The position in the present Parliament could change in the event of 'unforeseen circumstances'. But the Chancellor's intent was clear: the issue was off the agenda until after the next election.

The five economic 'tests' set by Brown for entry were as much about politics as economics. Even the most ardent supporters of the single currency agreed with the commonsense requirement of the first – for a settled and sustained period of convergence between the UK and continental European economies. But whether Emu, as three other tests required, would be good for investment, employment and the City of London, would always be a subjective judgement. The final test – that European economies demonstrate sufficient flexibility in labour and product markets to adapt to a one-size-fits-all monetary policy – could also be answered however the Treasury wished.

Brown declared that the tests had reframed the issue of Emu entry as one of 'national economic interest'. But it did not escape the notice of colleagues that, for all the emphasis on economics, Brown's statement had given him a veto over if and when the government recommended entry. Blair could not advocate a referendum on the issue unless and until his Chancellor decreed that the economic conditions were right. The Chancellor had given himself leverage – leverage that would be used in pursuing his ambition to succeed Blair in 10 Downing Street. By the early months of 2001, it was transparent that Brown's approach to Emu was conditioned above all by his own political ambitions.

On another level, the attempt to separate the economics from the politics of the single currency was disingenuous. Of course, a minimum level of cyclical convergence in terms of inflation, interest and exchange rates was a precondition for entry. But a debate focused on the economic arguments for and against the euro would always produce a stalemate. There could be no definitive answer to the question, for example, of whether the disadvantages of a single monetary policy (and the risks within the euro-zone of asymmetric economic shocks) would be outweighed by removal of exchange rate risks and the deepening of the single market. Joining the euro would involve surrendering monetary policy to the ECB, but how much freedom of manoeuvre would Britain have outside the euro zone? It was the essentially political nature of the decision – the implications for Britain's broader position within the European Union and Blair's ambition to establish it as a leading power – that led to the tensions between Prime Minister and Chancellor in the second half of the Parliament.

For all his own insistence on getting the economics right, Blair judged the political case for entry compelling. For the Prime Minister, participation in the single currency, albeit after the election, was central to his plan to establish Britain as a leading power on the European stage. It was, as he acknowledged in a private conversation in the summer of 2000, a question of the projection of British power. Robin Cook, whose support for the single currency had been lukewarm in opposition, came quickly to the same view at the Foreign Office. Peter Mandelson, the most instinctively Europhile member of the Cabinet, was equally determined that Britain should join at the earliest opportunity. In each case they agreed that the economics had to be right. By contrast, Brown, who had initially showed all the signs of being an enthusiast, seemed to cool as the Parliament progressed. The Treasury, far from being an active agent in securing the convergence necessary for sterling to join, positioned itself as a bystander. More than once Blair felt driven to seek reassurance from Brown that this stance was tactical – to take the euro out of the 2001 election campaign – rather than strategic. The position was further complicated by the intense personal animus between Brown and Mandelson, with the conflict between the two bursting frequently on to the front pages. When Mandelson was forced to resign for a second time in early 2001, there was undisguised glee in the Treasury.

The stand-off saw Blair unwilling to challenge Brown's October 1997 statement but occasionally anxious to reassure his European partners, and his Cabinet colleagues, that the government remained committed to participation. In a statement to Parliament on the national changeover plan in February 1999 he declared (at Mandelson's urging): 'We have stated today that as a matter of principle Britain should join a single European currency.'[21] It had originally been intended that Brown deliver this statement but Blair gave it himself when the Chancellor indicated that he was not prepared to put a more positive gloss on the prospects for entry. There was a similar spat in the autumn of 1999 at the launch of the Britain in Europe campaign, a cross-party pressure group of leading industrialists and senior politicians in favour of euro entry. The start of the new millennium saw Brown and Cook at odds over the single currency, with the Foreign Secretary arguing that the coming election campaign demanded a change in the emphasis if not the substance of the government's position. Stephen Byers, the Trade and Industry Secretary, also chose to present the cup as half full rather than half empty. On each of these occasions the Chancellor remained stubbornly immovable, protesting to the Prime Minister that the Foreign Office and Trade and Industry departments were trespassing on his territory. In the spring of 2000 Blair called the three ministers together to negotiate an agreed formula. Brown, it was agreed, would emphasise the primacy of the economic tests. Cook and Byers could take from the October 1997 statement the commitment to make an assessment 'early in the next Parliament'. It was an uneasy truce.

Publicly and privately, Blair stuck to his position that he favoured participation as soon as the economic conditions were right. But for all his determination to end the ambiguity over Britain's role in Europe, he was reluctant to confront the Eurosceptic press, particularly the virulently anti-euro *Sun*. For most of the time timidity ruled Downing Street. Brown meanwhile argued that there were good tactical reasons for caution. With William Hague's Conservatives committed to 'keeping the pound', at least for another Parliament, the Chancellor could argue that it was politically wise to put the issue on the backburner during the election campaign. The campaign for participation could then begin in the afterglow of a second victory. As to the economic tests, an objective judgement suggested that they were close to being met – save in one important respect. In terms of inflation, the level of interest rates, and growth Britain's economy was converging with those of its European neighbours. The important caveat was that sterling remained at an over-valued and unsustainable level against a weak euro. There would have to be a substantial adjustment before the pound could join.

The net result of all this was that public opinion was left to drift further in the direction of scepticism, with opinion polls in early 2001 suggesting that up to three quarters of the voters opposed British entry. And left unsaid was the suspicion that Brown, once an enthusiastic European, had obviously cooled on the euro. Some speculated this reflected simple stubbornness, an unwillingness to see the strategy he had announced in October 1997 overturned. Those with more Machiavellian minds concluded that the euro had become a pawn in the power struggle between Prime Minister and Chancellor. Others still that Brown simply did not like the European way of doing business. He made little secret of his lack of interest in the monthly meeting of the Ecofin council of finance ministers. Nor of his preference for trips to Washington over those to Brussels. Among Brown's aides there was certainly a view that participation in the euro could wait for another five or six years – perhaps until he had replaced Blair. So the question of British participation was effectively deferred to what promised to be an intense debate after the 2001 election.

First Lord and Chancellor

The Blair government's record of economic management was not without flaws. For all his intellectual rigour and political skills, Gordon Brown made mistakes. The decision, for example, to freeze public spending in the first two years of Parliament exacted a heavy price in terms of the quality of the public services. The expectations of the electorate were badly disappointed. In retrospect, Brown could have relaxed the spending targets without sacrificing credibility in the financial markets. Instead the funding of education, health and the rest went from bust to boom. There were other misjudgements. A decision to limit the rise in the basic state pension to 75 pence in 2000 cost the government considerable political capital and forced a much larger than otherwise settlement for the following year. Like the rest of the government the Treasury failed to see the building impact of high fuel duties once the world oil price began to rise. Brown was clumsy in handling benefit cuts imposed on lone parents and in the introduction of new tax incentives for savings. The expansion of the Private Finance Initiative had as much to do with political symbolism as with a serious attempt to improve the quality of public provision. And for all his Presbyterian instincts, the Chancellor could not resist reaching for headline-grabbing gimmicks on Budget day.

More seriously, Brown's refusal to warm to the euro encouraged the financial markets in pushing sterling to unsustainable levels. Manufacturing industry suffered badly as a consequence. In the first three years of the Blair government, manufacturing output rose by only 3 per cent. The start of the millennium saw many overseas investors – particularly the Japanese – seriously reassessing Britain's attractiveness as a base for production.

That said, the Blair effect on Britain's economic policymaking was profound. In this, Brown was the towering figure. The conversion of Labour to the market economy and orthodox macro-economic management erased the ideological dividing line which had defined left and right for most of the post-war period. The independence of the Bank of England and the framework for fiscal policy will long outlast their author. The government's stewardship of the economy also allowed it to do something else: to make the case for active as opposed to big government and for decent provision of essential services. Income tax cuts, for a time at least, lost their political magic. The public spending plans put in place in the summer of 2000 offered the prospect of sustained investment in health, education and transport, all badly neglected during the previous two decades. Blair's insistence that the extra resources be accompanied by significant reform of these services showed a commitment to modernisation unfamiliar to past Labour governments.

If there was a shadow on this record it was cast by the growing tension between Numbers 10 and 11 Downing Street. The relationship between Prime Minister and Chancellor is the essential hinge of effective government in Britain. When it snaps, as happened when Nigel Lawson quit Margaret Thatcher's administration in 1989, the consequences are momentous. Tony Blair and Gordon Brown could claim that their friendship was perhaps the closest in politics. But it was a marriage – and officials described the relationship thus – as tempestuous as it was vital to the remarkable shift in economic strategy over which they presided. When the journalist Andrew Rawnsley published an account of the feuding at the top of the government in the autumn of 2000, the reaction of friends of the Prime Minister and Chancellor was instructive.[22] They flatly denied much of the detail in the book but barely challenged much of the underlying thesis – that the Blair administration is as badly disfigured by personal rivalries and jealousies as any of its predecessors and, at the heart of these quarrels, stands Gordon Brown. Rarely has a politician been at once so powerful and so insecure.

The tensions over the euro became entangled with these personal rivalries. At one level Prime Minister and Chancellor divided the work of the government between them – Brown taking care of economic and welfare policy, Blair focusing his attentions on foreign affairs, defence, Northern Ireland, health and education. This was the bargain that Brown considered he had struck with Blair in 1994 when he stood down in the leadership contest after the death of John Smith. Blair frequently described his Downing Street neighbour as the most brilliant politician of his generation. He made it as clear as a Prime Minister can that he expected Brown to succeed him. The Chancellor and his aides, though, never dispelled the impression that they believed the party had made the wrong choice in 1994. Early in the Parliament Blair was disparaged by the Treasury team as non-executive chairman to Brown's chief executive. There was palpable scorn within the Chancellor's entourage at Blair's preoccupation with the opinion polls and the instincts of Middle Britain. Brown was the strategist, this critique said, Blair the politician tossed to and fro by the winds of public opinion. The Prime Minister had re-christened his party New Labour. It was a phrase that Brown rarely uttered. And if the making of the new economic policy was a joint enterprise, Brown never let go of his roots. Blair might lead the party, one close friend of the Chancellor once remarked, but, unlike the Chancellor, he was not *of* it. Here was a relationship that would need serious mending if it were to survive the rigours of a second term.

Notes

1 Gordon Brown, 'Responsibility in Public Finance', speech at the Queen Elizabeth Conference Centre, 20 January 1997.
2 Gordon Brown, 'Labour's Macro-economic Framework', speech to the Labour Finance and Industry Group, 17 May 1995.
3 Ibid.
4 Geoffrey Robinson, *The Unconventional Minister*, Michael Joseph, 2000.
5 Ibid.
6 The account in *Servants of the People*, by Andrew Rawnsley, Hamish Hamilton, 2000, is broadly accurate.
7 See 'A Talent to Bemuse', Alan Beattie, *Financial Times*, 29 June 2000.
8 *The Code for Fiscal Stability*, HM Treasury, March 1998.
9 Gordon Brown, Lecture to the Royal Economic Society, 13 July 2000.
10 See *Budget 98*, HM Treasury, HC620, March 1998 and *Budget 99*, HC298, March 1999.
11 See *Budget 2000*, HM Treasury, HC346, March 2000
12 Goldman Sachs, *UK Weekly Analyst*, 13 October 2000.

13 The IFS Green Budget, January 2000.
14 *Spending Review 2000*, HM Treasury, Cm8047.
15 *Budget* 97, HM Treasury, HC85, July 1997.
16 Gordon Brown, Anthony Crosland Memorial Lecture, February 1997.
17 Gordon Brown, Labour's MacroEconomic Framework, as above.
18 *Hansard*, 27 October 1997, Cols 583–588.
19 *Financial Times*, 7 May 1997.
20 *Hansard*, as above.
21 *Hansard*, 23 February 1999, Cols 179–186.
22 *Servants of the People*, ibid.

© Chris Riddell

Chapter 10

INDUSTRY

Geoffrey Owen

THE BLAIR GOVERNMENT'S policy towards industry was similar in many respects to that of the Conservative governments which preceded it. This was not just a matter of reluctantly accepting that privatisation and most of the other reforms associated with Thatcherism were irreversible. The new administration appeared to be wholeheartedly committed to competition as the principal spur to greater efficiency. As Gordon Brown put it, 'today we know that in a global economy greater competition at home is the key to greater competitiveness abroad. We know that it is the openness of the economy, not its closed nature, that is the driving force in productivity growth.'[1]

The contrast with Old Labour, with its penchant for protecting national champions and rescuing 'lame ducks', could hardly be more striking. But this did not imply a hands-off approach to industry. The Chancellor repeatedly drew attention to the productivity gap between Britain and other industrial countries, and did not hesitate to use his tax and spending powers to correct what he saw as the supply-side weaknesses – for example, inadequate investment in research and development – that were responsible for Britain's productivity lag. His aim was to combine macro-economic stability with micro-economic measures aimed at improving industrial performance and thus enhancing the economy's long-term growth potential.

This chapter looks, first, at the external environment in which industry was operating between 1997 and 2001, then at the impact of the government's policies. The concluding section assesses the state of British industry at the end of the government's term of office.

External Pressures and Opportunities

The 1997 election came at a time when the tide of structural change in British industry which had started in the 1980s was still running strongly. The forces at work were international competition, rapid technological change (including the rise of the internet), and an increasingly demanding stock market.

An additional source of strain for British firms for most of this period was the strength of the pound against the currencies of its principal trading partners in Europe. From its low point in 1995, three years after Britain's exit from the European Monetary System, sterling began to appreciate against the Deutschmark, and it continued to do so after the election. To the surprise of most commentators, the launch of the single European currency, the euro, at the start of 1999 brought no relief. The new currency declined in value against the pound and the dollar, and despite sporadic intervention by the European Central Bank, remained weak until the end of 2000. Despite some recovery in the early months of 2001, firms which exported the bulk of their production to Continental Europe found their profit margins painfully squeezed.

The effect of all these pressures was to force companies, especially manufacturers, to concentrate their efforts on businesses which had a realistic chance of competing profitably in an open world market, and to withdraw from those which did not. Some of the withdrawals were offset by foreign firms which built or acquired factories in Britain. Foreign investment continued to flow into Britain at a high level, as it had done under the Thatcher and Major administrations. Despite the problems arising from the strength of the pound, Britain was still seen – thanks to the reforms carried out during the 1980s and early 1990s – as an attractive manufacturing and exporting base.

For British companies the key to survival lay in specialisation – doing fewer things better, and doing them on an international scale. Take the case of the country's leading electrical/electronics group, GEC. Following the retirement in 1996 of the company's long-serving managing director, Lord Weinstock, the new management decided that the right strategy was not to maintain a broad spread of activities, but to focus more narrowly on telecommunications equipment. Defence electronics, which had been GEC's largest division, was sold to British Aerospace, and the proceeds were used to finance a series of acquisitions in the US. The name of the company was changed to Marconi, marking the transition from 'everything electrical' to a streamlined telecommunications business.

Another example was Imperial Chemical Industries (ICI). Having hived off its pharmaceutical division in 1994, this one-time bellwether of British industry was left with a collection of assets which did not constitute a coherent portfolio. The policy adopted in 1997 was to dispose of all its commodity chemical interests and to concentrate on high-value speciality chemicals. This involve an ambitious programme of disposals and acquisitions, and, at times, a dangerously high level of debt, but by the end of 2000 ICI had repositioned itself in sectors of the industry where it had good technology and a strong market position.

GEC and ICI, like many other British companies, were operating in global industries which were being reshaped through cross-border mergers and acquisitions. In some cases, such as pharmaceuticals, British-owned companies were well placed to take the lead. Thus Glaxo, having swallowed up Wellcome in 1995, entered five years later into an even bigger merger with SmithKline Beecham, while Zeneca (the pharmaceutical company spun off from ICI) merged with Astra of Sweden to form one of the world's largest pharmaceutical groups. In others British companies were on the receiving end of take-over bids from overseas; in the chemical industry, for instance, several medium-sized British manufacturers, including Courtaulds and Albright & Wilson, passed into foreign hands. While some observers regretted the increase in foreign ownership, on the grounds that it transferred decision-making power outside the UK, in most cases inward investment served to upgrade the competitiveness of the industries concerned and to integrate them more closely into the world market.

Restructuring was given further stimulus by the stock market. Underperforming firms found themselves facing demands from investors for a change in strategy, a change in leadership, or both. One target for attack was the old-style conglomerate – institutional shareholders were increasingly sceptical of the ability of managers to run a disparate range of businesses. Hanson, which had been one of the most successful corporate predators of the 1980s, split itself into four separate companies, and most of the other diversified groups which had flourished during that period were broken up or taken over.

The pressure on companies to maximise shareholder value had been gathering strength well before the Blair government took office. A new development was the shift in investor sentiment away from 'old economy' shares – mainly manufacturing companies in mature industries such as engineering, steel and chemicals – to the so-called TMT sector (telecommunications, media and technology). While the shares of internet-related companies boomed, those of profitable but slower growing manufacturing companies were driven down to low levels, often below the break-up value of their underlying assets. Although 'dot-com fever' abated in the second half of 2000, and many TMT stocks fell sharply in value, the shares of companies operating in traditional industries remained depressed, and many of them looked for ways of shifting resources into areas which had higher growth prospects.

These 'old economy' companies were also the ones most seriously affected by the strength of the pound against the euro. Manufacturers of commodity products which competed mainly on price suffered a drastic decline in the profitability of their exports. Thus Corus, the steelmaking group formed in 1999 by a merger between British Steel Corporation and Hoogovens of the Netherlands, was forced to make a series of cut backs, culminating in the decision to cut steel-making at its big Llanwery works in South Wales.

Another hard-pressed sector was textiles. A serious blow was the decision by Marks & Spencer, which had long been committed to buying most of its clothing from UK-based suppliers, to switch more of its purchases to cheaper overseas locations. Companies like Courtaulds Textiles and Coats Viyella which had been heavily dependent on the British retailer relocated more of their own manufacturing operations to low-wage countries, with consequent job losses in Britain. Meanwhile the Italian textile industry, the strongest in Europe, was able to take advantage of the weak euro to step up its exports.

The decline of the textile industry was not a new phenomenon; recent events could be seen as part of the continuing shift from high-wage to low-wage countries which had been under way for several decades. The motor industry was a different story. In the 1980s and the first half of the 1990s car production in Britain had been rising strongly, thanks partly to the decision by three Japanese companies, Nissan, Toyota and Honda, to build assembly plants in Britain as the base for supplying European markets. At the same time the old 'national champion' – British Leyland, now Rover – looked to be in a healthier state after many years of decline. When BMW bought Rover in 1994, this was seen as a vote of confidence in the British motor industry; the chairman of the German company declared that Britain had become 'the most attractive country among all European locations for the production of cars'. Yet six years later BMW had to admit that its investment in Britain had been a costly mistake. While it kept Cowley, the smaller of Rover's two assembly plants, for the production of the Mini, it sold the main Longbridge plant to a private consortium which hoped to keep the Rover car business alive until another foreign partner or acquirer could be found.

The strength of the pound was only one factor in BMW's decision, and probably not the most important. The German buyers had vastly underestimated the task of rebuilding Rover as an up-market, international brand complementary to, but not competitive with, BMW itself. Similarly, when Ford announced that it would be ceasing car assembly at Dagenham, its biggest British factory, the company insisted that the exchange rate was not the reason. Ford had been losing market share in Europe, capacity was far in excess of requirements, and at least one assembly plant had to go. Over capacity was also the main reason for Vauxhall's decision to end car assembly at Luton. Nevertheless, it was clear that exporting cars to Europe had become increasingly unremunerative. Nissan, now controlled by Renault, threatened to shift production of the new Micra small car to France, but eventually decided, apparently after receiving assurances from the government about exchange rate policy, to keep it in Britain.[2]

If the outlook for some of Britain's medium-technology industries was uncertain, new opportunities were opening up at the high-technology end of the spectrum. For most of the post-war period the world electronics industry, including computers, semiconductors and software, had been dominated by American and later Japanese companies, several of which had built plants in Britain. Most British-owned firms had either withdrawn from the race or sold out. More recently, however, a new generation of entrepreneurial British firms had emerged, targeting segments of the market where they had a unique technological advantage.

Two such firms were ARM, which designed high-performance micro-processors for use in mobile telephones and other portable devices, and Autonomy, which produced software for handling unstructured data. Both were part of a cluster of science-based firms situated on the outskirts of Cambridge and closely linked to the university. Although 'Silicon Fen' was far smaller than Silicon Valley in California, it grew at an impressive rate during the 1980s and 1990s; several of the leading firms were listed on the stock market, and achieved high market valuations.[3] Another promising contender outside Cambridge was Psion, which had specialised in hand-held computers but subsequently developed a new operating system for mobile telephones, allowing users to access the internet and exchange e-mail messages; the three leading mobile telephone manufacturers, Nokia, Ericsson and Motorola, invested in this system, with Psion retaining a large minority stake.

British firms were also doing well in biotechnology, an industry which had been pioneered in the US in the 1970s and spread to Europe in the following decade. By the end of the 1990s several British biotechnology firms had made the transition from high-risk start-ups, often dangerously dependent on a single drug, to strong, research-based groups with a promising pipeline of new products. The largest British-owned firm, Celltech, consolidated its position during 2000 with two sizeable acquisitions; two others, Cambridge Antibody Technology and Oxford GlycoSciences, were close to achieving 'critical mass' – and well regarded by investors.

A more remarkable success story was that of Vodafone, the mobile telephone operator. Created in the 1980s as a subsidiary of Racal, this company won one of the first British mobile telephone licences in competition with British Telecom. It was subsequently floated on the stock market, and embarked on a series of acquisitions outside Britain, culminating in the take-over of Mannesmann in Germany – the first-ever case of a German company succumbing to a hostile take-over bid from a non-German firm. With a large US acquisition already under its belt, Vodafone ranked as the largest mobile telephone network in the world.

Vodafone was one of several new firms which joined the FTSE index of the hundred most highly valued companies on the stock exchange. The changing composition of the index, while partly due to the fashion for TMT stocks which began to fade in the second half of 2000, reflected the process of 'creative destruction' which was taking place during this period. The rise of new companies and the redirection of old ones was transforming the British industrial landscape.

Part of this redeployment was a continuing shift in employment from manufacturing to services. Some observers bewailed what they saw as an unnecessarily rapid process of deindustrialisation. As one journalist put it, 'British manufacturing industry was once powerful, but must now adjust to the challenge of simply being a niche sector in a service-driven economy'.[4] Yet British experience over the last twenty years has not been far out of line with that of most other industrial countries (Table 1). Germany, with a significantly higher proportion of its labour force in manufacturing, is an exception, but this is at least partly due to the sluggish growth of its service industries, held back by an excess of regulation. In any case, the distinction between industry and services is becoming somewhat blurred; a growing number of manufacturing companies are seeking to provide their customers with 'total solutions', involving services as well as discrete products.

Table I Civilian employment by sector in the UK, US, Germany and France 1979–1999 (figures in per cent of total civilian employment)

		Industry	Agriculture	Services
UK	1979	38.6	2.7	58.7
	1999	26.0	1.6	72.4
US	1979	31.3	3.6	65.2
	1999	23.1	2.6	74.4
Germany	1979	44.2	5.4	50.4
	1999	34.5	2.8	62.6
France	1979	36.1	8.9	55.0
	1999	24.8	4.2	71.0

Source: OECD labour force statistics, 1979–1999, OECD Paris 2000.

The Role of Government

How did the Blair government respond to these changes? Did its policies help or hinder the drive by British companies to make themselves internationally competitive?

The starting-point was a fierce determination, most clearly articulated by Gordon Brown, to maintain macro-economic stability. Arguably the biggest failure of the Thatcher–Major era had been in the conduct of fiscal and monetary policy. The 'Thatcher recession' of the early 1980s had been extremely painful, and the boom that began in the second half of that decade had been allowed to go too far, leading to the severe downturn of the early 1990s. Entry into the exchange rate mechanism of the European Monetary System also turned out to be an error; the devaluation of sterling in 1992 was a humiliation from which the Major government never recovered. Tony Blair and Gordon Brown were anxious to avoid a repetition of the boom-and-bust cycle, and to demonstrate beyond any possible doubt that New Labour could be trusted to run the economy in a prudent and responsible manner.

The government was fortunate in taking office at a time when recovery from the recession was well under way. But the fact that the upswing continued, at a steady and sustainable pace, was due in part to New Labour's policies, including, most importantly, the delegation of monetary policy to the Bank of England and the strict control of public expenditure. By 2001 the British economy was in its ninth year of growth – the longest period of uninterrupted expansion since the war – and this had been achieved with low inflation and steadily falling unemployment.

This was a refreshing contrast from the crisis management that had characterised the Labour governments of the 1960s and 1970s. Hardly less remarkable was the new focus on competition. The government declared its intention to allow markets to work, and to intervene only where there was clear evidence of market failure. (If ministers needed further evidence that politicians and civil servants should not try to run commercial enterprises, it was provided by the embarrassing failure of the Millennium Dome.)

Competition policy was given a primacy which would have been inconceivable under Tony Blair's predecessors – Clement Attlee, Harold Wilson and James Callaghan. As the Treasury put it, 'effective markets and competition provide the best means of ensuring that the economy's resources are allocated efficiently'.[5] The Competition Act of 1998 strengthened the powers of the Office of Fair Trading to root out anti-competitive practices and increased the penalties that could be imposed on transgressors; it also allowed injured parties to sue for damages. Although some observers believed that the penalties were still too mild – there was no question of putting offenders in jail, as had long been the practice in US antitrust law – it was an important step towards a more competitive environment.[6] Another was the decision to eliminate the power of ministers to decide which mergers should be referred to the Competition Commission (the new name for the old Monopolies and Mergers Commission). This was part of a wider shake-up of mergers policy designed not only to prevent political interference in merger decisions, but also to ensure that in ruling on mergers the Competition Commission would be concerned solely with issues of competition; the vague public interest criteria which had guided the Commission in the past were scrapped.

With the new emphasis on competition came a downgrading of industrial policy, in the old sense of targeting particular industries or companies for support. Only in a few exceptional cases did the government seek to over-ride market forces for political reasons, and even here the scale of intervention was small. One such case was coal mining, where, in order to prevent an over-rapid contraction of the industry, the government intervened in the negotiations between the electricity companies and the privatised coal mine operator. Ministers claimed that the 'pool' through which electricity prices were determined was structured in a way which put gas-fired stations at an advantage over coal-fired stations; this was not only unfair, but also inconsistent with the promise contained in Labour's election manifesto that the government would maintain a diversity of energy supplies.[7] Some judicious arm-twisting of the generators secured a temporary reprieve for the coal mines, but this did not imply any long-term commitment to preserve the industry at a given level. The days when the coal miners could dictate to a Labour government were long since past.

A bigger test was the BMW/Rover crisis. Because of the deep involvement of past governments in Rover's affairs, it was inevitable that the Department of Trade and Industry should come under strong pressure to 'do something' to avert the threatened closure of Longbridge. The Secretary of State, Stephen Byers, went further than he should have done in apparently seeking to influence the negotiations between BMW and the potential purchasers of the factory. The successful bidder, the Phoenix consortium, received the Department's blessing, mainly because it promised to maintain Rover car production at a high level, while its rival, Alchemy, intended to scale back the Longbridge factory and produce only MG cars. The commercial rationale of the Phoenix plan looked dubious, and by the early months of 2001 the future of Longbridge was again in doubt. But, apart from redirecting to Phoenix the regional grants which had previously been offered to BMW for the redevelopment of Longbridge, the Department was in no position to offer large subsidies to keep the Rover operation alive. The contrast with the Chrysler/Rootes affair in the 1970s – when the Wilson government used taxpayers' money to prop up Chrysler's loss-making British plants – is instructive.

The one surviving element of old-style industrial policy – and on this there was continuity with the Thatcher/Major regimes – was the government's continuing willingness to support the aerospace industry. After some initial reluctance Tony Blair was persuaded in 1997 to make some £200m available to Rolls-Royce for the development of new engines. Ministers claimed that this arrangement was different from the 'launch aid' given by previous governments; it was, rather, an illustration of New Labour's commitment to public/private partnerships. (Since the investment, according to the government, was expected to earn a commercial return, it was not clear why it could not be financed from commercial sources.) A few months later the government provided British Aerospace with a £120m contribution to the development of wings for long-range versions of the Airbus A340 airliner. This was followed by a much larger subvention – more than

£500m – for the proposed 'super-jumbo' Airbus, the A3XX, designed to attack Boeing's long-standing monopoly in the market for very large airliners. Aerospace, it seems, is still a special case, whichever party is in power.

For 'normal' industries the rules were clear: companies could not expect to be bailed out because of their supposedly strategic value to the economy, or for reasons of employment. Although the Department of Trade and Industry continued to play its traditional role as 'sponsor' of industry – a role which had been upgraded, at least rhetorically, by Michael Heseltine during the Major government – sponsorship no longer took the form of selective intervention, but rather of broader programmes aimed at spreading best practice and encouraging the wider application of new technology. Outside aerospace, the government was moving from a 'mission-oriented' to a 'diffusion-oriented' industrial policy.[8]

New Labour's enthusiasm for freely functioning markets extended to the field of employment. The balance of power in labour relations had shifted decisively from trade unions to employers during the 1980s, and the Blair government made no attempt to turn the clock back; for the most part the unions were seen as one interest group among many, no more deserving of special favours than the CBI. The one significant gain for the unions was the Employment Relations Act of 1999, which set up new procedures for establishing trade union representation in firms where a majority of the employees wanted it. As Robert Taylor explains in Chapter 12, the unions got less out of the Act than they had hoped for, and it was not expected to have a major impact on the character of British labour relations. According to one careful survey of employment practices published in 2000, 'the prospect is for a further disintegration of what remains of the system of joint regulation and employee voice based on trade union representation'.[9] Despite the introduction of a minimum wage the labour market remained far less regulated in Britain than in most Continental countries, and this was widely seen – by Ministers as well as employers – as a competitive advantage which should be preserved.

Vigorous competition within a stable fiscal and monetary framework was a necessary condition for economic success. But competition on its own, in the government's view, was not enough; something more was needed to bring about the step-change in British economic performance which, ministers believed, was both desirable and achievable. The fundamental weakness, stressed by Gordon Brown from his earliest days as Chancellor, was low productivity.

The government accepted (though it did not often say so) that Thatcherism had been good for productivity. After lagging behind other European countries in the first thirty years after the war, Britain began to catch up in the 1980s, and the improvement continued into the early 1990s (Table 2). However, there remained a sizeable gap, both in relation to Germany and France, and in relation to the US (Table 3). Moreover,

Britain's productivity performance appeared to slacken, especially in manufacturing, during the second half of the 1990s. The government set itself the challenge of closing the gap, thus raising the UK's trend growth rate and the wealth of the nation; as the Treasury pointed out, if the UK were to match the productivity performance of the US, output per head would be over £6,000 higher.[10]

Table 2 Output per hour in manufacturing in Britain and France 1960–1999 (average annual rates of change in per cent)

	UK	France
1960–1973	4.1	6.6
1973–1979	1.0	4.4
1979–1985	4.1	3.0
1985–1990	4.1	3.4
1990–1999	2.4	3.6

Source: US Department of Labor, Bureau of Labor Statistics

Table 3 Britain's relative productivity position in 1999 (UK = 100)

	UK	US	France	Germany
GDP per capita	100	137	105	113
GDP per person engaged	100	129	126	126
GDP per hour	100	128	120	131

Source: Nicholas Crafts and Mary O'Mahony, *A perspective on UK productivity performance*, mimeo, July 2000

How much importance should be attached to the productivity gap? After all, Britain had been more successful than France and Germany during the 1990s in getting people into jobs. Measured on the basis of GDP per capita rather than output per worker, the lag behind Germany and France was much smaller. The impressive levels of productivity in the two Continental countries had been achieved in part at the expense of employment; a combination of high labour costs and an over-regulated labour market had stimulated capital investment and discouraged firms from taking on new workers. Comparisons with the US, on the other hand, showed that it was possible to combine a high rate of participation in the labour force with high output per worker. This was one of several reasons why New Labour tended to look to the US rather than Continental Europe for micro-economic lessons; the so-called 'Rhineland' model of capitalism was out of fashion.

The greatest American advantage lay in its large and highly competitive internal market. This conclusion was confirmed by studies from McKinsey, the US management consultants, and underpinned the Blair government's thinking about competition.[11] But academic research also identified two other important sources of Britain's productivity lag: a lack of investment in human capital (the training and education of workers) and a lack of investment in physical capital.[12] The typical British worker was less well trained than his counterpart in other industrial countries and had less power at his elbow.

The first of these deficiencies had been a matter of concern for successive governments since the 1960s. With the traditional apprenticeship system in decline, too many young people were entering work without qualifications and did not receive any systematic training from their employers. One consequence was a persistent British weakness, especially in relation to Germany, in skill-intensive industries such as mechanical engineering.[13] German firms benefited from a comprehensive and well-organised apprenticeship system, providing for regular training in vocational schools as well as at the workplace.

Extensive reforms of the training system were introduced under the Thatcher/Major governments, including the creation of employer-based Training and Education Councils at the local level, a new set of vocational qualifications, and, in the mid-1990s, the introduction of Modern Apprenticeships. This last was an attempt to recreate the virtues of the traditional apprenticeship – its training in broad, transferable skills – while eliminating its defects – the lack of externally monitored standards of competence.[14] Some improvements resulted; by the end of the 1990s the number of people with intermediate skills, as a proportion of the labour force, had significantly increased (Table 4). But the Blair government felt that progress was too slow: too many young people were receiving no systematic training, and, with unemployment coming down, skill shortages were appearing in several regions and industries.

Once again, new institutions were thought to be needed, and in 2000 the government set up the Learning and Skills Council to take responsibility for all post-sixteen education and training, excluding higher education. This

Table 4 Britain's skills deficiency

Stocks of qualified persons as % of all employees in the UK, the US and Germany

		UK	US	Germany
1978/79	Higher	6.8	15.8	7.0
	Intermediate	21.8	11.4	58.5
	Low	71.4	72.8	34.5
1998	Higher	16.6	24.1	13.5
	Intermediate	34.6	18.1	63.8
	Low	48.8	57.8	22.7

Source: Nicholas Crafts and Mary O'Mahony, *A perspective on UK productivity performance*, mimeo, July 2000

was an attempt to give a stronger national direction to the training effort, but it was not clear how the new central body would work with the local Learning and Skills Councils, and there was a danger of bureaucratic confusion in Whitehall. Some observers feared that yet another structural reform, following the bewildering series of changes that had taken place since the early 1980s, would create 'initiative fatigue' without solving the fundamental problem – the lack of incentives for employers to invest in workforce skills.[15]

The creation of the new Council was one of a range of policies aimed at raising standards in education and training. But the government was also criticised for neglecting what was once one of the country's greatest assets but was now in danger of decline – the universities. Although the number of people attending universities had increased during the 1980s and 1990s, this had not been matched by an increase in funding, and there was growing anxiety that the British higher education system was no longer delivering world-class research and teaching. Given the growth of 'knowledge-based' industries, this was arguably a more serious weakness than the deficiency in craft skills. The competitiveness of American firms in information technology and other new industries derived in part from the quality and diversity of the country's universities, most of which had much larger financial resources than their British counterparts. Although the Blair government announced in 2000 that funding for universities would rise by 10 per cent in real terms over the following three years, this was widely regarded as inadequate. In the longer term, a new system of funding, perhaps including the part-privatisation of some universities, would almost certainly be necessary, but this issue was left unresolved.

As for investment in physical capital, this, too, had been a long-standing source of concern in Britain. Throughout the entire post-war period growth rates of capital intensity had been below those of France and Germany.[16] In 1999, according to the government's figures, France had 40 per cent more capital stock per worker than Britain, Germany 60 per cent.[17]

Earlier Labour governments had tended to blame the financial system, and the City of London in particular, for failing to provide industry with capital on the terms that were needed; various proposals had been put forward to solve the problem, including the creation of a publicly-owned National Investment Bank. The Blair government took a different line, preferring to work with the City rather than against it. Although it saw 'a curious mismatch' between the dynamism of Britain's capital markets and the persistence of under-investment,[18] it was not persuaded that the short-termism of British financial institutions lay at the root of the problem. Indeed, it recognised that under-investment had been due in large measure to the volatility of the economy. Noting that since the mid-1990s business investment as a share of GDP had increased faster in Britain than in other countries, the Treasury commented: 'Greater stability in macroeconomic policy had produced greater certainty that interest rates would remain low and hence a more positive climate for investment in physical capital.'[19]

While the government ruled out radical change in the financial system, it believed that the system could be made to work better. Some of the improvements were in the government's power, and several tax changes were introduced to encourage investment. This included a reduction in the marginal rates of corporation tax, moving to a 30 per cent main rate and introducing a new 10 per cent starting rate for the smallest companies. The Chancellor also introduced a number of changes designed to increase the flow of funds into venture capital.

In addition, the government looked to the City for suggestions about how the system might be improved. Paul Myners, head of Gartmore Investment Management, was asked to conduct an inquiry into the behaviour of institutional investors, looking at such issues as whether the institutions were too prone to invest in established companies rather than high-risk start-ups, whether they had the right incentives to tackle underperformance in the companies in which they held shares, and whether the growth of indexation was exacerbating the bias towards companies with high market capitalisations.[20] The first results of the Myners inquiry were proposals to end the 'minimum funding requirement', which limited the ability of pension funds to invest in equities, and to make it easier for these funds to invest in private equity partnerships. Myners made it clear that the thrust of any further reforms would be to eliminate any factors that were distorting decision-making by institutional investors.

Another form of investment which attracted Gordon Brown's attention was research and development. Academics had pointed to the existence of market failure in this field. Investment in R & D often generates knowledge which is difficult to appropriate; because the benefits of one firm's R & D may spill over to other firms, less R & D gets done than would be optimal for society as a whole. Brown accepted this argument and, in his 2000 Budget, introduced a tax credit for small and medium-sized companies; this increased the existing 100 per cent relief on R & D expenditure to 150 per cent. In response to pleas from business, the government subsequently agreed to consider extending the tax credit to all companies.

These changes were part of a wide-ranging programme aimed at increasing the rate of innovation in the economy. Here, too, the US was the model, rather than Germany, and ministers' speeches were peppered with references to the dynamism of Silicon Valley and other high-tech clusters. In 2000 the DTI announced a £1bn programme in association with the Wellcome Trust to promote research in key new areas such as genomics. At the same time the government sought to strengthen links between universities and entrepreneurs through the University Challenge Scheme, providing incentives for scientists to commercialise their inventions.

In contrast to the egalitarianism of Old Labour, the Blair government was more than happy for successful British entrepreneurs to get extremely rich through their innovations. A fair number of them did so when their companies' shares were floated on the stock market, but the government was anxious to ensure that the financial attractions of working for start-up companies were as generous as in the US – hence a variety of moves to make it easier for these firms to grant stock options to their employees. The government's aim was to build a broadly-based entrepreneurial culture, in which more people of all ages and backgrounds started their own business. 'In the US entrepreneurship is widespread because entrepreneurs are highly regarded and well rewarded. In the UK entrepreneurs are still too often regarded as mavericks.'[21]

Whether entrepreneurs needed the additional incentives the government was providing was open to doubt. It was arguable that in the 'dot-com boom' of 1999–2000 too much money went to start-up firms, many of which had poor management and only the sketchiest of business plans. There was also a danger that in devising a variety of incentives for entrepreneurs the government was adding to the complications of an already complex tax system. Yet Gordon Brown was determined to press on with his productivity agenda, and constantly urged industry to rise to the challenge.

At the time of his Pre-Budget Statement in October, 2000, he wrote to the CBI and the TUC calling for a national productivity drive and suggesting that the two organisations should work together on 'an agenda for economic reform'. For employers this suggestion had a disturbing echo of 1960s tripartism, but the Chancellor also said in his letter that the main role of the government was to create an environment in which productivity improvements could take place. 'Within that environment,' the Chancellor wrote, 'government can sometimes do best by getting out of the way.'

Some businessmen felt that 'getting out of the way' was not something that came naturally to a Labour government, even a New Labour one. The director-general of the CBI warned that the government 'must shun new employment legislation and curb red tape and bureaucracy, or businesses will increasingly relocate overseas'.[22] There were also fears that in ' fine-tuning' the tax system to support particular kinds of business activity the government risked distorting behaviour and raising the costs of compliance.

British Industry in 2001

Some of the measures discussed in the previous section will have their effect only in the long term, and it is too early to say whether they will help to lift the economy onto a higher growth path. Even if some of them are dismissed as mere tinkering, it is not obvious that they will do much harm. When the record as a whole is considered, it seems fair to conclude that the Blair government has built on the reforms of the previous two decades, especially in macro-economic policy and in competition policy, and that, with one important reservation, the state of the British economy and British business at the end of its first term of office is healthy. The reservation concerns the exchange rate. The strength of the pound against the euro has clearly damaged parts of manufacturing. What remains uncertain is the extent of the damage, and what the government should have done about it.

According to a recent study by economists at the National Institute of Economic and Social Research, two important factors underlying the improvement in British economic performance since the early 1990s are the fall in inflation and the decline in the cost of capital to firms; the outcome is a more investment-friendly environment than has been seen since the 1960s.[23] 'These changes have been brought about by an improvement in the monetary policy framework in the UK, a world-wide reduction in budget deficits which have helped keep down real interest rates, and a generally helpful corporate tax regime.' The labour market has also behaved exceptionally well, although part of the reason for the absence of wage pressure has been the over-valuation of sterling.

Is this the platform from which the Blair government, if it is re-elected, can achieve its goal of raising the trend rate of growth? Many observers pin their hopes on the so-called 'new economy' – the surge of investment in information technology (IT) industries, including internet-related hardware and software, mobile telephones and computers. These activities are creating a raft of new businesses and altering the way existing businesses are run. The leading nation in the 'new economy' is the US, and the rapid increase in IT investment appears to be partly responsible for the improvement in US productivity growth since the mid-1990s.

There is no evidence as yet that the British economy is benefiting from a 'new economy' effect. Nevertheless, the size of the IT sector in Britain is relatively large compared with other European countries, and in other respects Britain seems well placed to follow the American path. An active and well-developed capital market is helping to shift resources from low-growth to high-growth sectors, and British universities, under-funded though they are, have the potential to make a big contribution to the new industries. In contrast to the days when Britain was the sick man of Europe, this country now has 'a culture and set of free-market policies that is generally supportive of new enterprises'.[24]

None of this brings much cheer to hard-pressed manufacturers struggling with the consequences of the strong pound. Some commentators believe that the Blair government made a serious error in not joining the single European currency immediately after the 1997 election, but the British economy at that time was at a different stage in the economic cycle from its Continental counterparts, and the interest rate appropriate for the euro-zone would have been quite unsuitable for the UK. In these circumstances the government was right to adopt a waiting stance. The subsequent weakness of the euro was unexpected, and it is not at all clear what the government could have done to minimise its effects. The euro began to recover in the early months of 2001, and, with the US economy slowing down, most forecasters expected the improvement to be maintained. Meanwhile the surprising strength of British exports suggested that, despite the problems in steel and cars, British industry as a whole was adjusting quite successfully to the high exchange rate.

The uncertainty over the currency should not detract from the good performance of the economy as a whole as the Blair government comes to the end of its first term. One may deplore the fact that Labour's acceptance of the market economy came in the 1990s, and not – as with the Social Democrats in Germany – in the 1950s. In the intervening period Britain's unreconstructed Labour governments inflicted serious damage on industry, and the legacy of some of those mistakes remains. Nevertheless, the conversion, when it came, was genuine and apparently irreversible.

Notes

1 Speech to the British Chambers of Commerce, 5 April 2000.
2 *Financial Times*, 26 January 2001.
3 *The Cambridge Phenomenon Revisited*, Segal Quince Wicksteed, Cambridge, 2000.
4 Barry Riley, 'The Long View', *Financial Times*, 27 July 2000.
5 *Productivity in the UK: the evidence and the government's approach*, HM Treasury, October 2000.
6 Irwin Stelzer, 'Time to get vigorous with the competition', *The Times*, 16 November 2000.
7 Geoffrey Robinson, *The Unconventional Minister, My Life inside New Labour*, Michael Joseph, 2000, Chapter 12.
8 This distinction is made in Henry Ergas, 'The importance of technology policy', in Partha Dasgupta and Paul Stoneman (eds), *Economic policy and technological performance*, Cambridge, 1987.
9 Neil Millward, Alex Bryson and John Forth, *All change at work? British employment relations 1980–1998*, Routledge, 2000.
10 *Productivity in the UK: the evidence and the government's approach*, HM Treasury, October 2000.
11 McKinsey Global Institute, *Driving productivity and growth in the UK economy*, McKinsey and Company, October 1998.
12 Mary O'Mahony, *Britain's productivity performance 1950–1996*, National Institute of Economic and Social Research, 1999.
13 S.J. Prais, *Productivity, education and training*, Cambridge, 1995.
14 Hilary Steedman, Howard Gospel and Paul Ryan, *Apprenticeship: a strategy for growth*, Centre for Economic Performance, London School of Economics, October, 1998. For a critical review of recent training policy, see Ewart Keep and Ken Mayhew, 'The assessment: knowledge, skills and competence', *Oxford Review of Economic Policy*, Vol 15, No, 1, Spring 1999.

15 Ewart Keep and Ken Mayhew, 'The assessment: knowledge, skills and competence', *Oxford Review of Economic Policy*, Vol 15, No 1, Spring, 1999.

16 Nicholas Crafts and Mary O'Mahony, *A perspective on UK productivity performance*, mimeo, July 2000.

17 *Productivity in the UK: the evidence and the government's approach*, HM Treasury, October 2000.

18 HM Treasury, the 1998 Pre-Budget Report, Cmd 4076.

19 *Productivity in the UK: the evidence and the government's approach*, HM Treasury, October 2000.

20 *Institutional investment: a consultation paper*, the Myners review of institutional investment, HM Treasury, May 2000.

21 *Our competitive future, building the knowledge-driven economy*, the government's competitiveness White Paper, Department of Trade and Industry, 1998.

22 Digby Jones, director-general of the CBI, quoted in *Sunday Business*, 5 November 2000.

23 Richard Kneller and Garry Young, 'The new British economy', paper delivered to the NIESR conference on 'Technical progress, economic growth and the new economy', 29 September 2000.

24 David Finegold, 'Creating self-sustaining, high-skill ecosystems', *Oxford Review of Economic Policy*, Vol 15, No 1, Spring 1999.

© Chris Riddell

Chapter 11

THE FINANCIAL SECTOR

Delegation, unification and optimism

Peter Sinclair[1]

1. Introduction

THE FOUR YEARS from May 1997 have witnessed several important changes in Britain's financial sector. The Bank of England gained the power to alter official short-term interest rates at the start of the period. This change highlights the theme of delegation in the chapter's title, and is discussed in Section 2 of this chapter. Section 3 turns to the issue of regulation and supervision of Britain's financial firms, responsibilities for which were united under a new agency, the Financial Services Authority. This represents the theme unification. After a brief survey of some major changes in the institutional geography of the UK financial sector in Section 4, we turn to Section 5 to the behaviour of Britain's financial markets for bonds, equities and foreign exchange, all of which displayed signs of volatility and euphoria in at least the first three of these four years. Hence the optimism in the chapter's title.

2. Granting Instrument – Independence to the Bank of England

A few days after taking office in May 1997, the incoming Chancellor of the Exchequer announced that henceforward it would be the Bank of England, not the Chancellor, that set key short-term official interest rates. This change had been mooted in previous policy pronouncements that the Labour Party had made in opposition. Doubtless the proposal had been agreed with the new Prime Minister. But the announcement took all observers by surprise.

A rise in the short-term interest rate tends to lower inflation over the following two years. By making credit more expensive, and increasing the attractiveness of saving, it dampens consumer demand, and tends to reduce firms' investment spending. Mortgage interest rates rise in response, so that implies weaker demand in the housing market. The foreign exchange rate for sterling should appreciate, exerting negative pressure on the trade balance, and moderating any rise in import prices. Lower aggregate demand for UK goods and services translates into a reduction in the demand for labour, so that pay increases tend to fall. The end result should be lower inflation.

Inflation is widely agreed to be a costly nuisance. Suppose its costs rise with its square, so that 10 per cent annual inflation does four times more damage than inflation at 5 per cent per year. This means that inflation at 1 per cent or 2 per cent per year is only a trivial irritant, but that rapid inflation must be avoided. Against this, suppose that *unexpected* inflation brings benefits, say at a constant marginal rate. Unexpectedly rapid inflation might imply lower unemployment and larger output, for example. Alternatively, it may lead to a fall in the real value of government debt because at least some of that debt is a fixed obligation expressed in money terms. This will be helpful because distortionary, welfare-reducing taxes (such as income tax) are levied to service government debt and meet the interest charges on it.

If expectations of inflation are always realised, there is no unexpected inflation; then inflation is unambiguously harmful, and an objective policy-maker will want to set it at a zero rate. (In what follows, we shall assume that inflation rates can be set costlessly and immediately, with no error. In practice, it is short-term official interest rates that act as the main levers to control inflation, but these levers work slowly, with far from predictable effects, exerting their main influence on the price level over a span of up to two years or more.) In the long run, expectations of inflation should be realised, on average at least, so optimal long-run inflation is zero. If expectations of inflation are initially fixed, however, a policymaker who is concerned only with welfare here and now – for the next period, say – will perceive benefit from delivering inflation at a positive rate.

In the next page or two, we shall consider a simple mathematical example that illustrates the key ideas. This part of the chapter will be in italics; some readers will wish to study it, while others may omit it if they want. In words, the essence of the argument is this. The policymaker is attracted by the temporary benefit that a little bit of unexpected inflation brings. But he will worry about the fact that if he does this, generating some unexpected inflation, market participants will expect higher inflation later. This is unambiguously damaging. For the present, the policymaker must make a statement of his intentions about inflation. The market will give him the benefit of doubt initially, but will only trust him if he adheres to the inflation rate he had promised. To be credible, an inflation promise must be such that what the policymaker gains from keeping to it is no less than what is lost, in terms of broken trust. By delegating inflation-control to an independent agency that is conspicuously less inflation-prone or more far-sighted than he is, the policymaker can ensure that lower credible inflation promises can be made. That way, the rate of inflation stays down at a lower level. Everyone can gain as a result.

Suppose that the 'short-term' optimal inflation will equal b if the policy-maker's objective is to maximise, $b(p - p^e) - (p^2/2)$, for instance. Here p denotes the rate of inflation, and p^e its expected value (taken as given). A myopic policymaker, who observes p^e is given, will set inflation at b in this example, while one with only long-run concerns will seek to deliver no infla-tion. Now imagine that the policymaker announced an inflation target, t. The private sector, let us say, gives him the benefit of the doubt, for one period, and sets p^e at t. If the target is met, p^e will remain at t. If the policymaker reneges on the target, delivering inflation at its short-term optimal value of b, the 'dis-cretionary' rate, then p^e will go up to b for the following period.

Having announced the inflation target t, the policymaker now considers the benefits and costs of sticking to it. The cost is the short-term gain from setting inflation at b, rather than t. Comparing the welfare function under the two cases gives costs of $(b - t)^2/2$. The benefit, on the other hand, emerges in the following period, when p^e will be t if the target has been met and b when inflation is set at the discretionary rate. If welfare in the following period receives a weight of c against welfare in the current period (c = 1 if there is no shortsightedness on the policymaker's part, but c<1 otherwise), the present value of the benefit from delivering inflation on target will be $c(b^2 - t^2)/2$.

An inflation target is credible if the benefit of honouring it is no less than the cost. The optimal credible target equates benefit with cost in present value terms. This will be where $t = b[(1-c)/(1+c)]$. As this formula shows, t will increase with the welfare weight on inflation surprises (b) but fall if the welfare weight for next period (c) goes up.

When a politician sets at a credible inflation target, then, and has respon-sibility for delivering it (for example, by setting interest rates), we should see inflation at the rate $b[(1-c)/(1+c)]$. The politician will be influenced by elec-toral considerations. Winning the next election may be uppermost in his or her mind. There is also the chance that the politician may be moved to another government portfolio, or be displaced. This can only make his per-sonal value of c less than one. If c = 2/3, t will be b/5 for example; with c = 1/2, t = b/3. With inflation delivered on target, welfare in any period will be $-b^2/50$ in the first case and $-b^2/18$, a larger number, in the second.

With control of interest rates delegated to a central bank with, let us assume, no discounting at all (c = 1), the minimum credible inflation target falls to zero, and welfare is higher (it will be zero, not negative as before). In general, if c^* is the central bank's weighting on next period's welfare, and b^* its weighting on the benefit of surprise inflation, the minimum credible inflation target is $b^*[(1 - c^*)/(1 + c^*)]$.

With $b^*<b$ and $c^*>c$, central bank interest-rate setting will permit a lower credible inflation target, less inflation, and higher welfare even from the politician's standpoint, than if control over interest rates is retained by the politician. In sum, everyone gains if interest-rate setting powers are delegated to the central bank.

This argument has been based on an extended version of a model first constructed by Barro and Gordon (1983). Barro and Gordon's model prompted a huge literature, in which the contributions of Backus and Driffil (1985), Rogoff (1985) and Vickers (1986) stand out. The first paper to study the benefits of delegating inflation-control and inflation-setting to a central bank was by Rogoff (1985). It is the ideas developed in these papers, and illustrated here, that form the cornerstone of Gordon Brown's decision to grant the Bank of England instrument-independence in 1997.

The case for doing this has not gone unchallenged. One objection has been political: should monetary policy not be controlled by a government answerable to Parliament and electors? Another centres on criticism of the notion that positive inflation surprises bring gains in the form of higher output and lower unemployment, while a third is directed at the econometric evidence about inflation adduced by proponents of the case for central bank independence. For a sceptical view expounding these arguments and others, the interested reader is referred to Forder (1996). A comprehensive recent analysis of the issues and worldwide experience can be found in Fry *et al.* (1996).

Post-1997 British arrangements represent something of a compromise between full central bank independence, and democratic accountability to Parliament. Interest rate decisions rest with the Bank of England's Monetary Policy Committee. This meets monthly, announcing its interest rate decisions on Thursdays at noon. The Committee has ten members. There is one Treasury member, who has no vote, but observes and participates in discussion. Of the nine voting members, four are external independents, chosen by the Chancellor of the Exchequer for terms of (up to) four years. The Committee is chaired by the Governor of the Bank of England, appointed by the Crown (that is, the Prime Minister). The remaining four Bank members consist of two Deputy Governors, again appointed by the Crown, and two senior Bank officials whose appointments are subject to Treasury ratification. All new members of the Monetary Policy Committee appear before a House of Commons Select Committee, but do not require its confirmation. All nine voting members have equal votes. Individual votes are published, as are minutes two weeks later.[2]

Currently, an inflation target is set by the Chancellor of the Exchequer. The Chancellor could choose to set some other target, for example for the value of sterling, or a target for the price level at some future date. Throughout the period since 1997, the target has been defined for the rate of inflation. The target has been set at 2.5 per cent per year. The rate of inflation is defined as the annual increase in a version of the Retail Price Index, from which the effects of mortgage interest changes have been removed (RPIX). Around the 2.5 per cent target there is a 2 per cent tolerance zone, 1 per cent above and 1 per cent below. Should the annual inflation rate stray outside this zone, and to date it never has, the Governor of the Bank of England would write an open letter to the Chancellor. Such a letter would explain why the target has been missed, how long the Monetary Policy Committee believes the discrepancy will persist, and what the Committee will do to bring inflation back to the target. So the target is symmetric – there is no inflation ceiling (as with the European Central Bank) – and overshoots above and below the range trigger an outcome, in the form of a Governor's letter.

Before May 1997, control of interest rates rested with the Chancellor, not the Bank of England. But the change is perhaps less radical than appears at first sight. After October 1992, a previous Chancellor, Norman Lamont, instituted an inflation target. Departure from the Exchange Rate Mechanism of the European Monetary System meant that some alternative anchor for the price level was now urgently needed. Later on, monthly meetings were instituted between the Chancellor and the Governor of the Bank of England. The Governor gave advice on interest rates. A summary of their discussion was published, making it plain to all when the Bank of England's advice was not taken. Furthermore, the Bank of England was charged with the responsibility of publishing a quarterly Inflation Report, the most recent of which appeared in February 2001. These important documents have appeared regularly ever since, changing format very little after the May 1997 changes.

The Inflation Report examines the course of inflation, present and past, and the behaviour of numerous macroeconomic variables to which it is linked (output, production, the components of aggregate demand, statistics for money and credit aggregates, exchange rates, equity and house prices, unemployment rates and many other variables). The Report concludes with 'Fan Charts' giving modal (most likely) forecasts for the course of inflation and real GDP over the ensuing two years, with anticipated possible deviations in 10 per cent probability slices. The Fan Charts give a concrete, numerical picture of the degree of confidence attached to the modal forecasts. There are always risks that inflation may rise or fall, and these risks may not be symmetric. A small chance of a large fall in equity prices, an increasing preoccupation for the Committee since 1999, makes for a lop-sided distribution, with some probability of much lower inflation a year or two later. A small chance of a large fall in the external value of sterling would have the opposite effect, as it feeds into much higher sterling import prices.

The official interest rate that had been controlled by the Chancellor until 1997 was Base Rate. Previously, until 1972, it had been known as Bank Rate, which was then replaced by Minimum Lending Rate. In 1998 the key interest rate for control purposes changed again: it was now the repo rate. This was the rate at which the Bank of England would effectively grant its open market counterparties a fortnight's credit against UK government bonds (gilts).

Long-term interest rates provide some measure of how the market reacted to the granting of instrument independence to the Bank of England. At the end of March 1997, the annual yield on index-linked, almost fully inflation-proofed Treasury bonds maturing in 2016 was 3.62 per cent. Three months later, after the change was announced, it was barely changed at 3.63 per cent. Yields on these bonds give a good measure of long-term real interest rates for the UK.

Hypothetical twenty-year unindexed bonds, stripped of their coupon, are calculated to have given annual yields of 7.8 per cent at the end of March 1997, and only 7.1 per cent three months later. The difference in yields between indexed and unindexed bonds provides a measure of the market's expectations of the annual average rate of inflation over twenty years. On this showing, expectations of the UK's annual inflation rate for this period fell by 0.71 per cent across the three months. Over the year from end-March 1997, the market's implicit inflation expectations fell even more, by 1.65 per cent.

Other things were happening in 1997 and early 1998. Perhaps the most important was the continued non-appearance of faster actual inflation, in the UK to some extent but more importantly in the US, despite large continuing falls in unemployment in both countries. This welcome development will have lowered further inflation expectations in the US and the UK, and contributed to large falls in long-term bond yields abroad. The Asian Crisis of 1997–98 also lowered UK inflation, because the sterling price of imports from the countries affected fell after their devaluations. Even allowing for these effects, however, there is still an appreciable fall in the unindexed-indexed bond yield differential. This indicates that the financial markets concurred with the Chancellor's decision to forswear the control of interest rates, and also with the logic, about the greater credibility of Central Bank inflation commitment, that underlay it.

3. The Financial Services Authority

Two weeks after announcing that interest-rate setting powers would transfer to the Bank of England's Monetary Policy Committee, the Chancellor unveiled radical plans to recast the supervision and regulation of Britain's financial institutions.

These responsibilities had hitherto been divided between no fewer than nine different agencies. Unit trusts, life insurance companies, and stockbroking firms for example all fell under the purview of different regulatory bodies. In the case of the commercial banks, it was the Bank of England that supervised, exercising this function for more than a century. In addition to the Bank of England's supervisory role, the Financial Services Authority was to absorb the Registry of Friendly Societies, the Friendly Societies Commission, the Building Societies Commission, the listing activities of the Stock Exchange, the Insurance Inspectorate (which had formed part of the Treasury), and three self-regulating bodies. These last were the Investment Management Regulatory Organisation, the Personal Investment Authority, and the Securities and Futures Authority.

Before 'Big Bang' in 1986 (which put an end to fixed brokers' commissions) and associated legislation in the early and middle 1980s covering other areas in Britain's financial sector, the City of London displayed strong lines of demarcation. Retail, deposit-taking banks were quite different from building societies which specialised in mortgage lending. Discount houses which bid in weekly auctions for Treasury bills were distinct from merchant banks that concentrated on advising companies on external finance, mergers and acquisitions. All these differed in their turn from stockbrokers or insurance companies. Horizontal links between financial firms in different sectors were not unknown, but rare.

By the late 1990s, such segmentation was becoming a fading memory. Financial supermarkets had emerged, offering a vast range of services, sometimes directly, sometimes through subsidiaries or affiliates. Some building societies were demutualising, opting instead for bank status as public limited companies. Banks had started to offer mortgages in the early 1980s, but now emerged as a major player in this market. Savings deposits which had previously been lodged with banks or building societies were confronted by growing competition from money market funds and other products.

In such a context, this blurring of boundaries made existing supervision and regulatory arrangements look increasingly anachronistic. This was especially true in the wholesale field, where mergers and associations between commercial and investment banks made the distinction less and less visible. It was also believed that some regulatory bodies had been rather too trusting of the companies in their charge, too apt to weigh suppliers' interests more heavily than consumers', or insufficiently insistent on immediate changes in the event of trouble. There was growing evidence, for example, of the gross mis-selling of private pensions in the early and mid 1990s, practices which the then regulators had apparently failed to detect or rectify.

So supervision and regulation of the separate, but now barely distinguishable, groups of financial firms, would now need to be brought together, perhaps best in a single institution.[3] But where? Possibly the Bank of England, but, in the light of the previous decision to grant it instrument independence, this might seem an unwarrantedly large accumulation of responsibilities. It may have been believed by some that regulatory or supervisory concerns might somehow infect or compromise the independence of key monetary policy decisions over interest rates with which the Bank had just been entrusted. And since failures of banks and other financial institutions can never be entirely eliminated, perhaps it is as well that those charged with responsibility for monetary policy are saved the embarrassment that such failures could otherwise bring. Furthermore, it will have been seen that a number of countries, including Canada, Denmark, Finland and Norway, had never placed regulation and supervision within the central bank. Against this, amalgamating monetary policy decision-taking with supervising and regulating the complete financial sector could have some advantages. Examples might include the rapid and dependable flow of crucial information, and the opportunities for coordination in activities which were so clearly related.

Chancellor Brown was persuaded by the first set of arguments, not the second. The Financial Services Authority was created, to begin operating in 1998. It was enshrined in legislation by the Financial Services and Markets Act, which passed in June 2000. The new Financial Services Authority's first head would be the Bank of England's then Deputy Governor, who took with him nearly five hundred colleagues from the Bank's supervisory wing. The FSA also inherited some 1000 staff members from the other separated regulators it replaced. By late 2000, no fewer than 9275 financial firms operating in the UK were operating under FSA regulation.

From the outset, the FSA was given four main formal responsibilities. One is to strengthen confidence in the UK financial system, and a second to secure an appropriate degree of consumer protection. The remaining two objectives are the promotion of public understanding about the financial system, and contribution to the reduction in financial crime. The FSA was to be funded by levies upon the businesses within its purview. The justification for this is the notion that all such firms have an important interest in ensuring that the British financial system as a whole should be safe, honest and dependable. Each, if left to itself, would, however, choose to devote a little less resources to ensuring that its own affairs were kept in perfect order, than it would like other firms to spend on this. So an element of collective action and monitoring is needed. The FSA's task is to provide this.

Formally, the FSA has four statutory objectives. These are:

(i)   to maintain confidence in the financial system;

(ii) to promote public understanding of the financial system, including the awareness of the benefits and risks associated with different kinds of investment or other financial dealing;

(iii) to secure the appropriate degree of protection for consumers, having regard to the different degrees of risk involved in different kinds of investment or other transactions, the different degrees of experience and expertise that different consumers may have in relation to different kinds of regulated activity, the needs that consumers may have for advice and accurate information, and the general principle that consumers should take responsibility for their own decisions; and

(iv) to reduce the extent to which it is possible for a financial services firm to be used for a purpose connected with financial crime.

Under the post-1997 arrangements, financial stability, as opposed to supervision and regulation, would be an area in which the Bank of England retained important responsibilities, particularly in respect of systemic risks, that could threaten the rest of the banking system when a single financial firm fails. Safeguarding financial stability in practice means several things. It entails trying to devise an infrastructure and a set of incentives within financial institutions, and ensuring flows of timely and accurate information, that protects the payments and banking systems from the ultimate disaster of a financial collapse. A further aspect of financial stability activities involves discussing and formulating revisions to international agreements on banks' minimum capital adequacy and risk exposures, together with the Financial Services Authority and similar supervisory and central banking authorities in other countries, through the medium of the Bank for International Settlements. The Bank would also co-operate with the Financial Services Authority and the Treasury in resolving a financial crisis. Collapses can and do happen: the United States saw a third of its banks fail in the early 1930s, greatly aggravating that country's then exceptionally prolonged and deep recession. Collapses also occurred, more recently, in Indonesia, Korea and Thailand in 1997–98, and chronic fear of them contributed to the distinct lack of sparkle displayed by the Japanese economy during the 1990s and the early 2000s. This aspect of Britain's new arrangements is still to be tested. Fortunately there have been no crises emanating from within the British financial system since 1997. So we have no experience of how the new system might operate in practice.

Whether this allocation of functions between the Bank of England on the one side and the Financial Services Authority on the other, is found to have enhanced competition, innovation, consumer welfare and confidence in Britain's financial firms only time will tell. What matters most in this respect is perhaps not so much who performs particular functions, as how well they are done. One factor that makes evaluation difficult in this area is the fact that more competition in the financial system, whatever its advantages, may bring greater risks.[4] In comparison with a more competitive industrial structure, a few better-padded banks may produce too little and charge too much, but their greater profits could well make serious financial crises less likely.

4. The Institutional Geography of Britain's Financial System

In 1998, the last year for which full figures are available, the top seven British banks had a total of £1079 billion of assets. This vast sum is equivalent to some sixty-one weeks of national income. It has been grow-ing by some 5.5 per cent faster than GNP at current prices. The largest of the seven banks measured by assets was Barclays, which held 20.3 per cent of the assets of all seven banks in 1998, as against 21 per cent a decade earlier. Barclays was not, however, the most profitable although its most recent annual profits, announced in 2001, climbed in £3.5 bil-lion). For some years the Lloyds-Trustee Savings Bank group has enjoyed this position, earning about a quarter of the seven banks' total pre-tax profits. In assets, Lloyds-TSB ranks fourth, with 15.5 per cent, behind not just Barclays but also National Westminster (17.2 per cent) and Abbey National (16.4 per cent). Abbey National's share of assets has more than doubled in the past twelve years, while National Westminster's has receded from 22 per cent. Fifth by asset size in 1998, with 13.4 per cent, came Halifax, which nearly doubled its share in a decade, followed by Midland with 9.7 per cent and the Royal Bank of Scotland, Scotland's largest bank, with 7.4 per cent.

Amalgamations, demutualisations and increasing foreign penetration of the UK banking sector, broadly defined, were the prominent trends in the mid and late 1990s. In 1997, Lloyds had recently merged with TSB, and Midland had just been taken over by the Hong Kong and Shanghai Banking Corporation (HSBC); but Midland's traditional logo and name were to disappear from Midland's 1700 branches only in 1999. In 1999, Barclays acquired the Woolwich, the Birmingham and Midshires Building Society was absorbed by Halifax and the Standard Building Society trans-ferred to the Mercantile Building Society. In 1997 Bristol and West was acquired by the Bank of Ireland, and the Greenwich absorbed by Portman. In 2000, the Royal Bank of Scotland won a contested takeover bid for the National Westminster group, beating its local rival the Bank of Scotland. The period saw several other mergers and takeovers too. Early in 2001, Lloyds TSB announced a bid for Abbey National.

Building societies, and many insurance companies, were traditionally owned by their customers. In the late 1990s, several converted to Public Limited Company status. Customers, whether policy-holders or deposi-tors, shared lump-sum payments on flotation of the firm's shares. This had begun in 1984 with Abbey National (formerly the Abbey National Building Society). Among mutuals to adopt PLC status in or after 1997 were the Alliance and Leicester, Halifax, Northern Rock and Woolwich Building Societies, and Norwich Union, a leading insurer.

From a strictly English perspective, the increasing foreign participation of the British banking industry was evidenced by the Royal's takeover of National Westminster in 2000, and HSBC's earlier acquisition of Midland. Among many changes in the merchant banking arena, Morgan Grenfell was acquired by Deutsche Bank, and Kleinwort Benson by Dresdner Bank, changing its name to Dresdner Kleinwort Wassestein in 2001. British mer-chant banks are now all but extinct. The City of London is now like

Wimbledon Tennis – a very celebrated institution, dominated by foreigners, that is located in Britain.

5. UK Financial Markets, 1997–2000

The period since mid-1997 has witnessed, as we saw in the context of the Bank of England's new powers to set short-term interest rates, a large rise in the prices of long-dated unindexed bonds. Since such bonds are claims on a stream of coupon payments, which are fixed, and a known sum of money when they are redeemed at maturity, a rise in market value goes hand-in-hand with a fall in the rate of return upon them.

The 1997–99 rise in British government bond prices, of up to 32 per cent on some of the longest maturities, was modest, however, in comparison to the gains on most UK shares. From 1 May 1997 to 1 January 2001, the *Financial Times* all-share price index advanced by over 50 per cent. This comprehensive measure is expressed in sterling, and is not adjusted for inflation (which registered 8.1 per cent for the period as a whole). On average real capital gain of some 11.1 per cent per year over this period. This is a little lower than in New York, where the Dow Jones grew at 12.8 per cent per year in constant dollars over this period. German shares also grew faster, on average, on a constant purchasing power basis, but registered a slower growth rate than the *Financial Times* Index in nominal sterling terms because of sterling's appreciation against the euro. While all the main North Atlantic economies witnessed strong share price rises in the late 1990s, this did not extend to Japan, where stocks drifted slightly downwards in real terms, nor to some other Southeast Asian economies, particularly Indonesia, where severe falls were observed.

In both Britain and the United States, where the boom has run a little faster still, share prices trended upwards, in real terms, for almost nineteen years. This makes it history's longest recorded bull run. The bull market faltered in 2000, with a slide in the value of telecommunication and equity stocks after March, but wider-based share price indices displayed only a minor weakening in late 2000 and early 2001, in both Britain and the US. The *FT* Index is currently nearly six times higher in real terms than its all-time low in January 1975, and more than 60 per cent above an earlier peak in May 1972.

Many factors could be offered as possible explanations and justifications for the big increase in share prices. There could have been a fall in long-term real interest rates, which would merit higher capital values of given dividend streams. There could have been a rise in the long-term growth rate of the economy, to which profits and dividends should ultimately respond one-to-one. There could have been a rise in the profit share of income. There could have been a fall in the apparent riskiness of shares, as evidenced, for example, in lower variance relative to trend, or 'volatility'.

There might have been a large fall in the current or expected future rates of tax on capital and capital income. Quoted companies might be accounting for a larger share of national income. The shares of household income devoted to saving and net equity purchase could have gone up. Each or any of these developments could have made the share price jump quite explicable.

Has any of these phenomena occurred? Most measures of real interest rates for the late 1990s and 2000, in the UK and more especially the US, suggest that they are not historically low. In the US, labour productivity has certainly been rising faster since the mid-1990s than in previous decades, but, in the opinion of many observers, the overall change is relatively modest, with most of the advance confined to durables and information-technology sectors. In the UK, the long-term growth rate of real GDP, now believed to be a little above 2.5 per cent per year, is very close to the 1991–95 average. It is, however, clearly an improvement on the considerably slower growth recorded in the decade from 1973, and in Britain and the US what has been surprising is not so much the rate of growth after 1992 but the fact that it continued virtually uninterrupted for eight full years. Britain's profit share of income did advance sharply on most definitions from 1991 to 1995, but it has slipped much of the way back since. Share price volatility on a daily or weekly basis has tended to rise, not fall. There have been some changes in relevant tax rates, but, in Britain's case, probably the most important has been the less lenient treatment of pension fund investment income. This change, announced in 1998, increased Exchequer tax receipts by £6 billion per year. The latest 1990s fashion for outsourcing and downsizing has tended to reduce the ratios of quoted companies' gross receipts and value added to national income. Finally, the household sector in the US and the UK does appear to channel a higher proportion of its savings into equities. But in 2000, the ratios of household saving to household income are historically very low, sharply down on their average values in the mid and early 1990s.

In other words, there is, unfortunately, rather scant support for the view that the higher equity prices of 1999 and 2000 are supported by fundamentals. If shares are correctly priced now in terms of these fundamentals, they must have been seriously mispriced – much too cheap – in the past. Alternatively, if it is long-term average share prices that were correct, Anglo-American equities are currently too expensive, and likely, sooner or later, to fall. The weakening of share prices, particularly in information technology and telecommunication sectors, that occurred in 2000 and early 2001 suggests that market sentiment has begun to pay more attention to this alternative view.

There was one recent period where the logic of the previous paragraph could have taken hold on UK market sentiment. This was in the late summer and early autumn of 1998. In both August and September, the *FT* all share price index fell by about 7.6 per cent. In October shares continued to slip but November saw a rally that cancelled over half of the previous three-months' decline. Broadly parallel movements were observed in Wall Street.

It was probably not so much worries about whether current equity prices could be reconciled with fundamentals that explained the share price slide in the late summer of 1998. More important was the fear, keenly felt but soon to fade, that the previous year's financial crises and recessions in much of Southeast Asia would puncture the bubble-boom in the North Atlantic economies. In the event, GDP growth in the UK and the US did slacken late in 1998, but growth was still positive, and soon resumed strongly in early 1999.

It was not just UK equity prices that appeared to defy gravity in the years 1997–2000. The same was true of sterling, at least in relation to the German mark and the other currencies that would melt into the euro.

There are some 180 currencies in the world, of which over 150 are independent of each other. Since over one half of Britain's overseas trade is conducted with Eurozone countries, the euro-sterling exchange rate is of paramount importance to the UK, followed by the US dollar (the United States accounts for an eighth of British trade). But the overall value of sterling against a trade-weighted average of foreign currencies can be affected by other exchange rates, too. An effective exchange rate (EER) for sterling is constructed to depict an appropriate average of all movements.

Sterling's EER had declined by some 14 per cent in the wake of its departure, on 16 September 1992, from the European Union's Exchange Rate Mechanism (ERM). When the Labour government assumed power on 2 May 1997, sterling's EER was back to its 1990 value, having appreciated sharply in the last quarter of 1996. By May 1997, sterling bought almost as many Deutschmarks as it had before leaving the ERM.

Sterling's subsequent movements, between May 1997 and January 2001, were complex, but the trend was broadly upward at least until the last four months. Sterling's EER climbed 4.4 per cent in the last quarter of 1997 and the first of 1998. It lost all these gains in the last nine months of 1998, only to see them restored in the course of 1999. In 2000, sterling advanced by a further 4 per cent against the euro, but fell 8 per cent against the US dollar, leaving the EER little changed.

The EER for the euro (and its predecessor, the European Currency Unit) fell by some 3.8 per cent in 1997, and a further 2 per cent in the first quarter of 1998. The last nine months of 1998 saw it rise by 6.5 per cent, but it fell steadily through most of 1999 and 2000 (recovering some lost ground in the last two months of 2000 and the first two months of 2001). These two years witnessed a total decline of over 12 per cent. By the end of 2000, the euro's EER was 10 per cent below what it had been in mid-1997. The US dollar's EER witnessed a 4 per cent rise between these points, and the Yen's EER, which was particularly volatile, climbed overall by nearly 10 per cent.

One central factor propelling sterling and the US dollar upwards against the German mark and other euro currencies between 1997 and 2000 was the higher level of UK and US short-term interest rates. Both averaged between 2 per cent and 2½ per cent above their German and ECB counterparts. In some respects this represents a puzzle: in tranquil conditions, one would expect a currency on which higher interest rates can be earned to *depreciate*, in the long run, at least, against those where interest rates are lower. Risks aside, wealth-holders should allocate their portfolio so as to earn equal total rates of return on all assets, so a higher rate of interest ought to be offset by the anticipated capital losses that come from depreciation. If one country has to offer higher interest rates on its currency than its neighbour, the argument runs, this is because its currency is expected to slide.

In the euro case, against sterling and the dollar, this normal long run relationship failed to materialise, therefore, particularly in 1999 and much of 2000. Why was this? When a country raises its short-term interest rate, the immediate effect is to attract capital inflows from overseas. Usually this generates appreciation. One way of viewing this is to reason that the currency has to jump, to create room for its subsequent depreciation in line with the new interest differential. There is also another mechanism at work. The ECB's reluctance to increase short-term interest rates on the euro in 1999–2000, despite a weak exchange rate, may have been interpreted, possibly wrongly (since it was explicitly not committed to any exchange rate target), as a signal that it was prepared to see the exchange rate stay low, and even weaken further. Foreign exchange market participants spend much time trying to read policymakers' minds. One element in the former's thinking in 1999 and 2000 may have been the fact that unemployment in Germany and Italy was at or close to historic highs, and showing little sign of falling. Unemployment in Ireland and the Netherlands was low and dropping quickly, and moving downwards (if still historically quite high) in both France and Spain. But the depressing state of German and Italian labour markets dominated these developments in the aggregate statistics for Euroland as a whole. The European Central Bank, on the other hand, is preoccupied above all by its 2 per cent ceiling for average inflation of the geographical area under its domain, and the aggregate statistics for monetary growth. In its estimation, it was not until the late spring of 2000 that these data warranted any increase in interest rates.

In broad terms, the Euroland macroeconomy was only in the early stages of a business cycle upswing in 1999 and 2000. In the UK, and the US, by contrast, real GDP had been growing at or above trend, with falling unemployment, since as far back as the end of 1992. Previous business cycle upswings in America and Britain had averaged three to five years' duration, and often less; the upswings that began in 1992–93 were already exceptionally longlasting. Short-term interest rates tend invariably to climb as upswings mature, because of the growing need to curb inflation as labour market pressures multiply. Interest rate increases would attract overseas capital, and almost inevitably trigger temporary upward pressure on exchange rates. By contrast, much as ECB officials might express disquiet at the slide of the euro, in public or in private, the sluggishness of the giant German and Italian macroeconomies would tend to deter them, until mid-2000 at least, from raising euro interest rates sufficiently to reverse it. In the autumn of 2000, and early 2001, a combination of higher ECB interest rates, and foreign exchange market intervention to buy the euros by the ECB and other central banks, the Bank of England among them, led to a 6 per cent rise in the euro's value in sterling.

Sterling's tumble in the autumn of 1992 had increased Britain's external competitiveness sharply. At what were then very high levels of unemployment, British money wage rates were rising very slowly. So the gains to Britain's competitiveness were not eroded by rising labour costs. Exports grew rapidly in response. Sharply lower interest rates through subsequent years, and a large recovery in profits, both contributed to a strengthening of investment. Higher levels of exports and investment provided the platform for Britain's long upswing in the years that followed. A decade and more earlier, sharp appreciation of sterling had generated a steep recession (from 1979 to 1981–82). There were therefore widespread fears in the later 1990s that sterling appreciation would strangle the recovery and trigger a return to high levels of unemployment.

Dearer sterling was indeed to cause serious difficulties, and large labour-shedding, in a number of sectors of the UK economy exposed to overseas trade. Agriculture lost over 75,000 workers between 1997 and 2000. Employment also declined sharply in steel, coal-mining and microchip production. In vehicle assembly, Japanese transplants continued to prosper, but large falls in employment began to be implemented in the two largest plants, at Dagenham (Ford) and Longbridge (the Rover works, sold off by BMW). In 2001, General Motors announced that it would close its Vauxhall plant in Luton. In all these cases, the high external value of sterling was a prominent consideration. There were also heavy job losses in the financial sector in these years, particularly the larger banks, where exchange rate appreciation was not an issue: the banks were anxious to maintain profits and reduce costs in the face of growing competition for depositors' funds from other institutions and financial instruments, and in anticipation of a future possible downturn. The 1990–93 recession had led to losses on bad loans of over £10 billion, so great as to threaten their very survival under existing ownership.

For much of the rest of the UK economy, the years 1997–2001 were a period of continuing strength in production and employment. Labour shedding in agriculture, coal, steel, vehicle assembly, microchips and banking was more than offset by employment increases elsewhere. Most of the service sector saw rapid employment growth. A high external value for sterling was no grave threat here. If anything, it was favourable in its effects, because importable inputs fell in price, and their products could be sold to a buoyant domestic economy, sheltered from any serious threat from imports. Cheaper imports also helped to increase workers' real wages, and relieve pressures for higher pay. Given that domestic expenditure was high in the UK in the later 1990s, the net effect of sterling appreciation on these 'non-traded' sectors was if anything probably a positive one. As the Governor of the Bank of England put it (George, 2000),

> . . . our problem – and it is a real problem, as we have recognised for some time – is the imbalance, within the overall economy, between the domestically oriented businesses and sectors, and those that are most internationally exposed.

Britain opted to stand aside from the European Monetary System in 1997, but to consider entering it at a later date. The Labour government's policy was 'Prepare and Decide'. It is not in principle opposed to entry, and will, if reelected, decide in the next Parliament whether to recommend it to the British people in a referendum. It announced that its decision is to be based upon five tests:

(i)   Has the UK economy achieved sustainable convergence with the twelve economies employing the single currency (Austria, Belgium, Finland, France, Germany, Greece, Ireland, Italy, Luxembourg, the Netherlands, Portugal and Spain)?

(ii)   Is there sufficient flexibility in the UK economy to adapt to change and other unexpected events?

(iii) Will joining the single currency create better conditions for businesses to make long-term decisions to invest in the UK?

(iv)   How would membership impact upon the UK financial services sector?

(v)   Would joining the single currency be good for employment?

The main benefits of joining the euro, in the view of the Governor of the Bank of England (George, 2000), would be twofold. There would be the effects of confidence in a fixed nominal exchange rate, and the reduction of the spreads, for example between lending and borrowing interest rates, that could come from the broadening and greater liquidity of an enhanced, integrated capital market. The first effect stems from the fact that some 55 per cent of British exports go to the twelve countries in the euro area, and joining the euro would bring the prospect of much greater stability in the gains from this trade. Furthermore, the costs of converting one currency into another constitute a barrier to trade, not a large barrier perhaps, but, unlike tariffs for example, not a barrier that gives the consolation of any government revenue. Lowering the gap between interest rates charged to borrowers and interest rates paid to lenders, which an enlarged financial market may bring, would constitute a major advantage to both groups, and could well stimulate faster long-run growth.

Against this, there is the problem of 'one interest rate fits all' in a monetary union. With member countries all at similar points in their business cycles, and with similar fiscal positions, this would bring no difficulties. But disparities, caused for example, by asymmetric shocks, good or bad, that affect these countries differently, would mean that some members of the monetary union would have to accept monetary policies that were less than ideal from their national standpoint. Deprived of the option of devaluing or lowering interest rates in response to an adverse shock, such countries would have to rely upon other mechanisms to combat it: adjustments in fiscal policy for example, or the possibly slow and untrustworthy devices of migration or wage adjustments.

Conclusions

Within the first weeks of the Blair government, two radical decisions were taken. These would entirely reshape the oversight and operation of policy towards Britain's financial and monetary system. One was to grant interest rate setting powers to the Monetary Policy Committee of the Bank of England. The other entailed amalgamating the supervision and regulation of all Britain's financial firms within a single authority, the Financial Services Authority. The first decision has commanded a very wide degree of approval, and for sound reasons. The second has much to justify it, too. Britain's financial sector experienced four years of broadly falling interest rates, a strong positive movement in equity prices, and a sharp rise in sterling. Only in the last year did equities begin to wilt, and then somewhat selectively, while sterling started to edge downwards only late in 2000. On perhaps the most important issue of the period, whether sterling should join the euro, the accent was on preparation, with decisions, by cabinet, Parliament and people, left until after the general election in the event of a Labour victory.

Notes

1 The author thanks Bill Allen for his many helpful comments, and exculpates him from any remaining errors.
2 Rodgers (1997) and its three annexes set out these new arrangements in full. They were passed into law in the Bank of England Act, 1998.
3 The arguments for amalgamating regulation and supervision of all financial firms within a single regulator are set out powerfully and discussed by Briault (1999). See also Goodhart (2000) and Briault (2000).
4 For more on all these issues, the reader is referred to Sinclair (2000) and Brealey et al (2001).

© Chris Riddell

Chapter 12

EMPLOYMENT RELATIONS POLICY

Robert Taylor

'UNIONS KNOW AND accept that from a Labour government they can expect fairness not favours, but fairness will be a big advance on the open hostility they have had from government in the past fifteen years. It will give unions a fair chance to adapt to the new world of work. It will give them an opportunity to work for new members and to campaign for the future in new areas of concern to people at work. Government will provide the framework. It is up to unions themselves to take advantage of the opportunities that that framework provides.'[1]

'Trade unions will have no special or privileged place within the Labour Party. It is in the unions' best interests not to be associated merely with one party. The influence of the trade unions will come from being a broad voice of working people, not a direct party political voice or one that is concerned for the narrow interest of individual unions.'[2]

'We will not be held to ransom by the unions. We will stand up to strikes. We will not cave in to unrealistic pay demands from anybody.'[3]

'I want to focus on an agenda for trade unions as authors for individual empowerment in skills, on the enhancement of individual opportunity so we can really build a platform for a second term. Where unions can play a part is in increasing people's skills, in issues of pensions, helping with financial and legal problems. And without getting back into old-style corporatism, there are some good things government and trade unions can do together.'[4]

A New Relationship

The above range of quotations from the public utterances of Tony Blair provide graphic evidence of his often cool, detached and ambivalent attitude towards the role that he thinks Britain's trade unions ought play in the political economy. It should therefore come as little surprise to know that as Prime Minister he devoted a considerable amount of his personal time and attention to the evolution of the government's employment relations strategy during its first term than to many other areas of public policy. Employment relations always threatened to become a sensitive area for decision-making in government, capable of provoking discord over the character of New Labour's modernisation project, which deliberately sought to develop a positive and intimate relationship with business and a more arms-length and unsentimental one with the trade unions. Moreover, his handling of employment relations provides an important test for any assessment of the authenticity of the Blair effect by making it clear just how far the Prime Minister was prepared to go in ensuring a decisive break was made with past Labour government practice in handling the trade unions.

In its relations with the Trades Union Congress, Blair was determined to emphasise that his government would neither seek out nor establish any special alliance with them on the lines pursued with varying degrees of enthusiasm by all his post-war Labour predecessors at 10 Downing Street – Clement Attlee, Harold Wilson and Jim Callaghan. There was to be no formalised and bilaterally negotiated Social Contract with the TUC comparable to that which had existed in the 1970s and definitely no return to the once familiar 'beer and sandwiches' routine of the past where Labour Prime Ministers, mainly under external economic pressure from international financial markets, sought to negotiate agreements with the TUC, especially requiring wage restraint in the supposed national interest.

As Mr Blair explained in the first speech he delivered to TUC delegates at the September 1995 Congress after his election as Labour party leader which he had won with overwhelming trade union numerical support: 'We have an obligation as a government to listen, as we do to employers. You have the right to persuade, as they do, but the decisions, however, as you know must rest with us. We will be the government and we will govern for the whole nation, not any vested interest within it. That will be the distinction between ourselves and the present Conservative government.'[5] Blair also used that famous occasion to warn the trade unions that if elected to government New Labour would not restore all the favourable industrial relations legislation they were supposed to have enjoyed before Margaret Thatcher's arrival in office in May 1979. 'There is not going to be a repeal of all the Tory trade union laws. It is not what the members want, it is not what the country wants. Ballots before strikes are here to stay. No mass or flying pickets. All those ghosts of the past,' declared Blair. The party leader won a round of applause from most delegates for saying so, a clear sign he would not have to face any rearguard action from the majority of unions, who accepted there would be no restoration of supposed lost glories.

In such pronouncements he was not really departing very noticeably from the public position of his two predecessors as Labour party leader – Neil Kinnock and John Smith. The party's 1992 general election manifesto had promised to create a 'fair framework of law for both employers and unions' if Labour formed the next government but it emphasised there would be 'no return to the trade union legislation of the 1970s'. Much of Labour's employment relations agenda in the early 1990s – a legally-enforceable national minimum wage; minimum individual and collective rights at work; an end to the UK's opt-out from the European Union's 1991 Maastricht treaty social chapter – was inherited by Mr Blair. Indeed, little of detailed substance except for the always sensitive issue of union recognition was added to the party's employment relations programme after 1994. But there was certainly a change in the tone and style in which it was presented to the wider electorate. The new leader was determined to exorcise any lingering belief that the trade unions would somehow dictate his agenda without pressing for any formal break in the party's historic links with them.

Blair's attitude to the trade unions was not only free of sentimentality about the collectivist ethos of Labourism but it also reflected his personal conviction that in much of their behaviour the trade unions were often more part of the country's problems than part of the solution. Indeed, a clear continuity was evident in Blair's acceptance of the fundamental characteristics of the Thatcherite industrial relations settlement of the trade union question which Labour had fought against in opposition. In fact, in his basic attitude towards organised labour, Blair shared many of the views which were held by Conservatives during the 1980s. He believed – like Margaret Thatcher – that her industrial relations reforms (especially the introduction of compulsory pre-strike ballots and postal ballots for union leadership elections; an end to mass and secondary picketing; abolition of the closed shop) had made a 'continuing and beneficial effect' on the quality of workplace life. Blair argued that it was not just that those legislative changes had provided management with the right to manage again and thus ensured investment was once more regarded as the first call on profits rather than the last. In addition, they also helped to ensure a positive change in the attitudes of employees in the businesses for which they worked and in which they increasingly held shares. Indeed, Mrs Thatcher's supply side reforms, designed to weaken trade union power and influence, were more or less explicitly accepted almost in their entirety by Mr Blair. There was never any suggestion that a Labour government might repeal the key provision in the 1982 Employment Act that made trade union funds liable to sequestration or unions open to fines in the case of behaviour by them deemed unlawful by the courts. This change was the crucial hinge from which all else had followed. Once trade unions found themselves subject to the threat of civil action in the courts with the loss of legal immunities they had enjoyed since 1906, they were compelled to tread with caution and restraint in their industrial behaviour. The realisation that New Labour had no intention of restoring that vital freedom of immunity from civil liabilities in unlawful industrial conflicts went a long way to convince the trade unions they would need to restructure themselves if they were to exercise any positive influence on Mr Blair.

His personal attitude towards them reflected deep-seated doubts about the role he believed the trade unions had played in the history of the Labour Party that they were responsible for creating. Blair believed, in particular, that Harold Wilson had made a strategic error when Labour Prime Minister in the summer of 1969 by not seizing the opportunity opened for him to push through industrial relations reforms designed to make trade unions legally responsible for their behaviour in inter-union as well as unofficial disputes. Blair's criticism of trade unions was not confined to what he saw as their often obstructive attitude to post-war Labour governments. He also believed too many of them remained trapped in a time-warp, hostile to his ideas of modernisation and yearning for a return to what they remembered fondly as the good old days when they were portrayed simplistically as overmighty subjects. In fact, Mr Blair wanted to see nothing less than a cultural revolution taking place inside the trade union movement, bringing an end to the block vote fixing and negative posturing many unions continued to display in what he was coming to regard as the long lost world of Labourism.

During his period as shadow employment secretary between October 1989 and May 1992, Blair grew to dislike what he saw as the often aggressive and arrogant ways of some trade unions, especially those who continued to defend the use of the closed shop as an acceptable method for enforcing their collective power in the workplace. Despite facing personal abuse from activists in the printworkers' union, the National Graphical Association, for his decision, Mr Blair accepted, in December 1989, the Conservative government's move to outlaw all closed shops (whether pre- or post-entry). As a quid pro quo, however, he agreed that all individual workers must have the legal right to decide whether or not they should join a trade union. This commitment was in line with Labour's endorsement of the European Union's social charter. Moreover, Blair stood out firmly against senior party colleagues during 1993 in his principled if isolated stand in support of the introduction of one member one vote in the selection of Labour parliamentary candidates to replace the use of the trade union block vote in the process. Although he was still prepared to tolerate the historic and organic link between the trade unions and the party, Blair was determined that New Labour must not be beholden to such vested interests when in government.

In fact, he had come to the conclusion that many trade unions were obstacles to the Labour Party's capacity to modernise itself successfully.

Their agendas – Blair believed – still often reflected a limited producer group self-interest which was not only irrelevant to the needs of the Middle England that Labour needed to accommodate in order to win general elections but were out of touch with what most of their own rank-and-file members actually wanted. Blair liked to point out he was not born into the Labour Party. He was untouched by the ethos of Labourism and impatient with the party's often arcane customs and traditions, especially those that related to its 'contentious alliance' with the trade unions. Indeed, he was convinced that the trade unions had made a strategic mistake at the TUC 1899 Congress in voting for the creation of a separate political organisation to represent the labour interest independent of the Liberal Party. In initiating the formation of the Labour Party – he maintained – they had helped to ensure Britain experienced a predominantly Conservative-dominated twentieth century because of the division in the forces of centre-left progressivism. Moreover, Blair's repudiation of the politics of class, with which many trade unions were still identified, was fundamental to his ideological outlook. His close political friend Chancellor Gordon Brown was as much a New Labour moderniser as he was but unlike Mr Blair he went out of his way to keep in close touch with many trade unions. It is true much of this looked more like a matter of symbolism and gesture than substance as he talked vaguely of an old-time and essentially romanticised form of socialism. But the earnest and austere biographer of James Maxton, the millenniarian Red Clydesider of the inter-war years, Brown at least made an effort to identify himself with the historic roots of the Labour Movement for all his equal commitment to New Labour's modernising cause.

In fact, Mr Blair wanted New Labour under his leadership to become much more closely identified not with the trade unions but with the aspirations of the business community, with entrepreneurial success, risk-taking and the new world of information technology, innovation and small and medium-sized enterprises. To him, the trade unions looked increasingly like potentially dangerous political liabilities, evoking a bygone age of cloth caps, mills and pits, of sunset not sunrise industries. Of course, his picture was often lurid, simplistic and exaggerated. It reflected a tabloid view of trade unions. But it was one that Blair shared with the coterie of New Labour modernisers – notably focus group impressario Philip Gould, his press secretary Alastair Campbell and cynical spin-doctor Peter Mandelson – who came to influence him more closely than others after his election as party leader.

Both Blair and Brown were keen to reassure corporate Britain that it would have nothing to fear from the election of a Labour government. In March 1997 they even produced a business manifesto, designed to spell out the employer-friendly strategy Labour would implement. There was no similar document for the trade unions or workers. Brown, in his foreword to the manifesto, promised Labour 'would not turn the clock back to the

1970s in industrial relations because we know that flexibility is vital for business to prosper'. 'It is business not government that creates lasting prosperity,' opined Brown. 'The job of government is not to tell people how to run their businesses but to do what it can to create the conditions in which business can thrive and opportunities for all can flourish.'[6]

In spelling out the very limited and modest nature of its plans for industrial relations reform, the business manifesto even went so far as to reassure employers they would not have to reinstate any employees to their former jobs who claimed and then won unfair dismissal compensation awards before an employment tribunal even if this had occurred as a result of perfectly lawful industrial action. It was clear that New Labour was quite ready and willing to ignore or flout international labour conventions signed by past UK governments that had sought to establish protections for the basic rights of workers who wanted to exercise their freedom to strike without facing employer sanctions for doing so.

The Prime Minister's deeply questioning attitude towards the trade unions was not always on public display. After all, he needed to establish a modus vivendi with them. But within four months of Labour's landslide election victory in May 1997, Mr Blair was repeating his familiar warnings to them that he would tolerate no return to the divisive industrial politics of the past. 'I will watch very carefully to see how the culture of modern trade unionism develops. We will keep the flexibility of the present labour market and it may make some shiver but in the end it is warmer in the real world,' he lectured the September 1997 Congress.[7] 'Let us not make people think trade unions are someone you have to be forced to talk to. By your actions let us make it impossible to dismiss trade unions as old fashioned, defensive, anti-progress and activist dominated.' His patronising remarks angered many delegates. More seriously, they incensed the TUC, because they seemed to ignore deliberately the genuine modernising effects that were being made by its general secretary, John Monks, since September 1993 to restore the credibility and influence of the trade unions after a long period of ineffectiveness on the sidelines of the political economy.

But Mr Blair remained unrepentant about what he had said. He revealed even stronger feelings about the trade unions that day soon after his Congress speech. He and Monks were standing on the balcony of his room at Brighton's Grand Hotel in the last glows of an Indian summer afternoon.[8] The TUC general secretary suggested to him that perhaps he had been a bit rough on the trade unions in his speech. But Blair replied that Monks ought to recognise the trade unions were still in deep trouble. Their memberships had been in decline for nearly twenty years. They were dominated by middle-aged white men from decaying sectors of the economy. They were suffering from a genuine delusion if they believed his government was simply going to ride to their rescue. Moreover, they seemed ill-equipped to meet the challenges of the new world of work. Their structures were often archaic and obsolete. They were prone to internecine

conflicts which might well worsen as rivalries grew more bitter in potentially damaging competition over trade union recognition. While he was
certainly impressed by some of the TUC's recent activities, Blair also questioned just how far Monks's New Unionism message was actually travelling
outside the corridors of TUC headquarters and had become genuinely
rooted among union activists in many workplaces. He even wondered
whether Mr Monks could really count on the enthusiastic support and
commitment of many senior union leaders of the TUC general council to
back him up in the implementation of his modernising project. At best, the
Prime Minister remained sceptical about the willingness of the trade unions
to reform themselves and turn their backs on their recent past. Mr Monks
sought to convince him that such a bleak analysis was wrong but he admitted that this was going to take time. Blair's reflections at Brighton's Grand
Hotel that September afternoon suggested he retained a serious doubt over
whether Britain's trade unions were really capable of revival to take a constructive role in the making of the new thrusting pro-enterprise society he
wanted to help create. The Prime Minister's opinion reflected his fear that
most union leaders were simply not prepared to come to terms with the fact
that they were not going to enjoy a return to the powers and influence they
had allegedly enjoyed under previous Labour administrations.

During his first term Blair always felt that he needed to be convinced
that most unions inside the TUC were genuine in their commitment to
New Unionism and that the ideology of social partnership and cooperation
that he also claimed to believe in was not merely confined to Mr Monks
and his close full-time colleagues employed in Congress House. His grudging, luke warm attitude towards them undoubtedly encouraged insecurity,
unease, irritation and frustration among many trade union leaders on
whether he could be trusted to carry out what he had promised in opposition. As a result, employment relations policymaking under Mr Blair often
turned out to be rather disorganised, hand to mouth, uncertain, a seemingly
endless process of backroom lobbying between competing vested interests
and government departments with no sense of any ultimate finality.

In fact, the Prime Minister's unyielding refusal to tolerate a return to the
reputedly bad old ways of industrial relations disguised the fact that New
Labour was committed to what many people regarded as a substantial
and wide-ranging agenda of workplace reform. Often to the pleasant surprise of many trade union leaders, Mr Blair was ready – though perhaps
often through gritted teeth and against his own basic instincts – to go a
substantial way towards the accommodation of their immediate policy
demands in line with what had been Labour policy before his election as
party leader. But it is important to acknowledge that he always made it
clear that his support for an employment relations programme should be
seen only as a vital part of a much wider modernisation agenda. This covered the entire political economy from prudent financial policies, a
commitment to modest levels of state spending to a more vigorous support

for training, from measures to maintain economic and fiscal stability and low inflation to those aimed at stimulating greater competition through forms of deregulation and tax incentives. Moreover, the envisaged employment relations strategy was not to be regarded as some kind of pay-back or reward for the trade unions or an attempt to restore their former legal privileges. On the contrary, Mr Blair's objectives for workplace change were to be made compatible with an ambitious project, designed to reward individual opportunity and success, to encourage innovation and technology, to ensure education and learning secured the highest priority, to stimulate partnership agreements between companies and their employees, to emphasise the need for yet more and not less labour market flexibility, and above all to seek a reconciliation between social equity and economic efficiency. This was a determined effort to resolve Britain's enduring if familiar problems of low productivity, poor rates of return on capital and supply side labour market restrictions on job creation. As the Prime Minister liked to argue, the partnership approach he favoured in the workplace was to be combined with 'the pursuit of strong markets, modern companies and the creation of an enterprise economy'. In fact, the Prime Minister's attitude to the trade unions in 1997 was undoubtedly helped by the relatively benign economic inheritance – low inflation, modest wage increases and falling unemployment – he was bequeathed by the outgoing Conservative government. There was simply no pressing need for him to turn to the TUC for any assistance in tackling the country's macro-economic ills. Nor was any obligation imposed on him to establish a formalised special relationship with the trade unions even if they had proved loyal and generous financial contributors in helping ensure his general election triumph.

The New Employment Relations Agenda

However, despite the Prime Minister's apparent lack of sympathy for them, the trade unions secured a substantial public policy programme of achievement from him during Labour's first term in office (see the appendix at the end of this chapter) even if few of their leaders were ready to demonstrate much more than grudging public gratitude for what they received and Mr Blair often tended to under-play the magnitude of what by UK standards turned out to be a quiet workplace revolution. The TUC described the 1998 Fairness at Work White Paper, which set much of the agenda, as representing 'the biggest advance in workers' rights for a generation'.[9] While they may have failed to secure the repeal of all the hostile legislation passed against them between 1980 and 1994, trade union leaders were realistic enough, except for the now ineffective and fringe figure of Mineworkers' Union president Arthur Scargill, to know a return to the 1970s era had never been remotely likely since the later years of Neil Kinnock's leadership.

In his preface to the Fairness at Work White Paper, Mr Blair claimed that even after the implementation of promised workplace reforms, the UK would continue to have 'the most lightly regulated labour market of any leading economy in the world'.[10] But this questionable assertion, which irritated many union leaders, did nothing to reassure many employers who complained that they were being compelled to swallow an array of regulations in their business establishments which might be of some minimal advantage to their employees but brought a burdensome cost to them in money and time that might be better spent in improving their corporate performance. No doubt, much of the rhetorical hostility levelled at the government's employment relations proposals by companies and employer associations was ritualistic and ill-directed. In most respects, workplace reform under Mr Blair turned out to be the minimum required to close the substantial gap in legal rights and obligations that existed between the UK and mainland Europe employment practice. As average productivity rates remained from 20 to 30 per cent higher in the business establishments of the UK's main European trading competitors, it did not seem that the existence of more comprehensive social regulations had acted as a severe barrier or disincentive to corporate achievement elsewhere in the European Union. However, Mr Blair was always determined to develop and maintain close and friendly relations with private sector employers and seek to bring them into his government's policymaking process. He did not regard the substantial programme contained in the White Paper as a threat to their primary business interests. On the contrary, he made considerable efforts to try and address the worries of companies and ensure they were not neglected.

The often tangled and complex procedures that led to the eventual implementation of the 1999 Employment Relations Act underlined the crucial importance of the Blair effect. What he was seeking to do was to try and encourage trade unions and employers into what was in the UK a new form of employment relations based on the concept of social partnership. The Prime Minister's implicit but clear aim was to bring an end to the old, sometimes adversarial, culture of voluntarism that had characterised relations between capital and labour for much of the twentieth century. Blair sought to stress the common interests that bound companies and their employees together and not their differences. He argued the government's important White Paper 'steered a way between the absence of minimum standards of protection at the workplace and a return to the laws of the past. It is based on the rights of the individual whether exercised on their own or with others as a matter of their choice. It matches rights and responsibilities. It seeks to draw a line under the issue of industrial relations law.'

From the outset, the Prime Minister sought out consensus between capital and labour over trade union recognition and the new worker rights imprecisely promised in New Labour's 1997 general election manifesto. He was keen to prevent accusations being made that the government favoured the imposition of heavy legal regulations to further the cause of trade unionism on the shoulders of unwilling employers. Mr Blair said he wanted to see agreement reached on a lasting industrial relations settlement that would survive beyond the lifetime of only one Parliament. But little of real detail had been decided before Labour's victory in May 1997. The union recognition issue had even threatened to destabilise the party's campaign on one occasion, revealing a lack of clarity about what was being proposed and raising misplaced fears that it was an Old Labour demand that would lead to the return of trade union power.

It was initially left to Ian McCartney, the MP for Ashton in Lancashire, to sort out what needed to be done as a Minister of State at the Department of Trade and Industry under a sympathetic Margaret Beckett as its President. Energetic, knowledgeable and incisive, McCartney had already displayed his diplomatic skills to Mr Blair by winning over an initially hostile business community to acceptance of the principle of a statutory national minimum wage through a shrewd campaign of persuasion. Given what seemed initially like a relatively free hand, he set to work by combing through Labour's previous employment relations policy commitments to draw up a substantial list of individual and collective workplace rights for implementation. He was helped in his task by John Cruddas, a party official, established by Mr Blair in 10 Downing Street specifically as a liaison officer or point-man with the trade unions, the TUC and the often-overlooked but crucial trade union group of Labour MPs that had been reconstituted before the election.

However, it was also evident from the beginning that McCartney at the DTI and Cruddas at Number 10 would not be drawing up the government's employment relations policy undisturbed by direct personal involvement from others. The Prime Minister's policy unit was never to be a coherent and unified force on this subject as on many others. On the contrary, the two men were faced with loyalist modernisers who were much closer to Mr Blair's sceptical views of trade unionism and who suspected they were too close to TUC thinking on the subject. Peter Mandelson – former TUC staffer himself in his post-Oxford University days – sought to press the business case against too much overtly pro-union legislation when Minister without Portfolio inside the Cabinet Office. Geoff Norris, a former party researcher, was appointed to the 10 Downing Street policy unit, paralleling Cruddas's role with the unions, with the task of keeping in close personal touch with employers' organisations and companies and filtering their thoughts through into the policy process. But with full backing from Mrs Beckett and most of the DTI senior civil servants, McCartney and Cruddas were determined to compile a maximalist reform agenda for employment relations as a tactical manoeuvre for later bargaining purposes. The more they proposed, they reasoned, the more difficult it would be for any internal opposition in 10 Downing Street to remove all of their proposals.

Indeed, McCartney was keen to ensure that the employment relations agenda was written up in the inclusive language of New Labour and seen as an integral part of the government's wider modernisation programme. Contrary to suspicions of some of the Prime Minister's personal advisers, he was neither a conduit for the TUC nor a passive go-between. On the contrary, he believed trade unions must not hanker for the return of former powers but become key representative agencies of transformation in the promotion of workplace change. McCartney wanted to test the genuineness of their declared commitment to reform. What he sought was not to give or return benefits to trade unions for their passive enjoyment but provide them with the opportunities to respond positively to the challenge of new legal rights in the workplace. In other words, he wanted to lock the trade unions into the Blair agenda by offering them a new legitimacy after years of often malevolent neglect. He was working towards the Prime Minister's limited conception of social partnership and not away from it.

At the 1997 Congress Blair called on the TUC and the CBI to try and work together in harmony by reaching a compromise agreement on future employment relations reform, particularly over the contentious issue of trade union recognition. It was clear that the Prime Minister was simply not prepared to rubber stamp the TUC's initial bargaining stance. In particular, he rejected the view that recognition in a workplace should be conceded to a trade union merely through its achievement of a simple numerical majority of those actually voting in a secret ballot. The Prime Minister insisted that trade union recognition by a company ought to require clear proof of a much broader base of rank-and-file support, necessitating a specific proportion of all workers voting in favour of the proposition. He also argued smaller companies should be exempt from the union recognition procedures. Perhaps inevitably the TUC and the CBI were unable to find enough common ground to negotiate a deal satisfactory to both sides. But this did not deter Mr Blair from making further efforts to gain a wider understanding that might assuage business discontents.

By the early spring of 1998 John Monks accepted it would be necessary for the TUC to go some way to meet the Prime Minister's views, fearing the whole recognition issue might be lost unless the unions were prepared to compromise in the face of Mr Blair's intransigence. This was fuelled by employer concerns, especially from the national newspaper industry where trade unions had been unilaterally derecognised in the late 1980s after News International's move from Fleet Street to Wapping and a new world of work practices free from the stranglehold of the print unions with their craft mentality towards technological change. Monks won the TUC general council's approval to what was a crucial shift in his organisation's bargaining position. Now he proposed that a trade union would need to secure a 30 per cent threshold of support from workers in a bargaining unit in order to win a recognition ballot. Inevitably the CBI rejected that threshold figure, arguing it was far too low and calling instead for a 50 per cent vote of those in the proposed bargaining unit.

In the event, the trade union recognition issue went to Cabinet in May 1998 for a collective decision. By splitting the difference between the TUC and the CBI positions on the voting majority required, ministers agreed to the proposal that a trade union would need the backing of 40 per cent of workers eligible to vote to secure recognition. Monks welcomed the outcome, describing the Fairness at Work White Paper as 'a comprehensive package with many real advantages for people at work'.[11] Once the TUC general secretary had shifted ground over the threshold figure for recognition, Mr Blair seemed to accept any further concessions to the business lobby would have undermined Monks's position, something he did not want to do. In fact, the final outcome of the White Paper brought some unexpected concessions to the TUC. It allowed, for example, a trade union to win automatic recognition from an employer where it could prove it already had over 50 per cent membership. This offered trade unions another more attractive route to recognition than going through a cumbersome and risky legal procedure by encouraging them to launch recruitment campaigns to gain the required number of members for recognition. The White Paper also gave all workers – whether they were trade unionists or not – the right to representation or accompaniment by a union official or somebody else when involved in disciplinary or grievance procedures. The overall balance of the document seemed to suggest that the TUC had secured more from the complex lobbying process than employers. By focusing on the mechanism for recognition ballots, attention had been diverted from the issues of automatic recognition and rights to representation that now alarmed the CBI and many employers.

In fact, the White Paper's publication was not the end of the struggle. During the rest of the year the CBI, the Engineering Employers' Federation, the Federation of Small Businesses and other business lobbyists battled on behind the scenes to convince the Prime Minister that too much ground had been conceded to the trade unions on recognition. Rupert Murdoch's News International hired a consultancy firm to pile on the pressure. The arrival of Mr Blair's close friend Lord (Charlie) Falconer at the Cabinet Office in the summer of 1998 strengthened those at the heart of government who wanted to minimise workplace reform in response to the business lobbying. Union leaders even feared Blair might now be persuaded to abandon the whole recognition issue in the face of stiff employer resistance. By December 1998 it was certainly evident that the employers had clawed their way back into contention through effective pressures being applied on the Prime Minister, Lord Falconer and Mandelson, who had replaced Mrs Beckett as Trade and Industry Secretary. The CBI's director-general, Adair Turner, claimed he had 'made considerable progress' in making the proposed legislation 'more workable'.[12] As a result of employer representations, the union recognition procedures were made much more complex, potentially litigious and time-consuming. A trade union would not be able to secure automatic recognition in a proposed bargaining unit by demonstrating it had 50 per cent plus one of the relevant workers in membership if the revamped independent Central Arbitration Committee believed such a move would 'not be conducive to sustainable and good industrial relations'. Employers would still be able to dismiss workers in lawful disputes if a conflict lasted more than eight weeks. The proposed bargaining unit in a recognition bid would have to be compatible with 'the need for effective management'. It was agreed the level of compensation to workers in cases of unfair dismissal would be capped at a maximum of £50,000 and not left open as had been proposed in the White Paper. Monks had fought hard against the watering-down of the White Paper, ending up with a particularly bruising confrontation with Mr Blair at 10 Downing Street and finding allies among many Labour MPs across the party's spectrum. But in the end he accepted the unions had secured more than perhaps many of them had felt would be possible at the beginning of the process. Of course, without Ian McCartney's diligent involvement it may have proved even more difficult than it turned out to be. The Prime Minister was particularly sensitive to any suggestion that he had somehow caved in to trade union threats. The willingness of the CBI to go along with the final settlement was perhaps more important to him than upsetting a few union leaders over the details of the recognition procedures.

New Labour and Social Partnership

The tangled policymaking process over the Fairness at Work White Paper proposals in 1998–99 demonstrated there was not going to be any exclusive bilateral arrangement between the government and the TUC. The support or at least the passive acceptance of employers was a crucial factor in pursuing successful workplace reform. This reflected the Prime Minister's keenness to draw successful entrepreneurs into his social and political circle. He was perhaps over-impressed by the glittering world of big business, convincing himself that the private risk-taking sector was much better able to manage and thrive than stuffy, hide-bound public administration. Mr Blair sought to utilise the talents of the rich and famous in his widespread use of patronage in appointments to innumerable task forces, study groups and other advisory bodies that sprang up under his government. It is not quite true that trade union leaders were completely deprived of the fruits of patronage. Bill Morris, general secretary of the Transport and General Workers' Union, was appointed to the Bank of England's governing body. Ken Jackson, loyalist general secretary of the AEEU engineering union was knighted. A number of other trade unionists were given peerages – most notably Bill Jordan, former AEEU president and general secretary of the Brussels-based International Confederation of Free Trade

Unions and David Lea, former TUC assistant secretary. Liz Symons, former general secretary of the senior civil service trade union – the First Division Association – was made a working peer and served as a junior minister at the Foreign Office and later the Ministry of Defence. Alan Johnson, once modernising general secretary of the Communication Workers' Union and then Labour MP for Hull West, became Minister for Competitiveness at the Department of Trade and Industry with particular responsibility for liaising with the TUC after McCartney was shunted into the relative obscurity of the Cabinet Office. But there was no substantial figure inside the Cabinet whom the union leaders could look to for consistent support in any policy differences they might have with Mr Blair. Neither the Chancellor Gordon Brown nor John Prescott, the Deputy Prime Minister were willing to play such a role.

Although the TUC was not compelled to use the tradesman's entrance into 10 Downing Street to see Mr Blair, formalised visits by trade union delegations were few in number during the early years of the New Labour government, although Mr Monks was often more in close, personal touch with the Prime Minister. Mr Blair, for understandable reasons, was keen to maintain good relations with the TUC general secretary, although these could on occasion be subject to considerable strain as he also appeared at the same time to seek out bilateral advice from selected members of the business community.

But Mr Blair was not prepared to revive forms of institutional tripartism that could bring together the TUC, the CBI, other business organisations and non-governmental bodies in self-standing new independent public bodies. In every other European Union country social dialogues and social pacts as well as macroeconomic national economic policy co-ordination, are commonplace, reflecting the continuing important role being played by trade unions and employer associations in the successful management of their political economies. But in Britain such ideas have found little favour with Mr Blair. It is true he raised the issue of creating a stakeholder economy in his famous 1995 Singapore speech but this was soon to be forgotten. Nor did New Labour in government display much early active interest in reforming corporate governance to make employers more accountable not just to their shareholders but to their employees, suppliers and customers. Little progress was made either in pressing for greater social responsibility to be displayed by companies. Mr Blair was noticeably silent over the massive pay rises secured by many company chief executives for themselves, fuelled by share options and gold-plated remuneration packages, that widened the already substantial earnings gap between the very top and the rest of the workforce. There is no reason to suppose he did not agree with the view of his close friend Mandelson when the Trade and Industry Secretary assured an audience of entrepreneurs in Silicon Valley, California that New Labour was 'intensely relaxed about people getting filthy rich'.[13] What limited commitment there was to any redistribution of wealth and income did not deflect from the Prime Minister's belief that the marginal income tax rate should go no higher than the 40 per cent figure he had inherited from the Conservatives for those earning £33,000 a year or more.

When discussions were held between Mr Mandelson and Bodo Hombach, German Social Democratic Chancellor Gerard Schroeder's adviser, in their preparation for a joint Third Way/Neue Mitte document in the spring of 1999, it was made quite clear that the Prime Minister was not interested in 'building a social consensus with the trade unions on urgent problems and current reforms' because such a national partnership would 'raise the spectre of the 1978–79 winter of discontent' which had characterised the final months of the last Labour government.[14] It was noticeable, however, that the Germans insisted on making an explicit reference to the fact that 'immediately upon taking office the new Social Democratic government gathered the top representatives of the political sector, the business community and the trade unions around the table to forge an Alliance for Jobs, Training and competitiveness'. Such an arrangement was far removed from Mr Blair's agenda or way of thinking. In his vision trade unions were to enjoy only a limited role in the workplace, mainly as an aid to adding value to companies.

The only kind of social partnerships New Labour often seemed willing to tolerate were those that were voluntarily negotiated between companies and trade unions with a commitment to workplace modernisation. It is true there were some piecemeal, ad hoc initiatives designed to bring the trade unions into certain policymaking areas. Mr Blair was keen to encourage TUC and CBI involvement in the development of a training and learning agenda as well as in holding joint one-off conferences on such pressing matters as the information economy. Chancellor Gordon Brown invited the TUC and the CBI, in October 2000, to participate in joint discussions with him on how to tackle the UK's productivity failures. But for the most part, Mr Blair preferred informal, bilateral arrangements to deal with specific industrial relations and employment issues. His personal dislike for even limited forms of institutional corporatism, co-ordination or social partnership at national level that were once commonplace in Britain during the 1960s and 1970s was partly driven by the Prime Minister's fear that such a development might be interpreted as a return to the perceived failures of the past by giving the trade unions a new legitimacy in macro-economic management.

There was, however, one noticeable and successful exception to Mr Blair's dislike of social dialogues and pacts. He agreed to the formation of an independent Low Pay Commission as an advisory body in determining the level of the national minimum wage. Its first chairman was George Bain, then head of the London Business School and later Vice-Chancellor of Queens' University in Belfast. With a distinguished record of public service achievement stretching back to the 1960s, Bain was trusted by the TUC as well as most employers. His colleagues on the Commission were drawn from the TUC, the CBI, trade unions and academia. They sought to work by consensus and they did so with considerable success over a subject that might have so easily divided them. Indeed, the pragmatic and empirical diligence of the Low Pay Commission with its old-fashioned commitment to evidence-gathering and inquiry seemed to reflect the professional public values of a long-gone era before the arrival of spin doctors and focus groups came to trivialise and debase so much of political life. To a considerable extent, the politics of the Commission were of more direct concern to Mr Brown than Mr Blair. The Chancellor's high-handed interference often proved to be arbitrary and imperious as he rode roughshod over Commission sensitivities. On occasion, the Commission even had to seek out support from 10 Downing Street in the face of Treasury intransigence. But for the most part, the Commission worked effectively and it quickly became a respected body. Certainly the TUC could point to its early work as clear evidence of how successful a broad-based approach embracing employers and unions could be in public policymaking. 'Unions continue to believe that change in the world of work is best delivered through dialogue and partnership,' explained Monks. 'It remains axiomatic for the TUC that major national questions of labour market policy are best solved through the engagement of government, the TUC and the CBI. This is not ancient dogma but has been reinforced by our experience since 1997.'[15] In his opinion, the social partnership approach to the formation of the national minimum wage had ensured its introduction with 'a minimum of fuss'. Monks contrasted this exercise favourably with the government's disorganised implementation of the European Union's working time directive that introduced a maximum forty-eight hour working week by agreement and four weeks' paid annual holiday. Here, parallel lobbying by the TUC and assorted employer associations on 10 Downing Street and the Department of Trade and Industry produced what Monks rightly called a 'canine repast of regulations', revealing what could result when 'no open or honest exchange of views occurred between the social partners'.

New Labour and the Business Lobbies

The existence of conflicting institutional sources of power and influence between the Trade and Industry department and the Prime Minister's policy unit was to lead to an often untidy, cumbersome, sometimes ineffective and prolonged method for reaching agreed decisions. The process of parallel negotiations and the prospect of bilateral deals aroused considerable unease and displeasure from the TUC which came to fear that the business community, especially the CBI, was being provided with too much influence over 10 Downing Street thinking. From their perspective union leaders had no doubt they had good cause for concern. Mr Blair always made no secret that he was determined to build a close and fruitful relationship with the CBI. In early 1997, while still in opposition, he held a private meeting with Adair Turner, the emollient CBI director-general and Lord Marshall, the organisation's president. It turned out to be a seminal moment in relations between New Labour and big business that was to have a direct impact on the trade unions. Mr Blair was keen to reassure the business leaders on that occasion that he believed, like them, in the virtues of flexible labour markets and that his promise to sign the social chapter of the European Union's 1991 Maastricht treaty, thus ending the UK's opt-out, would not lead to the opening of the floodgates to excessive pro-worker social regulation. He went on to assure Turner and Marshall that New Labour in government would pursue a 'sensible and prudent' path in implementing its industrial relations and employment agenda. 'Our aim at the CBI was always one of damage limitation,' admitted John Cridland, the CBI's director-general.[16] 'We found Blair very receptive to business arguments. Indeed, by 1997 we had come to the view that our absence from the EU's Social Chapter policy process was a weakness and not a strength for us because it marginalised our influence and kept us out of the key EU social policy decision-making.'

In its March 1997 business manifesto, New Labour told employers they would not suffer as a result of the ending of the UK's opt-out from the EU's Social Chapter. As it explained: 'We understand business concerns that in the future costly legislation could be imposed on Britain through the Social Chapter. But we have made it clear that in government we will not agree to extend qualified majority voting to social security or co-determination in the boardroom. We will keep matters concerning pay and the right to strike outside the scope of the Social Chapter. There is no appetite among other EU governments for significant new labour market legislation. Should any further proposals be made a New Labour government will make sure the issues of employability and competitiveness are central to the decision-making process.'

Under Turner's leadership the CBI decided, in Cridland's words, to pursue a strategy of 'constructive engagement' with Mr Blair after he became Prime Minister. Business leaders were convinced he was genuinely sympathetic to their point of view and keen to accommodate their interests. 'The government always had a strong centralising direction from 10 Downing Street on industrial relations and employment issues,' recalls Cridland. 'The Prime Minister showed a much closer interest than his predecessors. This led to results that would have been quite different if it had just been left to the Department of Trade and Industry and the Foreign Office to deal with us.' Cridland even admitted that the public accusation made at the 2000 Trades Union Congress by Bill Morris, general secretary of the Transport and General Workers' Union, that TUC delegations might walk in through the front door of 10 Downing Street but that the CBI could get in the back way was 'right on target'. Indeed, CBI leaders were astonished at just how far the Prime Minister was prepared to go in making pro-business arguments for them against his own government's industrial relations proposals that even they thought spurious. At a Fairness at Work conference held by the TUC in June 1998, Monks complained of what he regarded as the Prime Minister's 'kid glove' treatment of employers with his suspicious, if not downright hostile, attitude to trade unions. 'We are cast in the role of stooge – to be used as a contrast to New Labour – not modern, not new or fashionable,' the TUC general secretary complained. 'There is little public acknowledgement of change in trade unions or of the positive partnership role of unions in raising standards of performance as well as terms and conditions of work.'[17] The most substantial achievement of the tacit Blair–CBI understanding came in the Prime Minister's active willingness to block any attempt by the European Commission to introduce a legally binding European Union directive that would require all companies employing fifty or more workers in all EU states to create information and consultation committees. Mr Mandelson, accompanied by Roger Liddle, one of the Prime Minister's trusted Downing Street advisers, were able to win the support of Germany's Christian Democratic Chancellor Helmut Kohl in persuading the German employers' federation (the BDA) to oppose what the European Commission wanted. The secret understanding was to continue between the UK government and the Social Democratic/Green coalition government after it took office in Germany in September 1998. New Labour's resistance to the formation of workplace representative bodies by law proved to be unyielding. Mr Blair and his colleagues insisted their opposition reflected a commitment to the principle of subsidiarity, that such mandatory regulation constituted an unnecessary intrusion into national industrial relations practices. However, critics pointed out the UK had already accepted the introduction of legally-enforceable information and consultation arrangements for workers in the case of mass redundancies and ownership transfer of business undertakings. The European works council directive had also been accepted by larger UK-owned enterprises with business operations in two or more EU countries. But this appeared to be as far as Mr Blair was prepared to move.

By early 2001 the Prime Minister's stance was looking increasingly untenable. Trade unions were incensed at the ruthless behaviour of a number of companies operating in the UK – General Motors in closing its Luton Vauxhall auto plant without any warning; the sale of much of the Rover group by BMW; and the redundancies at the steel company Corus. It seemed the flexible labour markets of the UK were helping firms in difficulty to shut down plants or dismiss workers without any consultation. The TUC warned that British workers – unlike their continental colleagues – were being treated as second-class citizens. As Mr Monks argued in October 2000: 'The UK has the highest rate of company mergers and takeovers in Europe – probably because the UK workforce is seen as expendable. Maintaining a position where it is easy to dismiss British workers seems a contradictory way of attracting inward investment. It is simply not fair that the first casualties of a drop in profits in multinational companies are so often UK workers. It is high time the UK government ended its opposition to the EU directive.'[18]

In December 2000 at their summit conference in Nice the EU heads of government finally agreed to the passage of the European company statue. The trade unions welcomed this, not least because it promised to open up the possibility of seeing an early acceptance of the information and consultation directive. What Monks called the 'Faustian bargain' between Mr Blair and the German employers backed by successive German governments now seemed under threat. It was widely understood that Berlin's willingness to help provide the UK government with a blocking vote to prevent a qualified majority for passage of the directive had been dependent on the situation with the European company statute. As long as this had failed to progress into law, the German government backed the UK resistance to the mild information and consultation draft directive. After Nice, Mr Blair found himself more or less isolated in his opposition to that proposal. However, the French government was thwarted when it attempted to push through a decision at an emergency social affairs council meeting just before Christmas 2000. The UK government used a technical device to prevent any vote, arguing that not sufficient time had been provided before tabling the proposal at the meeting.

But the issue was not going away and it looked set to define relations between Mr Blair and the trade unions in the future. 'It is hard to explain the government's continuing opposition to rules that have not stopped other European countries becoming more prosperous and productive than the UK,' argued Mr Monks in his 2001 New Year message from the TUC. 'There is real and widespread anger about the government's inexplicable blocking of the European directive. Given the unacceptable conduct of General Motors, Coats Viyella and BMW, this issue is now long overdue for government action.'[19] However, there were no signs early in 2001 that Mr Blair intended to back down despite the spate of plant closures and redundancies across vulnerable manufacturing sectors such as steel-making, ship-building, auto-production and textiles. His understanding with the CBI to block further EU social regulation, made early in 1997, was one promise he intended to keep even if it meant leaving the UK much more vulnerable to an acceleration in deindustrialisation.

But Mr Blair wrote in his 1998 White Paper foreword, the government's approach to employment relations reform was designed to go with the grain of the free market and not against it. As he argued 'This steers a way between the absence of minimum standards of protection at the workplace and a return to the laws of the past. It is based on the rights of the individual whether exercised on their own or with others as a matter of their choice. It matches rights and responsibilities. It seeks to draw a line under the issue of industrial relations law.'[20] Not all of this pleased the trade unions. As Mr Monks questioned: 'For every real advance there is a fly in the ointment that the government's union detractors will advance. Statutory recognition, yes, but why such a high ballot threshold and so many small print concessions? The minimum wage, yes, but why reject recommendations endorsed even by employers on the Low Pay Commission? Signing up to the Social Chapter, yes, but why such a lack of enthusiasm for EU social policy – particularly a directive on information and consultation in all enterprises employing more than fifty workers? All these factors, combined with the sense that trade unions are, to coin a phrase "embarrassing elderly relatives" have contributed to a general sense of dissatisfaction.'[21]

Mr Blair's close relations with Spain's centre-right Prime Minister Jose Maria Aznar suggested he was less than enthusiastic about the existing European social market model. There is little doubt that the Blair effect was important in shaping the employment relations agenda across the European Union. 'It is on social Europe that we have had the most influence on the Prime Minister,' claimed Cridland at the CBI.[22] The March 2000 Lisbon summit conference on European social and economic renewal – with its new liberalising agenda on employability, entrepreneurship, investment in human capital, above all a shift from regulation as social protection to regulation as a means to stimulate competition – was hailed as a triumph for the Blair approach. The introduction of targets and bench-making for achieving lower unemployment, the new focus on employment rather than unemployment rates and the creation of national employment action plans inside the EU were also cited as evidence of the Prime Minister's influence in setting a different social agenda from the old one of job protection and worker rights. But Brussels was quick to point out that many of those ideas originated from the European Commission itself and had first been mooted in the competitiveness programme launched by Jacques Delors in his last years as EU president in the 1980s.

In fact, Mr Blair was less directly involved in the development of the UK government's successful jobs strategy. This was focused on the need to encourage and reward those at work through employment opportunities for all and was predominantly the responsibility of Gordon Brown, the Chancellor of the Exchequer. The so-called New Deal – the £4bn welfare to work programme funded by a one-off tax on the privatised utilities – was very much a Treasury-driven affair although Mr Blair was keen to emphasise its success in helping to reduce the level of long-term unemployment. The welfare to work programme was heralded as one of New Labour's prestigious flag-ships. But in many respects there was much more continuity in its development with past Conservative government practice than either Mr Brown or the Prime Minister were prepared to admit in public. The introduction of the Jobseekers' Allowance to replace unemployment benefit in 1996 had reflected a focused concern by John Major's administration on the need to encourage greater employability and provide a fresh emphasis on those without a job improving their active search for work.

The Conservative modernisation of the state employment services and the creation of experimental ad hoc schemes aimed at getting the long-term jobless back into paid work were well underway before Mr Blair reached 10 Downing Street. It is true the New Deal acquired a more substantial allocation of resources and was more nationally comprehensive than other schemes but it represented more of a step-change in the pace of labour market reform and not a dramatic shift in the direction of public policy. Moreover, it was very unclear just how important the New Deal was in the achievement of what amounted to 'full' employment by the end of 2000. The level of registered unemployment had begun to fall from a peak of just under three million in the early months of 1993. Indeed, the rate of job creation turned out to be greater during the last two years of Conservative government than it was in the first two years of New Labour's first term.

We Are All Modernisers Now

There is little doubt that most trade union leaders responded to the Blair effect increasingly in a positive way despite occasional outbursts of ill-feeling and suspicion that the Prime Minister was too over-concerned with business sensitivities. Indeed, they were anxious to prove to him that they were genuine modernisers. In September 1998 the TUC made a presentation in 10 Downing Street, showing Mr Blair how the trade unions could help solve the country's competitiveness problem by forming partnerships with companies. On that occasion, union leaders assured him, they want to make companies successful, help create high quality jobs and embrace learning and training. It was a formal declaration by the trade unions of their abandonment of any old-style approach to industrial relations.

But a more substantial public sign of the changing times was the extraordinary trade union response to the blockade of Britain's fuel supplies by lorry drivers and others, in September 2000, in a protest at high fuel taxes which threatened to paralyse the economy. That offensive provoked a robust reaction from the TUC. In a statement to its Glasgow Congress the general council denounced what was happening as 'not a legitimate form of industrial action but a challenge to democracy and a crude attempt to hold the country to ransom'. 'The blockades are an unconstitutional and unlawful attempt to bully the government into submission,' declared the TUC.[23] Mr Monks went further in his denunciation. He accused the drivers of 'holding the country to ransom' and he urged the Prime Minister to 'stand firm against the blockades and insist on the rule of law in the face of intimidation'. The TUC general secretary reminded delegates of another occasion when 'trucks and lorries were used by the self-employed and the far right to attack democracy' in Chile in 1973 that had led to the downfall of President Salvador Allende's regime through a coup d'etat by a military junta. 'You will not and should not shift this government – any government – with bully boy blockades and civic disruption,' argued Monks. 'These blockades are not blockades on fuel. They are a blockade of our democratic system.' The TUC's display of loyalty and support for the government on that occasion gave eloquent testimony to the new relationship. It was a clear answer to the Prime Minister's earlier doubts about New Unionism displayed privately to Monks at Brighton's Grand Hotel in September 1997. Such words seemed light years away from the TUC attitudes of the 1970s and 1980s. They suggested New Unionism had come to stay – limited and realistic in its aims, less sectionalist and inward-looking, more willing to address the new world of work shaped partly by globalisation and technological change.

The effect of Mr Blair was to finally help dispel the illusions of some that even a New Labour government would involve a restoration of trade union privileges. But there was little sign during his first term that the Prime Minister intended to build on the new employment relations agenda he had introduced. He continued to indicate the trade unions and employer associations would enjoy a rather limited role in the political economy. Indeed, despite an undoubted improvement in the public policy climate of employment relations since May 1997, Mr Blair was not prepared to contemplate bringing the trade unions and employer associations into a more formalised relationship with the British state. But the pressures of the contemporary world suggested the need for more and not less co-ordination and agreement, for the encouragement of practical networks of influence that could bring together employers, unions, non-governmental organisations, local authorities and other agencies bound by partnership principles. However, Mr Blair seemed content to avoid creating new social institutions. He had done the least possible to honour the employment relations agenda he had inherited from Neil Kinnock and John Smith. With his partial view of recent labour history, he remained sceptical that trade unions and employer associations had much of a role to play in resolving the deep-rooted problems of the British economy. However, in doing so Mr Blair implied that the trade unions in particular were still prisoners of their recent past, enfeebled by deindustrialisation and the erosion of collectivist values, unable to establish their credibility among the young employed in the new individualistic work culture of e-commerce and dot.com entrepreneurship.

On the other hand, events might be pushing New Labour and the trade unions much closer together in their mutual self-interest of survival. Mr Blair was quite prepared to resort to the undemocratic use of the union block vote, something he had derided in the past, to try and prevent Rhodri Morgan becoming First Minister in the Welsh Assembly and Ken Livingstone's election as London's mayor. Such unseemly antics might suggest the Prime Minister's principled commitment to the individual membership ballot in internal Labour affairs was highly selective. On the other hand, the trade unions continued to display remarkable loyalty and stoicism in their relations with Mr Blair, perhaps confident that the day would come when he would recognise who his true friends really were. Growing apparent coolness between 10 Downing Street and Digby Jones, the straight-talking and populist CBI director-general during 2000 might have suggested many employers were no longer ready to try and work in harmony with New Labour but return to a more critical and politically detached position, voicing discontent at high taxes and over-regulation as barriers to business.

None of these developments, however, pointed to any sudden reconfiguration in relations between Mr Blair, the TUC and the CBI. Perhaps the continuing pressures from social Europe would eventually force through change as worker rights and employer responsibilities filtered through the British employment relations system. In November 2000 the government announced its support for new forms of alternative dispute resolution through the Advisory, Conciliation and Arbitration Service under its new chairwoman, Rita Donaghy, former senior figure in Unison, the public service union. This suggested the trend to greater juridification of employment relations may be tempered by a fresh commitment to institutional voluntarism. There were also some signs of a revival of public interest values in the proposed reform of the tripartite Health and Safety at Work Commission – formed in 1975 at the height of Labour's Social Contract with the TUC. The former head of the TUC economic department, Bill Callaghan, was appointed as its part-time chairman in 2000. A new emphasis on enforcement of standards and 'the naming and shaming' of companies that committed health and safety crimes indicated a strategic shift away from the more business-friendly attitudes of the 1980s and 1990s. In efforts to outlaw sexual harassment in the workplace, discrimination against women, homosexuals and ethnic minorities as well as older and disabled workers, Mr Blair was paying more than lip service to the need to guarantee acceptable minimum standards in British workplaces. This may not have led the Prime Minister to a warm-hearted approval of the EU's fundamental charter on human rights and it failed to soften his neo-liberal rhetoric on the need for flexible labour markets across western Europe. But it did suggest external pressures, like those from Brussels as well as underlying occupational and social trends, were going to make a profounder impact on the future of the country's system of employment relations than the views, rhetoric and actions of Mr Blair alone.

Appendix: The New Employment Relations Achievement, 1997–2001.
1999 Employment Relations Act.

- Qualifying period for unfair dismissal reduced from two to one year.
- Unfair dismissal compensation raised to a new maximum of £50,000 and index-linked.

- Outlawing of waiver clauses for unfair dismissal rights in fixed-term contracts.
- Right to be accompanied by a trade union official or fellow employee to disciplinary and grievance hearings.
- Part-time workers to have equal rights to full-time workers.
- Automatic trade union recognition where over 50 per cent of the relevant workforce is in union membership.
- Union recognition by ballot when a majority and at least 40 per cent of the workforce vote yes.
- Derecognition procedures broadly mirror recognition procedures.
- Protection for workers from victimisation when campaigning for union recognition.
- Discrimination by omission or blacklisting on grounds of trade union membership, non-membership or activities made unlawful.
- Individual contracts for employees who want to opt-out of a collective agreement.
- Employers cannot recognise a non-independent (sweetheart) union to bypass the legislation.
- Where recognition has been enforced, the union must be consulted on training.
- Dismissal of strikers taking part in lawfully organised industrial action is automatically unfair for eight weeks and only fair after that if the employer has taken reasonable procedural steps to try and resolve the dispute.
- Removal of the requirement to name union members in notice of industrial action.
- A partnership fund to train managers and employee representatives. Family Friendly Regulations.
- Extension of maternity rights from fourteen to eighteen weeks leave with pay.
- A right to extended unpaid maternity absence and unpaid parental leave after one year's service.
- The right to return to one's job or suitable alternative after parental leave.
- Three months' parental leave for parents adopting children.
- A right to unpaid reasonable time off for domestic incidents for all employees.
- Introduction of a maximum forty-eight hour working week, though can work longer by agreement.
- Annual paid leave for four weeks.
- Restrictions on night work.
- Minimum daily and weekly rest periods at work.
- Measures to strengthen protection for workers under the age of eighteen.

- A change in the burden of proof, placing the onus on an employer to disprove an allegation when a prima facie case has been made.
- Protection of workers posted temporarily in another EU state under contracts of employment, providing workers with the same minimum terms and conditions enjoyed by workers in the relevant countries where these are mandatory or imposed by collective agreements.

Notes

I should like to acknowledge the help of Ian McCartney, John Monks, John Cridland and members of the 10 Downing Street policy unit in the writing of this chapter. The best short account of the relations between New Labour and the unions can be found in the useful P. Anderson and N. Mann, *Safety First: The Making of New Labour*, London, 1997 but also see D. MacIntyre, *Peter Mandelson and The Making of New Labour*, London, 2000.

1 T. Blair, Unions '94 conference, London, 19 November 1994, in T. Blair, *New Britain: My Vision of a Young Country*, 1996, pp. 136–137.
2 T. Blair, 'No Favours', *The New Statesman*, 18 November 1994.
3 *Sun*, May 1997.
4 T. Blair, *Unions Today* magazine, January 2000.
5 Trades Union Congress annual report, 1995, p. 110.
6 Business Manifesto, March 1997, foreword.
7 Trades Union Congress annual report, 1997, p. 103.
8 Author's interview with John Monks, 24 October 2000.
9 TUC press release, May 1998.
10 Fairness at Work White Paper, Cmnd 3968, May 1998, p. 1.
11 TUC press release, May 1998.
12 CBI press release, December 1998.
13 Quoted in A. Rawnsley, *Servants of The People: The Inside Story of New Labour*, Hamish Hamilton 2000, p. 213.
14 *Financial Times*, 1998.
15 J. Monks, 'Trade Unions and the Second Term', *Renewal* magazine, Summer 2000, p. 17.
16 Author's interview with John Cridland, 24 October 2000.
17 TUC Fairness at Work conference, June 1998.
18 TUC press release, 12 October 2000.
19 TUC press release, 22 December 2000.
20 Fairness at Work White Paper, p. 1.
21 *Renewal* magazine, Summer 2000, ibid., p. 17.
22 Interview with J. Cridland, 24 October 2000.
23 TUC general council statement and Monks speech, press release, 23 September 2000.

© Chris Riddell

Chapter 13

TRANSPORT POLICY

Christopher Foster

Transport and Elections

TRANSPORT POLICY HAS never lost an election, but it may do so now. It last came nearest to being a major election issue in 1964 after the Beeching closures but those directly affected were a minority. (Only 11 per cent of passenger journeys were by rail, now they are 6 per cent.)[1] One usually thinks of health and education as the public services people care most about and are therefore most likely to be important election issues. But normally education directly affects electors only during short portions of their lives, while health for most people is only a major concern in their later years.

By contrast most people make journeys every day. Until now they did not make an election issue of it because the irritations and frustrations did not vary much over long periods of time. Until recently they knew that speeds on motorways had been much faster than journey times on the old trunk roads were. They knew that in cities journey speeds had been much the same for over a century despite a huge increase in the volume of traffic and, if they reflected on it, they knew it was due to innumerable incremental measures of traffic engineering. Congestion could be frustrating but rarely passed beyond an acceptable level without something being done about it. Accident rates had come down and were, and still are, among the lowest in the world. Despite a few horrific events, and the need always to try to be better, travellers knew too that our railways were far safer even than our roads, as they still are. Aspects of rail travel had long been a joke and there have always been some frustrations in rail travel. Yet overall we were proud of our rail system, which is why in the Beeching era, but only when people lost the least used parts of it, it did become a considerable election issue.

Why is there now the chance of much greater electoral concern? Why could transport policy be a decisive factor in this election, or if not then, in the one after? Of course a major change in economic well-being, or the dramatisation of Europe as the over-riding inter-party difference, could swamp it in importance; but if prosperity continues and Europe is sidelined, then transport could become a decisive issue. The difference from the past is that while transport conditions are tolerable, people only grumble, but that if travel becomes substantially and progressively more difficult and expensive, so that they are regularly impeded in their daily lives, they then may show their resentment at what they may see as government incompetence as well as its remoteness in London from the lives of ordinary people. It seems to have been what has happened in 2000.

Increased Congestion on Road and Rail

The unexpectedly strong and sudden sympathy of so many people with the September 2000 fuel duty protests – in an RAC Foundation poll 82 per cent supported fuel duty cuts – shows how much the cost of motoring matters to the electorate.[2] As long as congestion is a nuisance, people do not take it out on the government. But, everywhere, congestion has been getting worse in recent years. In 2000 the government gave us a good Plan – which we will later discuss – but actions mean more than words. A regular commuter by rail knows, almost irrespective of the route he uses, that the trains have become progressively more crowded and uncomfortable as traffic has built up (though whether they have become more unreliable varies by route). Though railways remain the safest form of travel and cannot be made accident free, demands for yet safer travel are bound to reduce their capacity, in the short run as disruptive action is taken and in the longer run when capacity is reduced for safety's sake as at the approaches to Paddington. Someone who has commuted by road every day, say from Putney to High Wycombe, for the last five years, knows how much more strenuous, expensive and unreliable their car journey has become. Worse congestion on the roads makes bus travel worse (and cycle travel less safe). Recently, journey times have become less reliable for millions of commuters by road and rail. Motorists usually complain about fuel duty increases after a budget, but these complaints normally fade away after a few days. Strong reaction in 2000 was caused by a succession of increases at the pump which made motorists repeatedly aware that 74 per cent of the price goes to the Treasury.

But why transport policy is likely to be an even more important issue in the next than in this election, is that the electorate does not appreciate how much worse congestion will become before it can possibly get much better – despite government forecasts indicating just that (though there are some things in many areas which could be done quickly). They predict that traffic on the motorways will increase by some 29 per cent by 2011 and 56 per cent by 2021.[3] Over many years (and in many other countries too), travel has increased somewhat more rapidly than Gross Domestic Product. It does not have to be so – a future in which teleworking replaces rather than reinforces commuting – is a possibility. But it is not happening yet in richer and more advanced economies than our own. Confidently, one can be sure it will not happen quickly enough to relieve the apparently inexorable pressures on our transport system. The trouble is that at the margin increasing traffic has more than a disproportionately adverse effect on traffic speeds and flows.

Some take comfort from the fact that very recently traffic on all roads, while still growing, has not been growing as fast as a few years ago. But that is to mistake a symptom of the disease for the cure. Traffic is not growing as rapidly because it is deterred by congestion. It is growing enough and will continue to do so to make congestion worse. But increasing congestion is no 'solution' to our transport problem. It means greater misery, greater cost, more pollution, less productive effort, more wasted time, less economic prosperity all round. Rather, the only decline in traffic growth worth having is that brought about through achieving equilibrium of supply and demand by use of the price mechanism, that is, through road pricing, because it implies that traffic will move at acceptable speeds. However it is not the only possible solution – indeed the two could be tried in different places – but the alternative is also politically difficult. It is to add to capacity on any or all modes of transport so that congestion falls so that the use of pricing to ensure free flow might then be unnecessary.

Limits to Increasing Capacity

Those who believe that adding to capacity, if unrestrained by price, will only buy time because there are limits to the amount of capacity that can be added may not be as right as they seemed even a few years ago. Major advances in fuel and vehicle technology have reduced the adverse environmental impact of vehicles considerably. It is still an open question how much further such advances can continue to improve these impacts without severe measures of traffic restraint as well. Enforcement of action against gross polluters would also make a substantial difference. Moreover there are other sectors of the economy where it is arguable that measures to reduce pollution and conserve energy would be more cost effective than further measures in transport. Then there are ways in which noise can be reduced. (The Highways Agency has committed itself to covering 60 per cent of the strategic road network with low noise surfaces.) A more severe limit to increasing capacity in many areas is the physical difficulty of motorway and other road widening. However the government has already said there are many places where motorways could be widened.

Furthermore there are many areas especially in Scotland and the North where physical limitations are implausible and it becomes an issue whether agricultural land should be sacrificed (at a time when agriculture is in strong decline and the possibilities of enhancing the roadside environment through tree planting and other landscaping are considerable). All these matters need to be researched quickly and definite policies chosen. However in Britain with its high population density, there are physical limitations to increasing road and surface rail capacity, especially in built-up areas. (Rail and to a far greater extent road tunnels, are very costly and difficult to connect to the rest of the system.) Moreover, it remains true that over this century as oil runs out there will have to be substantial changes in transport which may involve substantial reduction in some sorts of travel if various kinds of environmental standards are not to be breached. The questions that need to be answered are first how long we have to plan and follow such a path with minimum economic, social and personal disruption; second what the optimal path should be and then how we should organise ourselves, nationally and internationally, to follow it, rather than leap into apparently attractive pro-environmental policies which are not economically, socially or personally, or indeed politically sustainable.

The Fuel Duty Protests

It was understandable that the silent majority supported the hauliers and the farmers in the September 2000 protests against high fuel duty, because the policy behind almost the highest fuel duties in the world is not working. It rests on the assumption that high fuel duties will deter traffic enough to solve the problem. The latest evidence suggests that a 10 per cent increase in fuel prices brings about a 7 per cent reduction in fuel consumption and a 3 per cent reduction in traffic in the medium term.[4] But the fuel duty escalator introduced by the last government in 1992 and abandoned last year, by which fuel duty rose, first at 5 per cent and then 6 per cent more than inflation, only reduced the rate of traffic growth and still resulted in increased congestion. Moreover, part of the problem is that any single rate of fuel duty is not an appropriate price in different circumstances. It results in fuel prices which are too high on economic, social and environmental grounds in rural areas and on uncongested roads generally, while too low to ration space effectively on such roads as the M6 and M25 and in congested city areas. It does not get enough traffic off the roads to allow the buses to run freely or cycles to operate safely. Moreover, while there has been a successful record of improvements in the environmental and safety impacts of transport, one can reasonably doubt if the best measures have been used to achieve the best feasible environmental outcomes.[5]

Above all, the apparently inescapable forecast that congestion will deteriorate over the next ten to twenty years suggests we are running out of the palliatives which have eased congestion in the past. It has been said before, but rising congestion shows we cannot go on much longer, muddling through. Some would argue that the obvious answer is to raise fuel duties even higher; but that would exacerbate the unfairness in terms of the impact on congestion and pollution, on lightly used roads and relatively uncongested areas like the North of England, Scotland and Wales. (Smuggling is already a problem in Northern Ireland and Kent.) Moreover the autumn fuel duty protests showed how deeply unpopular high fuel duties are in all sections of the community and all parts of the country. Perhaps the strongest basis for the objections was that people cannot see why we should bear so much higher a burden allegedly for the environment than other nations do. (Duty per litre is roughly 21p a litre less in the rest of the EU, 42p less in the USA.)[6] Even when motorists have arguments put to them about the possible consequences of fuel duty cuts on health and education expenditure or the alternative of income tax cuts, 72 per cent still wanted fuel duty reduction.[7] Rising fuel costs, because of successive oil price increases in 2000, were one reason, but it also became a trigger-point for farmers worse off because of falling farm incomes and hauliers, angered by what they saw as unfair foreign competition; but the widespread realisation among motorists that they were being asked to contribute higher fuel duty than in continental Europe was also important. The total disruption of the rail network following the Hatfield crash in October 2000 compounded by the further effects of the worst storm damage ever, has made transport still more of a political issue.

Why have we got ourselves into such a difficult position? Transport has always posed a virtually unique administrative problem for ministers. While there are areas of government which are unimaginable other than under public administration – e.g., foreign policy, defence, and law and order (though there are inputs which can be privatised with varying degrees of ingenuity) – and there are other areas like health and education which can be run virtually in isolation from the rest of the economy (though they could be marketised almost completely if that were what public opinion wanted), transport is inextricably part of the mixed economy. When in 1947 an attempt was made to nationalise all goods transport, it foundered on the rock of the substantial amount of own-account haulage owned and run by tens of thousands of firms all over the country. Soon that attempt at a public monopoly began to unravel. In 1968 another government tried to integrate urban transport policy by nationalising all buses but before long it was realised that another underestimated form of public transport, taxis, was in competition with them and carrying as many passengers. In recent times the tendency has been to privatise the means of movement – buses and trains – in the interests of diversity, efficiency and innovation. But to privatise road and railway track is not so easy. To privatise all roads is unthinkable. To privatise any part of the road system might be worthwhile in certain circumstances but would create a local monopoly which would require detailed intervention in the interests of consumer protection, safety, the environment, law and order and planning. Similarly Railtrack has been privatised, but it too is a spatial monopoly which needs government intervention for the same reasons. Moreover the railway system cannot exist without a government subsidy (at least without more or less universal road pricing). Safety, the environment and local planning issues are further reasons why government cannot extricate itself from transport.

Up to the mid-1970s the system was managed by the use of similar economic criteria for the main modes. Investments in road and rail were made broadly if the economic return were high enough (though the fact that roads are unpriced meant the returns calculated were not directly comparable). Traffic growth was the most important determinant of a high return (though safely improvements were allowed for and the criteria could and should have been developed to reflect environmental impacts). Most traffic growth was on and therefore investment was in the roads. Because rail traffic was not growing, most rail investment was for replacement. However because of the shortage of public funds, there was still profound underinvestment in both and insufficient attention to environmental impact. The public expenditure crises following the inflation of the 1970s and in 1998/9 led to severe cuts in both road and rail investment. In the 1980s the railway system, if anything, became still less well maintained.

The Major Government

By 1989 the inadequacies of the road system had become such a serious matter of public complaint that in *Roads for Prosperity*, the then government began a substantial new programme of extra investment – indeed doubling the roads programme – which continued until the early 1990s. It was hampered by several factors. First it takes ten years or more for a new road (or rail) scheme to go through all the design, planning, preparation and construction stages before it is ready for use. Stop-go – as in the late 1970s and again in the mid-1990s – empties the pipeline and slows down the resumption of investment. Second, insufficient attention was paid to environmental factors in the design of roads (cars and fuel) or on how to restrain traffic and avoid congestion on roads where capacity was inadequate. Third, anti-road campaigners became highly effective at public enquiries and in delaying construction. Fourth, the environmental campaigners were in their turn effective in putting about the crude message that immediate and drastic traffic restraint was essential to avoid pollution and global warming; and that therefore virtually no roads should be improved or built. Last, the decision which roads to improve became more political with ministers taking a greater hand, sometimes being influenced by what they saw as electoral considerations. A corollary was that where roads were not improved for political or over simple environmental reasons, congestion built up because of continued traffic growth. As a consequence from about 1994 there was then a change in transport policy which seeded the present crisis on the roads, to some extent imperceptibly at first but after seven years of little new capacity, resulting in levels of congestion we see now, made worse when an event like rail disruption congests the roads with more traffic or there are seemingly uncontrollable street works for cable TV or to reduce water leakages. The Conservative government started to make a virtue of what they were persuaded was environmental necessity and again simultaneously cut both road investment and maintenance expenditure while embarking on the fuel duty escalator. Economising on public expenditure was an important consideration. Mistaken justification had been drawn from a government report which said that when one increased road capacity, there would always be some traffic increase, which is no more of a point than to say that if the demand for any commodity is increasing strongly, there will be a demand for any new capacity to produce it, increased if the commodity is less than economically priced. However the report did make the fundamental point that excess congestion will always occur if the price mechanism is not used to equalise supply and demand.[8]

There had also been action on rail.[9] While there had been lengthy debates in the 1980s over whether and how the railways should be privatised, it was not until after the 1992 election that rail privatisation went ahead. Some aspects of the form it took – especially the arrangements for penalising late-running – were predicated on the then universally held assumption that rail traffic would continue to stagnate as it had for forty years. While safety and reliability were at first improved and then maintained, the surprise was that the innovations of the privatised train companies resulted in a 20 per cent growth in traffic with expectations of further growth in future.

The Blair Government

Was 1997 a watershed in transport policy? No. The opportunity was there, since the Major government went with its transport policies in disarray. The road programme had been cut back dramatically. So had road maintenance. It had taken up no position on road pricing. John MacGregor had announced motorway pricing as government policy in 1993 which should have been effective in helping control traffic demand; but his successors lacked the political courage to persist with it. Despite lengthy debate, and many publications, the government produced no coherent view on how to balance economic and environmental concerns in transport.[10] Earlier the buses had been deregulated, but because of ineffective regulation the concentration of bus ownership into four or five operators had worked against the expansion of bus services which had been hoped for. Unlike 1964 and

1974 the new government had not prepared a transport policy in opposition. Blair was not interested in either transport or environmental policy.[11] The manifesto had lumped these together with second order policies under the heading 'We will help you get more out of life'. Not to be underestimated in overshadowing the first three years of the Blair government was the carrying on of the previous government's restrictions on transport expenditure, already severely cut from previous levels. Prescott as Deputy Prime Minister and a team player was particularly reluctant to ask for more. The tensions between John Prescott and his first three Transport Ministers did not help. Neither did the Yes Minister suspicion of civil servants which as in so many departments stopped them from getting some quick wins: as here by taking steps to break up the bus monoliths or step up road maintenance. A rail privatisation which had been rushed to meet the election deadline badly needed bedding down. Another quick win would have been to revise the penalty formula between Railtrack and the rail companies governing the reliability of trains. Perfectly adequate for a system without traffic growth it would not have been difficult to alter it to reflect the very different circumstances already revealed by unexpected growth in traffic. Better procedures were also needed to make easier the co-operation needed to design, fund and implement rail investment. Neither were there any immediate benefits realised from joining up transport, environmental and planning policies in the creation of DETR.

The incoming government in 1997 at first continued the Major government's transport policy. Until the U-turn in 1999 there were not many real changes. In some areas – for example, airports and ports – there have been no new policies. In civil aviation, the only development has been to press slowly on with plans to privatise air traffic control which in the manifesto they said they would scupper. (They could have had an alternative scheme from the civil servants for the asking.) As so often a premium was set on minor organisational changes which, whether or not desirable in their own right, had a tendency to delay real change: the setting up of the Commission for Integrated Transport, the conversion of the Office for Passenger Rail Franchising into a Strategic Rail Authority, the detrunking of some roads. A Scottish white paper had just before the election stressed reducing dependence on the car, reducing the impact of road freight and shifting the emphasis from both to public transport, while still pressing ahead with only a few major road projects.[12] In July, shortly after the election, the first attention to transport came in Wales when a minister promised a 'radically different transport policy'.[13] It promised to stop most road schemes. In the same month a roads review was announced in England to consider all schemes in the pipeline, stressing environmental factors in their reconsideration.[14] Of twelve schemes considered especially urgent, five had been given the go-ahead, seven had been cut by September. The next roads event was the publication of a study by a government standing committee which argued rightly, there was no given or necessary relationship between higher gross domestic product and traffic growth; but did not feel able to say how much traffic could be reduced without affecting the economy adversely.[15] By May 1998, the government's plans for devolution were impinging on transport. The new London Mayor was to run what was described as a new powerful executive body, *Transport for London*, which would act out a transport strategy developed for it by the Mayor. It was to have day-to-day responsibility for buses, the underground, strategic roads and other transport services.

The 1998 White Paper

July 1998 brought the long awaited transport white paper.[16] Given there was no money, it is easy to criticise it as a document full of promises. However it did lay foundations. In particular it signalled a shift towards more co-ordinated planning of transport at regional and local level. Local transport plans and regional transport strategies were to be the engines of change. Public transport and road schemes were not only to be better integrated in transport terms but to be chosen with their effect in mind on local and regional economies and on the environment. It argued that the forecasts for traffic growth into the next century were unsustainable. It again said public transport must be improved and dependence on the car reduced. More money was promised for road maintenance, but arguably not enough to catch up on the backlog. (Not ring-fenced, it could be used for other local authority purposes, for example, education.) Local authorities were to be allowed to experiment with congestion pricing. There was to be more use of performance indicators to ensure value for money. There was to be more investment in public transport, but it was not clear in an imprecise document how far it was at the expense of road investment. In appraising investment about equal weight was to be given to how schemes affected transport integration, safety, the economy, the impact on the environment and accessibility. But perhaps what stuck out most was the lack of any sense of urgency. Only £22 million extra was to be invested in the transport sector over the next three years. Rather than a radical document, it was a collection of small initiatives which could equally well have been produced by the previous government. At the same time it was announced that a number of road schemes were being abandoned but in fact most were referred back for further analysis.[17] However it seemed as if funding arrangements for the Highways Agency implied it would be unable to fund any new schemes until 2000/01.

In September 1998 more light was thrown on the new methods of appraisal which were to be used to decide which road and rail schemes were to be chosen.[18] Schemes were not to be considered except against the background of a coherent transport policy covering all modes. Schemes should increase accessibility, making it easier to travel, increase safety, represent good value for money, show an ability to facilitate economic activity while allowance should be made for environmental impacts, positive and negative. However it was not clear how much weight would be given to each criterion. The need to strike a balance between them inevitably promised more political decision making on individual schemes which it would be difficult to make transparent.

In December 1998 the government began a consultation exercise on road user charging and workplace parking levies. At this stage concern was raised by the likelihood that much of the revenue from such charges and levies would go to central government rather than to be kept locally for transport and other local purposes. In the same month it became clearer that none of the few (thirty-seven) schemes which had been approved would start before 2000/01. The last would not be started until 2004/05. Meanwhile twenty-six multi-modal studies were to look at particular corridors. (There had been a multi-modal study to look at rail alternatives to the Newbury bypass. In that case it was judged increased rail capacity would have no effect on road traffic conditions around Newbury.) For all this to be defensible, it would have been far better if work had been started far earlier. Substantial delays before the studies could be completed seemed and still seem inevitable.

In March 1999 it was announced that there was to be a £43 million increase in money made available to local authorities for road maintenance but of course this money is not ring fenced for that purpose and can be and was used by local authorities to fund other activities. How long and drawn-out the process of preparation would be was shown by the approval after consultation of guidance for the drawing up of local transport plans in May 1999.[19] In particular it encouraged joint working between the local and other authorities in transport. In the same month similar arrangements were announced for Scotland. Another white paper on buses in the same month noted that bus use had declined throughout the post-war period and now accounted for only 6 per cent of all passenger kilometres, though they still carried two-thirds of all public transport journeys.[20] However one-third of all bus journeys were in London. Again there was a lot of advocacy of plans and partnership arrangements. It argued that congestion was perhaps the major factor in the decline of bus use. It suggested congestion pricing and bus-only lanes as the best solution. In October 1999 there was yet more guidance on transport planning.[21] While many sensible suggestions were repeated from the past, there was little real innovation in what was proposed. Many felt there had been at least twelve perhaps eighteen, wasted months.

The change of government did not bring about appreciable changes in railway policy. Despite threats to renationalise at the time of privatisation, the new government could not afford it. There were some changes in personnel. Apparently to give himself more power over the railways, John Prescott turned the office of the franchiser of train services into a stand-alone agency, the Strategic Rail Authority, with the somewhat perverse effect of giving him rather less power to achieve the renationalisation by the back-door which some people had hoped for. As years passed the demand for investment grew. The need for investment to recover the backlog of under-investment for years had been greatly understated. The unexpected growth in passenger demand led to many new schemes to increase capacity. Many local transport plans developed some plan for rail or light rail commuting. Railtrack's annual Network Management Statement in which it set out its investment proposals each year became more substantial.[22] A tragic accident at Ladbroke Grove led to still more demands for investment to improve safety even if it meant sacrificing capacity. To manage so many tasks was a huge management challenge. (The further accident at Hatfield tipped the balance towards safety but also to more capacity constraints, more speed restrictions, more overcrowding and less reliability, until the promised massive new investment comes to fruition.) While it must be right to avoid the recurrence of accidents, by 2000 there was a danger that the emphasis given to safety and the vast expenditure incurred for it, given the already good rail safety record by comparison with other modes of transport – let alone the greater reduction in mortality and disease achievable by the same amount of money being invested in the NHS – might jeopardise rail travellers' other needs, especially for investment to expand capacity to reduce overcrowding and to provide for greater traffic growth.

A Change of Direction

However during 1999, especially from the summer, the focus groups were telling Number 10 that the government's transport policy thus far was not popular. As a result the Prime Minister and his advisor Geoff Norris put pressure on John Prescott to adopt more road user friendly policies.[23] A new transport minister, Gus Macdonald, was appointed. By the end of 1999 an important U-turn in government policy was in sight. (A pattern was emerging which had merit. Number 10 would question policies and prospective policies as they played to the majority as revealed by focus groups. DETR needed to defend their policies by showing they had the support from the various transport, including motoring, organisations which for the most part were drawn together in policy networks emanating from the Commission for Integrated Transport. As had been true since the 1980s, Parliament and the civil service did not play as integral a part in the testing of policies.) The government's focus groups were showing how hostile the public was to worsening transport conditions. Going back before the election there had been legislation in progress to try to force road traffic reduction targets on local and national authorities. It had become law in 1998. It required government to report to Parliament by the end of 1999 whether it would set a national target for traffic reduction. However the Commission for Integrated Transport advised against it[24] and on 13

December John Prescott said no country in the world would cut traffic in absolute terms whilst its economy is growing. Therefore he agreed there should be no target. It as the first recognition that a policy of traffic restraint on the roads and the promotion of public transport was not going to be enough to solve the transport problem.

In the same month the Transport Bill was published.[25] On the rail side it provided for there to be a strategic rail authority and for a number of other minor changes. It made statutory the requirement for local transport plans and a permitted regime for road user charging as well as for a workplace parking levy. It would have been even more welcome if it had not taken as long as two-and-a-half years to effect after the election. It was long delayed because of the legislative log-jam and because Prescott as Deputy Prime Minister did not feel he should get greater priority for his Bill. A similar bill was introduced into the Scottish Parliament in March. More guidance, this time for multi-modal studies, appeared in May.

The Ten Year Transport Plan

However in July 2000 there was a new more practical departure in the publication of *Transport 2010: The Ten Year Plan*, made possible by the greater priority given transport in the 2000 Comprehensive Spending Review. In it, the government at last made a commitment to finding the funds necessary to achieve the increase in capacity, reliability and safety needed on both road and rail, which were to get an about equal share of the extra £140 billion provided. It was well grounded on forecasts and analysis. In its Technical Appendix it demonstrated how much improvements and expansions of capacity were needed in every transport mode, despite differences in cost effectiveness, if rising congestion were to be curbed. There was not the same commitment to proceed with road pricing to curb that congestion, but at the same time there was a firm commitment to allow local authorities, including London, to experiment with road pricing. Yet again it seems dangerously late since the policy will prove unacceptable unless much better public transport – mostly buses since trains are full and extra capacity usually takes years to provide – is introduced simultaneously.

Why with so much investment promised were there almost immediately fuel tax protests? And why does transport promise to be a critical factor in the election? The problem once again is that there is so much preparatory work to be done before all the new capacity comes into existence, so that there is plenty of time for traffic conditions to worsen before they become better. Moreover anti-road campaigners still have the opportunity – as at Twyford Down and Newbury – to delay proceedings at the many public enquiries which must be held. The Highways Agency in October 2000 announced measures to shorten the proceedings which in the past meant at least ten years passed before new schemes could be completed. However other developments almost certainly will to some extent counteract any such shortening. Any significant road or rail scheme will have to be assessed by a multi-modal study which must consider modal alternatives. This study must then go to the Regional Planning Chamber or body for evaluation who will then send its recommendations to ministers who may sustain or alter its recommendations before they issue their guidance on the schemes in question to be submitted to public enquiry. The issue which could still lose an election is just how the government manages the transition from a rapidly worsening position on road and rail to its new promised land of improved road and rail infrastructure and operations.

Problems Ahead

Transport is a policy area where it is not enough for a government to announce a policy, pass legislation or issue regulations. Several government agencies – for example, the Highways Agency, the Strategic Rail Authority and the Rail Regulator – have to be tasked and motivated. So do a host of local authorities to produce plans which are acceptable to the public and then implement them effectively and with minimal disruption. Unlike education, transport solutions are complex and unique for local authorities so results cannot be achieved by directives from above. There are also large numbers of private interests – bus and train operators, Railtrack, contractors and suppliers of many kinds who need to be motivated to follow the public interest while being able to make enough profit. At the same time the public interest is not to be secured solely by making travel quicker and more reliable, though these are important objectives, but also by making it safer and more environmentally friendly in a number of different respects which can and often do conflict. In every practical instance a balance must be struck between them. Because at no level can politicians take all the balancing decisions required with any likelihood of consistency, procedures and criteria are needed to help local and modal decision makers take decisions which as far as possible reflect what ministers want. The more ministers interact in an apparently random, arbitrary or doctrinaire manner, the more poor decisions at regional and local level will be blamed on them or, if they are lucky, on local politicians.

A political explanation of why the crisis has developed is that it arises in large part from changes in the nature of the government. There is the change from more technical and rational to more political decision making which is almost bound to give less consumer satisfaction. Second, there are other consequences of the severe shortages of public funds, for capital expenditure especially, which here were not escaped by privatisation, at all for roads and not until very late for railways. Third, there was the apparent pursuit of environmental and safety objectives without sufficient consideration of their repercussions on mobility (or the extent to which they could be achieved by other means with a less adverse effect on mobility). Lastly there has been a shift, noted by many political scientists, from government by hierarchy to government through policy networks.[26] With all their faults, hierarchies generally at their roots were sufficiently close to earth to make things happen. As they have developed, policy networks mean long and sometimes seemingly endless chains of consultation which may result in open support for government policy but which frequently get in the way of action. Therefore what is most likely to determine whether transport policy will revert to being a minor consideration at this and the next election, is how far the government is able to overcome the obstacles to implementing their widely acclaimed Ten Year Plan. Actions will speak louder than words.

Notes

1 *Transport Statistics: Great Britain*, The Stationery Office, October 2000.
2 Total motorway costs have been stable in real terms for many years while real public transport fares have risen, exacerbating the difficulty of shifting traffic from road to rail.
3 DETR, *Transport 2000: The Ten Year Plan*, July 2000. Figure for 2021 is from: National Road Traffic Forecasts (Great Britain), 1997, DETR, 1997.
4 S. Glaister and Dan Graham, *The Effect of Fuel Prices on Motorists*, AA, 2000.
5 An increase of 10 per cent was announced to be followed by 5 per cent thereafter, S. Glaister, J. Burnham, A. Stevens and T. Travers, *Transport Policy in Britain*, Macmillan, 1998, p. 267.
6 Information from Institute for Fiscal Studies. Figures for USA from *World Road Statistics*, International Road Federation, 2000.
7 RAC Foundation Poll conducted by NOP Automotive, September 2000.
8 SACTRA, *Trunk Roads and the Generation of Traffic*, HMSO, 1994.
9 Department of Transport, *New Opportunity for the Railways*, July 1992 Cm 2012, Railways Act, 1993, HMSO.
10 Glaister *et al.*, 1998, pp. 269–271.
11 A. Rawnsley, *Servants of the People*, Hamish Hamilton, 2000, pp. 296–8.
12 Scottish Office, *Keep Scotland Moving*, HMSO.
13 *Hansard*, 10/6/97, Column 1051, Mr Peter Hain.
14 *Hansard*, 19/6/97, Column 519, Ms Glenda Jackson.
15 Standing Advisory Committee on Trunk Road Assessment, *Transport Investment, Transport Intensity and Economic Growth*, Interim Report, 1997.
16 DETR, *A New Deal for Transport: Better for Everyone*, Cm 3950, HMSO, 20 July 1998.
17 DETR, *A New Deal for Trunk Roads in England*, 31 July 1998; Welsh Office, *Driving Wales Forward*, 28 July 1998.
18 DETR, *A New Deal for Trunk Roads in England: Guidance on the New Approaches to Appraisal*, September 1998.

19 DETR, *Guidance on Provisional Transport Plans*, November 1998; Scottish Office, *Guidance for Local Transport Strategies*, May 1999.
20 DETR, *From Workhorse to Thoroughbred*, May 1999.
21 DETR, *Provision of Planning Policy Guidance*, Note 13, October 1999.
22 Railtrack, *Network Management Statement*, 2000, contains schemes for every part of the network.
23 Rawnsley, ibid.
24 Commission for Integrated Transport, *National Road Traffic Trends: Advice*, January 2000.
25 DETR, *Transport 2000: The Ten Year Plan*, July 2000.
26 For example, M. J. Smith, *The Core Executive in Britain*, Macmillan 1999. Other countries saw similar developments, J. Pierre and B. G. Peters, *Governance, Politics and the State*, Macmillan, 2000.

Policy Studies

© Chris Riddell

Chapter 14

DEFENCE

Lawrence Freedman

I N ONE OF the leaked memos that embarrassed Tony Blair in the summer of 2000, he expressed his concern on 29 April that 'We need to make the spending review work for defence. Big cuts and you can forget any hope of winning back ground on "standing up for Britain".' This was a striking indication of his sensitivity to what had been an electoral liability for Labour, although in some ways defence might be considered to be one of the more successful aspects of his administration. Blair managed to undermine the assumption that Labour governments were bad for defence even though defence spending retained a relatively low priority. He personally took a key role in providing leadership to NATO during the Kosovo war, asserting general support for robust intervention in regional conflicts, and to the European Union in the development of its own defence capacity. The questions for his second term would be whether at some point an overseas military operation would go completely wrong and whether the European initiative would produce credible results.

In Opposition

Anybody who had been listening to Labour Party defence spokesmen during the years in opposition should not have been surprised that once in government it turned out to be defence-friendly. The anti-defence reputation was almost entirely based on the nuclear issue, combined with an historical ambivalence when it came to the use of force.[1] During the hopeless years of the early 1980s, the opposition to Trident missiles for the British nuclear strike force and the basing of American cruise missiles in Britain was the most pronounced feature of the lurch to the left. This was one of the key issues which prompted the formation of the SDP and also the disastrous showing in the 1983 general election. The problem was not only that it lay the party open to accusations of a lack of patriotism and naivety in the face of the Soviet threat, but that it also revealed considerable muddle, notably over the question of whether a commitment to unilateral disarmament was compatible with a promise to get reductions in Soviet strategic arms through arms control. The issue was only marginally less painful in 1987, when Neil Kinnock appeared to advocate taking to the hills as a serious defence policy.[2]

Part of the regrouping after these two defeats was to abandon the commitment to unilateral nuclear disarmament. The importance of this move was symbolic as much as substantive, a signal that the left was being marginalised. Soon the issue had lost its salience as the INF Treaty of 1987 made possible the removal of the cruise missiles and the end of the cold war reduced the risk of an outbreak of total war. During John Major's administration all short-range systems were reduced and Britain's nuclear arsenal was progressively cut until only submarine-launched ballistic missiles were left in place. Trident began to enter service in 1994.

The years of nuclear controversy had a significant long-term impact on Labour attitudes to defence policy. One of the more interesting was the strong support given, at least rhetorically, to conventional forces. During the 1974–79 Labour government the official view was that it was possible to make savings in defence expenditure precisely because nuclear deterrence meant that war was unlikely and if it came there would be scant scope for regular military operations. Although the 1974 defence review had a limited effect, the deteriorating economic situation meant that the defence budget was raided regularly, to the point where the Chief of Defence Staff complained that it had been cut to the bone. Spending began to revive after the 1978 NATO summit adopted a 3 per cent guideline for raising defence expenditure, but the overall impression left was that defence was at best a low priority, and that a substantial body of party opinion sought to shift spending priorities away from defence to health, education and welfare. A further impression was that Labour governments had little interest in using the military instrument in their foreign policy. This was a lingering perception left over from the failure to use force to deal with the Rhodesian UDI in 1965 and appeared to be confirmed almost immediately by passivity during the Cyprus crisis in 1974. The naval deployments connected with the Falklands were covert.

In seeking to compensate for the unilateralism of the 1980s the Labour leadership claimed that their support for defence would be manifest through supporting conventional forces. In this context one advantage of cancelling Trident would be to release funds for front-line conventional forces. This argument lost force after the early 1990s as Trident entered service and substantial funds had been spent and committed. Nonetheless by this time the party had reversed its traditional hostility to defence and so when the Conservative government began to introduce substantial cuts in defence in the early 1990s there was no compunction about arguing that the cuts went too far. This was widely seen as being opportunistic, obscuring relief that the Conservatives were taking decisions that would test severely a Labour government. Equally Labour's calls for a defence review appeared as a substitute for a policy.

The brief of the Shadow Defence Secretary, David Clark, was assumed to be to keep defence as low a profile issue as possible, and avoid attracting any fire. In this he succeeded.[3] The effort to develop links and some credibility in the defence community was largely taken up by his deputy, John Reid, who later carried on that role successfully in government. The presumption that Labour's approach to defence was largely determined by the desire to avoid any unguarded statement being used in evidence against the party during a general election also helped explain the generally supportive attitude taken by front-benchers towards the Major government's policies in the Gulf and the Balkans. Nothing was done to suggest that Labour was anything other than supportive of the service men and women facing combat.

In Government

There was still a credibility gap on defence because of past policies and practice. Few felt they really knew what to expect of a Labour government in this area. Not many clues could be found in the backgrounds and personalities of the key players. The new intake of MPs was drawn from the liberal professions. A decade earlier and they would have been assumed to be hostile to defence. Now they could be assumed to be ignorant. Few were left of the generation that had served in the war or could remember national service. Even those who had entered politics during the Vietnam period were among the veterans. None of the Labour front bench had any military experience or even much background in foreign policy. The two top players – Tony Blair and Gordon Brown – had made their names on domestic policy. Robin Cook was best known in defence circles as one of the most articulate exponents of unilateralism during the 1970s and 1980s.

The first signal that defence was to be taken seriously came with the appointment of the defence team. Instead of Clark, who had made little effort to develop any serious expertise in defence, Blair handed the portfolio over to George Robertson. A party heavyweight, Robertson had a long history in defence and foreign policy, although not recent. Unusually for many front-bench Labour politicians he had opposed rather than supported CND in the early 1980s. Reid, who had developed excellent contacts in opposition, became Minister of State for Armed Forces. Lord Gilbert, who had long been considered to the right of his party on defence, returned to his old job as Minister for Defence Procurement.

With a reassuring ministerial team in place, the defence establishment began to scrutinise carefully the plans for a defence review. The promise was that this would be Foreign Office led rather than Treasury led, that is it would reflect the changing international context rather than an instinctive demand for savings. At the same time the Strategic Defence Review (SDR), as it was soon called, was also going to be watched closely by party activists. Part of the promise was that during the period of the SDR's production there would be widespread consultation.

The consultation process was elaborate, with special seminars, invitations to submit evidence and an independent expert panel. The government never lost control of this process. In this it was helped by the inevitably self-cancelling aspect of the diverse submissions, and the lack of any bodies of opinion outside of government that combined marked differences from official views, articulate development and strong political backing. The expert panel, which deliberately included a number of non-experts, was used as a collection of individuals rather than as a group capable of forming a coherent view of its own. The author was a member of this group and can report a number of interesting and lively discussions with officials and ministers but very few with other panellists as part of the process.

The intense debates of the early 1980s had subsided. The public might have passionate views about health spending or the Millennium Dome, but, other than vaguely warm feelings about the services, little to say about whether the Air Force needed more front-line aircraft or the future role of armoured divisions. From the left there was residual hostility to all things nuclear and arms sales, and demands for greater support for disarmament, but these had a slightly ritualistic flavour and could be dismissed as the ultimate in 'Old Labour'. Where more notice could be taken of liberal opinion was in demands that the forces become in some way more socially inclusive, by tackling racism and homophobia. In the event it took a human rights case to ensure that known homosexuals were allowed to serve, but unlike the Conservatives there was never any serious support for senior officers opposed to this development. The policy was managed by instituting a new code of conduct to govern the attitude and approach to the personal relationships of those serving in the Armed Forces, applying 'across the forces, regardless of service, rank, gender or sexual orientation'.[4]

For those with any knowledge of the services the idea that homosexuals on the front line would be a novelty was always faintly ludicrous. The decision made no palpable difference to the effectiveness of the forces. The issue of whether or not the forces could or should represent the country's social mix prompted some of the livelier debates of the period. There was a tendency within the forces to simply moan about 'political correctness', and they could point to a tendency among some advocates to forget about the implications of combat. The best test in most cases was whether or not true fighting ability would be impaired. There could be little tolerance for the idea that the inclusion of fit and motivated members of minority groups would somehow interfere with group cohesion, although efforts to improve the ethnic mix of the forces showed only modest gains. On the other hand accepting people with disabilities seemed, at least for Sir Charles Guthrie in his December 2000 valedictory as Chief of Defence Staff, a reasonable place to draw the line. The difficulty here was that 'disability' includes a range of conditions, many of which are perfectly manageable in the most stressed circumstances, and it was possible to point to national heroes from Nelson to Douglas Bader who had fought bravely despite losing limbs. Out of this it emerged that people who developed disabilities in service could be kept on if they could cope, but few were prepared to argue for recruiting people whether or not they could cope with the rigours of service life. The most challenging issue was that of the role of women. In terms of recruitment they were of growing importance, and studies suggested that there was no inherent bar to effective battlefield performance. The issue was more one of whether men and women could work together professionally in the unusual and highly-charged conditions of military operations and exercises. This was not a new issue – the Royal Navy had both sexes serving on warships for some time – and the experience suggested the importance of clear rules if a series of scandals were not to result.

If there was a division in public opinion it was one which cut across party boundaries, and it concerned the degree to which it was appropriate for Britain to intervene militarily in distant civil wars and regional squabbles. The terrible events in Bosnia, which produced a rather stuttering response from Western countries, including Britain, had led many on the left to argue for the use of armed force in good causes, just as many on the right were highly dubious about dabbling in other peoples' problems when British national interests were not at stake.[5] At the same time those on the left who assumed that no good could ever come from Western military action opposed it instinctively, even when directed against oppressive regimes, while those on the right who strained for Britain to be a major player on the world stage were uncomfortable with the idea that Britain could fail to join any major military expedition.

This debate did not really take off until the Kosovo War of 1999, but it was bubbling away in 1997 as a result of the Bosnian experience. This had seen British troops deployed as peacekeepers in late 1992, when there was no peace to keep. This unsatisfactory operation, which had done much humanitarian good but little to bring the conflict to a tolerable conclusion, had triggered serious Trans-Atlantic arguments. It was only when more robust action was taken in 1995 that a peace settlement of sorts was reached. Given the supportive position adopted during the Bosnian operation, and the instincts of the leading players, there was never much doubt that the defence review would come down on the side of the interventionist, internationalist position. Although the 'ethical dimension' to foreign policy, proclaimed by Foreign Secretary soon after taking office, has normally been judged as if it was all about arms sales, at its core is a commitment to human rights.[6]

The Strategic Defence Review

This was the basis for the document that emerged in July 1998.[7] In the run up to its publication the question posed by the media, and the Conservative opposition, concerned the proposed spending profile and whether it betrayed a Treasury victory despite the earlier assurances. The answer was sufficiently equivocal to allow the government to claim that the package was indeed foreign policy driven. The Treasury interest was met through promises of asset sales and efficiency savings, but there were none of the harsh cuts to front-line forces that would have demonstrated a Treasury-dominated process. There were also relatively few big spending decisions in the pipeline. The major aircraft programme – the Eurofighter – was relatively close to completion, and a decision to stay in the tank business with Challenger 2 had been made. The most important issue in terms of future plans, although not immediate decision, concerned the possible replacement to the three Invincible-class aircraft carriers. It was the plan for more substantial aircraft carriers that served to convey both a positive attitude to defence and a coherent view about strategic priorities.

By the time Labour came to office much of the hard work in adjusting to the end of the cold war had been done. It was arguable that more could be brought back from bases in Germany, but by keeping two divisions close to the old cold war front-line the Conservatives had been able to make a convincing case for command of the allied reaction force. Since the collapse of the Soviet Union at the end of 1991 nothing had happened to support fears that somehow another antagonistic superpower might arise like a phoenix from the Soviet ashes. For a variety of reasons connected with NATO's enlargement and assertiveness in the Gulf and the Balkans, and a general sense of self pity in Moscow, relations between Russia and the West became increasingly sour during the course of the 1990s. Russia's military strength, however, was in steep decline. The officer corps was demoralised and often unpaid. Conscripts failed to report for duty. Equipment was neither maintained properly nor replaced. The most substantial military operation – to subdue the rebel province of Chechnya – was a shambles. Russia had become a source of worry less because of its strength than its weakness, that its economic failure could produce social and political chaos. It was hard to be confident that the problems of such a big country could be contained, especially when it was still responsible for a large and complicated nuclear arsenal.

In terms of defence planning it was difficult to make the case that a high state of readiness had to be sustained for World War Three. Even if Russia did turn itself round there would be plenty of warning time, and any future attempts to flex its muscles would be solitary as most of the former Warsaw Pact countries were either in the process of joining NATO or wished to be taken seriously as candidate members. On the other hand the 1991 Gulf War, and to a lesser extent the 1995 Bosnian campaign, had demonstrated that even lesser wars could require high-intensity capabilities, and that the best way to avoid having to fight such wars and conclude them satisfactorily when they had to be fought was to sustain a substantial margin of superiority over any likely opponent.

The experience of the 1990s had demonstrated that the world without the cold war was not necessarily peaceful and harmonious. Many regions, notably Africa and parts of post-communist Europe, were suffering from severe disorder. The two hate figures of the decade – Iraq's Saddam Hussein and Serbia's Slobodan Milosevic – had been contained but hardly tamed. In Asia China was proving to be something of a handful while North Korea presented itself as the ultimate failed state and potentially the ultimate rogue state at the same time.

The basic foreign policy question was whether any of this mattered to Britain, a country well placed by geography to avoid the most direct consequences of upheavals elsewhere. The consensus view in London was that Britain could not stand aside. This was largely because of the country's position within the international system. As one of the five permanent members of the Security Council it had a responsibility to support UN operations. As the leading European member of NATO it could not easily decide to opt out. Only France in Europe could be considered as serious a military power as Britain, especially in its readiness to take on the hazards of combat. The high costs of its nuclear capability, the problems of ending conscription (to produce a force structure, as President Chirac stated, emulating that of Britain) and its awkward relationship with NATO's integrated military command and the United States more generally gave Britain an edge in terms of leadership. If Britain was not prepared to act then in most cases the rest of Europe would not be able to pick up the slack. More seriously all the arguments that might persuade Britain that it had no reason to get involved would apply to the United States. Any effort to encourage Washington to remain engaged with the rest of the world would falter if Britain began to disengage as well.

Nor was it possible to identify parts of the world Britain could safely ignore. Early in the review process there was a view that Asia was an unlikely arena for British military action. It soon became clear that it was impossible to be dogmatic on this point. One scenario, for example, might be a Chinese blockade of Taiwan. If the Americans sought to break this blockade would it be that easy for Britain to hold back – and then expect a robust American response to some European crisis? So while it remained extremely difficult to envisage contingencies in which Britain would do much more than provide token support for the United States, some capacity to act in this region had to be assumed.

The basic strategic judgement that informed the SDR was that whatever the country's inclinations for a quiet life it could expect to play a role in wider international affairs, and that it was important for global order and stability that it did so. This meant that while it was possible to make do with fewer combat aircraft and frigates, capabilities for moving units to overseas troublespots had to be improved, notably with extra sealift and airlift. This was why large carriers suddenly seemed a good idea. They could be seen as floating air bases, geared to projecting power ashore, rather than the much more expensive role as the centrepiece of a large maritime battle group, geared to winning command of the sea. Joint commands had to become a norm rather than ad hoc arrangements to prevent the three services each fighting their own separate wars, with a joint staff college, doctrine centre, command headquarters and rapid reaction force. The latter became operational in April 1999, two years earlier than originally planned.

The SDR was well received.[8] Earlier generations of officers might have balked at presentations of the military as a force for the promotion of an internationalist good rather than a national interest, but the current generation understood that the national interest, narrowly defined, now argued for even smaller armed forces while two decades of support for the civil power in Northern Ireland and a few years of the Balkans had demonstrated a basic competence, often notably lacking elsewhere, in operations of this sort. Unlike a deterrent posture, however, where success can be proclaimed every day that nothing happens, an activist international posture requires both contingencies where outside intervention can improve matters and a capacity for the right sort of intervention. The requirements for particular operations could vary enormously, depending on factors of distance and terrain, the nature of the likely opposition and the quality of the contributions from others.

Kosovo

During the early months of 1998 it became apparent that the situation in Kosovo, which had been unstable for at least a decade, was deteriorating. In the summer of 1998 Blair was among the first Western leaders to urge that a strong stand be taken against Yugoslav President Milosevic whose forces were turning on the Muslim majority in Kosovo in response to an outbreak of violence led by the KLA. The situation was serious enough to introduce the crisis into NATO planning and by the autumn the alliance was beginning to threaten air strikes if the persecution did not stop and the Muslim Kosovars were not allowed to return home.

The events of this period had fateful consequences. Instead of insisting on a proper military force to monitor the return of the refugees and implementation of the ceasefire NATO accepted that civilian monitors from the Organisation for Security and Cooperation in Europe (OSCE) would take on this task. In the event this provided an inadequate presence and it failed to control matters. With a NATO threat hanging over Belgrade it was not surprising that the KLA saw an opportunity to provoke local Serbs into retaliation. At the same time the uncertain nature of the threat encouraged Belgrade to take a risk. Milosevic faced a stark choice. Either he accepted the steady erosion of the Serb position within Kosovo (where they constituted some 10 per cent of the population) or he made an attempt to assert Serb domination, which in his mind meant depopulating substantial parts of Kosovo in the belief that this would make it extremely difficult for the KLA to operate.

A summit called in February 1999 at Rambouillet near Paris attempted to impose a settlement on the parties. A variety of myths have developed around this conference and the proposed settlement. Initially the Serbian side appeared content with the political side of the settlement. This allowed for autonomy rather than independence for the province. It did not propose a referendum on independence after three years – just a rather complicated consultation process. Initially the Kosovar delegation was extremely unhappy and had to be persuaded to relent. The problem for the Serbs was with the proposal for a NATO peacekeeping force. It has been suggested that it was the provisions for the movement of this force through Serbia proper were the most unacceptable for the Serbs but it was the principle of having an effective force in Kosovo that was the real issue. In the full knowledge that air strikes were likely to result Milosevic refused to agree to NATO demands.

On 26 March 1999 allied air forces attacked targets in Serbia. It took until June for the campaign to conclude with Milosevic effectively conceding on all of NATO's demands. The intervening weeks were extremely painful for NATO. The basic problem was that the alliance had made a threat in order to coerce Milosevic. When that threat failed and the bluff was called, the planned strikes had only a limited impact. A combination of bad weather and priority targets including air defences and military command centres had little impact on the Serb campaign on the ground against the Kosovar people. This had been building up for a number of weeks but suddenly reached a crescendo, leading to a massive outflow across the province's borders into Macedonia and Albania. The war's opponents later argued that it was only NATO's bombs that prompted the onslaught against civilians. The start of the NATO campaign certainly affected the timing and the manner of the forced exodus – for one thing it suited Milosevic to have NATO ground forces (some of which had been moved into Macedonia in readiness for a peacekeeping role) taken up with coping with the refugees. When the onslaught began, however, Serb targets within Kosovo itself were hardly being touched and there is no doubt that the objective was not retaliation but a deliberate effort to change the demographic character of Kosovo once and for all.

The ruthlessness of the Serb action completely wrong-footed NATO initially, given that its response appeared wholly inadequate in comparison. The very process that it was supposed to be preventing was accelerating. At the same time this ruthlessness also sealed the Serb's fate. Instead of cowing the KLA it inflamed it, and provided opportunities to acquire and train new recruits. One reason for Milosevic's eventual capitulation was the evidence of the KLA's growing strength, signifying the failure of his underlying strategy. Second, whatever the misgivings expressed during the first days of the NATO campaign, outrage at Serb behaviour created a bedrock of popular support that saw the alliance through many difficult days.[9]

The basic problem for NATO was its lack of land options. One much publicised reason for this was the reluctance of many allies, notably but not solely the United States, to deploy ground forces in combat. Yugoslav forces were considered to be tough and capable of imposing severe casualties on Western forces. Even if there had been a greater readiness to prepare for land operations, however, Kosovo was a logistical nightmare, one of the worst places in Europe in which to contemplate a ground invasion. The Macedonian government was anxious not to be seen to be conniving in such an operation: the Albanians were happy to connive but their infrastructure was primitive.

Gradually it dawned on NATO leaders that publicly ruling out land operations had been a big mistake, and planning began. This shift may have been another contributory factor to the capitulation. For the course of the campaign, however, NATO only used cruise missiles and air power. The problem here was that the Serb campaign in Kosovo itself, carried out by small para-military units, was not easily disrupted from the air, especially when pilots were flying at high altitude for their own safety. Air power could make a difference when directed against the Serb political and economic system, but this was morally awkward for an alliance that claimed to be attacking military targets and seeking to avoid civilian casualties. In practice bridges, railway lines, power supplies and some factories, could be described as military-relevant, although the main consequences were felt by the Serb population. The intensity of this campaign probably surprised Milosevic and again may well have contributed to the capitulation. He was probably surprised that opposition within NATO capitals was not more successful in restraining its air power. There were certainly some notorious mis-hits, which caused civilian casualties and, in the case of the Chinese Embassy in Belgrade, a major diplomatic incident. In the end, however, the air campaign continued because there was a general feeling that the alliance's credibility would be in tatters if it failed to win, and there was nothing much else that it could do.

Blair's Role

From the start Tony Blair took a high-profile role in support of NATO action. With Britain providing the campaign's NATO spokesman (Jamie Shea) and major political cheer-leader, Britain was seen internationally to be taking a hawkish stance. Military briefings in London were listened to as closely as those in Washington and Brussels. As the issue of ground operations was debated there was no doubt which country was pushing hardest for a bold and decisive move. Yet for most of the time Britain's actual military contribution was modest, in line with other European countries. It was better prepared than others for ground operations, and so when the capitulation took place and NATO peacekeepers streamed into Kosovo British units were to the fore and led by a British General (Sir Michael Jackson).[10]

While the legacy within Kosovo was inevitably awful some modicum of stability was restored to the province. The prospect remained for many years of a NATO/UN protectorate. The many unhappy aspects of the Kosovo War and its aftermath did not persuade the government to back away from its activist stance. It considered Kosovo to have been worthwhile and ultimately successful. The positive glow was reflected in the growing profile and reputation of George Robertson. The combination of the SDR and his performance during Kosovo led to his ennoblement and appointment as Secretary General of NATO. Another high profile performer during Kosovo was Clare Short, Secretary of State for International Development, and one of the leading left-wingers in the government. The role of DFID has been missed by many commentators on the Blair government. It has moved quite decisively into the security field, as a natural consequence of the movement of arenas of conflict into the weakest states of the third world, on the argument that little can be achieved in terms of development when the potential recipients are fighting each other and whole countries are imploding. This analysis has bolstered the activist internationalism that has been the hall mark of Blair's first term. A clear statement was provided by Blair in April 1999, during the Kosovo campaign:

> We need to enter a new millennium where dictators know that they cannot get away with ethnic cleansing or repress their people with impunity. We are fighting not for territory but for values. For a new internationalism where the brutal repression of ethnic groups will not be tolerated. For a world where those responsible for such crimes have nowhere to hide.[11]

In April 1999, during one of the more difficult periods for NATO, Tony Blair set out his stall on military intervention in a major speech in Chicago.[12] One reading of the speech was that it was intended to answer the critics who argued that NATO seemed to be creating for itself the right to intervene wherever and whenever it chose. Five tests were set down: a strong case, exhausted diplomacy, realistic military options, a readiness to accept a long-term commitment and a link to national interests that would not be met that often. In late 1999 these tests could be used to explain why there was little that could be done in response to the rather vicious Russian campaign in Chechnya. By making the case as to why the traditional right of states to non-interference in internal affairs had to be qualified when used as a cover for genocide and oppression, the Chicago speech did provide a rationale for later interventions, and was used in this form with East Timor (where Britain played a minor role in an Australian-led UN operation) and, in the middle of 2000, in Sierre Leone. In Sierre Leone, contrary to expectations, British forces acted without allies, initially to provide a rescue operation for personnel caught up in a nasty civil war and then to shore up a separate UN mission that was falling apart at the seams.

A further consequence of Kosovo, although this goes back to the October 1998 crisis, was the determination of Blair to press ahead with a European Security and Defence Initiative. The American reluctance to put forces at risk was becoming a critical strategic weakness for an alliance dependent upon American support. Blair took the view that it was rather pathetic for a rich and populous group of European nations, with substantial numbers apparently under arms, consistently to fail to muster significant forces for actual operations. If European pretensions to a coherent foreign policy were to have any substance then something had to be done about the ineffectuality of its collective military response to crises. In May 1999, when he accepted the Charlemagne prize, Blair observed that:

> For Europe, the central challenge is no longer simply securing internal
> peace inside the European Union. It is the challenge posed by the
> outside world, about how we make Europe strong and influential,
> how we make full use of the potential Europe has to be a global power
> for good.

A move in this direction would provide a wider, and more credible, basis for British foreign policy and provide an area, other than the euro, in which Britain could take a natural lead. For this to succeed, however, Blair had to demonstrate that instead of an alternative to NATO and a rebuff to the United States, the virtue of the new force was that it would give Washington the European support that it claimed to crave. This was summed up by Robertson's successor, Geoff Hoon: 'At the heart of the European Defence idea is the central conviction that a stronger Europe will also mean a stronger NATO.'[13] This argument had to be sustained in the face of counter claims from the Eurosceptics, who, other than adopting the euro, could envisage no more inflammatory policy change.

The charge that this initiative was designed to turn Europe into a superstate even at the expense of relations with NATO had been pushed for some time without much impact by Shadow Defence Secretary Ian Duncan-Smith, but during November 2000, in the approach to the Nice summit, it was picked up by William Hague and the *Daily Mail*. Initially the government appeared wrong-footed, but as he felt on reasonably secure ground the Prime Minister decided this was a European issue on which he could fight back. His problem was that there was backdrop of French comments which suggested the force might be more independent of NATO than was the actual intention and warnings by the American Secretary of Defense William Cohen that NATO might indeed become something of a 'relic' if the French line was followed. There was also a contest to see who could line up the more impressive list of former generals and defence secretaries for and against the proposal. By and large opinion poll evidence was mildly supportive of the Euro-force, although this was very much an elite issue. The corollary of distrusting Europe for British public opinion is by no means enthusiasm for the United States. At Nice Blair was able to get the language he wanted stressing the importance of the Atlantic relationship, avoiding any suggestion that a definitive choice had to be made between NATO and the EU. The EU would still depend on NATO infrastructure and would not aspire to be able to cope with major wars.

All the talk of a Euro-force displacing NATO and providing the foundation for a super-state missed the point that the real risk was that, as with a number of other European initiatives in the area of foreign and security policy, the whole would be far less than the sum of individual parts. With French and then German support the move produced pledges of improved capability from members of the EU: by 2003, they should be able to deploy up to 60,000 personnel to undertake crisis management operations. They should be trained and ready to reach crisis spots quickly, and be prepared to stay there for up to a year (which would require a total force of some 180,000 once allowance was made for *roulement*). This could form part of a NATO-led operation or, where NATO as a whole is not engaged, the EU could lead a crisis management mission. Whether there would be much delivery on these pledges or whether the EU could act as a unit at a time of crisis remains to be seen.[14] Britain earmarked some 12,500 troops for the new force, slightly more than France (12,000) and less than Germany (13,500). From all potential contributors, including a number of non-EU Europeans, the total initially pledged came to 100,000, less than required.[15]

The problem was not displacing the United States in situations where Washington wanted to act but to ensure that European interests could be safeguarded in situations where Washington was lukewarm. When Washington was ready to act London remained more inclined than the others to join in, accepting the risk of encouraging European prejudices about Britain's over-eagerness to please Washington. This was particularly evident with Desert Fox, Anglo-American air strikes directed against Iraq just before Christmas 1998. These were supposed to coerce Saddam Hussein into letting in UN inspectors of his weapons of mass destruction, but they were inconclusive, and led to niggling activity over the following years as Iraq unsuccessfully attempted to control its air space.

The main Trans-Atlantic difficulty Blair faced was nothing to do with humanitarian interventions but a rather traditional issue of the Clinton Administration's flirtation with the concept of a National Missile Defence system to guard against ballistic missile attack from rogue nations. To most European, including the British, governments this seemed to be an unreliable solution to one type of problem, the nature of which was still uncertain, which at the same time risked causing other problems, in particular arguments with Russia over the impact on the 1972 ABM Treaty. The Blair government took the line of least resistance, asking polite questions in public without ever moving to condemnation while hoping that the problem might go away. This succeeded, at least for the duration of the Clinton Administration, as a result of an unimpressive testing programme in the United States. Another area of constant difficulty, again unrelated to intervention issues, was procurement. Every time the British went for European collaboration rather than an American purchase there was suspicion in Washington that this was to make a political point.[16]

Conclusion

Geoff Hoon was able to use his good relations with the Prime Minister to extract a small but symbolically significant rise in defence spending as part of the 2000 Comprehensive Spending Review.[17] In this he was helped by Blair's high regard for the Chief of Defence Staff, General Sir Charles Guthrie, with whom his relationship was the closest with a Prime Minister since Admiral Lewin worked with Margaret Thatcher on the Falklands. Guthrie could point to the things Blair wanted done: Sierra Leone type interventions and a lead in building up European defence capabilities and argue that this could not be achieved on a declining budget. One reason why Chancellor Gordon Brown was said to have acquiesced at this point was that MoD were able to establish links between its activities and a cause he holds dear, the wretched state of many countries in the developing world. One of the expectations arising out of the Comprehensive Spending Review was that the FCO, DFID and MoD would work together on the prevention and resolution of conflict in the third world.[18] At the same time, Guthrie felt obliged to point out that 'being a force for good does not just mean cuddling orphans and giving aspirins and cups of tea to old ladies' but was also about 'being the best fighting troops in the world'.[19]

The key question with regard to the sufficiency of the budgetary provision was whether the Labour government was any better than its predecessors in finding ways to prevent the delays and cost overruns that had long disfigured the equipment procurement process. The Smart Procurement Initiative was designed to produce forces that were 'faster, cheaper, better', by spending more money at the early stage of a project to minimise cost growth and slippage later on.[20] The initiative could not, and did not, have much to show for itself in the first few years.[21] The most serious equipment problems, by their nature, could be traced well back before Labour came to power. The most obvious example of this was the farce of the Bowman radio, which had failed to materialise as commercial systems went through a number of technological generations. Elsewhere the government was embarrassed by well-publicised problems with nuclear-powered submarines, the new Merlin helicopter and the SA-80 rifle. Against this the services could point to the success of the helicopter carrier, HMS *Ocean,* and Challenger 2, and the imminent arrival of the Eurofighter. In addition, the fact that so much development of new systems was taking place in the civil sphere increased the possibility for more off-the-shelf purchases in the critical area of information technology. The steady rationalisation of the defence industry internationally meant that many of the old debates about competition and national champions were becoming irrelevant, as national champions (such as BAe Systems and Rolls-Royce) could survive only because they were global players, and many systems could only be provided by transnational consortia. Despite all the problems with the equipment budget, British forces still appeared relatively well equipped compared to all allies other than the United States and certainly more so than most prospective enemies.

In immediate terms, the readiness to commit British forces put enormous pressure on manpower. At the peak of 1999 some 47 per cent of all personnel were committed to operations, more than double the 20 per cent that would normally be considered comfortable. Towards the end of 2000 the percentage was down to some 27 per cent, with the Bosnia contingent moving down to 2000 from a peak of 11,500 and the Kosovo contingent down to 3500 from 10,500. It is perhaps of note that the cut in the Northern Ireland commitment from 30,000 to 14,000 troops made possible the activity elsewhere. As it is these numbers have to be increased during the marching season, so that any return to the pre-Good Friday agreement conditions in the province could cramp the government's style.

The problem for the government was not that it lacked a strategic vision. The focus was clear and consistent. During the cold war when the emphasis was on deterrence a successful defence policy meant that nothing happened. There was no Warsaw Pact aggression and no nuclear war. When the objective of policy is to make the world a better place, or at least less bad, then the tests are likely to be regular. The government just about managed to pass these tests during its first term but there was always the risk that they would be caught out during the second.

Notes

1 Dan Keohane observes that historically 'Labour's stance on security issues is much less assured than the Conservatives.' *Security in British Politics, 1945–99,* Macmillan, 2000.
2 For background see chapter nine, Lawrence Freedman, *The Politics of British Defence, 1979–98,* Macmillan, 1999.
3 However see David Clark, 'Labour's defence and security policy', *Journal of the Royal United Services Institution,* 142:3, 1997.

4   Statement by Geoff Hoon MP, Secretary of State for Defence, House of Commons, 12 January 2000.

5   This is well brought out in Michael Ignatieff's exchange with Robert Skidelsky in *Prospect*, reproduced in *Virtual War: Kosovo and Beyond*, Chatto & Windus, 2000.

6   Robin Cook, 'British Foreign Policy', 12 May 1997, www.fco.gov.uk.

7   *The Strategic Defence Review*, Cmnd 3999, July 1998. Worth looking at for a number of supporting essays.

8   For an analysis see Colin McInnes, 'Labour and defence – the reality', *International Affairs*, 74:4, October 1998.

9   See Lawrence Freedman, 'Victims and Victors: Reflections on the Kosovo War', *Review of International Studies*, 26:3, 2000.

10   The government's analysis of Kosovo is found in Ministry of Defence, *Kosovo: Lessons from the Crisis*, Cmnd 4724, June 2000. A more critical, although still generally supportive analysis is found in the Fourteenth Report of the House of Commons Defence Committee, *Lessons of Kosovo*, 24 October 2000.

11   Tony Blair, 'Why the Generation of 1968 Chose to Go to War', *International Herald Tribune*, 13 April 1999.

12   Speech to the Economic Club of Chicago, Thursday 22 April 1999, www.fco.gov.uk.

13   Geoff Hoon, 'Making Europe Stronger', speech to Institute for Public Policy Research Conference on European Defence, 14 November 2000, www.mod.gov.uk. On the same site see speech by Policy Director, Richard Hatfield, 'The Consequences of St Malo', Paris Institut Français Des Relations Internationales, 28 April 2000.

14   For an excellent analysis of the issues surrounding this initiative see Francois Heisbourge *et al.*, *European Defence: Making it Work*, Chaillot Paper 42, Institute for Security Studies: Western European Union, September 2000; Presidency Conclusions, *Common European Policy on Security and Defence*, 10 and 11 December 1999.

15   *Economist*, 25 November 2000.

16   The choice was made more difficult by the fact that the UK is the only major European nation allowed access to the most sensitive US technologies and its leading companies were determined to get access to US market. See Henry Van Loon, 'British Behemoth: Talks on Broad European Defence Industry Consolidation Develop Slowly', *Armed Forces Journal International*, June 1999.

17   Hoon was described as 'Labour's stealth bomber' having risen 'without trace to land a big job in the Cabinet before showing up on anybody's radar'. 'Who Hoon is. And why he matters,' *The Economist*, 11 March 2000.

18   *Spending Review 2000*, Cm 4807. CSR in 2000 added almost £400m to previous budget for 2001–02, a 0.1 per cent real increase rise to £23.75bn, growing to 0.7 per cent in 2003–04. Brian Groom, 'SAS-style operation won rise in defence spending', *Financial Times*, 20 July 2000. This was the first planned increase in defence expenditure since 1989, although there had been occasional extra expenditure from reserves.

19   *Daily Telegraph*, 10 August 2000.

20 MoD Press Release 096/97, 'Strategic defence review seeks "smart pro-
    curement"', 30 July 1997.
21 The House of Commons Defence Committee did, however, conclude that
    there were 'it seems to us, some early signs of a more imaginative and
    robust approach emerging, and these offer a glimpse of what improve-
    ments the initiative may be able to provide'. Tenth Report, *Major
    Procurement Projects*, July 2000.

© Chris Riddell

Chapter 15

EUROPEAN UNION POLICY

Anne Deighton

Introduction

THE SORRY SAGA of Old Labour's postwar European policies is well known. By May 1997, the question was how New Labour would deal with the European Union (EU). The EU is one of the great but unloved issues of our time. It now permeates most arenas of public life, and the domestic debate on European integration has influenced and often infected British politics for more than forty years. There has been no major political party that has been consistently able to call itself pro-EU. Both the Labour and Conservative parties have at various times been split open over policy towards the EU. Public opinion has rarely shown active support for European integration, and there are consistently high polls recording indifference or opposition to the EU. Cultural dissonance, ignorance and confusion play a part: Brussels makes 'Directives' and 'Decisions', not 'Laws'; has 'Commissioners' not 'Civil Servants'; 'Directorates General', not 'Departments of State'. Terms such as Pillars, subsidiarity, and the *acquis communautaire*, leave most Britons uneasy – and queasy. Mischief from opposition parties can bring easy political gains. Some sectors of the press have fuelled this problem. Anti-EU tabloid headlines such as 'Up Yours, Delors', 'The Great Danes', 'The *Sun* meets the Hun', 'Wake up the old British bulldog pride', and 'EU're in the army now' reveal the triumph of sound bite talent over taste or maturity, and can undermine serious debate on both sides of the fence.

The Inheritance

By May 1997, the Conservative Party was split wide open on the EU. Having agreed to substantial measures of supranational integration during the 1980s and 1990s with the Single European Act and the Maastricht Treaty, the government was in trouble. The agonising process of ratification of the Maastricht Treaty from 1992–93, and the ignominious retreat of the government from the Exchange Rate Mechanism in 1992, when it is estimated that £20billion was lost, tarnished its image. The 1996 scare over BSE and the resulting 'Beef War' between Britain and its continental partners resulted in a three month British refusal to agree to EU measures which required unanimity, causing huge disruption to EU business as well as much bad feeling. By 1997, the Conservatives were also weary after eighteen years in power, reputedly down to their third division in terms of ministerial talent, and under relentless and hostile pressure from within their own party.

The EU itself was also in the doldrums by 1997. It had weathered the critical years from 1989–1992, when the cold war structure of the international system collapsed around it, but it now seemed that the Union itself was losing its way and its political will. It lacked effective leadership from the Commission after the departure of Jacques Delors, and the new Santer Commission was to fall amidst a crisis about corruption and its competence in 1999. The difficulties experienced in France and Denmark in their referendums to ratify the Maastricht Treaty had awakened fears in the 1990s that the EU was drifting away from a base of popular consensus, and public support for integration dwindled across the EU. Rising unemployment was a continual problem for EU member states. Progress towards Economic and Monetary Union (EMU) was frustrated over compliance with the economic convergence criteria that the EU had set itself at Maastricht, and it was not clear that the agreed target dates could be kept. Preparations for the June 1997 Amsterdam Intergovernmental Conference (IGC) were also stalling. The IGC had been called to reform the EU's own institutional structure before any states from the former Soviet bloc, who were anxious to join, could be admitted. But the appetite for reform was not great so soon after the Maastricht Treaty. German Chancellor Helmut Kohl, exhausted by the economic and political demands of German unification (October 1990), was experiencing considerable difficulties at home. Meanwhile, the EU had virtually no effective means at its disposal to deal with the open sore of violence and conflict on its Balkan borders. The civil wars that had engulfed the Balkan region since 1991 reminded everyone of the feebleness of the EU as an international actor, and of the perils of instability on the periphery of the European continent that could spill over into the EU.

The Bases of New Labour Policy

Although Prime Minister Harold Wilson had submitted an application for membership in 1967, and had then secured a referendum result that confirmed Britain's membership in 1975, by the 1980s Old Labour had a manifesto commitment to leave the European Community, as it was then known. During the 1980s and 1990s wilderness years the party was essentially re-invented under the leadership of Neil Kinnock and then John Smith.

What were the ideology and priorities of New Labour by 1997? Its ideology has shifted from socialism to a moderate social-democratic position – ambitiously, if vaguely, called the Third Way.[1] This approach has been developing incrementally since the 1990s, influenced by US Democratic thinking, by variants of continental socialism, by the collapse of the Soviet bloc and the perceived revolution of globalisation, and at home, by the Commission on Social Justice. Third Way thinking is, at root, non-combative, and is based upon a belief that the status quo should be accepted and 'managed', and that strategies can be evolved that enable social democratic values to flourish in a capitalist world that is itself rapidly changing. The preferred economic model is a variation of the so-called Anglo-Saxon or neo-liberal version, with an emphasis upon reducing central controls, upon flexibility, employability and competitiveness, and upon incorporating values of justice, rights and individual opportunities. As Blair has said, the vision of the British government was 'to find a new way, a third way, between unbridled individualism and laissez-faire on the one hand; and old-style government intervention, the corporatism of 1960s social democracy, on the other.[2]

Blair and his advisors worked with continental social democrats to try to establish this European Third Way position. Blair had long sensed that it would be important to have allies within the Union from the earliest moments of the new government, and he spent a considerable amount of time on the continent (as well as in the US) in conversation with like-minded leaders and parties. Once in power, Blair published a joint booklet with German Chancellor, Gerhard Schroeder, and had meetings to discuss ideology with French Prime Minister Lionel Jospin. However, their different cultural roots and historical perspectives, revealed more about the varieties of late twentieth-century socialism and social democracy, than about common ideological starting points. Much of their debate in fact mimicked long-standing debates on the continent between *laissez-faire* and *dirigisme* within the EU.

The British Third Way is certainly not conceived as a means to stand up to the weight of the US, and to American global capitalism. The Third Way's British guru, Anthony Giddens, has little to say on the EU specifically, which he interprets as a mechanism for addressing globalisation, with the potential to create a 'global cosmopolitan regime'. Integration is seen as part of a global set of economic, political, social and cultural trends that provide a context for all politics in industrial societies.[3] Third Way thinking emphasises the completion of the EU's Single Market while ensuring protection for workers' rights, as well as peoples' issues such as the environment, cross-border terrorism, and fraud, none of which can be dealt with effectively at the level of the state or region. Subsidiarity – dealing with issues at the most appropriate level of government – is the working model, or, as Blair, in his important speech to the French National Assembly explained: 'Integrate where it makes sense to do so; if not, we celebrate the diversity which subsidiarity brings.'[4] There is more interest in the 'Union' as a collective ideal, rather than the 'European' dimension of the EU; with this comes an emphasis upon economic prosperity, the protection of individual freedoms and the recognition of democratic rights, rather than the issues connected with a European 'identity'. If the Third Way has an EU agenda, this is to use its philosophy as the basis of a European reform programme to remould the existing European social and economic model.[5]

This last point is important, as it reflects very strongly the second powerful, but deeply conservative strand of New Labour thinking about overseas policy, and the relationship between Britain's traditional foreign policy and the future. New Labour publicly portrays itself as a party that has drawn a line under the past, and which represents new and modernising policies. But the images and priorities of the past still play a core role for New Labour. It has not dropped Britain's classic projection of itself as a great, if now post-imperial, country. It still has nuclear weaponry, and global interests, with responsibilities as a permanent member of the United Nations Security Council, and as the leading member of the Commonwealth. Britain is portrayed as an Atlanticist country that still has a particularly important relationship with the US, and a leading role in NATO. Much of this derives from the policies of the 1945–51 Labour government, but it also represents continuity across British foreign policy since the end of the Second World War.

Britain as a pivot, leader, and agenda-setter drives both the presentation and content of much of its overseas policy, including that towards the EU. Agenda setting demonstrates power in a leader. This has been crucial not only for Blair's image overseas, but also at home. For, as he has said, 'though Britain will never be the mightiest nation on earth, we can be pivotal . . . It means realising once and for all that Britain does not have to choose between being strong with the US, or strong with Europe; it means having the confidence that we can be both. Indeed, that Britain must be both; that we are stronger with the US because of our strength in Europe; that we are stronger in Europe because of our strength with the US . . . We battled together throughout the Cold War. We stood shoulder to shoulder in NATO . . . We have deluded ourselves for too long with the false choice between the US and Europe . . . Nations must maximise their influence wherever they can. To be a country of our size and population, and to be a permanent member of the UN Security Council, a nuclear power, a leading player in NATO, a leading player in the Commonwealth, gives us huge advantages which we must exploit to the full.'[6] The agenda of changing the EU could be possible for New Labour because of the habit of leadership that is the inheritance of Empire and Britain's own historic great power status. So, in foreign relations, New Labour ideology is bolted onto traditional – if not Churchillian – British thinking about its role in the world and its relationship with the US.[7]

The 1997 Manifesto and New Labour's EU Policy

This is nowhere clearer than in the 1997 election manifesto. It of course attacked the Conservative Party's EU policy. The fiasco over BSE symbolised the Conservatives' failure in Europe. Britain had 'for centuries been a leader of nations', but its influence under the Conservatives had waned – that would now end. The manifesto makes more than a dozen references to leadership in foreign policy. There is a full colour photograph, under the heading, 'We will give Britain leadership in Europe', of Blair in full-flow, with President Chirac staring up at him, amazed – no doubt fearful that the days of a comfortable 'l'Europe française' were about to end. New Labour would bring a new tone to European politics, as well as leadership and, with it, change. They would sign up to the Social Chapter, and would then shape it to bring employability and flexibility, but not high social costs, to the European social model.[8] They would introduce proportional representation for European parliamentary elections. The distance from 1983 is remarkable.

But continuity with the past also marked New Labour's approach, and there is more of substance – though not of style – in the manifesto that reflects continuity rather than radical change. With an Atlanticist Britain at its centre, there would be no federal Europe, but a Europe of independent nations choosing to co-operate to achieve the goals, including those of free trade, that they cannot secure alone. Subsidiarity would be used wherever possible, and the EU would be more open, more democratic, and closer to its peoples. Britain would stand up for its own national interests and use the national veto when required; Britain would not immediately join the EMU project, but would keep to the Conservative line at Maastricht until a referendum was held. Further enlargement of the EU was a high priority for Britain. In reality, none of these goals reflect a major shift from Conservative policy, but a less cautious manifesto would no doubt have lost New Labour electoral support. For the image of an internationalist rather than 'European' Britain is derived from an imperial and successful cold war past and is deeply embedded in the public psyche.[9]

New Labour in Power

The EU is part of the policy process in most areas of British life – from the FCO to the Treasury, Home Office, DTI, and beyond, as well as being an object of 'foreign' policy. EU policy has been dominated publicly by three members of the Cabinet: Blair, Chancellor Gordon Brown, and Foreign Secretary Robin Cook. The pro-EU preferences of Peter Mandelson have been influential in the internal debate, although he has not been a Cabinet minister over the whole period of the first administration. Blair has little interest in the formulation and pursuit of policy detail, so Brown has had a vital role in the EU game although he has become rather more cautious about Britain's role in the EMU process, so determined is he that New Labour should survive a second term in office. Cook, on the other hand, who came into office with a reputation as something of a euro-sceptic, has now emerged as more enthusiastic about the necessity of Britain being inside the EMU, if only to consolidate its political leverage within the EU generally. If the FCO has been in retreat since 1997 in the Face of Treasury dominance, it has also now managed to convince its Foreign Secretary of the political benefits of EU membership, the traditional FCO position.[10] Doug Henderson, Joyce Quin, and Geoff Hoon (Quin and Hoon had earlier been members of the European Parliament) in turn acquired responsibility for the EU dossier, until the post of Minister for Europe was taken over by Keith Vaz in 1999. There are monthly meetings between departmental officials and the Minister for Europe to ensure consistency and coordination of policy; while at the same time, the increasingly powerful Prime Minister's office challenges other Whitehall departments.

Blair has managed, so far, to hold the party together on EMU and on European questions. One socialist, the Mayor of London Ken Livingstone, (now expelled from the party, but leading a pro-New Labour policy of 'London in Europe'), has remarked that where Britain finds itself is not where he would like to be, but that is the hand with which Britain has to play. This is a view with which most MPs in the party would probably concur. Nevertheless, the EU was not the first priority for the majority of the New Labour Cabinet in 1997: ministers were trying to learn the job, were concentrating on domestic politics, and were motivated by a determination not to wreck their chances of staying in power for two full parliaments.[11]

Early Days

Early on, Blair scored high and scored easily. It was not hard for continental leaders to applaud a change from the Thatcher and Major years. Blair's optimism and enthusiasm as well as his massive parliamentary majority meant that he would be a force to be reckoned with. The moderate social democracy that the Third Way represented marked a decisive break from the hostility towards the Union's capitalist club of many in Old Labour, although some continental leaders disliked Blair's hectoring tone, and the assumptions that Britain could easily change the EU's agenda. The first heads of state meeting, and the conclusion of the Amsterdam Treaty in June

1997 were nevertheless both marked by public good humour. New Labour held fast to traditional views about defence and security, and the use of the national veto. But acceptance of the Social Chapter was a symbolic shift by the new government. They also accepted that some of the intergovernmental arrangements for Justice and Home Affairs would be quietly folded into the main Community pillar.[12] They were perhaps lucky that it was the Germans who proved to be obstinate about reforms to the qualified majority voting system, which took the pressure off the British. Blair on a group bicycle jaunt; Blair joking with other heads of state in the summer sunshine – these were the new images of Britain in the EU.

The EU Presidency, January–June 1998

Setting a European economic and social policy agenda based upon Third Way principles was never going to be easy. The EU policy process is slow, complex, and mediated by compromise. British officials know this very well, and indeed have considerable skills in working the system, but the ways of the EU came as something of a shock to new ministers. The Commission's Agenda 2000 proposals, plans for EMU, and a raft of existing legislation meant that British agenda-setting would require time, patience, and, above all, allies. The first opportunity for New Labour to make an impact came with Britain's tenure of the Presidency of the European Union between January and June 1998. The Presidency should give the country a chance to exercise some strategic leadership, and to push ahead with particular policy areas. Cook stated that the British Presidency's mission was 'to give Europe back to the people', with a focus upon unemployment, crime, drugs and the environment. However, despite being in the position of managing the Union's day-to-day agenda, and the advantage of chairing the myriad of Council meetings, the Presidency does not in practice give much leeway, and indeed, is not intended to be used to secure national advantage. What it does do is to give the incumbents a chance to put EU issues onto the domestic agenda, to give many speeches at home and abroad, and to try to shift the EU's programme. The mass of Presidency speeches and events sought to push old problems into the dustheap of the past and to reinvent the UK as 'Cool Britannia' in a changing EU. The launch of the Presidency in front of a Eurostar train at Waterloo Station (was this a spin doctor with either a weak sense of history, or just with a bizarre sense of humour?); the children's paintings on the Presidential logo; and Blair's Third Way speech in French to the National Assembly in Paris, all showed a desire to invent Blair as a leading EU player.

In practice the Presidency was disappointing – New Labour had not been in power long enough to set a viable agenda. During a Presidency much time is spent dealing with issues as they arise. The British Presidency was no exception, with agriculture, Kosovo, China, and inter-state disputes amongst the many items that crowded the EU timetable. Attempts were made, however, especially at the Cardiff Summit of June 1998, to assert new economic thinking concerning employability and social exclusion. The Europol Convention was ratified, and provision was made for an increase in mutual recognition of the decisions of each other's national courts on questions of cross-border crime.

Enlargement

The two major developments that took place during the UK Presidency were driven by the EU's own timetable, and not by British initiatives. Extending membership of the EU is its most important strategic issue, now that the question of EMU has been resolved by most other states. Britain has long championed enlargement, a position echoed by New Labour, whose strategy has been to encourage enlargement to a large number of countries – indeed, Blair has talked of this as a moral duty. Ironically, Britain found itself in a different position to many of its partners, who, despite public statements, were now in private increasingly fearful of the costs and consequences of enlargement. To add to this, Britain's largely uncritical approach has not added leverage to it as a player in the tactical manoeuvres surrounding enlargement. During the British Presidency, accession negotiations got under way with the first set of six countries: Cyprus, the Czech Republic, Estonia, Hungary, Poland and Slovenia, to be followed by a second five countries: Bulgaria, Latvia, Lithuania, Romania and Slovakia. Whilst the negotiations during the UK Presidency did not present any particular problems – apart from a flurry over Turkey's refusal to attend the conference for the hopefuls who were not to be considered as a priority – neither did they strengthen the UK's hand in this area.

Enlarging the EU requires the applicants to accept the Union's *acquis*, a formidable body of rules and norms. However, with the possibility of many new members, the Union has also to adapt its own decision-making procedures to accommodate larger numbers of states. The 1997 Amsterdam European Council failed to make substantive progress on how the EU member states would take decisions after enlargement. In February 2000, preparations got under way for another revision of the EU treaty to 'tidy up' after the Amsterdam summit and to try once again to prepare the EU for enlargement. Discussions on decision-making inevitably led to a debate on the wider purposes and aims of the EU. During the summer of 2000, both the German Foreign Minister, Joschka Fischer, and Chirac put forward proposals for rather more radical reform.[13] It was not until October 2000 that Blair added Britain's contribution to this wider debate. In what was rightly trailed as a key speech, Blair set out his position on the EU's political future while on a visit to Warsaw.[14] Drawing heavily upon historical references, and asserting that the time had come to overcome the legacy of Britain's own past, Blair's *tour d'horizon* tried to place Britain in the mainstream of EU developments, by deploying his now classic Third Way approach of marrying two apparently irreconcilable opposites – the EU as a minimalist free trade area, and a federal Europe. Whilst these depictions were caricatures, Blair then went on to argue that the EU could become a superpower whilst not developing into a superstate. He suggested that the constitutional arguments about the structure of the EU should mimic the fluidity of the British constitution, without requiring the *finalité politique* of a single legally binding document called a Constitution. He urged the citizens to take ownership of the EU, and not to feel it to be a controlling power over them. To enable this to happen, he proposed that the European Council should agenda-set for the EU on an annual basis; that the possibility of team presidencies should be considered; and that the European Parliament should have a second chamber tasked to review the EU's work. He met the earlier proposals of Fischer and Chirac by agreeing that certain groups of member states should be able to cooperate more flexibly on certain projects, but resisted any proposal that there should be a hard core, or pioneer group of states which excluded others.

The December 2000 Summit in Nice and the European Conference with the applicants that preceded it, was a bruising affair that extended beyond its allotted three days. It underlined the gap between the positive rhetoric about enlargement, and the private reluctance of existing member states to give way themselves, or to alter the status quo to enable enlargement to proceed. The British were represented by Blair, Cook, and Vaz, and were well briefed. They managed the extensive, indeed relentless, press coverage with considerable skill, by constantly referring back to their own negotiating bottom-line (or 'thin red lines'). They deflected attention from Britain's own difficulties, focusing instead upon those of the French (chairing the Summit), and the smaller powers who were fighting to save the status quo.

The contribution of the Nice Summit to the question of an enlarged EU is significant, although the Treaty will not enter into law until it has been ratified by each member state, and much of it will not be applied until enlargement finally moves ahead. The balance of voting and blocking powers between member states has shifted slightly; the applicants' future allocation of Council votes and powers, and their number of European Parliament seats has been agreed. Qualified majority voting has been extended in some areas to make decision-making easier, although it is not clear how these changes will contribute to the smooth running of a future, enlarged EU. The new members will each have a European Commissioner. Substantive policy issues, in particular the EU's agricultural policy, were not addressed at Nice, although this will be one of the most contentious policy areas to be decided before enlargement can take place.

Nice has made a psychological difference: the numbers game has been extended to the applicants; the member states have accepted that there will be new members and that decision-making structures will have to be modified as and when these new members finally arrive, perhaps in four to five years' time. So Blair can be pleased that, after Nice, the assumptions are now that there will be, not just that there should be, new members of the EU, despite the difficulties ahead over the nuts and bolts of the accession process. Advocacy of enlargement has proved so far to be a low cost, but also low-profile agenda item for New Labour.[15]

The Single Currency

The second important event of the British Presidency of the EU was also determined by the Union's existing agenda, and this has never been low-profile. At the beginning of May 1998, it was decided that eleven willing member states fulfilled the necessary conditions for adopting the euro on 1 January 1999. Wim Duisenberg was appointed President of the new European Central Bank after much political wrangling, and Brown was then in the position of launching a key committee, initially called Euro-X, a process from which the UK was itself excluded. The European Central Bank came into operation on 1 June 1998.

EMU presents the greatest challenge to New Labour and to Britain in the EU. Blair's difficulty is that EMU is highly politically sensitive – an 'act of faith', as Eddie George has called it, and yet very technical and deeply contested even between economists and business people. It is hardly surprising that public opinion is confused, indifferent, and antagonistic in equal measure. EMU is perceived to challenge an established icon of British identity, the pound sterling: losing this would be irrevocable. EMU is further seen as undermining national sovereignty, as monetary policy would be determined by the European Central Bank. Macro-economic policies would increasingly be negotiated and brokered at the European, not national, level and a visible sense of the control of the national economic agenda would be lost. Despite emphasis upon the national veto, and an insistence that fiscal autonomy would not be lost, the logic of a Single European Market however points to greater convergence, and to shared decision-making.

The government came into office with a manifesto commitment that any 'decision about Britain joining the single currency must be determined by a hardheaded assessment of Britain's economic interests. Only Labour can be trusted to do this: the Tories are riven by faction . . . What is essential for the success of EMU is genuine convergence among the economies that take part, without any fudging of the rules. However, to exclude British membership of EMU forever would be to destroy any influence we have over a process which will affect us whether we are in or out . . . there are three pre-conditions which would have to be satisfied before Britain could join during the next Parliament: first, the Cabinet would have to agree; then

Parliament; and finally the people would have to say "Yes" in a referendum.' It was the Conservatives, in 1996, who had first proposed a referendum on EMU, and Labour were forced to follow suit, a move that has boxed them into a very tight spot. Thus, a referendum would be essential, but remains a high-risk option.

Many in New Labour privately thought – and hoped – that EMU would not get off the ground, and that the problem would just go away. When they began to realise that their continental partners were indeed still serious, they contemplated privately requesting that the project should be postponed, until advised by senior British ambassadors that this would be disastrous, and would destroy efforts to build better relationships within the EU. In the meantime, measures were put in place that would allow for eventual membership, and the Bank of England was given the independence necessary to comply with the Treaty of Maastricht. There were government initiatives to prepare businesses and the public sector for a change-over to the euro after 2002, and to review the UK's strategy towards EMU. In October 1997, Brown's five conditions finally set a framework for subsequent debate, and it was made clear that a referendum would not take place during the lifetime of the first Parliament. The events surrounding the establishment of the five conditions were marked by bitter rows between Blair, Brown and their advisors.[16]

Should Blair have moved earlier, relied upon his massive majority, and gone for a referendum soon after 1997? The answer is no. Adopting a 'prepare and decide' policy towards EMU was inevitable, given that New Labour had failed to develop a clear strategy towards EMU before coming into office. Despite his massive majority and great personal popularity, an early referendum would have courted disaster and generated accusations of cynicism, given the consistently negative polls on the euro and the strength of the pound sterling. The general election vote anyway was, as is the case in most general elections, in part a vote against the Conservatives and their inheritance, and New Labour's electoral victory would not have guaranteed a referendum success in 1997.

It is now safe to predict that the government will stick with its five conditions as the sheet anchor of its tactics. In their 1975 referendum campaign over re-negotiated membership, Labour had emphasised the technical, apolitical aspects of the issues to be voted on. This time, too, the conditions that the UK itself has to meet before a referendum can take place are also vague and technical, and allow the government maximum flexibility. The government has chosen not to produce a running commentary on progress that has been made towards meeting the conditions for a referendum. So the EMU debate has now been kicked into touch, where it rests until two years after the general election. However, given the Danish referendum which rejected the euro, in spite of Danish elite support, it is a possibility that a technical approach that plays down the question of sovereignty and subsequent pressures for greater fiscal harmonisation will not be enough for Britain. The Conservative Party, certain newspapers, and sectors of the business community will inevitably focus upon the loss to a notional national sovereignty. This prospect will force Blair to decide whether this is an issue on which he will have to lead from his position as Prime Minister, or whether he will leave his Chancellor, or even his Foreign Secretary, to make the running and to take the risks, and perhaps then gain the advantage within the party hierarchy if a referendum in favour of joining EMU is successful.

Agenda Setting in the EU?

There is evidence that New Labour has made some headway with their agenda for employability, for flexibility within labour markets, and for adapting the European economy to technological change. These issues, and particularly unemployment in the EU, were however already under discussion, notably within the Commission's Agenda 2000 document. New Labour were able to put new so-called Broad Economic Guidelines for economic and social reform, along with employability, inclusion, social cohesion and lifelong learning, as well as the promotion of the interests of small and medium-sized businesses, onto the table at the Cardiff European Council in June 1998. These decisions, as well as the national Employment Action Plans (derived from the Luxembourg Council of December 1997), were again raised at the special Lisbon Summit of March 2000. Here the new strategy for a knowledge-based economy and for eEurope – was accepted. Further, the EU has set targets that devolve the responsibility to the states themselves for pushing change forward, with national reporting, peer evaluation and bench marking, working within the concept of subsidiarity. This method of working is administratively different, and has been much favoured by New Labour, which has also placed great store upon the outcomes of the Lisbon and Feira Summits in 2000. However, the effects of the new programmes have yet to be fully assessed. EU unemployment is more than fifteen million, and concerns about skill shortages have led to target-setting for training programmes, Research and Development, and lifelong learning schemes within the EU, as well as informal discussions to encourage more immigration of skilled workers.[17]

These policy arenas show that there has been some progress in the practical application of subsidiarity, as advocated by New Labour. Comparing best practice, benchmarking, and peer review are approaches that emphasises the role of states as well as the Commission in pushing through policy change. Comprehensive and detailed statistics are not yet available about how far these initiatives have altered national policies, and a House of Lords Select Committee has pointed out that the Lisbon Summit gives a higher priority to the Commissions role in this process than was favoured by the British. Indeed, Whitehall is aware that Britain itself has not performed as well as it might under the benchmarking systems. Relatively low British productivity remains a problem that gnaws away at the new government's economic record.

Opting into the Social Chapter has enabled New Labour to press for greater social inclusion at the EU as well as national level, based upon the premise that the best safeguard against social exclusion is a job. The government has advocated the increased use of Community Structural Funds to complement work done at the national level. Government ministers have refused to de-nationalise social policy questions, or to countenance French plans for a more intensive social agenda. But it seems that – as one Treasury official put it – the Social Chapter 'has no impact whatsoever upon any British decisions'.[18]

Turning to EU decision-making bodies, New Labour had agreed in the manifesto that the 1999 European Parliamentary elections would be run in Britain on a system of proportional representation. There was still an appalling turn out and the election brought disappointing results for the government. The government also supported changes in the administration of the European Commission after its sudden resignation in spring 1999, and encouraged the reforming efforts of Commissioner Neil Kinnock. This created a momentary panic amongst some Brussels bureaucrats, when British-style, if not Thatcherite, administrative reforms were suggested which appeared to be out of character with the working practices of the Commission.[19]

At the December 2000 Nice Summit, the President of the Commission was given greater managerial powers over his Commission. This can be seen as compensation for decisions which may, in the longer term, reduce the authority and influence of the Commission. For there will still be one Commissioner for each state for the foreseeable future, which will reinforce the role of the smaller states, the culture of national quotas for senior personnel, and the role of unelected officials through COREPER, rather than allowing the Commission to develop as an independent body. The Nice Treaty will also tip the balance of influence towards the Councils of Ministers, and within them, to the larger states (including Poland as and when it joins), which was an ambition of the British government. At Nice, Blair also ensured that small groups of states should not be able to develop policies that might exclude other countries, and ensured that the proclaimed Charter of Rights would not be incorporated as a 'constitution' in the new Treaty. A deal between France and Germany, however, means that this core issue will be revisited at another IGC in 2004.[20]

Meanwhile, the day-to-day business of the EU takes up the largest portion of government time, particularly over the Justice and Home Affairs legislation, and the Schengen provision, where Britain has an opt-out. Issues concerning borders, the movement of peoples, and the harmonisation of court procedures are unglamorous and arduous to negotiate. Like the detailed work on the single market, competition and regulation, they represent the nuts and bolts of Britain's policy within the EU. New Labour has been active in publicising its efforts to build coalitions and alliances with different states in these various policy arenas. Although it sounds unglamorous (and most EU activity is just that), this reflects a real concern that the working methods of the EU must adapt and that it must become more flexible. The Lisbon Special Summit was in part due to an Anglo-Spanish initiative, and good relations between Blair and the Spanish Prime Minister Jose Maria Aznar have meant that difficult issues connected with the Gibraltar problem have had a lower profile than might have been expected. The government has sought also to build a coalition with Sweden on the question of social exclusion, with the Italians on high-tech issues. Indeed, Vaz boasts of nine different bilateral initiatives relating to alliances constructed at the time of the Lisbon Summit.[21] But perhaps the most striking of these state-to-state alliances has been with the French, and this has been over one of the EU's most sensitive arenas: military security.

European Security

If the record of New Labour has not been visibly spectacular in the above policy arenas, the major shift in British policy towards the EU as a military security actor will have enormous long-term, but unpredictable consequences. For the EU has historically had no brief for military matters. Instead there has been a conscious emphasis upon economic and civil society issues. Britain has been one of the staunchest supporters of the view that the EU should not challenge NATO's remit. At the same time it has consistently sought to be an active player in the formulation of common foreign and non-military security policies.[22]

During the early months of the new administration, New Labour stuck to these traditional British postures on security. Burden-sharing issues in NATO were not new, and after the end of the cold war, Western European Union (WEU) had been increasingly squeezed as some partners sought to give the EU a greater role in the defence and security debate. Blair initially rejected the more ambitious and integrationist security plans of some partners at Amsterdam, and supported only the creation of a High Representative for EU foreign policy (a post given to the former NATO Secretary-General, Javier Solana); an early warning unit; and the terms of reference under which WEU or coalitions of the willing might be allowed to act. But during 1998, after intensive debates within Whitehall, the government shifted its ground. As early as March 1998, Blair talked publicly about the capacity for the French and British to act together with more energy in joint military undertakings. As 1998 progressed, the ongoing

Bosnian and Balkan crises exposed the shortcomings of the European powers; WEU appeared administratively clumsy and insignificant, and its members were reluctant to give it authority to play a role. There was now a growing disquiet about the extent to which the US would continue to sanction its presence through NATO as a peacekeeper in the region, and more generally, whether America might not in time have a more isolationist leader who would be less committed to the future of NATO as a security organisation.

At the informal EU summit in Pörtschach in Austria, Blair personally decided that the gridlock on European security had to be broken. After the summit he said that, as well as having NATO, an effective common foreign and security policy for the European Union was necessary, and that it was 'high time we got on with trying to engage with formulating it', with new institutions, capabilities and political will.[23] Although questions were raised in the House of Commons during November 1998 about this new security initiative, it was not until December that Blair and French President Jacques Chirac spearheaded a fundamental shift.[24] The Anglo-French St Malo Declaration of December 1998 was a diplomatic bombshell, for it asserted that 'The European Union needs to be in a position to play its full role on the international stage . . . To this end, the Union must have the capacity for autonomous action, backed by credible, military forces, the means to decide to use them, and a readiness to do so, in order to respond to international crises . . . acting in conformity with our respective obligations to NATO.'[25]

The Declaration created a storm. Now, at the stroke of a pen, NATO's most assiduous partner in Europe was publicly suggesting that the EU should extend its reach into the hitherto unthinkable arena of hard, military power. American Secretary of State Madeleine Albright responded through the pages of the *Financial Times*. She argued that NATO was itself preparing to reformulate its strategy to deal with twenty-first century missions: so it was not the lack of appropriate institutions that was the problem, but 'the lack of agreement to use the instruments we have'. She went on to warn of decoupling within NATO, of duplication of scarce defence resources, and of discrimination against NATO members outside the EU.[26] Some French decision-makers feared that this bilateral change was in fact a new move by perfidious Albion to draw France closer into NATO, and the Americans further into Europe: even in the EU, all partners are motivated by interests, not friendship. Applicant countries to the EU – especially Poland – feared that NATO might be undermined. The Conservative Party reacted with predictable hostility: three of its former Foreign Secretaries joined in the debate, and Thatcher boomed from the US about 'the utopian venture of creating a single European superstate', and that Blair was 'in pursuit of a doomed ambition to "lead Europe"'. William Hague, leader of the opposition, argued in the House of Commons that this 'momentous' decision had 'profound dangers'.[27] Nevertheless, the fact that this diplomatic *démarche* had come from the only two serious military powers in the EU could not but send a signal that the security landscape was about to change. Was Blair now charting a Third Way between the US and France?

Over the next two years, flesh has been put onto the bones of this proposal. By the end of 2003, the EU should have access to an ad hoc rapid reaction force or Military Security Pool of up to 60,000 personnel, complete with necessary command, control and intelligence facilities and, as appropriate, air and naval elements, within sixty days.[28] Any decision to take military action would be agreed by a unanimous vote of the European Council, and would be taken only when NATO had decided, as a whole, not to act. Where and in what scenarios this force can be deployed is still under discussion: its present terms of reference are the Petersberg security tasks – humanitarian and rescue tasks, peace-keeping tasks and tasks of combat forces in crisis management, including peace-making.[29] Global as well as European fields of action have not been ruled out – it has been suggested that such a force could have been deployed in Sierra Leone, and that, in time, its use would not be inconceivable even within the countries of the EU itself, if needed. Those not members of the EU, whether members or not of NATO, will also be able to participate in forward planning and military operations, but will not be involved in an EU Council decision. But the project suffers from confusion, first about defence (territorial defence is not covered by the proposals), and second about the popular misnomer of a European Army or Rapid Reaction Force. But the Military Security Pool is not a permanent force or standing army, and any mission would take two months to be agreed and set up.

Why has this major change, spearheaded by Blair personally, taken place? There were tactical as well as strategic reasons for Blair's thinking. He saw an opportunity to lead in the security sphere, and to create a military capability that worked, and had indeed even privately explored ideas of some kind of Commonwealth-based security force. He has never intended to undermine the core defence function of NATO. His actions can be understood in the context of the post-imperial strand of New Labour's foreign policy, and from his determination to be perceived as a leading actor in international relations. This leadership role was to be confirmed with the greatest clarity during the air war over Kosovo between March and June 1999, at a time when the US national security team was widely criticised for its hesitations. America's reluctance to commit itself to the use of ground troops seemed to spell disaster during the faltering air campaign, but the military deficiencies of the European contribution were also glaringly apparent. During those weeks, Blair was prepared to play a very public, leading role, and to stake considerable personal prestige upon the continued conduct of the war.[30] On European security, Blair has always emphasised the need to be effective – and has cast most of what he has said on this subject in terms of the capabilities of the Europeans to make a difference, rather than as a contribution to European integration. His important Chicago speech of April 1999, also made during the Kosovo war, then tried to set out a new agenda for intervention based upon principles of human rights, which gave an added dimension to the initiative.[31] Military security was thus one of the few arenas in which the UK could find political space for a new initiative – it was sidelined over EMU and Justice and Home Affairs issues, and enlargement was not seen as a vote-catcher. In January 1999 the euro would be launched, and Britain would be outside the charmed circle. At home, the Strategic Defence Review had already laid the ground for the more effective deployment of forces for lower-level security operations, and asserted the credibility of the UK as a flexible, hard-power player.

So St Malo is a leap in the dark for Britain and for the EU, and represents the greatest change that New Labour has made in EU policy. The taboo on military action by the EU has been broken: the initiative for security policies has shifted to the EU and away from the US. It sets the UK at the head of a very significant change in the international role of the EU, while the US has been caught on the back foot. At home, furious attacks from the Conservatives and tabloid press did not affect high positive consensus for the initiative in opinion polls, and Blair quite rightly decided to face the Conservatives and tabloid attacks head-on. Abroad, the impact upon NATO and the US is not clear – St Malo might in time be seen as the moment that led to the Europeans finally beginning to take real co-responsibility for military security – as some Conservatives fear; or it could lead to an even stronger US presence as part of a re-imagined Atlantic Community in Europe – the French nightmare. Blair talks with equal passion about Britain's Atlantic ties, and his commitment to a European vision. Although he is probably an Atlantic Community man, the question remains as to whether he can steer a way forward that remains both inclusive and effective. Blair's Atlantic versus European dilemma has been highlighted by the Anglo-American raids on Iraq, particularly in December 1998 and February 2001, which have been met with dismay by European allies.

The management of the European security agenda will remain an extremely sensitive issue for the next administration. There are still deep disagreements amongst EU and some NATO members about this initiative. Realising a Military Security Pool to carry out the Petersberg Tasks will require considerable political will and high-level management at a time when the new Republican President of the US, George W. Bush, is still finding his way, and is deciding upon the US's own role in security tasks. The willingness of the EU to play a part that is commensurate with its wealth and population must temper the Republican Adminstration's declared reluctance to support these developments with great enthusiasm. But even if the current initiative stalls or takes longer than anticipated to bring to fruition, the EU will one day take some active part in military security questions, and these will be further supported by additional EU-wide policing initiatives. The psychological 'glass ceiling' under which the civilian EU sheltered, not intruding into either NATO or national security and defence competences has been irredeemably shattered since St Malo.

Conclusions

The EU is an extraordinarily 'sticky' institution in which change is always deeply contested. Its original mandates stretch back over forty years, and its institutions survive, with modifications, from the 1950s. British commentators have long been anticipating the collapse of the so-called Franco-German axis in the EU. This axis has been weakened by the unification of Germany, and is now under considerable strain, not least because of the relative lack of interest of the current German Chancellor in EU politics compared with his predecessors. Yet this powerful reflex, driven by history, bureaucratic procedures, mutual (if different) benefits, and the habit of diplomacy still shapes the EU's agenda more powerfully than any other bilateral relationship. While the British have observed the rocky moments of the Franco-German *ménage à deux*, they have been unable to create a *ménage à trois*, although they have worked very hard to build an edifice of state-to-state alliances over specific issues. At the same time, the EU has displayed a remarkable policy momentum over EMU. So, for other members, Britain is an important partner, but it is not of vital importance. In the same way that the allies have accepted the incongruence of France's semi-detached position in NATO, the EU has learned to live with the inconveniences of Britain's own difficulties over the EU.

All this has made the New Labour mission of reform extraordinarily hard, and it is only during a second term that results may begin to emerge. In opposition, Blair and his predecessors worked to reinvent the party; they sought to build bridges with continental social democrats; and with American Democrats, they fashioned a so-called Third Way. With all these changes has come a more temperate view of the EU which is based upon perceived economic and social realities rather than ideological fervour. This is a real shift.

Blair himself, like most British Prime Ministers before him, has taken an increasingly active role in EU politics, and the growing power of the Prime Minister's Office has been remarkable. Blair is happy to wear a European, an Atlanticist, and also an internationalist heart on his sleeve. He refers to his own work experience in Paris, his wish that his children should see themselves as Europeans, and made passionate remarks during his keynote Labour Party conference speech in 2000 against latent xenophobia in certain sections of British society.[32] His personal popularity, and skilful press representations of his role, have helped to create a far more positive and proactive image of Britain's role in the Union. His major speeches given across the Union have explained British policy as it has evolved to those who have cared to read them.

The combined effect of party and personality changes has meant that the substance as well as the tone and presentation of Britain's EU politics do show a real sea change. The early acceptance of the Social Chapter, the reform of the European Parliamentary voting system, efforts to modernise approaches to the economy, with eCommerce, benchmarking and other initiatives, have been coupled with a determination to explain and project EU policies in a favourable light, as well as a continued support of traditional British strategies in favour of widening the EU. Britain's decision to champion a military capacity for EU members to project a military security presence beyond the EU's borders that has perhaps been the most remarkable, if not vote-catching, policy during the first New Labour term in office. Blair's own mission to lead and change has been enhanced by his personal performance at the Nice Summit, where he declared after four days of wall-to-wall negotiation, that 'we cannot go on like this'.[33] The lack of convincing Conservative Party alternatives for the EU will be helpful to Blair during the parliamentary ratification process of the Nice Treaty after the election.

EMU was approached with extreme caution by New Labour, and has been shaped by a classic British policy of conditionality. If re-elected, New Labour will have to make a decision when to risk a referendum on EMU. The transformation of Cook's position from doubter to proselyte for the EU and for EMU, is a classic example of how those in power are more convinced of the need for positive participation within the EU, while those outside are happy to criticise. However, a second New Labour administration would have to continue to push very hard for a version of the Anglo-Saxon economic model that it has promoted in the EU. Britain will be hard placed to lead on issues of constitutional reform, however good the ideas it brings, given its historical baggage as a difficult member of the EU, but this is an area in which any government must take a very active, agenda-setting role. And if New Labour truly wishes to create a 'peoples' Europe', domestic opinion will have to be convinced that further enlargement will bring strategic, political and economic benefits.

So the jury is still out on the Blair Effect on EU policies. Despite his personal popularity, Blair has failed to turn public opinion substantially over EMU or enlargement, or to shift the general indifference to the EU that still dominates polling figures.[34] This reflects the inherently conservative approach to foreign policy of a post-imperial country. Blair may be personally popular, but the EU certainly still is not. It remains a constant battleground, a hopelessly over-complex and alien institution. The challenge to a second administration will be to alter this. They will still have to convince the British public that the politics of rough and tumble, and of give and take, is the acceptable reality of European Union membership.

Notes

1 The term 'Third Way', has, however, generally fallen out of favour.

2 'A Modern Britain in a Modern Europe', Tony Blair, The Hague, 20 January 1998.

3 Anthony Giddens, *The Third Way: the renewal of social democracy*, Polity Press, 1998, p. 179.

4 'The Third Way', Tony Blair speech to the French National Assembly, Paris, 24 March 1998.

5 Gordon Brown has said of the euro, 'If a single currency would be good for British jobs, British business and future prosperity, it is right in principle to join. The constitutional issue is a factor in the decision, but it is not an overriding one. Rather, it signifies that, in order for monetary union to be right for Britain, the economic benefit should be clear and unambiguous'. HC Deb, 27 October 1997, Col. 584.

6 Tony Blair to the Associated Press Luncheon, London, 15 December 1998, www.fco.gov.uk.

7 Anne Deighton, 'Labour, New Labour, and European Integration', in Adolf M. Birke *et al.* (eds), *An Anglo-German Dialogue*, KG Saur: Munich, 2000, pp. 273–284.

8 This was psychologically very important for New Labour, as the Conservatives forced the eleven EU partners to adopt the Social Charter of 1986 by 'opting in' without them to a Protocol to the Maastricht Treaty in 1991. To agree to sign up to the Social Charter was also important for Blair's relations with his continental social democrat partners, and it shows the extent to which the earlier Kinnock reforms of the Labour Party had taken root.

9 Labour Party Manifesto, 1997.

10 The FCO have actively worked to inform the public about the EU, not least through the massive expansion of its website on fco.gov.uk, and links therein, especially to fco.gov.uk/eu.

11 Charles Grant, *Can Britain lead in Europe?*, CER, 1998, p. 5, quotes a member of the Labour government as saying that only four members of the Cabinet had any interest or knowledge of the EU.

12 The Schengen Agreement on borders was incorporated, with an opt-out for the UK and for Ireland. Civil law, asylum and immigration questions were transferred to Pillar One, with greater Commission involvement. Police and judicial cooperation in criminal matters remained in Pillar Three, allowing states greater flexibility in choosing the means through which they choose to implement agreed changes.

13 www/elysee.fr/disc/disc_.htm; www.auswaertiges-amt.de/infoservice/presse/index_html?bereic.

14 'Europe's Political Future', Speech by the Prime Minister to the Polish Stock Exchange, Warsaw, 6 October 2000; www.fco.gov/news/speech-text.asp?4215.

15 Robin Cook admitted as much, evidence to House of Lords, 21st report of Foreign Affairs Select Committee, 1998–9. The Nice Treaty provisional text proposes that, from 2005, the four large states, the UK, France, Germany and Italy, will give up their second Commissioner. Until the EU reaches 27 members, each state will have one Commissioner, 'The Treaty

of Nice', 12 December 2000, SN 533/00, at www.fco.gov.uk. On poor polling on enlargement, *Eurobarometer* polling for October 2000: europa.eu.int/ comm/dg10/epo/eb/eb53/eb53.html.

16 Andrew Rawnsley, *Servants of the People: the inside story of New Labour*, Hamish Hamilton, 2000, chapter 5.

17 At Lisbon, the Union set itself the target of becoming 'the most competitive and dynamic knowledge-based economy in the world capable of sustaining economic growth with more and better jobs and greater social cohesion', Lisbon Conclusions, March 2000, http://europa.eu.int/council/. UK Progress Report on Economic Reform, November 2000.

18 Private information. At the Nice Summit, Blair ensured that the social policy question would not undermine the government, no doubt mindful of the difficulties that this question had created for John Major at Maastricht in 1991.

19 *Le Monde*, 5 May 2000.

20 'The Treaty of Nice', provisional text, 12 December 2000, SN 533/00, www.fco.gov.uk.

21 See, for example, www.fco.gov.uk/news/speechtext/asp?4163.

22 For Blair's foreign policy, which is in large part managed through the Common Foreign and Security Policy of the EU, see the chapter in this volume by Christopher Hill.

23 Austrian presidency Informal Summit, www.number-10.government.uk.

24 HC Deb, 11 November 1998, cols 286–305.

25 'Joint Declaration on European defence': British–French Summit, Saint Malo, 3–4 December 1998, www.fco.gov.uk.

26 *Financial Times*, 7 December 1998.

27 The three foreign secretaries were Lord Hurd, Lord Owen, and Sir Malcolm Rifkind, although Hurd has been more supportive to New Labour than the other two. Margaret Thatcher, BBC, News online, 8 December 1999. Hague spoke to the House on 13 December 1999.

28 Anne Deighton, 'The Military Security Pool: Towards a new security regime for Europe?', *The International Spectator*, Vol XXXV, No 4, Oct–Dec 2000, 19–32. About 20 per cent of the military contribution comes from the UK.

29 The Petersberg tasks were formulated in 1992 by Western European Union (WEU). The scope of these tasks in effect extends as far as NATO-Article 5 defence of territory tasks.

30 For a fuller account of Blair's defence policy, see the chapter in this volume by Lawrence Freedman. Blair also gave rousing speeches in Romania and Bulgaria as the war was under way, and virtually promised them EU and NATO membership because of their support for the NATO action; Tony Blair, Sofia University, 17 May 1999; www.fco.gov.uk/news/ speechtext.asp?2436.

31 www.fco.gov.uk/news/speechtext.asp?2316; see further, chapter in this volume by Christopher Hill.

32 Tony Blair speech to Labour Party conference, 26 September 2000; www.labour.org.uk. He also repeated that, 'Standing up for Britain means know we are stronger with the US if we are stronger in Europe, and stronger in Europe if we are stronger with the US'.

33 *The Economist* reproduced a devastating transcript of a few minutes of the
    Nice bargaining process at Heads of State level, *The Economist*, 16
    December 2000.
34 See, for example, Eurobarometer polling for October 2000: europa.eu.int/
    comm/dg10/epo/eb53/ep53.html. This latest polling presents a dismal, but
    not unexpected picture, with Britain still the most doubting and hostile of
    member states. Higher support for the security initiative is unlikely to be
    an electoral vote-catcher; but it is anticipated within the Labour Party
    that the personal popularity of Blair would encourage voters in a referen-
    dum to vote in favour of membership of EMU.

© Chris Riddell

Chapter 16

FOREIGN POLICY

Christopher Hill

BRITISH FOREIGN POLICY is the last area where we might expect
radical change, particularly from a party which has taken patholog-
ical care to avoid controversy while in Opposition, for fear of
repeating the gifts to the Conservative Party of the 1980s. Nonetheless a
case can be made for saying that the Blair government has boldly gone
where their Labour predecessors *in office* had feared to tread and introduced major innovations, making some progress in reconciling foreign
policy with the values and principles of the party faithful. One Japanese
observer has referred to a 'diplomatic revolution', which is precisely what
is still being called for by the Foreign Policy Centre, set up with the blessing of Foreign Secretary Robin Cook and a reliable indicator of New
Labour attitudes.[1] On the face of things there is a long list of innovations:
foreign policy with an 'ethical dimension'; the creation of a strong new
Department for International Development (DfID); the new look towards
Europe, including a significant improvement in relations with France which
made possible the St Malo defence initiative of December 1998; the
Strategic Defence Review of earlier in the same year; Tony Blair's 'doctrine
of the international community' (the Chicago speech) during the Kosovo
intervention of spring 1999; and the new military commitments taken on in
the Balkans and Sierra Leone. These things together can be said to amount
to a very significant change not just in the usual stance of Labour in power
but also in the traditional continuity and bipartisanship of British foreign
policy since 1945.

A closer look at the record may lead us to qualify this picture of a pain-
less revolution in British foreign policy. Domestic critics on the left are not
slow to argue that nothing has changed, with the UK in pawn to NATO
and American interests, while it is difficult to believe that observers in
Damascus, Buenos Aires or Beijing would have noticed any seismic shifts in

London. What follows will examine the main planks of the Blair-Cook foreign policy outside Europe the ethical approach, the attitude towards humanitarian intervention, development policy and relations with the big three outside Europe (Russia, China and the US) in order to test the proposition that we are in the midst of a diplomatic revolution. The decision-making dimension will not be neglected, as Robin Cook has attempted to impose a new ethos on the Foreign and Commonwealth Office, while Tony Blair is accused of allowing Cabinet government to atrophy. Finally, an attempt will be made to evaluate the claims made by the government and to indicate the main points of vulnerability.

Ethics

New Labour hit the ground running in foreign policy, to the surprise of many who had noted the apparent lack of preparation as well as interest in the area in the run-up to the election of May 1997. The new Secretary of State Robin Cook wasted no time in making it clear that he wished to impart a new 'ethical dimension' to British foreign policy – a declaration which was predictably simplified into a commitment to run an 'ethical foreign policy'.[2] The attempt to base foreign policy explicitly on 'ethics' is in itself something of a revolution. Previous governments, while always in practice having to balance prudential and ethical considerations, have always preferred to do so behind the screen of a theoretically bland pragmatism, whereby interests have been deemed eternal and ideas a fatal distraction.[3] Robin Cook (for it is not clear how far the Prime Minister shared his wish to go public on this matter, and so soon) was determined that British foreign policy should face the new 'realities' of on the one hand an increasingly blurred line between the domestic politics of particular countries and the problems of the international system, and on the other the pressure from non-governmental organisations (NGOs) for Britain to take a moral stand on issues such as arms sales and foreign dictatorships. The Foreign Secretary also clearly believed personally that it was right that the balance should tilt in favour of what he terms 'progressive' causes and away from purely inter-state considerations.

Such a bold hostage to fortune has caused problems, since critics from all sides have drawn attention to every failure to live up to the highest standards. Nonetheless Mr Cook has not retreated into a more conventional posture or hidden behind the language of realism so congenial to ministers as they settle into power. Indeed, in September 2000 his speech to the Labour Party Conference was couched unashamedly in the rhetoric of cosmopolitanism, and made no attempt to damp down delegates' expectations over human rights issues. He claimed that 'we have put human rights at the heart of foreign policy'.[4]

In giving prominence to ethics, and explicitly requiring foreign policy to

be related to the values of domestic society (instead of playing to the supposedly Machiavellian rules of international politics alone), Cook was
changing at least the language of post-war British foreign policy. Values had
never been absent, as the anti-communism of the Cold War and the anti-
colonialism of previous Labour administrations had shown. But all British
governments had focused on the stability of the inter-state system rather
than on interventions in domestic affairs, and they had tried to temper the
crusading zeal of some American leaders by stressing the very principle of
non-intervention, and its corollary, peaceful co-existence. Thus both the
Labour and Conservative governments of the day had been willing to
recognise the post-revolutionary government in China after 1949, when the
United States delayed recognition until 1971.[5] The talk of ethics, therefore,
insofar as it related almost exclusively to the idea that Britain should try to
promote change inside certain other states, opened up a set of issues which
had previously been bracketed out of serious policy discussions, not least
because the international lawyers, governmental and academic, mostly
agreed that they were *ultra vires*.[6]

In this move the Foreign Secretary was not being wholly original. He
was clearly supported by the New Labour hinterland which looked eagerly
towards the huge majority of their government to make possible some radical change in foreign policy, as it had done in 1945. By contrast with
those war-torn days, moreover, Cook was in tune with the *zeitgeist* in
wanting to transform the very quality of international relations – as
opposed to confronting a new security threat, as Attlee and Bevin had
thought they had to do. Since the end of the Cold War the West had been
increasingly confident about making its foreign aid 'conditional' on internal change and about requiring 'democratisation', seen as a condition of
international peace and security as well as a value in itself. This, together
with traumatic events such as those in Bosnia, had fostered the growth of
domestic interest in foreign affairs and in the serious possibilities of global
human rights advances. Robin Cook was the first politician with the
courage to tie actual policy into the moral debate, but in doing so he was
hardly swimming against the tide. On the other hand his claims distanced
himself from his Conservative predecessors, and by definition implied
their amorality.[7]

Since May 1997 the Prime Minister and the Foreign Secretary have
formed one of the more effective foreign policy executives in recent British
history – that is, the pair of key individuals with ultimate responsibility for
deciding on Britain's reactions to key international events. The Chancellor
of the Exchequer and the Secretaries of State for Defence, and for
International Development, are also often part of this inner group of the
Cabinet, but Blair and Cook have a day-to-day responsibility which sets
them slightly apart. Both men have continued to articulate the discourse of
ethics in relation to foreign policy, and indeed to assume that Britain has a
special leadership role in this respect. Yet with experience, and the

perpetual flow of unforeseeable 'events' which Harold Macmillan labelled his greatest problem, has come a reversion to more conventional diplomatic language. Thus on the FCO's current web-site, 'Foreign Policy Achievements' are listed under conventional headings such as 'security, international peace and stability', or 'prosperity', although the detail discloses an impressive catalogue of such claims as 'agreed land-mines ban' and 'first ever FCO/DfID Annual Reports on Human Rights'.[8]

The central issue in terms of New Labour's ethical dimension to foreign policy is the extent to which it has changed the substance, as opposed to the presentation of policy. And if actual practice has changed, how deep does the transformation go, and with what results? Despite the short time which has elapsed since the arrival of the Blair government, a certain amount of academic work has already been completed on these issues, mainly by Nicholas Wheeler and Tim Dunne at Aberystwyth, and Richard Little and Mark Wickham-Jones at Bristol. Their findings are broadly favourable to the government, in contrast with denunciations in the press, from both right and left and on the grounds of both hypocrisy and ineffectiveness.[9] On the other hand, Wheeler's and Dunne's conclusion in 1998 that 'there has been a marked shift in the content and conduct of British foreign policy' had changed two years later into the view that there is 'a growing discrepancy between the moral rhetoric of the Blair government and its subsequent practices'.[10] In foreign policy the fact of the matter is that intentions, however sincere, are inherently difficult to translate into significant change because of the extent to which they depend on other people and other, often intractable, societies.

The evidence about the impact of a more ethically aware foreign policy is therefore inevitably mixed. On the negative side of the equation is the fact, deplored by many Labour activists, that little has been done to change the pattern of British arms exports, or indeed Britain's status as one of the leading arms manufacturing states. Britain had 10.7 per cent of the world's market share in arms in 1992, and 16.2 per cent in 1998.[11] This is probably because there are powerful interests, economic and security-related, behind the maintenance of national capacity in the defence industries. Production is increasingly characterised by multinational collaboration, but we are still far from the market conditions which obtain, say, in the car industry, or from a consolidated European arms industry – despite the government's clear moves to encourage the latter.[12] This is not necessarily a proof of ethical failings, but it does make it harder to cancel orders from governments which maltreat their own or others' citizens. Thus the Blair government has been sharply criticised for continuing to sell a range of arms to Indonesia throughout Jakarta's repression in East Timor, and it is vulnerable to a turn of events in the Gulf states, where Britain's military and political stake is extensive and the kind of democracy urged on Eastern Europe has yet to take root.

Arms are only one instance of the 'double standards' problem which besets any government trying to claim the moral high ground. It damaged Jimmy Carter as it is damaging New Labour. It was brave to confront head-on the difficult issues of how far a given country should accept 'duties beyond borders' in relation to the internal affairs of others as well as to their purely foreign policy behaviour, but probably foolish to raise the flag of an ethical stance before it had been even half thought through. The way was clear for critics to score easy points and for inconsistent decision-making. The government does not have to connive in other governments' repressive policies; mere inaction or inattention is enough to open it up to criticism. This was true in East Timor, where the government was quickly accused of not doing enough, or in time, to prevent Indonesian militias from terrorising the population during and immediately after the election of 30 August 1999 which voted for independence. There is no doubt that Cook and Blair deplored Indonesian actions, and pressed for the liberation of East Timor, in sharp contrast to their predecessors in 1975, when the Wilson government had tacitly condoned Jakarta's annexation. Equally, they allowed other states, in particular Australia, to take the lead in organising a peace-keeping force. This might make good sense in terms of Britain's limited resources and a division of labour approach to the world's problems (as it had done in Albania in 1997) but once public expectations of moral leadership have been excited such an approach seems like foot-dragging. This is true even where Britain has not had formal responsibility; how much more difficult would have been the government's experience if the first years after the hand-over of Hong Kong to China had produced serious clashes over human rights? Here the UK has prime moral responsibility but very little practical capacity to help, so that the gap between philosophy and action would have been all too evident.

China itself has been another case of the government not seeming to do enough to live up to its ethical aspirations. If the Foreign Secretary has wished to enter into dialogue over human rights, so as to avoid both 'row' and 'kow-tow', then he has had to tread the thinnest of tight-ropes.[13] In practice he has done little more than British governments did with communist regimes throughout the Cold War, and particularly after the Helsinki Accords of 1975: draw attention to some abuses, particularly behind the scenes, and hope that détente at the intergovernmental level would promote further change. The main concern has been not to endanger strategic dialogue and stability by pressing too hard on human rights. In the case of China during the 1990s there have been the additional factors, not present with the USSR, of nervousness about Hong Kong, and of the commercial incentives not to rock the diplomatic boat. In this context it has been surprising not only that criticisms of China's often brutal system have been muted, but that President Jiang Zemin was granted a visit with full honours to Britain.

There have been other issues on which New Labour's foreign policy has seemed laggardly or culpable by omission. In Nigeria the complaints of the Ogoni people against the misrule of their province, dominated by the Anglo-Dutch oil multinational Shell, have largely gone unheard in Whitehall. The death of the military dictator Sani Abacha in June 1998 removed the worst dilemmas about cooperation with a corrupt and brutal regime, but economic interests and the need for Nigerian cooperation over the wider crisis in West Africa have continued to inhibit comment on the internal affairs of the region's major state. In this case quiet diplomacy might be the best strategy, but in the new, self-induced climate of transparency it gains few brownie points with public opinion.[14]

It was the extraordinary saga of General Pinochet, however, which best illustrated both the wish of the Blair government to live up to its human rights-based values and its practical difficulty in so doing. It is difficult to imagine a British government of any colour before 1997 allowing a foreign head of state to be detained in Britain while the legal case was argued as to whether he should be extradited to Spain on charges of having been responsible for the torturing and deaths of his own and Spanish citizens over two decades before. Pragmatism, *realpolitik* or diplomatic immunity would have lead to the General being allowed to return freely to Santiago from his private shopping trips to London, as he had done several times before.[15] It was therefore remarkable that Pinochet should have been detained at all – albeit in comfortable, nursing home conditions – and not surprising that it was the one issue on which the Conservative Opposition furiously dissented from New Labour's foreign policy. For sixteen months, from October 1998 until 2 March 2000, Pinochet's presence in Britain alternately embarrassed the government and kept attention fixed on the ethics of foreign policy. A series of highly publicised court rulings made it impossible to play the issue down while illustrating the technical problems of international law inherent in attempts to be a 'good international citizen'.[16] On balance, and from a narrowly political point of view, the British government came out of the whole affair quite well. Their ethical reputation had been dramatically enhanced by the publicity over Pinochet's detention, while they had been able to keep responsibility at arms length by stressing the independence of the judicial process. They also prevented the nightmarish prospect (in terms of relations with Latin America) of Pinochet dying in custody by allowing his return home on medical grounds – which even at the time seemed dubious. Whitehall clearly facilitated his immediate exit before any further obstructions could be created. The Spanish government was also quietly relieved, and precedents for the future treatment of travelling dictators remained ambiguous.[17] In the end everyone took something from the affair.

More serious in terms of the damage which has been inflicted on the image of a more ethical foreign policy have been those instances where the government has been prepared to act, but has seemed deliberately to rank propriety below more traditional foreign policy criteria. This was the case with the Sandline affair in Sierra Leone, the Russian war on Chechnya and the continued Anglo-American pressure, military and economic, on Iraq.

Sierra Leone has been the government's biggest bilateral problem, and one which has been virtually coterminous with it – the crisis having begun with a military coup on 25 May 1997. The dilemmas over intervention, and mission creep, which continue to commit British forces in west Africa to this day, will be dealt with below. The first difficulties for Robin Cook and his colleagues, however, arose over the Sandline affair which burst into view in the spring of 1998. This complex set of issues will rate only a footnote in history. Nonetheless, as the Foreign Secretary himself acknowledged, it 'took its toll' on his standing as a minister, and led to criticisms of the FCO by the (Labour-dominated) House of Commons Foreign Affairs Committee (FAC) which were extremely severe.[18] In short, it involved the British 'private military company' Sandline providing arms to the exiled (constitutional) President of Sierra Leone so as to help him return to power. This involved the breaking of a UN arms embargo which the British government had supported. Sandline had acted with the knowledge of the British High Commissioner to Sierra Leone and of some FCO officials – although not, it seems, that of the Foreign Secretary. Undeniably, some parts of the official British foreign policy machinery were involved in breaching international law, thus at least showing consistency with the behaviour revealed by the Scott enquiry over the Iraqi supergun affair, and indeed with a scandal over illegal arms supplies to Rwanda in 1996.[19]

The Sandline affair was a murky business, and the FAC's report was frustrated by not being able to investigate the role of the intelligence services in it.[20] The British government's policy was to restore the legal government of President Kabbah by peaceful means, bizarrely allowing the High Commissioner to go into exile in Guinea with the President. Kabbah himself and some of his friends were clearly willing to use all means available (one of these individuals epitomised globalisation in his own person: 'an Indian businessman, travelling on the passport of a dead Serb, awaiting extradition from Canada for alleged embezzlement from a bank in Thailand').[21] Once the Kabba government had been restored to power (in March 1998), but with the British government coming under fire over Sandline, this led Tony Blair to observe that what mattered was the justice of the end, not the means. Yet as the prime minister was to discover, in a conflict between them, law cannot so easily be subordinated to a consequentialist morality. The deception, muddle and sheer risk-taking of British conduct during Sandline damaged the country's general policy in west Africa, and undermined its domestic support in what has become a dangerous and long drawn-out conflict.

The FAC report came within an ace of calling for the resignation of the Head of the Diplomatic Service. It referred (para. 64) to 'a remarkable admission of professional incompetence' by Sir John Kerr, and concluded (para. 70) that 'the Permanent Under-Secretary failed in his duty to Ministers'. This damning indictment went well beyond the studied conclusions of the earlier Legg Report and was treated with disdain by the Secretary of State. Yet the Diplomatic Service came out of the Sandline affair with its reputation for professionalism besmirched. It should also not be forgotten that insofar as British officials were playing the Thomas à Becket game over Sandline they were doing so because they wished to support Nigerian troops in ECOMOG (Economic Community of West African States Monitoring Group) who were working to the same end, of restoring President Kabbah. But Nigeria was itself the subject of an arms embargo at the time, because of the behaviour of its own military dictatorship, and keeping such company, particularly given the further shared goal of keeping Sierra Leone's valuable diamond mines out of rebel hands, was hardly the stuff of the 'ethical dimension'. Furthermore the indirect use of force by giving a green light to mercenaries risked plunging the whole region into chaos.[22] In short, Sandline was a serious failure of British policy, in terms of both conduct and regional consequences. The Blair government has only emerged as unscathed as it has because the affair occurred early in its period of office, because media attention to foreign affairs is shallow and because Parliament has few instruments of pressure. It was, in a way, Robin Cook's Bay of Pigs. Like John Kennedy in 1961, however, Cook learned from the experience. He admitted errors, publicly defended the officials who had landed him in the mess and used the opportunity to set in motion various reforms in the FCO which, if fully implemented, should make decision-making both more efficient and more accountable.[23]

In the other two areas where New Labour has seemed deliberately to prefer traditional balance of power considerations to its own ethical agenda, Britain has not had the primary responsibility which faced it in Sierra Leone. In Chechnya, the outbreak of a second war in 1999, not long after NATO's victory in Kosovo (and not, perhaps, coincidentally) faced all western states with the dilemma of whether or not to condemn the iron hand approach of the Russian government, eventually legitimised by Vladimir Putin's election as President, when this risked alienating further a chaotic state already digging itself into a bunker over the Balkans. Predictably, Putin has not been able to win the war quickly, and a bloody stalemate has ensued. For London this means a constant reminder of the double standards problem, given an extra twist by Moscow's claim to be behaving in much the same way as NATO did over Kosovo, and by the decision to seek a special personal relationship with Putin through reciprocal visits.[24] Yet if Putin decides in the end to go for military victory, which might be possible if he were willing to sanction a further massive loss of life, the British government would have to condemn Russia and to impose some form of sanctions upon it.[25]

So far as the continued bombing of Iraq is concerned, it is possible for the British government to make the case – as indeed it can be made over

Russia – that the polarity between ethics and *realpolitik* is a false one, because the need to achieve arms control, in this case of chemical and biological weapons, is a supreme necessity.[26] Britain continues to act with the United States (and in the face of growing disquiet from some EU partners) to enforce the 'no-fly zones' in northern and southern Iraq, and to insist on the maintenance of comprehensive sanctions against Iraq, despite the evidence that they are damaging the Iraqi people more than the Hussein regime. It does this no doubt partly because of the perceived benefits of being continually seen in Washington as the United States' most loyal friend when things get tough (although the same perception world-wide brings the UK significant costs) and partly because of the genuine belief that Saddam Hussein is a threat to the stability of the Middle East and will take advantage of any latitude shown to him. The further measures, of first threatening and then initiating air attacks on Iraq (the latter in Operation Desert Fox, in December 1998), were the logical consequence of the game of 'chicken' in which both sides were ensnared. Just as with Milosevic over Kosovo, once the Iraqi leader had passed a certain point in his failure to comply with the demands being made on him (in this case over access for the UNSCOM inspectors) the UK and the US were left with no options other than backing down or military escalation. The result was the unedifying spectacle of high-tech attacks on a defenceless target and a widening credibility gap between defensible aims and indefensible means. Military action also made it much more difficult to get off the hook of the increasingly unpopular sanctions policy, and easier for Saddam to exploit divisions among and within the western states.[27]

The 'ethical dimension' has certainly changed the language of British foreign policy, and language is not simply a neutral transmission belt. It helps to shape the thought being expressed through it, and it affects how those who hear or read of it perceive an issue. At the most superficial level, public relations do sometimes work while politicians often come to believe their own rhetoric. In the case of New Labour's foreign policy, however, things cut deeper. In terms both of the government's own objectives and of any liberally-minded view of the need to promote human rights and/or a sense of international community, some real change has been achieved, and in less than four years. Superficial as they might be, and still far short of the hopes of many, decisions such as those to support an International Criminal Court, a ban on land-mines sale and manufacture, and the creation of an EU Arms Export Code of Conduct have all advanced the frontier of what is considered both ethical and realistic in international relations. Britain has persistently urged democratisation and human rights, risking the inevitable charges of double standards, when it could have chosen a lower profile. Its enthusiasm for EU enlargement, for example, although arguably flawed in its neglect of geopolitics and a failure to think through the long-term issues, is consistently geared to a view of a wider Europe able to share the freedoms and prosperity so far only available in the western part of the continent. The long-drawn out detention of

Pinochet in the UK was also a powerful symbol and focal point for all those who had been struggling for decades to ensure that human rights issues were taken seriously in international relations.

The real difficulty with even the modest goal of adding an ethical dimension to foreign policy is not the lack of impact in other countries, or the hypocrisy of pressing the weak and ignoring the strong – both are certain to happen.[28] More serious would be an indication that the discourse had come to exist for its own sake, that it was a routine form of window-dressing with no consequences for the standard operating procedures of diplomacy or for the strategic choices faced by the government. Only those already keen to rush to judgement would find the Cook–Blair foreign policy guilty on that charge now. On the other hand a serious verdict will be unavoidable after a second term, if granted by the voters.

Assuming a continued commitment on the part of Robin Cook or his successor, the central dilemma will continue to revolve around the fact that ethics are not, contrary to popular belief, synonymous with human rights. Quite apart from the tensions over international law during the Sandline case, the issue of the liberty of citizens is only one part of a moral view of world politics. R.J. Vincent showed how human rights must be understood to include economic as well as political rights, but beyond both lie the issues of justice and order raised by Hedley Bull, who saw them as both inherently value-laden.[29] Events inside states, and the pattern of inter-state relations, grate against each other at the moral as much as the practical level. Indeed, it should be a moral imperative for foreign policy-makers to be as concerned for issues of international peace, security and stability, as for those of genocide and oppression. While therefore we may disagree with the positions taken by Britain on nuclear non-proliferation, or by the US on the Middle East, we should not assume automatically that they represent moral-free zones. Most foreign policy decisions represent trade-offs between competing moral-political considerations, with the politics relating to the degree of perceived practicability and to the stake (or interest) of the actor concerned. But those very perceptions and stakes will be given life by the views of desired worlds (that is, the moralities) represented by the actors, and the strength with which they are held. Thus the British government will continue to wrestle with dilemmas which are inherently both ethical and political, whether they relate to human rights in Burma, sanctions against Iraq over weapons production or – most dramatic of all – the possibility of military intervention in an international conflict such as Kuwait or Taiwan.

Intervention

'Twenty years ago we would not have been fighting in Kosovo. We would have turned our backs on it.' This was the claim made by Tony Blair in his Chicago speech as a preface to his new 'doctrine of the international community'.[30] Despite the unhistorical nature of this claim, the speech repays close attention for the self-conscious way in which it attempts to signal a new departure in British foreign policy – indeed in international relations more generally. It is possible that the speech will be seen by future historians as a landmark in the way that Gladstone's 'Bulgarian horrors' pamphlet, the Eyre Crowe Memorandum or Churchill's concept of the 'three circles' all acted as reference points for debate about British foreign policy. Equally, it might turn out to have been an over-ambitious attempt to change international law – 'the principle of non-interference must be qualified in important respects' – which failed to attract the support of wider international society and became a millstone round the government's neck.[31]

What were the contents of the speech? Although its centrepiece is an attempt to rewrite the just war doctrine for the new millennium, this was set in the midst of a discussion of globalisation, political as well as economic, which was fostering, the Prime Minister argued, 'the beginnings of a new doctrine of international community'. By this he meant 'the explicit recognition that today more than ever before, we are mutually dependent, that national interest is to a significant extent governed by international collaboration and that we need a clear and coherent debate as to the direction this doctrine takes us in each field of international endeavour'. This might mean, in practical terms, focusing on reform of the international financial system through the G7, on free trade at the WTO, on reform of the UN Security Council, on Third World debt and on cooperation between rich and poor states over the environment.

Moving on to international politics Blair argued that 'the principles of international community apply also to international security' and correctly identified the key foreign policy problem of the modern state – at least, of those like Britain with the pretensions and perhaps the power to have a global role: how 'to identify the circumstances in which we should get actively involved in other people's conflicts'. The classical rule of non-interference (enshrined somewhat ambiguously in the UN Charter) needed qualifying in three ways: to justify action against genocide; to deal with 'massive flows of refugees' which became 'threats to international peace and security'; and to deal with regimes based on minority rule. Such changes would amount to the doctrine of 'humanitarian intervention' long canvassed in international law.[32]

Exceptions to the rule of non-intervention have been canvassed since ever John Stuart Mill first fixed on the problem, and most have proved highly contentious.[33] Blair's third category is so obviously problematical that it can be counted an aberration. His government has no intention of intervening in a state just because it is not a democracy. The other two provide more serious grounds, especially when taken in conjunction with the five conditions that Blair then argued should be satisfied before a decision to intervene could be taken: a strong case; the exhaustion of all diplomatic options; the practicality of the military option (for intervention here means military action); contingency plans for the long term; and our own national interests at stake. These conditions were sensibly introduced not as 'absolute tests' but as 'the kind of issues which we need to think about' in future decisions.

Whatever its fate, the Chicago speech is highly unusual in the history of British foreign policy for the explicit attention which it gives to the criteria for action and to conceptualisation. It amounts to a minor revolution against the pragmatic empiricism which has dominated the language of British foreign policy since the days of Cobden, Bright and Gladstone. It is to be commended for its thoughtful approach – in the midst of a major crisis – and for having opened up a debate rather than trying to close one off. Probably no Prime Minister of the twentieth century other than Churchill could have uttered a sentence like 'we need to focus in a serious and sustained way on the principles of the doctrine of international community and on the institutions which deliver them', in an attempt to go beyond the ad hoc.

On the other side of the coin, there has so far been little follow-through in terms of the doctrine or efforts to obtain international consensus around it. British policy has reverted, perforce, to making principles through cases: as well as Kosovo, there have been Sierra Leone and the continuing saga of Iraq. In part this is because of some large assumptions made in the Chicago speech which are inherently difficult to translate into both law and practical policy. One is that the struggle of right against wrong in international affairs can be equated to 'the cause of internationalism . . . against isolationism'. Yet isolationism is a straw man, espoused by few in current conditions, while 'internationalism' has so many different meanings that it provides no concrete guidance on the problem of getting involved 'in other people's conflicts'. Moreover the speech slides too easily between the idea of economic interdependence and that of international community. As Kenneth Waltz has powerfully demonstrated, not only does interconnectedness not guarantee common understandings, it may create new conflicts. In the case of British foreign policy, it has been evident for two centuries that as a trading nation the United Kingdom has fundamental interests in how the international system is organised. But the arguments have still raged as to what that should mean in terms of intervention or non-intervention, force or diplomacy, vicinity or globalism. The Blair tests have confronted the humanitarian aspect of these dilemmas more explicitly than ever before, but they still beg important questions about whether Britain should take a lead, whether it should act unilaterally or only multilaterally, and how far it should risk life and resources in the pursuit of such ends. There are elements of wish-fulfilment and ethnocentrism in the belief that international relations are becoming like society at home – the famous 'domestic analogy' – and accordingly the new 'doctrine of international community' is much a statement of preference as a guide to action.

Sierra Leone continues to illustrate the problems. Sandline was only the first of the foreign policy crises it precipitated. The breakdown of the ceasefire between government and rebels in May 2000 produced further savage fighting and a situation of anarchy into which British troops were sent, after initial denials, to train and sustain government forces. On a much smaller scale, it has been reminiscent of the 'quagmire effect' by which the US was drawn ever deeper into the Vietnam war, and indeed Robin Cook has had to face regular Conservative charges of 'mission creep'. The three humanitarian qualifications of the rule of non-intervention outlined in the Chicago speech do not convincingly account for this commitment. The violence is terrible, but it is not genocide; the flows of refugees are a threat to peace and security in the region, but not 'internationally'; and the action is in support of a government against insurgents – admittedly in an attempt to prevent the onset of a murderous version of minority rule. Of the five conditions which would also need to be met (see above) there has been little clarity on long-term plans, or on the nature of 'national interests' at stake. Quite probably the main motivations for intervening have been a sense of responsibility for one of the most British of ex-colonies in Africa, and a desire to restore order regionally not least in relation to the diamond mining industry. These are perfectly defensible reasons, but they do not derive from an emerging rule of humanitarian intervention. At best they relate to some tacit notion of a division of labour among the major powers in relation to humanitarian disasters. It is noteworthy that the UK has acted for the most part unilaterally in this crisis, rather than in the framework of the UN operation, while the EU has had no significant role at all.

The Blair attempt to carry forward both thought and practice on intervention, one of the most fundamental problems in international relations, has therefore predictably met with modest results so far. This is an area where law, morality and politics are intensely complex and entwined. It is possible that the Chicago speech will be left as a marooned outpost, with foreign policy reverting to more familiar and defensible terrain. Yet if New Labour, in a second term, is able to extend the discussion throughout the international community, with the prospect of shaping new norms in the EU and the UN, it will have exerted the moral leadership on the world scale which Blair and Cook have always sought.[34] In this they are typical of their country's foreign policy tradition. The contents of the Chicago speech, however, are new and ambitious. If they can be built upon, they will represent a radical change in the ideology of British foreign policy. The UK has submitted to the UN Secretary-General four rules on which it seeks general agreement. Three of these add nothing in essence to the UN Charter of 1945. But the fourth states that 'when faced with an overwhelming humanitarian catastrophe and government that has demonstrated itself unwilling or unable to halt or prevent it, the international community should act'. This is the humanitarian principle, which the government seems determined not to let drop.[35]

The Domestic Dimension

One of the problems of Labour's new thinking in foreign policy is that it has not always been 'joined-up' to use one of the party's favourite clichés. Although the Chicago speech dealt with the ethical issues so central to Robin Cook's approach, the FCO had not been consulted on its drafting, and the final result produced some shock and anger in King Charles Street – not least among the senior legal advisers, whose territory it blithely invaded. The speech seems to have originated from the Prime Minister's own foreign policy advisers, including some in the academic world. The Foreign Secretary himself is probably more wedded to a traditional Labour concern for the UN and for international law than to the new mixture of morality and NATO, while FCO officials have been attempting to reel in policy ever since the shocks of Kosovo and Chicago.[36] Cook must also have been ambivalent about the way in which Kosovo propelled Tony Blair to the centre of foreign policy-making, just as the Falklands had done for Margaret Thatcher.[37] On the other hand, personal rivalry has not been sharply evident, and the Blair–Cook foreign policy executive has evolved into a working relationship. Things have been easier since Cook weathered his first year, difficult because of his personal life and a series of gaffes abroad, notably on a state visit to India and Pakistan when the Queen was placed in an embarrassing position. During that first year it seemed increasingly that Peter Mandelson was the Foreign Secretary-in-waiting, making diplomatic visits to European capitals reminiscent of Neville Chamberlain's use of personal envoys, which finally led to the resignation of Anthony Eden in February 1938. Robin Cook was therefore the main beneficiary of Mandelson's demise, and his increasingly authoritative performance has further increased his standing, in the party, in the country and abroad. He now commands the substance of foreign policy even if the Prime Minister shares responsibility for setting the *grandes lignes*.

Relations with other ministers and departments have so far not caused insuperable problems, despite the rumours about poor personal relationships and the weakness of Cabinet government, which Tony Blair has not sought to disguise. Given the increasingly direct involvement in external policy of the Treasury, the Ministry of Defence, the Department of Trade and Industry and Customs and Excise, and the creation of DfID, there is considerable potential for bureaucratic politics and the deflection of policy. If foreign policy can increasingly draw on a wide range of instruments (from military training to Chevening scholarships for students to study in the UK) then this puts a premium on the capacity for coordination of the government machine. The achievement of a 'foreign policy-led' Strategic Defence Review shows what a determined effort can achieve, but the downgrading of the Cabinet, and possibly also of its key Defence and Overseas Policy Committee will make it much more difficult to sustain such efforts over time.

One area where Robin Cook sought immediately to make a difference was in the presentation of British foreign policy, where his audience was as much at home as abroad. Having finally managed to break the association between Labour and a weak or unpatriotic foreign and defence policy. Cook took the initiative to project an image of a modernising foreign policy more in touch with its own people and less defensive about 'abroad'. This partly involved the 'cool Britannia' image-making of the new Foreign Policy Centre, actively encouraged by Labour to debate a new agenda which straddled home and foreign affairs, and partly opening up the FCO itself to a wider range of citizens than had ever been through its grand portals before. A real effort has been made to broaden the base of recruitment into the FCO, and to dispel some of its mystique of exclusivity. There are limits to what can be done in this area, and certainly the pace of change will be slow if professional standards are not to be compromised, but there is no doubt that the historical process of making the FCO less like a gentleman's club is now moving on apace.[38] The danger from the government's viewpoint is that while easy points may be clocked up through declarations about multiculturalism and ethical diplomacy, this may heighten public interest in foreign policy to the point where the political impact is quite unpredictable.

Development and Foreign Policy

The fact that development policy has moved in and out of FCO control according to whether a Labour or Conservative government is in power suggests that its relationship with mainstream foreign policy is ambiguous and controversial. Broadly speaking those who want 'eliminating world poverty' (the title of Clare Short's White Paper of November 1997, the first on development for twenty years) to be the priority, insist on separate ministry with a Cabinet minister to defend its interests. They tend to be more often in the Labour Party. Those who wish to see aid related to the wider goals of foreign policy prefer the set-up of the last government, that is an Overseas Development Administration subordinate to the FCO. New Labour decided in December 1995 that they would set up a new Department for International Development, and after the election victory Clare Short was given the job of running it and a seat in the Cabinet. Over the last four years Ms Short and DfID have worked hard to ensure that British attention is not monopolised by Europe, and have taken advantage of the current stress on the importance of conflict prevention to involve themselves in a wider range of activities than would have been possible during the Cold War.[39]

A number of difficulties have arisen from the fact that development is a policy area in flux, and that it has become more obviously politicised over the last decade. Thus while pressure groups call for an end to tied aid, or for Third World debt to be written off, with governments like Britain seemingly often in agreement, those same governments insist increasingly on 'good governance' and on the need for aid to be 'conditional' on progress in political and economic reform. When poor countries step out of line, they are likely to be subject to economic sanctions, of which the first casualty will always be aid. Of the twenty-four countries in February 2000 subject to UK sanctions regimes, the vast majority are states suffering from the 'abject poverty' which DfID is aiming to eradicate.[40] Equally, while there is general agreement on the benefits of multilateralism, states continue to compete over the commercial orders which inevitably spin off from grants and loans – such as the 1500 Land Rovers, worth £25 million, due to go to the Zimbabwe police, which New Labour froze on entering office, then unfroze and finally cancelled midstream in protest against Mugabe's land policy.[41] At the same time the European Union, the world's largest aid donor and on the face of things the ideal platform for British development policy, has been severely criticised by British observers (including Chris Patten, External Relations Commissioner) for its inefficiency, while its once path-breaking Lomé Conventions have been allowed to stagnate and to fall into disrepute.[42]

Thus New Labour has been almost forced to go down the national path of development policy, with all the associated temptations of economic and political conditionality, at the same time as talking up multilateralism and aid-without-strings. The tensions thereby created have not yet shown up too obviously in policy-making, since the FCO has been absorbed with its own makeover and the MoD has been grateful for the new roles which have come its way. There have been turf wars, but these have mostly arisen from problems of coordination during crises, as between Cook and Short during the Montserrat volcano emergency, or during the floods in Mozambique in March 2000, when DfID and the MoD wrangled over whose responsibility it was to send helicopters. On the other hand, when Clare Short refused to use her visit to China as a vehicle for promoting British trade, it revealed fundamental divisions which can be expected to recur, notwithstanding New Labour's disavowal of slush funds like that which caused the Pergau Dam scandal.[43]

Although aid is now a priority again, after two decades of being run down, it is proving difficult to live up to the hopes of the committed and even to the government's own targets. Clare Short reaffirmed Labour's promise in Opposition to head for the UN target of official development assistance at the level of 0.7 per cent GNP, from the 1997 base-line of 0.23 per cent. Unfortunately that figure has still not yet been raised, while even the projection for 2001 is only 0.30 per cent.[44] The time-lags and problems of implementation turned out to be greater than envisaged. Britain is now well behind France and Japan as the main individual aid donors.[45] The same is true for the issue of debt relief. Although the government has enjoyed some good publicity about their willingness to cancel Third World debt, there was an element of gesture politics about the announcement, given that much debt could not have been reclaimed anyway, and that difficult problems remain over coordinating the financial burdens to be incurred by the various western states – Britain is not one of those states which will suffer most.[46]

Not all British activity in the Third World has revolved around development, as we have seen with Sierra Leone. The Commonwealth has continued its modest revival as a forum in which Britain is active and finds support. On the other hand, it has also continued to generate problems, post-colonial and otherwise. The explosions of nuclear devices by both India and Pakistan have exposed the limits of British influence – as indeed of every other outside power. The failing states of west Africa, including the looming presence of Nigeria, were a source of such concern to both Britain and France that they drove the historic rivals together in joint African initiatives not seen for decades. Foreign Ministers Cook and Vedrine visited Ghana and the Côte d'Ivoire together in March 1999, one month after a joint statement from the Development Ministers of the two countries (plus Germany) had tried to stir the EU into reforming its aid policies.[47] In South Africa, the Blair government's evident goodwill towards the ANC did not change much in the complex and long-drawn-out negotiations over an EU–South Africa Trade Agreement.

It was in Zimbabwe, however, where the limits of British influence were most sharply exposed, despite sympathetic support from EU partners and an apparent free hand as the ex-metropolitan power. Here President Mugabe's determination to hang on to power led him to encourage black squatters to take over the land of white farmers, in disregard of the law. The latter's protests were heard outside the country, and Britain responded with a clear and forceful condemnation, despite the obvious risks of being cast as the defender of an economically dominant white minority. The Foreign Secretary tended to take a back seat, leaving the conduct of the crisis to his Minister of State Peter Hain, well-known as a South African born radical opponent of Apartheid. This may have seemed an intelligent ploy at the time, but it soon back-fired. Not only did Hain's emotional involvement lead him to strain too far in the search for impartiality, as when he referred to Mugabe's behaviour as 'uncivilised', but the very fact of a white African instructing a veteran leader of a liberation struggle on democracy smacked of colonialism. It handed Mugabe the very card he needed, of black solidarity in the face of external intervention from the former overlord. British concern, and the attention of the world's media, helped to build up the democratic opposition, and may have prevented even worse atrocities against the white farmers, but ultimately Britain was shown up as having responsibility but not power. Once again the shibboleths of the Third Way turned out to be difficult to apply in foreign policy.

Special Relationships?

Under Tony Blair and Robin Cook Britain has not sought any exclusive, major relationship; it has not wished to choose between its many potential partners. Rather, New Labour has sought to be friends with almost everyone. They built a new relationship with the EU, while staying close to the Clinton White House. They have continued to revive the Commonwealth, and have sought 'critical engagements' with Russia, with China and with the erstwhile 'crazy states' such as Libya, North Korea and Iran. There has also been a general enthusiasm for multilateralism.

At one level this is wholly desirable. Jaw-jaw generally is preferable to war-war unless primary values have to be sacrificed, and there was too much hostile posturing towards presumed enemies in the Cold War when the real problem was more often than not a difference of socio-political system. New Labour has seen through the perpetual search for an Other, and to its credit has dispensed with one. Equally, there is little point in posing abstract choices between closeness to the US and friendship with EU or Commonwealth partners. International relations have in part always been about overlapping relations or cross-cutting cleavages, and the multiple dimensions of the modern system have made such a pattern the norm. In fact this is a much more familiar story than New Labour likes to believe. The talk of Britain's special roles in both the Atlantic and European spheres, plus its Commonwealth heritage, is nothing more than the familiar Churchillian image of the three circles, with Britain uniquely in the intersecting cusps.

It is thus not difficult to find traces of a philosophy of exceptionalism in Britain's current foreign policy, albeit one stripped of the old trappings of empire and hierarchy. Certainly there is no serious sense of the 'retreat of the state' coming out of the FCO or 10 Downing Street, for all the talk of the onward march of globalisation. In fact ministers tend to stress that 'for too long the politics of globalisation has lagged behind the economics', and to assume that in catching up they can be the 'spokesmen of the common good'.[48] Old Labour's UN and Commonwealth-based internationalism has been grafted onto a human rights discourse and to a more positive attitude towards the EU with barely a pause for breath, and no false humility about overstretch or cultural relativism. Moreover even the traditional geopolitical sense of responsibility for an indivisible international security has not been ditched. Britain, it seems, has emerged from the dark years of declining middle power and is once again at the centre of international deliberations. Little wonder that there is no sign of considering relinquishing the permanent seat on the UN Security Council. Blair has said that the EU should become a 'superpower', no doubt with the UK prominent in its guidance, given that the latter is 'a pivotal power in international affairs'.[49]

All this amounts to a vast range of commitments even when times are serene. It is impossible to please all partners all of the time, as the current row over Echelon indicates. The European Parliament has investigated allegations that the anglophone surveillance system has been used for commercial spying at the very time when the UK is supposed to be encouraging the development of the Single Market and a rationalisation of the European defence industry.[50] Emerging problems over Nuclear Missile Defence also show how UK–US cooperation over defence and communications has the potential to embarrass any British government which stresses its multiple friendships. Another kind of weakness has been evident in Africa, in the Indian sub-continent and over the Arab-Israel dispute, where ministers have gone beyond what might have been expected in efforts at mediation and peace-keeping, but where the limits of British influence, resources and domestic political support have soon been reached.

It would be wrong to argue that New Labour have generated a new, bullish language for British foreign policy while failing to achieve any changes of substance. The language and the actions are intimately connected, not least because the key figures in making foreign policy appear to have genuinely internalised the philosophy they articulate. Yet they are also at risk of being carried away by their own heady ambitions. On the one hand Robin Cook adheres to views which could almost have been expressed by Disraeli or Macmillan: 'Britain is best served by a foreign policy of enlightened self-interest' (as opposed to the crude self-interest he appears to believe was pursued in the past); or 'Britain has more to gain than any other state from an orderly international framework for the global economy'. On the other, he can state that 'the global interest is becoming the national interest'.[51] This considered assertion was made not in the first few days of office, but in late January 2000, and was backed up with serious arguments about the need to promote democracy and human rights. Leaving aside the philosophical problems, if it is really held to be true that Britain's interests are now difficult to distinguish from those of the world as a whole, then there can be no limit to the activism and dilemmas over intervention in the future. How can one decide on priorities? The Blair–Cook effect has been to bring a surprising degree of courage and ambition to British foreign policy, but it runs a distinct risk of hubris.

I am grateful to Martin Dahl for his most helpful research assistance during the writing of this chapter.

Notes

1 Shigeo Mutsushika (University of Shizuoka, Japan). 'The transformation of British foreign policy under the Blair government', unpublished research paper, September 2000. Also 'Public Diplomacy', by Mark Leonard and Vidhya Alakeson, in *Global Thinking: the Foreign Policy Centre Newsletter*, Spring 2000, pp. 1–2.

2 For the early days of New Labour and its foreign policy statements, see Nicholas J. Wheeler and Tim Dunne, 'Good international citizenship: a third way for British foreign policy', *International Affairs*, Vol. 74, 4, October 1998, pp. 847–70.

3 This section draws on the author's 'Rewriting foreign policy: Cook, Blair and the move towards intelligent internationalism', *Parliamentary Monitor*, Vol. 6, No 10, September 1998, pp. 64–66.

4 Robin Cook, speech on 'Foreign Affairs', Labour Party Conference, Brighton, 26 September 2000.

5 James Tuck-Hang Tang, *Britain's Encounter with Revolutionary China, 1949–1954*, Macmillan, 1992.

6 See Adam Roberts, 'Humanitarian war: military intervention and human rights', *International Affairs*, Vol. 69, 3, July 1993.

7 This implication did not go down well with such figures as Douglas Hurd, who felt that they were being painted as having connived at genocide in the Balkans. In general the Tories argued that 'the greatest ethical achievement of post-war foreign policy – victory in the Cold War, removing the greatest threat to world peace, restoring human rights in Russia and Eastern Europe and liberating nations – resulted from policies pursued by the Conservatives in the 1980s. Labour just as vigorously denounced those policies'. Michael Grenfell, *A Conservative Ethical Foreign Policy*, Bow Group Research Paper, 2000, p. 2.

8 http://www.fco.gov.uk/directory/. The full list of major headings is: Security, International Peace and Stability; Prosperity; Quality of Life and a Strong International Community; a Strong UK Role in a Strong Europe; Open Government/Projecting Modern Britain; Protecting British Citizens and Applying UK Immigration Policy Overseas (as of March 2000). Between them these headings cover a total of sixty-nine specific bullet points. This is a long way from the generalised reports to Parliament of previous governments, but it should be noted that the direct access provided by a web-page itself by passes Parliament and raises further questions about the operation of formal accountability.

9 On the right, the *Daily Telegraph* has been prominent. On the left, John Pilger continues to wage his heroic lone campaign against the Anglo-American conspiracy to run the world.

10 Wheeler and Dunne, *International Affairs*, October 1998, *op.cit.*, p. 850; and Tim Dunne and Nicholas J. Wheeler, 'Blair's Britain: A Force for Good in the World?', in Margot Light and Karen E. Smith (eds), *Ethics and Foreign Policy*, Cambridge University Press, 2001.

11 This last figure was a drop from the 1997 peak of 19.6 per cent, but it is probably too soon to see any impact of New Labour one way or the other. *The Military Balance, 1999–2000*, International Institute of Strategic Studies, 1999, p. 281. See also 'UK arms exports figures give lie to "ethical" foreign policy', *The Independent*, 1 October 1999.

12 Britain is one of the six 'Letter of Intent' countries (LoI) which agreed on 6 July 1998 to attempt to harmonise their regulations regarding arms procurement. Little has yet been achieved, however. See Burkard Schmitt, *From Cooperation to Integration: Defence and Aerospace Industries in Europe*, WEU Institute for Security Studies, Chaillot Paper No. 40, July 2000, especially pp. 59–78.

13 *Daily Telegraph*, 14 November 1997, cited in Dunne and Wheeler, (in Light and Smith). The following paragraph draws on the analysis of the China case provided by Dunne and Wheeler.

14 Kurt Barling and Sola Akinrinade, 'The Edge of the Abyss: Nigeria', *The World Today*, Vol. 54, 8–9, August/September 1998, pp. 200–202.

15 It should be noted that although some British citizens were among those

killed by Pinochet's regime, neither British prosecutors nor Her Majesty's Government ever sought to arraign the General for these crimes. Insofar as they were willing to envisage him facing trial, it was only in respect to the charges laid by Spanish magistrates.

16 The idea of 'good international citizenship' derives from Gareth Evans, Australian Minister of Foreign Affairs from 1988–96. It is analysed in the works of Wheeler and Dunne cited above.

17 For the legal issues, see Marc Weller, 'On the hazards of foreign travel for dictators and other international criminals', *International Affairs*, Vol. 75, 3, July 1999, pp. 599–617.

18 *New Statesman*, 13 November 1998, cited in House of Commons Foreign Affairs Committee, Second Report, *Sierra Leone*, 3 February 1999, para 4 (http://www.publications.parliament.uk).

19 The Report of Sir Richard Scott on Arms to Iraq can be found in HC (House of Commons) 115, Session 1995–96. For the Rwanda affair see FAC Report, *op.cit.* para 25. It should also be noted that the UK was at this time participating in the formulation of a European Union 'Common Position' on the control of Dual-Use Goods, as a means of conflict-prevention, and of a Code of Conduct on Arms Exports. The Common Position dates from 1994 (decision 94/942/PESC of the EU) and has been continually modified. For the latter, see Christopher Hill and Karen E. Smith (eds), *European Foreign Policy: Key Documents* Routledge, 2000, pp. 460–65.

20 The earlier Legg Report, commissioned by the Foreign Secretary, records that of all the 102 relevant intelligence reports, only one was relevant to that investigation. See Sir Thomas Legg and Sir Robin Ibbs, *Report of the Sierra Leone Arms Investigation*, HMSO, 27 July 1998.

21 *Ibid*, para 26, the businessman was Mr Rakesh Saxena, and the description was Robin Cook's.

22 For a good analysis of the west African context see Funmi Olonisakin, 'Mercenaries fill the vacuum', *The World Today*, Vol. 54, 6, June 1996, pp. 146–48.

23 House of Commons Foreign Affairs Committee, Session 1998–99. *Response of the Secretary of State for Foreign and Commonwealth Affairs to the Second Report of the Foreign Affairs Committee*, April 1999, Cmd 4325.

24 President Putin's first overseas visit was to London, probably because French and German criticisms of the war were more vocal than those from London. See Helen Womak, 'Putin rewards Blair's stance on Chechnya', *Independent on Sunday*, 16 April 2000.

25 See Pavel Baev, 'Deadly Decisions: the Russia–US Summit in Moscow, June 2000', *The World Today*, Vol. 56, No. 6, June 2000. In this article Dr Baev predicted the kind of accident that befell the nuclear submarine *Kursk* two months later, and saw Tony Blair as helping to prepare the agenda for a summit which emphasised arms control and kept Chechnya as a low priority for discussion.

26 This case was indeed made by Robin Cook in 1998. See Rhiannon Vickers, 'Labour's search for a Third Way in foreign policy', in Richard Little and Mark Wickham-Jones (eds), *New Labour's Foreign Policy: A New Moral Crusade?* Manchester University Press, 2000, pp. 40–41.

27 John Moberly, 'Deterrence: the last weapon', *The World Today*, Vol. 55,

No. 3, March 1999, pp. 16–17. Sir John Moberly's careful criticism is the more notable for coming from an ex-British Ambassador to Iraq and Jordan. For an interesting discussion of Tony Blair's initial willingness to seek Parliamentary approval for the use of force, in February 1998, and his later taking of that approval for granted, see Matt Lyus and Peter Hennessy, *Tony Blair, Past Prime Ministers, Parliament and the Use of Force*, Department of Government, University of Strathclyde Papers on Government and Politics No. 113, 1999, pp. 1–2, 16–18.

28 Although it is worth noting that the EU states, with Britain not dissenting, have begun for the first time to criticise the USA for its use of capital punishment.

29 Hedley Bull, *The Anarchical Society: A Study of Order in World Politics* Macmillan, 1977, pp. 77–78 and 93–98

30 Tony Blair, Speech to the Economic Club of Chicago, Hilton Hotel, Chicago, 22 April 1999. http://www.fco.gov.uk/news/speechtext.asp?2316 Although made in the adopted city of Hans Morgenthau, the speech made no mention of that major thinker about international relations.

31 Ibid.

32 First of all by Hugo Grotius, according to H. Lauterpacht, cited in the classic work on nonintervention, namely R.J. Vincent, *Nonintervention and International Order*, Princeton University Press, 1974, p. 283. The case for humanitarian intervention is made in Nicholas J. Wheeler, *Saving Strangers: Humanitarian Intervention in International Society*, Oxford University Press, 2000.

33 Ibid. pp. 54–56.

34 The Strategic Defence Review of 1998 included the phrase 'we have a responsibility to act as a force for good in the world . . .'

35 Speech by Robin Cook to the Royal Institute of International Affairs, London, 28 January 2000 http://www.fco.gov.uk/news/speechtext.asp?3259.

36 For Cook's personal concern not to by-pass the UN and international law see his interview with Rachel Sylvester in *The Independent on Sunday*, 13 June 1999.

37 Mark Wickham-Jones, 'Labour party politics and foreign policy' in Richard Little and Mark Wickham-Jones (eds), *New Labour's Foreign Policy: A New Moral Crusade?*, p. 109.

38 For an interim assessment, see House of Commons, Select Committee on Foreign Affairs 1999–2000, *Fifth Report: Annual Reports of Foreign and Commonwealth Office and British Trade International 2000*, 4 July 2000, paras 17–18.

39 See the chapter in this book by Lawrence Freedman.

40 *List of sanctions regimes and arms embargoes implemented by the UK as at 10 February 2000*. FCO . . . The only exceptions to the 'abject poverty' category are Bosnia, Croatia, Yugoslavia, Iran, Iraq and Libya.

41 *Africa News*, 13 May 1997. Also *Zimbabwe Standard*, 30 April 2000, both accessed through http://allafrica.com.stories.

42 The Cotonou Agreement of June 2000 closes a chapter by admitting the failures of Lomé and the need for retrenchment.

43 Geoffrey Lean, 'The giving age has been postponed: decreasing foreign aid', *New Statesman*, 18 December 1998.

44 *Statistical Release*, DfID, 3 May 2000, http://www.DfID.gov.uk/public.

45 At the Okinawa G8 meeting Tony Blair apparently became 'visibly agi-tated' after being told by Jacques Chirac and Japanese Prime Minister Mori that he had no standing for his criticisms of French and Japanese programmes of tied aid, *Japan Weekly Monitor*, 31 July 2000.

46 Britain is owed $2,100bn by the Highly Indebted Poor Countries, com-pared to Japan's $10,500bn. Neither sum, of course, is trivial. Richard Lloyd Parry, 'Blair airs frustration over progress on debt relief', *The Independent*, 22 July 2000.

47 *Manchester Guardian Weekly*, 28 February 1999; *The Independent*, 8 March 1999.

48 The first phrase is Clare Short's, in the *New Statesman*, 16 August 1999. The second is Hedley Bull's, see *The Anarchical Society*, p. 85.

49 Tony Blair, Speech to the Polish Stock Exchange, Warsaw, 6 October 2000, and Speech at the Mansion House, 13 November 2000. See 'Speeches' at http://www.number-10.gov.uk/news.

50 Echelon is a system run by the US, the UK, Canada, Australia and New Zealand. The nature of its membership, and the obscurity of its purposes, illustrates the difficulties of living up to protestations about European cooperation in the areas of security and intelligence.

51 The quotations in this paragraph are all from Speech by Robin Cook to the Royal Institute of International Affairs, London, 28 January 2000 http://www.fco.gov.uk/news/speechtext.asp?3259.

© Chris Riddell

Chapter 17

CRIME AND PENAL POLICY

Terence Morris

The Origins of the Estate

THE BRITISH GENERAL election of 1997, after almost twenty years of unbroken Conservative government, produced a landslide victory for the Labour Party. The superficial observer could be forgiven for thinking that the direction of British politics was about to alter by 180 degrees, for the size of the Labour majority encouraged comparisons with the situation in 1945. Closer examination of contemporary history reveals that situations are often altogether less simplistic. Much of the programme of the Attlee government built upon the foundations of the political consensus that had emerged in wartime; its Criminal Justice Act of 1948[1] was based upon the Conservative bill of 1938 abandoned at the outbreak of war while the broad thrust of its legislation on health and social security had been anticipated by Liberal administrations before 1914. In 1997, not only had the Labour Party been re-launched as 'New' Labour but in eschewing virtually all connection with its socialist roots had presented itself to the electorate less as the purveyor of radical change than as a new and more competent steward of those remnants of Thatcherism that Middle England still cherished.

For the greater part of the twentieth century and certainly until 1950, allegiances in British politics had been determined along class lines.[2] But the electorate that gave Blair his astounding victory in 1997 was unlike that which had sent Attlee to Downing Street in 1945, Wilson in 1964, or Callaghan a decade later. The affluence of the 1960s which had heralded a new sense of identity among both manual and white-collar workers had been followed by the progressive demise of Britain's industrial base and the rise of a service economy. A wholly new pattern of social stratification had emerged and a correspondingly novel sense of political choice; most importantly, such choices were to be characterised by volatility rather than fidelity at election times. 'Middle England' was newly confident and no longer deferential towards the homiletics of the Great and the Good. Above all, it was concerned to cherish its property and its security. Whereas in the past voting behaviour mirrored the voter's perception of his or her class identity and its corresponding interest, by the end of the twentieth century it had become a matter of perceived self interest.

It was from this new source of political building material, if not perhaps that marble from which Disraeli thought working class Conservatives were fashioned,[3] that the building blocks of two decades of Thatcherism were to be quarried. And while important distinctions must be drawn between the phenomena of crime and criminal justice during different periods of the Thatcher era – and that of John Major – there was a consistent and discernible pattern in the approach to criminal justice that was to form part of Labour's inheritance in May 1997. It reflected not only a widespread fear of crime (as distinct from a direct experience of it) but a distinct intolerance of it and a resentment towards those who committed it.

The Reading of the Will

Elsewhere[4] I have argued that whereas crime and penal policy, like foreign affairs, were the constituents of the consensus politics that formed the core of the post-war 'settlement' between the Conservative and Labour parties, by the late 1970s crime and its management had become one of the most important foci of interest for the New Right in Britain and the United States and in much of the remainder of the western industrial world. In Britain, not only was this concern straightforwardly generated by a rise in levels of crime, especially offences against property – itself increasing in volume as a function of growing affluence – but by a consciousness among the newly affluent that the conspicuous proprietorship, by which their newly acquired status was demonstrated to the world, was being violated. The traditional working class, living in their rented terraced houses, had for generations little more than their bicycles or the coins in their gas meters to lose; Essex Man,[5] in contrast, was already eschewing rented housing for home ownership and the once prized 'All Steel' Raleigh that had graced the factory bicycle rack had long since been replaced by the lovingly washed and waxed Cortina in the now obligatory works car park. While crime became feared, not least since the popular image of crime, especially among the growing numbers of the elderly, is one in which violent offences are in an overwhelming majority, crime was becoming *resented*. More accurately, it was criminals who were resented; an attitude wholly consistent with that powerful strain of working-class authoritarianism that has nourished enthusiasm for capital and corporal punishment and hostility towards 'scroungers' and foreigners and more recently, asylum seekers.

To begin to identify the 'Blair Effect' upon crime and penal policy since 1997 it is first necessary to consider the position of the Blair government in relation to those of John Major and Margaret Thatcher. It is perhaps simplest to begin by recognising the extent to which it was legatee of its predecessors in the sense that it inherited, *faute de mieux*, the expectations as well as the anxieties of the electorate. In the early days of the Thatcher era, traditionally liberal-minded Tory Home Secretaries like William Whitelaw had been regularly baited at the annual party conference; later incumbents were to recognise that the promise of more repressive policies were as *panem et circenses*[6] not only to the party faithful but to a wider public audience. Blair's portion was entailed in the ideological appetites of a new constituency within the polity; it had no strong allegiance to party as such but in its place a commitment to values that were both derivative and consonant with the widespread affluence that had been acquired in barely a generation since the war. Those appetites, while encompassing equality of opportunity in the context of competitive individualism, had little room for social altruism, not least if it had implications for direct taxation. Its focus which Margaret Thatcher was succinctly to identify was upon individuals and their families, not upon the less immediate, more abstract notion of society. It had little time for what it perceived as failure among its own kind and even less for the condition of those groups which the tabloid media had come to portray not as the legitimate beneficiaries of welfare but a parasitic growth upon the efforts of individual enterprise.

Why, then, did not only Essex Man but other traditionally cautious voters desert the Conservative Party at the polls in 1997? Not, I would suggest, because they were now wholly disenchanted with the various legislative manifestations of the ideology of the New Right (the possible exception being the disastrously unpopular poll tax). Nor, in the absence of persuasive evidence to the contrary, that they were newly enchanted with those manifestations of liberal egalitarianism that appeared in Labour's manifesto. What for Labour is likely to be the uncomfortable truth, is that the Conservative government under John Major had suffered the devastating loss of its credibility. Divided both publicly and privately, ill at ease in its relations with Europe and besmirched by sexual and financial scandal, it was no longer seen as providing safe pairs of hands. Far from representing, therefore, a mass conversion to democratic socialism – the latter term not one in common usage by the architects of New Labour – the result could be characterised as the appointment – conscription, even – of a new management team. In short, disenchantment with sleaze and peccadillo notwithstanding, the electorate had demanded more competent delivery of what had for nearly two decades been the essence of Conservative election promises. And where 'law and order' was concerned, there was little ambiguity about what the public wanted.

The Inheritance

Labour was still in opposition and Blair Shadow Home Secretary when he employed the famous slogan 'Tough on crime and tough on the causes of crime'. Like Norman Tebbitt's injunction to the unemployed to get on their bikes, it readily entered that lexicon of political quotations whose substantive meanings are less relevant than the historical context in which they were uttered. Since 'law and order' had been established as one of the concerns of the New Right by the late 1970s, reference to crime control in such terms could have but one meaning; that Labour intended to be more successful on that front than the Conservatives had been. And more than that; it indicated that Labour had now adopted the same rhetoric of 'toughness' that had been adumbrated in the early 1980s during Leon Brittan's time at the Home Office and which had come to full flower during the incumbency of Michael Howard in the last months of the Major administration. Had John Smith led Labour to victory in 1997 it is likely that it would have been Blair and not Jack Straw who would have found himself Home Secretary, but one effect of Smith's death, apart from precipitating Blair into the leadership, was to promote Straw into the shadow Home Office post. In the run-up to the election Labour's room for manoeuvre on the law and order front was limited by the straitjacket of public expectation that had developed during the Major years and openly fostered by Howard.[7] Unlike the Wilson government thirty-five years before, neither Straw – nor Blair – had the advantage of having had a moderately detailed blueprint for criminal justice policy already to hand.[8] Nor, perhaps, would one have been of much utility since the task with which the Blair government was faced was essentially to satisfy this expectation. Labour, on criminal justice as in other areas, has been driven less by original thinking than by the necessity of being reactive to public opinion.

The Shadow of Crime

Politicians, both in and out of office, are now permanently sensitive to the fact that the fear of 'crime' occupies an important place in the litany of public anxieties. Yet included among those who fear crime most are significant numbers of those who are least likely to experience it: moreover, public knowledge about the magnitude of the crime problem and the frequency of particular offences is notoriously deficient. In general it is believed that violent crime forms a greater part of the total of all crime than is the case and that the sentences passed by the courts are more lenient than they are.

But if the public is ill-informed about the nature and extent of crime and its punishment, politicians are prone to aver, if not to believe, that the level of crime can be directly affected by legislative initiatives. In opposition, Labour blamed the Conservatives for the incidence of crime throughout the Thatcher years but the boot was soon to be on the other foot. Indeed, since 1997 the Conservatives in opposition appear studiously to have ignored the fact that crime levels have been falling overall since before they left office and have continued to portray the situation as one of undiminished if not increasing gravity.

In reality, crime levels are less related to either government policies or the substantive law than to other much more general social, economic and demographic factors.[9] To what extent policies have a bearing upon these more general factors is less easy to assess. The collapse of Britain's industrial base reduced many communities previously dependent upon mining or manufacture to a state of disintegrative *anomie*. Like the invasive weeds around the derelict factories, the drug culture, car theft and vandalism on the equally derelict housing estates grew, seemingly unchecked. And while a generation of young people came to maturity largely ignorant of the disciplines or dignity of the world of work, a synthetic culture of short-term hedonism flourished. The poverty of the poorest, which has continued to grow under the Blair government is, nevertheless, a problem susceptible to positive and redistributive fiscal remedies, unlike that of drug and alcohol abuse which has co-existed with it and has had disproportionately deleterious effects upon those at the margins of society.[10] Yet to what extent Britain is now host to an 'underclass', excluded from the mainstream of the social market, like that of the worlds described by Defoe, Hogarth or Dickens is arguable; what appears highly plausible is that some kinds of crime are a function of what is now more fashionably termed 'social exclusion'.

'Tough on the causes of crime' might be taken as a statement of legislative intent. But it presupposes that the 'causes' of crime are readily identifiable. The simplistic approach popular with religious (and for that matter political) fundamentalists is that criminals choose to commit crime but can be deterred when they are persuaded that the combination of a high likelihood of being caught and being subjected to severe punishment makes it a less attractive option. An alternative view is that crime is a behavioural response to situations faced by individuals who are disadvantaged in a variety of ways. In reality, the conditions which stimulate criminal behaviour are various, complex and above all, by no means of the same order. Nevertheless, since the majority of crimes are those against property, it is not unreasonable to look if not for causes, then for correlations with movements within the economy. In the third quarter of the nineteenth century the expansion of the economy and the increased demand for labour, including that of the unskilled variety (since many tasks still depended upon muscle rather than machinery) was accompanied by a reduction in the prison population. What faced the Blair administration was not merely the challenge of re-integrating those sections of the population which had become progressively excluded from the world of work; it extended to that of addressing the social alienation of large numbers of young people, some already into their thirties who had been sucked into the bleak vortex of a life dominated by poverty, drug and alcohol abuse, prostitution, petty crime and not infrequently, homelessness. The scope of the task extended altogether beyond the confines of the criminal justice system and in a sense beyond that of the straightforward provision of welfare. Although the slogan 'Education, education, education' was readily derided by the government's critics as yet another example of political rhetoric likely to be unmatched by delivery, it indicated an awareness that without education there could be little or no hope that those most disprivileged would ever find the kind of employment that would lift them from the pit of poverty. But although drug and alcohol abuse have been known as the partners of despair from Gin Lane to the bleakest run down estate the task of setting free those imprisoned by addiction requires a different kind of investment. Although not strictly Home Office initiatives, the Blair government has attempted to address these issues, quite apart from pursuing pro-active policies against the traffic in drugs and their abuse by offenders.[11]

Yet in some degree any attempt to eradicate the 'causes' of crime, even if it is limited to eliminating the conditions in which crime flourishes, is a labour of Sisyphus. Over time it has been possible for the culture of civilisation to reduce the extent of barbarism but the flawed nature of humankind makes its elimination impossible. What is likely to be more successful in the short run is the promotion of various measures of crime control, notably those deriving from 'designing out' crime. Improved vehicle security, street lighting and CCTV cameras have each contributed to crime reduction.

But while it is possible for government to formulate policies directed towards eliminating social exclusion, those directed towards deterring individuals from criminal and anti-social behaviour are likely to have less immediate effects. When crying new legislation in the criminal justice field in the course of seeking to allay public concern, ministers, no less than opposition spokespersons, seldom if ever remind their hearers that penalties for crime are effective only insofar as significant numbers of criminals are caught. And while the clear-up rate for most serious offences against the person remains relatively high, that for property crimes if anything is given to decline from an already dismally low figure. It is conceivable that most middle-class citizens have a genuine fear of the consequences of conviction; the loss of reputation and employment quite apart from the deterrence of financial or custodial penalties. But for the majority of those for whom passage through the criminal courts is already a commonplace, their lifestyles are such that jobs and reputations apart (in themselves generally rare commodities), fines and incarceration are often an all too familiar part of a social experience which tends to breed a resigned fatalism.

But public perceptions are all important, and among the images of crime that are most sharply projected on to public consciousness are of the offences which are committed in what is known as public space and for which the clear up rates are low. Any passenger arriving at a mainline station in a big city is aware that almost every lineside structure or item of equipment has been sprayed, frequently with weird hieroglyphics in a style known as 'hip hop'. The streets of any moderately sized town on a Friday or Saturday night are commonly the scene of loutish behaviour in the form of urination in the street, overturned rubbish bins and fighting. Cars parked on residential streets through which the revellers make their way homeward offer targets for theft or the display of the athleticism required to leap on the bonnet of one and then from roof to roof of those parked behind, leaving a trail of ruined and expensive bodywork. Yet no matter how frequently it is stated that the perceived fear of crime is generally greater than the reality and that those who fear crime most are likely to be those least at risk, the general public belief is that crime is both extensive and continually increasing.

Ministerial antennae have been aware of the fact that although such things as burglary and vehicle crime have been decreasing, public perception of crime is stimulated by its awareness of incivility in public places. For this reason, by late 2000 the government was investing time in exploring ways of dealing with unruly behaviour including the notion of fixed penalties.

Measuring String: Estimating the Extent of Crime

It is now widely accepted that the figure of crimes reported to the police can represent an under-estimate of its true volume. There are some crimes, such as homicide, in which the figures are likely to approach parity while in others the divergence will be wide. In recent years the British Crime Survey has, in parallel with traditional criminal statistics, provided a useful corrective. Thus between 1987 and 1997 crime as a whole as measured by the BCS rose by some 20 per cent compared with 18 per cent for recorded crime.[12]

Contrary to popular belief, the crime rate measured by offences per hundred thousand of population has been falling since 1994 and has continued to do so. In 1998–99 violent crimes, burglaries and thefts of and from vehicles all fell between 10 and 2 per cent though sexual offences rose slightly. None of these data, however, have wide currency in the public domain, least of all among the readers of the tabloid press who remain unshaken in their belief that the tide of crime rises inexorably from year to year while the courts continue to pass ineffectual sentences of increasing leniency. The reality is otherwise in that while the proportion of sentences involving fines or community penalties remained roughly constant, the numbers sentenced to immediate custody rose by some 7,500 (or 7 per cent) compared with 1997.[13] Nor is this the end of the matter for while predictions vary from 7 per cent to 20 per cent, the expectation is that the prison population will continue to rise as new legislation provides offenders with fewer chances of avoiding custody and increases the chances of their remaining behind bars for longer. What is largely obscured from public view is the cost of incarceration; like water from an unmetered supply, it is only too easy to work on the assumption that imprisonment is to all intents a freely provided service.

Tough on Crime: Remedies from the New Pharmacopoeia

If crime rates have actually been falling since 1994 as would appear to be the case, then those who applauded the policy of 'tough on crime' (if not always on the 'causes' of crime) would seem to have had their confidence justified, for it was in 1993 that Michael Howard set out his famous twenty-seven points of policy for criminal justice and in the context of the slogan 'Prison works!' declaimed, 'Let's take the handcuffs off the police and put them on the criminals where they belong!' On assuming office, Straw was not only bound by Blair's earlier promise to be tough on crime and its causes but by the knowledge that if he did not continue to recognise the expectations of that section of the electorate which might be termed the 'tabloid' constituency he would be immediately vulnerable to the charge of being 'soft on criminals'. Little ability is required to decipher so lightly encoded a political message and realise that by 'tough on crime' is meant 'tough on criminals'. Howard's colourful references to 'yobs who break the law' was to be matched by Straw's imprecations against 'squeegee merchants'. And lest the departure of Howard into the political night were to have suggested that the pressure was off, his successor, Ann Widdecombe, soon proved to be every bit as strident in maintaining the political heat.

Several issues need to be identified here. First, there is the assumption upon which all these 'tough' policies are predicated, namely that crime will be followed by punishment. But since so many of those responsible for crime (and the majority of property offences) are never identified, let alone prosecuted and convicted, for a significant number of lawbreakers penalties of increasing severity are mere empty threats carried on the wind of political rhetoric. Second, there is the assumption that those offenders who are detected and subjected to 'tough' measures will be deterred from crime in the future. However, the re-offending rates of young men released from Young Offender institutes and prison indicate a more dispiriting outcome. Even among the far smaller numbers of juveniles held in the specially secure unit at Medway around 25 per cent are in trouble again within five days of release. To expect behavioural change in consequence of simplistic penal intervention is analogous to the idea that a dog can be trained to be compliant by nothing more than a period of structured deprivation.

Third, and perhaps most significant among these issues, is the real possibility that even if tough measures are not rewarded with success, to the extent that they will have delivered a measured dose of misery to the criminal the remedy will not have been in vain, at least in the eyes of the tabloid voter; in a situation not unlike that which used to arise in the days of capital punishment when many enthusiasts for the gallows would argue that even if it did not deter murder, murderers individually deserved to die.

Michael Howard had proclaimed that 'Prison works!', a variant of the theory of incapacitation by which it can be demonstrated that a criminal taken off the streets is one criminal fewer committing crime. In the United States the massive expansion of the prison population combined with mandatory sentences of the 'three strikes' variety has become an alternative to the provision of welfare: the social exclusion of imprisonment renders the provision of schemes for education and social regeneration in the community superfluous. Almost all the measures that were either introduced or about to be implemented in the last days of Conservative rule have been continued or adopted by New Labour. Respected observers of the prison scene such as Morgan have argued that Straw has acted quietly to manage the prison population at its currently high level.[14] All these measures are distinctive in being predicated upon the objective of *control*. Perhaps the most publicly visible of all is the CCTV camera which, for all its varying degrees of grainy unreliability and periodic malfunctioning, sends out a confident public message of omniscience.

In the pursuance of what has been termed 'populist punitiveness'[15] the Home Secretary has become the hostage not only to that fortune which formed New Labour's inheritance from the outgoing Conservatives, but to what may prove to be an electorally deadly combination of that punitive (if unintelligent) authoritarianism and volatility of preference which has come to characterise the tabloid voter. The criminal justice system now provides for mandatory minimum sentences for burglars, drug dealers and certain categories of violent offenders and for Anti-Social Behaviour Orders in which the distinctions between criminal and civil processes are sufficiently blurred to give rise to the possibility of a conflict with the European Convention on Human Rights which was incorporated into English law in October 2000 and into Scots law at the time of devolution. Other more arcane measures, such as reducing the threshold for offenders being returned to court for breaches of probation orders and the automatic withdrawal of social security payments for up to six months have come on to the agenda.

More sinister, in the view of some critics, has been the proposal to amalgamate the Prison and Probation Inspectorates, it being suspected that the hidden agenda is to bring to an end by a 'GLC style' solution the constant publication by the Chief Inspector of Prisons of reports that have ranged in recent years from the critical to the condemnatory. The first Chief Inspector of Prison in modern times,[16] Judge (later Sir) Stephen

Tumim, became something of a disappointment to Michael Howard on account of his liberal approach and constant criticism of prison policy. When Sir David Ramsbotham was appointed as his successor it was undoubtedly in the hope that the professional soldier who had acquired the nickname of 'Rambo' as a result of his 'no nonsense' reputation would be altogether more sympathetic towards the government viewpoint. Events proved him to be as robust as his reputation had promised but only too ready to express quite fearless and independent judgment. It was not long before it became clear that far from being a docile incumbent of the post his 'Rambo' qualities were now manifest in his approach to prison inspection. From time to time he was thought to have seriously exceeded his brief as when, for example, in October 1999 he openly urged the release of the youths Thompson and Venables once they had reached eighteen. Jack Straw was not pleased and Ann Widdecombe left no-one in doubt about her view, saying that it was none of his business and it was not for him to second guess the decisions of the courts or the Home Secretary in such matters. Interestingly, a year later when the task of determining their tariff fell to the Lord Chief Justice, Lord Woolf, the decision was precisely in accord with Ramsbotham's view.

New Labour has found it no easier to manage the prison system than its predecessor and in particular the sector providing for young offenders has been particularly troubled. The institution at Portland came under scrutiny following complaints of systematic abuse of young inmates by staff, a matter currently still unresolved. That at Feltham, which has a long and unenviable record of bullying by inmates, self-harm and suicide was again in the headlines in November 2000 when an Asian youth, due for release, was brutally murdered in his sleep by his cell mate who emerged at his Old Bailey trial as a racist with severe personality problems, neither of which was unlikely to have been unknown to the management of the institution. In May 2000 the adult establishment at Blantyre House which had operated a relaxed and liberal pre-release regime was raided by officers from other prisons on the pretext of searching for contraband material. Some £6000 worth of damage was done in the course of doors being smashed down and other violence and inmates complained of provocation and intimidation. The governor had been earlier removed at short notice. Critics of the raid have suggested that the trivial volume of unauthorised articles found suggested that the real agenda was related to the inside politics of prison management and a desire to bring the regime to an end. The Prisons Minister, Paul Boateng, was fielded to answer awkward questions by Paxman on the *Newsnight* programme on television and maintained (somewhat unconvincingly) that the raid had been related only to a need to protect the public.

Meanwhile the extension of the commercial sector of the prison estate, which has had its share of difficulties, is an issue no longer open to debate, while easily the most controversial of New Labour's proposals has been the attempt to limit the right of election of jury trial which, interestingly, has attracted criticism from across the political spectrum. Even those who seek to be tough on criminals have recognised in the jury system a presumed safeguard against wrongful conviction. On the issue of refugees (or 'asylum seekers') Home Office policy under New Labour has not discernibly diverged from that of its predecessor, being based upon the assumption that application for such status is bogus until proved otherwise, although in order to escape oppression travel on false passports – or none – has often been a necessity for those involved. Parallels have been drawn with the attitude of British governments between 1933 and 1939 towards the acceptance of Jewish refugees from Nazi Europe in which general suspicion is accompanied by a policy of detention difficult to distinguish from imprisonment without trial. When in 1939–40 those designated by the Defence Regulations as 'enemy aliens' were rounded up and imprisoned they included numbers of German nationals who had just made it across the Channel and thus escaped the coming Holocaust; somewhat insensitively, they were forced to share the prison yard along with Mosleyites who had been incarcerated under the same legal mandate. Those contemporary asylum seekers permitted to await their fate in the community have endured not only social hostility in the areas in which they have been settled but have become the victims of racist attacks. Such marginalisation has not been offset by the shift in policy that resulted in their subsistence payments in cash being substituted for vouchers for which shops were not obliged to tender change. By the time of the New Labour party conference in September 2000 it was becoming increasingly difficult to defend the use of this symbolically degrading device, yet criticism of it was largely limited to liberal opinion. When some months earlier fifty-nine young Chinese illegal immigrants died what must have been a terrifying and painful death in the back of an airless lorry trailer that had arrived off a ferry at Dover, public concern was focused upon their illegal status rather than the manner of their deaths. The contrast between this incident and the death of a smaller number of British nationals in an Australian backpacker hostel at about the same time was striking. Reforms in the administration of the courts continued under the Blair administration, largely esoteric and removed from wider public view. Not so the attempts to reduce the scope of trial by jury. A measure intended to limit the number of offences triable 'either way' twice failed in the Lords, the defeat being notable by the role played by Labour rebels whose allegiance to New Labour has otherwise been beyond question.

New Labour/Blue Labour: Home Secretary as Hostage

As commander in chief of New Labour, Blair has been compelled never to shift his gaze from the demands of those 'Middle Englanders' who gave him his mandate. So too, Brown as Chancellor went freely into the first two years of government bearing the fetters of Conservative fiscal restraint not merely with dignity but at times what seemed to be pride. Similarly, Straw has continued along the furrow to which the plough was first set by Leon Brittan during his time at the Home Office in the 1980s and behind which Michael Howard followed with energetic enthusiasm. In that New Labour has accepted the gift of the heavy horse, unconcerned about the state of its teeth, the Home Secretary can hardly be described as having been on a frolic of his own since 1997.

In the last days of opposition New Labour continued on grounds of principle to voice criticism of the policy of contracting out imprisonment to the commercial sector and resisted the idea of negotiating any new contracts with the prison companies. Within a month of the election Straw had done just that, but there was more to come, for it was but a short time before he admitted a personal conversion to a preference for this particular variant of private finance initiative. To the extent that the issue of law and order is an essentially populist phenomenon the Blair government has needed little persuasion that its fate at the polls is not in the hands of its traditional supporters but upon a volatile tabloid constituency. Straw has remained its hostage.

By January 2000 it had become clear that the law and order issue was now perceived by Conservative strategists as a front on which New Labour might be potentially vulnerable. William Hague embarked on a series of 'hardline' speeches on law and order. Addressing the annual conference of the Police Federation on 18 May he argued for the right of victims to appeal against the imposition of what they believed to be 'over-lenient' sentences for such offences as grievous and actual bodily harm, burglary and racially aggravated crimes. He remained unapologetic for his earlier assertion that asylum seekers should initially be held in custody. These were not the only proposals in a package which he described as setting out 'the most concerted attempt by any British political party to challenge the failed post-war liberal consensus and to win the war against crime'.

Examined in detail, Hague's proposals were carefully crafted to address a series of concerns, some of which had been demonstrated by recent events. The pledge to abolish the rule whereby a defendant cannot be tried twice for the same offence upon substantially the same evidence[17] was a clear reference to the case of those who had been indicted for the murder of the black teenager Stephen Lawrence in the course of first a public and later a private prosecution, both of which had failed. Combined with his suggestion that those convicted of racially aggravated offences should be at risk of having their sentences increased should their victims appeal against their alleged lenity, he gave a clear indication that criminal justice was for everybody and certainly not limited by racial prejudice. His reference to wanting criminals 'to be fearful of getting caught and fearful of punishment so they will choose not to commit crimes' was followed by a wish for 'the law abiding millions in our country to feel free from fear in their homes and on the streets'.

Earlier, in April 2000 a Norfolk farmer, Tony Martin, had been convicted of the murder of a teenage boy who with an accomplice had entered his farmhouse in the course of an attempted burglary. Martin, who had been burgled before, had turned his home into a virtual fortress and had opened fire with a shotgun on the intruders. One was killed and the other wounded. While it would be an understatement to say that public sympathy for the dead youth was markedly conspicuous by its absence there was widespread support for Martin who was popularly portrayed as victim rather than offender. Later in the month when making a speech during a visit to Alcester, a small Warwickshire village with a very low crime rate but which had experienced a substantial rise in burglaries during the previous year, Hague suggested that: 'The Tony Martin case lit a touch paper that has led to an explosion of anger and resentment among millions of law-abiding British people who no longer feel that the state is on their side.'

While unequivocally excluding vigilantes as having no place in a civilised society he went on to pledge that 'the next Conservative government will overhaul the law with a strong presumption that, in future, the state will be on the side of people who protect their homes and their families against criminals'.

Both Hague and Widdecombe kept up an unrelenting pressure on law and order issues throughout 2000, which could be read as affirming that crime had risen under New Labour and continued to do so, not least as a consequence of the fall in police manpower. By the early months of 2001 it had become increasingly clear that as the opposition returned again and again to the issue, New Labour was forced to react by making it clear that crime control was going to occupy a significant priority in the legislative programme in the second term it confidently expected to enjoy. On 8 February 2001 Blair chose the venue of a London school to make a critically important speech setting out the government's intention not only to pursue radical change in secondary and higher education but to make law and order a no less important priority. Prior to the speech it was becoming clear from various statements what the salient points of policy were likely to be. Major changes in the lay magistracy (which presently attends to the overwhelming majority of criminal business before the courts) following the Auld Report are likely to consist of lay magistrates being reduced to sitting with a presiding District Judge (the new appellation of stipendiary magistrates). One likely effect of such changes would be to limit the number of cases in which the defendant would have the right of jury trial, thus reaching through another door the objective of limiting jury trial in which the Lords had already frustrated the government's desire. A second probability is that the end result of the sentencing review already underway in the Lord Chancellor's department, is a further shift towards greater severity rather than innovation *per se*. A third serious possibility is the idea of disclosing the past criminal record of defendants, favoured by some senior police officers and thought to be far from unattractive to Straw. In

these two areas, the shift of balance away from the defendant to the pros-
ecutor is consonant with the 'tough on criminals' approach thought to
appeal to the tabloid voter. Finally, there is the issue of reform of the police.
At present Chief constables exercise considerable autonomy which some
critics see as being at variance with further moves towards regional and
centralised management of crime control in the face of organised crime. It
is difficult to escape the impression that as the count-down to the election
began, the back room strategists of New Labour, no less than the Home
Secretary himself were determined to impress upon the electorate the image
of superiority in both the ability and the will to deal with crime.

Sparks from Crossed Wires?: Spliffs on the Bournemouth Agenda

At the Conservative Party Conference in October 2000, much was made of
Labour's alleged failure to deal with crime while the Shadow Home
Secretary, Ann Widdecombe, seemed eerily to echo the approach of
Michael Howard. The centrepiece of her speech to the Conference was the
announcement that a new Conservative government would legislate to
provide for fixed penalty minimum fines of £100 for the possession of
cannabis. Though applauded by her audience, the policy began to unravel
within hours as confusion reigned over whether members of the Shadow
Cabinet had been fully seized of the proposal in advance, in particular the
Shadow Chancellor, Michael Portillo,[18] for whom the cost implications of
its policing would have been critical. As the subsidiary issue emerged about
whether there was a distinction in law between a criminal record and a
police record, journalistic questioning over the following weekend revealed
that no fewer than seven members of the Shadow Cabinet had admitted to
having smoked cannabis in their younger days.

In response to the calls for the legalisation or 'decriminalisation'[19] of
cannabis which the Widdecombe proposals generated, Straw remained
firm notwithstanding that at least one former senior police officer argued
in favour of a liberalisation of the law as did some of the government's
back-bench supporters. His 'Drugs Tsar', Keith Halliwell, in a prominent
interview on the BBC's *Today* programme, emphasised that cannabis was
four times as carcinogenic than tobacco. Clearly, Straw was not to be put
in check, let alone checkmated by the Widdecombe proposal which
appeared uncommonly similar in the way it was made public to a suggestion made by Tony Blair some months earlier to an audience of reportedly
perplexed German theologians at the University of Tübingen. Addressing
the issue of dealing with drunken louts who disturbed the evening peace of
urban centres, he had somewhat oddly suggested the imposition of on-the-
spot penalties in satisfaction of which they might be taken by a police
officer to the nearest cash point machine. History may yet identify the

triviality of this transparently impractical proposal as among the earliest signs of the decline of Blair's high standing as a man of trustworthy common sense, aware of life in the real world.

More Crossed Wires?: Blair's Secret Memorandum

On the Martin issue Hague had appeared to suggest that an incoming Conservative administration would either broaden the extent of the law of self-defence in homicide or in some other way provide for a more flexible penalty than that of life imprisonment. But Blair too, had been moved to express a view, albeit in a private memorandum identifying 'touchstone issues' dated 29 April 2000 circulated within government but leaked to the *Sunday Times* in early July. Of five constituent topics, the first three were dedicated to Home Office issues. Thus: 'i) Possibly on the Martin case, asking a senior judge to look at changing the sentencing law, i.e. to allow lesser sentences than life . . .'

For a lawyer who had been a Shadow Home Secretary, this was on the face of it as astonishing as it must have been embarrassing to the incumbent Home Secretary. Parliament had, in fact, already looked at the mandatory penalty of life imprisonment for murder not once but twice in the shape of detailed investigation by Committee. While as long ago as 1989 the Nathan inquiry in the Lords had recommended a change, the House of Commons Home Affairs Committee in the last days of the Major government, chaired by the practising Conservative lawyer Sir Ivan Lawrence, had come down firmly in favour of the *status quo*, save for removing decisions about the tariff from the political sphere of the Home Office and handing the task to the judiciary. Meanwhile in 1993 the Lane Committee, set up by the Prison Reform Trust but chaired by the former Lord Chief Justice, Lord Lane, and whose members included a retired Lord Justice of Appeal as well as a former senior Conservative Home Office minister, re-affirmed the judgment of the Nathan inquiry. Blair could hardly have been unaware of all this material on the mandatory penalty which Parliament had decreed in the Murder (Abolition of Death Penalty) Act of 1965 and it is unclear from his musings what sort of advice he hoped a senior judge might be able to provide.

Presently, the English law relating to homicide is fraught with anomaly and, in the public view, inconsistency.[20] In murder, the crime with which Martin was charged, it is not necessary for the prosecution to show that the accused intended to kill, only do his victim serious harm. Allowing a trial judge to determine the sentence in cases where the circumstances were extenuating would undoubtedly go some way to meeting the kind of public disquiet voiced after the life sentence on Martin. Straw, however, has made it abundantly clear that like the then members of the House of Commons Home Affairs Committee, his opposition to the abolition of the mandatory life sentence for murder remains implacable.

Michael Howard had rejected the findings of the Lane Committee and when, in May 2000, Straw was asked to what extent he advanced the arguments that had been set out by Howard in his response to the Lane Report he replied that in his view Howard had made all of the major points that need to be made in favour of the retention of the mandatory penalty and the setting of tariffs by the Home Secretary. This he later confirmed, could be taken as a statement of government policy.[21] From this it can be inferred that holding fast on this issue when Hague seemed to be offering some flexibility gave a clear indication that in no way was New Labour about to offer a vulnerable flank either to its political opponents or its tabloid critics which would suggest anything resembling a 'soft' approach to what is widely regarded as the gravest of crimes. With regard to the tariff, however, the Strasbourg court produced a ruling in the cases of Thompson and Venables (the child killers of the toddler James Bulger) requiring a decision on release from detention at Her Majesty's Pleasure under the 1933 Childrens Act to be made by a judge and not the Home Secretary.[22]

Nor, apparently, were asylum seekers by any means flavour of the month in Downing Street that April. The second 'thought' appearing in the leaked memorandum of 'touchstone issues' began:

> On asylum, we need to be highlighting removals . . . plus if the April figures show a reduction then a downward trend. Also, if the benefits bills really start to fall, that should be highlighted. Plus some of the genuine asylum claims should be given some publicity.

From this we may infer a view, consonant with both the perception and word association of the tabloid voter, that asylum seekers are to be regarded as 'bogus' until demonstrated to be otherwise. Saloon bar opinion characterises them as burdens on the taxpayer and the source of problems for local authorities needing to be sent back whence they came. But following the logic of the memorandum *some* (but presumably not all) of the genuine asylum claims should be given *some* publicity (author's italics) which would admit to the possibility that the uncovenanted arrival of certain of these indigent aliens might, after all, have been triggered by torture or persecution.

The third 'thought' related to the need to

> . . . highlight the : compulsory tests for drugs before bail . . . report on the confiscation of assets; the extra number of burglars jailed under 'three strikes and you're out'.

It continued in increasingly innovative vein:

. . . as ever, (*sic!*) we lack a tough public message along with the strategy. We should think now of an initiative, e.g. locking up street muggers. Something tough, with an immediate bite, which sends a message through the system. . . . and I, personally, should be associated with it.

Blair was again to thrust himself forward on the criminal justice front in January 2001. In a TV interview with David Frost (widely regarded as the opening salvo in the general election campaign) he asserted;

Within four years I want to have more police employed in this country than ever before – and we have got the money to do it.

At a stroke he sought to wrest back a central issue from Hague, presenting a criminal justice initiative that was pro-active and not re-active, while at the same time reminding his audience of New Labour's competent management of the economy.

What appears very clear both from the public speeches of Hague and the contents of Blair's private memorandum is that the leaders of both parties, conscious of the Presidential style that now characterises British politics, perceived that they could not concede an inch to the other, whatever the logic might be, for even the context of Hague's suggestion of a more flexible approach to the sentencing of householders defending their lives and property was no less unambiguously hostile to criminals. The Victorian jurist Fitzjames Stephen had remarked in his great *History of the Common Law*; 'I think it highly desirable that criminals should be hated, (and) that the punishments inflicted upon them should be so contrived as to give expression to that hatred.'

Both leaders would be only too aware that, though likely to be couched in less elegant language, these sentiments could be expressed by any tabloid columnist. In spite of the criticism that William Hague's speeches reflected a sense of political opportunism it can be argued that he was no less a hostage to authoritarian sentiment and public whim. And to the criminals identified by Fitzjames Stephen are now added football hooligans, drunken louts and all their like who disturb the peace of public places.

Odile and Odette: One Dancer in Two Roles

In the ballet *Swan Lake* there are two anthropomorphised creatures of identical appearance; one symbolising the 'good' and the other the 'bad'. Traditionally, both roles are danced by the same *prima ballerina*. Critics of New Labour's criminal justice policy found to the left of the party were dismayed to find that it appeared indistinguishable in its general tenor from that of the Conservatives. Political consensus in the form of the convergence of policies, while attractive to those who experience a distaste for what they perceive to be extremism has a tendency to bring down if not always the wrath then often the derision of those with greater enthusiasm for definitively distinct positions. In the 1950s the discernible similarity of general outlook between R.A. Butler, sometime Conservative Chancellor of the Exchequer (and arguably one of the greatest Home Secretaries since Peel) and Hugh Gaitskell (by similar token one of the greatest Labour Prime Ministers never to hold office) caused the *New Statesman* to identify the character of Mr Butskell. New Labour's Home Secretary has suffered a not dissimilar fate in being dubbed by his critics as Michael Straw, the *alter ego* of Jack Howard.

This has been particularly unfortunate for Straw since by the time he left office Howard, in the eyes of his numerous critics had come to be a figure who symbolised an approach to criminal justice that was essentially authoritarian if not downright reactionary; at once anathema to the left and a potential source of embarrassment to the centre right. Simply to regard Straw as Howard politically re-incarnate is not a view that sustains close scrutiny, any more than that which regards New Labour's policies on crime as representing a seamless continuity with those of the administration that went before. The difficulty in discerning the differences, though considerable, is less pronounced when the public approach of the two men is compared. For while Howard appeared constantly aware of the retributive preferences of the tabloid voter, Straw has always striven to present his policies in a constructively pragmatic light. Not that this has always succeeded in mollifying his critics.[23] In spite of the pursuit of a 'tough' and uncompromising set of policies for the control of crime there are, on the other side of the balance sheet, some remarkable entries. The Youth Justice programme involving better cooperation between local agencies and funded projects aimed at crime reduction among disaffected youths has received little public notice. Not involving such controversial activities as taking juvenile delinquents on safari or voyages down the Nile, there has been little to attract the macro lenses of the tabloid press and generate the condemnation of those whose preferences are for essentially punitive rather than restorative criminal justice.

Perhaps the most politically courageous act of New Labour's Home Secretary was to establish the Macpherson Inquiry into the death of Stephen Lawrence. His murder in a brutal racist attack at a suburban bus stop in south-east London was followed by a criminal investigation by the Metropolitan Police that could be most kindly described as deeply flawed. It was followed by prosecutions, both by the Crown and the Lawrence parents that failed to achieve the conviction of those widely believed to have been Stephen's killers. At the time one newspaper published their photographs, named them as the murderers, and challenged them to sue for libel.

The Macpherson Inquiry was able to establish that the police investigation had been fatally handicapped by an initial delay in arresting suspects whose identity had been suggested to them almost immediately that evening, allegedly allowing incriminating material to be dumped. The victim was of Afro-Caribbean descent while those suspected of his murder were not only white but believed to harbour extreme racist views. It was suggested to the Inquiry that the absence of any sense of urgency in the initial investigation arose from what the subsequent report described as 'institutionalised racism' in the Metropolitan Police.

The Macpherson Report, while it did little to stimulate morale among the lower ranks of London's police, did much to galvanise government thinking about the police generally, quite apart from the issue of 'institutionalised racism'. Throughout New Labour's first three years of office the problem of police manpower was one that would not go away. Police officers, like nurses, have been and remain in short supply. Police recruitment has not simply been related to paying enough to attract recruits and housing costs, especially in urban areas though it has been a contributory factor. But just as many teachers have become dispirited by the continuous torrent of criticism directed at their performance and perceive themselves to be undervalued servants of the community, so too many police officers faced with a range of criticism from incompetence to racism have done little to discourage the idea that theirs is hardly a worthwhile job. The clamour is for more officers on the beat but more police, in spite of the widely held public belief, would not by themselves have much effect on the general level of crime.

The issue of the Macpherson Report and policing in London came alive again in November 2000 when Damiolola Taylor, a 10 year old Nigerian boy, was mortally wounded on his way home from school, it is thought by a slightly older group of youths. The North Peckham estate, where the tragedy occurred is among the most deprived areas of Inner London and the large numbers of police who seemed suddenly to be in the area – Straw himself made a point of visiting in person – were contrasted by some critics with what was alleged to be a normal paucity of police in the area, noted for its violence and drug related crime. Hague was quick to intervene in the public debate, but was equally quickly accused of attempting to play the 'race card' to his political advantage. The issue of police numbers came again to the fore although by early 2001 it was evident that the numbers of police had begun to increase across the country following the provision of additional funds to police authorities. As with the question of whether the overall level of crime is falling or rising, it is likely to be what the tabloid voter chooses to perceive, rather than the statistical reality, which will decide the electoral input on law and order issues.

Paedophiles out! Truckers Rule, OK?

In the summer of 2000 as Blair's popularity still soared higher in the polls than that of Hague, a small girl, Sarah Payne, was abducted from near her grandparents' home in Sussex and her violated body subsequently found in a field in another part of the county. The police, having initially determined on a high profile campaign to find the child, the case took on a national dimension. It was assumed that she had been the victim of a paedophile offender. Part 1 of the Sex Offenders Act of 1997 requires an offender convicted of certain specific sexual offences to register with the police and notify them of any subsequent change of address. There is no provision for such information to be generally available within the public domain. Further, under the terms of the Crime and Disorder Act of 1998, the police may, if they consider the offender is behaving in a way that gives rise to concern that he (or she) may be a danger to the public, apply in a magistrates' court for an order imposing restrictions on the individual concerned.

As public fears about the missing child grew the *News of the World* announced that it proposed to publish, week by week, the names, addresses and photographs of every convicted paedophile in the country. Although the newspaper vigorously denied any suggestion that this was intended other than to allow anxious parents to have intelligence of what dangerous individuals might be lurking otherwise unsuspected in their neighbourhoods, it was criticised as providing the basis for vigilante action quite apart from driving such offenders underground and making their supervision more difficult or even impossible. Trouble was not long in coming and a variety of men were attacked and their homes and cars subjected to criminal damage, several cases involving men who were completely innocent of any crimes against children. Matters reached a flashpoint on a council estate in Portsmouth where a group consisting mainly of women marched nightly to the homes of suspected offenders, some with small children in push-chairs, holding placards inscribed among other things with 'Don't house them; hang them!' To these unedifying spectacles were added arson attacks by delinquent elements attracted to the scene. What is notable about the events on the Paulsgrove estate is less the fact that the trouble soon died down but rather the absence of any high profile action by the police, even though one officer had sustained injury from a missile, motor vehicles had been set on fire and numbers of individuals subjected to terror and intimidation.[24] The events, examined in terms of the law relating to public order, suggested *prima facie* evidence for several kinds of criminal offence and later, in October, more than twenty individuals appeared before a District Judge in Portsmouth charged with a range of serious offences of this nature.

The reaction of Home Office ministers to the issue was, in essence, emollient. Discussions took place with the Payne family about how information about sex offenders might be disseminated in the future and criticism of the action of the *News of the World* was limited to observing that if paedophiles were driven underground it would become impossible to keep them under observation thus increasing rather than diminishing their danger to children. But these localised disturbances were not more than that and disappeared with onset of the autumn rains.

Not so the events that were to convulse the country at the summer's end. In France groups of fishermen, disgruntled at the high price of fuel, disrupted the ferries bringing British families home from their holidays. Soon they were joined by groups of lorry drivers. It was the sort of thing that British holidaymakers had met many times before, no doubt re-inforcing a national stereotype. True to that stereotype the French government acceded to some of their demands. It was therefore a matter of great surprise when, without warning, a group of equally disgruntled Welsh farmers having met at Ruthin market decided, with a number of private hauliers, to blockade the Shell oil refinery at Stanlow on Merseyside. Within a matter of hours almost every major fuel refinery and depot in Britain was paralysed by the presence of tractors and trucks at the gates. The effect was to promote a public panic and within hours long queues at filling stations had resulted in the emptying of their underground tanks. It was an effect that had been achieved by almost no effort other than the presence of the demonstrators at the refinery entrances. In terms of political analysis, these events can be considered as a form of extra-Parliamentary opposition, building upon the discontents of country people about the growing problems of rural life. The Blair government had earlier undertaken to permit a free vote on the subject of banning hunting with dogs and although the Countryside Movement (as it styled itself) voiced concerns about a range of rural issues, its central concern was to ensure that fox hunting continued as a country 'sport'. Outside the refineries the talk was less of hunting and the closure of rural post offices and more of the costs of rural motoring[25] and the diesel needed to power tractors. The truckers, mostly lone or small operators, were no less concerned with the effect of their operating costs upon their profit margins and the degree to which they were disadvantaged in comparison with their European competitors. In yet another sphere, the spectre of Europhobia was projected upon the backdrop of public debate. The theme of the protesters' media interviews was remarkably similar to the Countryside Movement's slogan 'Listen to us!' it was that the Blair government 'wasn't listening'.

While Blair's personal reaction was to appear apologetic almost to the point of contrition and though Brown maintained that budgetary matters were for government and not for pickets, all the indications were that the government had been taken completely by surprise. By the time it was taking the first steps to employing emergency powers panic buying had had its effect. The fuel blockade not only threatened the country with economic paralysis; it produced a cataclysmic fall in Blair's personal popularity and a corresponding rise in the fortunes of the Opposition as the Conference season opened.

From the perspective of public order policing, while the anti-paedophile protests were localised and could be relied upon as burning themselves out, the blockades of the refineries and fuel depots were of a different order of magnitude. These demonstrations were unlike the industrial disputes at Orgreave or Wapping, political riots against the poll tax or capitalism, or the eco-protests at the sites of new road developments. First, they involved not one but police forces across the country, each of which had to make its own operational decisions. Second, the protesters were not trade unionists or eco-warriors, groups who had been readily marginalised to the edge of the political spectrum during the Thatcher years. These people, as William Hague was quick to observe, were identified as upstanding and respectable citizens; certainly they purported to speak on behalf of that very part of Middle England burdened by a heavy tax on vehicle fuel and which had grown accustomed to using its motor cars to travel to work and convey its children to school (often in off-road vehicles sensibly protected against wandering bulls) – the very constituency most able to send shivers through the corridors and lift shafts of Millbank. Third, there was no centrally co-ordinated effort to deal with the problem comparable with the way in which the Association of Chief Police Officers had managed the miners' strike.

Those on the Left recalled images of trucks laden with newsprint being driven at speed past the lines of impotent pickets at Wapping but this time there were only those movements which the protesters permitted to leave to supply essential services which they identified as hospitals and ambulance depots. In addition to the blockade of the fuel depots, numbers of large trucks drove slowly along major roads and city centres to produce traffic congestion but only in London was there any report of direct police inter-vention to frustrate such demonstrations. At the Saltley coking plant in the days of the Heath government, protesting miners had simply overwhelmed the police; in these demonstrations the physical interaction between police and protesters was close to zero and reports suggested that intimidation was so minuscule as to be virtually non-existent.

The fuel protesters, having given Gordon Brown an ultimatum to come up with a solution to the high cost of petrol and diesel in sixty days (until in effect the time of the autumn budget statement) threatened further action. While various spokesmen for the fuel protesters (whose leadership was by now fragmenting) uttered vague imprecations about the nature of forthcoming protests should their demands remain unsatisfied, the gov-ernment began its strategic planning, ensuring that the oil companies, the large haulage firms and the relevant trade unions were 'on side'. It launched an information counter-offensive to convince the public that far from their having been only the most isolated acts of random intimidation, it had in reality been widespread. In his autumn statement Gordon Brown was able to announce a package of measures that were not only initially attractive to the private motorist but were also appealing to many within the road haulage industry. In the event, the remnant of the protesters decided to drive a convoy of heavy vehicles down the motorways system from the north of England to London. One spokesman infelicitously dubbed it a new 'Jarrow Crusade' thus outraging those Labour stalwarts who, remembering the suffering of the unemployed men who walked to London in 1936, denounced it as a kind of blasphemy. Meanwhile, the Metropolitan Police declared an exclusion zone within the M25. By the time the convoy of one hundred or so vehicles reached London it was decided to require them to park on the closed elevated section of the M40 from which fewer than three hundred demonstrators walked to a thinly attended meeting in Hyde Park. Meanwhile, another small group of demonstrators drove from the north of Scotland to block the streets of Edinburgh.

Just as the miners' strike had been first a political and only secondly a public order issue, so too the fuel protests acquired a political profile elevated above the considerations of policing strategies. The fuel protesters were initially dubbed by some sections of the Left as Poujadist but the comparison was largely superficial. The protesters were quick to recognise that while the motorists of Middle England were initially happy to see farmers and truckers pulling chestnuts from the fire on their behalf, if fuel at the pumps disappeared their apparent goodwill would evaporate with equal rapidity. Although the widespread flooding following the autumn rains and the dislocation of railway services following the Hatfield disaster might be said to have pushed the issue from the news headlines, the combination of political skill and low profile policing contributed significantly to restoring the *status quo*.

Bringing Justice Home: The Human Rights Act

In 1950 the Council of Europe agreed a Convention on Human Rights and Fundamental Freedoms. For fifty years British citizens have been able to use the European Court of Human Rights in Strasbourg as a court of last resort with regard to claims under the Convention but only after having exhausted all domestic remedies, for successive British governments have, until now, doggedly declined to incorporate the Convention into domestic law. Whatever might befall the fate of bills designed to ensure the right to roam or the end of hunting with dogs, this objective has been one which the Blair administration determined to reach. Having much sympathetic support in the Lords, human rights under the Convention became enforceable in the courts of England and Wales and Northern Ireland on 2 October, 2000. In this sense they have been 'brought home' since litigants had previously to take a long and expensive road to Strasbourg to claim them.

The changes most readily marked in the criminal courts will be that even at the lowest level written reasons will need to be given for decisions such as the granting and withholding of bail, for the finding of guilt or innocence, and for why a particular sentence or course of action has been taken after conviction. In the pre-trial stage police powers and practices will be subject to closer scrutiny. A further consequence is the assurance that standards of performance on the part of the lay magistracy, already now well trained, will be driven upwards still further towards a virtual para-professional status. This is provided that it continues to exercise its present jurisdiction.[26]

But the incorporation of the Convention has by no means been a bi-partisan venture. While wholeheartedly supporting the content of the Convention the Conservative lawyer and Shadow Lord Chancellor, Lord Kingsland, opposed the incorporating Bill in the Lords because of his belief that adverse domestic constitutional consequences would flow from it. The judges, in his view, would become perceived as part of the political process. Part of this argument enters the highly technical realms of statutory inter-pretation but in simple terms suggests that major social and political change will become driven by judges rather than legislators. In response it must be said that there is little evidence of this in those countries in which the Convention has been long domestically incorporated. Less erudite crit-icism has been more hostile. The myth that 'human rights' will now virtually guarantee immunity from prosecution for every speeding motorist who declines to identify the driver of the car caught on camera, or every thief suspected of handling stolen goods if only he has the wit to keep absolutely quiet and answer no incriminating questions, is likely soon to evaporate as cases begin to go to the Appeal courts. More importantly, just as there is considerable misunderstanding of the distinction between the Council of Europe and the European Community, so too the European Court at Brussels and the European Court of Human Rights at Strasbourg are often confused. For enthusiastic Europhobes things 'European' are the devices of Johnny Foreigner, forming a continuum from such absurdities as outlawing other than straight cucumbers to the near blasphemy of remov-ing the image of the Sovereign from the coinage. Needless to add, quite a few of the judges at Strasbourg appear to be just the kind of outsiders who would want to overturn 'our' laws.

The Blair Effect: Questions of Change

What changed in the area of crime and criminal justice? In short, not a great deal. Aside from changes in the level of crime which are largely beyond the immediate effects of political activity, it is the case that in the area of policy there was for the most part, more of the same. Rather than identifying what or who drove the changes it is more relevant to identify the sources that ensured this continuity and as this essay has attempted to show, while all politicians perceive the need to assuage public anxieties about crime, those in government ignore them at their peril.

How far have these continuities been the positive choice of New Labour? Traditionally, the Labour Party never had a clearly discernible approach to penal matters that formed part of its ideological centrality and a deeply entrenched strain of working-class authoritarianism was frequently in conflict with the vein of progressive liberalism manifested in much of its middle- and upper-class membership. Currently New Labour seems in little danger of ceasing to be an ideology free zone in which pragmatism – or what its critics might perceive as opportunism – is identified as a universally guiding principle.

How effective have these continuities proved to be? The question cannot properly be answered until both opinion polls and the result of the next general election confirm New Labour as the party inspiring the greatest trust on the issues of crime and criminal justice. If New Labour has abjured ideology in the sense of such prescriptions as Clause 4 it has replaced it by an assiduous desire to please. In the area of criminal justice this has consisted in seeking to identify the concerns of an essentially populist agenda. Judged most harshly, it will be seen to have satisfied them less by rational choice than by having been driven by them.

Notes

1 Public concern about crime formed no significant part of the political agenda in 1945 since crime and punishment had never been a matter of partisan concern.

2 *See* M. Benney, T. Gray and R. Pear, *Politics and Social Class: The 1950 General Election in Greenwich*, Routledge and Kegan Paul, 1953.

3 His famous description of the newly enfranchised working-class Conservatives in 1868 was 'angels in marble'.

4 In *Crime and Criminal Justice In Britain since 1945*, Blackwell for ICBH. Oxford, 1989. See also *The Major Effect*, D. Kavanagh and A. Seldon (eds) Macmillan, 1994.

5 A term originally deriving from the fact that traditional Labour supporters, now newly affluent, had turned to support Margaret Thatcher in the new towns in Essex like Basildon and Harlow.

6 Roman Emperors when in trouble with the dissatisfied plebians often resorted to the diverting provision of free bread and circus amusements.

7 Notably in his famous speech to the Conservative Party conference in 1993. See Kavanagh and Seldon (eds) *op.cit.* at p. 310.

8 The driving force behind the Wilson government's major programme of reform in law and criminal justice had been his Lord Chancellor, Gerald Gardner. Unlike either Blair or Straw he had behind him a long and distinguished practice at the Bar and a deep involvement in the politics of penal reform. Essentially a humane and far seeing lawyer, he was often ill at ease on the rialto of politics.

9 The relatively low rates of juvenile crime in the 1930s and early 1940s were a consequence of the demography of the period which was

characterised by the one child family. Likewise the post-war rise in the birthrate produced a subsequent increase in the number of young offenders before the courts.

10 The need to satisfy drug dependency has had a direct effect upon domestic burglaries in many areas while the irresponsible over-consumption of alcohol is closely related to a substantial proportion of crimes of violence among young males and to those forms of criminal damage that are popularly identified as 'mindless vandalism'.

11 The Drug Treatment and Testing orders now available to the courts represent a new approach to constructive control.

12 *Criminal Statistics England and Wales, 1988*, Cmnd 4649, March 2000, Stationery Office Ltd.

13 *Criminal Statistics England and Wales. 1998. op.cit.*

14 Quoted by D. Downes in 'The Macho Penal Economy' in *Punishment and Society*, January 2001.

15 A. Bottoms, 'The philosophy and politics of punishment and sentencing' in C. Clarkson and R. Morgan (eds) *The Politics of Sentencing Reform*, The Clarendon Press, 1995.

16 The first Prison Inspectors were appointed in the mid-nineteenth century before the prison system was unified in 1877.

17 The rule of *autrefois acquit*.

18 Some commentators have placed the Widdecombe speech in the context of a potential leadership contest between herself and Portillo, should Hague fail to lead the party to victory at the forthcoming election.

19 A term of some legal dubiety but generally taken to indicate a matter going to penalty while being largely indemnified from the stigma of a criminal conviction.

20 While causing death by dangerous driving of a motor vehicle carries a maximum sentence of ten years, that for manslaughter is discretionary, with a maximum of life. Only for murder is the life sentence mandatory yet the line between the latter two crimes is often blurred.

21 Private communication of 30 June, 2000.

22 While this decision does not instantly affect the case of Myra Hindley whose appeal to the House of Lords against her 'whole life' tariff was rejected in March 2000, the matter will almost certainly go to Strasbourg as a human rights issue. The fate of that application in the light of current Strasbourg jurisprudence is, however, by no means a foregone conclusion.

23 When interviewed on Radio 4 at the end of November 2000 on the proposals to extend electronic tagging to offenders as young as 10, and confronted with the criticism of Harry Fletcher of the Probation Officers union, Straw somewhat wearily replied that no matter what he proposed there seemed to be no pleasing Harry Fletcher.

24 Contrasts were drawn with the way in which the Metropolitan police neutralised demonstrations by Tibetan exiles at the time of the visit of the Chinese president and particularly with the way in which the ancient offence of 'besetting' was handled during the miners' strike of 1984.

25 Research on the comparative costs of insurance, parking and vehicle efficiency (which is limited by urban congestion) suggests that it is actually

urban dwellers who are worse off in terms of what they are obliged to spend on private motoring.

26 If following the Auld Report lay magistrates cease to sit independently of presiding District judges it is likely that there will not only be a substantial exodus from the lay magistracy but that it will become more difficult to recruit able candidates. The office is unpaid, and as one lay chairman of many years experience put it 'It will be very hard to find many people who will want to be trained only to be unpaid book-ends'.

© Chris Riddell

Chapter 18

SOCIAL POLICY

Howard Glennerster

What Was New?

HOW WILL BLAIR'S social policy be viewed in the long sweep of history? My guess is that it will come to be seen to be as significant as that of the 1945 Attlee government – though for very different reasons.

- The Blair government's social policy strategy marks a decisive shift from the dream of previous post-war Labour administrations. It is a move away from an all-inclusive universal welfare state – never achieved in practice but always a dream.
- It retained many of the structural reforms to welfare institutions initiated by the previous Conservative government and hence solidified them.
- But Blair and Brown aimed to reverse that government's policy on poverty and income distribution – to reduce the growth of social exclusion.
- It concentrated additional public spending on health and education which looked likely to survive whoever wins the 2001 election.
- This new social policy strategy adds up to one of 'selective universality'. (The education element is covered in Alan Smithers' chapter, public spending more generally in Philip Stephen's chapter and family policy in that by Jane Lewis.)

As I have argued elsewhere[1] the two Wilson administrations of the 1960s and 1970s essentially continued the social policy agenda set by the post-war Attlee government. The issues, the priorities and the policy tools employed by those governments would have been recognisable to any member of Attlee's Cabinet. Many of those of the Blair government would not. The economic crisis of the 1970s and the legacy of two decades of Thatcherism broke the mould. They challenged assumptions about the best means of achieving the old social policy ends and about what was possible in terms of public spending. Moreover, the economic, demographic and social structure of the country changed profoundly in the last quarter of the century. Social policy, as it was conceived in the 1940s, had to change fundamentally or die – to be interred by the next Conservative government.

Three central dilemmas faced Blair as they did social democratic governments elsewhere.

- First, the demands on the welfare system were outpacing the electorate's willingness to pay.
- Second, growing inequality in the labour market was making it more difficult to achieve the goals of a fair and inclusive society. In the post-war period up to 1976 economic growth had gradually narrowed the gap between rich and poor. Now instead of working with the grain of social policy the wider economy was working against it.
- Third, voters were demanding much more of their social service providers. Consumers' means of communication, banking and shopping had been revolutionised. They expected equivalent changes in their social services. Those services had been slow to produce real improvements in quality or responsiveness to consumers.

In short, voters wanted more but showed little willingness to pay.

Mrs Thatcher's administration had begun to provide its own answers to these pressures but it had done so in ways that actually made some of the problems worse – notably income inequality. Deep structural changes in the economy produced widening gaps in earnings and much higher unemployment. But these were sharply exacerbated by tax and benefit policies. As a result the United Kingdom moved from being one of the more equal societies in the advanced world in the 1970s to one of the most unequal in the 1990s as the Rowntree Commission on Income and Wealth[2] so clearly demonstrated. The United States used to be the most unequal advanced economy in terms of income distribution. By the mid 1990s the UK had caught it up, if that is the right expression. At the 1997 election worries about that division in society reached unprecedented levels of concern in public opinion surveys. Poverty and deprivation in certain areas reached levels not known since the 1930s. One in five families with children had no earner by the mid 1990s, four times the figure in 1968. If the Blair government proved successful in providing answers to these new challenges it would, indeed, be ground breaking. I discuss each of these central problems in turn.

1 The Tax Constraint

During the period 1946 to 1976 British governments of both parties took, in tax revenue, about a third of all the additional incomes individuals earned and spent the proceeds on social policy. They took another third and spent them on other items of public expenditure. Thus the major part of Britain's economic growth went to fund public services of one kind or another and not into people's own pockets. In the mid 1970s taxation rose *faster* than earnings. Individuals' real take home pay fell. Voters had had enough. That was the end of an era. No government that has significantly increased taxes in the past quarter of a century has survived.

Public attitude surveys do suggest the electorate is willing to pay more for public services even if that means higher taxes. However, on closer inspection the room for political manoeuvre is very small. The surveys suggest that voters are only prepared to see taxes go up a little, and mainly for education and health spending, not for benefits to the unemployed. Indeed, the public thinks such benefits are too generous and discourage work.[3]

Opinion polls are only one kind of evidence. Actual political decisions driven by what politicians think the electorate will stand are another. This is, after all, a politician's job. If we look at the share of incomes taken by all kinds of tax over the past twenty-five years we find they have varied very little, mostly between about 33 per cent and 37 per cent. It is difficult not to conclude that there really is a severe tax constraint in the UK, however much some in the social policy community would like it to be otherwise. Britain is a low tax preferring country. Given that constraint, how should a Labour government, which wants to give social policy a high priority, respond? The answer had to be a strategic shift in approach to universal social services.

Previous Labour administrations acted as if the UK was a high tax preferring country when it was not. They promised high quality universal services, including pensions, and could not deliver. That 'old' Labour fudge was no longer tenable. In reading the Labour manifesto in 1997, however, we gain no clue about the answer to this strategic dilemma. The reduction of unemployment will solve all. The reason for this lack of an answer seems to be that the party did not have one. The appointment of Frank Field as the minister in charge of welfare reform supports that conclusion. He shared Blair's values – his stress on duties as well as rights to welfare, notably the duty to work and not to cheat – but he favoured generous universal benefits across the board and especially in pensions. In the ensuing long internal debate, and with Field's departure, a strategy was worked out. It was one that owed a great deal to the Treasury, now freed from running monetary policy, and to a Chancellor intensely interested in social policy, and his young advisors.

The logic runs something like this. There are basically four extreme positions any country can occupy in the tax and benefit world (Figure 1).

Figure I Tax and social policy worlds

	Universal services	Selective services
High tax	*Sweden*	*Rawlsian ideal*
Low tax	*UK old style*	*Australia*

A country can be a high tax accepting society with good universal services for everyone. Sweden is that kind of country. It can be a high tax country where the average voter is prepared to see most of that money going to the poor – a pure Rawlsian state. I do not know of one. It can be a low tax tolerating country and target its taxes on the poor. Australia is an example. Or it can be a low tax country that spreads that tax income thinly over everyone. That is not a good place to live if you are a poor person. That was Britain after 1976.

Where are Blair and Brown positioning Britain today? Voters thought Labour was in favour of a generously financed old style welfare state. But they said they wanted to keep taxes relatively low. The problem is there is no place on the map for that combination. Over the first four years of Blair's administration a clear strategy emerged. It may not be popular but it is robust and it is different. Right or wrong it will set Britain on a distinctive new social policy course whoever wins the 2001 election.

Selective universalism

The essence of the new Blair/Brown strategy is what my colleague John Hills has called 'selective universalism'. Some key universal services are being given priority to grow but the rest of the social policy budget is now increasingly targeted on the poor. The strategy begins with the central objective that the overall level of taxation as a share of total income should remain at around 37 per cent. This distinguishes New Labour clearly from the new Conservative Hague/Portillo strategy of steadily reducing that ratio but it poses a real constraint. Within the total, social policy is taking a growing share of public spending and will take more. The two key universal services that still serve the majority of the population – health and education – are benefiting from substantial rates of real growth, but only since April 1999. They paid a high price for the commitment to hold spending for two years to the very tight 1997 Conservative spending plans. During that period public spending actually fell as a percentage of the GDP. But following the first Comprehensive Spending Review, whose results were announced in 1998, education spending was to increase at an annual real rate of 5.1 per cent a year, health spending by 4.7 per year. All other spending programmes were to increase by only 1.8 per cent. In the outcome these growth rates have been exceeded. This is in marked contrast to all previous post-war Labour governments, all of whom were forced to cut back on ambitious social spending plans by economic crises.

The Comprehensive Spending Review announced in July 2000 extended that pattern. Education and the NHS will have gained an extra 1 per cent of the GDP each while social security loses 0.4 per cent. The NHS with a planned growth rate of just over 6 per cent a year for four years from 1999 will end its apparently inexorable fate of being the least well endowed health care system in the western world. Education spending will also increase in real terms by over 6 per cent a year in the same period while social security spending – the largest component of the social policy budget – will grow by only 1.2 per cent a year – if all goes well. However, all this has come late in the electoral cycle. By the time really big results begin to feed through it will be past election day. Such are the costs of prudence.

The fall in social security spending as a share of the GDP has been partly the result of an improving economy, partly the result of holding many benefit rates constant in real terms while increasing benefits for those on income support, especially for those with dependent children. The firm resolve not to increase the basic pension in line with earnings has been a key part of this strategy. The tussle between the veteran Barbara Castle and Gordon Brown on this goes to the heart of the strategy and we discuss it more below.

Benefit costs have also fallen as a result of getting people off benefit through the various New Deal welfare reform efforts. The numbers going through these programmes are not huge – half a million young people gaining jobs in four years – but they have two side consequences. One is that it becomes much more difficult to earn on the side and draw benefit. Second, they send a message about expectations of life on welfare. Estimates suggest that youth unemployment is perhaps 40 per cent lower than it would have been without the New Deal. Numbers on benefit seem to have fallen faster than in previous post recession periods. The purely voluntary advice to single parents about finding work led to a drop in numbers claiming benefit of 3 per cent after eighteen months.[4] It was especially effective in areas of high unemployment. The scheme paid for itself – just about – in the short term. If working and the income associated with it have long-term benefits to the women and children involved, then the programme will bring long-term gains (see Jane Lewis' chapter for a fuller discussion of this policy). Both pensions policy and disability benefit policy are good illustrations of the broader strategy.

Pensions policy – a test case

In one sense British pension policy was doomed from the point that Beveridge penned his famous report. Post-war state pensions were set so low that they would never have been generous enough for the average worker to live on let alone the growing middle class. Labour governments have always dreamed of providing adequate basic pensions and never did so. Workers found their remedy in private occupational pensions until Mrs Thatcher added private personal pensions to the menu. The Wilson government's attempt to provide an attractive state pension – the State Earnings Related Pension Scheme (SERPS) – came too late. Only a year after it was introduced Mrs Thatcher took office. She reduced its generosity and encouraged people to opt out with generous tax breaks. Most of the population had already opted out of SERPS when New Labour took office. Only 30 per cent of the working population were members and most of these were from lower income groups. Blair and Brown could have tried to resurrect SERPS as a universal state pension scheme as the American scheme is today. But that would have meant either requiring most people to be members of both private and public schemes or leave their private schemes. This was never on. More could have been forced to leave private schemes by removing the tax privileges they enjoyed. To have an impact these tax penalties would have had to be so harsh as to be politically impossible. Merely to strengthen SERPS and increase the flat rate state pension in line with earnings would have meant raising National Insurance contributions to 25 per cent of pay rolls, as the Government Actuary pointed out.[5] Thus trying to resurrect SERPS as a universal scheme was never feasible.

Alternatively the universal flat rate pension could have been made far more generous so that it produced a livable income well above the means test level. But that would have taken much of the available funds Brown had to spend for this and the next Parliament. To have raised the basic pension to £90 a week would still not have lifted most pensioners off means tested benefits and would have cost £11 billion or a fifth of the cost of the NHS. If the government wanted to save the NHS and give priority to education the only route was to give up any pretence that adequate universal state pensions were affordable. The government stubbornly refused to up-rate the basic state pension in line with earnings despite the public outcry that followed the 75p pension increase in 2000 which was low only because inflation was low. The outcry was a perfect example of what economists call the money illusion – people partly think in terms of cash not what the cash buys. But it mattered politically. Even so Gordon Brown stuck to his guns in the November 2000 pre-Budget statement and did not promise to return to the automatic link between the basic pension and earnings. That would have destroyed his whole pensions and social policy strategy.

- Over the Parliament the Blair government significantly increased means tested income support for old people on lower incomes (the so-called Minimum Income Guarantee) and promised to continue to raise it in line with average earnings. When the Blair government came to office the Minimum Income Guarantee for the poorest pensioners was £68.80 for a single pensioner and £106.60 for a couple. That rose to £92.15 in April 2001 and will rise to £100 a week in 2003. The married couple level will rise to £154 a week. Given the relatively low levels of inflation in the period these are large increases (nearly a third in real terms with the winter fuel allowance) and would have been impossible on the old spread-it-thin universal principle.

- The great problem with such a means test strategy is that those who have saved or have small occupational or private pensions see little or no gain from their lifetime savings efforts. This is where the second element comes in. The savings a pensioner can hold and still draw MIG was increased. More fundamentally there will be a new pension tax credit and a higher starting point for paying tax as a pensioner from 2003. Those in the band of incomes up to about £200 a week will benefit. The level of the credit will rise with the level of earnings in the economy. As in the rest of social policy the tax system is gradually taking over as the means of delivering income support. In the interim the basic state pension is being increased in 2001 by £5 for a single pensioner and £8 for a married couple with more in 2002.

- The new Second State Pension legislated in 2000 came to terms with what SERPS had already become – a pension for the poorer worker. It concentrates National Insurance Contribution revenues on enhancing the pensions of those with low incomes. Employers are paying a percentage of their payroll with no top limit. Employees are paying a percentage of their incomes with a ceiling. There is a relatively small reduction for opting out into a private scheme but a lot of this revenue will go to enhance the pensions of the low paid – those with incomes below £9,000 and to a lesser extent those below £18,000 for an interim period. The accrual rate for those earning at the rate of £9,000 a year will be doubled. In other words the value of the pension earned for working a given number of years will be doubled. The rules will also enhance the pensions of those with caring responsibilities and with children under five. In short, the Second State Pension will be targeted on the poor and those with caring responsibilities. But it will come to fruition only slowly.

- The near poor are being encouraged to become members of the heavily regulated private Stakeholder Pension Schemes. Employers with no employer based pension scheme will be required to make a Stakeholder Pension Scheme available to their employees through a private pension company. No employer contribution will be required. Government sets minimum benefit standards and limits to the administrative charges these schemes can make. The pension contributions will attract tax relief up to a ceiling.

This whole policy will give individuals in the UK a greater responsibility for their own retirement than in almost any other western country including the USA. Now, this pension strategy has its problems. It will only raise those on the Second State Pension above the means tested system of support if they have very long paid working lives or very lucrative ones. Many will still end up drawing means tested pensions and will get no reward for saving. This is most likely to be true of women. The steady decline in the value of the old basic pension relative to earnings means there that will be little room between the means tested 'guarantee' and this new pension. Some people will not gain a great deal, by contributing for a lifetime. The whole system is very very complicated. It will take a long time to phase in. In short, I cannot see it lasting in its present form without modification.

But the strategy will cost the UK public budget less than any other European or North American state pension scheme despite our aging population. It is a strategic shift for a Labour government of very great significance. It can assuredly be improved upon and simplified. The flat rate first pension and the new second pension will no doubt get absorbed into a single scheme at some point. Entitlements need to be made more generous for women and others with shorter careers. There is a strong case for targeting tax relief less generously on the rich pension contributor and more on the poorer stakeholder pensioner. The whole complexity of the schemes needs simplifying and good advice for the lower paid secured. People do not know their way around the present pension maze let alone this more complex one. But the whole strategy *is* economically sustainable, which many other countries' pension systems are not and it is heavily targeted on the poor.

Disability

By 1997 spending on cash benefits for the disabled had come to take over a quarter of the social security budget compared to less than 15 per cent in the early 1980s. These benefits help to meet the costs of disability by paying carers, help replace earnings lost as a result of disability or help the poorest with means tested benefits. The cost of all these had increased substantially – trebling since 1974. This was partly because the previous government had deliberately encouraged people to apply for these benefits to keep down the unemployment count. There were other incentives to gain disability status and disincentives to return to work but recent work suggests there was a real increase in disability as well and the government needed to deliver something to the disability lobby whose cause it had championed in opposition.

This dilemma led the Labour government to redefine the principles underlying the benefit structure. Once again it was driven to a more selectivist solution. It is possible to argue that all disabled people should be compensated for their disability regardless of their financial circumstances –

horizontal equity. Though not implemented at all generously that principle had lain behind several benefits introduced in the 1970s. Now the government decided that if it was to improve benefit levels, especially for children, it would have to rein back incapacity benefit which was seen as subsidising unemployment and early retirement as well as going to higher income disabled. When the chips were down spending money on the poor disabled won out over the idea of equity between the disabled and non disabled sections of the population. The disabled wanted to work and be part of mainstream society. Incentives not to work had become part of the benefit system. They had to be removed and disabled people helped back to work if at all possible. This approach fitted easily into the dictum 'work for those who can and security for those who cannot' which Blair had enunciated in launching the government's welfare reform green paper.

So:

- Incapacity benefit was retained but the process of qualifying was sharpened. New claimants were allocated to an advisor to ensure they were unable to work and to help those who could to return to work. The benefit becomes means tested so that income from a private pension scheme, for example, will be taken into account and the benefit reduced accordingly.
- The Severe Disablement Allowance was abolished. Those in need can apply for income support but at the same time benefits for those with young children were improved.

This shift of principle provoked anger from disabled groups and saved tiny sums of money in the short run. But it did fit as part of the overall approach to social security – target the poor, check abuse and encourage paid work.

Long-term care – universal or selective?

The same kind of tension between a selective or a universal model had to be faced in the case of long-term care. Here the dilemma was different. The existing system of care for elderly people derives more or less directly from the poor law. It is only available free to those on low incomes and with very limited capital assets. Local authorities are the main providers or at least purchasers of these services. Yet they interact daily with services provided free by the National Health Service. People move between these services all the time from hospital back into the community and vice versa. The clash of principles affects vulnerable individuals day to day and is damaging to sensible and humane service delivery.

As many of those who gave evidence to the Royal Commission on Long Term Care[6] put it – why should we be able to receive care free if we are unfortunate enough to be dying a lingering death from cancer but not if we are suffering from Alzheimer's disease? Essentially the boundary line problem could be resolved either by turning the NHS into a means tested service, too, or by extending the principles of NHS funding to long-term care.

The economic case for long-term care to be part of the universal set of services is powerful in its own right, as the Royal Commission on Long Term Care argued. Market failures associated with private insurance for long-term care are even greater than in the case of health insurance. An insurance company finds it very difficult to predict far into the future what kind of care will be available, what it will cost and what will have happened to the elderly population's level of incapacity. Much care is now provided by spouses and relatives. A promise to pay for care may make these informal carers less willing to care. That is what economists call moral hazard and is very difficult to predict. Insurance companies are not in business to take uncertain risks. Premiums on private policies are therefore high. Most people, while young, do not lay awake at night worrying about their time in an old person's home, though it is only when you are young that these policies are at all attractive. Hence very few people take out private long-term care insurance even in the US where ordinary health insurance is the norm. The private insurance route is not a feasible or efficient solution for long-term care.

Yet, to extend the NHS to cover all the care needs of old people would be expensive and might mean that families would come to rely on it rather than look after their spouses or parents. The main gainers would be the non poor. The Royal Commission was divided precisely on these grounds. The majority on the Royal Commission proposed doing what both Germany and Japan have just done in a similar situation – merging the funding of health and long-term care. This would make the receipt of care free, paid for by taxation. Individuals would have to pay for their food and accommodation in a home as they do if they are living in their own home. But it would have moved long-term *personal care* into the category of a universal service. The total cost of the Royal Commission's plans would be about a half of one per cent of the GDP, it claimed, or what the government had put into the education service in five years. Where would the government draw the line between selective and universal principles?

In July 2000 the Westminster government came down on the side of the minority report. It agreed to fund nursing care from taxation in whatever setting it was provided. Those in nursing homes would have their fees reduced. Personal care would be charged subject to a means test. There would be a period of grace before the charges were levied and the level at which they applied would be raised. They could be put off until death!

The tax funding of nursing care *is* an extension of the universal principle, but stopping short of funding personal care will not help solve the problems of integrating social and health care. In February 2001, the

Scottish Parliament came down in favour of the Royal Commission's Solution. This would prove an interesting experiment in devolved government like the equivalent divergent policy on student fees.

Housing

Housing has never been a universal service. In the 1940s it was the aspiration of many working-class people to live in a decent council house and move on from substandard private landlord rented housing. The great boom in owner occupation made council housing a clearly residual sector largely catering for the poor and very poor and vulnerable. Mrs Thatcher speeded the process with the right to buy, which richer council tenants in better property took up. Here too, as in pensions only more so, there was no way back. The failure of many local councils to manage their often huge stock of housing effectively doomed them. Increasingly ministers moved to encourage the voluntary transfer of the council stock to self standing organisations – housing associations or housing cooperatives.

Perhaps the biggest single change was to complete the process of abolishing the tax relief that owner occupiers received which the Conservatives had begun. At its height this was the biggest public subsidy to any form of housing and a massive middle-class benefit. It also sparked off a massive and economically dangerous housing boom. The Labour government's biggest failure was the inability to reform housing benefit. This gives perverse incentives to those out of work, making it costly to return or enter the labour market. It is appallingly administered by local councils. After labouring for over two years the review of the system failed to come up with a better one.

Post-war Labour governments had housing as one of their major concerns. It has now all but disappeared off the political map. It has been replaced, if at all, by the plight of the modern city. That is a far more relevant concern. The scale of housing construction is not as it was for so much of the post-war period. In many parts of the country we suffer from *excess* housing stock. These issues were addressed by Lord Rodgers' Urban Task Force and many of his recommendations, especially tax incentives to build in cities and revive many of them, were followed up in Gordon Brown's 2001 budget and elsewhere.

Does it add up?

The political reasoning behind this whole new selective universality strategy, which is distinctively Brown's and the Treasury's, may be clear but does it make deeper sense? Is 'selective universality' just a clever phrase? My view is that it does add up. Indeed, it is the only means we have to save our health and education systems from becoming residual services for the poor like housing.

The case for universality has always had several elements to it. First, there are what economists call neighbourhood effects. Poorer or less advantaged children gain by being taught in schools and classes with more able and advantaged. This is now a well established finding. A heavily segregated private – or public – system reduces the achievement levels of the whole population. Some similar effects apply in health care. Effective preventive strategies rely on universal free access to health services to be effective. There is no real equivalent public good gain with cash benefits.

Second, we know that private insurance markets work very badly in health care. For a host of well accepted reasons health markets fail for rich and poor alike. The same cannot be said about private insurance for old age. There are issues about administrative costs of private pension insurance but the market works. It may, indeed, promote more individual savings. The case is not conclusive but on balance the argument for public funding of pensions is not as powerful as is the case with health care.

Third, there is the more political argument that a service for the poor becomes a poor service, as Richard Titmuss put it. Once a service loses the personal interest of the average voter it will not get funded adequately. The problem is that this happened a long time ago with social security. Social policy is a one-way street. Once lost, this support cannot be regained by forcing people to re-join a universal service. Nor does a universal pension scheme necessarily benefit the poorest. The current US pension scheme is a case in point. It is universal and quite generous for the average person but not for the poorest.

In short, free markets work least well in health, education and long-term care. Private pensions have disadvantages but nothing like as great. If I were adrift on the ocean and could steer my boat towards a country with a decent pension scheme and a high preference for taxation I would set my sail for Sweden. As a resident of the UK with its relatively low propensity to be taxed, the Brown/Blair strategy looks like a sensible compromise that will help secure the future of the NHS and state education and improve the income of poorer pensioners. But it is a strategy that will need some selling. Selling its strategic social policy vision is something this government has been surprisingly bad at.

2 Redistribution to the Poor

The sharply growing inequalities of the past quarter of a century have already been remarked upon. Here again New Labour has set out in a distinctive new direction and set itself a surprisingly difficult policy goal – to abolish child poverty in a generation, as Tony Blair put it, or halve it in ten years, as Gordon Brown put the same pledge. This strategy has several parts to it.

- For the first time in the UK a minimum wage was introduced in 1999 to put a floor under the very lowest wages. Though not primarily benefiting poor families it did make possible the next and most important part of the plan – a wage supplement for low earners with children.
- The Working Families Tax Credit replaced an existing cash benefit for low income families. It is more generous and it tapers off less sharply than the old cash benefit as a family's income rises. It can be received either as an enhanced wage packet or as a cash payment to the mother. For a low paid worker these benefits will add more than a hundred pounds a week to family income. The aim is to put an income floor under poor single earner families of £214 a week.
- A child care tax credit meets 70 per cent of the cost of child care up to a reasonable ceiling.
- A new tax credit for families with children worth £10 a week per child was trailed for April 2001. It will be gradually withdrawn for those paying the higher rate of tax.

These are significant improvements to the incomes of poor families who are in work. The use of the tax system to deliver benefits is meant to be less stigmatic and easier for families to access. It has become a key part of the government's benefit strategy. How far it will ease access is too early to say. But already significantly more families are claiming these credits than did the previous cash benefits. For those in transitory jobs with small employers there may be problems we are yet unsure about.

The alternative?

What we have, then, is a real and substantial boost to the incomes of the poorest working families. Was there another way of doing this? Assuredly there was. The way favoured by the Child Poverty Action Group was a much larger increase in child benefit for every child. The government did raise the level of child benefit by 36 per cent for all first children. But they could have raised the benefit far more so that all families got as much as those now receiving WFTC. That would have avoided extending the range of the poverty trap. Take up would have been near 100 per cent. But the cost to the tax payer would have been vast – rivaling that of the NHS.

One advantage of making such low wage supplements part of the tax system is that it makes it more difficult for Conservatives to oppose. It is after all a reduction in taxation. For the same reason the costs do not count as public expenditure. In a world of pure economics these things do not matter but in the real political world they do. American experience, heavily drawn on by Brown and his advisors, bears this out. A small Earned Income Tax Credit for poor families introduced in the USA in the mid 1980s was turned by Clinton into the biggest programme of support for poor families the USA has. The Republican Congress dared not oppose it. By the end of the 1990s it was costing more than the whole of welfare. Recent research suggests that it has been more important in attracting people back into work, along with the buoyant economy, than US welfare reform – the threats to cut benefit off after two years or less.

Other child benefit changes

Blair's government also introduced a range of other benefits for families with children:

- A higher level of child benefit – up £3.15 for the first child to £15 a week and up £0.40 to £10 a week for other children.
- Most important, but hardly recognised, there have been significantly higher benefits for those with children who are on income support. Income support rates for children under eleven have been increased by over 70 per cent. The government's best kept secret!

Tax changes

There have been a series of other measures that have reduced the tax burdens on the poor and taxed the rich more heavily.

- The starting point for income tax levied on lower income groups has been raised.
- There is a 10 per cent initial tax rate band for the lowest paid – down from the old 20 per cent band.
- National Insurance Contributions paid by the low paid have been reduced.
- Tax relief on buying a house has been abolished as we mentioned above. Once, when tax rates were higher rich people could get much of the interest on their mortgage paid by other, often poorer, tax payers. The gradual reduction in this perverse benefit began with the Wilson administration in the 1970s. Further reductions were outlawed by Mrs Thatcher. Only after her departure did Kenneth Clarke begin again to reduce the tax subsidy. Gordon Brown has gone the whole way abolishing mortgage tax relief altogether.
- The tax bands – the income at which you begin to pay different rates of tax have not been increased in line with rising earnings, especially high earnings. More people have therefore been drawn into the top band of tax. Increasing the incomes at which the various tax bands begin to bite in line with earnings would have reduced income tax by about two billion pounds. Or to put it

another way the government is taxing the higher income groups significantly more even though it is not shouting about it. Perhaps one reason for the government's unpopularity is that those affected have tumbled to what is going on.

- Married couples used to receive tax relief whether they had children or not. This too has been abolished and the extra revenue used to give higher rates of child benefit and the new Child Tax Credit. The value of the married couples' tax relief was worth nearly twice as much to a high income group couple as it was to a low income one. Child benefit is a flat sum received by all couples with children, child tax credits do not go to the rich.

Taken together these measures have been markedly pro poor.

Making work pay

The Blair government's aim has not just been to redistribute cash to poor families but to get them into work. Once again this looks like the only robust long-term policy that will significantly reduce inequality. One of the most striking trends in the recent past has been the rise in the number of non earning families with children. One in five of all families with children were in that category when the government took office: 60 per cent of single parents and 10 per cent of married couples. This was twice the levels of 1979 and four times that of 1968. Worklessness had become a much bigger and a longer term phenomenon than it was. Yet, we have the tightest labour market since the 1960s. A great deal of the government's early efforts were understandably spent trying to set up the New Deal Programme that would help get people back into work with intensive advice and some sanctions. The tax and benefit changes were a necessary complement to that strategy.

The result will be to lift most working families off Housing Benefit and Council Tax Benefit and reduce the sharpness of the poverty trap. More people, though, will be brought within some means tested benefit. The government judges that a lesser disincentive, affecting more people, is the right trade off.

The result?

During the first year of the new government overall inequality *rose*. Those are the latest figures we have from *Economic Trends* in April 2000 and may be all we have before the next election. Wages and salaries of those in work at the top continued to rise fast as the economy grew. Yet, none of the measures to increase benefits were in place. The claim that the poor get poorer under Labour looked as if it would run again. Yet in the longer run when the policies begin to bite what will be the result? Colleagues David

Piachaud, John Hills and Holly Sutherland have modelled the impact on
families. The policies in combination should reduce the number of children
in poverty by one million by 2001. Official estimates including the later
measures in the 2000 Budget put the figure at 1.2 million. That still leaves
two million more poor children.[7] Hills[8] shows that poor households with
children (the poorest fifth) will be between 10 and 12 per cent better off as
a result of the Budgets 1997–2000. They gain far more than any other
income group. The highest income groups lose (see Figure 1). The reason
most households, except the richest, gain is that the scale of spending on
items like defence which cannot be allocated between households has
fallen.

Hills concludes:

> One assessment of the government's record is that it has
> simultaneously delivered as much to low income groups as more
> expensive Old Labour policies would have done while . . . reforming
> the structure of the system to improve work incentives overall and
> delivering (an) improvement in the public finances. In these terms it is
> a very impressive achievement. Alternatively one could say that the tax
> and benefit reforms have only barely delivered enough to the lowest
> income groups as a whole to prevent inequality from rising.

The forces of inequality are much more powerful than they were either in
Attlee's or Wilson's time.

The Working Family's Tax Credit and the minimum wage took two
years or more to establish. The Child Tax Credit will not be in place until
April 2001. Pause, and the tide of inequality will drive you before it. The
Annual Poverty and Social Exclusion Report the government is producing
will be a continuing challenge if it wants to report good news.

Figure 1 Impact of Labour budgets 1997–2000 (compared to statutory indexation)

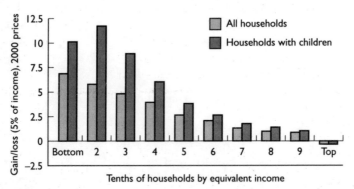

Source: POLIMOD & Hills 2000

Social exclusion

The high demand for labour had its positive side though. Evidence from small area statistics collected by the LSE Centre for Analysis of Social Exclusion suggests that the good economic climate is now beginning to affect the very poorest areas. Again the story, though positive, is not dramatic. These areas have suffered such a long-term battering that recovery will take decades. The whole range of action zones the government has introduced – health, community, education – can be sneered at but are providing a stimulus to new work, new approaches and some enthusiasm. Many are also rather top heavy in senior officer time and committee work for the sums involved.

The work at the centre of government – the Social Exclusion Unit – is promising. A very lively and able group of staff has thrown itself into trying to get departments of state to work across territorial boundaries on poor neighbourhoods, on family break-up, on truancy. Their work is much more focused than past cross-departmental efforts like the Central Policy Review Staff and more high profile. Again, the size of the task government has set itself is daunting. Whitehall is difficult to move. The early reports of the Unit were good. They drew on outsiders from the field as members of the task groups. Good evidence was marshaled and sensible policy prescriptions resulted. However, a full assessment of their impact is too early to call. As far as machinery for social policy goes this looks as if it could become one of the more successful models.

3 Quality Health Services

The National Health Service turned out to be one of the government's most difficult testing grounds. Labour has always been seen as the party best fitted to run the NHS even when the electorate thought it no good at running the economy. Expectations were high and were raised in the election campaign with talk of 'saving the NHS'. Yet, at the same time, the government made it difficult for itself. In line with its election promise health service funding was held to the very tight limits the previous Conservative government had set. Some small respite was given in the early Brown budgets but the rate of real growth in health spending was held well below that of earlier years in the decade.

Labour had also fulminated against the Conservative's market reforms to the NHS. Yet, whatever their deficiencies, they had been designed to improve the responsiveness of the service to consumers, to foster innovation and challenge the monopoly power of hospitals. Evidence both from academic research and managers on the job suggested that the reforms were working to some extent – notably the purchaser provider split and the devolved budgets to GP fundholders. Labour began by revoking the power of GP fundholders to make separate contracts with hospitals and paused before it tried to make its own changes. The NHS was weary with change. The consequence was that the NHS fundamentally trod water for two years. The pressures on hospitals to improve and speed their services exerted by the old fundholders were removed. An almost audible sigh of relief could be heard from hospitals relapsing into their old ways. Most noticeably waiting times rose. In the end the NHS white paper team made a good job of keeping the major features of the Conservative reforms that had worked. To ease the pain the changes did not come into operation until April 1999 and even then were to be gradually phased in. Specifically:

- The purchaser provider split between those funding services and those providing them was to stay.
- Hospital trusts would remain running hospitals.
- Fundholding would go. Individual GP practices would lose their capacity to buy services for their own patients from hospitals or other providers.
- In Scotland fundholding disappeared unlamented. In England most of the NHS budget would be devolved gradually to new primary care groups. These groups would comprise general practitioners and other primary care staff serving populations of about 100,000. They came into being in April 1999. In time most would merge into Primary Care Trusts including community health services. They would contract with hospitals of their choice to provide care for their area. These groups' budgets are capped and cover pharmaceutical costs as well as all other aspects of care. The independence of fundholding has gone.
- A new central body was created to set down clinical guidelines to ensure common standards of treatment were set for the whole of the NHS. This body is called the National Institute for Clinical Excellence (NICE). Ever since the NHS's inception the term 'National' has been a misnomer. The funds have come from a central source but each clinician has gone their own way professionally. Wide differences in standards and practices have been permitted. Now good practice ways to treat a disease or condition are to be agreed with leaders of the profession using the best available research. NICE looks at the clinical efficacy *and* the cost effectiveness of new and existing drug and other therapies and gives advice to ministers about whether they should be paid for on the NHS.
- A Commission for Health Improvement acts as a kind of quality inspectorate offering advice to ministers and to local health authorities about the quality of their local services. If necessary it can recommend corrective action.

Taken together these changes constituted a bigger challenge to the professions working in the NHS than any thing that the Conservatives did or anything that has happened since 1948. Decisions about what hospital to fund are to be tipped right down to the bottom of the service and put into the hands of those who see patients day by day – general practitioners and other primary care workers. For the very first time government has accepted that a tax financed service cannot provide everything that drug companies and others invent whatever their efficacy and cost. Rationing was something politicians denied could be done or even contemplated in the NHS. Now it is being done, explicitly. Past Ministers of Health have shied away from 'inspecting the NHS' for quality of service provided by individual practitioners, despite the fact that other services have had quality controls since the early Victorian era. Now a Commission for Health Improvement has been created to do this.

But this was all new machinery, not new cash. Health economists have taken pride in the fact that the NHS has been the lowest funded service amongst advanced economies. Only Spain, Portugal, Greece and the Czech Republic spend less per head and the UK does not do badly when you look at broad health indicators like expectation of life. But these measures have little to do with the quality of health care. When you come to look in detail at areas of medicine like cancer or the quality of outpatient facilities the UK does very badly. It has far too many avoidable deaths. There is too much variation in treatment from one area to another for no good reason and the standard of facilities and equipment are often poor. The crisis of expectations, I mentioned earlier, was waiting to blow up.

It was the flu epidemic of Christmas 1999 that triggered an explosion that was really inevitable at some point. Blair presumably saw this. His pledge to raise UK health spending to that of the rest of Europe in January 2000 was highly significant as are the detailed plans for spending the increment that followed in July 2000. Blair and his staff got heavily involved in drawing up that plan just as Mrs Thatcher had in the 1989 counterpart.

Perhaps for the first time ever in an NHS white paper document, real practical issues are addressed. There is a research-based programme for treating coronary heart disease, a detailed plan for mental health and early intervention and support for those with psychotic episodes. There will be a single primary care setting where old people and families can go to get help. Clinicians are to undergo an annual appraisal! All of this betokens some real involvement by people in the service who understand the day to day detail as opposed to structures and budgets. But in the end many of the means come down to targets and standard setting, not letting people at the bottom have their head.

Local actors need good information and incentives to produce results. It is still not clear that this centralist minded government is willing to do that.

Critical will be their attitude to primary care groups who wish to switch provider because they believe they are not doing a good job.

The Labour government has chosen to put itself in the firing line of one of the most intractable problems modern societies has to face. You can leave medicine to the private market and let 'managed care organisations' take the heat – as is happening in the US right now. Or you can try to explicitly handle the health care dilemma as a national responsibility. Few try to do that. Where they do they have usually failed and got egg all over their faces. If the Blair government succeeds in introducing openly debated health service rationing and standard setting it will be a remarkable achievement. As I heard a senior health service manager say at a meeting: 'This is the Service's best chance ever. If we f. . . this up it is curtains for the NHS.' But changes of this kind, as with much of social policy, take decades to come to fruition. Therein lies the electoral problem.

Overall

The Blair administration, against all my pre 1997 predictions I must say, has put together a coherent social policy package that is distinct both from its Conservative and Labour predecessors and different from other European countries. It has contained the demands of an aging population on the tax payer but shifted much of the burden onto people's own pockets. It has made room for major health and education spending within a budget that is tax constrained by British voters. It has a commendable and effective policy of redistribution to the lower income working poor and their children. It has produced a promising reform to the structure of the NHS and promised a major infusion of funds that will reverse the UK's long standing place at the bottom of all the league tables for health spending. The attack on inequality may still look small in comparison to the powerful economic forces at work but it does move in the opposite direction to nearly two decades of budget policy.

Yet taking the public with the new strategy will not be easy. It emerged in the process of governing. It is a break with past expectations. It only came to be expounded forcefully late in the term. Social policy is now more difficult for a party of the left to get right than it is for a party of the right. Populist attacks on welfare win votes. Crafting a solid future for welfare institutions within a severe tax constraint against attacks from traditionalists on the left and the critics on the right is much more difficult. Blair is paying a high price for the mistakes of the first year. But though I could pick quarrels with individual answers to particular questions I am forced to give Blair's social policy an alpha minus. Alpha for the strategy, gamma for presentation, beta for some of the detail.

Notes

1 H. Glennerster, *British Social Policy since 1945*, Blackwells, 2000.

2 *Joseph Rowntree Foundation Inquiry into Income and Wealth*, Joseph Rowntree Foundation, 1995.

3 J. Hills and O. Lelkes, 'Social security, selective universalism and patchwork redistribution' in *British Social Attitudes: the 16th Report: Who shares New Labour values?* R. Jowell, J. Curtice, A. Park and K. Thompson, Ashgate, 1999.

4 C. Hasluck, A. McKnight and P. Elis, *Evaluation of the New Deal for Lone Parents, Department of Social Security Report No 110*, Corporate Document Services, Leeds, 2000.

5 *The Actuary*, June 1998, pp. 22–23.

6 Royal Commission on Long Term Care, *With Respect to Old Age: Long Term Care – Rights and Responsibilities*, The Stationery Office, 1999.

7 D. Piachaud and H. Sutherland, *How Effective is the British Government's Attempt to Reduce Child Poverty?* CASEpaper 38, London School of Economics, 2000.

8 J. Hills, 'Taxation for the Enabling State' *Public Policy for the 21st Century: Social and Economic Essays in Memory of Henry Neuburger*, N. Fraser and J. Hills (eds), Policy Press, 2000.

Chapter 19

EDUCATION POLICY

Alan Smithers

T HE BLAIR GOVERNMENT came to power with education at the top
of its agenda. 'Education, education, education' seems destined for
the *Oxford Book of Quotations* (though perhaps not John Major's
retort, 'My priorities are the same, but in a different order.')[1]. The new
Secretary of State, David Blunkett, who had shadowed the post for three
years, immediately embarked on a whirl of activity. Within a week of
taking office a new Standards and Effectiveness Unit was established and,
within two, ambitious targets for the literacy and numeracy of eleven-year-
olds had been declared. The Queen's Speech announced a wide-ranging
Education Bill (later divided) to give effect to the manifesto pledges, and
also an enabling bill to phase out the previous government's assisted places
scheme. Just sixty-seven days into the Parliament a White Paper, *Excellence
in Schools*,[2] was published, closely followed by another proposing to
extend the use of Lottery money to, among other things, education.[3] The
reforms and initiatives of the first few months gathered pace in the first full
calendar year in office for two decades. The School Standards and
Framework Bill and the Teaching and Higher Education Bill made it to the
statute book (though not without a struggle in the House of Lords over
tuition fees), and major Green Papers on lifelong learning[4] and the teaching profession[5] were published. The Parliament drew to a close much as it
had begun with another education Green Paper, this time essentially an
election manifesto focusing on secondary schools.[6]

Change, But No Change?

What is remarkable about all the apparent change is how little it differed at
root from the policies of the previous Conservative administrations. Many

of the education reforms which the Conservatives had introduced from 1988 onwards, and which were bitterly attacked by the Labour opposition of the time, now became the backbone of the Blair programme. The National Curriculum, tests and league tables, financial delegation to schools, and a beefed-up inspection service were all enthusiastically embraced by New Labour. Indeed, Tony Blair pledged before the election to keep Chris Woodhead, the Chief Inspector of Schools, in office, disappointing the fervent hopes of many of Labour's traditional supporters. The sense of change, but no change, was heightened by the pre-election promise to adhere to Conservative spending plans for the first two years.

It was not only the central planks of Conservative policy that were assimilated. The Specialist Schools programme, which the Conservatives had happened on following the failure of business to support the City Technology Colleges in the numbers expected, became part of New Labour policy (which also sees an attempt to create more CTCs as City Academies). Even the literacy programme which New Labour counts as one of its great successes was initiated by Gillian Shephard, the outgoing Secretary of State. Such was the extent of the take-over that the Conservatives were hard pressed to establish 'clear blue water' in the election campaign, and John Major was left somewhat desperately promising 'a grammar school in every town'.

Blair's Team

The dramatic turnaround in Labour education policy can be clearly identified with Blair himself. Five days after his election as leader of the Labour Party, he was called upon on 26 July 1994 to present the party's new education policies. These were the fruits of its Education Commission which had deliberated long and hard under Ann Taylor in the aftermath of the 1992 defeat. It was proposed, among other things, to scrap league tables, to place City Technology Colleges under LEAs and, most radical of all, to abolish A-levels and replace them by a grouped award to be called the General Certificate of Further Education. This awkward name had been lighted upon because GCFE was thought to resonate with GCSE. The decidedly traditionalist stance was not to the new leader's taste and, amazingly, he was able to spin the launch so that the news headlines the next day proclaimed that Labour was proposing to retain and broaden A-levels.

When Blair came to appoint his shadow Cabinet in the autumn, he replaced Ann Taylor with a political heavyweight, David Blunkett. Blunkett, from the centre left with a background in local politics, had had to undergo his own Damascine conversion. At the Labour Party Conference in 1995 he famously rescued the leadership from losing a vote on selection when he said: 'Watch my lips. No selection, either by examination or by interview, under a Labour government.' But by March 1996, in supporting the party's new policy of fast-tracking the most able and allowing grammar schools to survive, he found himself saying 'the comprehensive school should have focused on every pupil reaching their full potential instead of developing an unfortunate association with rigid mixed-ability teaching'. Still later this most adroit of verbal communicators was having to confess that by an unfortunate slip of the tongue he had missed out a word, and what he thought he was saying, was 'Watch my lips. No *further* selection . . .' Both in opposition and office Blunkett has served Blair loyally and has become his mouthpiece not only on education but other issues. One suspects, however, that many of his instincts lie elsewhere and that as a canny and ambitious politician he has been biding his time.

Much more in tune with Blair's thinking, and responsible for refining much of it, is the group of Oxford-educated men that he has gathered around him. At Number 10 he has installed his own education team led by David Miliband, state-school educated but looking every inch a public school boy. He has been joined by Andrew Adonis who, like Blair, is independent school, Oxford and Islington. A journalist with the *Observer* and the *Financial Times* he came to Blair's notice when before the election he wrote an impassioned article urging Blair to become his own Secretary of State for Education. Such has Adonis' influence grown that it is said that he, not Blunkett, controls education policy.[7]

At the DfEE as head of the newly created Standards and Effectiveness Unit, Blair appointed Michael Barber. Barber is also very much in the same mould as Blair himself. Both were public school and Oxford educated, and both eschewed the local comprehensive for their children – in Barber's case preferring an independent school. Barber had been plucked from the relative obscurity of NUT official and unsuccessful Labour candidate for Henley to become an education professor first at Keele, then the London Institute of Education. The extent of his admiration for Blair came through in his inaugural lecture at the Institute when he said, 'If Tony Blair had not existed, he would have had to have been invented'.

Also very important to Blair has been the Chief Inspector of Schools, Chris Woodhead, originally appointed by the Conservatives and credited with getting them to move literacy and numeracy up the agenda. Answerable only to the Prime Minister himself and bolstered by the evidence of his inspectors, he became a very powerful critic of the *status quo*. Articulate and unconcerned about his popularity he proved an ideal bludgeon for Blair. His initially surprising alliance with the Prime Minister did not, however, extend to the DfEE. His relationship with Blunkett was cool and polite. As head of a government department, albeit non-ministerial, Woodhead regarded himself as the equivalent of Blunkett (he was certainly paid more). Much of what he criticised was dear to the hearts of DfEE officials. In particular, local education authorities became a battleground. Ofsted acquired a statutory right to inspect them and presented a series of highly critical reports. It is said that Blair hoped that this would create a climate in which they could be abolished.[8] But while there have been some gestures towards outsourcing, the LEAs have emerged largely unscathed. Perhaps in frustration, or perhaps feeling that he had taken his brief as far as he could, Woodhead resigned on 1 November 2000, to write for *The Daily Telegraph*. He was replaced by the more emollient Mike Tomlinson who in his first annual report published in February 2001 was careful to find things to praise. Although in his dealings with the DfEE Blair holds most of the cards he has not always got his own way. Some of the inconsistencies which we shall be laying bare reflect the compromises that have had to be made.

A Distinctive Strategy

The changes that New Labour did make in that early flurry of activity – phasing out assisted places, re-positioning grant maintained as foundation schools, placing limits of the size of infants' classes – were relatively minor compared with the broad thrust of policy that had been accepted. But as the education strategy has been rolled out it has become clear that it differed from what had gone before in at least three important ways. First, the government itself has sought to *manage* the education system by setting targets, assessing performance and offering money on 'a something for something basis'. Second, in pursuit of standards it has seen itself as maintaining 'the high challenge' of the Thatcher approach, but providing much more support. And, third, it has made 'inclusiveness' a twin goal alongside economic competitiveness.

Government as management

The Conservative administration in 1988 had radically altered the relationship between central government and the schools. From the inception of Local Education Authorities in 1902 governments had contented themselves with laying down the legislative framework. The real power was in the hands of the LEAs, funded through the rates, which could often choose whether to respond to what central government wanted. The present government's difficulties over grammar schools stem from a small number of authorities which refused to implement the 1965 Circular[9] to reorganise on comprehensive lines. What to teach and how it should be taught were left to the professional judgement of schools and teachers, but within the context of LEA arrangements which differed considerably. Parents of school-age children often found it hard to move from one part of the country to another without upsetting their children's education.

The Conservatives became increasingly frustrated with the role of the LEAs, particularly the largest, the Inner London Education Authority. The

1987 manifesto promised a major shake-up, transferring the bulk of the funding to schools and the break-up of the ILEA. Kenneth Baker, Secretary of State at the time, was fond of using the analogy of the wheel with power shared between central government at the hub and schools as the rim (though presumably linked through the thin spokes of the LEAs). Conservative administrations had already begun systematically stripping away the responsibilities of the LEAs – polytechnics, training, and later further education and sixth-form colleges – and placing them under agencies of various kinds. But they still did not feel strong enough to abolish them – something which would have been interpreted as a fundamental assault on local democracy. Eventually, it was thought the answer had been found in the grant maintained policy whereby schools could opt to receive their funding directly from a government agency, including what the LEA would have received so there was a cash inducement. So confident was John Patten, the then Secretary of State, that schools would flock to opt out and leave the LEAs to wither away that, in June 1994, he made the unwise boast that 'I will eat my academic hat garnished if by the time of the general election we haven't got more than half England's secondary schools grant-maintained'. This was never honoured even though *The Guardian* had a nice mortarboard-shaped cake baked for him by Jane Asher.

New Labour found itself with a partial transformation. The traditional administrative arrangements whereby the government legislated, the LEAs managed and the schools complied had become the government legislating, agencies implementing, the schools managing – and the LEAs alive and kicking but with no clear role. The radical shift New Labour has made is to take on a large part of the managing itself. It has set targets for eleven-year-olds, for sixteen-year-olds, for nineteen-year-olds, for twenty-one-year-olds, and for economically active adults. These National Training Targets are monitored annually. The targets are nested in Plans which extend down from central government through the LEAs to the schools to the individual teachers. LEAs have been required to submit Education Development Plans, schools have to have Plans in which there is a statutory duty to set targets, and teachers are to be 'performance managed' against individual objectives. So pleased has the Blair government been with this managerial stance that new targets – as for fourteen-year-olds – are continually being added.

The schools are now treated as producers of qualification output. The extent to which they meet the relevant targets is published. Schools are also issued with 'performance and assessment reports' (PANDAs) by Ofsted which compare how well they are doing in comparison with schools having a similar mix of pupils. Schools which are judged to be failing on the basis of their inspections are expected to cooperate with 'a special measures recovery scheme' (SMART). The government first 'named and shamed' the failing schools, but in response to widespread criticism tried counterbalancing with 'naming and acclaiming',[10] then quietly dropped the announcements altogether.

The Blair government's approach to the management of the education system has been underpinned by 'something for something' funding. A significant proportion of new government money for schools is tied to specific projects and agreed outcomes rather than, as in the past, distributed to be used at the discretion of local authorities and schools. They now have to bid and, if successful, receive money from the Standards Fund, the New Opportunities Fund (from the Lottery) and other particular pots, like Excellence in Cities. They can also make a case to become Education Action Zones, Beacon Schools and Specialist Schools. Nowadays, schools and local authorities have to spend a lot of time, and become very skilled at, bidding if they are to do their best for their children.

Support

The Thatcher and Major governments had been right, in Blair's view, to challenge education, but wrong not to provide the support to enable schools to meet raised expectations. To deliver that support a Standards and Effectiveness Unit under Michael Barber, was established in the DfEE immediately after the election. Like a cuckoo in the nest it grew rapidly to employ over one hundred people. The Unit's main tasks are to improve attainment, promote innovations and monitor performance, intervening where necessary. It is responsible for the National Literacy and National Numeracy Strategies and most of the two or three word acronyms with which New Labour has transformed the educational landscape, or at least its language – Education Development Plans, Education Action Zones, Special Measures, Fresh Start, Beacon Schools, City Academies. Much of this was foreshadowed in Barber's book, *The Learning Game*,[11] which was personally endorsed by Blair.

Inclusion

The third distinctive feature of the Blair approach to educational reform has been to make inclusion a twin goal alongside competitiveness which had been the organising principle for the Conservatives. The DfEE revised its mission statement, 'the Aim' in civil service parlance, to incorporate the new emphasis. In November 1998 it declared that its purpose was 'to give everyone the chance, through education, training and work, to realise their full potential, and thus build an inclusive and fair society and a competitive economy'.[12] Three objectives were specified, one to do with education to sixteen, the second, lifelong learning, and the third, work. Significantly, there is no mention of higher education.

The stress on inclusion represents the mainstay of the Blair government's approach to re-balancing the educational agenda in favour of social justice. The unifying feature of much of what the previous Conservative administrations had attempted was that the concerns of parents should be harnessed to lever up standards. A quasi-market whereby money followed pupils was established. Schools were put in a position of having to compete for pupils to fill their places to receive full funding. They therefore had to be very sensitive to parents' views. Part of the point of the publication of schools' test results and inspection reports was to enable parents to make informed judgements. Schools reacted pragmatically to this regime in trying to present the best possible face to the public. This could sometimes mean that under-performing and disruptive pupils were not especially welcome. School exclusions rose dramatically and persistent truanting was tacitly accepted.

As a counterbalance, the Blair government established a cross-departmental Social Exclusion Unit reporting directly to the Prime Minister himself. Its task as explained by Blair at the launch in December 1997 is to develop 'joined up solutions to joined up problems'. Its report *Bridging the Gap* led to a new ConneXions (sic) initiative designed to keep more young people in education and training at least till age nineteen. Not an easy task given that many young people, 50,000 a day on government figures, have made it plain by truanting that they don't want to be involved in formal education even to the official school leaving age of sixteen. But the government hopes that through a whole raft of measures including on-site attendance officers, Learning Mentors, Learning Support Units, off-site Pupil Referral Units and 'Truancy Buster' awards, not to mention police truancy sweeps,[13] it will be able to keep more young people in school. It has therefore been tough on truancy, but what of the causes of truancy? Could it be that young people bunk off when they do not see the point of what is on offer? And if the limit of their horizon is one or two poor GCSEs which lead nowhere who is to say they are wrong? The creation of worthwhile goals for the non-academically minded lags some way behind the commitment to containing them behind school railings.

It is these three elements, management, support and inclusion, plus a determination to retain and develop many of the Conservative reforms of the 1980s that characterise the Blair approach to education. This has enjoyed some notable successes in improving pupil performance, but it has also come up against some intractable problems, made the mistake of over-elaboration and been guilty of wilful neglect. It can only really be evaluated in relation to England, because as a consequence of Blairite devolution, education in Scotland, Wales and Northern Ireland became the responsibility of their own administrations (in Northern Ireland, Martin McGuiness, of Sinn Féin and allegedly a former IRA commander, became education minister).

Successes

The major success of Blair educational policy has been where it mattered most to both the children themselves and the government – pupil performance. It has also shown great skill in resolving a split within itself, as well among educationists, over an appropriate qualifications structure for sixteen- to nineteen-year-olds. There has also been some subtlety in the way it has adapted and refined the reforms of the previous administration to its own purposes.

Pupil performance

In introducing the *Excellence in Schools* White Paper, David Blunkett laid the government's educational priorities on the line, 'standards matter more than structures, intervention will be in inverse proportion to success and there will be zero tolerance of under performance'. In setting precise targets for improvements in the literacy and numeracy of eleven-year-olds he said, 'We will be judged on how we meet those targets'. During questioning from the media this was intensified into an offer to resign if they were not met.

Admittedly, the target date became 2002, always likely to fall after the next election, but it was nevertheless a bold and determined commitment. In 1995, when the results for eleven-year-olds were first published, 48 per cent in English and 44 per cent in maths obtained at least a Level 4. This was not as bad as it might seem since Level 4 was set as the *average* level of performance, so that about 50 per cent could have been expected to have reached or exceeded it. But New Labour interpreted Level 4 as something that could be expected of *all* eleven-year-olds and declared targets of 80 per cent for English and 75 per cent for maths as steps towards this. The targets were even bolder than the government perhaps realised.

Having framed them it pulled out all the stops. It pressed ahead with the Literacy Task Force which it had set up in opposition and established a Numeracy Task Force. Both arrived at detailed programmes of study for about an hour each day which would form part of primary school inspections. In specifying its requirements so precisely, the government crossed the line between telling schools what to teach and telling them how to teach. The drive to literacy and numeracy was under-pinned by a number of other measures. Literacy and numeracy summer schools were organised, detailed guidelines were established on how much homework was to be undertaken, support for parents was provided, and Lottery funding was made available to extend the network of homework clubs initiated by the Prince's Trust.

The good news from the test results is that the strategies seem to be succeeding brilliantly. The results for 2000 show that the percentage reaching Level 4 in English had been raised to 75 per cent and, in maths, to 72 per cent, so the targets look to be well within reach. The improvements have been so dramatic that the feasibility of raising *average* scores by that amount without lowering requirements has been questioned. But leaving that aside there seems little doubt that through concentrated effort the government will have succeeded in helping to rectify an appalling weakness in English primary education – large numbers of young people emerging after six years of formal schooling unable to use words or numbers properly.

Improved performance at GCSE, A-level and degree, particularly by girls, has continued under New Labour, so that the other National Learning Targets look as if they will be passed relatively easily. In GCSE the 'target' is struggling to keep up with improving pupil performance and it has been raised by four percentage points for 2004. The continuing rise in GCSE and A-level results has been greeted with annual cries in the press of dumbing down. But if one accepts that the Qualifications and Curriculum Authority has been making strenuous efforts to hold standards constant, and an inquiry by its predecessor and Ofsted found little evidence of any lowering, then it does look as though real improvement is taking place. Incontrovertibly, on paper we are becoming a better-qualified nation. So many students now get As at A-level that the grade is no longer sufficiently distinctive for the top universities to base their entry requirements on it alone. Advanced extension tests are to be introduced to help identify the best.

Qualifications sixteen to Nineteen

When New Labour came to office its predecessor's response to the Dearing Report[14] on the reform of qualifications sixteen to nineteen was in the early stages of implementation. Dearing had offered three options: keep separate qualifications for academic, applied and occupational studies; underline the equivalence of the different qualifications by making them routes to an overarching certificate; or devise a diploma based on prescribed combinations of subjects. The Conservatives had accepted the first and pressed on in the hope of pre-empting the incoming government. But New Labour immediately called a halt, on the grounds that headteachers had advised that it was not possible to keep to the schedule, and put the Dearing proposals out to consultation.

This bought the new government time to resolve the differences within itself. As we have seen, Blair gave his own A-level spin to the report of Labour's Education Commission which was recommending their abolition. His pro-A-level stance was supported by the then Minister of State, Stephen Byers. But Lady Blackstone, Under Secretary for Higher Education, had been Chairman of the Trustees of the Institute of Public Policy Research which had strongly advocated a new grouped award, the 'British Bac'. Its most fanatical supporters at the Institute of Education were over the moon during the first weeks of the new government believing their time had come. It only slowly dawned on them, and us, that the government was really being rather clever.

What emerged from the consultation in which only the first two of Dearing options were offered (the 'Bac' idea had already been dropped) was strong support for a half-way house to A-level and that General National Vocational Qualifications should be more like A-levels. On the strength of this the Qualifications and Curriculum Authority was able to recommend a structure whereby it would be possible to take five subjects. This repaired the major deficiency of A-levels, which was that it was not possible to achieve real breadth across just three subjects, and it did this without imposing the same version of breadth on everyone. As the details emerged, however, there were complaints from schools and pupils about the extra workload. The QCA also recommended that the revamped GNVQs should be called Applied A-levels but it was sent away to think again and eventually settled on the less accurate Vocational A-levels. Supporters of a 'Bac' were quieted by the interpretation that the different qualifications would soon grow together and then it would seem natural to combine them into the sort of grouped award they were looking for.

Adaptation of Conservative Policies

The Blair government could also claim as one of its successes the way that it adapted and developed the policies of the previous government to its own ends. The early Conservative version of the National Curriculum was unworkable because it was over-loaded and over-prescriptive. It had already been slimmed down and revised under Kenneth Clarke as Secretary of State, but it was New Labour that finally got it bedded in. In order to allow sufficient time for the literacy and numeracy programmes, the statutory curriculum for primary schools was reduced to a core of English, maths, science, information technology – and swimming. Schools are required to teach the other subjects, but it is for them to decide how much time to spend on each and how to fit them in. The curriculum post-fourteen was also made more flexible around a core, partly to allow the development of a vocational pathway. New National Curriculum Orders were laid for September 2000 and, in stark contrast to the uproar which greeted the first Orders, these were accepted almost without a murmur. Less quietly accepted has been the continuing and expanded role of Ofsted. In addition to its scrutiny of schools and teacher training colleges, Ofsted, in keeping with its importance to Blair, acquired a statutory right to inspect local authorities, nursery education and sixteen to nineteen provision.

Missed the Point

The Blair government has put a lot of energy and effort into a number of other areas, but here the returns have been less obvious because it seems to have missed, or been unwilling to recognise, the central point. There are three clear examples of this. The way it has used the fig leaf of diversity as a cover for its unwillingness to get to grips with the organisation of secondary education, its constant references to 'modernisation' to distract us from its disinclination to face up to the costs of ensuring adequate teacher supply, and the emphasis on nursery places without settling what the children will be doing there.

Secondary education

England has a monstrously untidy and unfair secondary education system. The 1944 Act held out the prospect of order of a kind, with three types of maintained school to reflect academic, applied and occupational strengths. But the technical pathway was never fully implemented, so maintained secondary education became divided between the 'haves' of the grammar schools and the rest. The Labour government of the 1960s tried to rectify this by reorganising to neighbourhood schools for all abilities and aptitudes, but it did nothing to address the main fault line – that between independent and maintained education. In any case, some local authorities resisted the change and retained the grammar schools. Others created eleven to eighteen comprehensives, or eleven to sixteen comprehensives with those beyond the age of compulsory schooling going to sixth form or tertiary colleges.

The Thatcher administration added to the untidiness. It was persuaded by business that the key to both under-achievement in the inner cities and the shortage of scientists was to establish two hundred City Technology Colleges and it would fund them. In the event, only a small part of the money for some fifteen CTCs (which, in fact, have been very successful) was forthcoming. In an attempt to rescue the policy and to deflect demands for its new curriculum subject, technology, to be funded properly across all schools, it worked its way to the idea of Technology Schools. From this emerged a Specialist Schools policy with languages, sport and the performing arts also regarded as specialisms. The Conservatives also added to the confusion in secondary education when in pursuit of a policy of weakening the local education authorities they allowed schools to opt out of LEA control and transferred the sixth form and tertiary colleges to the further education sector.

When New Labour came to power secondary education was crying out for reform. What has it done? Very little beyond setting out its aspirations at the very end of the Parliament. It is true that the grant maintained schools have been reabsorbed into the local authorities as foundation schools, and some money has been put into partnership schemes to enable some independent and state schools to work together. (New Labour is on record as saying it likes independent schools.)[15] But it has hardly tackled any of the real issues. Its mantra has been that it is standards, not structures, that matter. It has also adopted the Conservative's argument that diversity is necessary to allow parents to express their preferences.

Absolved in this way, it has done nothing on grammar schools, or at least has handed the issue over to parents with such difficult ballot conditions that even the most ardent campaigners have given up. It has taken over the notion of Specialist Schools, but with the twist that they will be able to select only 10 per cent of the intake on talent. So specialist here seems to mean receiving a bit more money from government and business. It is trying to revive the idea of CTCs as City Academies. It has also contributed to the divisiveness by inventing Beacon Schools. Identified by the school inspectors, Beacon Schools receive a small amount of money to enable their staff to raise standards in the 'poor relations' down the road, whether the help is wanted or not. Intentional or otherwise the message goes out to parents that some comprehensives are better than others.

This jumble of a system is supposed to work through parents expressing their preferences. But according to where they live there may be available to them grammar schools, secondary moderns, comprehensives from eleven to sixteen, or eighteen or other variants, City Technology Colleges, Specialist Schools, Beacon Schools, City Academies, which may be foundation, community or aided, coeducational or single sex, with a religious affiliation or not. Even if parents understand this, and there is in the vicinity a school which they feel would be right, there is no guarantee that their child will get in. Local authorities have the duty to ensure that there are enough school places, but have no control over the type of places and admissions policies of foundation and aided schools. Parents have the right of appeal which they are using increasingly, but there have also been a few instances where parents have been so dissatisfied that they have felt they have had no option but to try and start their own school in a local hall.

Faced with a seemingly intractable set of issues and deeply divided on selection, the Blair government has taken refuge in the notion that diversity is a desirable end in itself. In its Green Paper, *Schools: Building a Success*, it seems to be saying 'let all the flowers bloom'. But diversity is a cop-out. Some *shape* has to be put on secondary education.

Teacher supply

Teacher supply is another area where the Blair government has ducked the main issue. The nub is that insufficient people of the right calibre are coming forward to train as secondary teachers.[16] This is almost certainly because the pay and working conditions are not good enough. The profession is in competition with all the other opportunities open to graduates for a large proportion of the output of the universities each year (11 per cent overall, but rising to above a third in subjects like maths). By the time of the 2001 pay settlement the government had belatedly accepted that there was a serious problem, if not a crisis. But instead of making sufficient money available to restore the earlier status of teachers, it only allowed the School

Teachers' Review Body[17] to make adjustments with the limit of the rise in average earnings.

The government, as it announced in its Green Paper, *Teachers: Meeting the Challenge of Change* in December 1998, has preferred to go down the track of merit pay. Teachers able to cross a performance threshold will be paid an extra £2,000. This threshold is only part of a set of appraisals and assessments which the government calls 'modernising' the profession. There are to be career entry profiles on completing induction, fast-tracking, performance management of individual teachers each year, assessment for placement above the threshold, a grade of advanced skills teacher and, conversely, capability procedures for removing the incompetent. Although David Blunkett has maintained in his speeches that everyone can recognise a good teacher, the government has evidently had great difficulty in coming up with the criteria for these assessments, because they are on a different basis in each case. Eight *standards* in five groups have been arrived at for the threshold, performance management will be against *objectives*, fast-tracking will be on *competencies* and advanced skills teachers will be selected on excellence in eight *areas of performance* (which are different from the threshold standards). This disconnectedness betrays a lack of understanding and seems certain to both increase paperwork and lead to litigation from the disappointed. Whether this 'modernisation' will make teaching as attractive as the government hopes remains to be seen.

As well as its restructuring, and consistent with its 'something for something' approach, the government has also introduced training incentives. It first tried 'golden hellos' in the shortage subjects but in March 2000, halfway through the recruitment cycle, moved to salaries of £6000 for all trainees with £4000 on top for the shortage subjects. More recently, it has proposed paying off student loans over time and foreshortening the training period. It is also seeking to identify able graduates who can be fast-tracked and they will receive an extra £5000 and a laptop. It is also expanding the school-based training route and targeting potential mature entrants or returners. Relocation packages to help with housing costs are being considered. Following on from the first Green Paper, it is working towards bonus payments to schools based on pupils' performance; an improved working environment, including the 'staffroom of the future'; employing 20,000 extra qualified classroom assistants; sabbaticals for teachers (but which they may have to pay for by accepting a lower salary in the preceding years); and a further drive to reduce bureaucratic burdens (though its idea of reducing paperwork seems to be to put more onto its overloaded website, confusing the medium with the message). The Teaching and Higher Education Bill contained provision for a General Teaching Council overcoming years of resistance from the DfEE which did not want teachers to 'get away' like the doctors and lawyers had done a century before. No one could accuse the Blair government of inactivity on teacher supply. But one wonders how effective all the measures can be if the central question is not addressed: how to strike an appropriate balance between the interests of the taxpayer who will have to fork out any salary increases and the money necessary to make teaching an attractive profession?

Pre-school education

Pre-school education is a third area where the Blair government has been active but has shied away from the key question. In this case it comes in two parts. Should we lower the school entry age to three and, if so, what is it that we want the children to be doing? On taking office the government honoured its election pledge to scrap the nursery vouchers scheme of the previous administration and it had made available by 2000 a free nursery place for every four-year-old. By 2002 it hopes to have places for two-thirds of three-year-olds, and by 2004 places for all whose parents want one. It also carried forward the Conservatives' intention to assess children on entry to school.

Under Margaret Hodge pre-school education has enjoyed a high profile. She spotted its potential while joint Chairman of the House of Commons Education and Employment Committee, and on being appointed Minister for Employment and Equal Opportunities managed to persuade Estelle Morris, the Minister of State, to devolve it to her. She has overseen a National Childcare Strategy to integrate childcare and early years education and Sure Start to offer help and support to parents and children under four in some of the most deprived parts of the country. But it is still not clear where early years education has been heading. It takes place in an enormous variety of public, private and voluntary settings, for periods ranging from a couple of mornings to the whole week, and provides very different experiences.

In an attempt to achieve some consistency a new Foundation Stage to the National Curriculum was introduced from September 2000. It is defined by Early Learning Goals which include various social skills, but also a number of the basics of English and maths. As such, they seem to be an uneasy compromise between the views of those like Chris Woodhead who wanted to press ahead with literacy and numeracy as early as possible, and those who point to the success in international comparisons of countries like Hungary, Switzerland and Belgium, where children do not begin the formalities of learning to read till age six or later. The Select Committee, chaired by Margaret Hodge's successor but one, Barry Sheerman, has come down in favour of postponing the formalities at least to the start of compulsory schooling.[18]

During their first year of compulsory schooling children also take tests which, in effect, serve to further define the early years curriculum. Called baseline assessment, it might be assumed they are mainly about attempting to measure the value added by schools, but they are also said to be diagnostic, enabling teachers to plan appropriate tuition. It is doubtful whether these very different purposes can be encompassed within the one set of tests. As in several other examples we have considered, early years education seems to be facing several ways at once. The Blair government seems unsure whether it wants the school entry age to be lowered to three, whether it wants that education to be formal or informal, and whether it wants children to have reached a certain level of achievement before entering infants' school. These are important questions because many of the inequalities in education, linked to parental income and gender for example, can be traced back to the earliest years.

Over-Elaboration

We have seen that the Blair government has been extremely active in education sometimes with great success, sometimes missing the point. On occasions, it has been guilty of blatant over-elaboration. Perhaps the most obvious example is in the new provision for further education and lifelong learning embodied in the Learning and Skills Bill which received Royal Assent in July 2000. Another example is testing. Having bitten the bullet New Labour has greatly extended the use of testing, targets and tables.

Local co-ordination

As we saw, in the DfEE's revised 'Aim' the Blair government has been making a bold attempt to recast all education beyond compulsory schooling as lifelong learning. One of the achievements of the previous administration was to give further education a clear identity through its own funding council. New Labour has sought to broaden that remit by establishing a Learning and Skills Council responsible for the planning, funding and quality assurance of all post-sixteen learning and skills delivery in England.

This is an enormous task, but the LSC will operate mainly through forty-seven Local Learning and Skills Councils. It is an approach intended to give coherence and reduce bureaucracy, but the local arms of the LSC will have to work with the Regional Development Agencies established by the Blair government to give more say to the regions of England (as part of the package which led to the Scottish Parliament and the Welsh Assembly). They will also have to work with Local Learning Partnerships set up to enable the various parties with an interest in lifelong learning to come together. In the June 1999 White Paper, *Learning to Succeed*, which laid the ground work for the Act, this was described as 'a family of organisations – not a hierarchy'. But there seems considerable potential for confusion and duplication which means that the clear identity that further education was establishing as the third sector of education alongside schools and universities could be dissipated.

A further complicating element in the local co-ordination of learning is the local education authorities. Surprisingly, Blair seemed no more enamoured of them than his immediate predecessors, but they have been stoutly defended by the DfEE. An uneasy compromise has emerged in which their roles have been defined as: allocating funding to schools locally; ensuring a supply of school places and securing fair admissions; devolving targets from the Education Development Plan to schools and monitoring their performance; transport; excluded pupils; and special educational needs. As such, they would look to be important intermediaries between central government and the schools. But since they have been opened up to inspection by Ofsted they have been under pressure, though they have not been confronted as Woodhead would have liked. Some authorities judged to be failing, like Islington, have had to hand over their responsibilities to private organisations (often consisting essentially of LEA retreads) although seemingly able to keep decision-taking in the Town Hall. Others, like Liverpool, have been obliged to contract out some of their services.

In an attempt to ginger up the LEAs, the Blair government introduced Education Action Zones, and more recently mini-EAZs. Consisting of consortia of schools they receive funding from central government and are expected to receive income in cash or kind from business. They are intended to act as test-beds for innovation in raising standards, but somewhat to the government's disappointment most of the early bids came from the LEAs or they were prominently involved in them. So far they have failed to make much impact. Ofsted's annual report[19] for 1999–2000 concluded, 'there is little evidence of zone programmes contributing to any improvement in secondary schools' test and examination results'. In the light of the Inspector's criticisms and the lack of support from industry the government has rowed back on EAZs though not the mini-zones.

There seem to be too many cooks involved in the broth of the local co-ordination of learning. We haven't yet mentioned all the partnerships in which the providers have to engage, which prompted one further education college principal,[20] to comment that there wasn't a day when at least one of her staff was not out at a partnerships meeting. This over-elaboration seems to stem from the Blair government's uncertainty over how much of the power it wishes to devolve from itself. A plethora of semi-competing bodies poses less of a challenge than a streamlined set of arrangements. It could be, however, that the government is less Machiavellian than it seems and it is simply unsure of what it is doing.

Testing

A second area where it could be argued there is too much of a good thing is testing. From the demise of the general Eleven Plus to the 1988 Act there was no national testing of England's pupils until the very end of compulsory schooling. In the teeth of determined opposition from the Labour

Party of the time, the Thatcher government forced through the testing of seven-, eleven- and fourteen-year-olds. Not only did the incoming Blair government accept these tests, but it continued with the publication of the results of eleven-year-olds and used them as the basis of its targets.

With the zeal of the convert, the government has introduced more and more testing. It has encouraged the Qualifications and Curriculum Authority to develop and sell to schools tests for the intermediate years of primary schooling and the first years of secondary schooling. These are ostensibly voluntary, but since so much hangs on the league tables schools are naturally keen for their children to get as much practice as possible. It also has gone ahead with the baseline assessment of five-year-olds. There is now hardly a year between the ages of five and eighteen where pupils are not taking some nationally devised test or examination.

This enthusiasm for testing seems partly to be about improving pupil performance (and it appears to be working), but it is also not unconnected with a wish to have the numbers to judge the effectiveness of schools. Coming up with a reliable value added measure is proving very difficult and the government has already had to abandon its progress indices. The essential problem is that gain scores in education are almost invariably inversely correlated with initial scores.[21] In other words, tables based on gains will tend to be the opposite of those showing the best results. In its desire to manage education the government seems to be seeking a numerical precision which is just not possible. The danger in the emphasis on testing is that schools will turn out practised test takers rather than the truly educated.

Neglect

The Blair government made no bones about it. On election its priority was school education. But even so its treatment of higher education which has left both students and universities impoverished amounts to wilful neglect.

Higher education

During the election campaign there was a tacit agreement between the parties to put higher education on hold while Sir Ron (now Lord) Dearing completed his third major education inquiry. *Higher Education in the Learning Society*[22] appeared in July 1997 as a massive document containing ninety-three recommendations covering all manner of things to do with learning, teaching and quality assurance. But crucially it addressed the financial position. Dearing took the view that there was a funding crisis (since 1989 there had been a 25 per cent per capita cut) that could only be met by asking students to contribute towards tuition fees. His proposals had a certain logic to them. All students would be loaned the money to pay a flat-rate fee that would become repayable when their salaries showed they were beginning to profit from holding a degree. Students from low-income homes would continue to receive a maintenance grant.

Although the government responded immediately and accepted the need for a student contribution, curiously, it rejected Dearing's carefully thought-out proposals for a version of its own. Maintenance grants were to be abolished and fees means-tested. Having acted in haste it then had to spend the best part of a year sorting out the ensuing muddles – among them how gap-year students already accepted by universities would be affected, the different arrangements in Scotland, and the effects on teacher training. Later in the year the government took reserve powers to stop universities charging top-up fees in case an Ivy League emerged.

The upshot was that the universities found themselves with little extra money, but the support system for students has been dismantled. Under the Blair government, as during the preceding Conservative administrations, the universities have cut back on support workers, run down their libraries and scrabbled around for full-fee foreign students. Students arriving in recent years will have found the universities very different from those that the previous generation had been able to enjoy. For the privilege they will be having to pay more, probably running up substantial debts, and in all likelihood having to fit in studying around part-time jobs.

Into this sorry state of affairs both the Prime Minister and the Chancellor of the Exchequer have stepped with pronouncements. At the Labour Party conference in 1998, seemingly to the surprise of the DfEE, Blair announced that higher education was to be expanded to provide for an extra 500,000 places by 2002. It has all the appearance of a target just plucked from the air. It has subsequently been reinterpreted to include further education and there is to be a revamp of the Higher National Diploma to create a new foundation degree, but nevertheless the universities are expected to fill upwards of an extra 50,000 places a year. Not surprisingly, with the scrapping of maintenance grants and introduction of tuition fees, some universities have been struggling to increase their recruitment and they face funding penalties which will exacerbate their situation.

The Chancellor's intervention was even more surprising and wider of the mark. In May 2000 at a trade union reception he berated Magdalen College, Oxford, for not admitting Laura Spence from Tyneside who was predicted to get a clutch of A grades at A-level and who had been offered a scholarship to Harvard. He suggested that this was because with 'these old universities all that matters is the privileges you were born with, rather than the potential you actually have'. The facts turned out to be rather different. Laura Spence comes from a posh bit of Tyneside, had not been given one of the very few medical places at Oxford but had been offered places at other medical schools, and was going to Harvard to study bio-chemistry for which she would have been accepted at Oxford. But by the time these details emerged the whole access debate had been set running. Here again the facts do not support Brown. When A-level performance is taken into account there is not much of an admissions gap with school or social background to the leading universities. But there is a wide applications gap and massive gap in the performance of the different types of school. In so far as there is any truth in what Brown was saying it redounds to him as Chancellor in presiding over the under-funding of state education.

One wonders therefore why he did it. It is said that he wanted to deflect attention from the Conservatives' assault on his niggardly pensions policy. How better to do it than attack some bastian of apparent privilege. He could also indulge himself in having a go at Oxford the *alma mater* of Blair and so many of his education team.

The Commons Education and Employment Committee in its long awaited report[23] in February 2001 was hard put to find any evidence which supported the Chancellor. But it nevertheless went on to recommend a substantial increase in the postcode premium to wider access. Blair also weighed in by targeting £18 million over three years to raise the proportion of state school pupils at the top universities.

Funding

The sense of continuity with Conservative education policies was heightened by the pre-election promise to keep to outgoing administration's spending plans for the first two years of the Parliament. This meant that many of the early announcements were mainly rhetoric because they could not be backed by serious money. Class sizes, for example, went up during the first two years. In terms of funding it could be argued that the Blair government's real education programme did not really start till April 1999.

Brown was keen to mark the arrival of Labour funding with a bang and announced that an extra £19 billion had been found in the Comprehensive Spending Review for education. It looked too good to be true, and it was. The £19 billion was arrived at by triple counting and made no allowance for inflation. On these plans, education spending would have remained lower as a share of gross domestic product than it was in 1995. Nevertheless, it did represent an increase of just over 5 per cent in 1999 and that is not to be sneezed at. Schools though received a lot less, because so much was held back for initiatives from the centre and the 'something-for-something' approach to funding. Direct payments to schools were introduced in the 2000 budget, but this amounted to only £9000 for a typical primary school and £40,000 for a typical secondary school. They have, however, been supplemented in subsequent budget statements.

There were indications in the July 2000 Spending Review[24] that there was to be an attempt to increase the funding of education on a sustained basis. It was announced there would be an annual growth in the money for education of 6.6 per cent per year in the four financial years from 2000–01 to 2003–04. Characteristically, the DfEE, under the Blair government, made it clear that the planned increase in spending was to be 'matched by tough targets'. There will be new targets for fourteen-year-olds and new minimum targets for children aged eleven, fourteen and sixteen. The managerial net ever widens. Inclusion gets another whirl through 'the ambition' to extend participation in higher education to 50 per cent of eighteen- to thirty-year-olds. Brown's predilection comes through in 'a new objective to widen university access and provision to help leading universities recruit more of their students from state schools and colleges and widen access to students from a broader range of backgrounds'.

This apparent largesse has come late in the Parliament and it will be the next before most of the effects of the extra funding, assuming that the plans are confirmed, show through. Over the lifetime of this Parliament education spending will have risen less than it did between 1991 and 1995. No wonder for all the large sums being bandied about education still feels cash-strapped.

Conclusion

In a major speeches[25] in September 2000 and February 2001 Tony Blair restated his education credo. The creation of New Labour 'was and is a project to deliver lasting change in Britain'. Its first two objectives are 'to shift the balance of power from the few to the many' and 'to extend opportunities to all'. Education has a central role to play. 'I don't just want education to be the number one priority of the government. I want it to be our passion as a party.' Our aim is 'a world class education system' which means specifically 'first class nursery education for all parents who want it'; 'smaller infant class sizes for all'; 'primary schools teaching children to read, write and add up'; 'excellent secondary schools for all' and 'a 50 per cent target for university participation among young adults'. In Blair's view excellent secondary education will require the 'modernisation of the comprehensive principle'. Maintained neighbourhood schools will come to rival the independent and grammar schools in their achievements through 'first-rate teaching and facilities, rigorous setting and personalised provision'. A Green Paper in February 2001, *Schools: Building a Success*, set out a wide range of proposals for, among other things, greater diversity in secondary education, more provision for developing pupils' individual talents and new teacher recruitment incentives.

How well do New Labour's achievements measure up to its aspirations? We have argued there have been some notable successes particularly in developing and refining what was there before and in pushing forward with the literacy and numeracy programmes. But elsewhere, though there has been a lot of activity, the Blair government has not always got to the heart of the matter. The word 'modernisation' is often used to provide a gloss in these circumstances. In order to 'modernise' comprehensive schools as Blair aspires, for example, New Labour will have to become clear where it stands on selection and to provide the funding (independent schools receive more than twice as much per pupil as state schools). It will also have to find the money to attract the teachers where again the project is to 'modernise' the profession.

If I had to highlight one aspect of the Blair government's approach to education, I would say that it has desperately wanted to be seen to be doing good things. Every day without a new education headline was regarded as a day wasted, particularly when Stephen Byers was Minister of State. Press notices issued by the DfEE went up by more than 50 per cent during New Labour's first year in office. When there was nothing new to be announced old stories were recycled. The literacy and numeracy strategies, the reform of A-levels and various packets of education spending must each have been announced half a dozen times. So many hares have been set running that it has been hard for even the professional government-watchers to keep track, let alone those responsible for making education happen.

What are we to make of all this activity? Has the Blair government really had 'a big picture', with the many initiatives necessitated by the numerous faults in the system? Or has it tended to dissipate its political capital by failing to focus sufficiently on the main issues, rushing off in all directions? As we have seen, there is some truth in both these propositions, but if I had to incline to one, it would be the latter. In his educational policy-making Blair has surrounded himself with a group of ideas-people whose roots, like his own, are not in maintained education. Idea after idea seems to have come tumbling out, often encapsulated in a catchy two- or three-word phrase, without a full appreciation of the education system's capacity to absorb them or their relevance to ordinary pupils. After a decade of continual reform in education, there was a stronger case for concentrating and consolidating than the Blair government would seem to have allowed.

Notes

1 Sources of the quotes from politicians may be found in the chapters on education I contributed to the annual volumes of the Institute of Contemporary British History, originally called *Contemporary Britain: An Annual Review* and from 1997, *Britain in* . . . P. Catterall and V. Preston (eds) (later joined by A. Cryer), Blackwell, Dartmouth and ICBH, 1991 onwards.
2 DfEE, *Excellence in Schools*, White Paper, Cm 3681, The Stationery Office, 1997.
3 Department for Culture, Media and Sport, *The People's Lottery*, White Paper, Cm 3709, The Stationery Office, 1997.
4 DfEE, *The Learning Age: A Renaissance for a New Britain*, Green Paper, Cm 3790, The Stationery Office, 1998.

5 DfEE, *Teachers: Meeting the Challenge of Change*, Green Paper, Cm 4164, The Stationery Office, 1998.

6 DfEE, *Schools: Building on Success*, Green Paper, Cm 5050, The Stationery Office, 2001.

7 F. Beckett, 'Which of these two men is the real education secretary? (not the one you think) *New Statesman*, pp. 11–12, 16 October 2000.

8 M. Phillips, 'Farewell Woodhead – and goodbye to raising standards', *The Sunday Times*, 5 November 2000.

9 Department of Education and Science, *The Organisation of Secondary Education*, Circular 10/65, DES, 1965.

10 DfEE, 'SMART expertise on hand for failing schools – Blunkett', *DfEE News* 110/97, 20 May 1997; DfEE, 'Byers "names and acclaims" as 73 schools celebrate success', *DfEE News* 52/98, 2 February 1998.

11 M. Barber, *The Learning Game: Arguments for an Education Revolution*, Gollancz, 1996.

12 DfEE, *Learning and Working Together for the Future: A Strategic Framework to 2002*, DfEE, 1998.

13 DfEE, 'Blunkett and Straw pledge more police sweeps as funding increases to tackle truancy', *DfEE News* 453/00, 19 October 2000.

14 R. Dearing, *Review of Qualifications for 16–19-Year-Olds*, School Curriculum and Assessment Authority Publications, 1996.

15 Anthony Seldon Interviews Estelle Morris, *Conference and Common Room* Autumn 2000, 17–19.

16 A. Smithers and P. Robinson, *Attracting Teachers: Past Patterns, Present Policies, Future Prospects*, Carmichael.

17 School Teachers' Review Body, *Tenth Report* 2001, Cm 4990, The Stationery Office, 2001.

18 Education and Employment Committee, *Early Years*, HC33, The Stationery Office, January 2001.

19 Ofsted, *The Annual Report of Her Majesty's Chief Inspector of Schools 1999–2000*, The Stationery Office, February, 2001.

20 J. Gravatt and R. Silver, 'Partnerships with the community'. In A. Smithers and P. Robinson, *Further Education Re-Formed*, Falmer, 2000.

21 R.S. Soar, D.M. Medley and H. Coker, 'Teacher Evaluation; a critique of currently used methods', *Phi Delta Kappan*, 1983, 239–246.

22 R. Dearing, *Higher Education in the Learning Society*, Report of the National Committee of Inquiry into Higher Education, NCIHE, 1997.

23 Education and Employment Committee, *Higher Education: Access*, HC205, The Stationery Office, February 2001.

24 HM Treasury, *Spending Review 2000: Prudent for a Purpose*, Cm 4807. The Stationery Office, July 2000.

25 T. Blair, Speech, 8 September 2000, reported widely, for example, A. Grice, 'Blair calls for sweeping changes to comprehensives', *The Independent*, 9 September 2000, T. Blair, 'The government's agenda for the future' speech, (http://www.number-10.gov.uk/) 8 February 2001.

Wider Relations

THE MONARCH

© Chris Riddell

Chapter 20

THE NATIONAL QUESTION

Iain McLean

What Changed?

ONE BLAIR EFFECT will certainly not be reversed, although it will be significantly modified. And its ramifications will continue to spread through all corners of national life, affecting the 75 per cent of the UK population to whom it does not apply directly almost as much as the 25 per cent to whom it does. That effect is the introduction of devolved government to Northern Ireland, Scotland, and Wales, coupled with a directly-elected Mayor and Assembly in London[1]. Northern Ireland is treated fully in Brendan O'Leary's chapter of this book, but is relevant to this chapter as well.

It may seem odd to call devolution irreversible, only two years after it was enacted and scarcely one year into the operation of the devolved assemblies. In 1994 John Smith, then Labour leader, sonorously proclaimed devolution to be 'the settled will of the Scottish people'. The Scottish referendum of 1997 settled the will of the Scottish people to change things, but there was no consensus on what sort of change the people wanted.[2] The Welsh referendum was held a week after the Scottish one in the hope of generating a bandwagon. Whether it did so or not, the result could not have been closer. Until the very last county reported, it looked all evening as if the *Noes* were going to win. The National Assembly of Wales was approved by just over 50 per cent of those who voted in the referendum, on a 50 per cent turnout (Table 1). Thus, as its enemies never tire of pointing out, only a quarter of the Welsh electorate voted for it.

Table 1 Scotland and Wales: referendum results, 1997

	Yes to parliament	No to parliament	Yes to tax powers	No to tax powers	Turnout
Scotland 11.09.97	74.3	25.7	63.5	36.5	60.4
Wales 18.09.97	50.3	49.7	n/a	n/a	50.1

The devolved government of Northern Ireland faces similar deep problems of legitimacy to all its predecessors back to 1921. All three assemblies have had a rough start. The Scots and the Welsh both got into unedifying rows about the cost of their new Parliament buildings. The Welsh threw out a leader imposed on them from London and chose one whom Tony Blair had been trying to block for over a year. So did Londoners. The Scots temporarily lost their First Minister, Donald Dewar, through illness. He never fully recovered, and died suddenly of a brain haemorrhage in October 2000. While he was off sick, a little-known Liberal Democrat, the head of the smallest party in the Parliament, led the Scottish Executive. Both the Scots and the Welsh got into bruising rows with Whitehall departments unwilling to accept in practice that they had in theory devolved power to the territories. The Ministry of Agriculture authorised field trials of genetically modified crops in a Welsh field whose postcode was that of the nearest English town. The Department of Education tried to force performance-related pay on Welsh teachers, using a piece of secondary legislation which the courts ruled it had no power to use. The Scots faced the wrath of the evangelical Christian Brian Souter (head of Stagecoach, one of Scotland's most successful companies) and of Cardinal Thomas Winning, the head of the Roman Catholic Church in Scotland. Both took violent exception to the Executive's proposal to repeal the so-called 'Section 28', which forbade local authorities to promote homosexuality. Souter financed a referendum that showed that a majority of those who voted in it (but not a majority of the electorate) opposed repeal. The Executive pressed ahead and repealed the section. Winning sourly denounced the Scottish Parliament as 'an utter failure'.

Most unsettling of all, devolution called into question the spending formula the UK government uses to allocate public spending on devolved services among its territories. This is the much misunderstood Barnett formula. The problem goes back to Gladstone's Irish Home Rule Bill of 1886. He had to devise a formula for revenue transfers between the Imperial Parliament (as it was then called) and the proposed Home Rule administration in Ireland. Gladstone's badly drafted formula was not put to the test, because the Bill fell. In the succeeding Unionist government, Chancellor of the Exchequer George Goschen proposed that public spending in Scotland should reflect its share of UK population. This 'Goschen formula' became the floor, not the ceiling, for Scottish public expenditure.

When Northern Ireland got devolved government in 1921, both the Northern Ireland and the UK government maintained the fiction that the former would make a net 'Imperial contribution'. In fact, the transfers flowed the other way, far above the Goschen proportion. By the 1970s Scotland, too, was getting far above the Goschen proportion of public spending, because Secretaries of State for Scotland could always threaten Treasury ministers in Cabinet, saying that if Scotland did not get the public spending they demanded, Scottish nationalism would grow and the union would be imperilled. The supreme practitioners of this were Tom Johnston and Willie Ross, Secretaries of State in the Second World War and Wilson governments respectively.

In the 1970s, this started to breed resentment in poor areas of England. The Northern region, centred on Newcastle-upon-Tyne, has a long border with Scotland and similar problems of poor health, housing, and unemployment. But public spending per head in Scotland was far above that in the region. This led regional leaders to persuade some of the region's MPs to revolt against the Callaghan government's Scotland and Wales Bill. The guillotine revolt of February 1977 killed that bill, and set in train the process that led to the arrival of Margaret Thatcher and the ditching of devolution in 1979.

Just before the Callaghan government was swept away, Chief Secretary Joel Barnett proposed the formula that now bears his name, in order to head off future bouts of Geordie (or other English) resentment. The Barnett formula regulates, not (as Goschen did) the absolute level but *changes* in the level of transfers from the Exchequer to fund devolved services. The idea was that, over time, most of public spending would come to consist of incremental changes on top of the 1978 baseline. In 1978 spending per head in Scotland, on the domestic services that would have been devolved, was perhaps 25 per cent ahead of its level in England. Over time, as the original baseline dwindled away, the Barnett formula would lead to convergence – spending per head in Scotland and Wales would equate to that in England. The Barnett formula was not to apply to Northern Ireland.

When the Blair government came to power, it announced that the Barnett formula would stay in place, and it is now embodied in the devolution arrangement for Scotland and Wales. So what is the problem? The same as in 1977–78, but now more conspicuous. Public spending per head in Scotland on devolved services is far above that in England, including in the deprived regions of England. All the candidates for Mayor of London pointed out that London pays more in tax than it gets in earmarked spending (though actually London is if anything a winner in regional spending. It pays a lot of tax because it is rich. It gets more back in identifiable spending than some poorer regions). In summer 2000, the *Journal* newspaper in Newcastle-upon-Tyne highlighted the stark disparities across the Anglo-Scottish border. The secondary school in Duns (Borders region) has a pupil:teacher ratio of 13:1 and one computer per five students. The secondary school in socially identical Alnwick (Northumberland) has a pupil:teacher ratio of 18:1 and one computer per thirteen students. Health spending per head, in fiscal year 1998/99, was £692 in Northumberland and £945 in the Borders. If you fall ill in Northumberland, you had better stagger over the Tweed into Scotland before you call an ambulance. Can devolution withstand such stark numbers? Below we look at the evolution of Barnett since the Scots and Welsh got their feet under the table.

And yet, and yet. In spite of all the problems listed above, the Scottish, Welsh, and London elected bodies are here to stay. The best signal of this is the reaction of the Conservatives, who campaigned vigorously against them. In the 1992 and 1997 general elections, John Major warned that Labour's devolution proposals threatened the Union itself. He may prove to have been right, but the Conservatives have modified their unionism. The 1997 election left them holding not one Westminster seat in any of the three devolved territories. However, proportional representation (which the Conservatives still deplore) led to them getting seats in both the Scottish Parliament and the National Assembly for Wales. In both, they have voted for proposals that would increase the autonomy of the parliaments. In Scotland they are now calling for 'full fiscal freedom'. In Wales, they got the following resolution passed by a majority of one against the minority Labour administration:

> The National Assembly for Wales calls upon the government of Wales to request Her Majesty's Government at Westminster to allow the National Assembly for Wales to decide on the question of hunting with dogs in Wales . . .

There is no inconsistency here. It would be suicidal for the Conservatives, having scrambled into both parliaments because of PR, to use these platforms to denounce the bodies themselves, despite the dubious initial legitimacy of the National Assembly for Wales. Were they to persuade the Welsh people to abolish the National Assembly, the Conservatives would be left with the UK Parliament, elected under first-past-the-post (which Conservatives support), in which they have no seats. Far better to join all the other parties in demands to extend its powers to issues (such as hunting with dogs) that were deemed to be for the UK government when the legislation was drawn up. This illustrates *path dependence*. The path that the Scottish and Welsh Tories have taken is rational given the institutions they now face. Likewise, all lobby groups and other civil society organisations, whatever they thought initially about the two parliaments, now rationally deal with them rather than with the UK government on devolved matters. The Blair government came in with a commitment to legislate in the first year; some saw this as an albatross; in fact it turned out to be an advantage. Had the devolution legislation been postponed, it might have been derailed.

So the devolved administrations will stay. But will they lead to the break-up of the Union? We cannot return to this question until we have reviewed how they came into existence.

What or Who Drove the Changes?

Is devolution an Old Labour or a New Labour policy? Or neither? It is Old Labour only on the oldest view of Old Labour. It is emphatically not Middle-Aged Labour.

The first generation of Labour leaders, including the Scots Keir Hardie and Ramsay MacDonald, were Home Rulers. MacDonald, indeed, began his political career as secretary of the London General Committee of the Scottish Home Rule Association. But Home Rule vanished from the Labour agenda in the 1920s, as Labour approached power under the same MacDonald. The simple reason is path dependence again. Labour began life as an appendage to the Liberals. The Liberals, and hence Labour, were strongest in peripheral Britain. It is a mistake to see late Victorian and Edwardian politics as essentially class politics. It was religious and centre-periphery politics more than it was class politics. For all general elections up to 1910 inclusive, the proportions of Nonconformists, and of Roman Catholics, in the local population are better predictors of the Unionist vote than the proportion of working-class people in the local population.[3] Home Rule for Ireland, Scotland, and Wales was therefore in the programme of Gladstone, Lloyd George, and Ramsay MacDonald. But centre-periphery and religious politics were much diminished by, and during, the First World War. Ireland was removed from British politics at last (it seemed) in 1921. Labour was a contender for national power. Devolution then became a hindrance, not a help, especially as Labour became a party concerned with national standards of health and welfare. In a Middle-Aged Labour perspective, these should not depend on geography. Therefore, Middle-Aged Labour opposed anything that would tend to lessen the grip of Whitehall and Westminster over the territory in question. The last Scottish Home Rule bills were promoted by Labour back-benchers in 1924 and 1928, and got nowhere.

Labour's most eloquent centrist was the Welshman Nye Bevan. He frequently recalled how he thought he had reached the levers of power when he was elected to Tredegar Town Council, only to find that real power resided in Monmouthshire County Council. Once there he found that power really lay in Parliament. But not on the back-benches, as he duly found out in turn. As his colleague Richard Crossman said, Bevan was interested not in detailed management but only with 'achieving Power, with a very big and very vague P'. That remark is not fair to Bevan the architect of the NHS, but it aptly illustrates the centralism of Middle-Aged Labour. No Labour minister between 1945 and 1979 seriously dissented from Bevan's view.

Why then did Labour sponsor an abortive plan for devolution to Scotland and Wales between 1974 and 1979? Out of pure political expediency. The two Labour administrations of 1974 both had a perilously narrow majority – actually a minority of seats from February to October 1974 and again from 1977 to 1979. One of the biggest threats to them came from the Scottish National Party, which won seven seats in February and eleven in October. In that election, it gained 30 per cent of the Scottish vote, more than the Conservatives. The electoral system gave the Conservatives more seats than the SNP, and preserved Labour's hegemony of forty-one (57 per cent) out of seventy-two Scottish seats on a minority (36 per cent) of the Scottish vote. The SNP was very close to the tipping point. On 30 per cent, it got eleven seats; on 35 per cent, evenly spread throughout Scotland, it would certainly have won more than half of the seats in Scotland. It had announced that it would take this as the trigger for starting independence negotiations. Therefore government had to be seen to be doing something about devolution. Wales was added to the original bill just for consistency, although the Welsh nationalist party Plaid Cymru, which was concentrated in Welsh-speaking Wales, posed no comparable threat. As related above, this bill fell in 1977, to be replaced by separate bills for Scotland and Wales. Further back-bench revolts imposed first a referendum on each territory, and then a requirement that a *Yes* vote would not bind the government unless 40 per cent of the electorate in the relevant territory voted *Yes*. The logic of this Cunningham amendment is at one level hard to justify. No government since 1935, and no Labour government ever, has crossed this threshold at a general election. The only time the Labour Party has ever done so was when it lost the general election of 1951 on a higher share of the vote than the winning Conservatives obtained. But the political logic of the Cunningham amendment was devastating. The Welsh proposals were thrown out by four to one – the assembly proposal being associated with the 20 per cent of the population who spoke Welsh, the other 80 per cent evidently thought that they would become a privileged minority. The Scottish proposals were approved, but the majority in favour fell far short of the 40 per cent threshold. The government abandoned its proposals; the Scottish Nationalists moved a motion of no confidence; the government lost by one vote; the reign of Mrs Thatcher began. Devolution disappeared from the domestic agenda.

One of many things to cripple these proposals was the 'West Lothian Question', henceforth WLQ, invented by the anti-devolution MP for that seat, Tam Dalyell. Why, he asked rhetorically, should he as a Scottish MP be able to vote on housing in Blackburn, Lancashire but not on housing in Blackburn, West Lothian? The easy answer is, 'Because that is what asymmetric devolution entails'. If Scotland and Wales get devolved parliaments and England does not, then the UK Parliament and government must also double as the Parliament and government of England. Some pointed out that the anomaly had existed in Northern Ireland since 1921 and had attracted almost no attention. But every possible answer to the WLQ stymied the Callaghan government. To grant devolution to England as a whole would be to hand over the government of England to the Conservatives, most of the time. (Only in 1906, 1945, and 1997 have governments of the left won a majority of seats in England.) To grant devolution to each region of England would be to withdraw permanently from power over domestic politics in, at least, the south-east and the south-west, and to have a tenuous hold over power in many other English regions. To adopt Mr Gladstone's 'in-and-out solution' (Scottish MPs at Westminster only to vote on non-devolved matters) would, again, deprive Labour of power over domestic policy after every election except a 1906 landslide. Labour's seat tally in Scotland and Wales has normally exceeded the Labour government's overall majority. One practical, albeit illogical, solution to the WLQ is to reduce the numbers but not the powers of MPs from the territories at Westminster. Scotland and Wales were, by 1978, quite heavily over-represented there due to population movements and the embedding of their seat totals in the Boundary Commission legislation[4]. But to reduce them even to their population proportion of seats, let alone below that as an answer to the WLQ, would be again to undermine the whole political point of devolution. The whole political point of devolution was to preserve a Labour governing power at Westminster. Therefore the WLQ was unsolved and insoluble.

Only two Labour ministers out of all those involved in that unhappy story actually came to believe in the devolution project. One of them was John Smith, who as a Minister of State at the Privy Council Office was in charge of the second Scotland Bill. Even Smith was initially hostile, having taken part in the notorious 'Dalintober Street coup' of August 1974 in which the Scottish Labour Party had said it was against devolution, only to be overruled by the national Labour Party (not much devolution there). But his conversion seems to have been genuine. Therefore, when Smith became Labour leader in 1992, it was only natural that devolution should return to the Labour programme. Smith, not Blair, was the father of the Scotland and Wales Acts. Blair inherited the commitment when he succeeded Smith as Labour leader in 1994. He did not initiate it. It should count as New Labour only if John Smith is to be counted as New Labour.

But we need to delve a little deeper. Scottish devolution was on the Blair programme for deeper reasons than John Smith's conversion. And we have not yet explained why Welsh devolution returned from the grave. Once again we need to study politicians doing what was rational given the institutions they faced. The Conservatives last won a majority of seats in Scotland in 1955. For twenty-seven of the thirty-eight years between 1959 and 1997, a majority UK Conservative government therefore ran Scotland with a minority of Scottish seats. In 1986 the government introduced the poll tax in Scotland a year ahead of England, having been bounced by outraged Scottish Conservatives faced with a long-overdue rating revaluation of their expensive houses. All the Scottish ministers who had piloted the tax lost their seats in the 1987 general election, but the legislation was imposed regardless. Only the riots of 1990 and the fall of Mrs Thatcher brought the poll tax to an end. This obviously damaged the legitimacy of the one and indivisible British state in Scotland.

Labour's turn to devolution in the 1980s was therefore home-grown and rationally explicable. In the 1970s, the Labour Party in London had had to override an anti-devolution Labour Party in Scotland to force devolution on it – a manoeuvre made possible only by the total lack of devolution in the internal organisation of the Labour Party. In 1988, by contrast, the Labour Party in Scotland helped promote a Claim of Right for Scotland, followed by a Constitutional Convention. The Claim of Right intoned:

> We, gathered as the Scottish Constitutional Convention, do hereby acknowledge the sovereign right of the Scottish people to determine the form of government best suited to their needs, and do hereby declare and pledge that in all our actions and deliberations their interests shall be paramount.

Labour worked together with the Liberal Democrats, the churches, trade unions, and other civil society bodies on the Constitutional Convention. The Scottish Nationalists hesitated but stayed outside. The Conservatives stayed out without hesitation. The Constitutional Convention's final report in 1995 recommended a 129-seat Parliament elected by an additional member system of proportional representation (AMS). It would have a power to vary the UK rate of income tax up or down by 3p in the pound. Public finance should continue to be governed by the Barnett formula. All of these provisions went into the Labour manifesto and, almost unaltered, into the Scotland Act 1998, so that they now govern the Scottish Parliament.

There was a wobble, however. The Conservatives denounced the tax-varying power as a 'tartan tax'. Tony Blair and his advisors were so determined that Labour could never again be branded as a 'tax and spend' party that they sprang into action to rebut this. Blair insisted – again, over the head of his reluctant Scottish executive, although this time each side was facing the opposite direction to 1974 – that the tax-varying power must not be given to the Parliament unless it was first supported in a referendum. And, on a Scottish tour just before polling day in 1997, he told the *Scotsman*:

> '[S]overeignty rests with me as an English MP and that's the way it will stay'. Mr Blair also ruled out the use of a Scottish Parliament's tax-varying powers, which he likened to those of an English parish council, in the first term of a Labour government . . . [H]is five-year pledge of no rise in the basic and standard rates of tax applied to 'Scotland as well as England'[5].

This speech caused a brief furore in Scotland but did not prevent Labour from winning fifty-six (78 per cent) of its seventy-two seats, on 45.6 per cent of the vote, at the general election. The double referendum led to a convincing 'Yes – Yes' majority (Table 1). The Parliament, and its power to tax, were thus both legitimised; the Act was passed in 1998. The first elections to the Scottish Parliament took place in 1999. As expected, Labour was the largest party, but the Additional Member System deprived it of an overall majority. Were the SNP to have been the largest party, AMS would equally have deprived it of an overall majority – a consideration which smoothed the path of AMS through the Labour policy machine. Proportional representation is death to Bevanite Labour at Westminster, but could be the life-saver of Bevanite Labour in preserving the United Kingdom (or at least Great Britain) intact. A Labour–Liberal Democrat coalition was formed, reviving the alliance that had produced the Constitutional Convention.

But Blair's interview with the *Scotsman* is not just the normal froth of an election campaign. To his enemies it denotes total failure to comprehend what devolution is all about. Especially, how could he possibly be in a position to bind the Scottish Parliament on tax? Even if he could bind the Scottish Parliament by controlling the Labour policy-making and nomination process, there were two deadly problems. First, how would the Scots react to a party that took its orders from London? Second, did Blair not realise that his own manifesto promise of AMS for the Scottish Parliament meant that Labour would not have a majority, so that it would have to bargain over tax and all other policy with a coalition partner? Was this not mindless control-freakery? Blair's friends insist that the speech was really meant for English consumption and that it was part of the subtle plan. Events were to give more credence to the 'control freak' than to the 'subtle plan' interpretation.

Meanwhile in Wales, attitudes had changed radically since the crushing defeat of the 1979 referendum – and essentially for the same reason as in Scotland. The Conservatives have been in a minority there for even longer than in Scotland – never since 1868 have they been the largest party in Wales, let alone held a majority of seats there. As long as Wales had no political self-consciousness, that mattered little in UK politics. But in 1964 Wales was given administrative devolution in the shape of a Welsh Office and a ministerial team. Some have suggested that this was simply a ruse to enable Harold Wilson to get rid of a popular but ineffective Welsh politician (Jim Griffiths). Certainly it merited but a single sentence in the Labour manifestoes for the 1959 and 1964 elections and seems to have attracted almost no attention even in Wales. But institutions create path dependence. The Welsh Office began life with few powers and its ministers had little status, as the aftermath of the Aberfan disaster (21 October 1966) was to show only too brutally.[6] But there was only one way to go. No party and no lobby had anything to gain from proposing to reduce the powers of the Welsh Office.

In 1979, as described above, Wales faced a deep political division between those who spoke the language and those who did not. Other issues followed exactly the same line. The Welsh-speaking areas were also the areas of active chapel-going, of Sunday closing of pubs, and of marginal family farming. This has always ensured, before 1999, that the Plaid Cymru vote was corralled in the Welsh-speaking areas, where it could do no harm to the UK parties. Even though majority-Welsh language constituencies have much smaller electorates than average (because they are in remote rural areas), there are only six of them. Only once, in 1979, when the failing Callaghan government had lost its majority, were Plaid Cymru able to force a concession from it (namely, giving the slate quarrymen of Bethesda and Blaenau Ffestiniog the same rights to silicosis compensation as the coal miners of Gwaun cae Curwen and Tredegar). And that was in the same year that the Welsh Assembly crashed to defeat in a referendum.

But things changed between 1979 and 1997. Not as much as in Scotland, but for some of the same reasons. First of all, UK politicians realised that language concessions in Wales were what the economists call cheap talk. They did not cost much to implement, and most of the costs could be spread thinly around the rest of the UK. The most costly innovation by far has been Welsh-language television. S4C (Sianel Pedwar Cymru) has been a great political, as well as broadcasting, success. It increased the visibility of the language, gave non-Welsh speakers for the first time an attractive incentive to learn it – and most of the costs were absorbed by the 95 per cent of UK licence payers and consumers of advertising who are not in Wales. Likewise, the Welsh Language Act 1993 has proved to be successful cheap talk. And the inclusion of Welsh in the National Curriculum, although it causes problems in recruiting primary school teachers, was an enormous step in safeguarding the future of the language The language, so explosive (sometimes literally) in the years up to 1979, had ceased to be an issue by 1997.

And as in Scotland, non-Conservative politicians and voters became sufficiently irked by the Conservative hegemony to consider putting their differences aside. In fact, the split over Welsh devolution in the 1990s was not between the three anti-Conservative parties but within the Labour Party. Plaid Cymru was an easier stable mate than the SNP because its nationalism has always been cultural rather than political. It has been downplaying Welsh independence for many years now, and its current leaders claim (implausibly) that it has never demanded sovereign independence for Wales. However, the Labour Party contained proportionately more descendants of Bevan in Wales than in Scotland. Neil Kinnock, who was born in Bevan's constituency, led the Labour No Assembly campaign in 1979, although his line softened as Labour leader (for the usual reasons of path dependence – if Labour seemed remote from power in the UK, it could at least secure power in Wales). The leader of the Labour Party in Wales in the 1990s, Ron Davies, faced a bruising internal fight between pro- and anti-devolution forces within his party. As a result, the commitment to Welsh devolution that appeared in the 1997 Labour manifesto was no Claim of Right, but rather a bargained compromise – the most that the antis in the Labour Party would accept, and far less than the pros wanted. As for Scotland, the National Assembly for Wales was to be elected by AMS. But it would have far fewer powers. The line in the sand drawn between Labour pros and antis gave it the power to make secondary legislation but not primary legislation. That sounds a sufficiently clear distinction but it was to cause endless trouble, which has by no means been resolved.

It was thus no surprise that the referendum campaign was more muted than in Scotland. The death of Diana, Princess of Wales, during the campaign stopped both campaigns for a week. This surely had no effect in Scotland, where minds were already made up, but may have done in Wales. The hairsbreadth *Yes* has already been reported. The *Yes* strongholds were in the strong Plaid Cymru and strong Labour parts of Wales. The *No* strongholds included the capital, Cardiff (although it was to be the greatest material beneficiary of devolution, and as the largest unit in Wales it contained the most *Yes* voters as well as the most *No* voters), and the whole English border area.

How Effective have the Scottish and Welsh Parliaments Been?

The outcome of the first Scottish elections, in which Downing Street did not intervene, was as expected. The outcomes in both Wales and London, where Downing Street did intervene, were not as expected. In both, the Labour Party did far worse than anybody had predicted before the Downing Street interventions. The votes and seats secured by the parties in Scotland and Wales were as shown in Table 2.

As Table 2 also shows, the votes and seats going to each of the four parties were very similar in both countries. However, that similarity conceals more than it reveals. In Scotland, Labour won more seats than the Nationalists, but fewer than an overall majority. However, it was always expected that the governing coalition would involve Labour and the Liberal Democrats, the two Constitutional Convention parties, as they were the two ideologically closest. The arithmetic would have permitted a Lab/SNP coalition, or a Cons/LD/SNP coalition against Labour. Both of these rival coalitions would have spanned too much ideological space to be stable. As elsewhere, much of the tension in the early months was intra-Labour, but in Scotland it was between Donald Dewar, the First Minister, and John Reid, the Secretary of State remaining in the UK Cabinet. Their proxy battle was fought through sackings and briefings, but had petered out by the end of 1999.

Table 2 Votes and seats, first elections to devolved parliaments 1999

Scotland

| | Constituency votes | | List votes | | |
	Vote share	Seats	Vote share	Seats	Total seats
Cons	15.5	0	15.4	18	18
Lab	38.8	53	33.6	3	56
Lib Dem	14.2	12	12.4	5	17
SNP	28.7	7	27.3	28	35
Other	2.7	1	11.3	2	3

Wales

| | Constituency votes | | List votes | | |
	Vote share	Seats	Vote share	Seats	Total seats
Cons	15.8	1	16.5	8	9
Lab	37.6	27	35.5	1	28
Lib Dem	13.5	3	12.5	3	6
Plaid Cymru	28.4	9	30.6	8	17

Wales was different entirely. Everybody had expected that Labour, which had got over half the Welsh vote at the 1997 general election, would win an overall majority in the National Assembly. This vision started to fall apart on Clapham Common. Ron Davies, the architect of Welsh devolution and first Secretary of State for Wales in the Blair government, was assaulted there in October 1998 in still unexplained circumstances. In an ideal world this might be thought to be irrelevant to Welsh devolution (and in passing note that the Blair administration, with three openly gay Cabinet ministers, has marked a new public acceptance of gay men in politics). But it led to Davies' resignation and replacement by the little-known Alun Michael. The majority of Labour Party individual members in Wales voted for Rhodri Morgan, who was not acceptable to Tony Blair (perhaps because he had been indecisive on some controversial Welsh issues), so the union block vote was resurrected to vote Michael into office, and thence to the First Ministership. Popular resentment at this manoeuvre led to a huge swing from Labour to Plaid Cymru in the first Welsh election. Plaid Cymru won three formerly rocklike Labour seats (Llanelli, Rhondda and Islwyn). Ironically, it was only Labour's dreadful performance that enabled Michael to win a seat at all. Too late to be nominated for a constituency seat, he stood as a list candidate in west Wales. Normally, Labour would have won too many constituency seats there to be entitled to a top-up list seat. But its unexpected collapse in the constituencies let Michael squeak in. He formed a minority Labour administration, but in February 2000 was forced out anyhow after losing a vote of no confidence, with all the opposition parties combining in protest at his autocratic style. The substantive issue at stake was whether the UK Treasury would promise to release matching funding to allow Wales to claim all the European Union money it had won by getting the former mining valleys and the rural west of Wales declared as 'Objective One' (that is, among the poorest regions in the EU). Michael, torn between Cardiff and London, felt unable to guarantee that. None of the three other parties, nor Morgan as leader of the Labour opposition, were so constrained. At the third attempt, Rhodri Morgan became the leader of Labour in Wales. In October 2000, he changed his administration from a minority Labour to a coalition Labour–Liberal Democrat one, and appointed Liberal Democrat ministers.

If this is not enough to support the 'control freak' against the 'subtle plan' hypothesis, events in London confirm it further. From early in the Blair government's plans for London, it became clear that they were determined to block at all costs a revival of the old Greater London Council under its charismatic left-wing leader Ken Livingstone. In the 1980s, so the analysis ran, Livingstone had helped make Labour unelectable at national level through his devotion to various wacky left wing causes. His administration had sharply cut public transport fares in London, but had neither budgeted to meet the deficit nor anticipated a successful court challenge brought by the borough of Bromley (which turned on the simple fact that the Livingstone administration's subsidy to London Underground represented a massive financial transfer from the parts of London, such as Bromley, without Tube lines to the parts of London that had Tube lines). He had entertained gay, lesbian, ethnic minority and Irish republican groups at County Hall. In fury, Margaret Thatcher's government had simply abolished his council, and all the other metropolitan county councils in England.

The Blair government wished to recreate democratic government across London without recreating a Livingstone GLC. So the district boundaries for the new Assembly for London were deliberately drawn not to be identical to borough boundaries – in order to prevent either their members being borough advocates, or borough Labour parties nominating candidates in the Livingstone mould. The mayoralty was a tougher nut. Labour put its faith in its nomination process, feeling confident that it could deny Livingstone, who by now was a Labour MP, the nomination. It did; Livingstone then promptly decided to run as an independent, and won by an overall majority, forcing the official Labour candidate into third place. The electoral system for the mayoralty, which had been carefully crafted to force a run-off between the top two candidates (the system designers having assumed that these would be Conservative and Labour) thus turned against its designers, and the run-off was between Livingstone and the left-wing Conservative Steve Norris.

Away from the fireworks, how have the devolved governments performed? Above all, will they weaken or strengthen the Union? Of course it is too early to say for sure. But enough has happened to analyse the strengths and weaknesses of devolution, and hence the Blair effect on the national question.

Both parliaments got off to a bad start. Both spent a lot of time in the first few months on their expensive proposed buildings and on members' allowances and holidays. But these are froth (albeit the buildings will be expensive froth – but even the dome-like building under construction in Edinburgh will never be a patch on the Greenwich Dome for blackholery). The Scottish Parliament now has quite an impressive list of legislative credits. That the Abolition of Feudal Tenure etc (Scotland) Act 2000 was passed in May speaks for itself. It had never reached the head of the legislative queue at Westminster since 1707. The AMS electoral system permitted the election of two MSPs to the left of Labour.[7] One of them, Tommy Sheridan, a Militant who was expelled from the Labour Party in Neil Kinnock's days, promoted an Abolition of Poindings and Warrant Sales Bill. A back-bench Labour revolt ensured that this survived the Executive's attempt to defeat it. It is in committee as this book goes to press. The European Convention on Human Rights was incorporated in Scotland from the beginning, ahead of its incorporation in England and Wales in October 2000. It has already produced a ruling that temporary sheriffs may not be appointed by the administration, as this would be a violation of the separation of powers. Scotland is sidling towards a written constitution ahead of the rest of the UK.

Most of these worthy matters were overshadowed by the bruising row over 'Section 28' (actually section 2A of the relevant Scottish Act). Perhaps the most important thing to say is that Section 28, alias 2A, is now repealed in Scotland, in accordance with the wish of a majority of the members of the elected house. In the rest of the UK it is still on the statute book despite the votes of the majority of the elected house, because repeal was defeated in the unelected House of Lords. The Winning and Souter attacks on the Scottish Parliament actually demonstrate the value to the centre of the founding idea of devolution – namely that accountability would be shifted from London to Edinburgh.

The National Assembly for Wales has achieved less. Some of this may be put down to the initial disruption of the Davies/Michael/Morgan succession and the inexperience of some ministers. But much of it is due to the Act that created it. The definition of its powers in terms of secondary legislation is unworkable. Secondary legislation (that is, Ministerial orders and Statutory Instruments) is not at all the same as legislation on subject areas which are devolved. The Act gives no instrument to the National Assembly whereby it may take responsibility for its subject areas. Also, it has not even the limited financial autonomy that the tax-varying power gives to the Scottish Parliament. In the circumstances, it is remarkable that Wales has busted its way out of the Barnett formula and Scotland remains within it.

The Welsh row about Objective One had to be resolved by the Chancellor's Comprehensive Spending Review (CSR) in July 2000. The bruising Michael battle may have forced the UK government's hand to produce the following remarkable joint statement by First Secretary Morgan and the Secretary of State for Wales:

> the Government has accepted our special case for funding outside the Barnett formula. In England the Objective One area only constitutes eight per cent of the population . . . In Wales 65 per cent of the population . . . are in Objective One areas. That is why Wales' case for different treatment was so strong. (*Western Mail* 19.07.00).

It is remarkable because after Barnett has been busted once, it can be busted again. Informed sources in Wales predict that the next battle will be over NHS spending. As explained above, the mechanical effect of the Barnett formula is to cause public spending per head to converge over time. But, in 1979, when Barnett was first calibrated, Wales was a poor area of the UK, which was receiving proportionately less in public spending than its Treasury-determined 'needs'. It is still, unlike Scotland, a poor region. In so far as Barnett has worked, it will have pushed Welsh health and education spending further below Wales' 'needs'. Therefore, the intellectual case to bust out of Barnett in Wales is strong. In Scotland the intellectual case is weak, but the political case is strong.

Scotland had no lever comparable to Objective One, and was held within Barnett. This makes life difficult for Scottish Ministers, especially the Finance Minister. Jack McConnell, who held that post until the death of Dewar, managed it adroitly. Facing north, he denied that there was a Barnett 'squeeze', as the SNP call it. But there is, and he knew it. McConnell lost the election to succeed Dewar as First Minister to Henry McLeish, regarded as a safe but uncharismatic performer. McConnell then moved to education, whose previous minister had been damaged by a scandal over botched exam results. His successor, the previously unknown and unblooded Angus MacKay, will have a very difficult job on Barnett. Cabinet Office and Prime Minister's Office sources brief conference speakers that the Barnett formula is now (for the first time?) working as Lord Barnett and his civil servants intended it to. The CSR announced a large real increase in public spending, most of it on services that are devolved in the three territories. That gave the Blair government the best chance that any government has had since 1979 actually to operate the Barnett formula without dire consequences. Scottish Ministers can announce that there has been a large real increase in their health and education budgets without having to concede (what is true) that the per head increase is not as great as that in England. Nevertheless, it will take many years of Gordon Brown CSR's before the number of computers per pupil in Alnwick matches the number in Duns.

Towards Quebec – or Slovakia?

Is devolution a slippery slope towards independence, or a stable resting point? Conservatives and nationalists, for their opposite reasons, assert the former; supporters of the Blair administration, the latter.

In Wales, devolution looks like an equilibrium outcome, although much remains to be sorted out in the powers of the National Assembly. There is no serious pressure, even from Plaid Cymru, for Welsh independence. Although there remains a mystery as to why Wales was offered her institutions of administrative devolution in 1964, and then of political devolution in 1997, the fact remains (just) that the latter won support in the 1997 referendum. The fact that Yes then won by a hair's breadth is now irrelevant. We have shown that even the Conservatives now believe that their interest is served better by the Assembly continuing than by its abolition. Until 2000, Wales had not actually been a beneficiary of the regional distribution of public money. When Barnett was first contrasted with each territory's 'needs' (an essentially contested concept) in 1979, Wales' public spending per head was shown to be behind its 'needs', and Scotland's and Northern Ireland's both well ahead. There is a social scientific explanation for this. Scotland and Northern Ireland can point credible threats to the Union. The Scots may threaten to walk away, depriving Labour of much chance of a UK majority, and depriving Conservative governments (who care about it most) of the continued 1707 Union. The credible threat potential of Northern Ireland has always been too obvious to need spelling out. Welsh nationalism has posed no comparable threat, apart from relatively minor outbursts of militancy around the time of the investiture of Prince Charles as Prince of Wales in 1969, and again with arson in English-owned second homes in the 1980s. It took the loss of Tony Blair's First Secretary to convince Downing Street that Wales needed a disproportionate increase in public spending. In that perspective, Welsh devolution has been a great success.

Scotland is much harder to call. It could become Britain's Quebec – always about to break way, never quite doing so. Or it could become Britain's Slovakia, where having bluffed its larger partner for many decades with threats of separation, suddenly one day that threat is taken seriously, and it finds itself unexpectedly independent, to its short-run disadvantage. In this matter, there is no obvious Third Way. Tertiavia is an imaginary country.

The Quebec Scenario

One striking similarity between these two cases is that the nationalist party consistently does better in lower-tier elections than in upper-tier ones. In both countries, voters are more willing to vote for the nationalists in the local Parliament than for, respectively, Ottawa and Westminster. The rapid decline of the Scottish Nationalists from a peak just after the October 1974 General Election resembles the repeated failure of the Quebec nationalists to gain majority support for independence. People came to the brink, assessed the economic consequences of going it alone, and walked back in trepidation. Whether Scotland would actually gain or lose from independence is of course a large and contested question. Nationalist economics are more plausible now than in the 1970s. Then and now they claimed implausibly that Scotland subsidised England. The truth is the reverse, in spades. Then, they claimed that Scotland would float free on oil revenues. Now, they prefer to claim that Scotland could thrive as Ireland has since the late 1980s – that is, as a small open English-speaking entry point to the European Union which is particularly attractive to inward investors. Scotland shares much of Ireland's romantic history of emigration in dire circumstances to the USA; maybe Scots-American capitalists would be attracted to an independent Scotland as Irish-American ones have been attracted to independent Ireland.

Other aspects of the Quebec scenario are just the inverse of those about to be discussed in the Slovakia scenario. In Quebec-City-on-Forth, the parties will not outbid one another in their denunciations of the Scrooge-like UK government. Either future Chancellors will conceal that a Barnett squeeze is in operation, or they will get away with operating it. Or, thirdly, they will continue to pass off Barnett goodies to Scotland without arousing English ire, even in Alnwick. The English will not get, or not develop, the institutions that will enable them to get regional public spending discussed in the open. The West Lothian Question, which has been remarkably little asked since 1997, will remain unasked and will become as much of a historical curiosity as Gladstone's Irish Home Rule Bill.

If the Quebec scenario unfolds, devolution will come to be seen as a jewel in Tony Blair's crown. In time, the embarrassments of his attempts to control what he had just set free will fade and he will be hailed as the saviour of a new flexible Union. Except, of course, by the Scottish Nationalists.

The Slovak Scenario

This scenario starts with some uncomfortable numbers. In 1978, when the Barnett Formula was invented, Scottish income per head was around 85 per cent of the UK average. It is now about 98 per cent – a tribute to the revival of the Scottish economy (without devolution, the crusty may observe). The Treasury's so-called 'needs assessment' of 1979 showed that Scotland's 'needs' per head (for the services that the Callaghan bill had proposed to devolve) were 16 per cent ahead of England's; spending on them per head was 22 per cent ahead of England's. Twenty years of Barnett should have converted this 'overspend' into an 'underspend'. If Barnett had

worked as expected, it would have severely undershot by now. Scotland's
spending per head would be at the same level as England's, whereas her
'needs' are probably still ahead of England's. Not by much, since Scotland
is now, unlike then, a part of the UK with average income. But it still has
cold weather, sparsely populated areas, and midges. What has happened to
Scottish public spending per head? It has not converged; it has diverged. On
the latest independent estimates, identifiable public spending per head in
Scotland, excluding social security (which is and will presumably remain a
service provided by the UK government) is 31 per cent ahead of the GB
average.[8] This, recall, in a territory that is now averagely prosperous. The
reason is probably that successive Secretaries of State, especially the last
two Conservative Secretaries Ian Lang and Michael Forsyth, used the credible threat of the breakup of the Union to extract more money for Scotland
than Barnett would have allowed.

   None of this will matter unless the English start to notice. If they do not,
the Quebec scenario beckons. But we have seen that they have already
started to notice in London, which has devolved government, and in
Newcastle, which does not. It was a Geordie revolt that killed devolution
in 1977–79. No comparable Geordie revolt has yet occurred this time,
and it may never do. But Barnett increases the pressure for democratically
elected regional bodies in England. The Blair government has not been
keen to offer these; a future government may or may not.

   In the Slovak scenario, the English reaction will force the UK government to put a firmer and firmer Barnett squeeze on Scotland. All the parties
in the Scottish Parliament except the party which forms the UK government
will protest furiously, and demand at least a restoration of Scotland's
spending advantage. The Scottish Nationalists will point out that you can
never trust the English. Meanwhile, the English will once again notice the
West Lothian Question. Although the number of Scottish MPs at
Westminster will be reduced after the next boundary redrawing to
Scotland's population share, it will not be reduced below that. These MPs
will have the power to vote on public spending in England, but English
MPs will not have the power to vote on public spending in Scotland. If
these MPs (perhaps with their Welsh cousins) form the pivot between the
English majority and the UK majority, the WLQ will recur in all its painful
complexity. Finally, the UK government will say 'All right, you don't like
the Union. Off you go then, and save us the money'. And Scotland will sail
off into the uncharted waters of independence.

   If the Slovak scenario unfolds, devolution will come to be seen as Tony
Blair's biggest mistake. Except, of course, by the Scottish Nationalists.

*With grateful thanks to seminar attenders, Oxford, September 2000, and
to Martin Johnes, Dylan Griffiths, James Mitchell, and a member of the
Prime Minister's policy staff for comments. The author takes sole
responsibility for all interpretations and any errors.*

Notes

1 The much more qualified manifesto commitments to explore regional government in England, and to experiment with elected city mayors outside London, had produced nothing firm by the time this book went to press.

2 D. Denver, J. Mitchell, C. Pattie and H. Bochel, *Scotland Decides: the devolution issue and the 1997 referendum*, Frank Cass, 2000, ch. 7 *passim*, esp. pp. 168–69.

3 K.D. Wald, *Crosses on the Ballot: patterns of British voter alignment since 1885*, Princeton University Press, 1985; I. McLean, *Rational Choice in British Politics: an analysis of rhetoric and manipulation from Peel to Blair*, Oxford University Press, 2001, ch. 4.

4 I. McLean, 'Are Scotland and Wales overrepresented in the House of Commons?', *Political Quarterly*, 66, 1995, pp. 250–68.

5 J. Penman, 'Real power will stay with MPs in England, Blair tells Scotland', *Scotsman*, 4 April 1997. A longer discussion of this episode is in I. McLean, 'The Semi-Detached Election: Scotland' in A. King ed., *New Labour Triumphs: Britain at the Polls 1997*, Chatham House, 1998, pp. 145–76.

6 I. McLean and M. Johnes, *Aberfan: government and disasters*, Welsh Academic Press, 2000, ch. 2.

7 Ongoing surveys of MSPs show that, judging by their issue positions, SNP MSPs are also to the left of Labour, but when identifying themselves on the left-right spectrum, Labour MSPs put themselves to the left of their SNP counterparts. Letter from Professor James Mitchell, September 2000.

8 See the tables in I. McLean, 'Getting and spending: can (or should) the Barnett Formula survive?', *New Economy*, 7, 2000, pp. 76–80.

Perfidious Britannia: Nicola Jenning's response to Mr Mandelson's handling of the Patten Report.

© Nicola Jennings

Chapter 21

THE BELFAST AGREEMENT AND THE LABOUR GOVERNMENT

Handling and Mishandling History's Hand

Brendan O'Leary

T HE BELFAST AGREEMENT of 10 April 1998, reached within a year of its general election victory, was the most surprising co-achievement of the new Labour government. The new government should not be praised too much, however. Credit was largely owed to others: the two men awarded the Nobel Peace Prize, John Hume and David Trimble, and their party colleagues and advisors; the representatives of republicans and loyalists, notably Gerry Adams, Martin McGuinness, David Ervine and Gary McMichael; two Irish governments, the Fianna Fáil-Labour coalition of 1992–94, and the Fianna Fáil–Progressive Democrat coalition of 1997 – including their officials in Ireland's Department of Foreign Affairs (DFA); and an array of others, including significant Americans. Tony Blair and his colleagues contributed no fresh ideas to the Agreement, despite courtier Charles Leadbetter's claim that it exemplified 'the Third Way'. Most of the ideas were articulated or prefigured before Blair took office. The Labour government's role was that of an enthusiastic first time midwife.

Before History's Hand

The bulk of the design of the political architecture agreed in Belfast on 10 April 1998 originated with Irish nationalists of all hues, within and without the SDLP, Sinn Féin, and the Irish government. Their demands were sculpted into a coherent negotiating package by the Irish DFA, acting under the skilful leadership of diplomat Sean O Huiginn, now the Irish ambassador in Washington, and embedded in the Irish contributions to the Joint Framework Documents (JFDs), agreed by the Irish and British governments in February 1995.[1] The JFDs arose from an established 'three-stranded' negotiating process in which matters internal to Northern Ireland, North-South issues, and East-West issues, were respectively addressed.[2] The JFDs anticipated a power-sharing Assembly and Executive in Northern Ireland, extensive consultative, harmonising and executive functions for an all-Ireland North-South body, and an innovative model of 'double protection' of rights. They also anticipated referendums in both parts of Ireland, the brainchild of Hume, to give expression to Irish national self-determination. The Belfast Agreement was the baby of the JFDs, though its conception and birth were long and painful, and even though it was mildly genetically modified by the Ulster Unionist Party's negotiators, who diminished the powers and autonomy of the proposed North-South Ministerial Council, and added the British-Irish Council.

The outgoing Conservative government deserved little credit for innovative ideas. Fortunately, and partly because of President Clinton's pressure, it avoided its instincts and refused to kill outright the political opportunity created by the antecedents and the materialisation of the IRA cease fire of 31 August 1994. Whitehall's civil servants, but not the local Northern Ireland Office, contributed positively to the agenda for the multi-party negotiations. Quentin Thomas, best known for leading the initial exploratory talks with Sinn Féin's Chief Negotiator Martin McGuinness, was crucial. In drafting the British contribution to the JFDs, he split the differences between the UUP's and the SDLP's preferences for the internal government of Northern Ireland from the previous inter-party negotiations of 1991–92.[3]

Labour's first Prime Minister for eighteen years had no profound agenda on Ireland, North or South – even though much was made of the fact that he had an Irish mother and a Catholic wife. 'New' Labour's role in Opposition had apparently been simple. It had supported the peace process, and offered bi-partisan support for the Major government in its death-throes. Behind the scenes the story was less perfumed. Blair's priority was to win the next general election, and Northern Ireland policy, like all others, was utterly subordinated to that objective. In 1994–95 his closest advisors believed some of Labour's existing policies, viz. support for Irish unification by consent and opposition to the draconian powers in the UK's anti-terrorism legislation, were electorally counter-productive. Not in themselves, but because they thought they were gifts to the right-wing press, identifying Labour with being soft on terrorism, and with political extremism. In fact, polls showed that weakening British sovereignty over Northern Ireland, and indeed troop withdrawal, enjoyed consistent majority support in Great Britain.[4] But Blair's coterie was driven by the fear that the party might appear soft on crime and terrorism. Blair had established himself with the mantra that he would be tough on crime and tough on the causes of crime. In the summer of 1994, apparently on Peter Mandelson's counsel, he unilaterally ditched Labour's policy of seeking Irish unity by consent – without the formal approval of the Party Conference – and modified the party's stance on the Prevention of Terrorism Act (PTA). Then he supported whatever the Major government did, whatever contradictions it created.[5]

There was a *prima facie* case for Labour's policy shift. Dropping the policy of encouraging unity by consent appeared to move Labour to a neutral stance on the future of Northern Ireland, at odds with the Sinn Féin demand that a British government become a persuader for Irish unity. Thereby it made unionists more likely to enter into negotiations with republicans and others. This *prima facie* case was not, however, the determining factor in the policy shift, though it would be used retrospectively by the leader's spin doctors. The case was also doubtful because the Conservatives were persuaders for the Union, and New Labour's shift meant that both the UK's 'parties of government' favoured maintaining the Union, albeit in different formats and with different intensities, and thereby de-stabilised one of the premises of the republican initiative.

In October 1994 Blair replaced Kevin McNamara in the Northern Ireland portfolio with Dr Marjorie (Mo) Mowlam – an elected member of the Shadow Cabinet. McNamara concluded that Blair deemed him too Old Labour, and too 'fat and bald and green'.[6] His able number two, Jim Marshall, was dismissed. Roger Stott MP, another junior spokesman, who had unintentionally embarrassed Blair when he was Shadow Home Secretary by opposing the PTA, also suffered loss of office, and went into a downward spiral that led to his premature death. Clive Soley MP, a former spokesman on Northern Ireland, soon to be a sycophantic Chairman of the Parliamentary Labour Party, rationalised Blair's policy shifts as designed to support Major against right-wing conservatives opposed to the peace process.[7] That appeared plausible, but it was misleading. The Labour leadership's focus was entirely electoral. Northern Ireland policy was wholly constrained by the objective of minimising enemies in the right-wing press – which supported the right-wing conservatives opposed to the peace process. Blair would take no risks for peace while in Opposition. Notes of meetings with Dr Mowlam record her prosaic and characteristically honest appraisal in 1995: 'They [Blair and Mandelson] think we should be so far up Major's **** that he can never accuse us of not being behind him'.[8]

Removing McNamara, on the pretext that he did not win a place in the Shadow Cabinet elections, eased the Labour leadership's parliamentary relations with the UUP, whom they hoped might one day support them in bringing down the Major government in a parliamentary 'no confidence' motion, or at least remain neutral. Mowlam, in contrast to McNamara, was a reluctant appointee, telling me that she would have preferred the Education portfolio. But she embraced the post with characteristic energy, mental sharpness, and superb networking skills. She had been appointed a junior Northern Ireland frontbench spokesperson by Neil Kinnock in 1988–89, at McNamara's suggestion, and knew the terrain. She was, in

contrast to Blair, not a unionist as far as the Union of Great Britain and
Northern Ireland was concerned. She believed that Irish unification by
consent was fine in principle but not feasible within this generation. In
1988 with McNamara and others she deliberated over how best to achieve
either a negotiated settlement, or, failing that, a system of shared British
and Irish sovereignty which would involve a devolved component – work
that was later developed and encouraged by Neil Kinnock, and later by
John Smith.[9] She had no time for Labour's electoral integrationists – who
claimed that bringing Labour's organisation and message to the region
would salve working-class divisions and transcend sectarianism and nationalism.[10] In private her sympathies lay with the SDLP, though she found its
leader, John Hume, remote and unapproachable.[11] Though many of the
UUP's MPs called for McNamara's dismissal, Mowlam was not exactly
what they wanted; though some unionists harboured illusions about her.
On becoming Shadow Secretary of State she supported the agenda of the
emerging JFDs, and endorsed them upon their publication. She was fun and
pragmatic, but had settled principles on the peace process: the priority was
an inclusive agreement with which peaceful republicans, nationalists and
moderate unionists would be content. She was schooled in political science
and political anthropology. She was knowledgeable about consociational
and federal principles, and had a PhD dissertation on referendums. She was
unusually skilled at making warm connections with people, irrespective of
nationality, class or sex, and mastered her new brief. She did not go down
well with the UUP's older males, for whom the flirtatious Redcar MP was
the embodiment of secular, profane, and liberated woman.

   Blair's support for whatever Major did had one negative consequence.
After the IRA ceasefire of 31 August 1994, and its reciprocation by loyalists six weeks later, there was a long hiatus of eighteen months, and no rush
to start the inclusive negotiations for parties with democratic mandates that
had been promised by Major and Albert Reynolds's joint declaration of
December 1993. Instead Sinn Féin was put in quarantine in the UK. The
blockage to negotiations was simple: Unionists and some Conservative
MPs strongly opposed negotiations commencing without prior decommissioning of its weapons by the IRA and without a declaration that its
ceasefire was permanent. The blockage strengthened as Major's majority
diminished. Blair did not offer, and Major apparently did not seek, his support to bypass these obstacles to negotiations, even though there would
have been a cross-party majority in the Commons for such an initiative.
The blockage eventually won a name, viz. 'Washington 3', after a clause in
a speech made by Secretary of State, Sir Patrick Mayhew, in March 1995,
which demanded some prior decommissioning before inclusive
negotiations.

   The Irish government, under Taoiseach Reynolds (1992–94), and most
Irish nationalists, north and south, took the view that the IRA ceasefire was
permanent, and that decommissioning should be left until negotiations

were completed. The two governments, steered by Irish officials and with American good offices, agreed to establish an international body, composed of former US Senator Majority Leader George Mitchell, Canadian General Jean de Chastelain, and former Finnish Premier Harri Holkeri, to propose ways out of the impasse. On 23 January 1996 they did the obvious, but in lucid and effective language. They proposed six peaceful and democratic principles to which parties to the negotiations would be obliged to commit themselves. They also proposed that 'parallel decommissioning' begin *during* the negotiations rather than *before* (the British suggestion) or *after* (the Irish suggestion).[12] Major responded by appearing both to accept and reject the Report. If prior decommissioning was not to happen, a certainty, then he would call for elections to a Forum, playing fast and loose with a clause in the Report,[13] so that parties would have mandates for negotiations, and then decommissioning could be handled as Mitchell had proposed. This was playing with fire. It required Sinn Féin (and the SDLP), who already had mandates, to legitimate a new forum, and thereby the status of Northern Ireland, in advance of negotiations, and to agree to elections which they regarded as an excuse for delaying engagement.[14]

Blair supported Major's manoeuvre. Their myopic consensus had predictable consequences: the IRA went back to war, bombing Canary Wharf on 9 February 1996, killing two British citizens. It was a re-start of bombing to force negotiations to begin, rather than a complete republican exit from their new strategy. But the breakdown of the IRA ceasefire deeply damaged the peace process, both in the short and longer run. It heightened distrust all around, and confirmed unionist presumptions that the ceasefire was purely tactical. The same events confirmed republican suspicions that the British political class would behave as perfidiously and as slowly as it could, despite the good offices of international mediators. Fortunately, however, the IRA's bombing campaign in 1996–97 was limited, both in the sense of being largely confined to small scale operations in Great Britain, and in its impact on the public (with several IRA personnel proving incompetent).[15] Elections to the Forum took place in May. Sinn Féin increased its vote share significantly – see Table 1 – while the unionist vote fragmented, a significant pointer for the future.[16] Negotiations, in principle open to the top ten parties with democratic mandates, began in June 1996, with Sinn Féin excluded. Negotiating teams were separated from the Forum, and nationalists boycotted the Forum. The negotiations remained procedural until the Westminster elections were called in May 1997. In Northern Ireland – see Table 2 – they led to a further rise in Sinn Féin's vote share, and confirmation of the thesis that the vote for overtly unionist parties was in secular decline.[17]

The functional, but not entirely intended, consequence of Blair's constant following of Major was mildly to relax the UUP's fear of a new Labour government. Its London supporters started to have fond memories of the Callaghan premiership, and of Callaghan's royalist, unionist and

Table 1 Parties' Shares of the Vote and of Seats in the 30 May 1996 Elections

Party	Votes (%)	Seats	(%)
UKUP United Kingdom Unionist Party	3.7	3	(2.7)
DUP Democratic Unionist Party	18.8	24	(21.8)
UDP Ulster Democratic Party	2.2	2	(1.8)
PUP Progressive Unionist Party	3.5	2	(1.8)
UUP Ulster Unionist Party	24.2	30	(27.3)
APNI Alliance Party of Northern Ireland	6.6	7	(6.4)
Lab (Northern Ireland) Labour	.8	2	(1.8)
NIWC Northern Ireland Women's Coalition	1.0	2	(1.8)
SDLP Social Democratic and Labour Party of Northern Ireland	21.4	21	(19.1)
SF Sinn Féin	15.5	17	(15.5)

Election System: PR-list system (using the Droop quota, followed by d'Hondt, equivalent to pure d'Hondt) with two seats guaranteed to the top ten parties (four parties achieved representation solely through this mechanism). Deviation from proportionality was quite high, $(d = (1/2) \sum [s_i - v_i]$ = 7.85) and led to the DUP winning more seats than the SDLP on a lower share of the vote.

Source: O'Leary and Evans (1997).

Table 2 Parties' Shares of the Vote and of Seats in Westminster Elections, 1997

Party	Votes (%)	Seats	(%)
UKUP United Kingdom Unionist Party	1.6	1	(5.6)
DUP Democratic Unionist Party	13.6	2	(11.1)
UDP Ulster Democratic Party		—	
PUP Progressive Unionist Party		—	
UUP Ulster Unionist Party	32.7	10	(55.6)
APNI Alliance Party of Northern Ireland	8.0	—	
SDLP Social Democratic and Labour Party of Northern Ireland	24.1	3	(16.7)
SF Sinn Féin	16.7	2	(11.1)

Election System: Plurality rule in 18 single member districts.

Source: O'Leary and Evans (1997).

brutish Secretary of State, Roy Mason. This worried the party's Irish nationalist sympathisers, but they were relaxed because Mowlam had the key portfolio, and was patently the best prepared prospective office holder since the post was invented in 1972. Blair privately promised Irish officials that once elected he would deliver; he did not disappoint.

Taking the Cards Dealt by History

In the summer of 1997 the new government, with Blair and Mowlam at the helm, orchestrated the renewal of the IRA's ceasefire as the first significant non-economic initiative of the new regime. They correctly judged that the IRA's campaign had been intended to persuade the UK government to change its stance, and to force Sinn Féin's entry into negotiations, rather than to dictate the outcome of the negotiations. The government's judgement would make Sinn Féin's entry into negotiations possible, and was preceded by a speech made by the new Premier in Belfast to assure unionists of Blair's commitment to maintaining the Union as long as a local majority so wished. He declared that 'A political settlement is not a slippery slope to a united Ireland',[18] and that he did not expect the latter within his lifetime. The message was intended to keep the UUP at the negotiating tables while bringing Sinn Féin to join them. It would succeed. 'The settlement train is leaving', Blair told republicans, 'I want you on that train . . . So end the violence now.'[19]

The Labour government facilitated the eight parties which would make the Agreement – the UUP, the loyalist PUP and UDP, the SDLP, Sinn Féin, the Alliance, the Women's Coalition and (Northern Ireland) Labour. It was not distressed by Paisley's DUP and McCartney's UKUP decision to withdraw from the negotiating process after Sinn Féin was admitted – it eased the making of the Agreement. The government's unsung hero would prove to be Minister of State Paul Murphy, the future Secretary of State for Wales, who chaired long months of negotiations about negotiations between the summer of 1997 and the spring of 1998. The crucial performance of the new government, especially of its Premier, was to exhort, cajole and persuade the UUP, and its leader David Trimble, to negotiate and make the Agreement. Trimble had succeeded James Molyneaux after the latter's resignation – the production of the JFDs had been a green bridge too far for his party colleagues. He had been elected because he was seen as a hard-liner, the 'hero of Drumcree', and the brightest of the UUP's Westminster MPs.[20] He was also sensitive, underconfident, prickly, and terrified, sensibly, that he might face the fate of previous UUP leaders who had decided to accommodate Irish nationalism, such as Terence O'Neill, Brian Faulkner and Bill Craig. The government's delicate task, with its Irish counterpart, was to encourage Trimble to negotiate on the basis of the JFDs while enabling him to maintain that he had repudiated them. Blair's charm mattered. Trimble had sworn he would not fall for the same trap as Molyneaux, i.e. seduction through bilaterals with Number 10. Instead he resolved always to be accompanied by party colleagues when he met the PM. This was a resolution that Blair would wear away, partly because Mowlam's relations with Trimble deteriorated radically.

Blair's government got off to a good start with the Irish government and its officials, and neither Blair nor Mowlam displayed the same sensitivities to America's benign interventions as their Conservative predecessors.[21] This ensured that there were three governments strongly mission-committed to the success of the negotiations. The replacement of the rainbow coalition in Dublin (1994–97) with a new Fianna Fáil led coalition invigorated the Irish commitment because the new Taoiseach, Bertie Ahern, enjoyed the confidence of Northern nationalists, unlike his predecessor, Fine Gael's John Bruton.[22] The British and Irish governments' decisions to act through Senator Mitchell, the chair of the negotiations, when they concurred, and their decision to set a deadline for completing the negotiations,[23] were important components in delivering a successful outcome.

When the IRA renewed its ceasefire in July 1997 Mowlam took responsibility for monitoring it with the understanding that Sinn Féin would join the negotiations in September if the IRA's conduct withstood scrutiny. At Mitchell's initiative in August the two governments established an Independent International Commission on Decommissioning, chaired by de Chastelain. This was intended to facilitate the UUP's acceptance of Sinn Féin's presence at the negotiations, and, tacitly, to enable decommissioning to be parked while other substantive issues were addressed. In September Sinn Féin signed up to the Mitchell principles. Despite the provocation occasioned by an IRA statement that it did not accept the Mitchell principles and was not a party to the talks,[24] and a bomb planted by the dissident republican faction, the Continuity-IRA, the UUP, flanked by the loyalist parties, agreed to participate in negotiations with Sinn Féin.

A tacit division of labour developed. The Prime Minister was seen as more empathetic to unionists, the Secretary of State to nationalists – a correct perception. This would mean that in the final negotiations of April 1998 Blair's role was visibly more important, since nationalists bargained on behalf of themselves with the back-up of the Irish government, whereas the unionists looked to Blair for sympathy. Before and during the negotiations Blair and Mowlam overrode the timidity of some of their ministerial colleagues, accepting that the full-scale release of all paramilitaries on ceasefire must form an essential component of the peace process. Mowlam in particular displayed political courage and *nous* in visiting the Maze prison to calm loyalist paramilitaries in January 1998, earning the sobriquet 'Mighty Mo'. In the new year the two governments produced 'Heads of Agreement', prefiguring the eventual settlement, while Mowlam and Mitchell successfully managed temporary suspensions of the UDP and Sinn Féin from the negotiations because of violations of their ceasefires by the UDA and the IRA respectively.

The final negotiations were held in late March and April 1998, with a deadline of Thursday 9 April. Strand One, the internal government of Northern Ireland, was negotiated head-to-head by the SDLP and the UUP, with the SDLP making the proposals, and the UUP choosing to reject them or accept them. In Strand Two Blair and Ahern agreed to dilute the powers and scope of the proposed North-South Ministerial Council previously agreed by their officials to meet Trimble's and the UUP's requirements. They resisted an explicit linkage between inclusive executive formation in the North and prior decommissioning by the IRA. In Strand Three the governments negotiated constitutional and other peace and confidence-building measures, sometimes with loyalists and republicans. The Agreement was finally produced on 10 April, Good Friday, but not without difficulties. Jeffrey Donaldson MP of the UUP walked out because he was not satisfied that the Agreement required decommissioning before executive formation, and two independent commissions had to be established on policing and the administration of criminal justice because the parties could only agree their terms of reference. Nevertheless the Agreement was made, and justified Blair's comment that he had felt the hand of history upon his shoulder. Now what was required was to have it endorsed in referendums and implemented, without fear or favour.

Building Institutions or a House of Cards?

The Agreement was endorsed in both parts of Ireland, with a 95 and a 71 per cent 'Yes' vote in the South and North respectively. Blair, posing as a fully fledged unionist, was successful in persuading at least some unionists to vote 'Yes' – though he also gave hostages to fortune inconsistent with the text of the Agreement, he had almost done the same on the day of the Agreement in an ambiguous letter to Trimble, who suggested that the Prime Minister agreed that decommissioning of its weapons by the IRA 'should' commence before the new Executive could be formed with Sinn Féin's participation. The 'should' was indicative: the text of the Agreement, by contrast, did not warrant Trimble's position, or that of Blair in some of his later statements, and, in any case, the words of a UK Premier are not law, outside the ranks of New Labour. After the Agreement was made and ratified in the two referendums Mowlam helped override obstruction from some of her Northern Ireland Office's officials and ensured that the full content of the Agreement was eventually faithfully reflected in the Northern Ireland 1998 Act.[25] But in general the Blair government would prove much better at managing the making of the Agreement than in managing its successful implementation.

In part, of course, this was because implementation was more difficult. The government could not be faulted, initially, on the hours it put in. Blair was astonished at the time he had to devote to Irish matters, and so were his advisors. At one stage, Jonathan Powell, to his chagrin, ended up trying to micro-manage the Drumcree dispute, occasioned by the Orange Order's demand that its members should be able to parade down the Garvaghy Road without the prior consent of local (mostly nationalist) residents. The government's difficulties in implementation were not, of course, entirely of its own making. The deep polarisation that the Agreement occasioned within the unionist bloc as a whole, and more particularly within the UUP, were obviously not Labour's responsibilities. In the elections to the new Assembly in June 1998 – see Table 3 – the SDLP outpolled the UUP, the 'No Unionists' performed slightly better than they had in the referendum, and Trimble's Westminster parliamentary colleagues mostly opposed the Agreement. Trimble's responses to these intra-unionist crises were to be a key source of tension in the Agreement's implementation. Republican (and loyalist) dilatoriness on the matter of decommissioning would be another.

The proportionality of the election results was evident, both with respect to blocs and with respect to parties. But the deviations in seats won compared to the first preference vote benefited the pro-Agreement parties. The UUP was the principal beneficiary of the transfer of lower order preferences taking its seat share (25.9 per cent) significantly above its first-preference vote-share (21.3 per cent) – though these lower order preferences came from voters who voted 'No' as well as those who voted 'Yes' to the Agreement. The net transfers by voters to the pro-Agreement candidates, though not as significant as had been hoped, converted a bare 'Anti-Agreement' majority of the first preference vote (25.5 per cent) within the unionist bloc of voters into a bare 'Pro-Agreement' majority (27.8 per cent) amongst seats won by unionists, a result that was essential for the Agreement's (partial) stabilisation. The Labour government could hardly be faulted for the palpably evident intra-unionist divisions, but it would significantly contribute to the difficulties in implementing the Agreement, not least in managing its own responsibilities, and the new institutions. This would become especially manifest in a series of unilateral and ill-judged actions, inactions and public lies on the part of Peter Mandelson who replaced Dr Mowlam as Secretary of State in October 1999.

Table 3 The June 1998 Elections to the Northern Ireland Assembly

Party/Bloc	First preference vote (%)	Seats	(%)
SDLP	22.0	24	(22.2)
SF	17.7	18	(16.7)
Other nationalists	0.1	–	
All nationalists	39.8	42	(38.9)
APNI	6.4	6	(5.5)
Women's Coalition	1.7	2	(1.8)
Other 'Others'	1.3	–	
All Others	9.4	8	(7.3)
UUP	21.0	28	(25.9)
PUP	2.5	2	(1.8)
UDP	1.2	–	
Other Yes Unionists	0.3		
All Yes Unionists	25.0	30	(27.7)
DUP	18.0	20	(18.5)
UKUP	4.5	5	(4.6)
Independent No Unionists	3.0	3	(2.8)
All No Unionists	25.5	28	(25.9)

Source: O'Leary (1999). Per cent figures for votes and seat shares rounded to one decimal place.

Mandelson was Blair's best known and least liked confidante, his Prince of Darkness. In 1999 Blair wanted to rehabilitate him after his sins committed in the Notting Hill housing market with the pockets of Geoffrey Robinson. He hoped Mandelson's appointment would spare him endless unionist deputations – largely occasioned by their refusal to engage Mowlam, who had been suffering from treatment of a benign brain tumour, and had, partly in consequence, become immensely popular, more popular than the PM, but whom some UUP MPs nevertheless treated with a mixture of political and sexist disdain. Mowlam had wanted to be promoted to the Foreign Office, which Blair would not entertain, and at one stage contemplated requesting that she have Mandelson as her deputy. Mandelson saw Northern Ireland as the route to his rehabilitation – given that other ministers would be happy with his 'relegation'. He also thought of it as a route to the ministry he most coveted, the Foreign Office. He had once been friendly with Mowlam – they had holidayed together in Spain – but now was said to regard her as 'terminally undisciplined'.[26] He, by contrast, tended to be terminally disloyal to past friends, commitments, and the truth. In the spring and summer of 1999 he and his associates, including Labour's unionists, started to damage Mowlam's reputation in the press in much the same manner as they had once defamed David Clark, when Mandelson had coveted his Cabinet position.

Mandelson came to Northern Ireland with no obvious preparation in Opposition, unlike Mowlam, though his more credible supporters, such as Donald MacIntyre of the *Independent*, span the line that he had made programmes on the region for *Weekend World* in his days as a TV producer. That at least was accurate. Some in the UUP, including Trimble, called for Mandelson's appointment – much as some had once called for Mowlam to replace McNamara. The DUP, by contrast, were not pleased: 'we do not want a sodomite' as one of its typically homophobic members put it to me.[27] Blair calculated that it was more important to calm Trimble and his party than to continue with the balanced ticket of a soft unionist PM and a soft nationalist Secretary of State. Indeed 'saving Trimble to save the Agreement' would become the government's priority in 1999–2000. The world was told that Mandelson possessed remarkable negotiating skills and diplomatic finesse. This was not evident in his opening parliamentary statement when he described himself as Secretary of State for Ireland – rather than Northern Ireland. He would also quickly demonstrate that he lacked one important element of the normal job description of a normal Foreign Secretary, the capacity to get on with and be appreciated by foreigners. If Blair deserves credit for making the Agreement with Mowlam, as he does, then he must also share with Mandelson the blame for mismanaging its implementation.

The Nature of the Agreement(s)

The Belfast Agreement, incorporated in the British-Irish Agreement, an international treaty in 1999, was an exemplary constitutional design. Internally it was 'consociational'.[28] Externally it established confederal relationships, and prefigured imaginative federalist relationships and a novel model of double protection. If the Agreement fails debate will arise over whether flaws in its design or in its implementation were the principal factors. The rest of this chapter anticipates that debate. By contrast, if the Agreement is fully successful, albeit outside of its scheduled timetable and its own agreed procedures, I hope it will become an export model for conflict regulators. What follows appraises the Agreement's novelties, possible design flaws, and the contributions of Labour's decision-makers to its implementation. Three evaluative arguments are advanced:

1. The Labour government correctly grasped that the conflict required external as well as internal resolution, and realised that the sovereignty and self-determination disputes needed to be resolved. But it failed to follow through on its treaty commitments, and broke international law when it unilaterally suspended some of the Agreement's institutions between February and May 2000, and thereby destabilised the Agreement by making all its provisions and commissions negotiable.
2. The novel dual premiership, designed by the major moderate parties, the SDLP and the UUP, in the heat of the negotiations, has proved its major institutional weakness, suggesting, paradoxically, that moderates are not always the best designers or caretakers of power-sharing systems.
3. The Labour government's, especially Mandelson's, mismanagement of policing reform has severely threatened the stability of the Agreement, and, thereby, the prospects of peace.

These propositions require a prior analysis of the Agreement as a 'constitution'.

A Consociational Federacy

The Agreement met all four standard consociational criteria:[29]

A. *Cross-community executive power-sharing.* This was manifest in:
1. The creation of a quasi-presidential dual premiership, elected by a concurrent majority of unionists and nationalists in the Assembly, and expected to preside over

2. The inclusive grand coalition ten-member executive cabinet of ministers, whose portfolios are allocated according to the d'Hondt voting procedure.

B. *Proportionality norms.* These were evident in:
   1. The d'Hondt procedure used to determine the composition of the cabinet – which resulted in five unionists (three UUP, two DUP) and five nationalists (three SDLP and two Sinn Féin) holding ministries between November 1999 and February 2000, and again from May 2000;
   2. The electoral system (the Single Transferable Vote in eighteen six-member districts) used to elect the Assembly;
   3. The d'Hondt procedure used to allocate Assembly Members to Committees with powers of oversight and legislative initiative; and
   4. Existing and additional legislative provisions to ensure fair and representative employment, especially throughout the public sector, and the promise of a representative police service.

C. *Community autonomy and equality.* These commitments were evident in:
   1. The official recognition of 'unionists', nationalists' and other's political identities, notably in the Assembly's cross-community consent procedures, and in a declaration of 'parity of esteem' between the communities and a promise of 'rigorous impartiality' in administration from the current and possibly future sovereign states;
   2. The decision to leave alone the existing separate but recently equally funded forms of Catholic, Protestant and integrated schooling;
   3. The renewed outlawing of discrimination on grounds of political or religious belief;
   4. The replacement of an oath of loyalty to the Crown with a pledge of office for Ministers;
   5. The establishment of a Human Rights Commission tasked with protecting individual equality and liberty, and identity rights;
   6. The entrenchment of vigorous equality provisions, eventually incorporated in Section 75 of the Northern Ireland Act (1998);
   7. The promise of better legislative and institutional treatment of the Irish language and Ulster Scots – both of which became languages of record in the Assembly; and
   8. The promise of a civic forum, and 'participatory norms of governance', to facilitate the representation of voices that might not be heard purely through electoral or party mechanisms.[30]

D. *Veto rights for minorities and mutual veto rights.* These were evident in:

1. The legislative procedures in the Assembly which require 'key decisions' to be passed either with a *concurrent majority* (under the 'parallel consent' procedure) of registered nationalists and unionists, or with a *weighted majority* (60 per cent majority including the support of at least 40 per cent of registered nationalists and registered unionists);

2. The mutual interdependency of office-acquisition and maintenance by the First Minister and Deputy First Minister; and of the running of the Northern Ireland Assembly and the North-South Ministerial Council; and

3. The legal incorporation of the European Convention on Human Rights and Freedoms in UK public law and (the promise of) other legal enactments to give Northern Ireland a tailor-made Bill of Rights.

The Agreement led to a devolved government,[31] with full executive and legislative competence for economic development, education, health and social services, agriculture, environment and finance (including the local civil service), though plainly it is constrained by both UK and EU budgetary and other policies in these domains. Non-devolved powers remain with Westminster and the Secretary of State, who continues to be appointed by the UK Premier. The form of devolved government originally envisaged few limits on Northern Ireland's capacity to expand its autonomy. Through 'cross-community agreement' the Assembly is entitled to agree to expand its competencies; and, again through such agreement, and the consent of the Secretary of State and Westminster, the Assembly is empowered to legislate for non-devolved functions. Security functions, policing and the courts, were not devolved, but could be if sought by 'cross-community' consent. Maximum feasible autonomy was therefore within the scope of the local decision makers. A convention may have arisen in which the Secretary of State and Westminster 'rubber stamped' the legislative measures of the Assembly. Indeed public policy in Ireland, North and South, might eventually have been made without direct British ministerial involvement.

For these reasons and others had the Agreement been fully implemented and developed Northern Ireland would have become a specimen of what Elazar terms a 'federacy'.[32] A federal relationship exists where there are at least two tiers of government over the same territory, and when neither can unilaterally alter the constitutional capacities of the other. Such a relationship is a necessary element of a federal system, but whether it is sufficient is controversial. Normally a federation has sub-central units that are co-sovereign with the centre throughout most of the territory and population of the state. Plainly it would be premature to call New Labour's reconstructed UK a federation. But any system of constitutionally entrenched autonomy for one region makes the relationship between that region and the centre functionally equivalent to a federal relationship, and following Elazar, I call such a region – and its relationships with the centre – a federacy. The term 'federacy' captures how Irish nationalists understood the Agreement's institutions.

Through standard legislative majority rules the Assembly is empowered to pass 'normal laws', though there is provision for a minority, of 30 of the 108 members, to trigger procedures that require special majorities. Controversial legislation, 'key decisions', including the budget, require these special procedures demonstrating 'cross-community' support. Two rules, parallel consent and weighted majority, were designed for this purpose (see D1 above). There is also one super majority rule, which was not explicitly concurrent, cross-community or consociational. The Assembly is entitled by a two-third resolution of its membership, to call an extraordinary general election before its four-year term expires. This was agreed by the parties, after the Agreement, in preference to a proposal that the Secretary of State should have the power to dissolve the Assembly.

This distinctive consociation, or consociational federacy, as it would and should have become, challenges the conventional wisdom of the post-1945 political science of ethnonational questions. For a long time 'external' self-determination, in law and political science, as well as political practice, was accepted solely as a once only right of colonial territories. The Agreement was, in part, a striking rejection of this wisdom. It contained agreed procedures on how a border might be changed, or rather abolished. The Agreement accepted the legitimacy of an irredentist aspiration: the desire of the Irish nation in both parts of Ireland to unify in one state, though its realisation was made conditional upon the consent of majorities in both current jurisdictions, and the recognition of the aspiration was accompanied by the removal of an irredentist territorial claim-of-right in the 1937 Irish Constitution. The Agreement, like the negotiations that preceded it, contained recognition by the UK of the right of the people of Ireland, North and South, to exercise their self-determination to create a united Ireland. The UK has never officially recognised Northern Ireland as a colonial territory, but its employment of the language of self-determination in the making of the Agreement was an interesting departure. In addition, the Agreement established elaborate cross-border arrangements explicitly seen by nationalist parties as mechanisms to facilitate national reunification. Lastly, the Agreement contained features of an externally protected minority rights regime, a tacit 'double protection model' – laced with elements of co-sovereignty, and designed to withstand major demographic and electoral change. The UK and Irish governments promised to develop functionally equivalent legal protections of rights, collective and individual, on both sides of the present border, promising protection to Northern Irish nationalists now on the same terms that would be given to Ulster unionists if they ever become a minority in a unified Ireland. National communities were to be protected whether they were majorities or minorities, irrespective of the sovereign stateholder – whence the expression 'double protection'. The two governments affirmed that 'whatever choice is freely exercised by a majority of the people of Northern Ireland, the power of the sovereign government with jurisdiction there shall be exercised with *rigorous impartiality* on behalf of all the people in the diversity of their identities and traditions and shall be founded on the principles of full respect for, and equality of, civil, political, social and cultural rights, of freedom from discrimination for all citizens, and of *parity of esteem and of just and equal treatment* for the identity, ethos and aspirations of both communities' (*author's emphases*).

If conventional post-war political science was correct, then all these linkages, between an internal consociational settlement and measures that envisaged the possibility of a transformation in borders and of sovereignty regimes, should be the key sources of instability in the Agreement, raising expectations amongst a national minority and arousing deep fears amongst the local national majority. Indeed for nearly ten years after the collapse of the 1973–74 Sunningdale settlement it was an axiom of faith amongst UK policy-makers that an internal consociational agreement – power-sharing – should be reached without an external agreement – an Irish dimension. Alternatively, it was held that an internal agreement should precede an external agreement. This thinking was reversed in the making of the Anglo-Irish Agreement. Recognising that the absence of an Irish dimension facilitated republican militancy, the two governments established an inter-governmental conference, giving the Irish government unlimited rights of consultation over UK public policy on Northern Ireland, while encouraging the local parties to agree internal power-sharing. This combination of external and internal arrangements and incentives, 'coercive consociation', was unacceptable to unionists, in the short term. But since they could not destroy the Anglo-Irish Agreement, through strikes, paramilitarism, civil disobedience or conventional parliamentary tactics, unionists eventually negotiated the Belfast Agreement in return for the modification of what they regarded as deeply unsatisfactory external arrangements.

Northern nationalists certainly had their expectations raised, and unionists certainly had, and still have, anxieties about the Agreement's external dimensions, but both the making of the 1998 Agreement and its stalling in 2000 suggest that the post-war wisdom of political science needs revision. Consociational arrangements can be effectively combined with cross-border regimes, which enable a change in sovereignty, without engendering massive instability. The 'No Unionists' who rejected the Agreement did not like its external features, but they focused their rhetorical fire on the prospects of gunmen getting into (the internal) government, terrorists being released early from jail, the failure to secure the decommissioning of (republican) paramilitaries' weapons, and on those parts of the Agreement, including proposed policing arrangements, which implied the full equality of nationalists with unionists within Northern Ireland. By contrast the 'Yes

Unionists' trumpet some of the external aspects of the Agreement, pointing out that the Agreement had led to changes in the Irish Republic's constitution, which now requires the active consent of majorities in both parts of Ireland before Irish unification, and claiming that they had 'negotiated away' the Anglo-Irish Agreement of 1985. 'Yes Unionists' defend the cross-border institutions as minimal rational functional co-operation between neighbouring states, and observe, correctly, that they had succeeded in trimming down the more ambitious cross-border institutions advocated by the Irish government, the SDLP and by Sinn Féin. In short, the primary unionist concerns with the Agreement, and which materially contributed to its unilateral partial suspension by the UK in February 2000, and its current instability, cannot reasonably be said to have lain with its external dimensions.

Con/federalising Arrangements

Confederations exist when political units delegate powers and functions to bodies that can exercise power across their jurisdictions, while retaining veto and opt-out rights. Two confederal relationships were established under the Agreement: the North-South Ministerial Council and the British-Irish Council.

The North-South Ministerial Council (NSMC) brings together those with executive responsibilities in Northern Ireland and in the Republic. Nationalists were concerned that if the Assembly could outlast the NSMC, it would provide incentives for unionists to undermine the latter. Unionists, by contrast, worried that if the NSMC could survive the destruction of the Assembly, nationalists would seek to bring this about. The Agreement was a tightly written contract. Internal consociation and all-Ireland external confederalism went together: the Assembly and the NSMC were made 'mutually interdependent'; one could not function without the other. Unionists were unable to destroy the NSMC while retaining the Assembly, and nationalists were not able to destroy the Assembly while keeping the NSMC. The NSMC satisfactorily linked northern nationalists to their preferred nation-state. The Irish government successfully recommended a change in its constitution to ensure that the NSMC, and its delegated implementation bodies, would be able to exercise island-wide jurisdiction in those functional activities where unionists were willing to co-operate. The NSMC functions much like the Council of Ministers in the European Union, with ministers having considerable discretion to reach decisions, but ultimately accountable to their respective legislatures. The NSMC meets in plenary format twice a year, and in smaller groups to discuss specific sectors on a 'regular and frequent basis'. Provision was made for the Council to discuss matters that cut across sectors, and to resolve disagreements. In addition, the Agreement provided for 'implementation' bodies. The scope of these institutions was somewhat open-ended. The Agreement, however, required a meaningful Council. It stated that the Council *'will'* (not 'may') identify at least six matters, where 'existing bodies' will be the appropriate mechanisms for co-operation within each separate jurisdiction, and at least six matters where co-operation will take place through implementation bodies. The latter were subsequently agreed to be inland waterways, food safety, trade and business development, special EU programmes, the Irish and Ulster Scots languages, and aquaculture and marine matters. The parties further agreed on six functional areas of co-operation – including some aspects of transport, agriculture, education, health, the environment and tourism, where a joint North-South public company was established.

The NSMC differed from the Council of Ireland of 1974. The name change was significant: a concession to unionist sensibilities. There was no provision for a joint parliamentary forum but the Northern Assembly and the Irish *Oireachtas* were asked 'to consider' one. Nationalists wanted the NSMC established by legislation from Westminster and the *Oireachtas* – to emphasise its autonomy from the Northern Assembly. Unionists wanted it established by the Northern Assembly and its counterpart in Dublin. The Agreement split these differences. The NSMC and the implementation bodies were brought into existence by British and Irish legislation, but during the transitional period it was for the Northern executive and the Republic's government to decide how co-operation should take place, and in what areas the North-South institutions should co-operate. Once agreed, the Assembly was unable to change these agreements – except by cross-community consent. The signatories to the Agreement promised to work 'in good faith' to bring the NSMC into being. There was not, however, sufficient good faith to prevent the first material break in the timetable scheduled in the Agreement occurring over the NSMC – but this was patently a by-product of the crisis over executive formation and decommissioning. The signatories were required to use 'best endeavours' to reach agreement and to make 'determined efforts' to overcome disagreements over functions where there is a 'mutual cross-border and all-island benefit'.

A second weaker confederal relationship was established, affecting all the islands of Britain and Ireland.[33] Under the new British-Irish Council (BIC) the two governments of the sovereign states, and all the devolved governments and neighbouring insular dependent territories of the UK, can meet, agree to delegate functions, and may agree common policies. This proposal met unionists' concerns for reciprocity in linkages – and provides a mechanism through which they might in future be linked to the UK even if Northern Ireland becomes part of the Republic. Unionists originally wanted the NSMC subordinated to a British-Irish, or East-West, Council. This did not happen. There is no hierarchical relationship between the two Councils. Two textual warrants suggest that the NSMC is more far-reaching than the BIC. The Agreement required the establishment of North-South implementation bodies, leaving the formation of East-West bodies a voluntary matter, and stated explicitly that the Assembly and NSMC were interdependent, making no equivalent provision for the BIC.

The Agreement opened other linkages for Northern Ireland, one within the UK, and another possibility with the Republic, which held federalist as opposed to confederalist promise. The Agreement, unlike Scottish and Welsh devolution, was embedded in a treaty between two states, based on the UK's recognition of Irish national self-determination. The UK officially acknowledged that Northern Ireland has the right to join the Republic, on the basis of a local referendum, and it recognised, in a treaty, the authority of Irish national self-determination throughout the island of Ireland. The Agreement's institutions were brought into being by the will of the people of Ireland, North and South, and not just by the people of Northern Ireland – recall the referendums and the interdependence of the NSMC and the Assembly. In consequence, under the Agreement, the UK's relationship to Northern Ireland, at least in international law, in my view, has an explicitly federal character: Northern Ireland had become a federacy. The Westminster parliament and executive could not, except through breaking its treaty obligations, and except through denying Irish national self-determination, exercise power in any manner that affected Northern Ireland's autonomy inconsistent with the Agreement. The author first composed this last sentence immediately after the Agreement was made. Plainly the suspension of the Agreement by Mandelson in February 2000 showed that the UK's authorities did not feel constrained by its reasoning.

The Agreement also opened federalist avenues in the Republic – one of the most centralised states in Europe. The Irish government and its people did not abandon Irish unification. Instead it became 'the firm will of the Irish nation, in harmony and friendship, to unite all the people who share the territory of the island of Ireland, in all the diversity of their identities and traditions, recognising that a united Ireland shall be brought about only by peaceful means with the consent of a majority of the people expressed, in both jurisdictions in the island' (from the new Article 3). Irish unification cannot be precluded because of present demographic and electoral trends – which have led to a steady rise in the nationalist share of the vote across different electoral systems. The unification envisaged in the re-drafted Irish Constitution is, however, now different. It no longer resembles a programme of assimilation. The Republic is bound to structure its laws to prepare for the possibility of a con/federal as well as a unitary Ireland. Northern Ireland is a recognised legal entity within the Irish Constitution, and its elimination as a political unit is no longer a programmatic feature of *Bunreacht na hEireann* (Constitution of Ireland).

Externally Protecting the Agreement

The two states signed a treaty and created two intergovernmental devices to protect their respective national communities. The most important was the successor to the Anglo-Irish Agreement's, viz. the new British-Irish inter-governmental conference (BIGC) that guarantees the Republic's government access to policy formulation on all matters not (yet) devolved to the Northern Assembly or the NSMC. The Irish government retains rights of consultation in those Northern Irish matters that have not been devolved to the Assembly, as was the case under Article 4 of the Anglo-Irish Agreement, and as with that agreement, there continues to be an intergovernmental conference, chaired by the Minister for Foreign Affairs and the Northern Ireland Secretary of State, to deal with non-devolved matters, and it continues to be serviced by a standing secretariat. The new Agreement, moreover, promised to 'intensify co-operation' between the two governments on all-island or cross-border aspects of rights, justice, prison and policing (unless and until these matters are devolved). There is provision for representatives of the Assembly to be involved in the intergovernmental conference – a welcome parliamentarisation – but they will not have the same status as the representatives of the governments of the sovereign states. The Anglo-Irish Agreement fully anticipated these arrangements, so it is as accurate to claim that it has been fulfilled as to say it has been deleted.

Formal joint sovereignty over Northern Ireland was not established, but the governments guaranteed the Agreement, and embedded it in an international treaty. Irish officials had been wary since the early 1990s of trading likely irreversible constitutional changes in exchange for institutions that might share the same fate as the Sunningdale settlement. That is why they argued that the Agreement should be incorporated in a treaty. The official Irish belief, and the Irish nationalist belief, was that the Agreement, like Northern Ireland's constitutional choice between membership of the UK and the Republic, now rested on the consent of the Irish people, through the joint act of self-determination of the North and South. The UK government would not, on this view, have the authority to do anything that was not legitimate under the Agreement's procedures. The UK government, under Mowlam, shared this understanding. Under Mandelson it did not. In February 2000 Mandelson obtained from the UK Parliament emergency statutory powers to suspend the Assembly and Executive. In doing so he acted in classic Diceyian fashion, using the doctrine of parliamentary sovereignty to arrogate to himself the power of suspension – which had not been granted in the making of the Agreement, or in its (UK) legislative enactment. The UK government's officials knew that suspension would breach the formal Agreement – because in the summer of 1999, when both governments contemplated a suspension mechanism, Mowlam's officials proposed that the treaty that was about to be signed by the two governments, which incorporated the Belfast Agreement, should be amended, to make it compatible with suspension. No such amendment was made.

Mandelson's justification of suspension in February 2000 was that it was necessary to save the First Minister, David Trimble. His threat to resign because the IRA had not delivered on decommissioning, in advance of the deadline mandated by the Agreement, would have become operative in an environment in which 'Yes Unionists' no longer commanded an absolute majority of the registered unionists in the Assembly.[34] Therefore, it was feared, Trimble could not have been resurrected as First Minister if he did resign. This reasoning was false: the Assembly, by weighted majority, was entitled to pass any measure to amend its current rules for electing the dual premiers, and to send this measure to Westminster for statutory ratification. So there was a mechanism, within the Agreement, under which Trimble could have regained the position of First Minister. But even if Mandelson's justification was true, which it was not, for the reason just given, the suspension was an unconstitutional and a partisan act. It was unconstitutional in Irish eyes because the suspensory power had not been endorsed with cross-community consent through the negotiation of the Agreement, or in the referendums, or in the UK's legislative enactment of the Agreement. It was partisan because neither the Agreement, nor the Mitchell Review of the Agreement that took place in late 1999, required Sinn Féin to deliver decommissioning by the IRA because of a new deadline set by the leader of the UUP. The then formally agreed deadline for decommissioning required all political parties to use their best endeavours to achieve full decommissioning by 22 May 2000.

One passage of the Agreement referred to procedures for review if difficulties arose across the range of institutions established on the entering into force of the international treaty: 'If difficulties arise which require remedial action across the range of institutions, or otherwise require amendment of the British-Irish Agreement or relevant legislation, *the process of review will fall to the two governments in consultation with the parties in the Assembly. Each government will be responsible for action in its own jurisdiction*' (italics mine). The italicised passages, read in conjunction with the whole Agreement, suggest that the UK government was obligated formally to consult the parties in the Assembly and the Irish government over obtaining any power of suspension, and that any remedial action required the joint support of the two governments, especially as regards their treaty. That each government would be 'responsible for action in its own jurisdiction' was not taken by the Irish side to mean that the Westminster Parliament had unilateral discretion to alter, amend, suspend or abolish the institutions of the Agreement. It merely meant that for agreed remedial action there would not be joint sovereignty but rather parallel legislative procedures.

The central purpose of the UK's agreement to delete section 75 of the Government of Ireland Act of 1920, and of the Irish state's agreement to modify Articles 2 and 3 of the Irish Constitution, had been to show that both states were engaged in 'balanced' constitutional change, confirming that Northern Ireland's status as part of the UK or the Republic rested with its people alone. The UK's Diceyians, including Ulster Unionists, have obviously interpreted the UK's deletion of section 75 of the Government of Ireland Act as meaningless because in their eyes Parliament's sovereignty remains intact in a given domain even when it removes a statutory statement which says it remains intact! Irish negotiators obviously should have been more careful: the UK's 'constitution' is Ireland's British problem. Had the Agreement fully bedded down perhaps Northern Ireland status as a federacy would have developed the status of a constitutional convention – the UK's mysterious functional poor cousin of constitutionality.

The suspension had four messages. First, it made plain that every aspect of the Agreement is vulnerable to Westminster's sovereignty. Everything in the Agreement – its institutions, its confidence building measures, its commissions, the promise that Irish unification will take place if there is majority consent for it in both parts of Ireland – is revisable by the current Parliament, and any future Parliament, and that Parliament's Secretaries of State, irrespective of international law, or the solemn promises made by UK negotiators in the making of, the Agreement. No UK parliamentarian can look an Irish nationalist or republican in the eye and say that Northern Ireland's status and its institutional arrangements rest upon the consent of its people. By its actions the Westminster Parliament has affirmed that it regards its sovereignty as unconstrained by the Agreement. Had it sought and obtained the assent of the Northern Assembly – by cross-community consent – to its possession of the power of the suspension that would have been a different matter. It did not. Even if the Secretary of State's motives were entirely benign – and that has been questioned – his decision to obtain the power of suspension destroyed the assumptions of nearly a decade of negotiation.

Second, the suspension spells out to official Irish negotiators, and Northern nationalists, the necessity, in any new round of major negotiations, of entrenching Northern Ireland's status as a 'federacy', perhaps in the same manner as the UK's courts are instructed to make European law supreme over law(s) made by the Westminster Parliament, through full domestic incorporation and entrenchment of the relevant treaty. Without such protection the Agreement cannot be constitutionalised consistently with Irish national self-determination, North and South. This will require Ireland's negotiators to require Westminster to repeal the suspension Act and to declare that its sovereignty is circumscribed by the Agreement.

Third, unionists must, eventually, consider the constitutional consequences of suspension. The 'Yes Unionists' embrace of the doctrine of parliamentary sovereignty forgets that they may one day suffer from the consequences of the sword they urged Westminster to deploy. What Westminster did on unionists' behalf it may take from them tomorrow –

including membership of the Union. Mandelson's action means that the Union does not rest on the consent of its component parts, but rather upon Westminster's say so: Westminster is free to modify the Union in any way it likes, for example, through full-scale joint sovereignty over Northern Ireland with the Republic, or through expelling Northern Ireland from its jurisdiction.

Lastly, the suspension spells a blunt warning to the Scottish Parliament and the Welsh Assembly – bodies created with smaller proportions of popular support and lower electoral turn-outs than their Northern Irish counterpart. Sovereignty remains indivisibly in Westminster's possession: even under 'modernising' New Labour.

The Dual Premiership

Among its institutional novelties the Agreement established two quasi-presidential figures, a dyarchy, to preside over an Executive formed through the d'Hondt allocation process.[35] An executive presidency is an executive that cannot be destroyed by an assembly except through impeachment; the dual premiership has presidential characteristics because it is almost impossible to depose the two office-holders, provided they remain united as a team, until the next general election. The First and Deputy First Minister are elected together by the *parallel consent procedure*, an idea that flowed out of the making of the Agreement which required propositions to have the support of a majority of parties, including parties representing a majority of nationalists and of unionists. The carry-over of this concurrent rule of negotiation into the election of the two premiers gave very strong incentives to unionists and nationalists to nominate a candidate for one of these positions that was acceptable to a majority of the other bloc's members. It also meant that the respective unionist and nationalist moderates were guaranteeing their control of these positions. In the first elections for these posts in *designate* or *shadow* form pro-Agreement unionists in the UUP and the Progressive Unionist Party, who between them then had a majority of registered unionists (thirty out of fifty-eight), voted solidly for the combination of David Trimble of the UUP and Seamus Mallon of the SDLP. Naturally so did the SDLP, which enjoyed a majority among registered nationalists (twenty-four out of forty-two). (The 'No Unionists' voted against this combination, while Sinn Féin abstained).

The Agreement and its UK legislative enactment, the Northern Ireland Act (1998), made clear that both posts had identical symbolic and external representation functions; indeed both have identical powers; the sole difference is in their titles: both preside over the 'Executive Committee' of Ministers, and have a role in co-ordinating its work. Their implicit and explicit co-ordinating functions, as approved by the Shadow Assembly, were elaborated in February 1999. A Department of the First and Deputy

First Ministers was created. It was to have an Economic Policy Unit, and an Equality Unit, and was tasked with liaising with the NSMC, the BIC, and the Secretary of State on reserved and excepted UK powers, EU/International matters, and cross-departmental co-ordination.

The prime ministerial dyarchy is quasi-presidential, because neither the First nor the Deputy First Minister formally appoint the other Ministers to the Executive – save where one of them is a party leader entitled to nominate the Ministries to which his party is entitled. Posts in the Executive are allocated to parties in proportion to their strength in the Assembly, according to a mechanical rule, the d'Hondt rule. The rule's consequences were simple: any party that won a significant share of seats and was willing to abide by the new rules established by the Agreement had a reasonable chance of access to the Executive. It creates a voluntary grand coalition government because parties are free to exclude themselves from the Executive Committee, and because no programme of government has to be negotiated in advance. The design created strong incentives for parties to take their entitlement to ministries because if they did not the seats would go either to their ethno-national rivals or to competitors in their own bloc.

This dual premiership critically depends upon the personal co-operation of the two holders of these posts, and upon the co-operation of their respective majorities (or pluralities – under the weighted majority rule). The Northern Ireland Act (1998) reinforced their interdependence by requiring that 'if either the First Minister or the Deputy First Minister ceases to hold office, whether by resignation or otherwise, the other shall also cease to hold office' (Article 14 (6)). This power of resignation has been strategically deployed by both elected office holders.

In the summer of 1999 the SDLP's Mallon resigned as Deputy First Minister (designate), complaining that the UUP were 'dishonouring' the Agreement, and 'insulting its principles' by insisting upon decommissioning before executive formation. He did so to speed an inter-governmental review of the implementation of the Agreement. The question immediately arose: did Mallon's resignation automatically trigger Trimble's departure from office, and require fresh elections to these positions within six weeks? The Initial Presiding Officer's answer to this question was that it did not, because the Assembly was not yet functioning under the Northern Ireland Act. This answer was accepted, and in November 1999 Mallon's resignation was subsequently rescinded with the assent of the Assembly with no requirement that the two men would have to re-stand for office.

Shortly afterwards, however, when the Assembly and Executive came fully 'on line' in November 1999, and ceased to be in designate form, David Trimble was to use the threat of resignation, helping thereby to precipitate the suspension of February 2000. He wrote a post-dated resignation letter to the chairman of his party who was authorised to deliver it to the Secretary of State if Sinn Féin failed to achieve IRA movement on the decommissioning of its weapons – in the form of 'product' – within a specified period after the Ulster Unionist Party had agreed to full-scale executive formation. As we have seen, the fear that this resignation would become operative was the proximate cause of the Secretary of State's decision to suspend the Assembly.

How should we appraise the executive design in the Agreement? The skill of the designers/negotiators was to create strong incentives for executive power-sharing and power-division, but without requiring parties to have any prior formal coalition agreement – other than the institutional agreement – and without requiring any party to renounce its long-run aspirations. The dual premiership, by contrast, was designed to tie moderate representatives of each bloc together, and to give some drive towards overall policy coherence. It was intended to strengthen moderates and to give them significant steering powers over the rest of the executive. The d'Hondt mechanism, by contrast, ensured inclusivity and was carefully explained to the public as achieving precisely that. Distinctive coalitions could form around different issues within the Executive, permitting flexibility, but inhibiting chaos (given the requirement that the budget be agreed by cross-community consent).

In these respects and others the Agreement differed positively from the Sunningdale experiment of 1973. Yet the Executive, and the dual premiership in particular, have proven unstable – and for reasons that go beyond the holders' personalities. Two causes have mattered: the precariousness of the 'Yes Unionist' bloc, and the potency of the resignation weapon available to each premier. Arguably the inter-moderate party deal was a weak spot in institutional design. Had the first and deputy first premiership been allocated according to the d'Hondt procedure, and had parties which threatened not to take up their Executive seats, simply lost access to Executive power, then there would have been very strong incentives for the Executive to be sustained, especially if the Secretary of State had decided to take a hands-off approach to any threats of non-participation in the Executive.

Using the d'Hondt rule to allocate the dual premierships, with the same Mitchell-inspired ministerial pledge of office, perhaps modified by a rule that one premiership had to go to the unionist party with the highest number of seats and the other to the nationalist party with the highest number of seats, would, however, have had the consequence of making more likely the future success of harder-line party leaders, such as Paisley or Adams. That, of course, was one motivation behind the construction of the dual premiership. However, the prospect feared by the moderates may not have spelled disaster: the prospect of the highest offices might have further moderated the stances of the respective hard-line parties. It is a heretical thought.

What was not foreseen was that failure to timetable the formation of the rest of the Executive immediately after the election of the premiers would precipitate a protracted crisis of executive-formation. Trimble availed of this loophole to prevent executive formation until November 1999. If the Agreement survives, amendments to the Northern Ireland Act (1998) could be adopted by the UK Parliament, or by the Assembly, to prevent any recurrence of this type of crisis. In future candidates for First and Deputy First Minister could be obliged to state the number of executive portfolios that will be available, and the formation of the Executive should be required immediately after their election. That would plug this particular constitutional hole. It may, however, be unnecessary. It is unlikely that future candidates for First and Deputy First Minister will agree to be nominated without a firm agreement on the number of portfolios and the date of cabinet formation.

The crisis of executive formation, which dogged the implementation of the Agreement between June 1998 and November 1999, arose for political and constitutional reasons. Trimble insisted that Sinn Féin deliver some IRA decommissioning before its members would take their seats in the Executive: 'no government before guns'. Under the text of the Agreement, Trimble had no warrant to exercise this veto:

1. No party can veto another party's membership of the Executive, though the Assembly as a whole, through cross-community consent, may deem a party unfit for office (it has not done so).
2. The Agreement did not specify a starting date for decommissioning though it did require parties to use their best endeavours to achieve the completion of decommissioning within two years, that is, by 22 May 2000;
3. Any natural reading of the Agreement mandated executive formation as the first step in bringing all the Agreement's institutions 'on line'.

Trimble's concern was to appease critics of the Agreement within his own party, and he was initially facilitated in exercising this tacit veto by the UK and Irish governments who were sympathetic to his exposed position. One flexible provision in the Agreement gave Trimble time to stall. The Agreement stated that there must be at least six 'other Ministers', but that there can be 'up to' ten. The number of ministries was to be decided by cross-community consent and that gave an opportunity to delay executive formation. It would be December 1998 before the parties reached agreement on ten ministries.

In mid-November 1999 it looked as if the crisis over executive formation would finally be resolved. The UUP accepted that the running of the d'Hondt procedure to fill the cabinet could occur after the *process* of decommissioning began – with the IRA appointing an interlocutor to negotiate with the IICD – while actual decommissioning, consistent with the text of the Agreement, would not be required until after executive formation. Senator Mitchell in concluding his Review of the Agreement, and with the consent of the pro-Agreement parties, stated that 'Devolution should take effect, then the executive should meet, and then the paramilitary groups should appoint their authorised representatives, all on the same day, in that order'. This was an honourable resolution to what looked like becoming a fundamental impasse – though the Ulster Unionist Council fatefully rendered it problematic. To get their support Trimble offered the previously cited post-dated resignation letter to become operative within a specified period not negotiated under the Mitchell Review. The IRA did not deliver, at least not in the way that Mandelson believed was required; suspensory powers were obtained and used. Had the Agreement been followed to the letter the parties in the Assembly could have determined by cross-community consent that Sinn Féin and the PUP were not fit for office because they had not used their best endeavours to achieve comprehensive decommissioning. That avenue was not deployed.

Suspension did not completely save Trimble from the wrath of his party: 43 per cent of whom voted for a stalking horse to replace him, the Reverend Martin Smyth MP. Trimble remained leader but bound by a mandate for reformation of the Executive that neither the UK government or republicans seemed likely to deliver. The 'Yes Unionists' had failed decisively to rout the 'No Unionists', partly through misjudgement and mismanagement, and partly through the over-representation of 'No' and 'soft Yes' unionists amongst the UUP's activists as opposed to its voters. Their failure was, of course, rendered more likely by the republican position on decommissioning. They were locked in a ghetto of insecurity – determined that, at best, the decommissioning of their weapons would be the last or joint last act of implementation.

In May 2000, however, republicans promised to deliver a 'confidence-building measure', viz. inspections of some of the IRA's arms dumps, by two international observers, Cyril Rhamaposa, the former ANC negotiator, and Marti Ahtisaari, the former Finnish General and Premier. It also seemed clear that they would re-engage with the Independent IICD. In return Trimble promised to lift his resignation threat and Mandelson took the Executive and Assembly out of suspended animation. It was agreed that completing decommissioning be delayed for one year. Republicans appeared to be engaging in the decommissioning process in return for the restoration of the Executive, side-payments for their prisoners and those still facing extradition, and for assurances on demilitarisation and police reform: Mandelson appeared vindicated in the eyes of his supporters. Blair gave assurances that the UK government would implement the Patten Commission's proposals on policing, which Trimble was known to oppose. Trimble warned republicans to engage with the IICD; republicans warned Mandelson to deliver on his obligations under the Agreement, and that takes us to the present crisis over executive maintenance and policing reform.

Policing Reform and Spinning out of Control[36]

The institution building of the Belfast Agreement was flanked by confidence building processes involving ceasefires by paramilitaries, the release of their incarcerated prisoners, and commitments to protect human rights, entrench equality, demilitarise the region, assist in decommissioning, and the reform of the administration of justice and policing. As I write just four of these items await full or effective beginnings in implementation: decommissioning by paramilitaries; the reform of the system of criminal justice; demilitarisation; and policing reform. These items are inter-linked. Full demilitarisation and full decommissioning are mutually interdependent. And decommissioning is seen in republican circles as conditional on the UK government fulfilling its promises to implement the Patten Report on policing, given in May 2000.

The Labour government initially welcomed the Patten Report for charting 'the way forward in the interests of all'. Blair, Mandelson, and the 'Explanatory Notes' issued by the Northern Ireland Office accompanying the Police Bill put before the UK Parliament in the spring of 2000, flatly declared their intention to give effect to Patten's 175 recommendations. That was not true, and is still manifestly not true. The UK government also implied, usually in off-the-record briefings, that it could not implement the Patten Report in full because of the 'security situation'. This position, in dissembling contradiction with its official one, would have had credibility if the necessary preparatory steps to implement Patten in full when the security situation was satisfactory had been taken. They were not.[37]

Policing was so controversial that the parties to the Agreement could not concur on future arrangements.[38] They did agree the terms of reference of a Commission, eventually chaired by Christopher Patten, a former minister in the region and now a European Commissioner. To have effective police rooted in, and legitimate with, both major communities was vital to the settlement. Eight criteria for policing arrangements were mandated in the Commission's terms of reference. They were to be impartial; representative; free from partisan political control; efficient and effective; infused with a human rights culture; decentralised; democratically accountable 'at all levels'; and consistent with the letter and the spirit of the Agreement. The Patten Commission engaged in extensive research and interaction with the affected parties, interest groups and citizens, and published its report in September 1999. It did not, and could not, meet the hopes, or match the fears, of all, but the Commissioners undoubtedly met their terms of reference.[39]

The Patten Report was a thorough, careful and imaginative compromise between unionists who maintained that the existing RUC already met the terms of reference of the Agreement and those nationalists, especially republicans, who maintained that the RUC's record mandated its disbanding. However the Police Bill presented to Parliament in the spring of 2000 was an evisceration of Patten, and condemned as such by the SDLP, Sinn Féin, the Women's Coalition, the Catholic Church, and non-governmental and human rights organisations, such as the Committee on the Administration of Justice. It was also criticised by the Irish government, the US House of Representatives (H. Res 447, 106th Congress), and Irish Americans, including President Clinton.[40] The veracity of the critics' complaints can be demonstrated by comparing some of Patten's recommendations with the original Bill:

1. Patten recommended a neutral name, the Northern Ireland Police Service. The Royal Ulster Constabulary was not a neutral title so it was recommended to go. Patten also recommended that the display of the Union flag and the portrait of the Queen at police stations should go. Symbols should be 'free from association with the British or Irish states'. These recommendations were a consequence of Patten's terms of reference, the Agreement's explicit commitment to establishing 'parity of esteem' between the national traditions, and the UK's solemn commitment to 'rigorous impartiality' in its administration. The original Bill, by contrast, proposed that the Secretary of State have the power to decide on the issues of names and emblems.

2. Patten recommended affirmative action to change rapidly the proportion of cultural Catholics in the police. Even critics of affirmative action recognised the need to correct the existing imbalance – in which over 90 per cent of the police are local cultural Protestants. The original Bill reduced the period in which the police would be recruited on a 50:50 ratio of cultural Catholics and cultural Protestants from ten to three years, requiring the Secretary of State to make any extension, and was silent on 'aggregation', the proposed policy for shortfalls in the recruitment of suitably qualified cultural Catholics.

3. Patten proposed a Policing Board consisting of ten representatives from political parties, in proportion to their shares of seats on the Executive, and nine members nominated by the First and Deputy First Ministers. These recommendations guaranteed a politically representative board in which neither unionists nor nationalists would have partisan control. The original Bill introduced a requirement that the Board should operate according to a weighted majority when recommending an inquiry, tantamount to giving unionist and unionist-nominated members a veto over inquiries, i.e. partisan political control, and a direct violation of Patten's terms of reference.

4. Patten avoided false economies when recommending a downsizing of the service, advocated a strong Board empowered to set performance targets, and proposed enabling local District Policing

Partnership Boards to engage in the market testing of police effectiveness. The original Bill empowered the Secretary of State, not the Board, to set performance targets, made no statutory provision for disbanding the police reserve, and deflated the proposed District Policing Partnership Boards, because of assertions that they would lead to paramilitaries being subsidised by tax-payers.

5. Patten proposed that new and serving officers should have knowledge of human rights built into their training, and re-training, and their codes of practice. In addition to the European Convention, due to become part of UK domestic law, the Commission held out international norms as benchmarks (Patten, 1999, para 5.17). Patten's proposals for normalising the police – through merging the special branch into criminal investigations – and demilitarising the police met the Agreement's human rights objectives. The original Bill was a parody. The new oath was to be confined to new officers. No standards of rights higher than those in the European Convention were to be incorporated into police training and practice. Responsibility for a Code of Ethics was left with the Chief Constable. Patten's proposed requirement that the oath of service 'respect the traditions and beliefs of people' was excluded. Normalisation and demilitarisation were left unclear in the Bill and the Implementation Plan.

6. Patten envisaged enabling local governments to influence the Policing Board through their own District Policing Partnership Boards, and giving the latter powers 'to purchase additional services from the police or statutory agencies, or from the private sector', and matching police internal management units to local government districts. The original Bill, by contrast, maintained or strengthened centralisation: the Secretary of State obtained powers that Patten proposed for the First and Deputy First Ministers and the Board, and powers to issue instructions to District Policing Partnership Boards; and neither the Bill nor the Implementation Plan implemented Patten's proposed experiment in community policing.

7. Patten envisaged a strong, independent and powerful Board to hold the police to account, and to replace the discredited Policy Authority (Patten, 1999: para 6.23). The police would have 'operational responsibility' but he held to account by a powerful Board, and required to interact with the Human Rights Commission, the Ombudsman and the Equality Commission. The Bill watered down Patten's proposals, empowering the Secretary of State to oversee and veto the Board's powers, empowering the Chief Constable to refuse to respond to reasonable requests from the Board, and preventing the Board from making inquiries into past misconduct.

8. Patten was consistent with the terms of reference and spirit of the Belfast Agreement. The original Bill was not, being incompatible with the 'parity of esteem' and 'rigorous impartiality' in administration promised by the UK government. Manifestly it would not encourage 'widespread community support' since it fell far short of the compromise that moderate nationalists had accepted and that Patten had proposed to mark a 'new beginning'.

What explains the radical discrepancy between the Patten Report and the original Bill? The short answer is that the Northern Ireland Office's officials under Mandelson's supervision drafted the Bill. They appeared to 'forget' that the terms of reference came from the Belfast Agreement, and that Patten's recommendations represented a rigorous compromise between unionists and nationalists. They treated the Patten Report as a nationalist report, which they had to modify as benign mediators. Although Patten warned against 'cherry picking' the Secretary of State and his officials believed that they had the right to implement what they found acceptable, and to leave aside what they found unacceptable, premature, or likely to cause difficulties for pro-Agreement unionists or the RUC. The Bill suggested that the UK government was: determined to avoid the police being subject to rigorous democratic accountability; deeply distrustful of the capacity of the local parties to manage policing at any level; and concerned to minimise the difficulties that the partial implementation of Patten would occasion for Trimble, by minimising radical change to mere reforms of the RUC.

Under pressure Mandelson beat a partial retreat, whether to a position prepared in advance only others can know. Some have speculated that he designed an obviously defective Bill so that nationalists would then be mollified by subsequent improvements. That is to make the characteristic error of endowing him with greater political intelligence than his record suggests: all that the defective Bill achieved, according to Mallon, was to 'shatter already fragile faith in the government's commitment to police reform'.

Accusing his critics of 'hype', 'rhetoric', and 'hyperbole' Mandelson promised to 'listen' and to modify the Bill. He declared that he might have been too cautious in the powers granted to the Policing Board. Indeed the government was subsequently to accept over sixty SDLP-driven amendments to bring the Bill more into line with Patten. The Bill was improved in the Commons and Lords, but insufficiently. The quota for the recruitment of cultural Catholics is now better protected. The Policing Board has been given power over the setting of short-run objectives, and final responsibility for the police's code of ethics. Consultation procedures involving the Ombudsman and the Equality Commission have been strengthened, and the First and Deputy First Ministers will now be consulted over the appointment of non-party members to the Board. The weighted majority provisions for an inquiry by the Board have gone. Yet any honest appraisal of the Act must report that it is still not the whole Patten; it rectifies some of the original Bill's more overt deviations, but on the crucial issues of symbolic neutrality and police accountability, vital for a 'new beginning' it remains at odds with Patten's explicit recommendations.[41]

Symbolic neutrality

Patten wanted a police rooted in both communities, not just one. That is why he recommended that the name of the service be *entirely* new: The Northern Ireland Police Service. The Act, because of a government decision to accept an amendment tabled by the UUP, styles the service 'The Police Service of Northern Ireland (incorporating the Royal Ulster Constabulary)'. The Secretary of State promised an amendment to define 'for operational purposes', to ensure that the full title would rarely be used, and that the parenthetic past generally be excluded. He broke this commitment at Report Stage. Mandelson was mendaciously misleading in declaring that he was merely following Patten's wishes that the new service be connected to the old and avoid suggestions of disbanding. Patten proposed an entirely new and fresh name, and proposed linkages between the old and new services through police memorials, and *not* the re-naming adopted by the government. We will see whether, as critics fear, there develops a police with two names, the Police Service and the RUC, just as Northern Ireland's second city has two names, Derry and Londonderry.

Patten unambiguously recommended that the police's new badge and emblems be free of association with the British or Irish states, and that the Union flag should not fly from police buildings. The Act postpones these matters. Avoiding responsibility, the government has passed the parcel to the local parties to reach agreement while providing reassuring but vague words in Hansard. Since Mandelson had already ruled that only the Union Jack, albeit just on specified days, should fly over the buildings of the devolved administration, nationalists lacked faith that he would deliver on cultural neutrality and impartiality.

Why do these symbolic issues matter? Simply because the best way to win widespread acceptance for police reform was to confirm Patten's promised new beginning by following his proposed strategy of symbolic neutrality.[42] Full re-naming and symbolic neutrality would spell a double message: that the new police are to be everyone's, and the new police are no longer to be primarily the unionists' police. This symbolic shift would mightily assist in obtaining representative cultural Catholic recruitment and in winning consent for the new order amongst nationalists as well as unionists. Not to follow Patten's recommendations in these respects has spelled a double message: that the new police is the old RUC re-touched, and linked more to British than Irish identity, i.e. a recipe for the status quo ante.

Oversight and accountability

Patten recommended an Oversight Commissioner to 'supervise the implementation of our recommendations'. The Labour government – under pressure – put the Commissioner's office on a statutory basis, which it did not intend to do originally, but confined his role to overseeing changes 'decided by the government'. Had Mandelson and his colleagues been committed to Patten they would have charged the Commissioner with recommending, now or in the future, any legislative and management changes necessary for the full and effective implementation of the Patten Report. That they refused to do so speaks volumes. Patten recommended a Policing Board to hold the police to account, and to initiate inquiries into police conduct and practices. Mandelson in effect prevented the Board from inquiring into any act or omission arising before the eventual Act applies. This was tantamount to an undeclared amnesty for past police misconduct, not proposed by Patten. Personally I have no objections to an open amnesty, but this step was dishonest, and makes it much less likely that 'rotten apples' will be rooted out, as promised. The Secretary of State will additionally have the authority to approve or veto the person appointed to conduct any present or future inquiry (clause 58 (9)). Patten also recommended that the Ombudsman should have significant powers (Patten, 1999: para 6.42) and should 'exercise the right to investigate and comment on police policies and practices', whereas in the Act the Ombudsman may make reports, but not investigate (so it is not a crime to obstruct her work). The Ombudsman is additionally restricted in her retrospective powers (clause 62), again circumscribing the police's accountability for past misconduct.

Mandelson suggested his critics are petty, arguing that they are ungrateful, pointing out just how much he has done to implement Patten, and how radical Patten is by comparison with elsewhere. This 'spin' is utterly unconvincing. The proposed arrangements effectively seal off past, present and future avenues through which the police might be held to account for misconduct, e.g. in colluding with loyalist paramilitaries or covering up assassinations; and are recipes for leaving the police outside the effective ambit of the law. And be it noted: Patten is not radical, especially by the standards of North America. Canada and the USA have long made their police democratically accountable and socially representative. Patten is only radical by the past standards of Northern Ireland.

There is a small ray of hope here: if the implementation plan on policing brings the government strongly into line with Patten then there may be the promised 'new beginning'. But failure to deliver on police reform, as proposed by Patten, in my judgement is likely to herald disaster, in two forms. Its weakest form is taking shape. Without quick and radical steps by the Labour government the SDLP, Sinn Féin and the Catholic Church are unlikely to recommend that their constituents consider joining the police, and may well boycott the Policing Board and District Policing Partnership

Boards – even though pressure is being exerted on them, including by Patten, to accept 'Patten life'. That will leave the police without Patten's promised 'new beginning', lacking full legitimacy with just less than half of the local electorate. Over three hundred police were killed in the current conflict, but outsiders tend to forget that the outbreak of armed conflict in 1969 was partly caused by an unreformed, half-legitimate police service, responsible for seven of the first eight deaths. In its strongest form disaster will de-couple nationalists and republicans from the Agreement, and bring down its political institutions.[43] Failure to deliver Patten will mean that Sinn Féin will not even try to get the IRA to go further in decommissioning than their current arrangements for the inspection of arms dumps. The argument has already been advanced in republican circles that the UK government has reneged on a fundamental commitment under the Agreement so the IRA must not disarm, leaving nationalists to be policed by an unreformed service. Given Sinn Féin's response to what the UK government has done with the Patten Report, the IRA will, in any case, find it difficult to prevent further departures to the Real and Continuity IRAs, except by refusing to budge on arms. In turn, however, that will lead to a repetition of unionist calls for the exclusion of Sinn Féin from ministerial office, with further threats of the UUP's withdrawal from the Executive.

More generously disposed analysts might believe that Mandelson's conduct on Patten was motivated by the need to help Trimble and the UUP who are in a precarious position. It was, in part. 'Saving David' may account for the tampering with Patten's proposals on symbolic matters, but it hardly accounts for the blocking of the efforts to have a more accountable service – here the Secretary of State succumbed to lobbying by security and his civil servants, presumably concerned, amongst other things, to avoid the unearthing of past and present scandals. But whatever his motivation, he forgot, again, that it was not his role unilaterally to abandon or re-negotiate the Agreement, or the work of Commissions set up under the Agreement, either on his own initiative, or at the behest of any party.

Avoiding a Meltdown?

In January 2001 it was difficult to avoid pessimism about the prospects for the Agreement. The passage of the Police (Northern Ireland) Act in November 2000 had left the SDLP, Sinn Féin and the Irish government strongly dissatisfied. Even though the final Act was better than the original Bill it was still 'Patten lite'. The IRA had not formally re-engaged with the IICD, partly, it seemed, to put pressure on Mandelson to deliver on Patten and de-militarization – though it did facilitate a second inspection of its arms dumps. The UK government was refusing to move fast on de-militarization because of its security concerns, especially about dissident republicans, who were strongest in areas which have historically been vigorously republican – and where there is the greatest demand for demilitarization. The discipline of loyalist paramilitaries was breaking down: there was internal feuding, and sections of the UDA were targeting vulnerable Catholics with pipe-bomb attacks in predominantly unionist towns.

On top of all this David Trimble had decided to play executive hardball. At the end of 2000, besieged by internal party critics demanding a fast exit from the executive because of the IRA's obstinate stance on decommissioning, he decided to take what was called proportionate action. Acting on poor legal advice he availed of a technical clause in the Northern Ireland (1998) Act and refused to nominate the two Sinn Féin Ministers to carry out their obligations under meetings of the North-South Ministerial Council. Sinn Féin's two Ministers, Bairbre de Bruin and Martin McGuiness, and the deputy First Minister, Seamus Mallon, announced they would test the legality of Trimble's decision in the courts. Trimble's lawyer justified his action as intended to put pressure on Sinn Féin to get the IRA to deliver on its obligations. Judge Kerr ruled Trimble's action unlawful on 30 January 2001, partly because Trimble could not inhibit or frustrate one part of the Agreement, cross-border co-operation, to ensure progress on another, viz. decommissioning. He also ruled that Trimble had acted beyond his powers. Trimble immediately decided to appeal. When ministers take one another to court in any coalition government, prospects for co-existence look ominous.

The political stalemate and legal showdown suggested an acrimonious and messy meltdown. However, on 24 January 2001 something unexpected happened. Peter Mandelson was forced to resign as Secretary of State because of events that had nothing to do with Northern Ireland. He was replaced by Dr John Reid, the former Secretary of State for Scotland. The DUP were not distressed at Mandelson's departure; the UUP's reaction was more cautious – some felt they had lost a friend at court. But his exit left nationalists, republicans and the Irish government almost as happy as Labour's backbenchers, and hopes were restored that a final deal could be reached.

Plainly at least four things have to be done if the Belfast Agreement and the supplementary prime ministerial and joint governmental statements of May 2000 are to be successfully implemented, in whole.

1. The two Governments and the pro-Agreement parties must agree that the remaining items for effective implementation, including decommissioning, police reform, criminal justice reform, and demilitarisation, are resolved to their mutual satisfaction. This will require Blair and Reid to unravel at least some of Mandelson's stances on policing reform.
2. Republicans will have to move from the inspection of the IRA's arms dumps to accomplish wholly credible disarmament.

3. Action and discipline is required from the major loyalist parties and paramilitary organisations – whose obligations on decommissioning tend to be forgotten in UK circles.

4. Lastly, the UUP must be satisfied with republican action on decommissioning, and accept that the UK government has obligations to deliver on demilitarization and the full-scale reform of criminal justice and policing – in ways that are against their preferences.

It is a tall order – though not impossible. We will know soon whether a final deal can happen. There is continuing public support for the Agreement, including, on balance, amongst unionists.[44] There are two tacit deadlines on current negotiations: the next one that the UUP may try to impose, and the beginning of the next UK general election. The pro-Agreement parties have an interest in tying up such a final package before the Westminster election, because without it the UUP is likely to be damaged at the polls. There is, however, one agreed deadline, June 2001. Meeting that will require more trust and multi-lateral co-operation than has so far been evident. New Labour's one constitutional miracle is in mortal danger, but not in the same danger as when it was under the custody of its Prince of Darkness. If the Agreement does collapse then Blair and Mandelson will have to take a full measure of responsibility for their part in endangering what Blair and Mowlam helped put together.

Notes

1 Brendan O'Leary, 'Afterword: What is Framed in the Framework Documents?' *Ethnic and Racial Studies*, 1995, 18 (4): 862–72.

2 The origin of most of the ideas for the internal government of Northern Ireland, in Strand One, also stemmed from Irish nationalists, led by the SDLP, and advised by Irish officials and others.

3 See Brendan O'Leary and John McGarry, *The Politics of Antagonism: Understanding Northern Ireland*, Athlone, 1996, pp. 327–69.

4 One article, confirming this proposition, was made available to Labour's leadership, viz. Brendan O'Leary 'Public Opinion and Northern Irish Futures', *Political Quarterly*, 1992, 63(2): 143–70.

5 For a mildly jaundiced but accurate overview see Brendan O'Leary, 'The Conservative Stewardship of Northern Ireland 1979–97: Sound-Bottomed Contradictions or Slow Learning?' *Political Studies*, 1997, 45(4): 663–76.

6 See Julia Langdon, *Mo Mowlam: The Biography*, Little, Brown & Company, 2000, p. 269.

7 According to Langdon, Soley was 'acting as a secret and unacknowledged emissary between the Conservative British government and the leaders of Sinn Féin', p. 271 ff. In fact he was one of numerous channels through which Sinn Féin attempted to persuade the UK's parties of government that they were serious about negotiations.

8 Personal notes kept in my capacity as advisor to Mr McNamara and Dr Mowlam, 1988–1995.

9 See *inter alia* Brendan O'Leary, Tom Lyne, Jim Marshall and Bob Rowthorn, *Northern Ireland: Sharing Authority*, Institute of Public Policy Research, 1993.

10 McNamara's salvo against Labour's electoral integrationists led the party's unionists to argue that he was unfit for office, see Kevin McNamara *et al.* 1992, *Oranges or Lemons? Should Labour Organise in Northern Ireland?* Westminster, House of Commons: the Authors. Electoral integrationists were especially salient amongst Scottish MPs (convinced that the Scottish sectarian question was the same as the Irish national question), members with communist pasts, those influenced by Ireland's Workers' Party, and those who are Northern Irish cultural Protestants. They campaigned against McNamara, much as they would later campaign against Mowlam, by the politics of 'malicious gossip', a trait they shared with New Labour's principal apparatchiks – for a sharp statement see Ken Follett, *Observer*, 2 July 2000.

11 Evidence of her empathy with Irish nationalists was manifest in her willingness to use Ken Livingstone to inform her of Sinn Féin's positions, and her (rejected) proposal to Blair that Livingstone become part of her ministerial team at the NIO, *Mo Mowlam*, p. 4.

12 George J. Mitchell, John de Chastelain, and Harri Holkeri, 'Report of the International Body on Arms Decommissioning (The Mitchell Report)', 1996. For the Senator's account of matters see George J. Mitchell, *Making Peace*, updated with a new preface from the 1999 edition, University of California Press, 2000, especially chapter 3.

13 The International Body's text had suggested elections if they were widely agreed, viz. 'If it were broadly acceptable, with an appropriate mandate, and within the three-strand structure, an elective process could contribute to the building of confidence'. An elective process was not 'broadly acceptable' to the SDLP and Sinn Féin.

14 Mitchell puts matters with characteristic tact: Major's response 'wasn't support, but it wasn't exactly a dumping. It was a temporary sidestep to get to negotiations by a different route', *Making Peace*, p. 39.

15 At a meeting with Adams and McGuinness in 1997–98 Blair is said to have told them that he would do everything he could to find an agreement, 'But if you ever do a Canary Wharf on me, I will never talk to you again', Andrew Rawnsley, *Servants of the People: The Inside Story of New Labour*, Hamish Hamilton, 2000, p. 123. The irony would not have been lost on them. Canary Wharf prompted the two premiers, Major and Bruton, to specify the date on which negotiations would begin, and the modalities through which negotiations would take place. A year and half's relative inaction by the UK government after the IRA's ceasefire ended three weeks after the bomb. None other than Tony Blair supported the two governments' rapid volte-face.

16 For the details, and the state of public opinion at that time, see Geoffrey Evans and Brendan O'Leary, 'Frameworked Futures: Intransigence and flexibility in the Northern Ireland Elections of May 30 1996, *Irish Political Studies*, 1997, 12: 23–47.

17 Brendan O'Leary and Geoffrey Evans, 'Northern Ireland: La Fin de Siècle,

The Twilight of the Second Protestant Ascendancy and Sinn Féin's Second Coming', *Parliamentary Affairs*, 1997, 50: 672–80.

18 Speech by the Prime Minister, Belfast, 16 May 1997.

19 Ibid.

20 For a hasty biography of the UUP leader see Henry MacDonald, *Trimble* Bloomsbury, 2000, and for a critical notice see Brendan O'Leary, *Sunday Business Post* (Dublin), 13 April, 2000.

21 For a treatment of the Clinton administration on Ireland see Conor O'Clery, *The Greening of the White House*, Gill & Macmillan, 1996; he does not miss the significance of the Morrison delegation, Clinton's undeclared 'envoy'. See also Mitchell's *Making Peace*, passim.

22 Irish Labour leader, Dick Spring, Tánaiste (deputy prime minister) 1992–97, was an essential figure in shaping the Agreement's focus on the protection of rights in both parts of Ireland.

23 The legislation establishing the Forum envisaged its termination in May 1998. Though it did not require the negotiations to be concluded by that date the government argued that since the negotiators' mandates stemmed from their elections to the Forum it was the authorised deadline.

24 *An Phoblacht* (Republican News), 11 September 1997.

25 Some NIO officials sought to dilute or block the potentially far-reaching equality clauses, mandated by the Belfast Agreement, and now embedded as section 75 of the 1998 *Northern Ireland Act*. Mowlam was critical in blocking these efforts. Her conduct was in striking contrast to that of her successor who allowed his officials to dilute the proposals of the Patten Commission.

26 *Sunday Telegraph*, 27 July 1997, cited in *Mo Mowlam*, 8.

27 Ian Paisley had once run a campaign to 'Save Ulster from Sodomy'; his party is notoriously homophobic.

28 See Brendan O'Leary, 'The Nature of the Agreement', *Fordham Journal of International Law*, 1999, 22: 1628–67, and 'The Nature of the British-Irish Agreement', *New Left Review*, 233: 66–96.

29 Arend Lijphart, *Democracy in Plural Societies: A Comparative Exploration*, Yale University Press, 1977.

30 See Christopher McCrudden, 'Mainstreaming Equality in the Governance of Northern Ireland', *Fordham International Law Journal*, 1999, 22: 1696–1775.

31 Northern Ireland's devolution arrangements may be contrasted with those of Scotland and Wales, described in Iain McLean's chapter. In Northern Ireland inter-party power sharing and proportionality are required and UK Labour has no party interest at stake. The Northern Ireland Assembly is larger and more powerful than the Welsh National Assembly and may, by the agreement of its blocs, expand its autonomy to the same degree as the Scottish Parliament, and indeed beyond. Northern Ireland's autonomy is both more open-ended, and more constrained. It is tied to the all-Ireland North-South Ministerial Council. It has a specified right of secession, to join a unified Ireland. See also Robert Hazell and Brendan O'Leary, 'A Rolling Programme of Devolution: Slippery Slope or Safeguard of the Union?', in Robert Hazell (ed.), *Constitutional Futures: A History of the Next Ten Years*, Oxford University Press, 1999, pp. 21–46.

32 Daniel Elazar, *Exploring Federalism*, University of Alabama, 1987.

33 The NSMC also linked Ireland, North and South, to another confederation, the European Union. It required the Council to consider the implementation of EU policies and programmes as well as proposals under way at the EU, and made provisions for the Council's views to be 'taken into account' at relevant EU meetings.

34 The resignation of one UUP member from the party whip meant that 29 'Yes Unionists' exactly matched 29 'No Unionists' in the Assembly.

35 For a fuller discussion of the d'Hondt allocation process see O'Leary, *The Nature of the Agreement.*

36 I draw on evidence I presented, viz. 'Why Failing to Implement the Patten Report Matters', Testimony for the Hearing of the Commission on Security and Co-operation in Europe (the Helsinki Commission), entitled 'Protecting Human Rights and Securing Peace in Northern Ireland: The Vital Role of Police Reform', Friday 22 September 2000, International Relations Committee Room, Raeburn Building, Washington DC.

37 Despite the Omagh atrocity of 1998, the key indicators of political violence demonstrate that the security situation has been much better in the period since 1995 than it was in the period running up to 1994, and significantly so by comparison with the entire period of fully active conflict which preceded the first IRA ceasefire (i.e. 1969–1993). The death toll during 1995–99 more than halved by comparison with 1990–94.

38 See John McGarry and Brendan O'Leary, *Policing Northern Ireland: Proposals for a New Start*, Blackstaff, 1999. A former Irish prime minister, Dr Garret FitzGerald has described policing in Northern Ireland as having the status of Jerusalem in the Israeli-Palestinian peace process, 'Watering Down of Patten Unnecessary', *Irish Times*, 12 August 2000.

39 See Christopher Patten *et al.* (1999) *A New Beginning: The Report of the Independent Commission on Policing for Northern Ireland*, Belfast and London, September. See also Brendan O'Leary, 'A Bright Future and Less Orange (Review of the Independent Commission on Policing for Northern Ireland)', *Times Higher Education Supplement*, 19 November 1999.

40 I described it as betraying Patten's 'substantive intentions in most of its thinly disguised legislative window-dressing', Brendan O'Leary, 'What a Travesty: Police Bill is Just a Parody of Patten', *Sunday Business Post*, 30 April.

41 For the defects in the Bill and the accompanying implementation plan with regard to community policing see Paddy Hillyard of the University of Ulster, 'Police Bill is Not Faithful Reflection of Patten', *Irish Times*, 2 August 2000.

42 An alternative path, legitimate under the Agreement, would have been to pursue a fully bi-national symbolic strategy (McGarry and O'Leary 1999). However even if the police were to have both an English and Irish title in each case the name should be neutral: Northern Ireland Police Service or Coras Siochana Thuaisceart Eireann.

43 The careful and detailed denunciation of Mandelson by Mitchel McLaughlin, Sinn Féin's leading moderate, suggests the depth of the crisis, 'The Mandelson Factor', *Belfast Telegraph*, 1 December 2000. It specifically accuses Mandelson of failing to deliver on explicit commitments and obligations.

44 See e.g. Geoffrey Evans and Brendan O'Leary, 'Northern Irish Voters and the British-Irish Agreement: Foundations of a Stable Consociational Settlement?' *Political Quarterly*, (71): 78–101.

© Chris Riddell

Chapter 22

WOMEN, MEN AND
THE FAMILY

Jane Lewis

POLICIES EXPLICITLY ADDRESSING families have been put at the centre of the Labour government's work. This is new. The family has always tended to be a sideshow in British politics and what goes on within it has been viewed a private matter, unless there was evidence of gross malfunction. Explicit 'family policy' has historically been associated with the continental European countries and has not been the favoured approach in any of the English-speaking countries.

Certainly, it is extremely difficult to get the politics of the family right. The last Conservative government had a go at family policy in the context of a stern defence of 'family values', most notably at the 1993 Party Conference, when Peter Lilley's (the then Secretary of State for Social Security) 'little list' included lone mothers who were charged time and again by Conservative ministers with deliberately having babies and then supporting and housing them at the expense of the taxpayer. However, the fact that the Conservatives made no attempt to disentangle the social and moral issues badly backfired. Lone mothers turned out to be a disparate bunch, a majority being divorced (like many Cabinet members) and not necessarily the feckless, young unmarried mothers of Lilley's 'little list'. Even when governments are more cautious and less eager to endorse traditional family values, the issues are both fraught – everyone thinks they know about the family – and hard to unravel. As was pointed out a quarter of a century ago in this country and in the United States, there are many different kinds of family and the interests of family members – men, women and children – differ. Since then the pace of family change has been the most dramatic of all social trends. In one generation, the numbers marrying have halved, the numbers divorcing have trebled and the proportion of children born outside marriage has quadrupled. The roles of men and women have also changed considerably, particularly in respect of paid work, with women contributing proportionately more to the family economy and men less. It is no wonder that politicians in the 1990s felt that they had to say and do something about 'the family'.

Broadly speaking, the Conservatives reached for traditional models: men should provide, which in a period when the order in which cohabitation, childbirth and marriage took place seemed to be increasingly uncertain, was translated into the idea that men should pay for their biological children and embedded in the most unpopular piece of legislation after the poll tax: the 1991 Child Support Act. If women did not marry and secure support for their children from husbands, then they should not expect to do so from the state. And if absent fathers could not be relied upon, which despite changes to the child support legislation in the mid-1990s, seemed to be the case, then it was deemed that they should receive less favourable treatment from the benefit system than married couples (presumably as a deterrent) and that they should be prepared to support themselves by entering the labour market. The classic issue of how to reconcile paid work and care for children was not addressed. This had always been considered a matter for private individuals to work out in post-war Britain and it remained so under the last government. Nor were other signs of family stress acknowledged or addressed, particularly the huge rise in child poverty between 1968 and 1995/6, from 10 per cent to 33 per cent.[1]

Labour has waded into the family arena on a variety of fronts. Blair's pledge in the 1999 Beveridge Lecture to end child poverty in twenty years was enormously significant given the size of the problem (affecting 4.4 million children) and given the extent to which it demands that employment, tax and social security policies become more child centred. It is almost twenty years since Anna Coote asked how the world would look if policy centred on the best way to care for and to support children. Labour has not taken up this challenge in full, because (as will be seen in section III below) it has not addressed the issue of care with the same vigour as it has issues to do with cash. Nevertheless, its focus on children is new and radical.

However, many would associate Labour with a very similar 'family morality' to the Conservatives. It seems that many Cabinet members, Blair and Straw at the forefront, view married couple families as the social glue for a healthy society and are just as worried about the decline in marriage in particular as many Conservatives. Labour has been much more careful not to condemn other, fast-growing family forms, but the tightrope is a difficult one to walk.

Alongside a regard for traditional families, has come as much or more emphasis than previously on 'family responsibilities', particularly of parents for children, which is in line with the much broader desire of Labour to stress the importance of responsibility rather than either rights and entitlements, or a self-seeking individualism. For example, parents have continued to be targeted in respect of policies to deal with crime, disorder and truanting among children. There has been a tendency to define parental responsibility in traditional terms, with men being seen as responsible above all for financial support and women for care. Responsibility for adult family members in need of care has not been talked about explicitly, but given the lack of policy development in respect of long-term care outside Scotland, despite the 1999 Royal Commission Report on this subject, this is also extremely significant. However, in parallel with the emphasis on the importance of good parenting, supported by initiatives such as the setting up of the National Family and Parenting Institute, has gone another set of responsibilities increasingly assigned to all adults: the obligation to work and to be self-supporting. Parental responsibility for men has traditionally translated into the provision of cash, which fits with the injunction to work. But the 'good mother' has traditionally stayed at home to care for her children. Thus from women's point of view, there is a major tension in Labour's 'responsibilities talk'. This results from two separate but related issues: first, the assumption that all adults are now in the labour market and that policy can therefore be made on the basis of an adult worker rather than a male breadwinner model, which for women especially comes into conflict with the model of the good, caring, female parent; and second the emphasis in Labour policies on cash, whether in the form of earnings, benefits or tax credits, and the relative neglect of care.

In short, Labour has made family issues mainstream policy issues, but the policies are far from consistent. It would be extremely surprising if this were the case. From the time of the classical social contract theorists, liberal political theory has always assumed the individual to be the basis of society, alongside an assumption about the separation of public and private spheres that has resulted in the individual being defined as a male head of household. The separation of spheres has become less rigid over time, and as women have entered the public sphere – as voters and increasingly as paid workers – so the problem of what to do about the private sphere of the family and of care has loomed larger. Socialists such as Engels wanted to commodify the work of the household, a solution that has found favour with some, but not all, feminists and most recently with some defenders of continental European social insurance welfare states, who see the contributions of women employees as crucial to ensuring the affordability of social provision. But the point is that 'all or nothing' female employment solutions have not proved popular. Just as people seem increasingly reluctant to prescribe a particular family form for others (even though they may state a 'general' preference for marriage over cohabitation), so they are reluctant to say that all mothers should be in the workforce, or all at home. The point is that people's views about family and the behaviour of adult family members is messy, and to this extent the refusal of the government to condemn non-traditional family forms is wise. Nevertheless, there is a tension (at best) in Labour's obvious preference for the traditional family and willingness to talk about it in moral terms, while pursuing a determined policy to ensure that all adults, male and female, are in the workforce.

I Marriage and Morals

This is the trickiest terrain of all for ministers. The central concern of Labour has been the enforcement of personal responsibility. Within the family, the emphasis has been on parental responsibility, but the issue has been raised as to whether mothers and fathers who are also husbands and wives carry out this responsibility better, the reasoning being that marriage is a better guarantee of commitment and stability for children. In the face of high and stable divorce rates, the fact that first marriage rates were lower than they had been at the beginning of the century, and emerging evidence (from the 1992 British Household Panel survey data) that cohabitants with children were four times as likely to break-up as married couples,[2] politicians from both major political parties have asked whether government should play more of a role in encouraging marriage and discouraging other family forms. Labour had to decide how to deal with a major piece of family law, the 1996 Family Law Act, and whether and how to address the issue of marriage in social policy. These matters were complicated by the fact that support for a more determined line on marriage came from many points on the political spectrum, some of them influential with New Labour.

During the last part of the twentieth century, issues to do with intimate relationships have increasingly been privatised to the individuals concerned. Lord Devlin was the last person to argue fiercely in public debate in this country for the imposition of an absolute moral code during the 1960s, but the majority of Establishment opinion took the view that morality could no longer be imposed from without, but had to come from within the individual. Major reform of the law affecting abortion, homosexuality and divorce followed.

The Conservatives had initially been divided between a more libertarian and a more authoritarian approach to the family. Ferdinand Mount, Mrs Thatcher's family policy adviser in the early 1980s had after all defended the autonomy of the family and had described it as being in 'permanent revolution' against the state. Nevertheless, faced with heated debates about the causes of the rapid increase in lone mother families, the majority of whom are divorced women, and anxieties about the growth of selfish individualism, Lord Mackay, the then Lord Chancellor, seemed to revert to the older desire to make morality a top down exercise when he announced his intention of introducing measures to cut the rate of divorce.

The desire to try and stem the tide of family change was supported by a much broader Anglo-American chorus of voices that were leftist, liberal and communitarian as well as conservative pressing for a more explicit moral lead from politicians. In Britain, A. H. Halsey, Norman Dennis and George Erdos all argued from the political left that the successful socialisation of children required the active involvement of two parents.[3] The decline of the married two parent family and the rise of the lone mother family was in their view responsible for at best irresponsible and at worse criminal behaviour in the next male generation. William Galston, the American liberal philosopher, argued that the modern liberal state is committed to a distinctive conception of the human good and must therefore promote it: 'My guiding intention is that the US is in trouble because it has failed to attend to the dependence of sound politics on sound culture' (p. 6). Galston quoted Walter Mondale, failed Democrat contender for the Presidency as saying in 1984: '"The answer to lax morals is not legislated morals. It is deeper faith, greater discipline, and personal excellence"', a classic statement in favour of morality from within.[4] Galston was far from convinced that this would be sufficient. Communitarians, whose ideas influenced leading Labour politicians in the mid-1990s, shared this view.[5] Anutai Etziani as much as the right-wing commentator, James Q. Wilson[6] deplored the reluctance to talk about morality; both have been visitors to Downing Street. Philip Selznik, another American whose communitarian ideas can be traced to New Labour[7] suggested that 'a robust community, however pluralistic, must embrace the idea of a common good' (p. xi).[8] While accepting that the kind of absolutist morality espoused by Devlin had become impossible to impose, Selznik rejected the kind of moral relativism that does not admit objectivity. In other words, he argued that values are not reducible to subjective preferences. But how to define what is acceptable to 'the community', whether by appeal to past experience and institutions, or to contemporary dialogue, is extremely problematic, especially in the field of adult intimate relationships.

In the case of Lord Mackay, it seemed that he had thought better of any attempt at direct social engineering when he introduced his 1995 White Paper on mediation and the ground for divorce, which proposed a collection of measures intended to make divorce less expensive and more amicable, while ensuring that the obligation of husband and wife as father and mother to take responsibility for, and to secure the position of, children was fulfilled. In many respects, this was to apply the new regulatory approach taken in respect of the public services to the family: drawing up a framework of control that endeavoured to ensure self-regulation and self-governance. In the public services this consisted of a whole variety of measures associated with the 'new public management', for example, performance indicators,[9] while in the family it consisted of making couples think about their position and negotiate their desired outcomes. As the 1993 Green Paper had put it:

> If changing the law cannot save irretrievable marriages, it can slow down the divorce process and enable the parties to do as much as possible to prevent the marriage from finally ending . . . it can make sure that people are made to realise the full consequences of divorce for themselves and their children . . . In that way they can take personal responsibility for their decisions.[10]

The Family Law Act of 1996 sought to embody both the idea that the decision to divorce should rest with the couple, and the notion that men and women should take responsibility for sorting out their affairs, particularly in respect of their children. To the latter end, couples were required to settle their affairs before seeking divorce, a complete reversal of the procedure required prior to the 1969 legislation, when any such move would have been regarded as evidence of 'collusion' and a bar to divorce.

The Act finally abolished fault-based divorce. The sole proof of irretrievable breakdown in the new legislation was to be a waiting period of one year, which was to apply to couples without children as well in order that marriage should not be devalued. This signalled a preoccupation that became much more pronounced as the legislation made its way through Parliament: saving marriage. In other words, law as a means to controlling behaviour in intimate relationships came back on to the agenda, mainly, but not exclusively because of the concerns of far-right Conservatives. The large and complicated debate about the legislation revolved around the place of marriage. Opposition to the complete abolition of fault came from MPs who felt that it would, as John Patten put it, 'empty the marriage contract of any meaning' and 'turn a contract for life into a probationary matter' (*Daily Telegraph*, 9 September 1995). The underlying fear was that marriage would become indistinguishable from cohabitation. The Family Homes and Domestic Violence (FHDV) Bill had already been lost in 1995 as a result of a rebellion by Conservative MPs determined that cohabitants should not have an equal legal status to married people. Part III of the Family Law Act, which sought to cover the same ground as the lost FHDV Bill, called upon the courts to have regard when making an occupation order for a cohabitant to the fact that they had not given the commitment of marriage. This together with other clauses that rendered cohabitation 'less eligible' than marriage were, according to the Lord Chancellor, intended to 'emphasise the important general message that marriage is special in a way that no other relationship is' (House of Lords, Debates, 30 January 1996, c. 705).

The Conservative government, which, for the first time in the twentieth century, had assumed responsibility for legislation dealing with the grounds for divorce, had to accept many amendments in order to get the legislation through. No-fault divorce was not intended to be permissive, and the one year waiting period was intended to promote reconciliation. The general principles underlying the legislation set out in section 1 of the Act and formulated at a relatively late stage in the Bill's passage through Parliament, referred explicitly to the fact that 'the institution of marriage is to be supported' and that the parties to a marriage 'are to be encouraged to take all practicable steps whether by marriage counselling or otherwise to save the marriage'.[11] The Labour Party's spokesman on the Bill in the House of Commons, Paul Boateng, is said to have described the legislation as a 'dog's breakfast'[12] however, Boateng had spoken strongly in favour of marriage saving, urging that the new legislation 'should not be simply a vehicle for the dissolution of marriage, but a means by which marriage might be supported'.[13] Boateng's role shows how blurred party lines became over the discussion of the aims informing the Family Law Act; it is hard to distinguish party politics and strategy from the espousal of principle.

Those parts of the legislation dealing with divorce were always going to be difficult to implement, with their complicated requirements for consideration, reflection, conciliation and mediation on the one hand, and the likely opposition of those wishing to divorce to the wait involved on the other. The legislation represented the most ambitious family law project since the 1969 Divorce Act. But in mid-1999 the Labour government signalled that it would abandon parts of the Act related to divorce. Lord Irvine stressed the fact that the pilot schemes had been disappointing in terms of encouraging mediation, but the reason for abandoning the legislation probably had much to do with the difficulty of persuading (and paying for) large numbers of people to be put through a lengthy process designed to promote conciliation if not reconciliation.

So has Labour 'backed down' on marriage? Many commentators, academics included, would say no. In particular they would cite the consultative document, *Supporting Families*, issued from the Home Office's new family policy unit in 1998, which while stating that many lone parents and 'unmarried couples' raised their children successfully, also stated that 'marriage is still the surest foundation for raising children'.[14] Thus marriage is best, but other family forms are not condemned outright. The document stated firmly: 'Neither a "back to basics" fundamentalism, trying to turn back the clock, nor an "anything goes" liberalism which denies the fact that how families behave affects us all, is credible any more'.[15] While endeavouring to avoid out and out prescription, the document was very different to the report on marriage prepared by the Home Office and the Department of Social Security under the last Labour government (*Marriage Matters*, 1979), which accepted the then dominant idea of marriage as a means to 'personal growth' and made much less of responsibilities and obligations.

It seems that Labour, particularly influential Cabinet members such as Jack Straw and Tony Blair himself, share the concern of Conservatives about the implications of family change, especially in respect of the increased instability faced by children. Teaching the value of marriage to children, if not dealing so prescriptively with adults, is on the agenda and became part of the *quid pro quo* for the (failed) attempt to abolish 'Section 28' of the Local Government Act, which forbade 'the promotion' of homosexuality in schools. However, Labour has shown that they are sensitive to the difficulties of prescribing a particular family form in a society that no longer is willing to accept the imposition of morality from without. Nor is there any evidence that Labour is willing to try and use mechanisms other than family law to offer direct incentives to marriage. Thus the married couples' tax allowance was duly abolished in April 2000. The value of this allowance had been allowed to decline under the Conservatives, to the anger of some right-wing commentators,[16] who rightly pointed out the inconsistency of the Conservatives' position on this issue. Labour seem to have tried to make a virtue of steering an often inconsistent line between a traditionalist and more liberal line on marriage, although it is possible to interpret one of their earliest decisions to implement the Conservative plan to reduce lone parents' benefits in terms of a determination to signal disapproval of this family form as much as a desire to demonstrate strict control over public expenditure.[17] This interpretation gains force from the fact that subsequent budgets restored the value of the cuts to lone parents, but without advertisement.

Nevertheless, after its initial statements on marriage, *Supporting Families* referred to policies for 'families' rather than to 'family policy', which was something of a major departure. The significant back-bench revolt over the early cuts to lone parents' benefits probably increased sensitivities in regard to the vexed issue of family form. Critics may accuse Labour of a pick-and-mix post-modernism, but it may be as has been suggested,[18] that it is determined to take into account the often demonstrably contradictory state of public opinion on different issues to do with the family. It is an area of policy making about which people have finely honed notions as to what is appropriate, and yet these may differ profoundly between generations, classes, ethnic groups and regions. A mid-1990s Eurobarometer survey showed 60 per cent of Europeans choosing the 'not for others to judge' option when asked about the desirability of cohabitation.[19] Similarly, an *Observer*/ICM poll indicated late in 1998 that a majority of people believed that government should steer clear of telling them how to conduct their private lives. However, while views tended towards the non-judgemental, they were not necessarily permissive: 47 per cent agreed that divorce should be made more difficult, as opposed to 44 per cent who disagreed (*Observer*, 25 October 1998, p. 16).

II Feckless Fathers

Nowhere was the ease with which government legislation could trample these deeply-held popular ideas about obligation underfoot felt more keenly than in respect of the ill-fated 1991 Child Support Act. In the words of Peter Lilley, the Child Support Act was intended to reverse 'the inadvertent nationalisation of fatherhood'. Michael Howard, then Home Secretary, said in a speech to the Conservative Political Centre in 1993:

If the state will house and pay for their children the duty on [young men] to get involved may seem removed from their shoulders . . . And since the state is educating, housing and feeding their children the nature of parental responsibility may seem less immediate.

Conservatives were as worried as any feminist about male irresponsibility and the 'flight from commitment'.

Thus under the child support legislation, all biological fathers, unmarried and divorced, were given a persistent obligation to maintain. The legislation was billed as a means of securing greater provision for women and children, but research showed that they made few gains. Any money raised from fathers was deducted pound for pound from the mothers' benefits. This together with an increasingly punitive approach taken by Conservative governments in the 1990s, suggested that the main preoccupation was with enforcing private parental responsibility rather than with the welfare of the mothers and children. By 1996, mothers who refused to cooperate with the Child Support Agency by naming the father lost 40 per cent of their benefits. The Conservatives were unprepared for the enormous hostility on behalf of 'absent fathers' and their second families to the legislation. After all, in 1990, when the British Social Attitudes Survey asked respondents whether they thought a father should pay for his children after divorce 90 per cent of men and 95 per cent of women said yes. The legislation was sold in terms of doing something about the problem of 'feckless', absent fathers. Men who were already paying something (no matter that it was in all probability a fairly small amount) and middle-class men did not think of themselves as feckless, and did not expect to come into contact with the new Child Support Agency. Given that women and children gained little from it, it was a measure with no supporters.

In face of the massive protests by fathers and manifest administrative failure of the Agency, the Conservatives increasingly targeted parents-with-care who were drawing state benefits. By 1997, 88 per cent of the parents-with-care on the Agency's caseload were drawing benefits. Better-off parents avoided the system and used the courts. Second, in 1994 and again in 1995 the scheme was modified to lower the level of payment required from fathers. But by 1997, the Agency was owed over a billion pounds and more than half of this was reckoned to be uncollectable. Labour inherited a child support system that many reckoned had put the whole cause back a generation.

However, with the importance Labour attached to parental responsibility, it was unlikely to abandon the idea of making fathers pay. Indeed, maintenance payments had always been insisted upon, but, until 1991, had usually been set at a low level and often not enforced. In 1999, there were 1.5 million children on the books of the Child Support Agency. Only 40 per cent of non-resident parents paid all that was due; 30 per cent paid nothing at all. In a sample survey[20] of non-resident fathers, it was found that 63 per cent of non-payers could not pay. Labour's White Paper on the subject was issued in 1999 with the title: *Children's Rights and Parents' Responsibilities*

(Cm. 4349). The legislation that followed tried to take the heat out of the issue. 'Absent parents' become 'non-resident parents' and the tone towards men was conciliatory. The formula applied in order to determine the liability to pay is substantially simplified, thereby reducing the level of the average assessment. It also takes into consideration a variety of circumstances, for example, the needs of all children of the non-resident parent and whether the non-resident children stay overnight on a regular basis. A child maintenance disregard of £10 is introduced, which will ensure that some money goes to the parent with care. Alongside the intention to make the formula 'fairer', there is also the promise of stricter sanctions. This is all sensible as far as it goes and is very much a case of making the best of a bad job.

Interestingly though, the trend away from a universal administrative system for child support towards something that focuses on those parents-with-care who are drawing state benefits is continued by Labour's legislative initiative. People drawing the new tax credits available to people in low income employment will not have to register with the Child Support Agency. It seems that people who are prepared to fulfil the personal responsibility criterion by entering the labour market are deemed sufficiently deserving to avoid the CSA. Thus Labour's divide on the issue of child support is between those in work, whether well-off or not, and those out of work, which draws attention to the central place accorded the responsibility to engage in paid work.

III Mothers or Workers

The rapid pace of family change produced a large group of lone mother families (accounting for just over 20 per cent of all families with children by the mid-1990s), and it was these families that prompted concern in the late 1980s and early 1990s among Conservatives about morals, marriage and child support. There are, broadly speaking, only three sources of income for lone mothers – men, earnings and state benefits. Faced with the doubling of expenditure on lone parents' benefits and the fact that by 1989 the children of lone parents accounted for three-fifths of all children of income support claimants (compared with under half in 1986), the Conservatives turned first to men as an alternative source of support, introducing the Child Support Act. However, when this measure proved a conspicuous failure, the Department of Social Security announced in 1996 a new incentive to assist lone mothers into paid employment, providing individual help with job search and assistance with training for work.

Lone mothers in the UK have lower employment rates than most European countries. Indeed their employment rate had been dropping during the 1980s while that of married mothers had continued to rise. In the United States, Charles Murray made a similar pattern of behaviour central to his argument that lone mothers could not expect to be exempted from work requirements given that it was now accepted that adult women would be in the labour market. The Netherlands, which had been the only other EU country to share both the UK's low labour market participation rates for lone mothers and the lack of a requirement to register for work so long as they had a child under sixteen, also passed legislation to get lone mothers into the labour market in 1996. British Conservatives were less than wholehearted in their support of such policies, harbouring traditional ideas about the place of mothers with young children being at home. Labour took up this particular baton with more vigour, in large measure because it fit with its conception of 'active citizenship' grounded in the responsibility to work. Modern welfare states have always been constructed around the paid work/welfare relationship, but Labour made its new mechanisms for securing 'welfare to work' the centrepiece of its social policy. Tony Blair's introduction to the document on welfare reform has been widely quoted: 'Work for those who can, security for those who cannot'.[21] Social inclusion has been defined in terms of access to paid work. But how to draw the boundary between those who 'can' and those who 'cannot' is a major issue. In respect of parents, particularly women given the traditional gendered division of labour, there is the issue of how far care work constitutes a valid reason for not going out to work.

Even in the early years of the century, Labour insisted that wages were the best form of welfare. It is hard to dissent from this position, just as it is difficult not to acknowledge that, given greater longevity and higher risk of family breakdown, women who spend any amount of time out of the labour market put their welfare in danger. Nevertheless there is much care work for young and old to be done, and Labour has also attached a premium to parental responsibility in the form of caring for children. The first problem stems from the fact that while rewards have been attached to the willingness to take up the responsibility to earn and a coherent set of policies erected around what might be termed an 'adult citizen worker model', less attention has been given to the needs of those fulfilling caring responsibilities. The second problem stems from the assumption, as per the argument first made so strongly by Charles Murray, that all adult women now expect and are expected to be workers.

To take the second of these first, according to the General Household Survey, in 1975 81 per cent of men aged sixteen to sixty-four were economically active and 62 per cent of women. By 1996 this figure was 70 per cent for both men and women. Indeed, the contribution by men to family income fell from nearly 73 per cent in 1979–81 to 61 per cent in 1989–91.[22] However, the vast majority of the post-war increase in women's employment has been accounted for by part-time employment. While it is true that the difference in the activity rates between women with and without dependent children has halved in the period 1973 to 1996, almost half of all women workers are employed part-time. Furthermore, almost a quarter of women with children under ten work fifteen hours or less.[23] The point is, that while families supported by a single male bread-winner are now undoubtedly in a minority, the division of paid work in dual-earner couples takes a variety of forms. Dual *career* couples like the Blairs are relatively rare. The norm in the UK, as in most other western countries, has become the 'one-and-a-half-earner household'. In addi-tion, because of the high proportion of women in the UK working short part-time hours, together with the low hourly rates of pay for part-time women workers, in many dual-earner households the woman does not achieve half the man's income. Ward *et al* found that 78 per cent of thirty-three-year-old women contributed less than 45 per cent of the joint household income and 46 per cent did not earn enough to be self-suffi-cient.[24] It cannot be assumed that women are or can be in any near future economically self-sufficient.

The vast majority of dual-earner couples rely mainly on relatives and childminders to provide childcare; among mothers with children aged five to eleven, 37 per cent only work while the children are at school. Furthermore, Labour Force Survey data report that 90 per cent of women with children who work part-time did not want full-time work.[25] Indeed, it has been forcibly suggested by researchers that 'alternative moral ration-alities' underpin women's greater commitment to family work and that to press them to take up paid work instead of staying at home to care for chil-dren would violate their sense of moral obligations.[26]

There is very little information on what happens on the care side of the equation in dual breadwinner families. Where the female earner works long part-time hours or full time, but not necessarily in a job that she regards as a 'career', a large amount of care may be supplied by kin, and a smaller amount by the state and the market. Where the female earner works short part-time, she will probably continue to provide the bulk of care, together with kin and her partner. The fastest growing provider of child care since the late 1980s has been the private sector.[27] However the most important source of child care, especially for pre-schoolers, remains kin, followed by childminders. The literature on the division of resources in the household has revealed the way in which money earned by the woman tends to be earmarked for expenditure on child care, reflecting the extent to which provision is believed to be the responsibility of the female partner.[28] We are very far from a fully individualised, adult worker model and this has major implications for social provision more generally and Labour's commitment to an adult worker model in particular. The new 'contract' for welfare is premised on a fully individualised adult worker model that takes insufficient account of care.

The New Deal for Lone Parents made lone mothers part of the welfare-to-work strategy. This New Deal programme offering advice on entering the workforce was not made compulsory. However with the introduction in 2001 of a 'single gateway', ONE, which combines the Employment

Service and those parts of the Benefits Agency that pay benefits to people of working age in 2001, benefit will become conditional on an interview. The hope is that lone mothers will become workers, although only just over half the lone parents attending an initial New Deal interview by December 1999 came from the target group of women with school-age children.[29] Indeed, as Katherine Rake has pointed out, the New Deal actually embodies a degree of confusion about the extent to which women are in the end conceptualised as fully individualised.[30] The New Deal for the Partners of the Unemployed (mainly women) treats them both as having an independent relationship to the labour market and as dependants. Their access to the programme is dependent on their being the partner of an unemployed man. The 1.4 million women with employed partners who say that they would like to be in paid work are not included in the New Deal because the aim of government in this instance is to do something about workless families rather than the needs of women *per se*.

Similarly, the Working Families Tax Credit (WFTC), the centrepiece of Labour's policies to 'make work pay', seeks to encourage labour market participation, especially by lone mothers, but might actually have the opposite effect in respect of women with partners. This may be an unintended outcome, but reflects the deep-seated traditional assumptions that continue to pervade the mechanisms for delivering social security. WFTC, like its predecessor, family credit, is designed to help those in low paid jobs, but is considerably more generous. It is administered by the Inland Revenue and employers rather than the benefits agency and is intended to be less stigmatising than other means-tested benefits. It is delivered via the wage packet, which threatened to transfer money from 'purse to wallet'. After protests, the government agreed to pay it to the nominated person in one earner, couple families, although in practice it is unlikely that a non-earning female family member will be nominated. However, when the promised 'integrated child credit' is introduced, the promise is that this will be paid to the carer, like child benefit. It is also possible that because WFTC is administered on the basis of joint earnings, that it will reduce the incentive for partnered women to enter employment.[31] Again, while it is now assumed that women will enter the labour market rather than be part of a 'male breadwinner model family', means-testing does not operate on the same premise.

The WFTC includes a separate child care tax credit, which meets 70 per cent of the cost of care for one child to a maximum of £100 and £150 for two. However, it is paid only to those in work and assumes that employment precedes child care. In fact arranging work and child care is chicken and egg for the women involved. In addition the child care tax credit is only available for registered childcare, but a majority of women in low paid employment make use of informal, unregistered care.

The tax credit shows that care has not been ignored by Labour. Indeed this and the National Child Care Strategy are important initiatives, especially in a country where the issue of reconciling work and family responsibilities has historically been ignored. There are also proposals for second pension credits for those caring for young children or adults, albeit on a much more restricted basis than for the basic pension. However, these efforts are limited. Some £470 million was set aside for the provision of child care over a five year period. Four-year-olds have an entitlement to a place and the aim is to offer two thirds of three-year-olds a place by 2002. But the UK still comes near the bottom of the European child care league, in terms of quality as well as the number of affordable places. In addition, given that working time has become considerably more flexible, the limited and usually inflexible hours of child care providers pose problems.

Labour has also taken steps to promote parental leave, in line with the European Commission Directive on the issue (EC 96/34), but the very short thirteen week leave has been confined to the parents of children born after December 1999 and remains unpaid. The 2001 Department of Trade and Industry's Green Paper on *Work and Parents* does not offer the option of paid parental leave.[32] Other European countries have shown considerable concern about the issue of care and its gendered dimension. Parental leave has been taken disproportionately by women, even in those countries paying generous sums to those taking it, and many Northern European countries have experimented with periods of leave available only to men – 'the Daddy month' – and with the right of men and women to work a shorter working day or a four day week while they have young children. Again, individualisation of leave is important if gender equality in the division of work, paid and unpaid is to be promoted. But the UK has seemingly had difficulty in addressing care. The opt-outs from the European Commission's Directive on working time (EC 93/104) allow the very British male 'long hours culture' to persist. Men are still regarded as a source of support in terms of cash rather than care. Even in regard to mothers, the government seems more comfortable in providing cash than time to care. The maternity grant has been doubled to £200 and will rise again, but British women still get some of the shortest maternity leaves in Europe.

While Labour has made clear its concern to promote both parental responsibility and the responsibility to work, more effort has gone into facilitating and enforcing the latter. In respect of the former, most effort has been devoted to financial support, with the attempt to reform the child support legislation as the stick. The WFTC and other measures, including a largely unadvertised rise in the amount of benefits paid in respect of children under eleven, may be seen as considerable carrots, enabling parents to provide financial support, as well as acting as the vehicle for implementing the adult worker model. A million children have been lifted out of poverty already and the stated aim is to take 1.2 million out of poverty by the end of the Parliament (although it must be cautioned that more than three and a half million will be left and may prove a more intractable problem). But in all this care has tended to be the poor relation, and given the gender inequalities in its provision, this in turn has significant implications for the overwhelmingly important assumption that all adults who can will be in the labour market.

Conclusion

It is all too easy to make a case that Labour has in essence continued Conservative policy in respect of the family, whether the issue is marriage, child support, or the obligation to engage in paid work, which is thrown into sharp relief in the case of lone mothers. But, on the first two of these, policies have been soft-pedalled. Labour has, like most politicians and policy makers, a not unreasonable concern about the extraordinarily rapid pace of family change. But its recognition that it is impossible to turn the clock back appears genuine. Given the erosion of the major prescriptive frameworks that helped to determine how adults thought about and carried out their roles in 'the family' – through family law based on a strict external moral code and the male breadwinner model family model – Labour faces an extremely difficult task in trying to balance the very different and often contradictory views people have about how to organise intimate relationships and family life. Traditionally both major political parties in the UK have tried to steer clear of these issues; the fact that the Family Law Act was a piece of government legislation made it a major departure. Despite abandoning this particular piece of legislation, Labour has signalled that it is unwilling to ignore family change. Reform of the law affecting cohabitants and the rights of unmarried fathers are high on the agenda and will affect rapidly increasing numbers of people. On the obligation to engage in paid work, a much firmer line has been taken. In the US, Mead[33] identified the trend towards enforcing personal responsibility, which is the thread running through all these dimensions of policy, as 'the new paternalism'. However, in Labour's imagination, responsibility probably has more resonance with George Orwell's hankering after 'decency'.

It is indeed impossible to come to conclusions about the degree to which Labour represents continuity or change without considering motivation. After all, in the 1980s and 1990s child support policies were introduced in the US and Australia as well as the UK. The basic policy was very similar, but the reasons for it and hence the way in which it was implemented and received varied enormously. Labour inherited a commitment to an American-style low wage, flexible labour market, to which it has joined both its own seemingly genuine lack of enthusiasm for anything resembling a continental European welfare state, and a commitment to an adult worker citizen model. Given the inheritance, the movement towards a minimum wage and in-work benefits (which is what the working families tax credit most closely resembles) makes sense. There is substantial evidence that Labour wants to implement this using means that are redistributive and will take children out of poverty. Labour has given every impression of wanting a more engaged society, more 'active' to use its own term, characterised above all by responsibility, inclusion and opportunity.[34] Its approach is positive whereas that of the last administration tended to be negative and often punitive. The importance of this context should not be underestimated. Labour is also convinced that we must and should expect to do more by way of self-provisioning in the future, particularly regarding pension arrangements (around which there is considerable room for debate). For all these reasons the centrepiece of 'personal responsibility' has become translated as the willingness to engage in paid work. People who can work must do so and will be helped. Policies focus on cash and on work. The needs of children are defined mainly in terms of cash. The major absence in all this is care. And the family members who find themselves in most difficulties are women (and by association, children). Care is in danger of being defined as 'non-active', which is as unfortunate as it is ridiculous.

An adult worker model is not in and of itself a bad basis for erecting a new settlement. More individualisation and the high risk of family breakdown makes it prudent for women to provide for themselves. The model becomes problematic, just as assumptions regarding the existence of the old male breadwinner model did, when more is assumed that the empirical evidence warrants. The UK has at best a one-and-a-half-earner model, and women remain responsible for the bulk of the unpaid care work. In addition, the rationale for moving towards an adult worker model is not wholly at one with the way in which the social security mechanisms work. The new focus on subsidies to the low paid in the form of tax credits actually assumes that lone mothers will be adult citizen workers, but will in all likelihood tend to treat married women as dependants. The tensions that result for women and for carers from the assumptions regarding a fully individualised adult worker model and the much greater focus on cash than on care can only be addressed if the logic of a more care-centred approach is acknowledged and if more is done to graft the implications of this approach – in respect of working time, for example – on to the adult worker model. After all, there are two western societies in which an adult worker model has prevailed for some time. One is the United States, in which care has remained a private responsibility and where family problems and juvenile criminality is rife. The other is Sweden, where care has been treated as more of a collective responsibility and the able-bodied citizen worker is permitted to exit from the labour market to care with wage replacement. Social glue and possibly social capital is derived from care and more attention needs to be paid to it.

Notes

1 J. Bradshaw, 'Child Welfare in the UK: Rising Poverty, Falling Priorities for Children'. In C.A. Cornia and S. Danziger (eds) *Child Poverty and Deprivation in the Industrialized Countries, 1945–1995*, Clarendon Press, 1997; P. Gregg, S. Harkness and S. Machin, *Child Development and Family Income*, Joseph Rowntree Trust, 1999.

2 J. Ermisch and M. Francesconi, *Cohabitation in Great Britain: Not for Long, But Here to Stay*. Working Paper 98-I, University of Essex ESRC Research Centre on Micro-Social Change, 1998.

3 A.H. Halsey, 'Changes in the Family', *Children and Society* (1993) 7 (2), pp. 125–36; N. Dennis and G. Erdos, *Families without Fatherhood*, IEA, 1992.

4 W. Galston, *Liberal Purposes, Good Virtues and Diversity in the Liberal State*, Cambridge University Press, 1991.

5 A. Etzioni, *The Spirit of Community: The Reinvention of American Society*, Touchstone Books, 1994.

6 J.Q. Wilson, *The Moral Sense*, Free Press, 1993.

7 A. Deacon, 'The Green Paper on Welfare Reforms: A Case for Enlightened Self-Interest?' *Political Quarterly* (1998) 69 (3), pp. 306–11.

8 P. Selznik, *The Moral Commonwealth. Social Theory and the Promise of Community*, University of California Press, 1992.

9 J. Kooiman (ed.), *Modern Governance. New Government-Society Interactions*, Sage, 1993.

10 Cm. 2424 *Looking to the Future. Mediation and the Ground for Divorce.* A Consultation Paper, Stationery Office, para 1.5.

11 S. Cretney and J. Masson, *Principles of Family Law*, Sweet and Maxwell, 1988, p. 327.

12 *Law Society Gazette*, 30 May 1996.

13 House of Commons, Standing Cttee. E, 25 April 1996, col. 4.

14 Home Office *Supporting Families*, Stationery Office, 1998, p. 4.

15 ibid., p. 5.

16 P. Morgan, *Farewell to the Family*, IEA, 1995.

17 A. Barlow and S. Duncan, 'Supporting Families? New Labour's Communitarianism and the "Rationality Mistake"', *Journal of Social Welfare and Family Law* (2000) 22 (1), pp. 23–42.

18 J. Baldock, 'Culture: the Missing Variable in Understanding Social Policy?' *Social Policy and Administration* (1999) 33 (4), pp. 458–73.

19 J. Reynolds and P. Mansfield, 'The Effect of Changing Attitudes to Marriage on its Stability'. In J. Simons (ed.) *High Divorce Rates: The State of the Evidence on Reasons and Remedies*, Lord Chancellor's Department, 1999.

20 J. Bradshaw, C. Stimson, C. Skinner and J. Williams, *Absent Fathers?* Routledge, 1999.

21 Cm. 3805 New Ambitions for our Country. A New Contract for Welfare, Stationery Office, 1998, p. iii.

22 S. Harkness, S. Machin and J. Waldfogel, 'Women's Pay and Family Incomes in Britain, 1979–1991'. In J. Hills (ed.) *New Inequalities: The Changing Distribution of Income and Wealth in the UK*, Cambridge University Press, 1996.

23 J. Rubery, M. Smith and C. Fagan, 'National Working-Time Regimes and Equal Opportunities', *Feminist Economics* (1998) 4 (1), pp. 71–101.

24 C. Ward, A. Dale and H. Joshi, 'Income dependency within couples'. In L. Morris and E.S. Lyon (eds) *Gender Relations in Public and Private*, Macmillan, 1996.

25 T. Thair and A. Risdon, 'Women in the labour market. Results from the spring 1998 LFS', *Labour Market Trends* (1999) (March), pp. 103–27.

26 S. Duncan and R. Edwards, *Lone Mothers, Paid Work and Gendered Moral Rationalities*, Macmillan, 1999.

27 H. Land and J. Lewis, 'Gender, Care and the Changing Role of the State in the UK'. In J. Lewis (ed.) *Gender, Care and Welfare State Restructuring in Europe*, Ashgate, 1998.

28 J. Pahl, *Money and Marriage*, Macmillan, 1989.

29 J. Millar, *Keeping Track of Welfare Reform. The New Deal Programmes*, Joseph Rowntree Foundation, 2000.

30 Katherine Rake, 'The Second Sex and the Third Way: Women, Gender Relations and New Labour's Social Policies', *Journal of Social Policy* (forthcoming 2001).

31 Rake, ibid; E. McLaughlin, J. Tewsdale and N. McCay, 'The Working Families Tax Credit: Some Issues and Estimates', *Social Policy and Administration* (forthcoming 2001).

32 Department of Trade and Industry, *Work and Parents: Competitiveness and Choice*. Green Paper, Dti, 2001.

33 L. Mead, *The New Paternalism*, Brookings, 1997.

34 R. Lister, 'From Equality to Social Inclusion: New Labour and the Welfare State', *Critical Social Policy* (1998) 18 (2), pp 215–25.

CHAPTER 23

THE MEDIA AND MEDIA MANAGEMENT

Margaret Scammell

Introduction

THERE CAN BE little dispute that New Labour has raised the business of political communication to a new plane. Consider the 'firsts' of Tony Blair's Labour. For the first time in its history Labour won the support of the majority of the national press at a general election (Figure 1). Blair is the first British Prime Minister to broadcast regularly on the world wide web. He is the first to meet weekly with his party's private pollster, the first to write regularly in the mass circulation tabloid newspapers. He is the first to model his Number 10 press machinery, in structure and personnel, on his party's election campaign team. He is the first to have, in addition to his press office, a strategic communications unit at Number 10. His press secretary, Alastair Campbell, is the first to regularly attend full Cabinet meetings, the first to make public the content of his briefings of political Lobby correspondents, the first to allow cameras into those once-secret meetings, albeit for a one-off documentary. Blair's Labour represents a landmark in communication terms, whose enduring transforming impact may well rank at least as importantly as Attlee's creation of the Central Office of Communication in 1946 and Thatcher's hiring of Saatchi and Saatchi.

If few dispute that we are witnessing a quantum leap, there is considerable argument about its significance. Tony Blair, in a BBC documentary about Campbell, put the case that presentation is simply part of the business of modern politics.[1] The news media are more extensive and demanding. The 1990s saw the emergence of twenty-four-hour dedicated TV and radio news channels and an explosion of news services on the internet. At the same time political journalism, 'the disillusionment industry' in Campbell's telling phrase, has changed. Journalists are no longer

Figure 1 Party votes and press partisanship

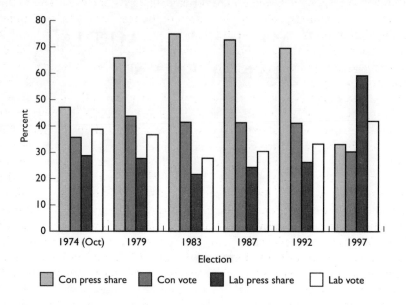

content with straight reporting of events, but have become increasingly critical analysts, ever alert to splits and spin. Governments, then, *must* work harder than before to stay on top of the news, or else become its victims, as indeed happened to John Major in his latter years. Stories, too often full of distortions, take on a life of their own and 'run off into the far distance', to quote Blair. All Labour has really done, he says, is to get 'on terms' with Thatcher's Conservatives. In short, Labour is doing nothing fundamentally different from its more successful predecessors; it has simply and sensibly adapted to the era of modern media and new communications technology.

It is a sympathetic argument on the face of it, not least because Labour does not deny its unprecedented attention to communications. It instead justifies it in the context of a rapidly changing media environment and a history of hostility towards Labour from much of Fleet Street. However, there is also considerable force in the claims of Labour's critics. In this view, Labour, more clearly than any of its post-war predecessors, is a permanently campaigning administration. It has attempted to re-create in government the rigid message discipline of its 1997 election campaign. To that end, it has strengthened the control of Number 10 over government departments. It has downgraded the role of Parliament, treating it as just another communications opportunity, in the process short-circuiting democratic debate. It has betrayed its own promises of freedom of information and open public debate and dialogue. Campbell and other of Blair's closest aides stand accused of bullying some journalists, blatantly favouring others and they are widely believed to have briefed against some of Labour's own government members, who for one reason or another are considered undisciplined or a threat to Number 10's control.

At root here, there is a mostly unspoken but clear sense that politics (governing and policy-making) and communications (news management and promotion) *should* be two separate entities. Politics is, or should be, the master and presentation the servant. Politics, properly and ethically practised, keeps communications in its place as a necessary, but definitely secondary, function. The extreme case against New Labour is that it has reversed this proper order. The demands of presentation overwhelm everything else, up to and including ideological commitment, the pursuit of principle and the making of policy. The reversal of the master-servant order is personified, critics claim, in the relationship of Blair and Campbell. Whereas Bernard Ingham, for all that he was a powerful Press Secretary, was clearly Thatcher's servant, Campbell appears as lordly as his master. Peter Oborne's biography calls Campbell 'the real deputy Prime Minister'.[2] He paints an extraordinary portrait of Campbell's status, with journalists hanging on to his every word while the Prime Minister stands unnoticed behind his shoulder.

These, then, are the opposing sides of the argument: first, that Labour is obsessed with news management, to the detriment of what one might hope for in governance and proper democratic debate, that New Labour is 'government by media and focus group'.[3] On the other side, there is Blair's view, that Labour is primarily reactive to the conditions of modern media, refusing to become victims to an ever-more voracious and cynical journalism and attempting to counter-act the traditional hostility of the national press. There is prima facie evidence to support both cases.

This chapter looks at the evidence, of the conditions of the media market, and of continuity and change in the approach and machinery of government communications. However, it is worth saying at the outset that judgements of the propriety of the Blair effect will probably not depend on the detail of the balance sheet. They will turn ultimately on one's political opinions. Those in sympathy with New Labour are likely to applaud its professionalism and forgive minor indiscretions, contrasting them to the Thatcher era when the government controversially spent many millions of taxpayers' money on advertising privatisation and 'action for jobs'. Those opposed will see propaganda rather than professionalism and will look cynically upon the mechanisms for measuring public opinion that Labour has introduced into government. Probably it was ever thus. Government publicity, energetically applied, is inherently combustible, especially when in combination with a remit for radical reform. It is no coincidence that prior to Blair, the periods of greatest controversy concerning government publicity have been the post-war Attlee and Thatcher governments. Nonetheless, let us focus on the evidence and see where it leads, starting with the media environment before turning to Labour's approach and use of government communications.

The Media Environment: Things Could Scarcely get Better?

Alastair Campbell's complaints at the 'disillusionment industry' are given short shrift by Sir Bernard Ingham. Compared to Ingham's time at Number 10, journalists are largely quiescent, almost 'poodle-ish' in their friendliness towards government.[4] Campbell, he says, is a 'whinging Pomme', who has no idea what it is like to be under sustained attack from the press. Doubtless, this partly reflects Ingham's own experience of his first few years at Number 10 when Mrs Thatcher was struggling in the polls, lagging behind the Social Democrats and undermined by leaks from her own Cabinet. Thatcher's successor, John Major, left Downing Street in May 1997 with scarcely a friend in Fleet Street, even among the traditional Conservative tabloids. The opinion polls and the press turned against Major following 'Black Wednesday', 16 September 1992 when Britain was ejected from the Exchange Rate Mechanism, and he proved unable to recover. So overwhelmingly critical was his press, that it was more fitting to talk of the 'media effect' upon Major, rather than the other way round.[5] Labour, by contrast, came into office buoyed by the support of most of the press, for the first time in its history (see Table 1). Soon afterwards, the *Express*, under the ownership of Labour peer Lord Hollick, switched camp from Conservative to Labour. The media honeymoon that is the normal due of a new government seemed to last unusually long.

Table 1 Newspapers: circulation, ownership and party preference

Paper	Owner	Circ. April 1997 (millions)	Circ. April 1999 (millions)	Circ. change %	Party pref, GE 1997
Daily Mail	Ass. Newspapers	2,151	2,336	8.6	Con
Mirror	Mirror Group	3,084	2,985	−3.2	Lab
Express*	MAI/United (Lord Hollick)	1,220	1,099	−9.9	Con (now Lab)
Daily Star	MAI/United (Lord Hollick)	648	605	−6.6	Lab
Sun	News Int. (R. Murdoch)	3,842	3,746	−2.5	Lab
Telegr'ph	Hollinger/C. Black	1,134	1,046	−7.8	Con
Guardian	Scott Trust	401	402	0.2	Lab
Times New Int.	(R. Murdoch)	719	744	3.5	No party
Indepen't	Mirror Group	251	224	−10.8	Lab
FT	Pearson	307	368	19.9	Lab

* From November 2000 Northern & Shell (Richard Desmond)

Partly this was Blair's luck. After eighteen years of unbroken Conservative rule, the whole country seemed willing to give the new government a chance. Partly it was determined courtship. The Blair leadership was convinced that tabloid hostility in 1992 had contributed significantly to the party's negative image and had helped set an anti-Labour agenda.[6] It was impressed too by the analysis of former *Guardian* journalist and now Labour MP Martin Linton, which correlated press support with vote shares at general elections (an updated version of this is shown in Figure 1). Where, in the Kinnock era, Labour's media relations were essentially a permanent exercise in damage limitation, Blair sought to turn the press to advantage. He set about fostering warmer relations with press proprietors and editors, especially with the Conservative tabloids and Rupert Murdoch's News International stable of papers. Famously, Blair in 1997, and Gordon Brown, as Chancellor of the Exchequer in 1998, flew to address Murdoch executives in Australia and Idaho. The policy claimed its first success when the *Sun* declared for Blair at the outset of the 1997 general election campaign. Since coming to office, it is no secret that the editors and proprietors are regular invitees to Downing Street and Chequers, while Campbell is a regular visitor to the tabloid newsrooms. Through courtship and good fortune there is now a Labour friendly climate in most of the major media boardrooms. Murdoch is pro-Labour and so too are Gerry Robinson at Granada which owns six of the 15 regional ITV licences and a 50 per cent share of OnDigital. Additionally, and in the teeth of strong objections from the Murdoch papers and the Conservative Party, Greg Dyke was appointed Director General of the BBC in 1999, despite his open support of Labour and donations to Blair's leadership and general election campaigns.

Things could hardly get better for Labour, or so it would seem. Yet, it *is* true, despite Ingham protestations, that the media market is changing in ways that make life more demanding and less predictable for parties. The news market has expanded significantly through twenty-four-hour news channels. Sky News and BBC 24 News were by the end of 1999 available in nearly 25 per cent of UK homes, while ITN in 2000 announced its plans for a twenty-four-hour dedicated news channel. Additionally, the BBC's 5 Live radio and the commercial station TalkSport both broadcast extensive news coverage and discussion throughout the day and night. One consequence is increasing pressure on politicians' time, for interviews and statements. A second is that media attention is both expanded and intensified. As Michael White, political editor of the *Guardian*, put it, if you are 'off message' now in an obscure village hall in Scotland, twenty minutes later 'it is down the satellite feed and on to the six o'clock news'.[7] At the same time, there has been a significant decline in the audience for news on the main terrestrial commercial TV network. Commercial television has all but abandoned hard news and current affairs in prime time. Most controversially, ITV dropped News at Ten in March 1999 in order to broadcast a more competitive entertainment-oriented schedule. Eventually, after prompting from the Independent Television Commission, it announced it would restore *News at Ten* three or four nights a week. This compromise ultimately may be upset by the BBC's decision to move its flagship *Nine O'Clock News* to 10 p.m. from October 2000. The one sure thing now is that in the new era of highly-competitive multi-channel TV, political news no longer has the secure, protected place in the mass-audience schedules that it had enjoyed for the previous thirty years. Thus, effectively politicians are being stretched across expanding news space while being less assured of a mass audience.

Insecurity is the watchword with the newspapers. Press partisanship is not as committed or secure as it was in the Thatcher era when the parties were split into clearly demarcated ideological camps. All the papers, even the tabloids, now have multiple columnists expressing a range of political opinions, which blur the once-clear line of the editorial page. Critical and often issue-contingent support has replaced unswerving loyalties. Where the *Mirror* was once virtually the propaganda mouthpiece of Labour, it is now a more detached defender with its columnist Paul Routledge, self-avowedly an 'old' rather than 'new' Labour man. It is willing to demonstrate independence and did so during the fuel crisis of the summer of 2000, supporting the demands for a petrol price cut. The *Sun*, following its 1997 conversion, is still warm towards Blair, but has never been convinced by his party. It remains, moreover, profoundly Euro-sceptic and not slow to remind Blair of the fact. 'Is THIS the most dangerous man in Britain?' it asked of Blair's willingness to 'scrap the pound' (24 June, 1998). New Labour is clearly nervous of the paper's influence with its huge audience of politically decisive voters. Campbell's oft-reported joshing of political correspondents significantly has *not* included the *Sun*'s reporters, who admit to being treated well. The *Sun* seems happy to keep Labour keen. Having dismissed the Conservatives as a 'dead parrot' in 1998, it was fulsome in its praise of William Hague's performance at the 2000 party conference. This was rather surprising given that the paper's political editor, Trevor Kavanagh, had appeared on television the previous night dismissing Hague's speech as probably the most curious he had ever heard from a leader at a party conference. It was an editorial warning to Labour that the *Sun*'s support cannot be taken for granted. Moreover, the political affiliation of the Murdoch press ultimately rests on its owner's calculation of his commercial interests.

New Labour and Political Journalism: More Spinned Against than Spinning?

There has been a marked change in style of political reporting over the last decade. Alastair Campbell has frequently lamented the drift from straight reporting of events to interpretation, often cynical at that, and bolstered by anonymous quotes 'real or imagined'. Journalists, not he, are the really powerful spin-doctors, Campbell claims. His description is essentially right in one respect at least. Content analysis of news coverage at successive elections confirms a trend from predominantly straight reporting to an increasingly analytical, evaluative and critical journalism.[8] This is particularly marked in the broadsheet papers. Of course, Campbell chooses to ignore his own responsibility in this process, because interpretative reporting, at least in part, is an entirely predictable response to politicians' intensified efforts at news management. As Michael Prescott, political editor of the *Sunday Times*, comments, reporters now see themselves as 'professional decoders' of the peculiar political language of spin. The more a journalist feels he or she is being 'spun', the less likely that an event will be reported at face value. A similar trend in the US has led to a phenomenon of 'strategic framing', in which political actions are evaluated routinely in context of their strategic intent and likely effects upon target voters, opinion polls and political alliances.

Much the same is now happening here and is manifested in the extraordinary upsurge in media interest in 'spin' (see Table 2). Mentions of spin doctors in a sample of national newspapers increased by close to 7000 per cent over the period 1989–99. In the early 1990s, spin doctor was a term unheard outside the political cognoscenti. If the terminology was new, the activity of news management was not and there had been significant interest in the 'marketing of Margaret' in the early Thatcher years, and attention to the power and role of her press secretary, Bernard Ingham, in her second and third governments.[9] However, by sheer volume of coverage there has been nothing to compare to the past three years. Spin-watching, by any name, is no longer confined to the fringes of academic inquiry, satire, radical and/or disgruntled journalists. It has spread to the mainstream and become *the* uniquely defining feature of press coverage of New Labour.

Table 2 Media attention to spin

Keyword search	1 Jan–31 Dec 1989	1 Jan–31 Dec 1999	
	Hits n.	Hits n.	% change (increase)
Spin	668	3921	587
Spin doctors	8	529	6610

Source: FT Profile Guardian, Daily Telegraph, Independent

Of course, communications was from the outset central to the party's transformation to New Labour. The party's media experts, especially Peter Mandelson and Philip Gould were among the leading architects of modernisation. When Tony Blair entered Downing Street, the communicators, Mandelson, Campbell and Gould, came with him among his closest advisers. Mandelson, as Minister without Portfolio, was given licence to put into practice some of his own recommendations, to strengthen the Cabinet Office and establish clear links between policy and presentation. Moreover, Labour appeared openly proud, sometimes even boastful, of the professionalism of its communications efforts. Campbell told the House of Commons Select Committee on Public Administration (1998): 'In opposition we made clear that communications was not something that you tagged on at the end, it is part of what you do. That is something we have tried to bring into government.' Gordon Brown's former spin doctor Charlie Whelan cheerfully admitted being 'economical with the truth' as he recalled details of his news management triumphs in a Network First television documentary aired within months of the 1997 election. In 1998 Philip Gould proclaimed his own role in his book, *The Unfinished Revolution*, immodestly sub-titled: 'How the modernisers saved the Labour Party.'

Not unnaturally, then, the role of the image-makers has always been a significant part of the press story of New Labour. At first this could be characterised as somewhat grudging admiration of the spinners' skills, the 'on message' discipline of the party's election campaign and Campbell's ability to contrive headline-catching soundbites, most famously 'the people's princess' line which Tony Blair delivered in eulogy of Princess Diana. However, over the last two years spin coverage became more abundant, more routinely part of everyday political reporting and more cynical. The spin doctors themselves became headline news, conducting 'proxy wars', according to the press, between the feuding camps of Brown and Blair. The resignation of Charlie Whelan in January 1999, amid suspicion that he had leaked against Peter Mandelson, took more coverage in some broadsheet papers than the launch of the euro the same day. Even, and perhaps especially, the personal lives of politicians were reported as part of the game. Was the Blair's child, Leo, the first baby in Number 10 since 1848, 'conceived by a spin doctor', the BBC's correspondent Nick Assinder asked, with tongue only partially in cheek. Although most media commentators stopped short of so cynical a judgement it was a striking sign of the times that 'the people's baby' was discussed publicly at all in such terms.

Since the image-makers claimed and had been given much credit for Labour's success, it was no surprise that they were among the first to be blamed when the opinion polls finally turned against Labour. The spring and early summer of 2000 were miserable months for the government. For the first time since 1997, it endured a relatively lengthy period of sustained setbacks. The London mayoral contest was deemed a public relations disaster from start to finish, ending with Frank Dobson, Labour's official candidate, beaten into third place. Heavy losses in the May local elections were followed by a summer of presentational failures, including the rare indignity of the slow hand clap for the Prime Minister during his speech to the Women's Institute. The government's robust refusal to succumb to protestors' demands for fuel price cuts brought mixed reviews among the commentators but a general verdict of clumsy presentation. Was Blair losing his touch? Voices from within and without the party blamed the spin doctors for the mess.

Novelist and former Labour fund-raiser Ken Follett accused Campbell and Mandelson of stirring trouble in the heart of government, spreading 'malicious gossip' against certain ministers, notably Gordon Brown and Mo Mowlam. A few days later, 9 July, leaked correspondence revealed that John Prescott, the Deputy Prime Minister, was demanding weekly Cabinet inquests into why the government seemed to have lost its grip on the media. A succession of leaked memos written by Philip Gould brought further embarrassment for Blair and blame for the spin doctors. According to Gould's focus group research, the 'New Labour brand' had been badly contaminated, the object of constant criticism and ridicule and 'undermined by a combination of spin, lack of conviction and apparently lack of integrity, manifested by the [London] mayoral selection process'. One of Gould's leaked memos concluded: [Tony Blair] 'lacks conviction, he is all spin and presentation, he says things to please people not because he believes them.' The irony was as irresistible as it was obvious: New Labour, the masters of presentation, hoist by their own petard. The only surprise, for some commentators, was that Gould had taken so long to discover this. As Roy Greenslade put it in the *Guardian*: 'what use are these focus groups if they are so slow to catch on?' (19 June).

Campbell, over the three years since 1997, has employed multiple strategies to cope with the media. He energetically sought to strengthen and professionalise the Government Information Service, recruiting sympathetic journalists to top posts in government departments (see below). He continued in government the policy begun in Opposition to rationalise ministerial appearances, essentially to limit appearances to those media outlets considered to have sufficiently large and/or influential audiences. He has tried to by-pass what he sees as the corrosive cynicism of the political journalists in a number of ways. He encouraged the Prime Minister to use alternative media, such as daytime television, women's magazines, regional papers and the ethnic press. He fed articles signed by the Prime Minister and other Cabinet members to the tabloid press in particular. A total of about 150 Blair by-lined articles were published in his first two years in office. One was almost as likely to read Blair in the *Sun* as hear him in the Commons. From February, 2000, Campbell has used the Number 10 website to publish summaries of his briefings to the Westminster Lobby journalists and to broadcast Prime Ministerial speeches and a regular audio package of Blair's views on leading issues and policy matters.

He has tried to shame political correspondents into changing their ways, arguing publicly with them that the modern fashion for reporting spin is lazy and incestuous journalism that short-changes the public's need for news about the really important issues of the economy, health and education. He has tried greater openness, putting the once-secret Lobby briefings on the record and by granting extraordinary access to certain journalists. The BBC's Michael Cockerell was given unprecedented access for the making of the documentary *News from Number 10*, allowed to film in Downing Street and at Lobby briefings over the course of four months. The *Observer*'s chief political columnist, Andrew Rawnsley, was given near-total co-operation in the writing of his inside account of New Labour *Servants of the People* (2000). In neither case, according to these journalists, did Campbell attempt any untoward interference in their editorial decisions.

Eventually, however, the Prime Minister decided that the best approach was to withdraw Campbell from the day-to-day fray with journalists. From June 2000 the twice-daily Lobby briefings were taken mostly by Campbell's civil service deputy Godric Smith. Campbell was to take a more detached role, overseeing government communications strategy. According to Number 10 sources, Blair had wanted this for some time, believing that Campbell's capacity to take the long view was undermined by the pressure of preparing for the equivalent of Prime Minister's Questions twice a day with Lobby journalists. Campbell had been more reluctant. For all his open contempt of journalistic standards, he seemed to enjoy the high adrenaline of daily confrontation with his former Lobby peers. However, Campbell himself had come to accept that he was now part of the government's image problem. Campbell agreed that he had got himself into a situation with journalists 'where combat was the only language being spoken'.[10] Never one who needed pushing into a fight, his relations with Lobby journalists were 'bloke-ishly' abrasive from the outset. 'Explain to me just why I should waste my time with a load of wankers like you . . .' were Campbell's first words to the Sunday newspaper lobby after the 1997 election victory. He has never been slow to tell journalists how to do their jobs, either in person or in letters to the editor. Cockerell reported that several Lobby correspondents proudly produced furious personal letters of complaint from Campbell. While some journalists seemed to enjoy sparring with Campbell, others, notably Nicholas Jones of the BBC and his brother George at the *Telegraph*, describe him as a less than jocular bully and resent what they see as an abuse of his power. Paul Routledge, now on the *Mirror*, claimed that his impending appointment as political editor on the *Sunday Express* was blocked by Campbell, although this was denied by its editor, Rosie Boycott. Campbell's typical response to pressure is the counter-attack and defiant justification of his methods. Thus, for example, in response to criticism that government ministers were avoiding confrontational interviewers such as Jeremy Paxman, he wrote to *The Times* (30 June, 1998). He agreed that ministers were reluctant to appear on *Newsnight* 'with its dwindling audience' and added: 'As one minister said to me recently . . . "What is the point of me traipsing out to W12 late at night so that Jeremy can try to persuade the public that I'm actually some kind of criminal?"'

Has Campbell really behaved so differently from his predecessors? In his forthright demeanour he has more in common with Sir Bernard Ingham than with the three rather anonymous civil servants who successively served John Major. In fact, Peter Riddell, of *The Times*, describes the commotion made about Campbell as no more than an updated version of the complaints of media manipulation made against Ingham ten years earlier.[11] There is a difference though. Ingham was a civil servant scarcely known to Thatcher before his appointment at Number 10. There was never any doubt that Ingham was Thatcher's faithful servant. Campbell's relationship is one of a more politically disconcerting equality with his master. Campbell and Blair are of similar age, have similar Oxbridge educational backgrounds, and are close family friends as well as political allies. Campbell was Blair's press secretary in Opposition. His partner Fiona Miller is employed as public relations assistant to Cherie Blair. He is the first press secretary to be permitted to attend regularly full Cabinet meetings, something that previously had happened only exceptionally or was confined to certain Cabinet committees. In short, he has a closer political and personal relationship with the Prime Minister than any previous press secretary. Campbell's critics, including his biographer Peter Oborne, Ingham and former Labour communications director Joy Johnson, contend that too often Campbell is the real leader of the pair: the 'ventriloquist to Blair's dummy', to quote Ingham. Some observers found credence for the theory in Michael Cockerell's documentary about Campbell, *News from Number 10*. It made Blair look like an actor not an actor-manager, according to Austin Mitchell's review for the BBC. Worse, it made the Prime Minister 'look a prat', according to Charlie Whelan's *Observer* column. Of all the complaints about government publicity, this is the one most resented by Campbell, according to one Downing Street adviser. It was a 'travesty of the truth', he said. Campbell was fiercely loyal and would be bitterly upset to think that he had ever behaved in a manner superior to his boss. Moreover, the same source said that he knew 'for a fact' that Blair treated Campbell as an adviser, albeit an unusually close and trusted one, and had effectively excluded Campbell from delicate political matters where the latter's views were not considered helpful. Critics such as Oborne, Johnson, Ingham and Whelan, all have political and/or personal axes to grind, and besides are in no position to judge. Ingham's views were particularly suspected. Given his track record of 'rubbishing and leaking' in Downing Street, he could hardly claim to be the touchstone of propriety.

Is Campbell the real deputy prime minister? In truth, there is no hard evidence to prove this and good reason to suppose not. We can say with confidence that he is enormously influential, and even some Downing Street insiders admit that he is probably more powerful than some of the Cabinet. However, Campbell's power depends completely upon Blair's favour and fortunes. Unlike the elected politicians, Campbell has no

capacity for independent support among the broad party or public opinion. Moreover, the greater his influence is perceived to be, the more he
risks undermining Blair's authority and thereby his own power-base. In
short, Campbell cannot afford to behave like the 'real deputy prime minister' if he wants a long-term stay in Downing Street. In the troubled
summer of 2000 even Campbell's Fleet Street supporters began to wonder
if his sacrifice was the only way to save Blair from further damage from
the 'all spin and no substance' accusations. Campbell survived and questions about his role dwindled into the background as Labour recovered in
the polls. He has adopted both a lower public profile and a more conciliatory tone with journalists, admitting at a speech to the Westminster
press gallery (November 16) that he had 'hung on . . . that little bit too
long' in government to techniques of spin that had seemed appropriate in
Opposition.

Government Machinery of Press and Public Communication: Continuity and Change

An examination of the apparatus of government press and publicity confirms Labour's dedication to communications. Table 3 shows innovation,
particularly with regard to media relations and the monitoring of public
opinion, and significant expansion of all the inherited areas. Blair's government has strengthened publicity services across the board. The most
notable developments have come in the influx of special advisers as political aides to ministers and in the Government Information Service (GIS),
now re-named the Government Information and Communication Service
(GICS). The number of political appointees, the special advisers, has more
than trebled in Downing Street since the Major era from eight to twenty-
nine by March 2000. Close to one third of these, including Campbell, have
an explicit presentational role (below). The numbers of government information officers have been on a rising trend over the last twenty years.
However, as Table 4 shows, Labour has continued the upward path with
added vigour. In several key departments the percentage increase in
information officer numbers has been as great in the two years since 1997
as over the previous twenty (notably Education and Employment, Cabinet
Office and Treasury). The increase is all the more striking given that civil
service staff numbers generally have declined in recent years.

The new government, and especially Alastair Campbell, were quickly
unimpressed with the efforts of the Government Information Service (GIS)
that it inherited. In Campbell's view the information service was not
equipped to deal with twenty-four-hour news media. It was often slow to
respond to media inquiries, insufficiently proactive and co-ordinated
according to the over-arching themes of government communications strategy. In October 1997 Campbell famously circulated a memo to Heads of

Table 3 Government machinery of press and public communications

General Press Relations		
GICS (until 1998 called the Government Information Service)	Inherited. Re-titled as GICS following Mountfield Report.	Significantly increased staff numbers in key departments and Number 10
Strategic Communications Unit	Created Jan. 1998, following Mountfield.	Staff 6. Co-ordinates govt. communications. Responsible for Annual Report. Writes ministerial speeches/press articles
Media Monitoring Unit	Created December 1997, following Mountfield.	24-hour monitoring of media coverage of govt. activity.
Chief Press Secretary (PM's press secretary)	Post inherited. Normally, but not always, recruited from civil service ranks.	Convention of anonymity changed. Identified as PM's official spokesman and by name from 2000. Summary of Lobby briefings on the Internet. Campbell the first to attend full Cabinet regularly.
Research and information unit	Created March 1999.	Provides briefs to PM and SCU. Known as 'rebuttal unit'. Runs the 'Knowledge Network' computer databank.
Public Communication Services		
COI	Inherited.	Handles govt. advertising and other publicity. Spending increased since 1997.
Web services	Open.gov.uk inherited from Major. Established in support of Citizens' Charter.	Significantly expanded. Averages 14m. accesses per week. Target: 25% of govt. services to be available electronically by 2002. PM regular webcasts.
Peoples' Panel	Part of 'Service First' initiative which replaced Major's Citizens' Charter.	Permanent opinion survey to gauge attitudes to govt. services.
Freedom of Information	FOI Act November 2000	

Information warning them that the GIS must 'raise its game' (reported in the *Financial Times*, 9 October 1997). Campbell instructed information officers on the service that government now expected: 'We should always know how big stories will be playing in the next day's papers. If a story is going wrong, or if a policy should be defended we must respond quickly, confidently and robustly.' Most importantly, the civil service generally needed to change its attitude towards communications. Whitehall press officers needed to be in at the start of policy development, Campbell said, not as he sensed then happened, kept out of the loop until the media plan was produced at a much later stage.

Labour's first few months in office brought a number of clashes with

Table 4 Numbers of information officers in government departments

	Dept. of Emp. *	Dept. of Envir.	FCO	DHSS**	Home Office	DTI***	Cabinet Office	PM's Office	Treasury
1979	23	65	19	24	27	38	–	6	12
1983	22	37	17	18	25	77	–	6	12
1991	78	34	20	57	37	62	10	6	9
1997	44	42	30	141	50	67	14	12	16
1999	96	97	46	171	54	74	23	14	20
79–97 %+/–	91	–35	58	488	85	76	–	100	25
97–99 %+/–	118	23	53	21	8	10	79	17	25

Source: Central Office of Information: IPO Directory – Information and Press Officers in Government Departments
*Department of Employment becomes Education and Employment from 1995.
**DHSS splits into two departments, Health and Social Security. Figures from 1989 include both departments.
***Departments of Trade and Industry are separate in 1979 and 1983. Figures include both departments.
Data adapted from: A. Davis *Public Relations Democracy* (forthcoming)

civil service information officers. If the new government was dissatisfied with the GIS's professionalism, there were complaints from within the GIS that government did not always appear to understand the civil service code of conduct which insists on the subtle but crucial difference between information and partisan advocacy. A memorandum written by the Association of First Division Civil Servants (FDA) noted that the transition from Conservative to Labour government had been rather 'less successful' for the GIS than for most of the civil service. Ministers, used to the professionalism of Labour's Millbank press operation, appeared to have 'little grasp of the role of the GIS and in some cases failed to appreciate the issues of propriety governing the GIS itself'. The FDA was particularly critical of the special advisers who were 'pushing at the boundaries' of the GIS cultural ethos of political impartiality. By the end of 1997, eight heads of information had left, notably Jill Rutter at the Treasury, who complained that Brown's special adviser Charlie Whelan had taken over three-quarters of her job. By the end of 1999 only two of the seventeen departmental heads of information inherited by Labour were still in place. The FDA reported that morale among information officers 'was very low' in the wake of the departures and not helped by the fact that the replacements were often external candidates.[12]

In September 1997, Robin Mountfield, Permanent Secretary of the Office of Public Service, was asked by the Cabinet Secretary (then Sir Robin Butler) to consider government concerns about how well the GIS was equipped to 'meet the demands of a fast-changing media world'. Mountfield's committee included Alastair Campbell and Mike Grannatt, head of the GIS. The resulting report in November 1997 was widely interpreted as a victory for Labour's brand of news management. It accepted the thesis that 'effective communication and explanation of policy and decisions should not be an after-thought, but an integral part of a democratic government's duty to govern with consent'.[13] It recommended measures to improve co-ordination of government publicity, most notably with the establishment of the Strategic Communications Unit (SCU) in Number 10 and similar 'strategic planning units' in all departments. It recommended the establishment of a twenty-four-hour media monitoring unit, to be based in the Cabinet Office as a service for all government departments. It noted the disdain with which civil service policy administrators sometimes treated communications, and recommended that information officers be included in all stages of the policy process. It suggested the name change to Government Information and Communication Service, to reinforce the change in attitude: from reactive information supply in response to media queries to pro-active communication as part of the normal business of government. Mountfield recommended further that the Chief Press Secretary's Lobby briefings be put on the record, and that the press secretary be identified as the 'Prime Minister's Official Spokesman'. In short, Mountfield delivered all the key changes that Campbell had wanted, within the overall proviso of civil service codes of propriety.

In the wake of the Mountfield Report and amid continuing concern at 'Millbankisation' of government publicity, the House of Commons Select Committee on Public Administration set up its own review of the GICS. Under the chairmanship of Rhodri Morgan, it took evidence from among others, Mountfield, Campbell, Ingham, Sir Richard Wilson (the Secretary to the Cabinet) and a number of Lobby journalists including Peter Riddell, of *The Times*, and Michael White, of the *Guardian*. The committee sought some assurances from government about a number of matters, such as transparency of publicity costs, codes of conduct for special advisers, career advancement for GICS staff and clarification of the role of the SCU. Broadly, though, its report (29 July 1998) endorsed the Mountfield reforms. It noted Sir Richard's comment that there was a more 'determined effort to co-ordinate in a strategic way presentation of the government's policies and messages in a positive light across the whole of government, than I can remember since the time I have been in the senior civil service'. The committee welcomed this new approach. 'Governments in the past have often been ineffective in explaining their policies; it is high time that a more professional approach were taken to these matters.'

The Mountfield Report is a landmark in the modern history of government presentation. Ingham, in his evidence to the Public Administration Select Committee (2 June 1998), suggested that there was 'no original idea' in Mountfield. In a sense he was correct. All recent press secretaries, most notably Ingham, have sought to co-ordinate publicity from Downing Street with varying degrees of energy and success. The official handbook for the GIS had, at least since its 1980 version, demanded that heads of information have a close working relationship with ministers and permanent secretaries and be fully informed of all proposals and policies. Ingham himself had subscribed to the view that it was the GIS's job to present government policy in the best possible light, consistent with the civil service code of impartiality. As press secretary he had argued that impartiality did not mean strict neutrality, but rather the avoidance of purely internal party matters and attacks on the opposition, and the willingness to serve equally governments of whatever hue. Nonetheless, Mountfield brought together long-desired aims of government communicators, codified them and stamped them with the authority of the Cabinet Office. Most importantly it upgraded the role of communications *per se*, confirming its central place in the business of government. It introduced mechanisms for increasing Downing Street control and coordination of Whitehall publicity as a whole. Further, it gave official sanction to the idea that it was the GICS's job to present government policy in a positive way. As Ingham admitted to the Select Committee, the Mountfield Report 'is a most valuable document and I wish I had had it when I was press secretary'.

The SCU is the key institutional mechanism introduced by Mountfield. Its brief is essentially to ensure that all departments are 'on message', in line with centrally-produced themes. Headed by a civil servant, James Humphreys, it is accountable to the Prime Minister through his press secretary. Its formal tasks include advising departments on media strategy, on content and format of policy documents, production of the Annual Report, drafting articles and speeches for the Prime Minister and the development of government websites. The SCU is staffed by a mix of policy and media specialists, civil servants and political appointees, including two Labour-sympathising journalists, David Bradshaw from the *Mirror* and Philip Bassett from *The Times*. Bassett is the key figure in the SCU with responsibility for forward planning of the presentation of government publicity. The SCU establishes a 'grid' schedule of all foreseeable newsworthy events, ranging from parliamentary announcements to celebrity court cases, into which the timing of government publicity is organised for optimal effect.

The unit's staff numbers and the scope of its work have steadily expanded since its introduction in January 1998. Bill Bush, formerly head of BBC's political research and a one-time press aide to Ken Livingstone at the Greater London Council, joined in March 1999 and is in charge of a special research and intelligence unit attached to the SCU. Bush's task was widely reported in the press as similar to the rebuttal and 'pre-buttal' functions carried out by the party's Millbank machine, to anticipate and respond to criticisms of government policy. Joe McCrea, formerly special adviser to Frank Dobson at the Health Ministry, was recruited to establish the 'Knowledge Network' database. According to the *Guardian* (Alan

Travis, 'Labour's message will bypass media', 7 January 2000), the Knowledge Network replicates in more powerful form the Excalibur computer database used at Millbank in Labour's election campaign. A Cabinet Office document, written by McCrea, explains that the network provides the government 'line' on key issues, full texts of ministerial speeches and press releases, key quotes and facts supporting government policy and breakdowns to regional and constituency level of departmental announcements and activity. Data is mapped to media regions and electoral constituencies in order that benefits of government policy may be described at local as well as national level. Part of the database is to be for public access and part is restricted and confidential. It is intended as an all-hours service for government members, officials and press officers and ensures a 'common joint script' of relevant information for all government departments.

Thus, overall the government machinery of publicity has changed significantly from that inherited by Blair. It is much strengthened in staff numbers, in institutional and technological apparatus of presentational co-ordination, and it works to a far more clearly defined promotional remit. There is a far more overt political input at the heart of the machine, manifested in the increase in special advisers. In addition to Campbell himself, there is Bradshaw, Bassett, Bush and McCrea and several others including: Hillary Coffman, former Labour Party senior press officer, Phil Murphy, formerly director of communications for the Labour Party, and Catherine Rimmer, a former colleague of Bill Bush at the BBC's political research unit. Major had eight special advisers in total in Downing Street, while Blair has the same number dedicated to publicity matters alone.

The special advisers have become an increasingly controversial part of Labour's style of government. Their role is notoriously ill-defined and can range from policy adviser, to spin doctor to more or less anything that may assist the government's operation. Across government as a whole, there were seventy-seven in 1999 at a cost of £4 million, compared to thirty-eight at a cost £1.8 million in 1996. Advisers are paid by the state and the terms of their contract debar them from activities that could provoke criticism that they are employed at public expense for purely party political purposes. Labour altered the guidelines to openly permit that which had probably always happened, liaison between special advisers and the government party. The rules now read: 'The government needs to present its policies and achievements positively. It would be damaging to the government's objectives if the government party took a different approach to that of the government itself, and the government will need therefore to liaise with the party to make sure the party publicity is factually accurate and consistent with government policy'.[14]

The role of the advisers is central to persistent complaints that Labour is politicising the civil service, or that the advisers have become almost an alternative civil service. Such protests have come primarily, but not exclusively, from the Conservative Party and from former members of the GIS. The sacked head of the Northern Ireland Office's information service, Andy Wood, accused some (unnamed) advisers of lack of discipline and propriety, claiming that they had 'trashed the reputations' of certain members of the GICS. Bernard Ingham resents what he calls 'the enormous effort to blame everything this government has done on me', that is to say that Labour is behaving no differently from him. There is a huge difference in approach, he says. Where he had sought departmental co-operation in government presentation, Labour has chosen 'control freakery'. Where he sought to professionalise the GIS through training and promotional structures, Labour has wielded the axe, appointed placemen and women and imported special advisers. Labour, of course, rejects Ingham's assessment. A Number 10 adviser complained that too many of the inherited departmental information chiefs were plainly incompetent. The charge of 'control freakery' provokes a frustrated response of 'if only': the machinery of government is simply too large and unwieldy and individual departmental agendas too strongly entrenched to be readily controlled. Continuing concern about the special advisers prompted the Neill Committee on Standards in Public Life to issue recommendations in January 2000 to limit their number and to construct a coherent and transparent code of conduct to clarify their role in relation to the work of the GICS. After some months, in July, the government finally announced that it accepted Neill's recommendations and would introduce a code and legislation to set limits on adviser numbers.

New Labour's Approach to Communications: Modernisation, Electoral Politics and Democratic Governance

Spin, news management and message discipline are now the hallmarks of Labour's communications. Yet Blair entered office pledged to a more open style of government, to debate, dialogue and inclusion of a broader public in the discussion of policy. Since 1974 Labour has had manifesto commitments to freedom of information legislation. Blair in Opposition enthusiastically endorsed this reform. In fact he went further, saying that freedom of information meant more for New Labour than an isolated constitutional improvement. It was fundamental to its view of modern democratic politics, an essential part of the open and honest dialogue it sought to create in government. In a speech at the Freedom of Information awards (25 March 1996) he said: 'A freedom of information act would signal a cultural change that would make a dramatic difference to the way that Britain is governed. The very fact of its introduction would signal a new relationship which sees the public as legitimate stakeholders in running the country and sees election to serve the public as being given on trust.'

The freedom of information Bill introduced in the Commons in May 1999 bitterly disappointed the hopes raised by the 1997 White Paper, 'Your right to know'. It significantly diluted rights to public access, preventing disclosure where it might 'prejudice' the workings of government. Freedom of information campaigners complained that Labour's proposals were now scarcely stronger than those implemented in the Conservatives' 1994 Code of Access. Despite all the bright promises we were now back, as the Campaign for Press and Broadcasting Freedom put it, to 'government as usual'. Norman Fairclough's analysis (*New Labour, New Language?*, Routledge, 2000) reinforces that depressing conclusion. He notes that Labour constantly talks of initiating 'great debates', but in reality public inclusion amounts to little more than focus group consultation and promotional methods for the engineering of consent.

So what then are we to make of Blair's promises of a different, more grown-up, open kind of politics? Was the claim really no more than sham and spin? Such a judgement seems too cynical by half. It would be churlish to deny that there is more government information in the public domain. Blair inherited open.gov.uk from Major and has expanded it significantly. Access to information about government activities and proposals is far more readily available now, especially via the web, than ever before. Campbell is self-evidently more open about his dealings with the media than any previous press secretary. His lobby briefings are on the record and available on the web for public scrutiny, something that would have been unimaginable in the Thatcher era, even if the technological means had existed.

There would seem to be a contradiction in the evidence of greater openness, on the one hand, and intensified propaganda, on the other. In fact, there is no real mystery here. A coherent New Labour analysis of the importance of communications is readily available in the public domain, in the statements and speeches of Tony Blair and in the writings of his advisers. It is propelled by two distinct and sometimes inevitably conflicting views of political communication in the modern age: the first stems from the demands of electoral politics and the second from a critique of modern democratic governance. The first is the better known and is most obvious in the desire to drive the news agenda with an aggressive promotional policy. After so many years of overwhelming animosity from Fleet Street, Labour is unsurprisingly sensitive to the need to handle the media. Underlying this though, is a more fundamental strategy to create and sustain trust in what Philip Gould calls 'the New Labour brand'. Gould especially, but also Mandelson and Campbell, have made no secret of their approach, nor that it is in essence a marketing effort, similar in fundamentals to that of a commercial firm attempting to establish market leadership. The modernisation of Labour could not be accomplished simply by adjustment of procedures and policy. It required deliberate re-branding, created from a distinctive style and tone. Style is as important as substance, Gould concluded in his 1993 reading of the lessons of Bill Clinton's successful election campaign.[15] Voters would not believe Labour had modernised unless change was supported by appropriate symbols, language and 'symbolic policies' and encapsulated underlying core values. He advocated a deliberately 'non-political' tone and language for Labour to connect with voters, who were increasingly turned off by the typical adversarial aggression of political rhetoric. Moreover, in keeping with business marketing theory, the nursing of political reputation was a continual process. It was not simply a means to power that can be more or less discarded when in office.

Some Labour insiders doubt the strength of Gould's influence with Blair. One called him 'an obsessive memo writer', whose research data is far more useful to Blair than his analysis. Gordon Brown dismissed the Gould memos as 'ephemeral things', when asked his opinion of the leaked Gould analysis that the 'New Labour brand' had been contaminated. John Prescott was less diplomatic on the same issue when questioned on the BBC's Today programme. 'All that glitters isn't Gould. I am not a great fan of that kind of talk', he said. Nonetheless Gould is a frequent visitor to Downing Street and attends the weekly 9 a.m. Monday strategy meeting with the Prime Minister, his political staff and advisers. In Kavanagh and Seldon's analysis of powers behind the Prime Minister, Gould ranks among Blair's closest political advisers.[16] Typically, British politicians tend to deny the influence of pollsters. Perhaps the real difference with Blair is less that he listens to his pollster, more that he admits it. However, by any standard it is unusual for a pollster to be so routinely close to the Prime Minister outside periods of election planning or crisis. It is indicative of a Prime Minister who, more clearly than his predecessors, seeks to include in the normal business of government reference to public opinion and political image.

The theme of public opinion also emerges clearly in New Labour's approach to democratic government. Its view stems from an analysis of 'crisis' of democracy in the developed world and is put most coherently in the 'antipolitics' critique of Geoff Mulgan, formerly of the left-leaning think tank Demos and now a leading policy adviser at Number 10.[17] According to Mulgan, the formal institutions of politics are now out of step with an increasingly democratic culture and a public that has greater than ever access to information. Politics is dominated by professional politicians who conduct debates among themselves and are largely disconnected from the public, except through periodic elections. The rare occasions when public concerns burst through, and demand government response, are usually experienced as 'crises'. Voters have come to feel increasingly disconnected and dissatisfied with the institutional processes of politics. The public is disenchanted with politicians who court voters with promises at election times and then prove poor at delivery. It is a fundamental clash between culture, which through education, technology and consumer choice, is becoming more democratic and centralised bureaucracies, which still behave on the premise of public passivity. Democracy, in Mulgan's phrase, 'has not yet learned how to remake government in its own image'.

The remedies he suggests are drawn from the lessons of the successful 'lean' organisations in manufacturing and service industries. Most importantly they are: a focus on problem solving of core tasks, openness to ideas from outside the organisation, an end to the pretence that any one organisation has all the answers and a willingness to take a lead 'from their customers'. Translated for politics, it means that governments should seek new ways for open and honest dialogue with citizens. They should take steps to ensure public opinion is more adequately represented in government through polls and citizens' juries. They should add direct mechanisms, such as referenda, to the processes of representative democracy and be willing to experiment with electronic democracy. Mulgan's views were echoed famously by Peter Mandelson's statement at a seminar in Bonn in 1998: 'It may be that the era of pure representative democracy is slowly coming to an end . . . Representative government is being complemented by more direct forms of involvement, from the internet to referenda.'

Labour in government has put many of these ideas into practice. The first few months in office saw a snow storm of task forces, advisory groups and policy reviews, as ministers reached out to wider civil society and private business and invited them to help shape new public policy.[18] Government has demonstrated willingness to use referenda for constitutional reform and the introduction of the euro. It has experimented with deliberative democracy, in the form of citizens' juries, at local and regional levels. It claimed a world first with the establishment in July 1999 of the People's Panel, 5,000 randomly selected voters who form a sort of permanent focus group on the delivery of government services. Jack Cunningham, then Minister for the Cabinet Office, explained the Panel as an essential part of the 'Modernising Government' project: government will make policy 'by listening to, and learning from, people's views'.[19] The willingness to listen is also expressed on the Number 10 website, which is planning to develop an 'e-mail the Prime Minister' facility and has a 'Your Say' section that includes an electronic speakers' corner and a policy forum discussion area. Summary reports are sent monthly to the Prime Minister and are fed into the policy process, according to the site manager.

The annual report is another New Labour innovation that flows logically from the antipolitics analysis. Blair explained in the introduction to the first report, 1998, that it was designed to help the public judge delivery of Labour's election promises. It was to be a new mechanism for openness and an example of the relationship of trust which the government sought with the public. In fact, of course, it has turned out to be a good exemplar of the conflicting aims of openness and political marketing. The report was produced by the Strategic Communications Unit, whose job is to present government policy in a positive light. It is hard to imagine how it could be viewed as anything other than public relations at best, and at worst as pure propaganda at public expense. Subsequent reports were noticeably more self-critical than the first, but were still received cynically by much of the press and the Conservative Party. One former Labour communications insider predicted that the government would eventually abandon the report. It could not possibly serve Blair's stated intentions, unless the government was willing to entrust it to authoritative independent assessors. Such a course is not beyond the bounds of possibility, but is a high risk strategy from a promotional perspective.

Labour's record on freedom of information is another example of the awkward relationship between the goals of electoral politics and democratic governance. In Opposition there seemed no conflict. Freedom of information was a key pledge and a good example of Gould's 'symbolic policy' notion, in that it symbolised Labour's core values and distinctiveness from the Conservatives. In government, the story has changed. Legislation has been a long time coming and has diluted early hopes of substantial reform, reducing the threshold for prevention of disclosure from 'substantial harm' to 'prejudice' against the working of government. Moreover, the government's history of disclosure under the existing code of access is mixed. A Home Office report claimed that 1999 was a record year for government openness, with only 27 per cent of requests for information being refused. However, the Parliamentary Ombudsman was called in to investigate twenty-one cases, and found that in seventeen of them the government had wrongly withheld information. The government's diffidence on freedom of information contrasts with its boldness in transforming the machinery of government publicity. Openness and marketing are both clear strands in Labour's approach to communications. It has pursued the latter with gusto. With the former it has been cautious and wary.

Conclusion

There is a cyclical theory of government publicity, which goes roughly like this. One government sets out with an aggressive presentation policy. It pushes at the boundaries of the acceptable until eventually constrained by public outcry. The following government behaves far more cautiously and makes a statesmanlike virtue of its moderation. Thus John Major reacted against the excesses of the Thatcher era: he cut the government advertising budget, was more tolerant of departmental independence and appointed smooth civil servants to counteract the abrasive relations that had come to exist between Ingham and the lobby journalists. He signalled both a clear change in style with Thatcher and a marked difference from the marketing obsessions of Labour. When Labour comes to office it completes the circle, reacting to Major's failures of communication and returning to a more Thatcherite style of news management. There *is* something in this. There certainly are echoes of the Thatcher era in the complaints of politicisation and party propaganda at taxpayers' expense. In many respects, Labour has merely intensified trends that were already evident, for example: the transformation of parties' media experts from technicians to key strategists, the upgrading of the role of communications, and the tendency for Parliament to decline relative to the mass media as the main centre for information and debate.

However, the cyclical theory seriously under-estimates Labour's approach to communications, which is significantly more than mere reaction or opportunism. It is a double-edged approach involving permanent marketing on the one side and enhanced democratic governance on the other. There is overlap between the two approaches. They both seek to establish bonds of trust between government and the people, they both seek effective government which is responsive to public concerns. Equally, there is tension between them when the goals of openness and free debate conflict with the marketing requirement for a strong, unified message which bathes government activity in the kindest possible light. When they conflict, marketing with its eye relentlessly on the electoral prize, is usually the winner.

Thus, there is abundant evidence of the promotional drive in Downing Street and in the GICS. Labour moved with vigour to ensure the central place of communications in government and to bring the GICS up to speed. It has reinforced the authority of Number 10 more clearly and firmly than any recent government, including Thatcher's. In contrast, the effort to establish a more open and democratic public dialogue has been more tentative and achievements more patchy. The record on freedom of information now looks tarnished, as does the task force initiative, which lying outside the normal rules for recruitment to public bodies, has been criticised for fostering 'cronyism' and for a pro-business bias in appointments. The deliberative democracy experiment with citizens' juries has been at best marginal, making scarcely a dent on public consciousness. Nonetheless, government is moving in the direction of greater access to information and public inclusion in policy discussion. The charge that it is 'government by spin and focus group' might be made to stand up, but only if one focuses on the promotional approach alone. It would be to ignore the democratising impulse and the measures to strengthen citizenship, through for example, increased rights in the workplace, devolution, the incorporation into British law of the European convention on Human Rights, and the move to include citizenship education in the school curricula.

Finally, what conclusions can we draw about the success of Labour's news management? This is almost impossible to judge in any satisfactory way because of the difficulty of proving cause and effect. The media texts are not sufficient evidence. A pro-Labour press is as likely to stem from the media's reading of the opinion polls or from editorial prejudice as it is from the most determined efforts of the spin doctors. Equally, a critical press is not evidence of spin failure. The spin doctors were probably excessively credited with success when Labour was riding high in the polls, and over-blamed when the tide turned. However, to the extent that spin has contributed to a spiral of cynicism and undermined Labour's credibility, it has failed. That concern clearly motivated Campbell to take a back seat and prompted the government to accept the Neill Committee's constraints on special advisers. The more lasting legacy of Labour's news manage-ment style will certainly include the Mountfield reforms, which represent a quantum leap in government publicity. Most likely it will also include Labour's marketing approach to strategy and image-building. This, though, depends greatly on Labour's success in the next general election. Given the difficulties of demonstrating effects with any precision, political practi-tioners tend to view the best campaigns as the winning ones. Electoral success, not political science, provides the models. If, as seems likely, Labour wins a second term, then its marketing strategy will be the model that others will copy, just as Labour had borrowed much from the Thatcher example.

Notes

1 *News from Number 10*, A Documentary by Michael Cockerell, BBC2.
2 Peter Oborne *Alastair Campbell* Aurum.
3 Bernard Ingham (2000) 'Reaping the whirlwind', *The Guardian* 'Media' Section, March 6.
4 Interview with Sir Bernard Ingham.
5 Colin Seymour-Ure, 'Media' in Seldon (ed.) *The Major Effect*, Macmillan, 2000.
6 M. Scammell, 'New Media, New Politics' in P. Dunleavy, A. Gamble, I. Holliday and G. Peele (eds) *Developments in British Politics 6*, Macmillan, 2000.
7 Select Committee on Public Administration Sixth Report 'The Government Communication and Information Service', 6 August 1998.
8 See Norris, Curtice, Scammell, Sanders and Semetko *On Message: Communicating the Campaign*, Sage, 1999.
9 See M. Scammell, *Designer Politics*, Macmillan, 1995.
10 Quoted in Michael Cockerell 'Lifting the lid off spin' (2000) *British Journalism Review*, pp. 6–15.
11 See Peter Riddell, *Parliament Under Blair*, Politico's, 2000, pp. 174–5.
12 Memorandum submitted by the Association of First Division Civil Servants to the Select Committee on Public Administration Inquiry into the GICS Sixth Report, May 1998.
13 Mountfield, *Report of the Working Group on the Government Information Service*, Cabinet Office, HMSO 1997.
14 Quoted in 'The Advisers: Modernisation or Politicisation' 12 January

2000. BBC Online. URL: http://news.bbc.co.uk/hi/english/uk_politics.

15 Patricia Hewitt and Philip Gould, 'Learning from success – Labour and Clinton's New Democrats', *Renewal* 1(1), pp. 45–51.

16 Dennis Kavanagh and A. Seldon (1999) *The Powers Behind the Prime Minister*, HarperCollins, 1999.

17 Geoff Mulgan (ed.) *Life After Politics: New Thinking for the Twenty First Century*, Fontana, 1997. See especially Mulgan's chapter with C. Leadbeater 'Lean Democracy and the Leadership Vacuum', pp. 246–259.

18 Tony Barker, *Ruling by Task Force,* Politico's, 1999.

19 Jack Cuningham, 'Public Management and Policy Association Lecture', 17 March 1999.

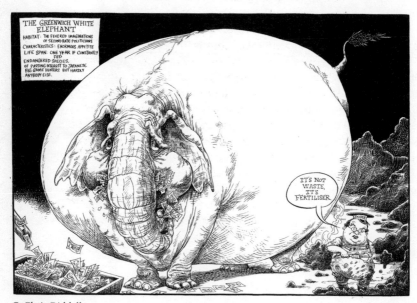

© Chris Riddell

Chapter 24

CULTURAL POLICY

Robert Hewison

IT IS WELL known that Tony Blair was lead singer in a rock band. The Ugly Rumours of 1973 were an unusually privileged group, public school rebels at Oxford playing cover versions of Mick Jagger and Captain Beefheart, but, at a period and in a political party where such things have powerful symbolic significance, to have an ex-rocker as Prime Minister was important. It reinforced the 'young country' image that Blair wished to project on coming into office, and it offered a counter-vailing glamour and populism to the puritanism associated with New Labour's commitment to family values.

It is difficult to legislate for creativity. Cultural policy does not occupy a great deal of any British government's time, cultural expenditure disposes of a pitiful fraction of its budget. Yet, as the shadow of the Dome lengthened over the first New Labour administration, the symbolic significance of Labour's attitude to the arts and heritage became as important as its practical effects. Arguably, at a time when symbolic goods – information, imagery, intellectual innovation – are more and more seen as the key to a successful real economy, the aesthetic and emotional consequences of the ideas and values that are addressed in cultural policy should have a higher priority than they have been afforded. This was the lesson of the Dome.

New Labour took more interest in cultural policy than any preceding government. A member of the Number 10 Policy Unit told me that on a scale of policy preoccupations from one to ten, cultural matters rated seven. Blair was personally alarmed when he learnt that the commitment to abide by Conservative spending plans across the board during the first two years of his government meant a cut in Arts Council funding. Yet politicians are the section of the elite with the least time to acquire cultural capital. In opposition Blair's speeches on the subject were few, and the word 'culture' only appears in *New Britain: My Vision of a Young Country* (1996) in the

context of a tribute to Sir Stanley Matthews.[1] The film of Blair exchanging
headers with the football coach Kevin Keegan in 1995 is the most powerful image we have of him in a cultural context. Blair's three receptions for
rock stars and show business personalities at Number 10 during his first
year of office underlined his populism, but alarmed traditional supporters
of high culture. One such was John Tusa, managing director of the
Barbican art centre in London, who wrote in 1998: 'The arts do not matter
to [Blair] personally because they are a marginal and thinly-rooted side of
his own experience. He is a true child of the sixties; the rock and pop
world is the one he likes instinctively; he is simply not at ease in the arts
world.'[2] The issue of populism versus elitism and the 'dumbing down' of
culture were to be an important theme. Blair's brushes with hedonism were
however more promising than the Calvinism and workaholicism of his
Chancellor Gordon Brown, who although an acknowledged 'film buff'
who made tax concessions to the British film industry in his first budget[3]
exercised a controlling influence. The power of the Treasury and Brown's
political strength made his cultural predilections as important as Blair's
own.

Blair's biographer John Rentoul calls him 'inaccessible' and 'unplace-
able' in the same paragraph. He writes: 'the personal tastes of the Blairs are
not easily classified'.[4] Tusa suggests that in terms of high culture Blair had
none, but Blair was not only a rocker at Oxford, he was also a successful
actor. It may be that as a politician he knew that it was better that his tastes
should be concealed, lest he should send the wrong signals in a field where
all cultural signals are wrong to some sector or other. (He is reputed to have
built up a small art collection under the advice of Lord Irvine.) The impression of a lack of cultural depth may be another way of expressing his
dislike of what he called – in spite of his predilection for Oxford-educated
advisors – 'the Oxford intellectual establishment'.[5]

Most of the cultural policy thinking in opposition appears to have been
done in and around the offices of the film producer David Puttnam's
Enigma Productions, although the opposition spokesman on the arts, Mark
Fisher, and the architect Richard Rogers collaborated on proposals to
improve the urban environment. At Enigma, Puttnam employed John
Newbegin, a former speech writer to Neil Kinnock, and Ben Evans, son of
Baroness Blackstone, who had undertaken research for Fisher, and who
had been an advisor to Jocelyn Stevens at English Heritage. Early drafts of
an arts policy devised by Fisher were abandoned after Blair's trip to
Australia to address the executives of Rupert Murdoch's News
Corporation. The Australian Prime Minister Paul Keating gave Blair a
copy of his government's 1994 policy document *Creative Nation*, which,
while promising to raise the status of the arts, argued that a cultural policy
should also be an economic policy. This idea evidently appealed to Blair, for
it appeared in Labour's much less sophisticated policy document *Create the
Future* in March 1997: 'We will re-focus the Department [of National

Heritage] to play a major part in the economic regeneration of our country, working with the cultural industries, local government and the private sector to create wealth and employment.'[6]

This idea gave shape to the most clearly New Labour institutional invention in the field of cultural policy, the Creative Industries Task Force, one of several such groupings set up in 1997 to generate a sense of dynamism and inter-departmental cooperation. In addition to civil servants from different ministries, participants included such New Labour luminaries as Puttnam, Richard Branson, Paul Smith, and the chief executive of Random House, Gail Rebuck, wife of the party's polls advisor Philip Gould. Also recruited was the record producer Alan McGee, a donor to the party who however rapidly became disenchanted with the government's policies on student fees, drugs and the dole. The 'creative industries' were defined as including software design, music, television and radio, architecture, advertising, designer fashion, crafts and the antiques market. A survey published by the Task Force concluded that collectively these generated a revenue of £60 billion a year, accounting for 4 per cent of the United Kingdom's GDP, greater than any manufacturing industry. The broad cultural definition that was applied, and the emphasis on economic value, accorded with Blair's cultural inclinations, even if the appropriation of the outward signs of a hedonistic culture of consumption was fundamentally at odds with the puritan instincts of both Blair and Brown. In 2000 the Secretary of State for Culture, Chris Smith, confided to his Irish counterpart that he had been successful in that year's Comprehensive Spending Review not by arguing for the value of the arts in themselves, but by emphasising their economic and educational return.[7]

'Things Can Only Get Better'

In 1997 there was a remarkable public appetite in Britain for the arts and culture in all forms. On a broad definition of what constituted the arts, 80 per cent of the adult population took part in some kind of cultural activity, with cinema going and country house visiting the most popular. On a narrower definition, restricted to the 'high' art forms – theatre, art, classical music, ballet, opera, jazz and contemporary dance – 37 per cent of adults, nearly 17 million people, enjoyed them in one form or another. More importantly, there was an indefinable buzz in contemporary culture. In May 1996, echoing the 'Swinging London' phenomenon of thirty years before, the *Sunday Times* ran a feature, 'Cool Britannia', proclaiming 'a cultural renaissance in the making', largely driven by younger people and led by a group known as the Young British Artists.[8] While they could take no credit for this phenomenon, both the Conservative Department of National Heritage and New Labour picked up the phrase and sought to appropriate its popularity.

The reason for this opportunism was that, however far from reality it may have been, the image seemed briefly to 'rebrand' Britain in the form of Blair's Young Country. The moment was indeed brief, and such manoeuvres only revealed the prevailing deep anxiety about national identity, an anxiety reinforced by the creation of a Welsh Assembly and a Scottish Parliament. These were welcome to the Welsh and Scots, but at the heart of the British state the English became increasingly uncertain about their purpose and security. The death of Princess Diana on 31 August 1997 produced a strange moment of national unity that Blair handled adroitly, yet it was an ephemeral moment, founded on a sense of loss and further weakening the national bond of respect for the monarchy. The wave of applause that swept into Westminster Abbey from the crowds outside in response to Earl Spencer's criticism in his funeral oration of his sister's treatment was a harbinger of the generalised disgruntlement focused by the fuel tax and farming protests of 2000. With Blair essentially playing for time over whether or not to signal closer European integration by joining the Euro, both Labour and the opposition felt it necessary to assert their versions of patriotism in the run up to the general election.

Ironically, the early feverish excitement associated with Cool Britannia contrasted with the very real difficulties experienced by what can be distinguished as the official cultural sector, the sector with which cultural policy was mainly concerned. In 1994/95 the Arts Council, in its last year as the Arts Council of Great Britain before its dismemberment as a gesture towards devolution by John Major, had received the first cash cut to its grant in aid since its formation in 1946. In 1996/97 the overall budget of the Department of National Heritage was reduced to £930 million, and cuts averaging 3 per cent were imposed on the budgets of the approximately fifty non-departmental bodies it funded. In January 1997 the Arts Council, now the Arts Council of England, released a briefing paper showing that the cut in grant in aid for 1996/97 to £186 million, followed by standstill funding at that level in 1997/98, meant a real terms reduction of £21.68 million since 1993/94. The Conservative government's Treasury plans projected a cut to £184.6 million in 1998/99, with a further reduction the following financial year.

The effect of the long-term attrition of behind-inflation funding, coupled with a parallel decline in local authority funding (the responsibility of the Department of the Environment) was demonstrated by the Boyden Report on English theatre, published in 2000, which showed that there was a vicious circle of fewer productions, smaller casts, declining audiences and greater indebtedness, which in the regions stood in 1997 at £8 million, rising to £10.3 million the following year. Regional orchestras were under similar pressure, and in 1998 the Hallé Orchestra narrowly avoided bankruptcy. The forecast indebtedness for regional and national orchestras by 2000 was £9.6 million.

The desperate revenue position, also felt by both local and national museums and galleries, contrasted surreally with the sudden availability of vast sums of money for capital projects from the National Lottery. Created by the National Lottery Act of October 1993, by 2001 this was to make available at least £10 billion for distribution to the 'good causes' identified by the Act, once prize money, operating costs and taxation had been deducted. The money was divided equally between the Arts Councils, the Sports Council, the National Heritage Lottery Fund, a charities board and the specially created Millennium Commission. The problem for arts, sports and heritage was that the money not only had to be unlocked by partner- ship funding, but that it could be used for capital projects only. The rationale was that this was the only way to guarantee the 'additionality' of these funds, the government having committed itself not to reduce revenue funding through grant in aid as the Lottery came on stream. As Richard Eyre put it vividly in his introduction to his 1998 report on the future of lyric theatre in London: 'the arts appear glutted with cash for substantial capital developments while they are famished for funds to sustain the work for which arts organisations exist. They are proud tenants of bright shining buildings in danger of becoming as redundant as stainless steel kitchens in a famine.'[9] By the close of the Major years the additionality principle was being ignored in practice, and desperate measures were being taken to create schemes using Lottery money for non-capital purposes. The National Lottery was none the less a significant creation by the Major government and a significant legacy to New Labour although, as we shall see, the abil- ity to fund the Dome also created a poisoned chalice.

The other important legacy was the creation of the Department of National Heritage, formed out of half a dozen disparate government departments and creating a new Secretaryship of State, giving responsibil- ity for cultural policy and media regulation to a minister of Cabinet rank. The minister's powers of media regulation were limited, in that the press was clinging on to its system of self-regulation, and broadcasting control was, in theory at least, at arms-length. Matters of 'taste and decency' were the province of the Thatcher-created Broadcasting Standards Commission. Commercial broadcasting was controlled through the Independent Television Commission and the Radio Authority. Commercial matters such as cross-media ownership were in the hands of the Department of Trade and Industry. The BBC was controlled through the appointment of the chairman and governors and setting the licence fee.

The Labour government was to signal its support for the cultural impor- tance of public service broadcasting by setting the BBC's licence fee at an annual increase of 1.5 per cent above inflation, thus encouraging the BBC to improve its content and continue to prepare to transfer to digital broad- casting. The appointment of Greg Dyke as Director-General produced a more bullish BBC prepared to go head to head with ITV over the timing of news bulletins, to the alarm of Chris Smith. In the rapidly changing televi- sion scene created by new technologies, the Labour government was to find itself behind the game, with new legislation as a result of the December 2000 White Paper not expected until 2002. The proposal was to replace the 'alphabet soup' of regulatory bodies with a single 'Ofcom', to regulate all forms of communication including telephone and internet, but the BBC governors would retain their responsibilities. The way would be clear for a single ITV network, Channel Four would not be privatised, but decisions on the thornier issue of relaxing rules on cross-media ownership were postponed.

In June 1997 the incoming Labour administration made an important symbolic change by changing the name of the Department of National Heritage – a title with backward-looking connotations – to the Department for Culture, Media and Sport. Blair placed it in the charge of Chris Smith, a Blair supporter and like him a Christian Socialist, who had clashed with Brown when opposition spokesman on Health. Although no attention was drawn to the fact, it was an important signal of Blair's social values that Smith was an acknowledged homosexual. Smith's service as Secretary of State can be divided into two distinct periods. A rocky first fourteen months until the outcome of the first Comprehensive Spending Review in the summer of 1998, and then a growing confidence marred by fall out from the disaster of the Dome and the mishandling of the renewal of the licence to run the National Lottery. Smith's early nadir was in May 1998 when he published a slim collection of recycled speeches as *Creative Britain*, which was greeted with almost universal derision.

Smith's difficulty was that while he declared in July 1997: 'Cool Britannia is here to stay', things did not get better. The Chancellor's commitment to the Conservatives' spending plans for the first two years meant that in 1997 Labour did nothing to increase the Arts Council of England's standstill grant in aid of £186 million, and then in 1998 enforced the Conservatives' cut of £1.5 million, although Smith was able to mitigate this with an additional £5 million specifically to develop new audiences. As Blair had appreciated, but too late for the cut not to go through, New Labour lost a great deal of the anticipatory goodwill in the arts community that it had generated in opposition.

The immediate problem for Smith on coming into office was that Labour's promise to 'review' admission charges at national museums in *Create The Future*[10] had given the impression that all charges would be removed. If Labour believed in 'access' and art 'for the many, not the few', it was axiomatic that the museums that had succumbed to Thatcherite economic pressure to introduce charging – the Maritime Museum, Science Museum, Natural History Museum, Imperial War Museum and (in 1996) the Victoria and Albert Museum – should be encouraged to be once more free, and that those teetering on the edge of charging should be held back. But the money to do so was not there, and in June 1987 the National Museums and Galleries on Merseyside joined the chargers. Over the following year there was hesitation until the Chancellor released fresh funds as a result of the 1998 Comprehensive Spending Review, with an extra £100 million for museums over the next three years. This ensured that the new Tate Modern at Bankside would be free when it opened to great popular enthusiasm in 2000. From 1999 charging museums were made free to children and from 2000 free to pensioners, but although 'universal free entry' was promised for 2001, the money allocated proved insufficient, and the charging museums showed themselves reluctant to abandon the advantage they had in being able to reclaim VAT. A compromise was reached that from September 2001 charging museums would, if their trustees wished, charge adults only £1, and be compensated from central funds. The museums' VAT status would be unaffected, but that agreement with Customs and Excise extended only to 2002, when there was to be a major tax review.

The difficulties over VAT hardly constituted 'joined-up government', and showed the limits of Smith's powers in relation to Gordon Brown. A relatively simple change to the rules under section 33 of the 1994 VAT Act could have solved the problem, but at the time of going to press the Treasury was unwilling. The March 2000 budget did however simplify fund raising by removing limits on Gift Aid, allowing tax relief on donations of shares and an improved payroll-giving scheme.

During 1997 and 1998 the fiscal and institutional aspects of cultural policy were thoroughly examined as part of the government's Comprehensive Spending Review. Blair indicated that he wished to see more money going to the sector, but only in exchange for institutional reform of distributing bodies. On 29 June 1998, amidst rising alarm about the funding of arts and heritage under Labour, twenty leading figures in the world of official culture (including John Tusa[11]) were invited to a ninety-minute seminar with the Prime Minister in Downing Street. Each was allowed to make their case for improved funding, to which Blair replied 'We must write the arts into our core script', (words echoed by Smith in the House of Commons on 25 July 2000: 'The arts are part of the core script of government'). This was a genuine consultation, for such had been the preparation by the delegation's chairman, Dennis Stevenson, the retiring chairman of the Tate Gallery, that the provisional figures agreed for cultural spending were subsequently increased by several million. Immense relief was felt on 24 July 1998, when Smith was able to announce substantial increases in funding as a result of the Review. The DCMS budget was set to rise by £78 million, with more modest rises in the following two years. This allowed the DCMS to tackle the problem of museum charging, already discussed, and to raise the Arts Council's grant to £219 million, an increase of £29.4 million. A return to three-year funding was as important as the increases promised. Comparative figures released by the DCMS, however, showed that at 1997/98 prices, this only brought ACE's grant back to just below where it had been in 1992/93.

The really significant increase in cultural spending came in the second

Comprehensive Spending Review, whose results were announced in July 2000. In 2001/02 the total DCMS budget would rise to £1.1 billion, and in 2002/03 to £1.2 billion. As a result ACE's grant in aid would rise to £252 million in 2001/02, £297 million in 2002/03 and £337 million in 2003/4. ACE calculated that this represented an increase in funding since 1998/99 of 78 per cent. This impressive statistic could be more than matched in sport (which had not been prioritised in the first spending review), where spending would increase by almost 100 per cent to £102 million in 2003/04. Sport is an important aspect of national identity for any government, and Britain's generally dismal performance in the game it had given the world was not a bonus for Blair, who seemed content to leave his representation at national events to the Deputy Prime Minister John Prescott. At the same time, the country's reputation for nationalistic football hooliganism meant that the attempt to secure the next football World Cup, led by Tony Banks who had served as Sports Minister from 1997 until July 1998, was a predictable failure. There was, however, some gratification at Britain's better performance in the 2000 Olympics, partially attributable to the benefits of Lottery-funded training.

Overall, the Blair government significantly increased spending in the cultural field, and when the contribution of the Lottery is added in, in 2001 the arts, heritage and sport were in a much better position than they were in 1997. Yet as a proportion of overall government spending, the DCMS's mite remained tiny: in 2000/01 it constituted just 0.27 per cent of total expenditure, in 2001/02 0.29 per cent, and 0.28 per cent in the following financial year. Though the overall increase in government expenditure meant that a tourniquet had been removed and blood would flow again through a withering funding system, there was no sign of an actual redistribution in favour of the cultural sector. As in other areas of government, such as the National Health Service, there was also the question whether the 2000 Comprehensive Spending Review had released funds into the system in time to make a difference in electoral terms.

A New Cultural Framework

On 14 December 1998 Smith was able to announce a series of significant institutional changes as a result of the internal review he had begun on coming into office. These changes were the price of the increased funding on offer through Brown's first Comprehensive Spending Review. The very first of his reforms had been the changes to the National Lottery, introduced by the new National Lottery Act of June 1998. This had been an election commitment. Smith began his regime by attempting to take on the 'fat cats' of the private company operating the Lottery, Camelot, over their large bonuses, and got nowhere. His White Paper, *The People's Lottery*, however, published in July 1997, while ruling out a state-run lottery, indicated the government's preference for a not-for-profit scheme when Camelot's operating licence expired in 2001. Smith altered the Lottery's regulatory system, placing it in the hands of a five person Lottery Commission, who would have the responsibility of awarding the new licence. Scandal surrounding one of Camelot's partner companies, G-Tech, over a disputed attempt to bribe Camelot's rival bidder Richard Branson and the concealment of failures in its software, put Camelot in a difficult position when competing for the licence in 2000, when Branson again bid, this time with the calculatedly-named creation, The People's Lottery. But the Lottery Commission botched the competition procedure by attempting to exclude Camelot. Camelot's successful appeal to law kept it in the race, causing delay in the final decision and provoking the resignation of the chair of the Lottery Commission, after the judge described the Commission's treatment of Camelot as 'conspicuously unfair' and 'an abuse of power'. In December 2000 the new chair, a retired Treasury mandarin Lord Burns, reversed the Commission's previous position by awarding the licence to Camelot, on the grounds that it was more likely to generate the £15 billion for good causes that both applicants had promised in the next seven year licence period. One commissioner, Hilary Blume, resigned in disagreement.

The chief purpose of the 1998 Lottery Act was to create a sixth good cause, the New Opportunities Fund, to join the other distributing bodies and take its share of the tranche going to the Millennium Commission, due to be wound up when its responsibilities – including funding the costs of the Dome – ended. The new good cause turned out to be the government itself, for in addition to the creation of the pet New Labour project, the 'talent-fund' NESTA, discussed below, its purpose was to fund schemes that arguably were a direct government responsibility: healthy living, cancer research, IT training for teachers, after-school care, access to learning and environmental projects. In addition to getting the Lottery to pay for these schemes, it transpired that the government-administered fund would absorb the entire funding stream of the Millennium Commission on its dissolution, taking a third of the total funds available, while reducing the share of the established four distributors to one sixth each.

The distributors were however now allowed to be pro-active, rather than merely responsive in their approach to Lottery-funded schemes. In order to localise decision-making, the Regional Arts Boards were given their own allocations to distribute funds for projects seeking less than £100,000, and the rigid distinction between Lottery capital funding and grant in aid revenue funding began to dissolve as the two funding streams started to merge.

The Act also brought into being David – now Lord – Puttnam's brain child, the National Endowment for Science, Technology and the Arts. This was radical and innovative in its conception and construction. Its purpose was to encourage creativity, broadly defined and in all areas, and, in a complete break with British cultural tradition, its intention was to identify and support individuals rather than organisations. Its method of funding was also radically different, in that it was set up with an endowment of £200 million of Lottery money, generating an independent income of at least £10 million a year. This was used to invest in new projects with commercial, cultural or social potential, in a collaborative educational programme, and in fellowships for individuals of up to £75,000 over three to five years. The award of a fellowship to the poet and academic Tom Paulin attracted the most attention in NESTA's early days, but a broad range of people from inventors to choreographers were also helped.

The institution most obviously in need of reform when Smith came into office was the Arts Council of England, which had been severely demoralised by cuts in funding, and the devolution programme imposed on it by the Conservatives, including the complete separation of the Scottish and Welsh Arts Councils in 1994. The Council's enfeebled state was demonstrated by its inability to deal effectively with its largest client, the Royal Opera House. The crisis of Covent Garden brought the fifty-year-old system for funding the arts into disrepute, and presented Smith with an immediate challenge to his capabilities.

In the summer of 1997 the Royal Opera House was preparing to close in order to carry out a £213 million redevelopment programme made possible by a £78.5 million Lottery award, one of the first to be made and immediately confirming populists' worst suspicions. In spite of this capital wealth, the Royal Opera House was carrying a £4.5 million deficit on its revenue side, a classic example of the Lottery conundrum. On 13 May the distinguished administrator Genista McIntosh, who had joined from the National Theatre in January, resigned as chief executive for unexplained health reasons, and the arts world was astonished to learn that she was to be replaced by none other than the secretary-general of the Arts Council, Mary Allen. This was a severe blow to the credibility of both institutions, and Allen was forced to resign the following March. The Opera House, meanwhile, was plunging towards insolvency. Other victims of the debacle were to be Lord Chadlington and his Opera House board, forced to resign in December 1997 following a damning report by Gerald Kaufman's House of Commons select committee, and Lord Gowrie, chairman of the Arts Council, who was so affected by Allen's apparent betrayal that he resigned in October 1997.

At first bounced by the Labour-supporting Opera House board member Lord Gavron into sanctioning the appointment of Allen as chief executive, Smith had attempted to regain the initiative in June 1997 by the customary device of setting up an enquiry. This was to be into the provision of lyric theatre in London as a whole, led by the former director of the National Theatre Richard Eyre. Smith called for the creation of a 'People's Opera' at Covent Garden, but by the time the Eyre report appeared in June 1998, confirming everything that was known about the under-funding of opera and the arrogance and mismanagement at the Royal Opera House, that idea, to which Smith had probably not attached much value, had been safely kicked into touch. The solution to Covent Garden's problems was an increased grant, the complete cessation of activities in 1999, and the appointment of the American administrator Michael Kaiser. Kaiser oversaw the reopening of the refurbished Opera House at the end of 1999, and Covent Garden appeared to return to a financial even keel, although Kaiser chose to return to America prematurely in 2001, leaving the Opera House as open to accusations of elitism as it had been before.

While Smith emerged undamaged from this crisis, the departure of Lord Gowrie from the Arts Council allowed him to appoint a new chairman more in Labour's image, who would make the necessary management changes. He was the millionaire businessman Gerry Robinson, chairman of the Granada Group and BskyB. He was only one of a number of Labour-friendly businessmen who moved into positions of cultural influence under Blair: Sir Colin Southgate of EMI as chairman at the Royal Opera House, Greg Dyke as Director-General of the BBC, publisher Matthew Evans at Resource, the developer Stuart Lipton at CABE (these latter new institutions are described below). Other figures sympathetic to Blair took on important chairmanship roles: Blair's former tutor at Fettes Eric Anderson at the National Heritage Memorial Fund, Neil Cossons at English Heritage, Helena Kennedy at the British Council.

Arriving at the Arts Council of England in January 1998, Robinson appointed a new chief executive, Peter Hewitt, and reduced the unwieldy membership of the Council itself to ten (now for the first time the new Council contained a majority of practising artists). Robinson pressed ahead with the devolution of ACE clients to the Regional Arts Boards, aiming for a 50 per cent reduction in the Council's staff while reconstructing the management. The formerly independent Crafts Council was partially merged with ACE. Robinson's business-like approach did not endear him to the arts community, whom he accused of regarding the Council as a soft touch, but he recognised that the arts were indeed under-funded, and his execution of government policy brought rewards in terms of increased grant in aid.

As part of the changes announced in Smith's policy document *A New Cultural Framework* in December 1998, equally important reforms were introduced in the field of heritage. English Heritage and the Royal Commission on the Historical Monuments of England were merged into a single body. Even more radically the Museums and Galleries Commission and the Library and Information Commission were wound up in April 2000 and replaced by a new body, the Museums, Libraries and Archives Commission, which under the chairmanship of Smith's publisher for *Creative Britain*, Matthew – now Lord – Evans, took the name Resource. Evans offended his new constituency, even before taking office, with a speech to the Association of Independent Museums in which he criticised museum professionals as regressive, isolationist, afraid of change and ignorant of new technology.

A similarly new body, the Commission for Architecture and the Built Environment, chaired by Stuart Lipton, was created in 1999 to 'champion' the cause of architecture, taking over the design review function of the Royal Fine Art Commission, which was wound up, and taking on the Arts Council's funding role in the field of architecture. A new Film Council was also created, chaired by the populist film director Alan Parker, to develop a coherent strategy for the promotion of film. The Arts Council, which had seen a return of only £6 million on the £97 million of Lottery money it had invested in sixty films, handed over responsibility to the Film Council which became a designated Lottery distributor, funding all film activities except the National Film School. In May 2000 the Film Council announced that it would be investing £10 million of development funds in 'popular mainstream' British movies.

Two further innovations completed Smith's new cultural framework. As part of the government's regional policy the DCMS set up a 'Cultural Consortium' in each of the eight English development regions established by Labour, to bring together representatives of the arts, heritage and creative industries. All local authorities were asked to produce a 'Cultural Plan' by April 2001. Finally, having conducted a significant rearrangement of the institutional landscape, reducing and realigning the number of non departmental bodies, Smith created a new watchdog to oversee their work and, in theory, also that of his own department. This was QUEST (Quality, Efficiency and Standards Team), a small body of arts administration specialists who would review questions of management and quality at his request. Although the overall effect of New Labour's reforms was to make arts institutions even more cautious of criticising the government, it was a measure of Gerry Robinson's independence that he described this potential star chamber for the DCMS's dependent bodies as 'a complete waste of time'.

The Dome

Overshadowing the entire period of the first New Labour administration was the Millennium Dome. Nothing could convey better the new economy of signs and symbols than 'the world of politicised show business' described by the Dome's official historian Adam Nicolson.[12] As a symbol, the Dome was Blair's Big Tent, and Blair's big disaster. It seemed to sum up many of the 'new' aspects of the New Labour project: it was an idea taken over from the Tories, it was regarded with suspicion by Old Labour opinion, it was intended to be a partnership between government and private enterprise, it was populist, it was managed at many levels by 'Tony's cronies', and they sought to apply to it the techniques of media control and manipulation that they had learnt in opposition. When the project went wrong, there was a marked reluctance to admit failure or take the blame.

As the largest Lottery project by far, the Dome also managed to encapsulate many of the Lottery's problems. While the design by Mike Davies for the Richard Rogers Partnership produced a superb piece of contemporary architecture, there were extreme difficulties in solving the problem of what to do inside it. As with so many Lottery projects, its business plan depended on wildly optimistic projections of visitor numbers, whose failure to materialise wrecked its finances. Originally set at 12 million, the final total for visitors was a humiliating 6,517,000, of whom one million did not pay, and two million paid less than full price.

Responsibility for the continuation of the Dome, launched under the Tories in 1995, must be laid entirely at Blair's door, for he could have stopped it even when he was in opposition. The planning of the project was already in deep trouble in the autumn of 1996, and Labour was happy to make political capital out of the difficulties of what was then seen as Michael Heseltine's project. In January 1997 the shadow Cabinet, steered by Brown, rejected the revised £750 million budget that had been accepted by the Millennium Commission. To secure the future of the project in the likely event of a Labour takeover, Heseltine broke with precedent by going to see Blair in his office, a humiliation during which he was forced to concede Labour's demands for a cap on spending and, most importantly, the right to review the project on coming into office. It became clear that the private enterprise aspects of the funding of the scheme would have to be underwritten by a government guarantee. This went beyond the original Blair/Heseltine agreement, and there were further crisis negotiations on 17 January 1997 before Blair could be persuaded to accept the need for an open-ended government guarantee. His endorsement was sufficiently enthusiastic for the Labour-friendly Bob Ayling, chief executive of British Airways, to agree to chair a new hybrid company, privately managed but government owned, the New Millennium Experience Company, which would be responsible for building the Dome and managing the exhibition. Jennie Page, chief executive of the Millennium Commission, would transfer to the new company. A millennium commissioner, the journalist Simon Jenkins, who had been closely involved in these telephone negotiations, told Alastair Campbell and Jonathan Powell: 'This is your first act in government.'[13]

As such, it was a hubristic one. The device by which the government would be able to apply to the state-owned Lottery for funding, using a private company whose single shareholder was a minister of the Crown, could not in practice protect it from responsibility for the disaster that followed, as Lord Falconer was to discover, although the careers of Ayling, Page, and senior managers of the NMEC were thrown to the wolves first. Driving all decisions on the Dome was the inexorable ticking of the Millennium clock. On coming into office Labour had to complete its promised review quickly. Responsibility was passed to the Cabinet's Home and Social Affairs committee, where Peter Mandelson became interested as Minister without

Portfolio. Mandelson's grandfather, Herbert Morrison, had been the guiding spirit of the successful Festival of Britain in 1951, and Mandelson, like Blair, could see the advantages to Labour of a triumphant event in the year preceding a general election. But the Cabinet was hostile. Chris Smith was in favour of a scaled-down, educational event at Greenwich but he told Nicolson: 'Quite a few of my Cabinet colleagues were virulently arguing that we should not go ahead.'[14] Brown, Darling, Blunkett and Dobson were against. While Page was forced to press ahead with construction, there was a real possibility that the project would be cancelled.

On 16 June Simon Jenkins wrote his 'Euan letter' to Blair, arguing that the event would be something the Prime Minister's children would enjoy, but the report prepared for the Home and Social Affairs Committee was largely hostile. Euan Blair did eventually visit the Dome; Downing Street refused to reveal his opinion. The decision was passed to the full Cabinet on 19 June. Before the meeting Blair discussed the scheme first with Mandelson, and then with Prescott, who came down in favour. The actual decision to proceed was taken in Cabinet with Prescott in the chair, as Blair had to attend a church service. Prescott reported Blair's desire for the project to go ahead, and though several ministers expressed their opposition, Brown, in spite of his concerns about the cost, agreed, and that afternoon Blair, Prescott and Smith appeared at the site of the Dome. There Blair declared: 'It is not the easy thing to do. It is the bold thing to do.'[15]

With hindsight, it was the wrong thing to do, but the risk had to be taken, and the Dome was a juggernaut difficult to stop. Blair did not however ease its course by imposing new conditions, that the Dome should be 'permanent' and that a million schoolchildren should be allowed in free. Having given the go-ahead – and there is no doubt that it was his personal responsibility – Blair was called upon to ensure its success. The commercial sponsors whose hoped-for £175 million contribution was essential to the budget were reluctant to come forward, and Blair was required to be at his most evangelical to drum up support. It was no surprise that Mandelson became the New Millennium Experience Company's single shareholder, a responsibility he retained when he moved to the Department of Trade and Industry in July 1998.

In February 1998 Mandelson declared 'the Dome will be like a gigantic mirror of the nation . . . I want the Dome to capture the spirit of modern Britain – a nation that is confident, excited, impatient for the future.' He was an enthusiastic advocate, but he was also the lightning conductor for much of the hostility to New Labour, so that his presence as single shareholder politicised the project. The NMEC wanted him to take a back seat, but as a 100 per cent political animal, this was impossible for him to do. The impression was given of 'New Labour control-freakery' and it proved very difficult even for Kaufman's Culture select committee to find out what was going on in the months leading up to the opening. While Mandelson talked about totally imaginary pursuits such as 'Surfball', the managers at NMEC, led by the untiring, domineering but uncreative Jennie Page were unable or unwilling to satisfy press curiosity as sponsors hesitated and designers came and went.

In January 1998 the design consultant Stephen Bayley, who had been hired as a creative director, resigned, accusing Mandelson of 'running the project like a dictator'. His function was taken over by a 'litmus group' of outside advisors, led by the media expert Michael Grade. Although the commercial sponsors, whose cash contribution finally came to £115 million (including Murdoch's BskyB, causing the *Sun* newspaper to reverse its policy of attacking the Dome) were not supposed to influence the actual contents of the Dome exhibition, commercial pressures led to a steady dilution of the higher ideals the Dome was expected to express in favour of populism. Using the metaphor of a newspaper, in 1999 the contents were thought to be too *Guardian*, and Ayling, Grade and NMEC directors Matthew Freud and Sam Chisholm wanted something more appealing to readers of 'red top' tabloids. As Nicolson records 'the push for a less highbrow tone to the content was coming at the designers and the NMEC team from all sides'.[16]

Mandelson was fortunate when he was forced to resign from the government in December 1998 though the Dome was to be his nemesis in 2001. He was replaced as shareholder by Blair's former flatmate, the New Labour ennobled Lord Falconer, whose efficiency as Blair's eyes and ears in Cabinet committees was not matched by the sort of personal charisma required of the 'owner' of the Dome. It was Falconer who had to face the outcry when the official opening on Millennium Eve went badly wrong because of chaotic travel arrangements to get VIPs to the Dome. By January 2000 almost the whole press and media was hostile to the Dome, the projected visitor numbers failed to materialise and having used up almost all of its initial grant of £449 million, the project was already in financial trouble. While many of those who did go pronounced themselves satisfied (having paid considerable sums for their 'one amazing day'), the exhibits were judged to be mediocre. At the end of January 2000 the government was asked to allocate an extra £60 million of Lottery money because of cash flow problems, with no guarantee that it would be repaid. Already hopes were being raised of securing funds in advance from the sale of the site.

At the beginning of February Page was sacked as chief executive, and a manager from Disneyland in France, Pierre-Yves Gerbeau, was placed in charge. In May the Dome asked for a further £38.6 million, of which it received £29 million on condition that Ayling resigned as chairman of the NMEC, and costs were slashed. Visitor projections were revised downwards to seven million. By May the NMEC was already technically insolvent, but was bailed out by a further £43 million in August, set against the proposed sale of the site for £105 million to Nomura International. In September the NMEC was given another £47 million and a third chairman, city specialist David James, was installed. An accountancy report commissioned by James revealed the depths of mismanagement, and shortly afterwards Nomura withdrew its offer to purchase. The Millennium Commission was forced by ministerial directive to produce a further £90 million guarantee. Falconer answered calls for his resignation and the immediate closure of the Dome with the argument that it would cost more to close than stay open, and that the regeneration of the polluted Greenwich peninsula was a significant legacy. His critics pointed out that the land on which the Dome stood was only partially decontaminated. In November a report by the National Audit Office concluded that wildly optimistic visitor numbers were the root cause of the Dome's failure, but that it had also been badly managed by people with no experience in the field.

The Prime Minister did not return to the Dome until 19 December. While a new group, led by the Labour-supporting property developer Robert Bourne and backed by two Irish businessmen, who wished to turn the Dome into a hi-tech business park was now identified as 'preferred bidder', there were doubts about the viability of their project. Following difficulties with Legacy, bidding was reopened in February; in the pre-election period the Dome stayed embarrassingly unsold. The group took the name Legacy, but the Dome was one inheritance Labour would prefer to forget. The day before Blair's second and final visit the life of the Millennium Commission was extended until August 2001 in order to meet continuing liabilities in connection with the Dome.

Blair's Contract Culture

In his speech to the Labour Party Conference at Brighton on 26 September 2000, Blair issued a half-hearted apology for the disaster of the Dome. 'Hindsight is a wonderful thing, and if I had my time again, I would have listened to those who said governments shouldn't try to run big visitor attractions.' This placed an odd construction on events, for unlike in 1951, when the Labour government had been closely involved in directing and financing the Festival of Britain, New Labour had attempted a quasi-commercial solution using Lottery money, business sponsorship and an arms-length Commission to distance itself from responsibility. New Labour and Blair's faith in the efficacy of the market lay at the heart of its confusions over cultural policy. These confusions are revealed in Chris Smith's foreword to his document *A New Cultural Framework* of December 1998. The four central themes of the DCMS were to be: 'access, excellence and innovation, education and the creative industries. They will be linked to the delivery of increased outputs, improved access and efficiency and increased private sector support'. There would also be 'a new emphasis on the public rather than the producer'.

The problem was that there was an inherent tension between the much-used buzzword 'access' – which implied that the arts should be economically available to all, and would therefore, in the face of market failure, have to be subsidised – and the notion that the arts had to see themselves as part of an 'industry', and therefore driven by market forces. There was also a tension between 'access' and 'excellence'. The demand for access was an expression of the market, since populism could only be measured through mass demand. Blairite appeals to 'community' were to a community that was market defined. Populism was opposed to elitism, so that access paradoxically became a way of excluding the non-homogeneous, redefined as 'elites'. Among the elite were those who had absorbed the dissenting values of modernist and post-modernist art, and acquired the cultural capital which allowed them to define what 'excellence and innovation' were – in effect the educated middle-class audience for the high arts.

The issue of access, which implied that the arts should not only be available, but somehow accessible to a mass audience, bore an important relation to the broader argument that British cultural life in general was 'dumbing down'. This was reflected in the increasing attacks on the Blair government from cultural traditionalists such as Tusa, Sir John Drummond, Sir Peter Hall and Sir Vidia Naipaul. In an interview in July 2000 Naipaul accused Blair of promoting a 'plebeian' culture. This was certainly not Blair's intention, and the seismic cultural shift that these rear-guard attacks revealed indicates the limits to which any government can legislate for cultural change. The writer Will Hutton observed: 'If our culture has become more plebeian, by which I guess [Naipaul] means that the masses have insisted upon entertainment they enjoy and understand, that is entirely because of the unstoppable rise of market capitalism and the buying power it gives ordinary men and women. This is not a plebeian culture being enforced by the state from above; it is a plebeian culture, if that it be, created from below by commercial values in a cultural marketplace.'[17]

Yet in spite of New Labour's faith in the operation of the cultural marketplace, when it sought to intervene, it imposed its will more thoroughly than any previous government. The means deployed were the funding agreements with client non departmental bodies, originally introduced in 1995 by the Department of National Heritage as a means of expressing what the government expected in return for the funding requested in the sponsored body's planning documents. These agreements had been gradually tightened, but according to a report by QUEST the 1998 Comprehensive Spending Review: 'marked a step change in the level of importance they were ascribed. A new regime of three year funding was introduced, in return for which the agreements would be linked to "clear responsibilities on bodies to deliver against demanding targets".'[18] The main drive behind this development came from the dominance of the Treasury with the introduction of Public Service Agreements for all government departments, along with the definition of key targets.

In terms of cultural policy this meant the replacement of the traditional attitude of 'response' by which funding bodies reacted to proposals made to them by the client organisations – a system driven more by the producer than the public as consumer – with a contract culture in which arts bodies had to meet pre-set targets such as an increase in attendances at museums and arts events. In July 2000 a confidential government 'peer review' of the DCMS concluded that the Department – characterised in the title of the report as 'a pale yellow amoeba' – over-managed the non departmental bodies for which it was responsible, collected too many statistics and spent too much time second-guessing its clients. The culture of control, together with a faith in market-defined 'efficiency', stemmed from Blair and Brown's ideological reform of Labour in opposition and government.

There were areas where New Labour's cultural policy appeared confused or unformed. Chris Smith was committed to the values of public service broadcasting, both at the BBC and in commercial television, and was keen to promote the technological changes associated with the spread of digital media. But technological and market forces were breaking up the patterns of regulation and ownership to which governments were accustomed, and a considered response would have to wait for legislation promised in 2002. Surprisingly, in view of Blair's emphasis on the importance of education, the Department of Culture's approach to the role of the arts in education was unclear. As QUEST commented in 2000: 'The DCMS's policy is still in development and desired outcomes not yet identified.'[19] This is partly attributable to the greater responsibility of the Department for Education and Employment, which did not appear to place much importance on the arts, severely squeezed in the National Curriculum. The two departments jointly commissioned a report by the National Advisory Committee on Creative and Cultural Education, which they had set up. But when the polemical *All Our Futures: Creativity, Culture and Education* was published in January 2000, it received a decidedly muffled response. The revision of the National Curriculum in September 2000 was a matter for the DfEE, the DCMS could only make extra-curricular contributions in sport and the arts, the most significant of which was the creation of the National Foundation for Youth Music, launched with £30 million of Lottery funding in June 1999.

The expectations placed on the DCMS in 2001 were a measure of the distance travelled since John Major set up the Department of National Heritage in 1992. Under Labour the National Lottery had been sensibly reorganised and as a result an experimental new institution, NESTA, formed. After a long and destructive period of under-funding, there was a promise of recovery and even expansion for the subsidised heritage, arts and sport. The institutions administering the government's cultural policies were significantly restructured, and the government itself tightened its grip on the creation and execution of cultural policy.

It was in the national interest that the significance of the social and political role of culture should have been more fully recognised. Yet if cultural policy means more than the efficient management of existing national resources, 'events', such as the humiliating failure of the Dome, threw into question the ability of any government actually to control cultural life. There were some grand buildings opened, visual art in particular seemed to thrive, but the country was no more 'at ease with itself' than when John Major had expressed his wish to see it so. Nor did it feel like Mandelson's 'modern Britain – a nation that is confident, excited, impatient for the future.' It was certainly impatient, as the Countryside Alliance, the hauliers and old age pensioners pressed their special interests, and floods and railway disruption gave an impression of growing chaos. The culture of individual consumption was also a culture of curmudgeonly complaint. Culture – in its broadest sense – could only reflect the impact of 'disorganised' market capitalism on a seemingly disintegrating nation state.

Notes

1　'Sir Stanley Matthews is a culture,' Tony Blair, *New Britain: My Vision for a Young Country*, Fourth Estate, 1996, p. 254.
2　John Tusa, *Art Matters: Reflecting on Culture*, Methuen, 1999, p. 77.
3　Paul Routledge, *Gordon Brown: The Biography*, Simon & Schuster, 1998, pp. 6–7.
4　John Rentoul, *Tony Blair* (revised edition), Warner Books, 2001, p. 446.
5　Quoted in Rentoul, *op.cit.*, p. 40.
6　The Labour Party, *Create the Future: A strategy for cultural policy, arts and the creative economy*, with preface by Tony Blair, London, The Labour Party, 1997, p. 7. The other brain child of the Enigma group, a 'talent fund', is discussed below.
7　'Smith's tips to get arts cash revealed', *Guardian*, 29 August 2000.
8　Robert Hewison, 'Cool Britannia', *Sunday Times*, 19 May 1996.
9　Richard Eyre, *Report on the future of the lyric theatre in London*, The Stationery Office, 1998, pp. 5–6.
10　*Create The Future, op.cit.*, p. 7.
11　For an eye witness account see Tusa, 'What happened at Downing Street', *Arts Matters, op.cit.*, pp. 79–92.
12　Adam Nicolson, *Regeneration: The story of the Dome*, HarperCollins, 1999, p. 149.
13　Adam Nicolson, *op.cit.*, p. 115.
14　Adam Nicolson, *op.cit.*, p. 136.
15　Adam Nicolson, *op.cit.*, p. 147.
16　Adam Nicolson, *op.cit.*, p. 230.
17　Will Hutton, 'Sir Vidia v. the plebs', *Observer*, 16 July 2000.
18　QUEST, *Modernising the Relationship Part One: A New Approach to Funding Agreements*, London, QUEST/DCMS, 2000, p. 8.
19　QUEST, *op. cit.*, p. 16.

© Chris Riddell

Chapter 25

BLAIR AND IDEOLOGY

Raymond Plant

I HAVE ALWAYS believed that politics is first and foremost about ideas. Without a powerful commitment to goals and values, governments are rudderless and ineffective, however large their majorities (Tony Blair)

In some respects it might appear somewhat paradoxical to link the name of Tony Blair with ideology since it is often assumed that the Prime Minister travels rather light in terms of ideological beliefs. After all, is not the Third Way which he espouses supposed to be a form of political thinking which is beyond the traditional ideological cleavages between Right and Left and which exalts a commitment to what works above the maintenance of ideological purity? Indeed, some have seen the present position of New Labour as being reminiscent of politics in the 1950s when thinkers such as Daniel Bell claimed the 'end of ideology'.[1] On this view, what matters is a pragmatic approach to politics rather than a political orientation and policy flowing from some fundamental and wide ranging ideology. It is argued sometimes that it is this flexibility and suppleness in political ideas that has allowed Tony Blair, to an extent at least, to break down the political tribalism of his own party – a tribalism which was underpinned by ideological beliefs even when the political practice of the Labour Party in both government and opposition had been some way distant from its professed and fundamental ideological beliefs.

The very important moment in this was early on in Blair's leadership of the party when he astounded most of his colleagues – even those who were sympathetic – when he announced to the Labour Party Conference his commitment to the abandonment of clause 4 which committed the party to the common ownership of the commanding heights of the economy – the means of production, distribution and exchange. Clause 4 embodied a commitment to a fully socialist programme – one which sought to replace the capitalist market economy with a planned and collectively owned socialist one. In 1959 Hugh Gaitskell, then Labour leader, had tried to get the party to abandon clause 4 and to accept the reality of the mixed economy. In this he failed decisively. Blair on the other hand succeeded and replaced clause 4 with a statement of values which marked a sharp difference from the socialist version. In Blair's view the Labour Party needed a constitution which indicated what Labour would in fact do, not one which linked it to what he saw as an outmoded collectivist economic analysis and prescription and which Labour governments in any case had never sought seriously to implement save in the Attlee government's nationalisation measures. The economic analysis on which clause 4 was based was no longer relevant. It had to be accepted that for most goods and services the market economy was the best available method for production and distribution. The need now was to ensure that the market economy could serve common interests and common purposes, but in order to achieve this, it was no longer necessary to replace it by a society with socialised ownership of the means of production. So did the abandonment of clause 4 and the embracing of the market economy mean that Blair had wholly jettisoned an ideological approach to politics in favour of a pragmatic serial problem solving approach?

To an extent the first part of this question about the role of ideology in Blair's conception of politics depends a good deal on what one means by 'ideology'. The term can mean anything from a fully developed 'grand narrative' as the French philosopher Lyotard[2] sees it: an account of the nature of society and politics that draws upon, for example, a theory of history as in Marx, or a theory of the destiny of a race as in National Socialism, or the historic mission of a religion as in some forms of Islamic fundamentalism; or it can mean something narrower, the importance assigned in politics and political orientation to a set of basic values but which are not fitted into such an overarching theory. It is only in this second sense that Blair can be said to have an ideological position, but it is surely not particularly useful to characterise his position in this way since while, as we shall see, he does have a clear value framework and one which does provoke some important questions to be asked, nevertheless his position is so far removed from ideology as grand narrative, it does not really serve any very useful purpose to call it ideological. So on the one hand Blairism is not an ideology in any useful analytical sense of that term, equally it does not thereby collapse into a form of rootless pragmatism such as is sometimes thought to be caught in the claim that 'what matters is what works'. So when critics such as Roy Hattersley bemoan Blair's lack of an ideology, they do not mean ideology in the grand narrative sense, they mean rather that his political views are not rooted in a set of fundamental political values. This view is mistaken. Blair does have a clear set of values. The interesting questions are about how defensible they are, how coherent they are, how recognisable they are as social democratic values, not whether or not he has them. Indeed a critic such as Roy Hattersley ought really to accept this point since what he regards in his own case as an ideological stance is in fact a linked set of basic beliefs.[3] There is nevertheless an important issue raised for social democracy by Hattersley's insistence on the importance of ideology as he calls it and this has to do with the importance of political values in the social democratic tradition.

This issue in fact goes back to at least one strand in the social democratic tradition in Eduard Bernstein's *Evolutionary Socialism* which is a basic text in this tradition. Bernstein's argument is that if socialism cannot be based upon a theory of history such as Marx's historical materialism because, as Bernstein[4] argued, such a theory was in his view no longer tenable, then socialism had to be defined in terms of its goals, purposes and values rather than its inevitability within the processes of history. Bernstein's own views on these basic values were heavily influenced by Kant's political and moral philosophy. The important thing however is the need for a party of the Left to be held together by values not by some pseudo historical explanation or a failed and synoptic economic analysis. So in the social democratic tradition, thinkers such as R.H. Tawney who wrote a good deal about equality and fellowship; E.F.M. Durbin who concentrated on democratisation; C.A.R. Crosland who argued for the centrality of equality – all in their different ways put values at the heart of the social democratic vision. In this respect Social Democrats are in a rather different position from Conservatives (at least pre Thatcher) in that as a radical movement social democracy could not take tradition, and an habitual way of doing things as an appropriate guide in politics as the Conservative could. The values have to be asserted and argued for as radical values they cannot be taken as being already an integral part of a political tradition.

At the same time however, the social democrat cannot avoid values by concentrating upon interests. No doubt social democratic parties in Europe and in the Labour Party in the UK have seen themselves as serving and advancing the interests of the working class, but this is not adequate as a political and social basis for social democracy. The working class in advanced capitalist societies is not large enough nor is it homogeneous enough to form the basis for a political party which sees itself as purely there to advance working-class interests. Social democratic parties have to reach beyond class interests if they are to be successful politically and in so doing they have to define their purposes in terms of values rather than of interests. These values have to transcend class and in a sense be universal (at least within that society) – they have to be concerned with citizenship rather than class. As universal values however, the social democrat assumes that they will be salient for the working class too, although as we have seen not defined in terms of their interests. So on this view Hattersley is quite right to argue that the Labour Party cannot just be a party of interests, but it is not particularly useful to couch this argument in terms of it necessarily being a party kept together by ideological beliefs, a term which as I have said might best be reserved for the grand narrative view of ideology rather than saying that it is a party held together by a set of values. It seems clear enough that Blair does hold to a firm set of values, but the real question is how far they are recognisably of a social democratic sort.

Before moving on to this point it is however important to lay to rest the idea that Blair's politics are a kind of unrooted pragmatism seeking to respond to changing circumstances rather than being grounded in strong beliefs. How robust these beliefs are is a genuine question which we shall address, but they certainly exist and for the reasons that I have already suggested they have a more than rhetorical purpose since part of the aim of New Labour under Blair has been to articulate a national agenda not one based upon class or sectional interest. Universal values are of great importance in giving this project coherence; 'Without them', as Blair says, 'we are adrift'. At the same time his own formulation of the claim that what matters is what works is instructive because in one dimension it does move away from what might be seen to be the pragmatism of the approach. He argues as follows:

> As I say continually, what matters is what works to give effect to our values. Some commentators are disconcerted by this insistence on fixed values and goals but pragmatism means just that. There are even claims that it is unprincipled. But I believe that a critical dimension of the Third Way is that policies flow from values and not vice versa.[5]

This passage is important for two reasons. First of all, he links what works with values. He is thus able to neutralise, at least in principle, the claim that his political stance is one of value free pragmatism. In his approach he is surely right. We cannot judge what works in a context free and a goal free way. Something works or does not work to promote some goal or end. There is no such thing as something 'working' in an ethical vacuum. Hence policies have to be judged finally in the context of the purposes they are designed to serve. So the claim that follows this passage is in tune with this basic idea because his claim is that markets can meet New Labour's social objectives, entrepreneurship can help create social justice and new technology can extend opportunity. So the goals such as opportunity, social justice and the social or the common good are indeed there and what is claimed to work has to be judged according to these goals. At the same time as Blair argues in the passage just cited, there has to be a degree of pragmatism about means. This accounts among other things for his antipathy to clause 4, namely that it turned a means, namely common ownership, which should be examined pragmatically on its merits, which he would now regard as being few, into one of the overall goals of social democracy and given his view about the relationship between means and ends, this reification of a means cannot be right.

At this point in the exposition three points become important. One is what are Tony Blair's values if they are as important to his project as I have said they are? Second, how consistent are they with the social democratic tradition? Finally, how coherent is the distinction that he wants to draw between means and ends? I will begin this section of the discussion by listing his values as he set them out in his Fabian Society pamphlet *Third Way: New Politics for the New Century*. I shall not at this stage discuss them in detail; rather I shall enumerate them and go on initially to discuss the other two questions. Tony Blair identifies his values as follows:

Equal Worth
Opportunity for All
Responsibility
Community.[6]

These are the basic values and policies have to be judged pragmatically in terms of how effective they are likely to be in realising these values. Let us for the moment concentrate on this latter point. First of all, it has to be said that Blair's insistence upon a sharp distinction between ends and means has been a feature of post-Second World War social democracy. In the 1950s, when Gaitskell and Crosland were campaigning against nationalisation as a defining aim of social democracy, exactly this distinction between means and ends was employed. In this sense Blair's insistence on the distinction is on all fours with a great deal of social democratic thought indeed since the time of Bernstein. While Blair does not invoke the history of this distinction or its great political salience, in the 1950s, nevertheless he is clear enough about the centrality of the idea so he argues as follows:

The Third Way stands for a modernised social democracy, passionate in its commitment to social justice and the goals of the centre left, but flexible, innovative and forward looking in the means to achieve them.[7]

The Third Way is not an attempt to split the difference between Right and Left. It is about traditional values in a changed world.[8]

What of policy? Our approach is 'permanent revisionism', a continual search for better means to meet our goals, based on a clear view of the changes taking place in advanced industrial societies.[9]

At the same time as there is this seeming clarity of distinction between ends and means, Tony Blair is somewhat less than fulsome in his praise for other revisionists such as Gaitskell and Crosland whose revisionism depended upon precisely the same distinction, so he says:

> Revisionists periodically tried to change the agenda, but their success
> was limited. The Third Way is a serious reappraisal of social
> democracy, reaching deep into the values of the Left to develop
> radically new policies.[10]

Thus there is a suggestion that while his own approach is within the revisionist tradition of the Left, nevertheless earlier forms of revisionism were
not very successful – perhaps he has in mind Hugh Gaitskell's unsuccessful
attempt to drop clause 4 in 1959–60. At the same time, there is perhaps a
hint of something more in the reference to the values of the Left to develop
radically new policies. There is a suggestion here perhaps that not only does
one have to be pragmatic about means, but also that there might be certain
ends/goals and purposes that the modern Left has lost sight of that also
need to be reinstated. This I think is true, but the discussion will wait until
I come more directly onto the values themselves.

At the moment, I want to concentrate on the question of how far this
distinction between means and ends is defensible in the form that Blair
states it. There are two issues here. He argues that the values are traditional
or constant with the means of achieving them being variable; secondly he
argues that it is possible to distinguish between constant values and pragmatic means. There are complexities around each of these rather
philosophical points which have always been of political importance to the
revisionist Left. One point might be worth making first in passing. In the
early days of Blair's leadership and premiership, a good deal was made of
the 'New' in New Labour. In the light of the passages already quoted from
Tony Blair's own understanding of his project, this could mean one of two
things. If the constancy of values is stressed then New Labour is 'new' in
respect of means only. Its revisionism extends only to means, not to ends.
If values are constant in the social democratic tradition then in terms of its
values New Labour is not new. It is new only in respect of openness, flexibility and pragmatism about the means of achieving these values. Certainly
this seems to be a perfectly reasonable way of reading Blair's point. In that
case it may be that there is a possible political price to be paid within the
Labour Party for the attempt to so sharply differentiate between New and
Old Labour. In so far as some Labour supporters are likely to think that
New Labour has forsaken many of the goals of Old Labour then on the
view that the difference between the two is about means only, then in
terms of the allegiance of its own supporters, it may turn out to have been
unwise to draw such a sharp distinction between New and Old which
looks very often as though it turns on values and not just on means. On the
other hand it is possible that talk about reaching deep into the values of the
Left to develop radically new approaches could mean that he wants to
draw a distinction between New and Old Labour in terms of values rather
than just means and argue that Old Labour actually lost sight of certain
values and misunderstood certain others with the implication that the

former (perhaps community) should be reinstated and that the latter (perhaps equality) should be reinterpreted.

However this assumes that the distinction between ends and means can in fact be maintained. It is however, not clear that this is so in any straightforward sense that does not itself involve value judgments. Let me take two examples from the history of Labour's approach to policy: nationalisation and comprehensive education. For the revisionist both of these are means to an end: social justice, greater equality etc. and each should be assessed in terms of how effective a means it is to those ends. Socialist critics of revisionism could however argue that means and ends in these cases are inextricably linked. The critic will argue in the case of nationalisation that common ownership is not to be seen as a means but rather part of the goal of socialism itself. The reason here is that social democracy is about the democratisation of the economy in the same way that liberalism had democratised the political institutions of society. This idea though, according to those who defend it, cannot be realised without the common ownership of the means of production, distribution and exchange. On this view collective ownership is not to be seen as one policy instrument among others, but rather as intrinsically linked to the possibility of the democratisation of economic life and the creation of a more equal society. So here it might appear that it is not clear how it is possible to arrive at some kind of political neutral way of distinguishing between constant ends and changing means if the critic argues that in this case nationalisation or common ownership is part of the framework of ends in social democracy. Precisely these points were made in the earlier debates about clause 4 in 1959–60. Similarly, it could be argued by protagonists of comprehensive education that it has to be seen not as just one means to a goal such as greater opportunity, but as an essential vehicle for developing a sense of common culture and a shared social experience which could not be achieved by the previous tripartite system. On such a view, if the social democratic goal is equality of opportunity alone, then it is conceivable that there could be a number of different means to the achievement of that goal, one of which might be comprehensive education. If however, the goal is broadened to creating a common culture and a common civic identity, then it could be argued there is at least a far closer if not an intrinsic link between comprehensive education compared with alternatives. The fact is that now, as was also the case in the late 1950s, the argument about means and ends does not turn on an academic distinction but on a political argument – namely to treat certain values or the interpretation of certain values as being crucial to a political project which then allows certain sorts of means to be discarded as not effective or not intrinsic to the achievement of that set of goals. This last point leads naturally enough to the constancy of the values of social democracy since Blair's argument is that values remain constant as part of the social democratic tradition while it is means that are being revised.

How plausible is this argument or how far is it the case that Blair's revisionism is about ends as well as means? This is actually a rather complex question that takes us to the heart of at least part of the Blair project, namely the relationship between social democracy and the social or 'new' form of liberalism developed in Britain at the end of the nineteenth century. This point is made very clearly by Blair in his Third Way pamphlet when he argues as follows:

> [The Third Way] is an attempt to split the difference between Right and Left. It is about traditional values in a changed world. And it draws its vitality from uniting two great streams of left of centre thought – democratic socialism and liberalism.[11]

This argument which seeks to unite both social democracy and progressive forms of liberalism has been important in sustaining Blair's keenness to maintain a good relationship with the Liberal Party in the run up to the 1997 election and since – a good many of the details of which are set out in Paddy Ashdown's *Diaries* (2000). However, for the purposes of this chapter it is more important to look at the more abstract issues of principle raised by this link between social democracy and liberalism. One point is obvious straight away, namely that it is difficult to see that Blair's approach here is not a revisionism about ends/goals/values as much as it is about means. If he was talking and arguing as a social democratic revisionist *simpliciter* then it could be argued that his emphasis on modernisation and revisionism is a revisionism about means to unrevised and constant social democratic goals. Given however, that his aim is to reunite around a set of common or agreed values, the social democratic and the social liberal tradition, then it seems clear that there has to be a degree of revisionism about ends as well as means. This is not really surprising since previous revisionists, if we take Gaitskell and Crosland as examples, had little or nothing to say about solidarity, fellowship or community, linked values which had been vitally important to an earlier generation of socialist and social democratic thinkers such as Tawney. It is a beguiling but I believe false idea to think that revisionism on the Left is entirely about means – it is about ends and values as well: some values are sidelined – as with community/fellowship in mid-twentieth-century social democracy; others are reinterpreted – as with Blair's account of equality; other values are relegated to means as with Crosland/Gaitskell's account of public ownership and with Blair's account of state power in the Third Way pamphlet:

> Liberals asserted the primacy of individual liberty in the market economy; social democrats promoted social justice with the state as its main agent. There is no necessary conflict between the two, accepting as we do that state power is one means to achieve our goals, but not the only one and emphatically not an end in itself.[12]

So in so far as it is accurate to say as Tony Blair does in the pamphlet that the Third Way is a 'modernised social democracy' then this modernised social democracy does I think have to be seen as embodying a revisionism about ends as well as means if for no other reason that he does want to incorporate into it insights from late nineteenth- and early twentieth-century liberalism which are not about means alone but values to and to do this in a way that either adds to social democratic values or leads to some degree of reinterpretation of existing or constant social democratic values. In a sense there is no surprise in this and indeed in some respects one might regard it as inevitable. Values such as liberty, equality, fraternity/fellowship/solidarity/community themselves contain internal tensions and contradictions and part of politics is about trying to establish the dominance of one interpretation of the meaning of a value over others. So, for example, liberty can mean negative liberty in the sense of freedom from interference and coercion; or it can be taken in a more complex way as certainly the New Liberals did incorporating negative liberty but also extending to positive freedom in which the emphasis would be on whether an individual had the resources and capacities to fulfil him or herself. This shift immediately linked freedom with the distribution of resources and with social opportunities – for example in education. A negative view of liberty does not carry this implication quite so clearly.

Similarly equality can mean equality of opportunity, or starting gate equality – equalising the opportunity to become unequal; or it can be concerned with greater equality of outcome seeking to constrain the gap between rich and poor which may still exist with equality of opportunity. Equality of opportunity itself may be seen in a minimalist way – for example in terms of removing discrimination; or it can be seen in a more maximalist way, that is to say by securing to individuals the resources and opportunities that they need to develop their potential. Community and its cognate ideas too can be understood in a variety of ways and some thinkers have indeed argued that it is one of the most indefinite social and political concepts and values. Given that these values are basic to Centre Left political attitudes and their theoretical elaboration and given their diversity of meaning, it is not at all surprising that a revisionist stance within social democracy, whether Blair's or anyone else's should also become, to a degree, a revisionism of ends as well as means. As I have said, this is even more true in Blair's case since he does see the Third Way as attempting to bring together the century long division between social democracy and progressive forms of liberalism.

So what then of Blair's own statement of values and their relation to social democracy? Perhaps if one wanted to describe them in highly general terms it would be through an emphasis on the need to strengthen society and the communities within it on the grounds that 'for most individuals to succeed, society must be strong'. While he recognises and indeed, puts at the head of the list of his values that of equal worth and this involves a recognition of individual uniqueness, nevertheless individuals can only flourish within strong families and communities which are essential for individuals to realise their potential. Indeed, on one occasion Tony Blair described that as his version of socialism – the emphasis on the quality of social institutions as essential for human fulfilment: 'We all depend on collective goods for our independence and all our lives are enriched – or impoverished – by the communities to which we belong.'[13]

This emphasis on community is perhaps the best example of what Blair means when he talks about 'reaching deep into the values of the Left' to ground his ideas, since it is undoubtedly true that the mid century Left in Britain rather undervalued the idea of community – for example Steven Haseler in his book on the Gaitskellites argues that the mid-twentieth-century revisionists did not really know what to do with ideas like community. This was certainly not always the case. The socialist and social democratic tradition has a very rich vein of thinking about community: Robert Owen, William Morris, R.H. Tawney, the Guild Socialists and so on all put the idea of community/fellowship/solidarity at the heart of their value framework. This was also a very important value in the writings and indeed the practice of many of the New Liberals. They were indebted to the writings of philosophers such as T.H. Green, Sir Henry Jones, Bernard Bosanquet[14] and others who emphasised the link between personality and the quality of social life. This had a profound influence on the university settlement movement: middle-class graduates going to live in a settlement in a deprived area to encourage the growth of skills and social development in those areas. They would have called themselves civic idealists but they are not very far from the idea of social entrepreneurs which the present government has promoted.

Blair argues that one of the things about the Left that he has wanted to change has been the way in which government has taken over more and more from civil society. He calls this the grievous twentieth century error of the fundamentalist Left and he wants to see a strengthening of civil society, in the voluntary sector and individual volunteering. This is a commitment that runs deep in the government and certainly also characterises the approach of the Chancellor of the Exchequer who has done a great deal to improve the tax environment for the voluntary sector and to encourage voluntary giving; it is also a deeply-held belief of David Blunkett who has made voluntary action one of the themes of his stewardship at the Department of Education and Employment. Indeed the most recent guidance to the Higher Education Funding Council is to place an obligation on universities to encourage students to play a full part in voluntary activity.

At the same time as the Prime Minister wants to strengthen civil society and in particular the voluntary sector, there are some dangers which need to be guarded against. If the government funds the voluntary sector more and more to act as its agent in delivering its policy objectives whether it be part of the New Deal or programmes such as Sure Start then if it wishes to preserve what it regards as the very valuable civil society aspects of the voluntary sector – its independence, its capacity for innovation, its volunteering side, its degree of trust and its local knowledge – it will need to ensure that government funding does not jeopardise the very features which New Labour values above direct state action and state provision. Nevertheless the central point here is that government wants to strengthen communities as a central aspect of enhancing social and human capital but equally it finds that government per se is not very well equipped to do this job directly lacking as it does the trust of the members of the communities it is trying to strengthen and also the local knowledge necessary to make policy effective. It therefore has to rely a great deal on the voluntary sector and the not-for-profit organisations in civil society to achieve its goals.

The link that Tony Blair makes between rights and responsibilities in the list of values cited earlier also in a sense follows from this recommitment to community. He argues that duty and responsibility have for a generation or more seen to be the preserve of the Right. The Left on the contrary had stressed rights and entitlements to the neglect of duties. The argument of the Left here would typically be that given that social democrats are in politics to extend democratic rights from the political sphere to the social and economic one and given that rights in the political sphere are unconditional, that is to say they arise from the status of being a citizen and not from the contribution that one makes (the only people exempted from political rights like the right to vote are peers, prisoners and lunatics), then there is no reason why rights in the social and economic sphere like rights to health, education, social security and unemployment benefit should be linked to the discharge of obligations. The rights of citizenship are seamless whether they are civil, political or social and there is therefore no case for making some depend on obligations and not others.

In this Third Way paper Tony Blair rejects this view. He argues two basic claims: that a reciprocal relationship between rights and duties has been a feature of the progressive Left which became obscured by the entitlement culture of the late twentieth century and secondly that 'the demand for rights from the state was separated from the duties of citizenship and the imperative for mutual responsibility on the part of individuals and institutions . . . The rights that we enjoy reflect the duties we owe: rights and opportunities without responsibility are engines of selfishness and greed.'[15]

The first historically based claim is certainly true and was a major theme of the writings of the late nineteenth-century liberal tradition as well as the social democratic one. In his book *Industrial Revolution* Arnold Toynbee, a prominent progressive liberal and ardent follower of T.H. Green in social philosophy, argued very strongly that rights without reciprocity were pernicious. In his view the pre 1834 poor law which had 'given relief without conditions had completely demoralised the people'.[16] Alongside these arguments though there was also the claim that modern society had to redevelop a sense of community in order to constrain a kind of dutiless individualism. So it is probably fair enough to claim that there is a link between Blair's endorsement of the idea of community and his critique of the culture of unconditional entitlement. This view that entitlements should become more conditional has been reflected in many of the government's reforms of the welfare state and indeed lies behind the New Deal. The link between rights and responsibility has also been a strong feature of Jack Straw's approach to strengthening the law particularly in relation to youth justice, curfew orders and the like which are aimed at strengthening the powers of the police and the courts to improve the quality of life in communities threatened with lawlessness. This critique of unconditional entitlement is set out by Blair in the context of unemployment benefit when he says that 'unemployment benefits were often paid without strong reciprocal obligations . . . This issue persists'. Again this sort of language has been also associated with Gordon Brown and David Blunkett. As in the case of community, this approach has partly been about reinstating a social democratic value that had been marginalised but also one which can draw into the argument ideas and insights from late nineteenth-century progressive liberalism.

In his catalogue of values Blair also stressed the importance of equality of opportunity or what he has called more circumspectly perhaps 'the widest spread of wealth, power and opportunity' or 'opportunity for all'. The issue of equality does mark one of those areas of the debate about values where it could certainly be argued that Blair is being a revisionist not only about means but also ends. The debate here is usually couched in terms of Blair and Brown particularly emphasising equality of opportunity and rejecting equality of outcome. The assumption is that traditionally social democrats – perhaps particularly Tawney and Crosland – did not believe that opportunity was enough. Rather there had to be an attempt to limit the scope of inequality. Crosland argued, for example in his pamphlet *Social Democracy in Europe*, that the job of a social democratic government was to use the fiscal dividends of economic growth to maintain the real incomes or the absolute position of the better off (otherwise they would not vote for social democratic governments because they would be voting to make themselves worse off) while improving the relative position of the worst off (i.e. diminishing differential equality of result). So while a social democrat such as Crosland thought that there was a strong case for differential rewards which would follow from the 'rent of ability', i.e. the sum of money needed to ensure that talents were mobilised and that unattractive work was done, nevertheless he was concerned with the issue of outcomes and clearly believed that there should be some attempt to limit the degree of overall inequality. He also famously argued in *The Future of Socialism* that equality of opportunity is not enough.

Blair and Brown have rejected trying to secure greater equality of outcome as a direct aim of policy. This is probably so for two reasons. One is that they do not believe that it is possible to go in this direction in a high tech economy in an open global competitive market because strong incentives to entrepreneurs and risk takers are needed and to secure differential rewards for those who gain extra skills. Secondly they have philosophical objections to it: it implies quite a high degree of state intervention in economic outcomes to try to constrain them by equality principles and it also means using the welfare state and public spending generally as a way of compensating for market-based inequalities of outcome. Blair and Brown on the contrary want the welfare state to work more with the grain of the modern economy rather than using it to reshape the results that such an economy throws up. Their emphasis is very much *pace* Crosland on equality of opportunity. There is both a moral and an economic case for their argument here. The moral one is based upon Blair's own invocation of the principle of equal worth. If people have equal worth and deserve equal respect, then also we have to respect and value what they are capable of and what their potential might be. Given that we all have potential and that we all have equal worth there is no antecedent moral case for one person having a greater degree of opportunity than another. The aim of government is to extend the widest degree of equality of opportunity to all and indeed throughout life to enable all to acquire new skills to extend their opportunities through such things as life-long learning.

The economic argument parallels this. It would be absurd to think that we know in advance the general sort of person who could do a particular job and it would be inefficient to rule out certain sorts of people, for example women or those from ethnic communities, without actually testing their abilities to do that sort of job. We should therefore extend opportunities to all so that society, business and commerce has the largest pool of talent to fish in and this must be economically efficient. Also if we are to reform the welfare state and to improve the position of the worst off members of society then we have to equip people with skills. There is falling demand for unskilled labour and if those at the bottom of the economic pile are to improve their position, it has to be through acquiring skills which are valued in the labour market.

The question of how the distribution of income and wealth will look when this programme has been running for some time, that is to say will equality of opportunity contribute to greater equality of outcome, cannot be answered except speculatively.[17] The more traditional social democratic critic will argue for example that a free market is likely to increase relativities. So while this programme of equality of opportunity may well improve the position of the worst off in the sense that they are likely to be better off than they would otherwise be, this does not mean that the relative position of the worst off will improve if nothing is done for example through the tax system to constrain relativities at the top of the income distribution. It seems fairly clear that the government is unlikely to go far down this road, if it goes at all for the economic and philosophical reasons against equality of outcome which were mentioned earlier. So this is perhaps the clearest case where the government has been revisionist about ends as well as means. This is not a criticism as I tried to make clear earlier, but it is doubtful if their proposals are best understood as looking for new means to realise traditional values unless we just say the value here is that of equality *per se* but as I argued earlier, values are more complex than this would imply and in the context of that complexity they do seem to be revisionists about ends. Indeed, despite his own characterisation of the position, Blair might in fact welcome this since revisionism about both means and ends might indicate a sharper division between New Labour and those aspects of Old Labour which he does not like, as well as opening up the possibility of a framework of values around which the progressive Left whether in the Liberal Democrat or Labour parties could unite.

Notes

1 For an interesting overview of this debate see A. MacIntyre *Against the Self Images of the Age*, Duckworth, 1971.
2 See F. Lyotard *The Post Modern Condition*, Manchester University Press, 1984.
3 See R. Hattersley *Choose Freedom*, Michael Joseph, 1987
4 E. Bernstein *Evolutionary Socialism*, Shocken Books, 1961.
5 Tony Blair *The Third Way: New Politics for the New Century*, Fabian Society, 1998.
6 Ibid.
7 Ibid.
8 Ibid.
9 Ibid.
10 Ibid.
11 Ibid.
12 Ibid.
13 Ibid.
14 For an account of those thinkers in relation to these themes see A. Vincent and R. Plant *Philosophy, Politics and Citizenship*, Blackwell, 1982.
15 Tony Blair *The Third Way*, op.cit.
16 A. Toynbee 'Are Radicals Socialists?' in *Industrial Revolution*, Reprint David & Charles, 1969.
17 For further discussion of this see R. Plant 'Crosland, Equality and New Labour' in *Crosland and New Labour*, Macmillan, 1998.

Commentaries

Chapter 26

AN INSIDE VIEW ON
BLAIR'S NUMBER 10

Michael Cockerell

THERE IS SOMETHING about Tony Blair that can bring out the beast in his critics – both in politics and in the media. A.A. Gill of the *Sunday Times* claims that the Prime Minister is 'an oleaginous, duplicitous douche-bag, with the manner of a Californian plastic surgeon and the sincerity of a Cairo carpet salesman'.

William Hague's view is that the Prime Minister leads a 'tax-raising, intervening, interfering, bossy, high-spending, over-regulating, trade union-funded, crony-run, hypocritical, amoral, arrogant Labour government. Tony Blair says he's in charge: when there's the slightest credit to be had – he is everywhere; but when the failures rack up – he's nowhere to be seen.'

The former socialist turned Thatcherite, Paul Johnson – at first a fervent Blair admirer – says, 'Tony Blair is just a clever actor: all things to all men, a chameleon, not to be trusted an inch.'

And there is devastating evidence from Blair's own words to support the view of his critics. In the notorious leaked memo on 'Touchstone issues' to his closest advisers in April 2000, the Prime Minister voiced his concern that he and his government were seen as 'out of touch with gut British instincts'. Blair proposed a series of 'eye catching' populist initiatives – 'tough with immediate bite' – on matters like crime and immigration. And he stressed: 'it is important that I personally should be associated with as much of this as possible'. The memo gave the media a field day. Michael Gove of *The Times* summed up the view that it revealed the PM to be nothing more than 'an image-obsessed, spin-driven, ego-absorbed, hucksterish, hypocrite'.

But there is another way of looking at it. As Blair suggested in his memo: public perception can sometimes be at odds with a government's long-term strategy. And in a media age where perception is at least half of the battle, symbolic corrective gestures are sometimes necessary. For Blair and his advisers are convinced they must retain the initiative from day to day, if they are to deliver in the long term. The Prime Minister's personal popularity is a central element in what they call the Blair project.

But the question of whether the project amounts to anything more substantial than holding on to power and winning a second term is fundamental to any assessment of the Blair government. To answer it requires an understanding and insight into the motivations and character of the Prime Minister himself.

To try to find what makes Tony Blair tick, I was lucky enough in the course of 2000 to have access to him and some of his closest associates for a number of months in making two television documentaries. It had taken me six years to persuade Blair and his press secretary, Alastair Campbell, to agree to my making these programmes. I had first approached them when Blair was elected Opposition Leader in 1994 and would repeat the request at regular intervals. Eventually they agreed to give me a limited access and a lengthy interview with the PM for a programme I suggested to mark Blair's thousand days in office in January 2000. After that they agreed – despite the opposition of some Downing Street political advisers and officials – to give me full access for a documentary about Number 10's relations with the media. Blair and Campbell did not ask for and were not given any editorial rights over the programmes, nor did they see them before transmission.

In the first half of 2000 I went so regularly into Number 10 that I experienced severe withdrawal symptoms when the filming had to stop. (High flying young civil servants who return to their ministries from an attachment to Downing Street suffer comparable cold turkey – which can stay with them throughout a career.)

Over the months I did a series of interviews with the Prime Minister and his advisers. We began in his study where I asked Blair how much of an actor he felt he needed to be as Prime Minister. 'Politics is a bit like the law or the media', he replied, 'in the sense that there's a part of it when you're on show – so there's a bit of it that's acting. But don't confuse it with real life – or with real problems and real solutions.'

As it happens, like John Major, Blair's forebears once trod the boards: his father's parents were Edwardian vaudeville artists and Tony Blair's own middle names – Charles Lynton – combine the real and stage names of his grandfather. And both at school and Oxford, Blair said his ambition was to go on the stage. I asked the PM: 'what about the view that some people have, that they don't know which is your real face – they think that your acting skills are all part of this, as your old friend Paul Johnson wrote.' Blair winced momentarily at the mention of his quondam admirer. 'People can think what they like. I am what I am within myself. The thing I'm quite sure about is that I will do this job to the best of my ability, whilst people want me to do it. I'll try and achieve the things that I believe I can achieve for this country. I have a very strong vision of where Britain needs to be and where the politics of this country have got to be for the twenty-first century. And I think I know some of the answers for that, which may sound a bit arrogant, but I think I do. But what I am as an individual – that's for me. And for anyone to come on television and say he was truly baring his soul – that would be the real acting.'

But what he is as an individual cannot be for Blair alone. His own formation, character and beliefs affect the public, as they help determine both his government's policy and how he reacts in a crisis. His early life provides some clues. At St John's, his Oxford college, Blair met a mature student and minister of the Church of Australia who was to have a profound influence on his thinking. Peter Thomson encouraged students to come to join him for meaning-of-life discussions that would go on into the night.

'They would smoke all my cigarettes and drink all my coffee and we'd get into religion and politics,' says Thomson. 'Tony Blair didn't have political ambitions at that stage; in fact all the time we were at Oxford, I thought he might have easily gone into the Church.'

Blair demurred when I put this to him, but he said 'Peter Thomson was very important because he reconciled what was a growing political awareness with my religious belief.' The PM then stopped talking and shifted uneasily on his sofa. I asked him why he seemed so uncomfortable when talking about his faith. 'Because you get completely misconstrued when you do. Either people think you are trying to wear God on your sleeve or paint God into the picture – and most people find that distasteful, including me: or alternatively it is somehow taken that you don't have a political grounding: well, I do have a political grounding.

'I am a practising Christian and that's part of me – there's no point in denying it; but I suppose that what I drew from Peter Thomson is the idea that your religious belief wasn't something that shut you away from the world, but something that meant that you had to go out and act.'

His Christianity remains one of the keys to Tony Blair. His former deputy press secretary, Tim Allan, tells how Blair would travel with his Bible among his papers and would become nearly frantic on a Sunday if it looked as if he might miss Holy Communion. He still prays every day. And on holiday he took a book on theology as part of his Tuscan reading. What makes his professed commitment to moral values hard to take for many people in a secular society is that Blair keeps company with both God and Mammon.

Soon after he became Labour leader, Blair attended a series of private dinners at safe mansions in ritzy parts of London where he met captains of industry. The man who organised the dinners for Blair was Lord (Dennis) Stevenson – now Chairman of the Pearson media group and the Halifax Building Society and listed by the *Sunday Times* as the eighth most powerful person in Britain. The aim of the dinners was to convince the tycoons that New Labour was a business friendly party and they had nothing to fear from a Labour victory.

'The point was to try and explain the nature of my political project,' says Blair, 'that we could get beyond the traditional boundaries of right and left, and you could have a pro-business, pro-enterprise but pro-fairness political party. We have to create a different type of progressive, political force, which has left the redundant twentieth-century battles between communism and capitalism behind; the new battles are about how you create a proper functioning civic society, in which opportunity is open to all. And I always thought that a lot of these business people would be important in us delivering our agenda.'

Stevenson says that Blair's performance at the dinners raised his credibility even among a number of the tycoons who were strong Conservatives. Since then he has observed the Prime Minister at close quarters and chairs the campaign that is close to Blair's heart to bring computers into every school, although Lord Stevenson is at pains to point out he is not a Labour party member.

Stevenson says of Blair: 'He is morally driven. He is highly intelligent, brighter than he comes across, because he seems so normal. He is a good communicator, rather cuddly. And he is completely ruthless – not in a pejorative sense, but he really goes for what he believes in. And to have that combination of qualities and not look like a ruthless shit: that is a good recipe for a leader – particularly a political leader.'

There are three 'Ms' in the Blair project: along with morality and mammon comes the media. From the moment Blair was elected Labour leader in 1994, he and his two chief media advisers, Alastair Campbell and Peter Mandelson, made it a priority to try to bring the traditionally Tory tabloids – the *Daily Mail* and the *Sun* – aboard. Campbell says: 'We were appalled by the damage the press could do to Neil Kinnock and others before him and determined they would not do that to Tony Blair.' Blair himself joked privately that if the *Mail* and *Sun* had written about him as they had about Kinnock he would himself have had difficulty in voting Labour.

'In the early eighties the Labour Party did not talk to most of the Fleet Street newspapers and that was silly', says Blair. 'I look back on the Thatcher government and the huge efforts they made to woo the media – including I seem to remember quite an array of knighthoods for various editors – and everyone says "fair enough". But when we attempt to get on terms with the newspapers it is considered some kind of great act of ground-breaking significance.'

Once they moved into Number 10, Blair and his press secretary echoed the view of President Clinton's chief spin-meister, James Carville: 'The politicians must always be ahead of the news cycle.' Says Alastair Campbell: 'We have to try to dominate the agenda, because good government demands it. We have to stay ahead of the media, finding new and creative ways to get our message to the public.' In practice that means ensuring a constant supply of positive pictures and messages from the

Prime Minister and, says Campbell, seeking to put across a coherent narrative of what the government is doing.

For the first six months it all went swimmingly. Blair's popularity reached record highs. But then came an event that threatened all this – the Ecclestone Affair. The uneasy cohabitation of morality and big money in the Blair project was metamorphosing into scandal. It appeared that a million pound donation to Labour funds had bought a government u-turn in favour of Bernie Ecclestone's Formula One and the tobacco companies. After some days trying to kill the story or at least limit the damage, Campbell and Mandelson decided the only way to bring about what they called 'closure' was to have Blair face a tough TV interrogation. Or as Campbell characteristically put it: 'You need to go and get a good kicking from Humphrys.'

At very short notice Blair agreed to appear on the BBC's *On the Record*. Blair prepared for the programme with Campbell playing the part of a belligerent interviewer in a style which – according to one of those present – made the programme's presenter, John Humphrys, seem a pussy cat in comparison. So long did the preparations last that Blair only took his seat seconds before the interview was due to start. And he appeared heavily rouged: apparently concerned about his pallid, strained appearance, he had insisted on the make-up artist adding an extra layer of slap to tint his cheeks.

While regretting the way the story had 'dribbled out' the Prime Minister adamantly denied any wrong doing. 'I would never do anything to harm the country or anything improper. I think most people who have dealt with me think I'm a pretty straight sort of guy – and I am.' Despite his blushing appearance, Blair's quasi-apology lanced the boil. 'Every story needs a full stop,' says Campbell, and the media spotlight turned elsewhere. But, as Andrew Rawnsley put it in his semi-authorised tale of the new Labour government, 'Blair's smile was still there but the PM had tobacco stains on his teeth.'

Blair's *On the Record* interview was a one-off. The Prime Minister has strictly limited his appearances on the traditional, heavyweight political programmes like *Panorama*. Campbell sees little percentage in his man going into a hostile TV environment to be given a hard time before a limited, upmarket audience. Blair has tended to prefer more relaxed TV encounters with David Frost, Richard Madeley and July Finnigan, or Des O'Connor. Downing Street calls this 'the Heineken approach': taking the Prime Minister and his policies to those parts of the voting public that other programmes cannot reach.

'I do think it is a good idea for someone in my position', the PM told Richard and Judy in 1999, 'to try to communicate directly and talk about things that really interest people in terms of the government's policies and programmes. And sometimes you can do that in better ways than just the traditional ways.' Blair says that he has taken part in more question and answer sessions with different sections of the public and appeared on more local radio and TV phone-ins than any previous Prime Minister in history.

The strategy is to try to connect directly to voters and not have every-thing filtered through the press, much of which the PM describes as 'corrosively cynical' and 'fundamentally dishonest' – determined to impose its own agenda. Both he and Campbell see themselves as more spinned against than spinning. That was partly the reason why they agreed to give us unprecedented access to make our TV documentary *News from Number 10*.

The PM and his press secretary felt the government could gain from an accurate representation of Downing Street's relations with the media. 'I may be making the biggest mistake of my professional career in letting you in', Campbell told us. 'But what I want to get across is that we fulfil a basic, necessary and legitimate function. We are not the horrible, Machiavellian people as portrayed. There is a huge range of information that we have to get out in a coordinated way. But the press – hand-in-hand with the Conservatives – say it's all just spin. It is all part of the strategy to say you can't trust the Prime Minister; that this guy doesn't really stack up, doesn't stand for anything.'

One day Blair seemed startled to see us filming when he paid an unan-nounced visit to his press secretary's bow-fronted office. It was a good place to ask Blair why his government placed such importance on its rela-tions with the media and on presentation. 'It's just modern government', he replied. 'Over the past twenty years the media has intensified – become twenty-four hours a day. So you have to try to be smarter, sharper and quicker off the mark than you used to be. I would prefer a situation where things happened in a far more deliberate, less frantic way than they do today – where what you wake up with in the morning is still happening at night. But nowadays, with the speed of the media it just doesn't happen like that. So it's important to have the capacity to get on top of the news, as far as possible; because otherwise a story can be out there saying you are doing something which you are not doing at all. And these stories then take on a life of their own and start running away in the far distance. So you have to be able to say: "hang on the facts are x and y".'

But, I said, it is reported that you and Alastair Campbell spend your whole time working out how you are going to spin things so that you will win the next election. 'That's rubbish', the PM replied, 'an awful lot of twaddle is talked about this. I'm supposed to have spent my holidays with him last year – now, much as I like him . . . I would be the happiest person in the world if I didn't have to give another thought as to what the presen-tation was. Of course when a specific controversy comes up, you have to manage the press angle and have answers for what they are going to be interested in.

'But the idea that I sit and think about presentation all day is nonsense. That is not what motivates us and it must not disturb me from doing the things that are really important for me – which are the things for this country; otherwise there is no point in doing this job. And people can believe this or not – but it is what I spend my time thinking about.' The impact of Blair's impassioned peroration was somewhat blunted when Alastair Campbell interjected with a laugh: 'So that's why you spent the last seven minutes talking to Michael Cockerell.' It was a vivid illustration of the relationship between the PM and his press secretary and a remark I subsequently learned that Campbell regretted having made on camera.

After the documentary went out Campbell said that he felt it had on balance justified the risk he and the PM had taken in giving us access: 'I would give it seven out of ten.' But from Number 10's point of view we had failed to portray the journalists as corrosively cynical enough. Nor had we dwelt sufficiently on what Campbell called 'the regular diet of trivia, froth, speculation and sheer invention that passes for so much political journalism these days'.

Throughout the filming the Prime Minister regularly said that he felt the media represented a barrier between him and the public: 'I would like to see the political debate focus on ideas and on the serious issues that I spend time thinking about – like how you reform the Health Service. The greatest frustration of modern politics is that – everyone talks about sound bites – on the main evening TV news you'll get thirty seconds, if you are very lucky – and twenty seconds, if you are not. So the number of times you can communicate with people so that they hear a structured argument is very limited. And it is partly I think because the media have become obsessed with themselves.' Do the media sometimes drive you mad? I asked. 'I think a no comment on that', he smiled.

At end of 2000 Blair agreed to appear on an ITV programme *Ask the Prime Minister* where he would face questions direct from a large studio audience and on the telephone. 'It's about the only time I get the chance to speak to people direct and not through the newspapers', he said. The questioners gave him a hard time over matters ranging from the single currency to fuel prices, crime, the health service and education. But by seeming to take the audience into his confidence, he drew the sting from many questions. The programme ended with numerous would-be interrogators noisily resentful at not having been called.

The television viewers did not see what happened next. Blair was on an extremely tight schedule – he was due to fly immediately to Belfast to meet the retiring President Clinton for a last minute round of talks with Irish political leaders to try to advance the peace process. But even though the programme's presenter, Jonathan Dimbleby, and Blair's own aides had left the studio, Blair had sensed the audience's frustration. He stayed on and conducted a further hour long question session off camera, with himself as chairman.

'Why,' asked one man, 'does Peter Mandelson seem to have a finger in every pie?' 'Oh, I must tell him that', replied Blair to laughter. 'Right, I'm coming to the group over there where you haven't had a question.' At first Campbell and the other aides wondered where the PM had gone, unaware that he was still in the studio. At the end of the impromptu session, where Blair had dealt with a whole range of domestic issues, the previously hostile audience which had been chosen for its tough questions, gave him a standing ovation. His performance showed Blair's skills at direct communication were unimpaired. Yet only two months later came an event that displayed in primary colours the *deformations professionelles* of the Blair project. Hindujagate contained many of the same elements as the Ecclestone affair: millionaire businessmen, allegations of cash for influence, initial attempts at cover-up and the unmistakable taint of sleaze. Yet this time, Peter Mandelson was at the centre of the story, which made his behind-the-scenes attempts to massage the media alongside Alastair Campbell much more hazardous.

The two men used many of the familiar instruments that they had both fashioned to try and defuse the story. It was Mandelson himself who had created a Clinton-style rapid rebuttal unit for New Labour. Now he produced for the Observer the first of what were to be a series of rapid rebuttals – sometimes of his very own words – down a mobile phone from the Museum of Asiatic Art in Paris. But the story of Mandelson's apparent involvement in securing a passport for Srichand Hinduja just kept growing.

Blair, Campbell and Mandelson all wanted, as they had with the Ecclestone affair, to bring what they called 'closure' to the story. Just as Campbell had successfully advised Blair 'to go and get a good kicking' on TV, now he advised Mandelson to do the same. But the two spin-meisters had not got their story straight and Mandelson's interviews only made matters worse. With the media screaming for blood the following morning over what it called 'Mandelson's lies', Blair acted on Campbell's dictum that 'every story needs a full stop'. Mandelson's rapid resignation along with the announcement of the Hammond enquiry were designed to lance the Hinduja boil.

But what had looked like a full stop turned out to be the first of three dots, followed by 'to be continued'. A vicious war of smear and counter-smear from 'Downing Street insiders' and 'friends of Peter Mandelson' broke out. Blair and Campbell were accused of blind panic and setting up a Kangaroo court that had destroyed an innocent man. Mandelson was branded a mad Queen. Outsiders wondered: if that is what they do to their friends, think what they do to their enemies.

Number 10's reaction to the Mandelson affair had been a classic example of the bunker mentality that afflicts all prime ministers – although it normally comes rather later in their terms of office and when they are well behind rather than miles ahead in the opinion polls. Blair himself had consciously sought to avoid the bunker mentality that afflicts Prime Ministers when they have been in office for some time. I was walking one night from my Westminster office and I looked up and saw the PM and his parliamentary secretary coming unescorted down Whitehall from Number 10 – clearly just wanting to walk the street to the Commons. 'The trouble with this job', Blair told me later, 'is that everything is a conspiracy against you leading a normal life. And that is why I spend a lot of my time going out and meeting people, away from the cameras and the press. And I find that every time you manage really to talk to people in a school or a hospital – you learn so much'.

I asked how different the job of Prime Minister was from what he had expected. Blair replied: 'The thing that has come home to me most clearly is the need not to be knocked off course by events and to pay not very much attention to the media barrage on a day to day basis. Because the moment you lose that focus of the big picture, then I think you have got a problem.'

Having had the chance to watch the Prime Minster close up and talk to him over a period of months inside Number 10, I reached some conclusions about what makes Tony tick. From the moment he and his team stepped into Downing Street, the over-riding aim has been to become the first Labour government ever to win a full second term with a good majority. But winning is not an end in itself for Blair; he genuinely wants to make his mark as a reforming Prime Minister. One of the famous leaked memos from his private pollster Philip Gould was entitled: 'Getting the Right Place in History – and Not the Wrong One'.

There was a certain irony here because I discovered that the Prime Minister's own knowledge of our political history is distinctly patchy. We filmed him talking to Sir Edward Heath at a party to celebrate the latter's half-century as an MP. 'When were you Chief Whip', asked Blair, 'was it in the fifties?' 'Yes', replied Sir Edward. 'What, not during Suez?' asked Blair. 'Yes, I handled the whole thing', replied the former Prime Minister to his successor's evident surprise.

Tony Blair is the first British Prime Minister to have been born in the second half of the twentieth century and was only three at the time of Suez. Yet it still seemed a remarkable gap in his knowledge – the more so since he likes to read political biography and history.

But he was very clear what he and his government needed to do to secure a positive place in history. 'If this government fails, it will be because we have been insufficiently radical in reform', Blair told me. 'And the next term – if we are lucky enough to win a next term – if the British people grant us that chance – there has got to be a big process of radical reform that we introduce. I've no doubt about that at all. Because I think the real essence of modern government is the speed at which things change and therefore the constant need to revitalise and modernise and keep up to date. And I think modern government is all about having a strong sense of values, but a completely open mind about how you deliver them.

'I have found that people can always give you a thousand reasons why something shouldn't be changed, and they find it hard to give you one reason why it should. And in the end you, as Prime Minister, have to be the person who drives that process of radical change through. And that can be very, very difficult indeed.'

Chapter 27

IMAGE AND REALITY
IN EUROPE

Timothy Garton Ash

Y ES, THERE HAS been a 'Blair effect' in Europe since May 1997. But
it has only been half what Tony Blair hoped for. And that half has
itself been only half due to the man and his government. But then,
he may be less than half way through his time in power.

Simplifying greatly, I see two major successes and two equally important
failures. The first success is that many continental Europeans are now convinced that Britain is a modern Western economy and state, with policies
worthy of study and sometimes even of emulation. We may forget how
novel this is. The best example is the joint paper signed by Blair and the
German Chancellor Gerhard Schroeder, outlining common approaches to a
modern, social democratic 'Third Way' or *Neue Mitte*. Woolly stuff, some
of it, to be sure. But ten or twenty years ago it was barely conceivable that
a German Chancellor would sign such a joint paper with a British Prime
Minister on fundamental questions of domestic economic and social policy.

Twenty years ago, Britain was still regarded in Germany as the sick man
of Europe. The talk was all of the 'British disease' and the 'German model'.
Ten years ago there was some grudging acknowledgement of the economic
recovery in the Thatcher years, but the Christian Democrat Helmut Kohl
would even have missed his supper (a notoriously terrible sacrifice for that
Gargantua) rather than sign such a document with Margaret Thatcher.
Now it is not just Schroeder but leading conservative German business-
people who study and admire British solutions in some areas, from
privatisation and deregulation to pensions and labour-market flexibility.
What is true of Germany is true also in other parts of Europe.

But is this really a Blair effect? After all, most of the hard, neoliberal
changes were made under Thatcher and Major. (One reason Schroeder cannot
be a Blair, is that Kohl was no Thatcher. So Schroeder has to be his own
Thatcher.) In this regard it is more realistic to talk of a Thatcher-Blair effect.

Indeed, one should probably add to that a Reagan-Clinton effect. For what has really happened here is that approaches developed in the world of Anglo-American capitalism have been partially and often reluctantly adopted in – or adapted to – that of Rhine-Alpine capitalism (to use Michel Albert's terms).

Yet even if one takes the jaundiced view that Blairism is simply 'Thatcherism with a human face', the human face matters. (As, indeed, the original 'socialism with a human face' of Alexander Dubcek was a whole lot different from the 'socialism' whose structures it inherited.) Without the Blair government's new emphasis on social justice and social inclusion, and its ready acceptance of a social dimension to the European project, the neoliberal economics would have been much less acceptable in Rhine-Alpine social-market Europe. And without Blair's initial charisma, personal charm offensive and active search for European partners, there could have been nothing like a Schroeder-Blair paper.

This brings us to the second success. Though you would never gather this from the British press, both the real policy agenda and the internal politics of the European Union are more comfortable for Britain in 2001 than they were five years ago – let alone ten years ago, at the time of Maastricht and in the heyday of Jacques Delors. The great exception to this statement is, of course, the eurozone, and the increasingly important coordination of economic policy by the (now, with Greece) Euro-12 committee of states belonging to the Economic and Monetary Union (EMU). But if you put that large and obviously important son-of-Maastricht to one side and ask what are the current policy priorities of the EU, you get a list with which Britain can be quite happy.

The Commission – still the great bogeyman of the British Eurosceptic press – spends much of its time pushing through a rather British agenda of economic liberalisation. The Nice summit made it clear that the biggest game for the next decade is enlargement, an undertaking with which Britain is now more comfortable than most of its current EU partners. Since the project of a European rapid reaction force originates in an Anglo-French initiative – and Britain has, for once, been 'present at the creation' – it is less at odds with Nato and our special transatlantic ties than it would have been if – like almost everything else in the history of Europe – it had initially been created without us.

As with the policies, so with the inter-state politics. Most of the British press still writes as if 'the European story' were Britain vs. the Rest. The Nice summit showed once again that this is not so. Unlike in the late Thatcher years, there is no racing certainty that the blocking minority will include Britain – and often be a blocking minority of one. As at Nice, different states are isolated on different issues.

Once again, only half the credit for this can reasonably be given to Blair and his government. There any many deeper causes at work. The post-Cold War fading of federalist enthusiasm all over Europe, after the high tide of the Delors years. The relative weakness of the Commission under Romano

Prodi. The weakening of the Franco-German axis, and united Germany's quiet, pragmatic pursuit of its own national interests. The very logic of enlargement, and the growing concerns of smaller states. But the Blair government's European policy has certainly contributed, by shaping the EU agenda (for example, in the Lisbon declaration on the knowledge economy for Europe), by building political alliances (notably with Aznar's Spain) and by taking joint initiatives, such as that with France on security and defence policy. To this extent, one can talk of a positive Blair effect.

These successes are qualified, however, by two failures, closely linked to each other. First, despite everything that I have said above, and despite several bold and imaginative European speeches by the Prime Minister, Foreign Secretary and other ministers, most continental Europeans are still not convinced that Britain is fully committed to what they think of (in their many different ways) as the European project. So long as that is the case, any ideas that the Blair government might have about assuming 'leadership' in Europe will remain illusory.

Second, and feeding the first, most Britons are not convinced that Britain should be fully committed to what they (often wrongly) construe to be the European project. Asked in the October 2000 Eurobarometer opinion poll the standard question as to whether membership of the EU is a good thing for this country, only 25 per cent of British respondents said yes. Only 22 per cent expressed support for the single European currency.

The 'Blair effect' in Europe is already much longer-lived and deeper than the brief honeymoon that was the 'Major effect'. But whether it is reinforced or subverted in his likely second term will depend on whether he can reverse these two failures. That in turn will depend, twist it how you will, on the readiness to pose what we still laughably call the $64,000 question – the EMU-question. At the end of Blair's first term, as at its beginning, the symbol, touchstone and litmus-test of Britain's European commitment remains its attitude to that single currency.

This is in many ways rather unfair. As I have indicated, the real European agenda is now only in part about working through the implications of monetary union. Monetary union was the central EU project of the 1990s, not of this decade. There are vast new tracts of European policy – enlargement, security, immigration, crime – where Britain has played a constructive part under Blair, without belonging to EMU, and can in fact do even more, whether or not it joins EMU.

British officials say, with obvious frustration, that this is 'the reality', as opposed to a distorted image in both the British and the continental media. But the truth is that, in European as in British politics, image and reality are just not separable in this way. For continental European opinion, as for British opinion, EMU-membership is the great symbolic test of Britain's European commitment. A government which has itself done much to blur the frontier between image and reality should not be surprised to find that in matters European the two can no longer be told apart.

Chapter 28

'NEW LABOUR' IN HISTORICAL PERSPECTIVE

Kenneth O. Morgan

HISTORIANS OF MODERN Britain dislike the cult of the new. Continuity rather than novelty seems to be the norm. 'New' is a word more commonly applied to American politics – Woodrow Wilson's New Freedom in 1913, Franklin D. Roosevelt's New Deal in 1933, John F. Kennedy's New Frontier in 1961. In Britain, the adjective 'New' has much less currency. But it has become commonplace since Tony Blair's first party conference speech as Labour's leader in October 1994. That repeatedly spoke of New Labour and New Britain. The word 'new' appeared thirty-seven times in that speech, and 107 times in the draft election manifesto. 'New Labour' was the ever-present watchword in the 1997 general election. When Tony Blair then took over the presidency of the European Union, he briefly proclaimed a New Europe as well, or alternatively (in another favoured usage) a People's Europe. Only after the departure of Peter Mandelson in January 2001 did 'New Labour' lose its sheen.

For cautious historians, it is not easy to spell out dogmatically what was new about New Labour policy. But in three quite different respects, the Labour Party today may fairly said to be different from anything that has existed before. First there is the matter of *leadership*. Tony Blair is manifestly the most dominant premier that Labour has ever had. Traditionally, the party has been suspicious of strong leadership. It has seen itself as a democratic body, a people's coalition in which power emerged from the grass roots, as enshrined in the 1918 party constitution. Keir Hardie, the first leader of the party in 1906–8, set the tone when he complained that leading it was a 'trial and a burden'. Until 1922, the designation of the party's head was 'chairman', not leader.

The one undeniably powerful Labour leader in its earlier years, Ramsay MacDonald (1922–31) was the exception that proved the rule. His conduct in August 1931 in resigning as Labour Prime Minister only to re-emerge as premier of a 'National government', was thought to be an act of treachery by an overmighty leader who betrayed his party in favour of the 'aristocratic embrace' (literally so in the case of Lady Londonderry). Labour leaders thereafter preferred a collective style; down to Neil Kinnock in the 1980s, they all vowed that they would never be 'another Ramsay MacDonald'. Attlee's uncharismatic but mostly effective style was utterly removed from a *führerprinzip*. Wilson did indeed project himself through the media, initially with much success. But he was a uniquely sensitive party leader. He was always hedged about with powerful colleagues such as Brown and Callaghan, and personally anxious to counter-balance rival factions of left or right, and neutralising Roy Jenkins or other possible challengers for the crown. Callaghan, as the last supposed Old Labour Prime Minister, was notable for a deliberately collective style of Cabinet government. In 1979, as always in the past, Labour offered the electors a team. Callaghan being located alongside Healey and Foot, as Attlee had been partnered with Bevin, Morrison and Cripps thirty years earlier.

No previous leader has ever come close to the degree of central personalised power exercised by Tony Blair today. Except on rare issues, he dominates his party, while the reform of conference and the National Executive means that they can no longer threaten the parliamentary leadership as in the past. For the first time in history (after all, even the revered Keir Hardie faced conference opposition over women's suffrage back in 1907), there is no left-wing threat to the leader. Parliament, with its enormous Labour majority in the Commons, is a passive forum; by contrast the Attlee government, with an almost equally large majority, had to give way to rebels on some occasions, notably over the length of national service in 1947 when the revolt was spearheaded by the normally centrist Jim Callaghan. Blair himself seldom turns up at Westminster. He also dominates his government. Only Gordon Brown is an alternative power broker of major stature, perhaps more so since the second departure of Peter Mandelson. New Labour's Cabinet tends to be almost a token assembly meeting once a week (one early Cabinet lasted only half an hour). The Cabinet committee system (despite a myriad of bodies run via the Lord Chancellor, Lord Irvine) is subordinate to the informal meetings of key ministers. The Lords might be a nuisance over Section 28 and foxhunting, but all the governments' many bills in the autumn of 2000 went through.

Blair himself has taken over a popular, or perhaps populist, style of leadership, through skilful image-making which emphasises his youth, energy, classlessness, and honesty. Spinmeisters like his press secretary, Alastair Campbell, emphasise the leader's detachment from Old Labour practices and class alignments. He is our first post-modern Prime Minister. Colin Crouch in a recent Fabian Society pamphlet (Fabian Ideas 598) offers the term 'post-democratic'. Tony Blair's media-sensitive, adroit response to the death of Diana, christened 'the People's Princess', underlined the change. Blair operates as a highly presidential Prime Minister, with a more secure base than the wartime premierships of Lloyd George and Churchill. The government is largely identified with him. When political difficulties occur, such as with its links with businessmen like the Grand Prix magnate Bernie Ecclestone, or £2 million donations from Lords Hamlyn and Sainsbury, it is the Prime Minister who appears on television to assure the electors (via David Frost) that he is still the same 'pretty straight kind of guy'. Of course, not even Blair is omnipotent. Abroad, on relations with Europe and over the Euro, at home on relations with the Liberal Democrats and the possible adoption of PR in future elections, the leader has to tread warily. An over-personalised leadership could yet present serious dangers: Harold Wilson's style of self-projection, Gannex raincoat and all, turned sour in due course, not least when the owner of Gannex went to gaol. Blair suddenly looked vulnerable in the summer and autumn of 2000 when he became the distinctly personal target of such varied adversaries as the jam-makers of the Women's Institute, road hauliers, Welsh farmers and railway travellers everywhere. But in general his leadership style has been astonishingly successful, more so than any Prime Minister in our history. Labour, which in 1983 gave us the longest suicide note in history, now offers us the longest honeymoon.

A second point concerns machinery. New Labour's commitment to the instrumentation of *technology* is genuinely new, indeed for any political party in our history. Traditionally, Labour has been suspicious of high-tech innovation: it has contrasted the honest strengths of its own grass-roots support with the Tories' use of money and image-making on the style of Saatchi and Saatchi. Its classic operators, Henderson, Morrison, Callaghan, cherished the patient house-to-house canvassing, the licking of envelopes on a wet evening, the drab committee rooms, the peeling walls, the stale tea. In 1979 Callaghan fought a low-key campaign which sought to contrast the premier's decency and folksiness with the strident dogmatism of Mrs Thatcher. Labour did move on under Neil Kinnock, for instance in remarkably successful projection of the leader on television, on *Chariots of Fire* lines. But under Tony Blair the embrace of high-tech has reached a quite new dimension. Peter Mandelson and Alastair Campbell have employed methods of technical management hitherto unknown. Politics flow not from policy-making committees as in the 1950s, but selected focus groups, the private polling of opinion, and interaction with journalists in the media. The 1997 general election was the most sophisticated ever, with such novelties as the Rapid Rebuttal Unit copied from the Clinton campaigns in the United States, and its pervasive spin-doctoring. Labour is now far ahead of the Tories in its use of information technology, part of its vision of its future is running a permanent election campaign. No longer is it, in Harold Wilson's words in the late 1950s, 'a penny farthing in the jet age'. It uses electronics to keep ministers and members 'on message'. Dissidence is firmly put down. Labour's fabled, often unfraternal, inner party democracy, which saw endless punch-ups and rebellions and which gave the party a unique reputation for being divided, seems a thing of the past.

Third, Labour's *social composition* is utterly changed. It is overwhelmingly a middle-class party. Indeed, Gordon Brown is eager to call Labour 'the party of business'. Its links with wealthy individuals from global corporate business, suggest that it now embraces the post-industrial ethic of Social Democratic politicians across the world from Marseilles to Melbourne. Keir Hardie called his creation in 1900 'the Labour Alliance', a partnership of a minority of socialists and the working-class masses in the trade unions. An early totem figure was Arthur Henderson, a giant in the TUC, long-term party secretary and ultimately Foreign Secretary, who invented the famous phrase: 'This great movement of ours'. Labour sprang from the maelstrom of industrial conflict. Its defining moments were Taff Vale, Tonypandy, Black Friday, the General Strike, the Jarrow March (the last still emotive enough in November 2000 to help out-manoeuvre the road hauliers' lobby). Even after 1945, the Labour Party still had authentic working-class figures in high office – Ernest Bevin of the Transport Workers as Foreign Secretary, Herbert Morrison, ex-miners like Nye Bevan, Jack Lawson and Jim Griffiths. An early measure in 1946 was the repeal of the Conservatives' 1927 Trade Disputes Act, moved by Ernest Bevin himself. Under Wilson and Callaghan in the 1970s, the unions stayed very close to the government in the Social Contract between party and TUC negotiated by Wilson and Jack Jones – an alliance that was to go horribly wrong in the 'winter of discontent' in 1979. Callaghan himself had been the general secretary of a white-collar union in his youth. The election of Neil Kinnock, son of a Welsh steelworker, as leader in 1983 owed much to the king-making of union bosses such as Clive Jenkins of ASTMS.

Today trade union membership has almost halved from thirteen million in 1979 to around seven million. The union reforms of the Thatcher years are wholly accepted by the Blair government. Despite the acceptance of the EU Social Chapter and the idea of a minimum wage, Labour seems quite as close to business and press magnates as to its natural supporters. The unions are marginalised by replacing the block vote with 'one man, one vote' at party conference, and the other reforms of the party's internal structure. Union leaders were invisible in the 1997 election. Only 13 per cent of the 419 Labour MPs are of working-class background: the 101 women MPs elected were almost wholly middle-class. Gender seemed to be replacing class as Labour's defining principle. There is still some correlation between class and politics: the most traditional working-class areas in Scotland, Yorkshire or South Wales swung to Labour in 1992 and even 1987, but the dissolution of the old industrial base and its replacement by a mainly service economy, has transformed the social structure even since 1979. Leadership and Cabinet, anxious to appeal to middle-class middle England, even to rural areas for all the outcries of the Countryside Alliance, represent a different kind of party from any version of Labour in the past. Tony Blair seems to have reinvented the Labour Party as Margaret Thatcher reinvented the Tories.

Beyond these structural matters, the policies of New Labour are dealt with elsewhere in this book. They are harder to classify. Tony Blair prefers to speak of broad 'values' with some emphasis on Christian metaphysics. There has been general talk of New Labour's pursuing Will Hutton's 'stakeholder society' or Anthony Giddens's 'Third Way', both of them shrouded in more than a little uncertainty. But clearly the claim that the whole of Labour's history prior to 1994 can be lumped together as homogeneous 'Old Labour' needs revision.

Labour has been in a state of change and renewal since it was founded in 1900. It adopted the flexible name of Labour, rather than Socialist Party to promote in a broad sense the interests of working people. Despite the contrary historical arguments deployed in Edmund Dell's fascinating book *A Strange Eventful History* (2000), Labour was always very loose in ideology. The socialist pledge in Clause Four in 1918 was symbolic and never taken literally. It was a compass, not a commitment. Since then there have been at least three 'new' shifts in Labour's history. There was first the economic programme of the 1930s when socialism was redefined to mean 'planning'. For the first time, Labour acquired a modern economic policy involving quasi-Keynesian techniques to promote growth and full employment. The thirties planners, Evan Durbin, Hugh Gaitskell, and especially Douglas Jay in *The Socialist Case* (1937) were light-years away from the ethical imperatives of Keir Hardie, who had had no interest in economics at all. Second, there was the revisionism of the 1950s, a shift away from the agenda of the Attlee years and the legacy from the 'people's war' of 1939. Instead of a programme of nationalisation, physical controls, universalism and rationing in the name of 'fair shares', the revisionists promoted the social agenda of greater equality. Anthony Crosland's *The Future of Socialism* (1956), with its belief that managed capitalism had solved the problems of growth, is of course the key text here.

Third, in 1963 Harold Wilson attempted to bypass the 'theology' of arguments over Clause Four or nuclear weapons by arguing instead that socialism was about science. He appealed to the ideal of modernisation, of the 'white heat' of a new industrial revolution created by white-coated workers. He emphasised supply-side skills such as new training and better education, and investment in computerised technology. It got Labour back into government in 1964 before disillusion with the Wilson government's planning machinery led to a decline in the party's fortunes.

Even the Wilson-Callaghan period of 1974–79 anticipated some key themes of New Labour today. They signified the first major reaction against Keynesian economics: Healey's cash limits, Callaghan's declaring that Britain could not spend its way out of recession, anticipated Gordon Brown's policy today. Second, it was Callaghan's Ruskin speech of October

1976 which first made 'Education, Education, Education' a supreme priority. Third, he tried to emphasise that Labour was truly the party of law and order; a former spokesman for the Police Federation, he rebutted the apparent anti-police attitudes of constituency militants. Fourth, Labour set itself up then as the party of the family. Barbara Castle pioneered child allowances, paid directly to mothers; Labour upheld the concept of the 'family budget', with tax and benefits brought together. Fifth, these governments, even if half-heartedly, were the first to promote Welsh and Scottish devolution; they never left the political agenda thereafter. Sixth, Wilson and Callaghan, both somewhat Eurosceptic by instinct, confirmed Britain's European role by orchestrating the successful referendum to confirm UK membership in 1975. Callaghan even appeared sympathetic to the idea of a single currency three years later.

In these respects, then, New Labour may be reclaiming policies, or perhaps policy positions, from its own past. Much of its social and economic policy, meanwhile, shows continuity with the neo-liberalism, privatisation and deregulation of the Thatcher regime. Its policies on law and order, its attitude towards civil liberties, have rivalled Michael Howard's tough policy. But there is the one great novelty. In the area of constitutional change, New Labour has been as radical as it has been cautious elsewhere – a Scottish Parliament with tax-raising powers, a Welsh Assembly, a Northern Ireland Assembly, an elected Mayor for London, the purge of the hereditary peers, the incorporation of European law, a Freedom of Information Act (admittedly limited). Perhaps in time might come electoral reform to establish some version of PR, even the supersession of our bicameral system in favour of a more full-blown federalism. All this has reversed that centralisation of government which marked British history since 1688, if not since 1066, in favour of greater pluralism, public accountability and the diffusion of power.

The priority given to constitutional change by the Blair government is indeed dramatic. It may be doubted whether the party has fully come to terms with the implications. *Dirigisme* and devolution have clashed, as in Millbank's unsuccessful interventions in the electoral process in both Wales and London has illustrated. The Scottish Parliament has posed a challenge by its distinctive policies on university tuition fees, teachers' pay and the cost of nursing care for the elderly, all contrasting with policies south of the border. It is true that Labour favoured forms of devolution in its early years, and contrasted its populism with the bureaucratic Prussian centralism of the German SPD. Keir Hardie and Ramsay MacDonald endorsed Scottish and Welsh home rule, along with Irish. Hardie sought to unite 'the Red Dragon with the Red Flag' – *Y Ddraig Goch a'r Faner Goch*. Meanwhile the Fabians and the ILP both championed 'municipal socialism'. But since 1918, Labour has been relentlessly unionist and centralist. Democratic socialism meant uniform social standards throughout Britain, and planning from the centre. To coin a phrase, the gentleman from

Whitehall (probably public school- and Oxbridge-trained) always knew best. So when Tony Blair has promoted constitutional reform, just as when he refers to an inclusive progressive Rainbow Coalition and included Keynes, Beveridge and Lloyd George amongst his heroes, he is pursuing lines unthinkable for previous Labour leaders from Clem Attlee to John Smith. In this key area, he has been the greatest revolutionary of them all.

Too much novelty, perhaps, can be claimed for New Labour's policies. Political parties have histories and living roots, they cannot disavow their past. Labour will always have its origins in the cultural weft and warp of modern Britain. Maybe there is really nothing new under the sun. And yet these constitutional reforms do imply a basic reformulation of the idea of the United Kingdom, and later perhaps of our relationship to Europe as well. The American historian (and my old mentor) Richard Hofstadter once called Teddy Roosevelt 'the Conservative as Progressive'. A future Hofstadter may see Tony Blair as 'the centrist as revolutionary' – not a candle in the wind, but the cybernetic premier, prophet of populism in our time.

Conclusion

THE NET BLAIR EFFECT

A FOUNDATION GOVERNMENT

Anthony Seldon

THE BLAIR GOVERNMENT of 1997–2001 was a surprisingly restrained government. Its caution was a puzzle for several reasons. The leadership had presided over a transformation of the Labour Party, and by 1996 and 1997 those same leaders were offering 'radically' to transform government and indeed, Britain, as it entered the new millennium. A new dawn appeared assured by the huge parliamentary majority for Labour on 1 May 1997 of 179, by the impression of a united Labour Party (even if divisions remained below the surface), quiescent unions, a friendly media, three years of solid work preparing for power, a very good economic inheritance, a prospectus that reached out to all sections of the country, and a weak and divided Conservative opposition. No Labour government in history had come to power with so many initial advantages, not even the Attlee government in 1945, the one Labour administration that Blair's Number 10 looks at with admiration, in contrast to the Wilson and Callaghan governments in the 1960s and 1970s which it regards as having squandered opportunities for modernising the economy and the Labour Party.

Where did this government make the most impact?

The greatest change from preceding governments came in the swathe of constitutional reforms, notably devolution, the Human Rights Act, proportional representation for all elections other than those to Westminster and local authorities outside Northern Ireland, and House of Lords reform. Number 10 were surprised and relieved by how well the reforms went through, and, in general, by how well they turned out in practice. Critics attacked the lack of coherence in the reforms, as well as their caution (leaving the House of Lords half reformed, the 'West Lothian question' unresolved, Westminster electoral reform and English regional assemblies ignored). Critics also pointed out that the reforms owed more to Liberal than Labour Party traditions. The biggest change with the policy of previous Labour governments came in economic policy. No Labour government had before established such a reputation for economic competence. The change was heralded by the announcement in the first week of the government's life of the Bank of England's independence, followed by the establishment of new fiscal and monetary frameworks. Other important, if not agenda-setting changes, came in education, especially at primary level, with the literacy and the numeracy strategies, and in a variety of other social policy changes, including welfare to work, the end to fund-holding, the reforms of widows' and incapacity benefits, as well as the integration of the tax and benefit system.

Major changes also came in the *style* of government. Cabinet was downplayed in importance, and control from Downing Street was enhanced. Number 10 grew in size from 130 staff in April 1997 to 200 in April 2001. Media management under Alastair Campbell reached unprecedented levels, with the Strategic Communications Unit being set up in Number 10, along with the Research and Information Unit and an expanded Policy Unit. The Cabinet Office adopted a new role in innovation and implementation, and the Performance and Innovation Unit and the Social Exclusion Unit were established within it. If 'joined-up government' did not live up to all expectations, it did work as a device for helping Number 10 obtain its way and helped departments work together on cross-cutting issues. Government, after five years of almost perpetual crisis from 1992–97, became more steady and assured, helped by the continuity of senior ministers – Blair, Brown, Straw, Cook, Blunkett, Prescott, Irvine, Short – which allowed it to weather the transport and flooding squalls of mid/late 2000 with a degree of equanimity. The modernised Labour Party was entrenched after 1997, with a downgrading of the power of the party conference, activists and militants in trade unions and local government, while the party became more national and classless and less of a sectional and class-based party, and it reached out as never before to embrace the establishment, including the City, business, the professions, the media and the Church of England, and even independent schools. The House of Commons was not Blair's natural *metier*, but he strove to take it seriously, as Number 10 ceaselessly observed.

Table 1 divides up the government's work into areas that saw major change, some change, and areas which saw broad continuity with the work of the preceding Thatcher and Major governments.

In sum, the Blair government of 1997–2001 was a moderately reforming government: the surprise was merely that, given its immense initial advantages, and its initial rhetoric, even more was not attempted. Its area of most striking policy change, the constitution, was not a traditional Labour theme, nor was it one calculated to advance its over-arching agenda of enhancing social justice and inclusiveness within a competitive international economic environment – the much-vaunted but ultimately abstract

Table I The net Blair effect

Major change	Some change	Continuity
Constitutional reform	Economic management	Public expenditure (until 1999/2000)
Labour Party	Secondary education (except performance-related pay)	
Public expenditure (from 1999–2000)		
Capacity of Number 10	The Arts	Public-private partnership
Steadiness of government	Europe – new agendas on defence and crime	Search for peace in Northern Ireland
Devolution – with Assemblies in Scotland, Wales and Northern Ireland	Civil service – some shift to 'joined-up' government and wider recruitment	Flexible labour market
Media management (unprecedented degree of central control)	Local government – with beginning of elected mayors	Single currency ('prepare and decide' replaces 'wait and see')
Primary education (literacy and numeracy strategies)	Defence/foreign/aid policy – higher priority to ethical rhetoric	Acceptance of much of Thatcher legacy
Monetary policy (independent Bank of England)	Criminal policy (especially in December 2000 Queen's speech)	
Selective universality in welfare	Family policy	
	Higher education (e.g. tuition fees)	
Employment (national minimum wage/union recognition)	Health (end fund-holding, new structures with primary-care groups)	

'Third Way'. Indeed, some of the constitutional reforms, by giving more potential authority to Scotland and Wales, and to local mayors, could be seen as cutting across central government's ability to establish national standards and policies. Britain did not join the Euro which might be seen with hindsight as a serious missed opportunity.

Number 10's own explanation for the caution of 1997–2001 is that this first Blair government was laying the foundations for the future. Maybe. To some extent it is a plea from hindsight, and contrasts with the confident claims of 1996–98. Only one of the preceding eight Labour governments, the first Attlee government (1945–50) could be called a success. No Labour leader in history has been re-elected after a full term with a working majority. Prime Ministers ruminate deeply on history, with daily reminders coming from the portraits of past premiers on the main staircase at Number 10. One can understand the caution. I will return to this question later.

A second theme of the book was to examine the effectiveness and quality of the government's work. Here the record is more positive. The government, as we have seen, gave an aura of competence and steadiness. External events, principally in mid/late 2000, and in early 2001 caused some wobbles. The impression of calm was also challenged by a series of leaks, many stemming from the Chancellor and those around him. Most damage was caused by Andrew Rawnsley's *Servants of the People*, published in September 2000, which revealed a certain naiveté on the part of those (many) in Downing Street who spoke to the author. Less noticed was Rawnsley's own naiveté. Had he known more history, he would have realised high-tension relations are the norm in Downing Street, and between senior Cabinet ministers: there was nothing unusual in this about the Blair premiership. Rawnsley's book also damaged trust between Downing Street and those who seek to write about it. Other, often poor, books, notably Geoffrey Robinson's *The Unconventional Minister* (November 2000), also caused ruffles, but did not unsettle the broad picture of competence at Number 10.

Any table of good governing and administration is bound to be more subjective than an assessment of those areas where a Blair effect was felt on policy. Nevertheless, Table 2 assesses those areas where Britain was better off in 2001 than in 1997.

Table 2 The quality of the government's work

Positive policy	Indifferent/Poor policy
Constitutional reform – though it might have gone further	Exaggerated promises (e.g. 1999 to be the 'year of delivery')
Economic growth and stability, and the rise in employment (e.g. through the 'New Deal')	Two year spending freeze produced lack of funding for public services (e.g. shortages of teachers, nurses, police)
Some redistribution of income and reduction of poverty (via the minimum wage, family tax credit reforms, etc)	Indecision on Euro allowed the pound to be pushed too high which damaged exports
Northern Ireland (with the 1998 Good Friday Agreement, and the Assembly established)	Lack of strategic clarity in some areas (e.g. transport and role intended for local government)
Industrial policy (though damage caused by the high pound)	Loss of opportunity radically to restructure the second chamber and introduce P.R.
Modernisation of the Labour Party (though sceptical and critical forces remain)	Failure to comprehend the limits of government action e.g. the Dome
Continuation by a Labour government of the enterprise culture without losing social/communal values	Obsession with meeting 'targets' (e.g. cutting NHS waiting lists, excessive paperwork for teachers)

The net record is positive. Some areas not listed above, such as crime, pensions and social security, saw considerable activity but positive progress was hampered by factors largely beyond the government's control. The government outshines in achievement over that of all other Labour administrations, except 1945–50. It can be most exactly compared with 1966–70, which also benefited from a landslide majority, and which produced some important liberal and educational reforms (especially the Open University), but became mired in unseemly political squabbling, trade union disagreements and economic difficulties. Critics from both left and right may attack the limited scale of change during 1997–2001: Labour from 1966–70 achieved much less, even acknowledging that the economy was much less favourable for earlier Labour governments.

The book then assesses the personal influence of the Prime Minister himself. His historical impact has been most felt in the establishment of Labour as a credible and sustainable governing force. He decided before coming to Number 10 to concentrate on education and welfare reform, to rebuild a better relationship with the EU than the Tories had achieved, a better relationship with industry and the City than any previous Labour administration had enjoyed, and that he would try to resolve the Northern Ireland dispute (little noticed was that these were broadly also John Major's priorities). Foreign affairs, notably Kosovo, periodically took much of his time, as did transport in 2000, despite him having little sustained interest in the subject, nor indeed in other broad swathes of policy, including the environment, agriculture, defence and the arts. Nothing unusual or bad in that: Prime Ministers need to focus on a few areas if they are not to squander their resources. The House of Commons, the civil service and local government also held no great interest for him. Economic policy he left largely to Gordon Brown, partly due to his own comparative ignorance of economics, partly due to the exceptional forcefulness and ambition of his Chancellor. Brown's and the Treasury's influence was keenly felt in other domestic policy areas too, notably in welfare to work and in pensions.

Every premier is the victim of circumstance. On balance, Blair enjoyed good luck. He was fortunate on the economy, on the ineptitude of the opposition, that he could contain differences and indecision on Europe, and that the Balkans did not become divisive (as did Suez in 1956), or an open-ended commitment (as Vietnam did for the Americans). He was unlucky in the death of Donald Dewar at a crucial moment: but it was less of a loss than other premiers have usually suffered (Bevin to Attlee, Macleod to Heath, Neave and Whitelaw to Thatcher and Christopher Patten to Major).

Blair was assisted greatly by an unusually harmonious (and large) Number 10 staff. The key figures – Jonathan Powell, Alastair Campbell, David Miliband, Anji Hunter – had all worked together in opposition. Also important among the newcomers was the young Treasury official, Jeremy Heywood, who in 1999 became Blair's Principal Private Secretary.

Heywood's predecessor, John Holmes, also proved invaluable to Blair, above all on Ireland and the Balkans. Prime Ministers are dependent upon the quality of their senior advisers. Not since Heath's premiership (1970–74) had Number 10 had such a close-knit and effective team. In one way Heath's Number 10, however, was more sophisticated: in Donald Maitland it had a more urbane and uncynical Press Secretary than Alastair Campbell. Blair certainly needed a rottweiler to knock the government's whole publicity apparatus into shape, and corral the bloodthirsty and coarse media hounds. Elements of the British press are appalling, and need a very proactive and brutal figure to cope with them. Campbell's rough demeanour in Number 10 was nevertheless paradoxical for a Prime Minister who sees himself as a moral and a religious man. Open questions remain whether his abrasive style could be counter-productive, and whether his forceful presence also encouraged short-termism to the detriment of strategic thinking. Campbell was a brilliant, pungent if increasingly flawed presence in Blair's Number 10.

Several reasons can be advanced for the government's comparative lack of radicalism between 1997–2001. Progress came most swiftly in those areas where most had been done to prepare for office between Blair's succession in 1994 until the general election in 1997. The planning focused on the areas of greatest political priority. What were those priorities? First, economic competence. Blair's team knew that they had to establish a new 'collective memory' of what a Labour government could achieve in office and that they had to demonstrate that they could be trusted to run the economy as well as or better than the Tories. Macroeconomic stability and getting the public finances in order, with the poor records of previous Labour governments ever-present, were *sine qua non*. Second, a new consumer focus had to be demonstrated in the delivery of public services, including in education (above all), as well as in health and law. Third, a new constitutional settlement had been advocated by progressive, centre-left forces for fifteen years and more. More recently, John Smith, Blair's predecessor as party leader, had had a deep commitment to it: action was now inescapable. Finally, after all the contortions of the Major government on European policy, it was obvious that a new relationship had to be achieved with EU partners, with a clear line not just on the Euro, but also with new agendas on defence, crime and other common issues.

Progress in office, therefore, was less conspicuous in areas where less thinking had taken place between 1994–97, which included housing, the environment, agriculture, transport, defence and foreign policy. Problems in some policy areas were underestimated, notably in health, where the full extent of the 'hollowing out' of personnel, infrastructure and funding had not been fully appreciated. Blair's core team also under-appreciated the complexity of EU politics – it described it as trying to play '15-dimensional chess' – and the immense investment of time and energy needed to achieve any movement. Complexity and intractability dogged progress in some other areas, such as crime. Again, the team had not fully appreciated the difficulties of bringing about reductions in crime, where up to half the crime in cities is drug-related, or improvements to the prison system. The decision to freeze fresh spending until 1999 hampered progress in the public services, notably police, education, health, and the rail and road systems. Progress came swifter in areas where ministers had a clear grip and a clear strategy, such as Blunkett and Straw, rather than in areas where ministerial grip was less tight or consistent for example, in health and industry.

The government's work after 1997 lacked a clear organising theme. Governments that radically change the agenda, as after 1906, 1945 and 1979, have a philosophical cohesion. The Third Way never translated into a practical programme for policy, in the way that Beveridge and Keynes informed the Attlee government's policy, and Friedman and Hayek the Thatcher governments. Claims were made such as by Blair at the 1999 annual party conference, about the 'forces of conservatism' impeding radical change. A more convincing explanation for the slow pace of change was the lack of Blair supporters in key positions, handicapped by a lack of clarity about what 'Blairism' meant in practical terms. On some issues, including having Liberal Democrats in Cabinet, a firm timetable on the Euro referendum and proportional representation for Westminster elections, he was blocked by Brown, Prescott and Straw. Fear of alienating the press, and hence the electorate, always loomed large, explaining prevarications from joining the Euro to banning fox hunting. Although too much was made by commentators of the claim that government policy was shaped by public opinion and focus groups, it was nevertheless still an unusually electorally-sensitive government. Number 10 defended itself by saying that by the late 1990s, all modern democratic governments had become avid and sophisticated opinion watchers, and they assert their use of focus groups and polling was less frequent than by most comparable governments. Blair's team, as it later realised, also allowed itself to make excessive claims, not least on its 'pledges', and to believe that its edicts would change outcomes more readily than they could. In reality, policy can be compared with an ocean-going supertanker. Achieving even a minor change of course requires considerable effort, and time.

Tony Blair himself, in 1994–97, and in office, promised much. In more reflective moments, he has said it would be a longer-term job to rebuild and modernise Britain, and is phlegmatic about how much has been achieved so far. Number 10 now believes that 1997–2001 should be seen as an introduction, a prelude, where some good things were done, but that one cannot draw up an ultimate balance sheet until one sees what happens after 2001. In the run up to the 2001 general election, they began to argue that the judgement on the first Blair government had to be on whether the legislative and non-legislative action had laid the foundations for the future.

One nevertheless has to judge governments as discrete entities, on what they have achieved between elections. The evidence of reforming governments of the last two centuries suggests that radicalism, where there has been radicalism, comes early on in a premiership or phase in office – for example, Peel (1841–46); Gladstone (1868–74); Disraeli (1874–80); Baldwin (1924–29); Attlee (1945–50); Heath (1970–74). The Liberal government after 1906 grew in confidence and radicalism, as did the Thatcher governments. Blair must hope that he can emulate their example, and that of F.D. Roosevelt's administration, which also began slowly, rather than the examples of Macmillan after 1959, Wilson after 1966 or Major after 1992, all of whom ultimately lost strategic focus. Some factors, including media support, public expectations, and party unity are unlikely to be as propitious after 2001 as they were in 1997. Nor will it be so easy to blame problems on past Tory governments.

The opportunity is certainly there for Labour to lead the country in a new direction and to establish a new consensus which other parties will be bound to follow. Everything does indeed depend upon what Labour does from 2001. The key factors are:

- **Individuals**: will there be clear leadership, or will energies be dissipated by personality conflicts, as they threatened periodically to do from 1997–2001, and as have damaged most administrations the longer they are in office? Will the leadership remain vigorous, or run out of steam? Will Brown remain containable?
- **Ideas**: will Downing Street successfully resolve the two core questions, of Britain's place in the EU (including the Euro) and its stance on public and private provision? If it can clarify its position on the latter question, while avoid being ensnared on the former, it could reshape the domestic policy agenda as radically as did the Attlee government. Will Labour continue to win the ideas battle?
- **Interests**: will old-style unionism and old Labour remain as ineffective and subdued as they were in 1997–2001? Will the press turn overwhelmingly hostile? Will business and financial interests remain as benign? Will the pro and anti EU/Euro interests remain balanced?
- **Circumstances**: will the majority be large enough to allow Downing Street rather than back-benchers to dictate policy? Will the country avoid a severe economic shock or economic downturn? Will the opposition remain as lame? Can the government avoid shocks/disasters (e.g. in public safety) for which the government will be blamed? Will the electorate become bored by Labour?

The edifice may prove more difficult to erect than the foundations have been to lay. Blair has succeeded in remodelling his party: he has yet to re-form his country. The future and the ultimate verdict of history on Blair and New Labour are wide open.

CONTRIBUTORS

Lewis Baston is a senior research fellow at Kingston University.
Vernon Bogdanor is Professor of Government at Brasenose College, Oxford.
Michael Cockerell is a political documentary maker.
Ivor Crewe is Vice-Chancellor and Professor of Government at Essex University.
Anne Deighton is a Fellow of Wolfson College, Oxford.
Sir Christopher Foster is an authority on transport issues.
Lawrence Freedman is a Professor of War Studies at King's College, London.
Tim Garton Ash is a Fellow of St Antony's College, Oxford.
Howard Glennerster is Professor of Social Policy at the London School of Economics.
Robert Hewison is a Professor in the English Department at Lancaster University and writes on the Arts for the *Sunday Times*.
Christopher Hill is Professor of International Relations at the London School of Economics.
Dennis Kavanagh is Professor of Politics at Liverpool University.
Jane Lewis is Professor of Social Policy at Oxford University.
Ian McLean is Professor of Politics at Oxford University and Official Fellow in Politics at Nuffield College.
Lord Morgan of Aberdyfi is Emeritus Professor of the University of Wales, Aberystwyth.
Terence Morris is Emeritus Professor of Criminology and Criminal Justice at the University of London.
Lord Norton of Louth is Professor of Government at Hull University.
Brendan O'Leary is Professor of Political Science at the London School of Economics.

Sir Geoffrey Owen is a senior Fellow at the London School of Economics.
Lord Plant of Highfield is Professor of European Political Thought at Southampton University.
Christopher Riddell is a cartoonist for the *Observer*.
Peter Riddell is Political Columnist and Assistant Editor at *The Times*.
Rod Rhodes is Professor of Politics at Newcastle University.
Maggie Scammell is a lecturer in Media and Communications at the London School of Economics.
Anthony Seldon is Headmaster of Brighton College.
Peter Sinclair is Professor of Economics at Birmingham University.
Alan Smithers is Professor of Education at Liverpool University.
Philip Stephens is Editor of the UK edition of the *Financial Times*.
Robert Taylor is Employment Editor of the *Financial Times*.
Tony Travers is Director, Greater London Group, London School of Economics.

CHRONOLOGY

1997

May

1   Labour wins general election with a huge 179 seat majority and over 43 per cent of the vote.

2   John Major resigns as Conservative leader.

4   The Foreign Secretary (Robin Cook) announces that the government will sign the European Social Chapter.

6   The Chancellor of the Exchequer (Gordon Brown) gives Bank of England 'independence'. The Bank's monetary policy committee becomes responsible for setting interest rates.

9   The format of Prime Minister's Question Time is changed from two fifteen-minute sessions on Tuesday and Thursday to one thirty-minute session on Wednesday.

29   The US President (Bill Clinton) meets Blair for the first time at Downing Street.

June

16   The Prime Minister meets EU counterparts for the first time at the Amsterdam Summit.

19   William Hague defeats Kenneth Clarke by 92 votes to 70.

30   Hong Kong returned to China after 156 years of British rule.

July

2   Gordon Brown's first Budget includes windfall tax on privatised utilities and £3 billion for education and health.

19   The IRA announces restoration of cease-fire broken on 9 February 1996.

22   Blair sets up a new Cabinet Committee on the constitution including Paddy Ashdown and four of his colleagues.

29   The government announces plans to create a Greater London Authority comprising a directly-elected mayor and assembly.

31   Conservative John Randall wins Uxbridge by-election with a 3,766 majority following the death of Conservative Michael Shersby.

August

2   Robin Cook announces that he is to leave his wife to live with his secretary.

31   Diana Princess of Wales dies in a car crash in Paris aged thirty-six.

September

6   Tony Blair reads a bible lesson at the funeral of Diana Princess of Wales.

11   Scotland votes in favour of Devolution in a referenda, with a turnout of 74.3 per cent.

18   Wales votes in favour of Devolution in a referenda, with only a 50 per cent turnout.

19   Southall (London) rail crash leaves seven dead and 160 injured.

30   Tony Blair's first Labour Party Conference as Prime Minister.

October

14   Keith Hellawell is appointed the UK's first 'drugs tsar'.

November

6   Labour retains seat in the Paisley South by-election after Gordon McMaster commits suicide.

10   The Labour Party promises to return a £1 million donation made by Bernie Ecclestone, President of the Formula One Association because of conflict of interest over tobacco sponsorship.

20   Liberal Democrat Mark Oaten retains his Winchester seat with a majority of 21,536 in a by-election caused by his Tory opponent's challenge to his two vote victory.

Conservative MP Jacqui Lait holds Beckenham with a reduced majority following Piers Merchant's resignation over his relationship with a Soho night club hostess.

December

1   The government sets up an independent commission under the Liberal peer Roy Jenkins to examine the first-past-the-post electoral system.

3   Government bans beef on the bone after scientific advice suggests it could transmit the BSE agent.

24   The *Mirror* newspaper 'entraps' the Home Secretary's son when a journalist reports she bought marijuana from the seventeen-year-old.

1998

January

12   Tony Blair visits Japan, where he receives an apology from Japanese Premier Ryutaro Hashimoto for Japan's treatment of British POW's during the Second World War.

14   Foods Standard Agency set up to monitor the safety of food.

29   Tony Blair announces a fresh inquiry into 'Bloody Sunday' killing of fourteen unarmed men by British paratroopers in Londonderry in 1972.

February

4   Tony Blair's first official visit to the United States as Prime Minister.

15   The media reports that the Lord Chancellor Derry Irvine spent £650,000 on refurbishing his House of Lords official residence.

17   Gordon Brown's second budget includes introduction of Working Families Tax Credit.

April

10   The UK and Irish governments and Northern Ireland political parties sign the 'Good Friday Agreement'.

June

18   Trade and Industry Secretary Margaret Beckett announces the National Minimum Wage to be set at £3.60 per hour for those over twenty-two.

20   Tony Blair announces the appointment of twenty-seven new life peers.

25   Elections take place for Northern Ireland Assembly (assembly first meets 1 July).

27   Tony Blair's first Cabinet reshuffle. Four Cabinet ministers sacked. Peter Mandelson promoted to Secretary of State, DTI. Margaret Jay becomes Leader of the House of Lords.

August

15   The Real IRA's Omagh bomb kills twenty-eight civilians and injures 120 others.

October

1   UK citizens ordered to leave Yugoslavia because of threat of NATO air strikes over conflict in Kosovo.

14   Government announces Royal Commission under Tory peer, Lord Wakeham, on the reform of the House of Lords.

17   Senator Augusto Pinochet, former Chilean dictator, arrested in London hospital following the Spanish government's extradition request.

27   Following 'a moment of madness' on Clapham Common, Secretary of State for Wales (Ron Davies) resigns. Alun Michael replaces him.

29   The Jenkins Commission publishes its report suggesting a new electoral system of 'alternative vote plus'.

November
16   Agriculture Secretary Nick Brown announces £120m aid package for farmers affected by price collapse.
23   EU agriculture ministers agree to lift ban on British beef imposed in March 1996.
25   Law Lords rule by three to two that Pinochet is not entitled to diplomatic immunity from extradition.

December
16   US and UK military forces launch Cruise missile and air attacks on targets in Iraq.
17   The Law Lords set aside their earlier decision in relation to Pinochet because of Lord Hoffman's links with Amnesty International, an interested party.
23   Peter Mandelson and the Paymaster General (Geoffrey Robinson) are forced to resign after publicity over Robinson's £373,000 home loan to Mandelson.

1999

1   The Euro becomes the national currency in eleven countries but not the UK.

February
6   Kosovo peace talks begin in Paris.
20   Secretary of State for Wales (Alun Michael) narrowly beats challenger Rhodri Morgan for leadership of Labour Party in Wales.
23   Tony Blair launches 'National Changeover Plan' which aims to prepare the UK for the changeover to the single European currency.
24   Macpherson report into black teenager Stephen Lawrence's death published which accused Metropolitan police of institutionalised racism.

March
9   Gordon Brown's third budget introduces new 10p income tax rate and promises to reduce basic rate to 22p.
16   European Commission resigns after reports of corruption and fraud.
24   Nato air strikes are launched against targets in Yugoslavia.

The Law Lords rule that Pinochet does not have immunity from extradition.

Italian politician Romano Prodi is nominated to succeed Jacques Santer as EC President.

April

13   Tony Blair tells Parliament that two thousand more British troops are to be sent to Macedonia to be deployed in Kosovo.

17   Nail bomb in Brixton injures fifty people.

24   Second nail bomb injures six people, this time in Brick Lane.

30   Third nail bomb explodes in Soho killing three and injuring seventy-three in a gay bar. (Loner David Copeland subsequently arrested and convicted of the murders.)

May

1   Amsterdam Treaty becomes law across the EU.

Over forty Kosovar civilians killed when Nato missile is mistakenly fired at bus.

3   Tony Blair visits refugee camps in Kosovo.

6   Elections held for Scottish Parliament and Welsh Assembly. In both Labour wins largest number of seats but fails to obtain overall majority.

Local elections see the Conservatives make modest recovery as Labour loses control of thirty councils.

17   John Reid becomes Secretary of State for Scotland as Donald Dewar becomes First Minister of Scotland.

20   Controversial proposals on welfare reform pushed through the Commons with a majority of 40 votes despite the opposition of 65 Labour backbenchers.

June

10   Yugoslav generals sign peace deal with Nato bringing an end to the Kosovo conflict.

European parliamentary elections held – Conservatives gain most seats but with a turn out of only 24 per cent.

Hilary Benn, son of Tony Benn MP, wins by election in Leeds Central.

July

12   Emergency legislation to establish a Northern Ireland Assembly. The Ulster Unionists boycott first session because of IRA approach to decommissioning.

22   Conservative Stephen O'Brien wins Eddisbury by-election.

28   Paul Murphy becomes Secretary of State for Wales replacing Alun Michael who becomes First Secretary in Wales.

31   Tony Blair again visits Kosovo.

August
1   EU lifts export ban on UK beef.

September
9   Chairman of Independent Commission on policing in Northern Ireland, Chris Patten, publishes his report.
27   Ban on gay men and women in the forces is lifted following European court ruling.
28   Labour Party conference at Bournemouth. Tony Blair promises to free UK of 'all forms of conservatism'.

October
5   Thirty people die in Paddington rail crash.
11   Cabinet reshuffle brings Mandelson back as Northern Ireland Secretary while Frank Dobson steps down to contest the London mayoralty.
19   Chinese President Jiang Zemin visits Britain and is greeted by public protests about Chinese human rights record in Tibet.
26   A deal between the government and opposition peers ends the right of hereditary peers to sit in the Lords although ninety-one will remain in the transitional house.

November
18   Cherie Blair announces she is expecting fourth child.
27   Labour MPs vote against government on Air Traffic Control Sell-off Bill.

December
10   UK blocks plans by EU to introduce European-wide tax on savings.
21   Scottish Parliament announces it will abolish tuition fees for students.

2000

January
1   Millennium Dome opening fiasco with many invited guests in lengthy queues to enter.
20   Lord Wakeham's Royal Commission on reform of the House of Lords reports suggesting a partially elected second chamber of 550 members.
30   Defence minister Kifoyle resigns to campaign on back benches.

February
8   Parliament legislates to suspend Northern Ireland Assembly.
9   First Secretary of Welsh Assembly (Alun Michael) resigns and is later replaced by Rhodri Morgan.

15 Government raises minimum wage from £3.60 to £3.70 for those over twenty-two.

20 Frank Dobson selected by college system to be Labour candidate for London mayor.

March

2 Pinochet found unfit to stand trial and finally leaves the UK for Chile.

6 Ken Livingstone is expelled from Labour Party for standing against the official Labour candidate.

11 Tony Blair visits Russia and is first EC leader to meet Acting President Vladimir Putin exciting some controversy because of Russia's actions in Chechnya.

21 Brown's fourth budget providing significant extra funding for the NHS – £2 billion extra for each of next four years.

25 Ulster Unionist leader David Trimble wins leadership contest beating his challenger Rev. Martin Smith.

31 Government announces thirty-three new 'working peers'.

May

4 Ken Livingstone wins London mayoral election running as independent.

Conservatives perform well in by-elections increasing their total councillors by 593 while Labour lose 573.

8 UK troops start to evacuate British EU and Commonwealth nationals from Sierra Leone after rebel forces make series of attacks.

20 Cherie Blair gives birth to baby boy.

June

1 Reinstated Northern Ireland Assembly meets again after 3 months.

7 Tony Blair is heckled at Women's Institute national conference.

23 David Lammy wins Tottenham by-election following Bernie Grant's death.

30 Tony Blair, speaking in Germany, proposes on the spot £100 fines for drunken or antisocial behaviour.

July

6 Tony Blair's sixteen-year-old son Euan is arrested for being drunk and incapable after celebrating end of GCSE exams.

17 The *Sun* and *The Times* newspapers publish leaked memo by Tony Blair saying his government is perceived to be 'out of touch' with gut British instincts.

18 The Chancellor of the Exchequer announces in the Comprehensive Spending Review that public services will receive an extra £43 billion over the next three years.

25   Lords crush attempt to repeal Section 28, Local Government Act prohibiting promotion of homosexuality.

August
1   Critical Select Committee report on the Dome.
2   Tony Blair unveils 10 year NHS blueprint.

September
17   Polls show Labour loses lead over Tories for first time in eight years and are less trusted than Tories to manage the economy.
18   Fuel protesters set government sixty-day deadline to bring down fuel prices.
26   Tony Blair admits mistakes over pensions and the Dome at Labour Party Conference in Brighton but pledges to make amends.
27   Labour leadership defeat after conference delegates backed a motion calling for the restoration of the link between earnings and pensions.
28   Former South African President Nelson Mandela speaks to the conference.

October
11   First Minister of Scotland Donald Dewar dies. (Later replaced by Henry McLeish.)

November
17   Hatfield rail crash kills four and injures more than thirty.
23   Heavy rain and floods add to transport chaos.
8   Brown's pre-Budget report provides for major pension rise and for cut in costs of motoring.
9   Critical Dome report increases pressure on Lord Falconer to resign.
24   Labour win three by-elections in West Bromwich, Preston and Glasgow Anniesland and Scottish Parliament seat on so-called 'Super-Thursday'.
25   Deputy Prime Minister (John Prescott) fails to secure agreement at climate talks in the Hague.
29   Lords allows bill to privatise National Air Traffic control after government concedes three months delay in sell-off.
30   Government uses Parliament Act to force through the bill reducing the age of homosexual consent.

December
6   Queens speech placed crime and health at the heart of the Government's agenda for its fourth year. Important measures on housing and education were also announced.
10   Nice Treaty removing most remaining institutional obstacles to enlargement.

14   George W. Bush becomes 43rd US President-Designate.
18   Richard Branson loses National Lottery bid to Camelot.

2001

January
1   Dome closes.
2   Lord Hamlyn revealed as mystery £2m donor to Labour Party.
4   Labour announced a further $4m from two individuals; Science Minister Lord Sainsbury and former Conservative supporter Christopher Ondaatje.
15   Prime Minister launched the next steps plan on neighbourhood renewal. Public fury as 7 bodies are left in an NHS chapel as mortuary full.
17   Parliament votes for the abolition of hunting with dogs. Tony Blair misses vote through involvement in Irish peace process.
20   Bush inauguration as US president.
24   Northern Ireland Secretary Peter Mandelson resigns over intervention in a controversial Indian tycoon's bid to secure British citizenship.

February
12   The government's education green paper.

March
7   Budget Day.

BIBLIOGRAPHY

Ainley, P. 'The Crises of the Colleges' (*Education Today and Tomorrow*, Vol. 49, No. 2, Summer 1997)

Alcock, P. *Social Policy in Britain: Themes and issues* (Macmillan, 1996)

Alderman, K. & Carter, N. 'The Labour Party and the Trade Unions: Loosening the Ties' (*Parliamentary Affairs*, Vol. 47, No. 3, 1994)

Alexander, G. 'Managing the State' in Brivati, B. and Bale, T. (eds) *New Labour in Power: Precedents and Prospects* (Routledge, 1997)

Alexander, R. *Policy and practice in primary education: Local initiative, national agenda* (2nd Edition, Routledge, 1997)

Allen, M. 'British Trade Unionism's Quiet Revolution' (*Renewal* Vol. 6, No. 4, 1998)

Amnesty International *UK Foreign and Asylum Policy: Human Rights and Audit* (Amnesty International, 1998)

Anderson, P. and Mann, N. *Safety First: The Making of New Labour* (Verso, 1997)

Anderson, P. and Blackburn, R. (eds) *Towards Socialism* (Collins, 1999)

Ashdown, Paddy *The Ashdown Diaries Volume 1, 1988–1997* (Allen Lane, 2000)

Atkinson, M. 'It won't always be Yes Minister' (*The Guardian* 6 June 1998)

Atkinson, T. 'Targeting Poverty' (*New Economy* Vol. 5, No. 1, 1998)

Backus, D. and Driffill, J. 'Inflation and Reputation' (*American Economic Review*, No. 75, 1985)

Baker, D. and Seawright, D. 'A "Rosy" Map of Europe? Labour Parliamentarians and European Integration' in Baker, D. & Seawright, D. (eds) *Britain For and Against Europe* (Oxford University Press, 1998)

Baker, D., Fountain, I., Gamble, A. and Ludlam, S. 'The Conservative Parliamentary Elite 1964–1994: The End of Social Convergence?' (*Sociology* Vol. 29, No. 4, 1995)

Baker, D., Gamble, A. and Seawright, D. with Bull, K. 'MPs and Europe', in Fisher, J., Cowley, P., Denver, D. & Russell, A. (eds) *British Elections and Parties Review Volume 9* (Frank Cass, 1999)

Bale, T. 'Managing the Party and the Trade Unions' in **Brivati, B. and Bale, T.** (eds) *New Labour in Power* (Routledge, 1997)

Bale, T. 'The Logic of No Alternative? Political Scientists, Historians and the Politics of Labour's Past' (*British Journal of Politics and International Relations* Vol. 1, No. 2, 1999)

Balls, E. 'Open Macroeconomics in an Open Economy' (*Scottish Journal of Political Economy* Vol. 43, No. 2, 1998)

Barber, M. *The Learning Game* (Gollancz, 1996)

Barker, Tony *Ruling by Task Force* (Politico's, 1999)

Barr, N. 'Towards a "Third Way?" Rebalancing the role of the state' (*New Economy* Vol. 5, No. 2, 1998)

Barrett-Brown, M. and Coates, K. *The Blair Relevation: Deliverance for Whom?* (Spokesman, 1996)

Barro, R. J. and Gordon, D. 'Rules Discretion and Reputation in a Model of Monetary Policy' (*Journal of Monetary Economics*, No. 12, 1983)

Bayley, S. *Labour Camp: The Failure of Style Over Substance* (BT Batsford Ltd, 1998)

Beck, Ulrich *The Brave New World of Work* (Aurum Press, 2000)

Bergounioux, A. and Lazar, M. *La social-démocratie dans l'Union Européenne* (Fondation Jean Jaurès, 1997)

Bevir, M. *The Logic of the History of Ideas* (Cambridge University Press, 1999)

Blackburn, R. and Plant, R. (eds) *The Labour Government's Constitutional Reform Agenda* (Longman, 1999)

Blair, Tony *Change and National Renewal* (Labour Party, 1994)

Blair, Tony *New Britain: My Vision of a Young Country* (Fourth Estate, 1996)

Blair, Tony *Leading the Way* (Institute for Public Policy Research, 1998)

Blair, Tony *The Third Way: New Politics for the New Century* (Fabian, 1998)

Brealey, R., Clark, A., Goodhart, C., Healey, J., Hoggarth, G., Llewellyn, D., Shang, C., Sinclair, P. and Soussa, F. *Financial Stability and Central Banks* (Routledge, 2001)

Briault, C. 'The Rationale of a Single Financial Regulator' (*Financial Services Authority Occasional Paper*, London, 1999)

Briault, C. 'FSA Revisited, And Some Issues for European Securities Markets Legislation (paper presented to European Union Conference in Fiesole, 2000)

Brivati, B. and Bale, T. (eds) *New Labour in Power: Precedents and Prospects* (Routledge, 1997)

Browne, A. 'Is Britain Now a Fairer Country?' (*Observer* 14 March 1999)

Brown, G. 'Equality Then and Now' in **Leonard, D.** (ed.) *Crosland and New Labour* (Macmillan, 1999)

Burch, M. and Holliday, I. 'The Prime Minister's and Cabinet Offices: An Executive Office in all but Name' (*Parliamentary Affairs*, 1999)

Butler, D. and Kavanagh, D. *The British General Election of 1997* (Macmillan, 1997)

Campbell, A. 'Beyond Spin: Government and the Media' (*Fabian Society Special Pamphlet 42*, Fabian Society, 1999)

Carlson, I. and Ramphal, S. 'Might is not Right' (*The Guardian* 2 April 1999)

Clarke, H. D., Stewart, M. C. and Whiteley, P. F. 'New Models for New

Labour: The Political Economy of Labour Party Support, January 1992–April 1997' (*American Political Science Review*, 92, 1998)

Coates, D. and Lawler, P. (eds) *New Labour into Power* (Manchester University Press, 2000)

Coates, K. 'Unemployed Europe and the Struggle for Alternatives' (*New Left Review* No. 227, 1998)

Cohen, Nick *Cruel Britannia* (Verso, 2000)

Colebatch, Hal *Blair's Britain* (Claridge Press, 1999)

Conservative Party *Our vision for Britain* (Conservative Central Office, 1997)

Cowley, P. 'The Absence of War? New Labour in Parliament', in Fisher, J., Cowley, P., Denver, D. and Russell, A. (eds) *British Elections and Parties Review Volume 9* (Frank Cass, 1999)

Crewe, I., Gosschalk, B., and Bartle, J. *Political Communications: Why Labour Won the General Election of 1997* (Frank Cass, 1998)

Crosland, A. *The Future of Socialism* (Cape, 1956)

Curtice, J. and Steed, M. 'The results analysed' in Butler, D. and Kavanagh, D. *The British General Election of 1997* (Macmillan, 1997)

Daniels, P. 'From Hostility to "Constructive Engagement": the Europeanisation of the Labour Party' (*West European Politics* Vol. 21, No. 1, 1998)

Darling, A. 'A Political Perspective' in Kelly, G., Kelly, D. and Gamble, A. (eds) *Stakeholder Capitalism* (Macmillan, 1997)

Deakin, N. and Party, R. *The Treasury and Social Policy. The Struggle for the Control of Welfare Strategy* (Macmillan, 2000)

Dennis, N. (ed.) *Zero Tolerance: Policing a Free Society* (Institute of Economic Affairs, 1998)

Denver, D., Fisher, J., Cowley, P. and Pattie, C. *British Elections and Parties Review, Volume 8: The 1997 General Election* (Frank Cass, 1998)

Draper, D. *Blair's Hundred Days* (Faber & Faber, 1997)

Driver, S. and Martell, L. *New Labour: Politics after Thatcherism* (Polity, 1998)

Eccleshall, R. 'Party Ideology and National Decline' in English, R. and Kenny, M. (eds) *Rethinking British Decline* (Macmillan, 2000)

Etzioni, Amitai *The Third Way to a Good Society* (Demos, 2000)

Evans, G., Curtice, J. and Norris, P. 'New Labour, New Tactical Voting? The Causes and Consequences of Tactical Voting in the 1997 General Election' in Denver, D., Fisher, J., Cowley, P. and Pattie, C. (eds) *British Elections and Parties Review Volume 8: The 1997 General Election* (Frank Cass, 1998)

Fairclough, Norman *New Labour, New Language?* (Routledge, 2000)

Field, F. 'A Hand-up or a Put-down for the Poor' (*New Statesman* 27 November, 1998)

Fielding, S. 'Labour's Path to Power' in Tonge, J. and Geddes, A. (eds) *Labour's Landslide: the British General Election 1997* (Manchester University Press, 1997)

Finkelstein, D. 'Why the Conservatives lost' in Crewe, K., Gosschalk, B. and Bartle, J. (eds) *Political Communications: Why Labour Won the General Election of 1997* (Frank Cass, 1998)

Finlayson, A. 'Third Way Theory' (*Political Quarterly* Vol. 70, No. 3, 1999)

Flinders, M. and Smith, M. J. *Quangos, Accountability and Reform* (Macmillan, 1999)

Foley, M. *The British Presidency* (Manchester University Press, 2000)

Ford, R. 'Lone Mothers, Work and Welfare' (*New Economy* Vol. 5, No. 2, 1998)

Forder, J. 'On the Assessment and Implementation of "Institutional" Remedies' (*Oxford Economic Papers*, No. 48, 1996)

Franklin, B. *Tough on Soundbites, Tough on the Causes of Soundbites: New Labour and News Management* (Catalyst, 1998)

Franklin, B. (ed.) *Misleading Messages: The Media Misrepresentation and Social Policy* (Routledge, 1999)

Freeden, M. 'The Ideology of New Labour' (*Political Quarterly*, Vol. 70, 1999)

Fry, M., Goodhart, C. and Almeida, A. *Central Banking in Developing Countries: Objectives, Activities and Independence* (Routledge, 1996)

Gamble, A. and Wright, T. *The New Social Democracy* (Blackwell Publishers, 1999)

Gamble, A. and Kelly, G. 'The British Left and Monetary Union' (*West European Politics* Vol. 23, No. 1, 2000)

Gardiner, K. 'Getting Welfare to Work' (*New Economy* Vol. 5, 1998)

Geddes, A. and Tonge, J. (eds) *Labour's Landslide: The British General Election of 1997* (Manchester University Press, 1997)

George, E. 'Monetary Policy and the Euro' (*Bank of England Quarterly Bulletin*, April 2000)

Giddens, Anthony *The Third Way: the Renewal of Social Democracy* (Policy, 1998)

Giddens, Anthony *The Third Way and its Critics* (Polity, 2000)

Goodhart, C. 'The Organisational Structure of Banking Supervision' (*Financial Stability Institute Discussion Paper*, 2000) and in **Brealey** et al.

Goodman, Geoffrey (ed.) and Blair, Tony *The State of the Nation* (Orion, 1997)

Gould, P. *The Unfinished Revolution: How the Modernisers Saved the Labour Party* (Little, Brown, 1998)

Gould, P. 'Why Labour won' in **Crewe, I., Gosschalk, B. and Bartle, J.** (eds) *Political Communications: Why Labour Won the General Election of 1997* (Frank Cass, 1998)

Grant, C. *Can Britain Lead in Europe?* (Centre for European Reform, 1998)

Gray, A. and Jenkins, B. 'New Labour, New Government? Change and Continuity in Public Administration and Government 1997' (*Parliamentary Affairs* 51/2, 1998)

Gross and Thygesen, *European Monetary Integration* (2nd edition, Longman, 1998)

Hall, S. 'The Great Moving Nowhere Show' (*Marxism Today*, November/December 1998)

Hamnett, C. *Winners and Losers: Home Ownership in Modern Britain* (UCL Press, 1999)

Hay, C. *The Political Economy of New Labour: Labouring Under False Pretences?* (Manchester University Press, 1999)

Hazell, R. (ed.) *Constitutional Futures: A History of the Next Ten Years* (Oxford University Press, 1999)

Heath, A. 'Social Change, Value Orientations and Voting Patterns since the 1980s' in **Kastendiek, H., Stinshoff, R. and Sturm, R.** (eds) *The Return of Labour – a Turning Point in British Politics* (Philo, 1999)

Heffernan, R. *New Labour and Thatcherism: Exploring Political Change* (Macmillan, 1999)

Hennessy, Peter *The Blair Revolution in Government?* (Polis, 2000)

Hennessy, Peter *The Prime Minister: The Office and its Holders since 1945* (HarperCollins, 2000)

Heseltine, Michael *Where There's a Will* (Hutchinson, 1987)

Hewison, Robert *Culture and Consensus: England, Art and Politics since 1940* (Methuen, 1997)

Hill, Christopher and Smith, Karen (eds) *European Foreign Policy: Key Documents* (Routledge, 2000)

Hillman, J. 'The Labour government and lifelong learning' (*Renewal* Vol. 6, No. 2, Spring 1998)

Hirst, P. *From Stalism to Pluralism, Democracy, Civil Society and Global Politics* (UCL Press, 1997)

Hobsbawm, E. 'The Death of Neo-Liberalism' (*Marxism Today* Special Issue, November/December 1998)

Hood, C. *The Art of the State* (Oxford University Press, 1999)

Hutton, W. *The State We're In.* (Jonathan Cape, 1995)

Hutton, W. *The Stakeholding Society: Writings on Politics and Economics* (Polity Press, 1998)

Jacques, M. 'Good to Be Back' (*Marxism Today*, November/December 1998)

James, S. *British Cabinet Government* (Routledge, 1999)

Johnston, R. J., Pattie, C. J., Dorling, D. F. L., Rossiter, D. J., Tunstall, H. and MacAllister, I. 'New Labour landslide – same old electoral geography' in Denver, D., Fisher, J., Cowley, P. and Pattie, C. (eds) *British Elections and Parties Review Volume 8: The 1997 General Election* (Frank Cass, 1998)

Jones, N. *Sultans of Spin* (Gollancz, 1999)

Jones, T. *Remaking the Labour Party: From Gaitskell to Blair* (Routledge, 1996)

Jordan, B. *The New Politics of Welfare: Social justice in a global context* (Sage, 1998)

Kastendiek, H., Stinshoff, R. and Sturm, R. (eds) *The Return of Labour – a Turning Point in British Politics?* (Philo, 1999)

Kaufman, G. *How to be a Minister* (Faber & Faber, 1997)

Kavanagh, D. and Seldon, A. *The Powers Behind the Prime Minister* (HarperCollins, 2001)

Kavanagh, D. 'The Labour campaign', in Norris, P. and Gavin, N. (eds) *Britain Votes 1997* (Oxford University Press, 1997)

Kanvanagh, D. 'R. T. McKenzie and After' in Berrington, H. (ed.) *Britain in the Nineties* (Frank Cass, 1998)

Kellner, P. 'Why the Tories were Trounced' in Norris, P. and Gavin, N. T. (eds) *Britain Votes 1997* (Oxford University Press, 1997)

Kelly, G. and Oppenheim, C. 'Working With New Labour' (*Renewal* Vol. 10, 1998)

Kelly, Gavin (ed.) and Blair, Tony *Is New Labour Working?* (Fabian Society, 1999)

Kenny, M. and Smith, M. J. '(Mis)understanding Blair' (*Political Quarterly* 68, 1997)

Kenny, M. and Smith, M. J. 'Reforming Clause Four: Hugh Gaitskell, Tony

Blair and the Modernisation of the Labour Party' in **D. Denver, J. Fisher, S. Ludlam and C. Pattie** *British Elections and Parties Review* (Frank Cass, 1997)

King, Anthony et al. *New Labour Triumphs: Britain at the Polls* (Chatham House Publishers, 1998)

King, D. and Wickham-Jones, M. 'Training Without the State: New Labour and Labour Markets' (*Policy and Politics*, 26(4), 1998)

Labour Party *Labour into Power: A Framework for Partnership* (Labour Party, 1997)

Labour Party *Partnership in Power* (Labour Party, 1997)

Labour Party *New Labour: Because Britain Deserves Better* (Labour Party, 1997)

Langdon, Julia *Mo Mowlam* (Little, Brown, 2000)

Lawson, N. *The View From Number 10* (Bantam, 1992)

Le Grand, J. 'The Third Way Begins With Cora' (*New Statesman* 6 March 1998)

Lee, P. and Murie, A. 'Targeting Social Exclusion' (*New Economy* Vol. 5, No. 2, 1998)

Leo, Abse *Tony Blair* (Robson Books Ltd, 2000)

Levitas, R. *The Inclusive Society? Social Exclusion and New Labour* (Macmillan, 1998)

Lewis, D. *Hidden Agendas: Politics, Law and Disorder* (Hamish Hamilton, 1997)

Leys, C. and Panitch, L. *The End of Parliamentary Socialism: from New Left to New Labour* (Verso, 1997)

Lightfoot, S. 'Prospects for Euro-Socialism' (*Renewal* Vol. 7, No. 2, 1999)

Lipsey, D. *The Secret Treasury* (Viking, 2000)

Lister, R. 'From Fractured Britain to One Nation? The policy options for welfare reform' (*Renewal* Vol. 5, Nos 3–4, 1997)

Lister, R. 'Social Inclusion and Exclusion' in **Kelly, G., Kelly, D. and Gamble, A.** (eds) *Stakeholder Capitalism* (Macmillan, 1997)

Little, Richard and Wickham-Jones, Mark (eds) *New Labour's Foreign Policy: A New Moral Crusade?* (Manchester University Press, 2000)

Lloyd, J. 'Third Way? They'll Do It *Their* Way' (*New Statesman*, 4 December 1998)

Ludlam, S. and Smith, M. J. (eds) *New Labour in Government* (Macmillan, 2000)

MacLean, Rory and D'Arcy, Mark *Nightmare: The Race For London's Mayor* (Politico's, 2000)

Mandelson, P. and Little, R. *The Blair Revolution: Can New Labour Deliver?* (Faber and Faber, 1996)

Marquand, D. *The New Reckoning* (Policy, 1997)

Marr, Andrew *The Day Britain Died* (Profile Books, 2000)

McIlroy, J. 'The Enduring Alliance? Trade Unions and the Making of New Labour, 1994–1997' (*British Journal of Industrial Relations* Vol. 36, No. 4, 1998)

McInnes, C. 'Labour's Strategic Defence Review' (*International Affairs* Vol. 74, No. 4, 1998)

McKenzie, R. *British Political Parties* (Heinemann, 1995)

McNair, B. 'Journalism, Politics and Public Relations: An Ethical Appraisal' in Kieran, M. (ed.) *Media Ethics* (Routledge, 1998)

McSmith, A. *Faces of Labour: the Inside Story* (Verso, 1996)

Mitchell, J. 'The Evolution of Devolution: Labour's Home Rule Strategy in Opposition' (*Government and Opposition* 33, 4, 1998)

Monks, J. 'Government and Trade Unions' (*British Journal of Industrial Relations* Vol. 36, No. 1, 1998)

Morgan, K. O. *Callaghan: A Life* (Oxford University Press, 1997)

Morris, D. *The New Prince* (Renaissance Books, 1999)

Nairn, Tom *After Britain* (Granta Books, 2000)

Nickell, S. and Layard, R. *Labour Market Institutions and Economic Performance* in Ashenfelter and Card (eds) *Handbook of Labour Economics* (North Holland, 1998)

Nicoll, A. 'Seeking a Level Battlefield' (*Financial Times* 3 June 1999)

Norris, P. 'New Labour, New Politicians? Changes in the Political Attitudes of Labour MPs 1992–1997', in Dobson, A. and Stanyer, J. (eds) *Contemporary Political Studies 1998, Vol. 2* (Political Studies Association, 1998)

Novak, Michael *Is There a Third Way?* (IEA, 1999)

Oppenheim, C. 'Welfare to Work: Taxes and Benefits', in McCormick, J. and Oppenheim, C. (eds) *Welfare in Working Order* (IPPR, 1998)

Peak, S. and Fisher, P. *The Media Guide, A Guardian Book* (Fourth Estate, 1999)

Perryman, Mark (ed.) *The Blair Agenda* (Lawrence & Wishart, 1998)

Peterson, M. 'The View From Sweden' (*Soundings* No. 9, 1998)

Philpott, J. 'The Performance of the UK Labour Market', in Buxton, T. et al. (eds) *Britain's Economic Performance* (Routledge, 1998)

Pilkington, C. *Issues in British Politics* (Macmillan, 1998)

Pimlott, B. *Harold Wilson* (HarperCollins, 1992)

Plant, R. 'So You Want to be a Citizen?' (*New Statesman*, 6 February, 1998)

Platt, S. *Government by Task Force: a Review of the Reviews* (The Catalyst Trust, 1998)

Powell, Martin (ed.) *New Labour, New Welfare State?* (The Policy Press, 1999)

Przeworski, A. *Capitalism and Social Democracy* (Cambridge University Press, 1985)

Pulzer, P. *Political Representation and Elections in Britain* (George Allen & Unwin, 1967)

Purves, L. 'Blair's Babes in the Wood' (*The Times*, 2 December 1997)

Ramsey, R. *Prawn Cocktail Party – The Hidden Powers Behind New Labour* (Vision Paperbacks, 1998)

Rawnsley, Andrew *Servants of the People: The Inside Story of New Labour* (Hamish Hamilton, 2000)

Recio, A. and Roca, J. 'The Spanish Socialists in Power: Thirteen Years of Economic Policy' (*Oxford Review of Economic Policy* Vol. 14, No. 1, 1998)

Redwood, John (MP) *The Death of Britain?* (Palgrave, 1999)

Reich, R. 'The Third Way Needs Courage' (*The Guardian* 21 September 1998)

Reisman, D. *Crosland's Future: Opportunity and Outcome* (Macmillan, 1997)

Rentoul, John *Tony Blair* (Little, Brown, 2001)

Rhodes, R. A. W. *Understanding Governance* (Open University Press, 1997)

Richards, D. and Smith, M. 'How Departments Change: Windows of Opportunity and Critical Junctures in Three Departments' (*Public Policy and Administration* 12 (2), 1997)

Richter, I. *Political Purpose in Trade Unions* (George Allen & Unwin, 1973)

Riddell, P. *Parliament under Pressure* (Victor Gollancz, 1998)

Riddell, Peter *Parliament Under Blair* (Politico's, 2000)

Riddell, Peter 'Does Anyone Listen to MPs?' (*The Times*, 23 March 1998)

Rivett, Geoffrey and Blair, Tony *From Cradle to Grave* (King's Fund, 1998)

Robertson, D. 'Lifelong learning: Can Labour deliver the unifying strategy we need?' (*Renewal* Vol. 5 Nos 3/4, Autumn 1997)

Robertson, G. 'Britain in the New Europe' (*International Affairs* Vol. 66, No. 4, 1990)

Robinson, P. 'Employment and Social Inclusion' in *An Inclusive Society: Strategies for Tackling Poverty* (IPPR, 1998)

Robinson, P. 'Literacy, Numeracy and Economic Performance' (*New Political Economy* Vol. 3, No. 1, 1998)

Rodgers, P. 'Changes at the Bank of England' (*Bank of England Quarterly Bulletin*, July 1997)

Rogoff, K. 'The Optimal Degree of Commitment to a Monetary Target' (*Quarterly Journal of Economics*, No. 100, 1985)

Rosamond, B. 'The integration of Labour? British trade union attitudes to European integration' in **Baker, D. and Seawright, D.** (eds) *Britain For and Against Europe: British Politics and the Question of European Integration* (Oxford University Press, 1998)

Rose, R. *The Prime Minister in a Shrinking World* (Polity, 2001)

Rossiter, D. J., Johnston, R. J. and Pattie, C. J. *The Boundary Commissions* (Manchester University Press, 1999)

Rossiter, D. J., Johnston, R. J., Pattie, C. J., Dorling, D., MacAllister, I. and Tunstall, H. 'Changing biases in the operation of the UK's electoral system, 1950–1997 (*British Journal of Politics and International Relations* Vol. 1, No. 1, 1999)

Roth, A. and Criddle, B. *New MPs of 1997 and Retreads* (Parliamentary Profiles Services Ltd, 1997)

Routledge, Paul *Gordon Brown: The Biography* (Pocket Books, 1998)

Routledge, Paul *Mandy* (Pocket Books, 1999)

Ruggie, J. 'International Regimes, Transactions and Change: Embedded Liberalism in the Post-War Economic Order' (*International Organization* Vol. 36, No. 3, 1982)

Ryan, H. B. *The Vision of Anglo-American: the US-UK Alliance and the Emerging Cold War, 1943–46* (Cambridge University Press, 1987)

Sanders, D. 'Government popularity and the next General Election' (*Political Quarterly* 62, 1991)

Sanders, D. 'Foreign and Defence Policy' in **Dunleavy, P. et al.** *Developments in British Politics 4* (Macmillan, 1993)

Sanders, D. 'Forecasting political preferences and election outcomes in the UK: experiences, problems and prospects for the next general election' (*Electoral Studies* 14, 1995)

Sanders, D. 'Economic performance, management competence, and the outcome of the next General Election' (*Political Studies*, 44, 1996)

Sanders, D., Ward, H. and Marsh, D. 'Government popularity and the Falklands War: a reassessment' (*British Journal of Political Science*, 17, 1987)

SAP 'Election Manifesto 1998: With a view to the future – the policy of the Social Democrats for the 21st century' (SAP, 1998)

Sassoon, D. 'The Union Link: the Case for a Friendly Divorce' (*Renewal* Vol. 1, No. 1, 1993)

Sassoon, D. *100 Years of Socialism* (IB Tauris, 1996)

Sassoon, D. *Looking Left: Socialism after the Cold War* (IB Taurus, 1997)

Sassoon, D. 'Fin-de-Siècle Socialism: The United, Modest Left' (*New Left Review* No. 227, 1998)

Saward, M. 'In Search of the Hollow Crown' in **Weller, P., Bakvis, H. and Rhodes, R. A. W.** *The Hollow Crown* (Macmillan, 1997)

Seyd, P. 'Tony Blair and New Labour', in **King, A.** (ed.) *New Labour Triumphs: Britain at the Polls* (Chatham House, 1998)

Shaw, E. *The Labour Party Since 1945* (Blackwell, 1996)

Sinclair, P. 'Central Banks and Financial Stability' (*Bank of England Quarterly Bulletin*, November 2000)

Smith, C. *Creative Britain* (Faber and Faber, 1998)

Smith, M. J. *The Core Executive in Britain* (Macmillan, 1999)

Spicker, P. 'The Welfare State and Social Protection in the United Kingdom' in **Mullard, M. and Lee, S.** (eds) *The Politics of Social Policy in Europe* (Edward Elgar, 1997)

Strange, S. 'The British Labour Movement and EMU in Europe' (*Capital and Class* No. 63, 1997)

Sully, Melanie *The New Politics of Tony Blair* (East European Monographs, 2000)

Taylor, G. *Labour's Renewal? The Policy Review and Beyond* (Macmillan, 1997)

Taylor, G. (ed.) *The Impact of New Labour* (Macmillan, 1999)

Taylor, M. and Cruddas, J. *New Labour, New Links* (Unions 21, 1998)

Taylor, R. *The Trade Union Question in British Politics: Government and Unions since 1945* (Blackwell, 1993)

Taylor, R. 'The Fairness at Work White Paper' (*Political Quarterly* Vol. 69, No. 4, 1998)

Taylor, Robert *The TUC: From the General Strike to New Unionism* (Palgrave, 2000)

Theakston, K. *Leadership in Whitehall* (Macmillan, 1999)

Tomlinson, J. 'Economic Policy: Lessons from Past Labour Governments' in **Bale, T. and Brivati, B.** (eds) *New Labour in Power: Prospects and Precedents* (Routledge, 1997)

Tomlinson, S. 'Sociological Perspectives on Failing Schools' (*International Journal of the Sociology of Education* Vol. 7, No. 1, 1997)

Tonge, J. and Geddes, A. (eds) *Labour's Landslide: the British General Election 1997* (Manchester University Press, 1997)

Toynbee, P. and Walker, D. *Did Things Get Better?* (Penguin, 2001)

Travis, A. 'Straw to target burglars' (*The Guardian* 13 January 1999)

Traynor, I. 'Peter's Passions' (*The Guardian* 16 March 1998)

Vickers, J. 'Signalling in a Model of Monetary Policy with Incomplete

Information' (*Oxford Economic Papers*, No. 38, 1986) and in *Prices, Quantities and Expectations* in **Sinclair, P.** (ed.) (Oxford University Press, 1987)

Weir, S. and Beetham, D. *Politcal and Democratic Control in Britain* (Routledge, 1999)

Weller, P. and Bakvis, H. 'The Hollow Crown: Coherence and Capacity in Central Government' in **Weller, P., Bakvis, H. and Rhodes, R. A. W.** *The Hollow Crown* (Macmillan, 1997)

Wheeler, N. J. and Dunne, T. 'Good International Citizenship: A Third Way for British Foreign Policy' (*International Affairs* Vol. 74, No. 4, 1998)

White, S. 'Interpreting the Third Way: Not One Road, But Many' (*Renewal* Vol. 6, No. 2, 1998)

Worcester, R. and Mortimore, R. *Explaining Labour's Landslide* (Politico's, 1999)

INDEX

The location of tables are shown in **bold**.